The Idiot and the Odyssey II

MYTH, MADNESS AND MAGIC ON THE MEDITERRANEAN

Joel Stratte-McClure

Cover Photo: Cliff walking in southern Italy.
(Credit: Judy Barnett)

The Idiot and the Odyssey II
Myth, Madness and Magic on the Mediterranean

Published by
Noble Creative & Freelance Ink Books

PO Box 994547
Redding, California 96099-4547

www.idiotandodyssey.com

ISBN: 978-0-9886961-1-2

Designed by Aaron and Jenni Elise Patterson, Slingshot Media,
Redding, California
Edited by Michael Knipe, London

ACCLAIM FOR

THE IDIOT AND THE ODYSSEY

"This is one of those seductive books that, as you read, slowly insinuates itself into your consciousness and becomes more and more compelling and entrancing....Stratte-McClure belongs to a generation that was entranced by the road journeys of Jack Kerouac and Robert Pirsig (*Zen and the Art of Motorcycle Maintenance*). These were journeys where the landscape and the exploration of the author's psyche were blended artfully....It is a high-wire literary act that is always in danger of collapsing into pretentiousness, but Stratte-McClure is so knowledgeable about the paths he walks and so sensitive to the history and landscapes around him that what he produces is not only an interesting travel book but a compelling story about a simple attempt to overcome a mid-life crisis and make some sense of the world." - *Bruce Elder, Sydney Morning Herald*

"American Stratte-McClure is that rare bird among writers who can write a memoir that addresses the universal without sounding pompous or self-indulgent. Here is a man who tackles the most fundamental subjects with wit and profundity in equal measure." – *Toni Whitmont, Booktopia*

"There must be simpler - and less strenuous - ways to get over a mid-life crisis following a divorce. Walking around the Mediterranean does seem to be a bit extreme. But American journalist and author Joel Stratte-McClure doesn't seem to be the type to take the easy way out." – *Diana Plater, Associated Press*

"A mid-life crisis prompts the US-born, France-based author to walk around the Mediterranean coast in the footsteps of his hero Odysseus. Overflowing with facts about the countries he visited and anecdotes from his three decades as a journalist, he is an entertaining, charming and erudite travelling companion." (****) – *WHO Magazine*

"From the turquoise-tinted water and zillion dollar yachts of Saint-Tropez to the intrigue of the Kasbah in Tangier, Joel Stratte-McClure takes the reader on a delightful spiritual journey around the Mediterranean that is filled with nudists and Buddhists, the obscenely chic and the exotic. *The Idiot and the Odyssey* is such a terrific antidote to the middle age melancholia that if Homer could do a sequel, Odysseus would probably jump ship to join Stratte-McClure's MedTrek instead." - *Craig Unger, Vanity Fair contributing editor, author of "Boss Rove: Inside Karl Rove's Secret Kingdom of Power"*

"The book's title suggests its tone: at once ambitious and self-effacing, literate and down-to-earth. Stratte-McClure is an erudite man whose lust for life is balanced by Buddhist wisdom, and he brings to each moment on his journey a genuine affection for all he encounters that is irresistible." – *Robert Speer, Chico (CA) News and Review*

"Facing a mid-life crisis and the collapse of your marriage after learning that your spouse has a lover half your age, what would you do? Get hammered? Not Joel Stratte-McClure. He'd already been there, done that, and quit drinking. Instead, the Stanford grad went back to basics — the very basics. He walked." - *Anneli Rufus, East Bay (CA) Express*

"Stratte-McClure describes the food and the hotels where he stopped while hiking more than 2,700 miles in the course of the book. While reading in airports and my living rooms, I was transported to parts of the world where I have traveled but not really known." – *Marilyn Hagerty, The Grand Forks (ND) Herald*

"Reading *The Idiot and the Odyssey* provides a hugely entertaining perspective of the world's oldest and greatest journey, conjured millennia ago by Homer. The book is a reminder that the Mediterranean, even today, is a wild and fascinating place." - *Tony Perrottet, author of "Route 66 AD: On the Trail of Ancient Roman Tourists*

"Joel Stratte-McClure's *The Idiot and the Odyssey* is a wonderful book. By turns whimsical and profound - and more than occasionally laugh-out-loud funny - it defies all the conventions. It is at once an adventure story, a work of history, a philosophical treatise and an unflinchingly honest memoir." - *Harry Stein, author of "The Girl Watchers Club: Lessons from the Battlefields of Life"*

"The whimsical author, a serial hiker in the midst of a mid-life crisis, embarks on an epic undertaking with determination, a sack full of Homeric quotes and Buddhist wisdom. You'll be glad you came along on a journey of discovery that is both entertaining and inspirational. Onward!" - *Tony Rocca, author of "Chianti on the Rocks"*

"In this mid-life 'coming of age' quest, we're invited to join Stratte-McClure on his extraordinary journey – trekking the Mediterranean through each creek and cranny as he weaves his observations of the physical world with his own inner contemplations. Readers are treated to meanderings filled with encounters, adventures and mishaps amidst a backdrop of musings abundant with wit and wisdom. An amazing and amusing read!" - *Elizabeth Billhardt, photographer/author of "Coastal Pleasures: Perusing the French Coastline"*

"Contemplative and entertaining, *The Idiot* traverses a very contemporary Mediterranean shoreline – though Greek gods and goddesses pop up along the way. Much more than a guidebook, Stratte-McClure's tale is saturated with history and humor. This mid-life meditation will appeal to adventurers and armchair travelers alike." - *Linda Phillips Ashour, author of "Speaking in Tongues"*

"Like slow food, the Herculean hike around the Mediterranean by Joel Stratte-McClure – no idiot, for sure – seems an improbable ambition. Yet, inspired by Odysseus, Chinese philosophy and his own mid-life crises, the account of his adventures is a triumph of travel writing – entertaining, witty, perceptive and informative. An enchanting read." - *Marion Kaplan, photojournalist/author of "Focus Africa" and "The Portuguese - The Land and Its People"*

"Joel Stratte-McClure maintains it would be unreasonable to think anyone can achieve Nirvana after walking less than 5000 kilometers. Wrong! I felt enlightened from the first page to the last of this inspiring and motivating book as I faithfully accompanied the author on every step and stumble of his remarkable journey. And it's a delight to see pesky French women finally taken off their pedestal." - *Margaret Kemp, editor at large/critic of Bonjour Paris*

"If, as the Greek physician Hippocrates said, 'Walking is man's best medicine,' then Joel Stratte-McClure's book proves it. Everyone who accompanies him will be healthier in mind and spirit. Slow down and read *The Idiot and the Odyssey*."- *Alex Belida, author of "Regrets Only: An Africa Journal"*

"Perhaps our perception of the world does not depend on the places we visit but the gait of our travelling. I never thought that, in an era obsessed with speed and technology, somebody could thrill me with his amusing observations, experiences and ruminations while tracing on foot the same route I travelled by car in 1968 to visit my aging grandfather at the other end of the Spanish coast. This is the best guide to the Mediterranean since Homer's *The Odyssey* and as informative as James Michener's *Iberia*." - *Princess Beatriz de Orleans Borbón from Spain.*

"This amazing account of human stamina and daring do, where mythological references merge with the author's experiences, creates a brilliant correspondence between past and present. Woven seamlessly in this tale are courage, curiosity and personal reflection, often against a historical or cultural context that shuns all pretence. The trek illuminates the human adventure, comprehension of the self and understanding of 'the other'." - *Constantine Christofides, Professor at the University of Washington and the Institute for American Universities in Aix-en-Provence, France.*

"Having reveled in the sun, storms and special characters of the Mediterranean, I can attest to Stratte-McClure's insightful clarity. Without being tedious or sanctimonious, he introduces people and places as stereotypical, fantastic and ridiculous as could only be true in the Mediterranean. From one audacious and adventurous *minga* to another, I compliment him on his stable stride in an unstable but captivating region." - *Ethan Gelber, Lonely Planet author and president of BikeAbout the Mediterranean*

"Reading *The Idiot and the Odyssey* made my feet hurt but my imagination soar. It sparked a long-dormant wanderlust that inspired me to hastily stuff a backpack and head for the Mediterranean. Then practicality set in and I realized the task is far too Herculean for a mere mortal. Luckily Joel Stratte-McClure, who must have been infused with the power of the gods, was up to the challenge and let me vicariously feel like an adventurer through his awe-inspiring exploits." - *Adam Rifkin, writer/director, (Look, Homo Erectus, Detroit Rock City, Mousehunt)*

"A delightful, soulful memoir-cum-guide of the birthplace of modern civilization. Veteran journalist Stratte-McClure takes readers along the sometimes rugged and often-urban coastline of the Mediterranean and, with his well-honed reporting skills, peppers the adventure with wise words from our greatest philosophers, history lessons of coastline sites, colorful descriptions of the characters he meets and tales of his own rugged life. It makes you want to put on your hiking boots and hit the path yourself. In search of what? As Stratte-McClure understands more clearly with each day of his years long trek, that is the eternal question." - *Dana Thomas, former Newsweek correspondent and author of "Deluxe: How Luxury Lost Its Luster"*

"Joel Stratte-McClure's didactic but sensitive voice simultaneously describes and contemplates the Mediterranean landscape he traverses and the individuals who inhabit it. He combines a knowledgeable guide's eye of historic and cultural detail with a tourist's awe of the fascinating scenery and people. Homer would love it!" - *Vince Tomasso, Classics Department, Ripon College*

"Homer and Lao Tsu may be the author's go-to guys, but as I read this enchanting book I was reminded of Cervantes. The humorous adventures, the piquant observations, the dreamlike buoyancy of memories jostled by travel - Joel Stratte-McClure is Don Quixote with his head screwed on right." - *Jeff Wheelwright, author of "The Wandering Gene and the Indian Princess: Race, Religion, and DNA"*

"Like travel writer Paul Theroux's *Happy Isles of Oceania: Paddling the Pacific*, journalist Joel Stratte-McClure's *The Idiot and the Odyssey* invites us along on a wonderfully entertaining pilgrimage around a legendary sea, undertaken by a recently-divorced middle-aged man hunting for fresh adventure, renewal and the meaning of life. The fleet-footed McClure finds his share of all three, and a dream experience of a lifetime. It's worth every ebullient, blistering step!" - *Tom Moore, former editor-in-chief, Reader's Digest Australia*

"One man's travel narrative becomes one woman's guiding light." – Judy Barnett, *The Sunday Examiner, Tasmania.*

FIRST BOOK

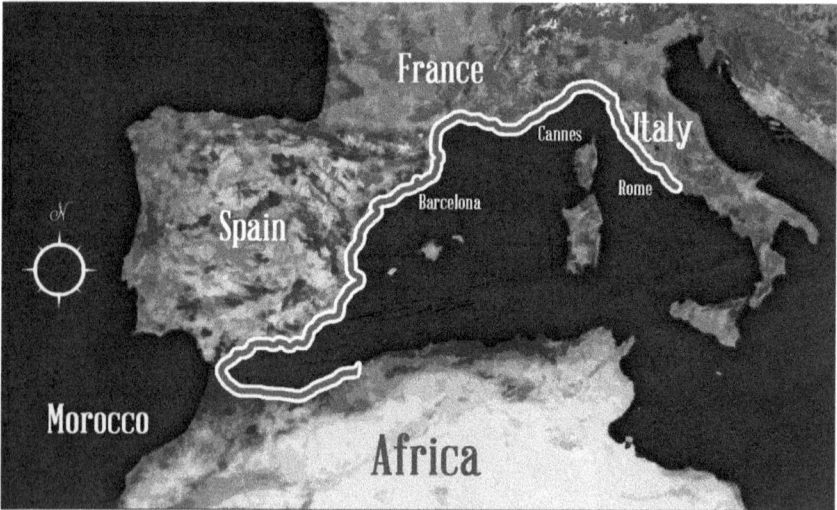

The Idiot and the Odyssey: Walking the Mediterranean took readers on a 4,401-kilometer MedTrek through Morocco, Spain, France, Monaco and down the Italian coast to Rome.

SECOND BOOK

The Idiot and the Odyssey II: Myth, Madness and Magic on the Mediterranean takes readers 4,401-kilometers from Rome to the boot of Italy, around the islands of Sicily and Crete, into the Peloponnese, up Mount Olympus, on to numerous Mediterranean islands and down the Turkish coast to Izmir.

CONTENTS

PREFACE

Gypsies Take Me Down

Sometimes I run into trouble during my ongoing 16,000-kilometer walk around the Mediterranean Sea.

After strolling 34 kilometers on the Italian seaside south of Salerno (or along "the shore of the tumbling clamorous whispering sea" as Homer so sweetly put it in *The Iliad*), I decide to abandon the sunny sandy beach and saunter through a dense and shady pine forest scented with wild thyme.

Big mistake.

When I encounter a small tribe of noisy nomadic Roma, three of the younger gypsies start cackling at me. Playfully attempting to bond and network with my fellow vagabonds, I retort with my patented Tule Lake goose call before realizing that I've put myself alone in the middle of the woods with a trio of taunting and intoxicated thieves.

"Domadoro, domadoro, DOMADORO!" they shout in a much-practiced threatening chorus as they approach me. "Give me gold, give me gold, GIVE ME GOLD!"

I realize immediately that, as Homer also pointed out in *The Iliad,* the shouting was "no invitation to dance but to a fight." I visualize the largest gypsy and me imitating Trojan warriors, scrapping in the sand "like two mountain lions over the carcass of a buck."

Their six glaring eyes look thirstily at the glimmering gold bracelets on my wrists and a white-and-yellow gold yin-and-yang pendant around my neck.

I instinctively remove two of these flashy ornaments when I saunter through urban areas and cities like nearby Naples, but never thought of taking them off on this rural stretch. "Not very smart for an experienced MedTrekker," I reflect as I make a buzzing beeline towards the beach and scream "Watch out!" in Italian. "I've got some friends with guns on the seashore!"

That ruse doesn't confuse the greedy gypsies for long. They know, much to my chagrin, that they've encountered, and are close to trapping, a solo peripatetic jewelry store.

"Domadoro, domadoro, DOMADORO!" they screech again and spit in unison when they confront me at the edge of the tranquil sea and stare, fixated, at my right wrist.

That's the wrinkle.

The gold bracelet on my right wrist is a permanent fixture. It's been there since I had it made in Vermont by jeweler Guy Cheng when I turned 21 in July 1969. That was when gold was still worth $32 an ounce and a few weeks before I wrote my first decent front-page newspaper story from the Woodstock Rock Festival, which was billed as "three days of peace and music."

To get the bracelet, they will have to cut off my hand.

The Idiot and the Odyssey II

PART ONE

MEDTREKKING ON ITALY'S ULYSSES RIVIERA

Onwardly Directions from Adorable Athêna in Rome
Myths and Madness on the March
Careening into Cannibals, the Underworld and Pompeii
The Magical Singing Sirens
Caught between a Rock and a Hard Place

Omwardly Directions from Adorable Athêna in Rome

"My life runs on then as the gods have spun it."
– The Odyssey
"The farther you go, the less you know." *– Lao Tsu*

Call me The Idiot. Despite a few dramatic mishaps and some tense missteps, I generally enjoyed the first 4,401-kilometer stage of my MedTrek, as I call my ongoing step-by-step stroll around the Mediterranean Sea. As I recounted in my first book – *The Idiot and the Odyssey: Walking the Mediterranean* – it took me through Morocco, Spain, France, Monaco and down the coast to Rome. On reaching the Italian capital, I decided to seek divine intervention to inform me what road would lead me out of Rome, where the first settlements date from the eighth century BC.

Should I continue my footloose promenade around the perimeter of the world's largest inland sea in the footsteps of *theios Homeros*, the divine Homer who, more than 2,700 years ago, wrote *The Iliad* and *The Odyssey,* the world's first travel narrative?

After all, it was this classic tale that inspired my slow walking adventure. But maybe, now, I should return to my day job as a columnist covering celebrities in Hollywood and forget my self-appointed role as a contemporary Odysseus. Or, considering the other end of the spectrum, perhaps I should practice the Buddhist principle of *apranihita,* or aimlessness, and quietly make random invisible footprints without thinking of a destination.

Perchance, in an effort to balance these extremes, I should simply keep calmly MedTrekking and continue experiencing the physical, emotional, spiritual and mental exercises that have enabled me to practice Lao Tsu's edict that "the goal is the path, the path is the goal."

A continuation of this mid-life project would give me a few more adventures and revelations while, at the same time, trying to adhere to another suggestion from Lao Tsu to:

> *"Achieve results, but never glory in them.*
> *Achieve results, but never boast.*
> *Achieve results, but never be proud."*

One enchanting aspect of MedTrekking is my frequent get-togethers, often in my meditative mind's eye, with the gods, goddesses, sea nymphs, warriors, villains, heroes, sorceresses and other supernatural, semi-supernatural and merely mortal beings that still inhabit the Mediterranean and meet me on my meanderings.

I am now confident that the grey-eyed, spear-carrying, Greek goddess Athêna will offer me some tips. It was she who also mentored the Greek warrior/king Odysseus during his eventful two-decade absence and slog back home to Ithaka after the Trojan War that ended in 1184 BC. You probably think that Athêna's entrance will be very dramatic, that there will be a thunderclap, a bolt of lightning, perhaps an eclipse. Or maybe a marble statue will miraculously come to life. But Homer's depictions of appearances by the gods are usually, though certainly not always, much more subtle.

Athêna who, contrary to popular belief, does not always have her pet owl perched on her shoulder, appears to me in Rome in the guise of a bubbly and ebullient 22-year-old American tour guide named Amanda. Sporting telltale Nike tennis shoes and a Hermês T-shirt, the Bryn Mawr grad looks like a typically contemporary young American woman and speaks with an American twang (think Scarlett Johansson with a Grace Kelly-like Philadelphia accent).

Amanda today deviously takes on the guise of Athêna, who frequently appears in *The Odyssey* disguised as Mentor, an old friend of Odysseus. But then, according to Homer, the burly Olympian gods and beatific goddesses "who eat no food, who drink no tawny wine and thereby being bloodless have the name of being immortal," can alter their appearance at the drop of a hat.

Homer makes it clear in *The Odyssey* that the immortal gods "go in foreign guise looking like strangers, turning up in towns and settlements to keep an eye on manners, good and bad" and Eidothea, the daughter of the sea divinity Proteus, says her father "can take the forms of all the beasts, and water, and blinding fire."

But I've learned some tricks that enable me to identify Athêna and other immortal visitors.

As I mentioned, the guardian goddess is grey-eyed. Her eye color never changes, despite different disguises and incarnations, and she always greets me with a distinguished left-eye wink. In *The Iliad*, Homer's dramatic epic that details a two-week period during the last year of the decade-long Trojan War, Athêna is described as a "tireless daughter of Zeus who bears the shield of cloud." That faint cloud cover is often a giveaway.

Another method of identifying goddesses like Athêna is by their walk. Homer wrote that "from his stride, his legs as he went off, I knew him for a god. The gods are easily spotted."

Whatever her guise and props, I love the way this wily and wise Greek goddess keeps popping up to influence the actions of cunning mortals like Odysseus, whom the Romans call Ulysses, and me, a sometimes bumbling idiot on a middle-aged odyssey, whom she once referred to as a barbarian, though in ancient times that word meant simply anyone who couldn't speak Greek.

I am obviously excited, maybe too excited, by Athêna's intervention in the Eternal City amidst its breathtaking classical, medieval, Renaissance and Baroque architecture.

But the crafty and cunning goddess, who gave Athens its name and whom the Romans called Minerva, doesn't really solve any existential problems when I serendipitously find her in the remnants of ancient Rome. (Actually it's never completely serendipitous when Athêna runs into me or vice versa). The dazzling daughter of high-thundering Zeus, the king of all gods, obviously senses that I require some guidance when we meet near the Pantheon, the Temple of All Gods, that was originally constructed by Agrippa in 27 BC to honor the seven deities of the seven planets.

Instead of providing an earthshaking augury on a sunny late

April morning as a saxophonist serenades passers-by, the delectable Greek deity simply directs me back towards the fish-breeding, salt-immortal sea and suggests that I spend a year in close consultation with Circe. This is the enchantress who turned Odysseus' crew into swine and now, apparently, Athêna wants her to give me some instructions.

Here's exactly the way Athêna put it when I taped her voice on my tiny Olympus digital recorder while exploring the Pantheon piazza:

"After a day of reflection in the Cemetery of the Capuchins on the Via Veneto, return to the shores of the Mediterranean precisely where you ended your last book and head south in the footsteps of Homer and Odysseus to Italy's Ulysses Riviera."

That sounds like fun because Italy's western coast has considerable credibility as a locale for Odyssean adventures and both Homer and Virgil mention it in their travel narratives, *The Odyssey* and *Aeneid*. Certainly most Italians are convinced that the Riviera between Rome and Naples is the appropriately named locale for the legendary journey and adventures of Odysseus/Ulysses. Those who aren't quite sure call it the Littoral Pontino, after the archipelago of islands just off the coast.

Athêna continues: "Then spend a year with Circe before you take another step and she, who helpfully advised Odysseus about his route and its perils, will have equally wise words for you about how to proceed on your mid-life walkabout."

A year with Circe, or Kirkê as Athêna prefers to spell it, will certainly enable me to reflect on why or whether I should keep walking around the Mediterranean's coastline. But I want a bit more detail.

"Can you please give me a hint where all this might lead?" I ask Athêna as we pass between the Pantheon's huge bronze doors and stand under the Great Eye in the center of the concrete dome. "After all, my footloose frolic around the sea is going much slower than Odysseus' did by ship. It's already been nine years."

"Sometimes you must sit before you step," Athêna/Amanda says as she gives me the same look that my grandmother in North Dakota used to flash me during a long driving trip when I asked "Are we there yet?"

But Athêna senses my angst and gratefully gives me a little more info about my proposed quest.

"Think Jason and the Golden Fleece meet the Twelve Labors of Hêraklês," the slender multi-tasking goddess of war, civilization, wisdom, strength, strategy, crafts, justice and skill says in a conspiratorial tone with her winsome but knowing smile. "Circe will give you all of the details about a twelve-step Mediterranean adventure and tasks that will lead you, if you complete them, to fulfill your own destiny and may end your decades-long exile as an American abroad. She may turn you into Odysseus himself and perhaps send you on an odyssey to your own home."

To my amazement *Tales of Brave Ulysses*, first performed by Eric Clapton's group Cream in the 1960s, is playing in a nearby café as a flock of starlings swarm overhead. The birds, always an omen of some sort in Homer's works, are flying west towards the sea and seem, perhaps only to me, demonstrative of the song's lyrics:

"You thought the leaden winter would bring you down forever,
But you rode upon a steamer to the violence of the sun.
And the colors of the sea bind your eyes with trembling mermaids,
And you touch the distant beaches with tales of brave Ulysses,
How his naked ears were tortured by the sirens sweetly singing."

Having Circe turn me into Odysseus will be interesting, I think, because Homer describes Odysseus as "master mariner and soldier" and "the peer of Zeus in warcraft and forethought." And Jason, who left the port of Volos in Greece with his Argonauts in their ship the Argo to seek the Golden Fleece in order to become King of Thessaly, was my childhood hero. I can, after living outside the United States for over thirty years, appreciate their journeys, both away and homeward, against so many odds and tests.

Hêraklês, whom the Romans call Hercules and whom many contemporary Greeks still consider their superhuman ancestor, was the son of Zeus and his name means "the glory (*kleos*)" of Hêra. But Hêra, Zeus' vengeful wife and Hêraklês' jealous stepmother, drove Hêraklês crazy and caused him to kill his wife and kids. As penance, the warrior born in Tiryns in the Peloponnese had to perform twelve difficult tasks, or labors.

I am sure my script won't be as challenging as his. Hêraklês voyaged into the underworld to combat the forces of death. He was able to hold the sky on his shoulders and traveled in Greece and to the ends of the known earth to encounter the Lion of Nemea, the Hydra of Lerna, the Hind of Keryneia, the Boar of Mount Erymanthos, the Birds of Lake Stymphalos, the Stables of King Augeas, the Bull of Crete, the Man-Eating Mares of Diomedes, the Girdle of Hippolyta, the Cattle of Geryon, Cerberus and the Golden Apples of the Hesperides.

I doubt this type of shopping list will be in store for me when I meet Circe, though Homer writes in *The Odyssey* "swine, wolves and lions she will make us all, beasts of her courtyard, bound by her enchantment."

Whatever eventually transpires, this sounds like a mad caper and a mythical and magical Mediterranean mystery tour!

The next moment, as though awakened from a dream, the young woman standing before me is no longer Athêna but is again a chirpy college grad working as a guide.

The following day I go to the Cemetery of the Capuchins on Via Veneto. I'd first run into the bony and macabre compositions in the crypt of the Santa Maria della Concezione Church that was commissioned by the 17th-century Pope Urban XIII when I co-wrote a guidebook to Rome in the early 1970s. The crypt contains the cleverly arranged skeletal remains of 4,000 Capuchin monks who died between 1500 and 1870 and the message above one of the bony displays is one of my favorite axioms: "What you are now, we once were; what we are now, you will be."

That simple statement certainly sums up the cycle of life. It also brings me down to earth and kicks me off on a resumption of my MedTrek with a proper dose of humility and reality. Homer had a warrior say in *The Iliad*: "You are made of mortal stuff like me," reminding me that I won't be able to keep wandering forever. An incident that occurs just after my visit to the church reinforces that awareness.

I am having coffee at a *caffeteria* on Via Veneto. A caregiver at the table on my left is spoon-feeding an octogenarian in a wheelchair while a baby at the table on my right is suckling at its mother's breast. The yin-and-yang of this scene makes me realize how lucky I am, right now, to exist somewhere between those two extremes.

I don't know what the old man is thinking, whether or not he realizes that I am comparing him to a babe in arms. But a phrase uttered by Lord Nestor in *The Iliad* runs through my mind: "Would god I had my young days back, my strength entire…Now let the young take part in these exertions; I must yield to slow old age, though in my time I shone among heroic men."

I recently found someone who had a copy of the 1972 *Insider's Rome* that I helped report and write for Pan American Airways.

It's been forty years but even today I can remember doing research for the book: the taste of my morning cappuccino at Caffé Greco on via Condotti; the rich chocolate *tartufo* ice cream at Tre Scalini in Piazza Navona; and walks near the graves of Keats and Shelly in the Protestant Cemetery. I thought I was brilliant (I was in my early 20s at the time) when I entitled one chapter *Roam and Ramble* (Roman ramble, get it?) and recall that my boss accused me of tipping too much (with his money) when I sampled various restaurants.

I returned to Rome quite a few times in the 1980s and 90s, reporting and writing about a number of subjects – European aerospace and telecommunications for *Scientific American,* a profile of an anti-Mafia judge for *People.* In those days of flourishing and unmonitored expense accounts I usually stayed at the expensive Grand Hotel on the via del Corso or the Hotel d'Inghliterra on via Bocca de Leone. Definitely way beyond MedTrek mode.

I have some vivid memories of over imbibing at those and other watering holes and often embarrassing myself here.

In the 70s I met Bill Tuohy, a distinguished *Los Angeles Times* correspondent who showed up at a dinner party on the Piazza Navona wearing a coat and tie, and I arrogantly told him how I didn't own a suit, would never wear a tie and didn't believe in using business cards.

"Wear a suit because you never know who you'll be interviewing and never leave a source without giving him your contact details," advised Tuohy. It was sensible advice that I adopted a few years later. In fact, I still have a Valentino suit that I bought in Rome in the 80s and I kept producing a creative line of *Freelance Ink - Have Computer, Will Travel* business cards until the Internet era.

However, I was such an inventive drinker in the 80s that one night in Rome I went to a dinner with journalist and author Robin Wright and pulled the tablecloth off in the middle of our meal in an attempt to perform a magic trick. It didn't work and was not my only transgression. Robin hasn't spoken to me much since.

My most memorable moment in Rome, though, occurred in 2011. I was returning from Greece and wanted to give my weathered sandals to a monk in need. When I couldn't find a monk at midnight I tossed the somewhat scruffy sandals over a locked gate towards the entrance of a church near the Trevi Fountain. They landed, miraculously, side-by-side and right side up as though mysteriously dropped from the heavens. I can still imagine the expression on the priest who opened the door in the morning and wondered how they got there.

"Jesus!" he might have said.

A Stroll in the Sand Turns into a Trudge in a Swamp

My son Luke, who has hiked more kilometers around the Med with me than any other human being, is with me the next afternoon when we return to the beach in Fregene, which was founded by the Romans in 245 BC, to begin the next stage of my MedTrek. It is often billed as the beach where "Rome goes for La Dolce Vita" because film director Frederico Fellini was a regular here. This is the precise spot that I ended my first round of MedTrekking and the beach is so civilized that we haven't made even a modicum of serious preparation for our return to the path.

Sure, I have sun block, a swimming suit, a baseball cap, a pedometer, an emergency whistle and the Day-Glo orange safety vest that I wear to be easily spottable by cars or rescue teams. But no water, no long pants, no extra shoes, not even a spare pair of socks. I'm sure that, starting in the middle of the afternoon for a symbolic kick-off, we'll simply have a good-natured beach hike to and beyond Rome's Leonardo da Vinci-Fiumicino Airport in the easy-to-walk *campi* or countryside.

Why bother with all of the sensible paraphernalia that an experienced hiker would be expected to carry? This late afternoon romp with my son in the verdant marshes will be a piece of pizza and lead me, in just a few days, to Circe's lair where I will chill for a year and determine the true purpose of my ongoing odyssey. This afternoon will not be a part of the MedTrek that, as Pema Chodron wrote in *When Things Fall Apart: Heart Advice for Difficult Times*, is "the moment-by-moment evolution of our experience, the moment-by-moment evolution of the world of phenomena, the moment-by-moment evolution of our thoughts and our emotions."

Or so I think as we casually take a left turn at the sandy seaside to kick off a meditative but adventurous 4,401-kilometer walk that will finally end, as this book does, a few years down the road in Turkey just beyond Troy, the site of the Trojan War.

After getting this much MedTrekking under my belt (though between you and me I rarely wear a belt), how can a veteran hiker like myself get into trouble on the initial ramble just outside Rome? Especially since I only need to make it three or four days down the coast before I spend 365 days with a tantalizing and tempting sorceress/nymph/witch/enchantress on Mount Circeo near Sabaudia.

Well, the crazy Greek gods perched on Mount Olympus in Greece are totally joking with, or provoking, Luke and me on a windy, rainy and blustery afternoon in Fregene. We alight near the Gilda on the Beach restaurant/nightclub, pass the Crazy Bull café, ignore the pine forest that dates from the 1600s when it was planted by Pope Clement IX to protect the land from the strong Mediterranean winds, and walk two kilometers on the sand before I choose to head up the bank of a wide canal entering the sea.

What an idiot!

Within minutes we encounter marshes, brambles, briars, spiders, sharp grass, brackish muck and bogs (and anything else you can name that makes walking more of a trudge in a swamp than a stroll on the sand). These conditions ultimately force us, after a frustrating forty minutes, to head back to the sea. That involves not a substantial loss of time but I am so bloodied, from head to toe, that I look like I just lost a contest to a bloodthirsty gladiator in the Coliseum.

By the time I admit temporary defeat, my legs are cut everywhere between my thighs and ankles, my new low-cut white socks are stained red, my arms look like a suicidal razor has been taken to them and I momentarily lose my glasses when a branch snaps them off my face into the murky water. In addition, there is a downpour of rain and we are both soaked from head to toe.

Why haven't I learned, after all this time on the path, that when a sign says *Fondo Chiuso*, or "Closed Area," not to climb over a barbed wire fence and presume that I can blaze a trail through an untended natural wetland?

Note to self: *chiuso* is *chiuso*.

I constantly tell Luke, and myself, to quit pursuing short cuts and detours like this but can't seem to take my own advice. And this is only one of the reasons that some people call me The Idiot.

When we return to the sea, on a part of the coast that's known as the *Area Protetta del Littorale Romano* (or the Protected Roman Seaside) which might help explain the impenetrable marshes, I am not at all concerned that we get wet up to the chest when we wade across the mouth of the canal because we are already wet from the top of our baseball caps to the bottom of our muddied hiking shoes due to the rain. In fact, I am relieved to get into the sea because the salt water cleans my dozens of cuts.

Luke hasn't fared much better. We look like two drenched, bloodied and defeated Trojan warriors as we quicken our barefooted pace along a beach that alternates between well-kept private sandy spots with umbrellas, *chaises longues*, and *salvataggi* (these are the blue life-saving rescue boats sponsored by the Red Cross found on many Italian beaches) and dirty, deserted, bedraggled, and oil-stained sand with lots of dead fish from the recent storm.

One benefit of this type of minor mishap is that it brings back a memory from my childhood when, on Saturday afternoons in Northern California, I used to wade in a patch of quicksand along the Sacramento River and relish cheating death, which Homer calls "the sleep of bronze" and the "destroyer of ardor," before returning home covered with mud.

"The cool thing about this kind of hiking is that it brings out the child in me," I mention to Luke. "This is fun!"

"Fun?" he asks morosely.

The beaches, despite our proximity to Rome, are relatively undeveloped and generally ignored by sunbathers, presumably because they are in the flight path of the Rome airport or are part of the protected coast. And every Roman knows that there is better sand and more sophisticated facilities a bit further south.

Waves, windsurfers and waterlogged driftwood are the primary attractions as we head through Focene, where we encounter beach shacks inhabited by a tribe of quasi-homeless folks who look like, well, who look like we do. A sad sight. When we arrive in Fiumicino, the town for which the airport gets half its name (it means "little river" but rolls off the tongue like a type of delicious pasta), we pass the Il Moro restaurant and meander through a number of markets selling fresh fish. Then, continuing on a beach with sand that's black due to its high iron content, we reach the banks of the Tiber and walk up along the quay until we stumble on a statue of two young babies and a wolf.

I vividly relate the story of Romulus and Remus and the founding of Rome to Luke as we cross the Tiber. Like many stories that I impart to my son, this one is partly based on historical fact but mostly on myths that I first encountered as a kid when I was a fervent reader of a book called *Myths and Legends of the Ages* that initially awakened my interest in myths and the Mediterranean. I orally relate, as *rhapsodes* did during Homer's time, the story to Luke, passing it from my generation to his. Also, because we're in no hurry, I spin it out in homespun fashion with what I consider just the right amount of detail.

"Many, many years ago (maybe around March 10, 753 BC), there was a town just up the river called Alba Longa with a good king named Numitor and an evil brother called Amulius who took over the palace and imprisoned the king's daughter," I begin.

"The princess escaped from prison and gave birth to twins before she drowned in the river. Bad King Amulius instructed a shepherd to throw the twins in after her but instead the shepherd put the babies in a wooden trough and pushed it into the stream.

"When the trough got to that little cove there and ran onto the shore," I say, pointing to what I consider to be the exact spot where this occurred, "a she-wolf who'd just lost her own cubs in the flood appeared and nursed them. Nearly nine months later a shepherd named Faustulus, looking for a wolf that had killed his master's flock, discovered the babies in a cave and took them home to his wife. They were raised as Romulus and Remus and Romulus often gets full credit for creating Rome, the Roman Legion, and the Roman Senate."

"It's good they named it after Romulus because there's already a Reims in France," Luke says.

We are told by one of the first townspeople we meet that Fiumicino is, territorially, the largest commune in Italy – stretching north to Fregene and taking in the airport and places like Maccarese, Focene and other communities – with a total of 213.44 square kilometers or 82.4 square miles. He adds that the average elevation is one meter above sea level and rattles off names of cities within the commune – Aranova, Focene, Fregene, Isola Sacra, Le Vignole, Maccarese, Palidoro, Parco Leonardo, Passo Oscuro, Testa di Lepre, Torrimpietra, Tragliata, Tragliatella and Aeroporto Leonardo da Vinci- Fiumicino.

I am wet and tired but I have enough active brain cells to recall that in the 1980s I once came here for a business lunch. However, this time, primarily because of our bedraggled appearance, we are not allowed to walk through a restaurant to an adjoining cheapo hotel where we seek a room for the night. Instead, we are politely asked to go through a back door to the lobby.

This would have been an appropriate time for Athêna to change my appearance, as she frequently did with Odysseus, her favorite mortal. She enabled "the raider of cities who had a full bag of traveler's tricks" to appear in various guises, from a beggar to a young warrior.

"Athêna lent him beauty, head to foot," Homer wrote. "She made him taller, and massive, too, with crisping hair in curls like petals of wild hyacinth but all red-golden."

And Odysseus gave her credit.

"As for my change of skin," he admitted, "that is a charm Athêna, Hope of Soldiers, uses as she will; she has the knack to make me seem a beggar man sometimes and sometimes young, with finer clothes about me. It is no hard thing for the gods of heaven to glorify a man or bring him low."

On this day, however, Athêna doesn't come to my assistance and alter my appearance. Instead I have to spin a story to the young receptionist about how we found a large dolphin on the beach and got bloodied pushing it back into the sea.

"*O Dio mio!*" she says as she checks us in. "That was so brave and kind of you."

Reader, if you make this walk, do not, repeat DO NOT, take a left turn when you reach the canal entering the sea. Get wet. Hire a boat. Walk on water. But forget about walking through the thick marsh. Otherwise, like us, you'll just get bloodied, frustrated and waste an hour. If you're stupid enough to ignore this advice and choose to pass the sign that says "*Fondo Chiuso*", at least carry water, long pants, gloves and everything else I tell myself never to walk without. And don't forget the stranded dolphin ploy when stymied by topographical challenges.

Just typing a variation of the word topography makes me eager to tell you that cliffs and rivers are the two most frequent obstacles that I encounter while walking around the Mediterranean. Both can lead to lengthy detours inland and diversions that add many kilometers to my continuing MedTrek, which involves staying as close to the sea as possible.

That's why, unless it's completely insane, I take cliffs in my stride and try to climb them or, occasionally, swim around them. It's also one of the main reasons that I travel as lightly as possible.

Traversing a seaside cliff near Taureana in southern Italy turned out to be a piece of cake. Climbing a much steeper cliff in the south of France got me in a scuffle with the bodyguard at the estate of Carla Bruni, the wife of a French president. And, after MedTrekking over 3,000 accident-free kilometers I took a very bad fall off a cliff in Morocco.

My MO, or *modus operandi,* is to find a room on the sea for up to a week and walk to it and beyond it, relying on public transport to get me to the path and back each day. All I ask for – at an average price of €30 a night – is a sea view and Wi-Fi. Then I take off with an easy-to-carry daypack rather than carrying my whole world on my back.

I tell Luke just after our experience in the marsh that my desire to walk and write was greatly influenced by a story by Laurie Lee called *As I Walked Out One Midsummer Morning* in the June 28, 1969, issue of *The New Yorker*.

"It was 1934," Lee wrote. "I was nineteen years old, still soft at the edges, but with a confident belief in good fortune. I carried a small rolled-up tent, a violin in a blanket, a change of clothes, and a tin of treacle biscuits. I was excited, vainglorious, knowing that I had far to go but not, as yet, how far. As I left home that morning and walked away from the sleeping village, it never occurred to me that others had done this before.

"I was propelled, of course, by the traditional forces that had sent many generations along this road—by the small tight valley closing in around one, stifling the breath with its mossy mouth, the cottage walls narrowing like the arms of an iron maiden, the local girls, whispering, 'Marry, and settle down.' Months of restless unease, leading to this inevitable moment, had been spent wandering the hills, mournfully whistling, and watching the high open fields stepping away eastward under gigantic clouds.

"And now I was on my journey, in a pair of thick boots and with a hazel stick in my hand….."

How easy and pleasant Laurie Lee made it sound. How easy and pleasant it is.

My own jaunt has hardly been a misanthropic one-man ego trip. Luke, good friends, bemused strangers, inquiring journalists and intrigued readers often accompany me. I had an engaging month strolling with a seductive sorceress in Spain and, as you'll discover a few chapters from now, I even sleep with Helen of Troy and have a relationship with a deceased princess. In retrospect, one of the most truthful sentences in my first book is that "....you never really know anyone until you walk together for a few days."

Join me. Get to know me. Let's walk together for a while.

Myths and Madness on the March

"Odysseus then you are, O great contender, of whom the glittering god with golden wand spoke to me ever, and foretold the black swift ship would carry you from Troy."
– *Circe in The Odyssey*

      The next morning, after trudging a mere eleven bloody kilometers the previous day, Luke and I cross the northern arm of the Tiber River in Fiumicino on a risk-free urban footbridge. Then we tranquilly march across the Isola *Sacra Lido del Faro* (which I translate as the Sacred Island of the Lighthouse Beach) with its pleasant horseshoe-shaped beaches. We energetically stride through a port with gargantuan ferries departing for Sardinia before arriving at the fabled lighthouse at the mouth of the southern branch of the Tiber, Italy's third largest river that got its name from the river god Tiberinus.

      It's an inspiring sunny dawn and, as though reminding us to respect the concept of impermanence, a complete change from yesterday's rain and drizzle, not to mention the sandy beach and paved promenade that replace cutting marshes and bruising brambles. I'm so excited about being back on the peaceful path that I begin singing "We're Off to See the Sorceress, the Wonderful Sorceress Named Circe" to the tune of *We're Off to See the Wizard* from *The Wizard of Oz*.

Luke knows Athêna instructed me to spend a year with Circe, whose father was the sun god Helios and whose mother was an Oceanid called Perse. I told him that an entire year of reflection with Circe illustrates that I'm not totally compulsive about getting around the sea but actually can stop, smell the roses and ponder one of the best parts of Homer's *Odyssey*.

He's a bit skeptical.

"Dad, you can't convince me that you're really going to spend a year with a witch who turned Odysseus' men into pigs!" said Luke, who had first heard bedtime stories about Circe as a child.

"First of all she's not a witch, she's an enchantress," I tell him, though many translations of *The Odyssey* do refer to her as a witch. "The first story I read about her to you was titled *Circe, the Enchantress* with the subtitle *A Sorceress is Outwitted*. Both terms are more applicable than 'witch.' Give her a break!"

Luke first saw a copy of *Myths and Legends of the Ages* when he was a toddler but undoubtedly doesn't remember the details of this written-for-children-in-a-gigantic-font text. It describes Circe as "the beautiful but wicked sorceress" and recounts how Odysseus was given a sprig of a plant that would prevent him from being turned into a swine when Circe commanded him to "Seek thy sty and wallow with thy friends."

We casually stroll past the Guru Lounge and the chic Florida Village complex which promises "*un pizzico* (pinch) *di divertimento* (fun) *in piu* (more)." Then we resist the allure of the Queen Mary Restaurant and the California Beach before making our way through the one-kilometer long pleasure boat port in Lido di Ostia (derived from the Latin *ostium*, which means mouth) and along the bustling seaside adjacent to omnipresent ruins constructed during the period when this was ancient Rome's principal port.

"Imagine this place as long ago as the fourth century BC, when the population could have been more than 100,000 people," I tell Luke. "The mouth of the Tiber, which is often called the yellow or blonde (*flavus*) river, has been extended about three kilometers since Roman times which is why old Ostia, or Ostia Antica, is now inland."

My appraisal of Ostia in my guidebook to Rome particularly described the 15th-century fortress built to defend the city from approaching pirates as well as "exciting excavations which offer a marvelous depiction of the fourth century BC seaport." I added that "the nearby Lido di Ostia is a popular beach among contemporary Romans."

Some things don't change much and today Ostia remains a beacon of contemporary leisure and historical wealth.

Virgil claimed that Aeneas, the Trojan hero whose voyage to what became Rome is recounted in *The Aeneid*, landed here but I had always thought things really got going with the Greeks. However, many contemporary archeologists insist the town's main foundation dates from the period when Rome ruled the Mediterranean. They contend that the original ramparts were erected by Sulla in 79 BC and that, like Rome, everything went downhill/downriver here after the legendary decline and fall of the empire in AD 476. What I find even more noteworthy than Ostia's start or finish is that it wasn't until 1909, after centuries of alluvium deposited by the Tiber were removed, that *Ostia Antica* was rediscovered.

When I visited the excavations forty years ago, I recall being especially impressed by the spacious baths with a detailed mosaic that depicts Poseidon, the blue-maned sea-god that Homer calls "the girdler and shaker of the earth," meeting his wife-to-be Amphitritê. I also noted for some obscure reason that then-modern brick apartment buildings here were built only a few stories high ("No elevators," I scribbled on my note pad decades ago) and that the largest temple, the Capitolium, was dedicated to Jupiter/Zeus, Juno/Hêra and Minerva/Athêna. "Talk about killing lots of gods with a few stones!" I wrote.

Back in the 1970s and 80s the sea was notably more polluted than it is today and I distinctly recall a fish dish I had at a seaside restaurant in Ostia with my pal Ken Melville in 1981. It tasted like cleaning disinfectant on a rotten sponge.

Some things on the Med change for the better and today the water is much clearer and cleaner, and the Ostia tourist port is much more animated, than four decades ago. The seaside is decorated and equipped, not unlike the port I described when I MedTrekked through Barcelona in Spain, "with everything from banks and a McDonald's to chic bars, sensual spas and inviting restaurants." Just beyond the harbor, along the promenade edging into town, a church has been converted into the Moby Dick nightclub, there's another McDonald's (this corporate invader puts other imperialists to shame), a remarkably contemporary glass-and-marble Sprintours building, and a hotel named Ping-Pong.

Luke and I stash our gear on the fourth floor of the Hotel Sirenatta in a room with a gigantic terrace and bay windows that simultaneously expose us to the refreshing breeze and pleasant murmur of the gently lapping sea. As you know I don't ask much from rooms, cribs or squats when I find a base camp for a few days. I almost never make reservations in advance. I love the serendipity of an unplanned outing and the Sirenatta fits the bill.

Our stroll on the promenade through contemporary *Lido di Ostia*

– which itself was founded in 1884 after the malaria-infested marshes on the seaside were reclaimed – takes us along the Roman Riviera that passes between the sturdy low-rise apartment buildings and well-tended beaches, with names like Village and Belsito. Besides the basic amenities (*chaises longues*, umbrellas, *salvataggi* rescue boats, lifeguard towers, sand, sweet water showers and bikini-bottom clad topless bathers) these sandy stretches feature elaborate swimming pools, cabanas, gyms, spinning centers, terraces and spas like the "My Body Beauty" club.

It's no wonder that much of Rome flocks here every weekend. And it's probably because of these pleasant beaches that they've let the cutting swamp survive up north. Yin and yang.

The sky is still clear, the sun is still out and the recent storms have completely faded from memory when we stop for delicious *panini,* that include all sorts of freshly grilled vegetables, at a mobile café-in-a-trailer at the bottom of via Cristoforo Colombo.

Shortly after that, however, our sand stroll is rudely interrupted when we reach the Lido Presidential. A spiffy army officer tells us that we'll have to hit the tarmac for three kilometers until we pass the military-controlled sector of beach. The fenced-off area is distinguished by six high tower outposts, not unlike those that the *Forces Auxiliaries* have on every hilltop in Morocco, to spy on interlopers daring enough to try to climb the two razor-wire fences and thrash through the daunting underbrush to get to the president, or whoever might be enjoying the luxury inside. The road, with not too much traffic, is the easier, softer way unless we want to dodge bullets from bored guards.

On the other side of the Lido Presidential we walk through the Paradise Beach Club and return to SandTrek through a long stretch of nudist and gay beaches, each with well-displayed recycling bins. There is a flurry of six-color rainbowishy gay pride flags and lots of naked guys not making much effort to conceal their packages or intentions in the undulating dunes. Luke and I catch (but, fortunately, don't capture on camera) what we agree is the most overt man-to-man blowjob that either of us has seen in public or private. One very tall, tanned and young man is standing on the top of a slightly elevated hillock, in plain sight, of not only us but also everyone else, while his partner is on his knees very energetically trying to suck the chrome off a human trailer hitch. The scene is outrageously brazen and I'm not sure I could play either role.

Not that I'm completely insensitive to playing the organ. In fact, blowjobs were a big part of my life when I co-founded a company called TastiCum. I co-developed a supplement that changed the flavor of natural semen to make it more palatable to women. The flavors included brazen banana, blissful blueberry, cheery cherry, sinful chocolate, calorie-free clove, crazy cranberry, honeyed hazelnut, kinky kiwi, magical mint, pulsating pineapple, reassuring raspberry, seductive strawberry, tangy tangerine, tempting tiramisu, very vanilla, and kicking kumquat. The vitamin-rich supplement, with its patented "TastiCum™ Semen Shooter" delivery system, was billed by one journalist as "the next Viagra" and by another as "revolutionary as the birth control pill."

"I've done a lot of outrageous things in public, but I don't think I'd have the balls to do that," I say to Luke as I can't help but watch the sexual ballet reach its uninterruptus finale. Then to change the subject I expand Deng Ming-Dao's philosophic contention that "going to the beach means walking in fresh air, listening to the sound of waves, feeling the grit of sand beneath our feet" by adding "and letting it all hang out while getting it off."

"What were the most embarrassing moments in your life?" Luke asks to avoid pursuing a pro-and-con discussion about the issue at hand and mouth.

"A few awkward incidents come back to me fairly frequently," I reply without hesitation. "I'll never forget how dumb I felt when I was sitting, stone sober, next to Joseph Stein, who wrote *Fiddler on the Roof*, in a packed auditorium at Columbia University in 1971 and mistakenly accused film critic Andrew Sarris at the podium of plagiarism. Another time I screamed at a guy for parking in a handicapped spot in Paris, which most people did at the time because they were never ticketed, and when he got out of the car he was missing a leg.

"Then there were all the things that involved drinking. I got nailed for pissing in the middle of Boulevard Saint-Germain in Paris, got caught shoplifting for Christmas presents at a bookstore in New York, and told a cop that 'I'm going to get you when I get out of here,' when I was tossed in the clink for a night. But now it seems I could give a blowjob on a gay beach and nobody would mind. I was born at the wrong time.

"I certainly never thought that at this stage of life I'd be taking a hike," I continue as I take a rapid inventory of my most embarrassing moments. "Heck, some people think walking around the Mediterranean is an embarrassment. I even think you were a bit ashamed at one point when you were younger because you said: 'You mean now I'm supposed to tell my friends that my father is walking around the Mediterranean as a job? Uh, I don't think so.'"

"Well, it did seem a little strange at first," Luke retorts. "And even though you told me it was creative, I spoke to some people who said you were having a mid-life crisis."

A mid-life creative crisis/venture, which some experts consider a key aspect of a healthy aging process, is either a complete contrast to the professional and personal existence that preceded it or a continuation of, and complement to, established personal and professional interests. In my case, luckily perhaps, it was the latter. I've always hiked in offbeat places, gone on retreats at monasteries throughout the world and usually written about my experiences and exploits.

The three-to-four months that I spend MedTrekking each year (it's too hot, crowded and expensive in mid-summer and frequently too cold in mid-winter so I prefer spring and autumn outings) are a constant educational experience as I improve my language skills, enjoy an ongoing history lesson and visit undiscovered territory, like virginal northern Morocco and locations straight out of the pages of *The Odyssey*.

The project gives me an opportunity to practice Deng Ming-Dao's adage that "experience is the ultimate teacher. That is why wise people travel constantly and test themselves against the flux of circumstance. It is only in this way that they can truly confirm their thoughts and compensate for their shortcomings."

As you'll see in this book, the flux of circumstance and experience is alluring, seductive and unpredictable. I exult when the gods sing to me at the top of Mount Olympus in northern Greece; I shiver when I'm serenaded by the sirens that tempted Odysseus while hiking the Amalfi Coast in Italy; and I have some Eureka "ahh omm" moments when I find Homer's purported birthplace on Chios and Zeus' cave on Crete.

But be forewarned that any worthwhile adventure has a downside and I'm now jobless and partnerless. MedTrekking and the travel time it requires is not, it turns out, conducive to marriage. Fortunately Athêna keeps me alive, smiling and on the path with very little distraction or down time. And now her terse words in Rome have me traipsing down the Italian coast to spend a year on a mountaintop with a sorceress.

Incidentally, a bit down the road I'll again meet up with Athêna, who was born from the aching head of Zeus. She'll be attired in a long white robe outside a temple dedicated to her in Paestum, Italy. And when we later meet at the summits of Mount Olympus in Greece and Mount Ida in Turkey she'll be wearing her "quadruple-crested, golden, double-ridged helmet enchased with men-at-arms."

I also have a great deal of respect for the goddess Circe. She's one of many key women in *The Odyssey* who, if you add them together, have a tremendous impact not only on the narrative and the fate of Odysseus but also on the depiction of women. Look at them all – Athêna, Circe, Kalypso, Klytemnestra, Helen, The Sirens – and you have what Froma Zeitlin, one of the many Homer scholars I meet on this journey, calls "archetypal forms of the feminine."

"I'm really much more enthused about running into Circe and

other women from Homeric times than these guys on the dunes," I tell Luke. "I'm fairly sure that they, not this, are key to my destiny."

The females depicted in Homer don't have much in common with contemporary Italian women who, to a great extent, are behind the times. Italian women still do most of the housework because the majority of Italian men, who unabashedly cherish their international image as self-indulgent mama's boys, don't know how to operate a washing machine. And Italian TV, which frequently resembles the Playboy Channel, is still replete with sexy, leggy, provocative women playing announcers, showgirls or dancers on most of the news shows, reality shows, game shows and commercials.

The anachronistic phenomenon and puerile fascination with sexy Italian women on TV has become such a custom and tradition in Italy that the on-screen girls, frequently known as *veline* (one translation for *veline* is "slips of paper" because the women are usually svelte and appear nearly naked), become national figures and wind up as models, on calendars or as wives of football stars. They've become so popular in celebrity-worshipping Italy that becoming a *veline* is still a frequent career choice for young girls.

Italian women are not only frequently denigrated and humiliated on Italian television shows, but Italy also ranks very low in terms of women's rights. Women in Italy constitute a smaller percentage of the workforce than in any other EU country and Italian working women make less than half the salary of their male counterparts.

Throughout his terms as prime minister, Silvio Berlusconi, who frequently gave political posts to former *veline* during his 17-year reign (the most appropriate word for his time in power), managed to insult the dignity of many Italian women with childish and politically incorrect antics both at parties and in politics. Yet he was frequently reelected.

Why?

I watched *Videocracy* – a documentary about the Italian fascination with Italian *veline*, television and the Berlusconi influence – and it's apparent that in many cases male looks, money, power and prestige trump common sense much more often in Italy than elsewhere.

The counterpart of this primitive and demeaning situation is that women still control much of what happens in the family in Italy. That influence lasts quite a while because over half of all Italians between the ages of 18 and 34 still live at home.

We get to the outskirts of Torvaianica. Although the sandy beaches are wide enough and there is an easy-enough-to-walk-on urban promenade, the city consists mostly of unattractive brick buildings that blemish the landscape for three or four blocks back from the sea. I'm not an investment adviser but personally I wouldn't buy any property here. It's not the next Montenegro, which I've recently been assured is THE place to invest, though I won't put any money there either.

Although Virgil mentions in the *Aeneid* that Aeneas also landed here, this place is deadly. In fact, we see a pool of fresh blood left by a pedestrian who was hit by a bus as it cruised into a bus stop. I'll find as time goes by that this image frequently haunts me and often zips through my mind whenever I see a bus near a stop.

Torvaianica derives its name from Torre del Vajanico, a now-demolished watch tower built here in 1580 to stave off Barbary pirates. The town was built in the 1940s and stretches along the coast for eight kilometers. The first advertisement we see on the beach is for the "We're Sorry Mama" tattoo studio. Good luck with that.

It brings to mind my own tattoo – a somewhat discreet blackish-and-reddish tramp stamp consisting of a yin and yang symbol surrounded by bluish Mediterranean waves. It made my own Mama gasp. I got needled during a "Thirty-Three Years Since Woodstock" party that I threw in the south of France in 2002 when the entertainment in my gigantic yard also consisted of folksingers, masseuses, piercers and dozens of kids handling the parking, bar and serving. I had to be the first to get a tattoo to kick off a memorable evening. Though I occasionally see the tat in photos, I'm rarely aware that it's there. I'm reminded of it, however, every time I meet someone who drunkenly picked up a tat during the night, and then I recall why I like my own. It was designed to honor the MedTrek.

"The ten thousand things carry yin and embrace yang," according to Lao Tsu in the *Tao Te Ching*. "They achieve harmony by combining these forces….For one gains by losing and loses by gaining."

Once we get back on the sandy path, Luke and I notice there's a construction project underway to repair portions of the washed-away promenade on the southern side of difficult-to-pronounce Torvaianica.

Fortunately we don't need a manmade promenade because this is perhaps the best walking sand I've encountered in Italy. Compact from being washed by the waves during a few days of stormy weather, it's easy to hike as the sea calms and retreats from the high water mark. There are no major rivers and we stroll peacefully for almost four hours on the Spiaggia di Rio Torto and along lidos/beaches with enticing names like Meduse, Lollia, Pini, Gigli, Enea, Cincinnato, Sirene and Marechiaro. We don't even really notice, as we maintain a speedier-than-usual 5.1 kilometer-per-hour clip, that we've walked through the small towns of Marina di Ardea and Lido di Lavinio because the buildings are set far back from the sea, though I do see a via called *Ulisse* (the first of many streets named after Odysseus/Ulysses) and a hotel called Kalypso. Lots of fit women and buff men, generally attired in what Luke calls "good thongs," are putting the final touches of the summer on their already dark tans.

The only minor disruption is that sometime, somewhere, Luke's cell phone fell out of his pack and he leaves me to backtrack for forty-five minutes before (1) miraculously finding his phone in the sand and (2) taking a bus to catch up with me. Without any telephone communication (his phone isn't charged which, I have to admit, is a frequent occurrence) he gets off the bus at the exact place I'm walking (Only I, not he, insist on walking every centimeter of the seaside during my MedTrek. Luke occasionally exercises his right of retreat if not cheat).

"Instinct and estimation," Luke claims when I ask how he found me so quickly. "I know everything about you after all this walking."

What he sees in me is a far cry from a mirror image of himself because we're not at all alike. I'm a recovering alcoholic who, despite decades of meetings, meditation and spiritual retreats, still has a habit, mentally anyway, of turning snails into dinosaurs. Luke, though he may occasionally be camouflaging his anxiety, has much greater equilibrium and a calmer disposition that enable him to shrink dinosaurs into snails.

We've chatted more than once about our genetic similarities and personality differences, often contrasting my outrageous behavior in the 1960s – a very free sex, cheap drugs, and loud rock & roll kinda decade – with Luke's much more balanced, polite, and faithful rolling stone approach to life in the 2000s.

"It was a different era," I said when we were enjoying *gelati* at the Tre Scalini in Rome's Piazza Navona the other day. "Extremism was encouraged. The wilder the better. Cops tolerated it, women tolerated it. Even your grandmother tolerated it. It tossed many lives upside down but also gave a lot of us the self-confidence to abandon traditional career paths and pursue numerous more adventurous lives. I mean, who thought that at sixty I would have given up my day job and be walking around the sea with my son? How glorious! But today I unquestionably agree with Deng Ming-Dao that 'an act that leaves destruction, resentment, or untidiness in its wake is a poor one.' And I had my share of those."

I hadn't planned to give up my day job writing a column in Hollywood when my first book about the MedTrek was published. After all, covering celebrities and premieres was a cushy life that provided a nice balance to walking on the Med. Balance, after all, is what I sought and that job certainly got the book a lot more coverage than if I'd been a mortician.

I blame my career change, and retirement from my Hollywood life and column, partly on a bookstore owner in Sandy Bay, Tasmania, who told me "an author's work really begins after he writes 'The End.'" That encouraged me to stop attending Hollywood events to completely embrace the relative unknown of the book world. I decided to dedicate myself to promoting *The Idiot and the Odyssey*.

I've never, even in Hollywood or the south of France, had so much fun "working" in my life.

Although many authors complain about the task and toil of marketing their books, I relish talking to the media, meeting bookstore personnel and chatting with readers and book clubs. In fact, I consider this to be one of the project's most enjoyable benefits. When I'm not walking/researching/reporting/writing on the Mediterranean, I'm talking about the MedTrek or keeping readers up-to-speed on my website, blog, Facebook, Twitter and other social networks.

This pleasant SideTrek (I add Trek to everything I do these days – MedTrek, SandTrek, TaxTrek, DogTrek….) has become almost as time-consuming as the walk itself. I visited more than a hundred independent bookstores in Australia, have given readings to crowds of various sizes from Paris to Shanghai, and even made presentations at sea while staying in a spacious stateroom on a Mediterranean cruise ship. More recently, I've had a blast talking to high school kids in Florida and Virginia (It takes a fairly adventurous school to let me loose on creative writing and critical thinking classes) and guest-guiding walking tours on the French Riviera.

This type of diverse reaction not only feeds my sometimes-inflated sense of self, though I must admit that it reminds me of something that T.E. Lawrence wrote: "There was a craving to be famous; and a horror of being known to like being known."

It also encourages me to MedTrek more than 8,800 kilometers, requiring more than ten million footsteps, to produce this book that you're now reading.

Luke takes pictures of portable lifeguard stands, fishing boats and a statement scrawled on a cement bench that says, in English, "Go Away." But his most intriguing shot is of a naked baby boy doll. "He's probably not Jewish," wrote one viewer about the dollish organ when I posted it on Facebook.

Photographs mark a major change between the first and second *Idiot* books. I shunned using a camera for most of the first 4,401 kilometers because I felt it would detract from my concentration on the hike itself. And I always felt I could get a professional photographer to collaborate with me and shoot the most interesting aspects of the

MedTrek. But Luke starts a trend that keeps me taking photos, the ones you'll see throughout these pages, until I get to Troy. My publicist created a blog called *Follow the Idiot* that has become the repository for my movements, self-deprecating thoughts, witty and wry observations and photographs. And I begin a separate project called "Athens (or whatever city I might be in) par iPhone" by creating Facebook photo albums in different cities.

Now I'm thinking of getting a number (50) of different photographers to shoot the Med based on different parts of, and anecdotes in, my books – the monkish monastery on Île Saint-Honorat, the good-bad-ugly-very ugly nudist colony in Cap d'Agde, the cliff I fell off of in Morocco, the sorceress in Spain, the thieving Roma in Italy, you get the drift. A contemporary rip-off of the old *Day in the Life of....* books that came out in the 1980s. I might even include a couple of my own pictures.

A number of the private low-rise apartment buildings can be entered by owners through tunnels on the beach if they have keys to the firmly locked, and often rusted, steel doors. This is a good way to keep out MedTrekking interlopers, though Luke and I do climb over a few fences to wander through private villas when the waves or rising water restrict our movement along the sea.

This reminds me that the Mediterranean region is likely to be hard hit by global climate change and a higher sea that could impact health, food production and tourism. I mention to Luke that a Mediterranean Climate Change Initiative is underway to jointly invest in the long-term health of the Mediterranean environment.

"I'm not holding my breath!" he replies.

We reach Tor Caldara on the outskirts of Anzio after 18 kilometers and continue along the beaches and cliffs until, just after a resort and restaurant called Saint-Tropez, we discover a remarkable *fin de trek* architectural site partially submerged in the sea.

Anzio, which greets us with an array of pleasant villas, is supposed to have been founded by Anteo, the son Odysseus may have had with Circe, though there's an equally strong argument that it's named after Ascanius, the son of Aeneas. Way back in the day, when it was known as Antium, this was the capital of the Volsci and the base for Coriolanus's rebellion against Rome. Then the Romans nabbed it and turned it into an upscale neighborhood with ostentatious villas along the shore. The popular location was just far enough away from Rome to avoid being impacted by riots in the capital.

The chic and in-demand Antium/Anzio dates from around the eighth century BC and is a namedropper's delight. Emperors Augustus,

Tiberius, and Caligula all lived in the much-recycled imperial palace here, and Cicero put his scrolls in the local library when he returned from exile. Nero, who like Caligula was born in Antium, built the sea-view villas that are now part of an archeological park near the lighthouse that we pass just as the sun is beginning to set. His own villa is thought to have taken up 800 meters of seafront and he also built a harbor and established a colony for war veterans.

Cicero called the nearby Torre Astura a *locus amoenus,* which means "pleasant place" in Latin, but Augustus and Tiberius both caught illnesses here that led to their deaths. Guess where artworks like the *Apollo Belvedere* in the Vatican and the *Borghese Gladiator* in the Louvre were found? Yup, right here.

Odysseus was supposedly here long before all this and one brochure contends that the "Big O came here on his way home after the Trojan War."

We reach the fishing port and, a few beaches later, the pleasure-boat port to see remnants of a fortress built in 1100 to defend the city against the Saracens. There's also a monument commemorating Anzio as the site of a bloody campaign during World War II in early 1944, where the Allies beat the Germans to ultimately liberate Rome.

After another three kilometers we arrive in Nettuno, which gets its name from (you guessed it) the Roman god Neptune and is twinned with Bandol in the south of France. Bandol, you might recall if you read my first volume, is the place where Luke, quite a few years younger than he is now, was too tired to walk after the 27 kilometers he marched on his first-ever MedTrek outing. Today we've both walked 31 kilometers into a town that was founded by the Saracens in the ninth century and I'm the one who's extremely stiff. This night we eat at Restaurant Elisio that serves *non sole pesce* ("not just fish") before checking into a beachside room in the three-star Hotel Marocca, twenty meters from the sea.

The next morning we visit the moving Sicily-Rome American Cemetery and Memorial before continuing down the coast. The cemetery for American military personnel killed during World War II is on 77 acres and contains 7,861 designated graves on impeccably kept green lawns with pines and cypress trees. Most of the soldiers died during the liberation of Sicily and at landings near Salerno and Anzio in 1943-44, and there are a number of maps depicting the different military campaigns. A cenotaph has the names of 3,095 missing combatants with rosettes indicating the deceased whose remains have been recovered and identified.

The cemetery is a humbling reminder of World War II's

devastation, and it's somewhat comforting to remember that the American soldiers are also credited with bringing baseball to Nettuno and its team, the Nettuno Baseball Club, is occasionally one of the best in the country.

I've always enjoyed the tranquility of cemeteries and the reflection they provoke. As I walk through this peaceful military burial ground I have a flashback to grave rubbing in New England in the 1960s, frequently getting lost in the maze that is Père Lachaise in Paris in the 1970s, and determining, in the 1980s, that some of my own ashes should be placed in the comparatively small, sloping, and comfortable cemetery near my home in Valbonne, France.

At the Sicily-Rome American Cemetery I have a fifteen-minute conversation with the caretaker, an American man about my age. We casually chat about the glory, if that's the right word, of the battles and burials during World War II compared to the general dishonor and disrespect shown to many soldiers who fought in Vietnam. The discussion evokes, as I quietly walk with Luke amidst the stark and severe white crosses, memories of my friends who lost their lives in Vietnam, both those killed in the war and others deadened in spirit for long afterwards by the trauma of the war. I make a commitment to walk for all of them.

I tell Luke about a ship I was taking from Southampton to New York in 1965 when I first met Americans who were vocally opposed to the Vietnam conflict and how I actively protested against it and refused the unjust draft, though I was ultimately exempted for both a bad knee with a big scar and a high lottery number drawn in a perverted selection system to determine who would fight.

"If you were white and upper middle class you could get out of that war and it was precisely that fact that made me realize how life worked in the United States," I tell Luke. "I told one recruiter that God didn't want me to fight and quoted Homer who had Menelàos proclaim in *The Iliad* that 'to enter combat when the will of gods is against you – to fight a man god loves – that's doom, and quickly' but that didn't help."

I describe how badly the troops were treated, mention how I was in Hong Kong in 1967 and met troops on a break who were either suicidal or convinced they'd be killed. I end the tale by describing how differently, and respectfully, soldiers are treated in the United States today.

The next morning at daybreak we leave the Marocca Hotel on the beach (we literally jump over the balcony outside our room onto the sand) and thank some immigrant workers cleaning the seafront. After our first pleasant kilometer, an intimidating fence makes it clear that it's forbidden to enter a *zona militario*. We speak to a guard who tells us that "shooting and explosion testing" will be occurring throughout the morning but "if you take responsibility for anything that happens you can enter at 1:00 p.m. Otherwise you'll have to walk on the inland road, the Via Acciarella, that abuts the *zona militario*."

Who can wait until one? We pass the entrance to this gigantic 12-kilometer long (as the bullets fly) seaside military zone, where there's even a sign in English announcing "Checkpoint: Show I.D." and take off on via Acciarella. Because it's narrow and a short cut for trucks, it's one of the more dangerous pedestrian roads in Italy and we've both seen enough of it after 15 kilometers, when we finally get around the coastal fortress to the seaside.

Luke is wearing the bright orange Day-Glo suicide smock while I sport a not-quite-so-bright orange T with "California" written in bold letters on the front. Neither provides much protection, even psychologically, as we pass the very-much-out-of-place Kinsale Irish Pub and keep seeing signs that remind us that we're walking next to a gigantic enclosure with *Esplosiones Improvise*. Those reminders, despite the traffic, make us happier to be on this side of the fence.

Our colorful garb does little to impress two Nigerian hookers we meet. In fact, they ask us for "a €10 *regalo*, or gift, because you're white and European and we're black and African."

This leads me into ruminations about hookers and I tell Luke about the role of prostitutes in history and literature, specifically in books like *Catcher in the Rye*, before relating my own somewhat limited experience with streetwalkers. I start with a description of how my first "date" in San Francisco cracked me up as much as anyone has ever cracked me up when we walked up two flights of stairs to her room, decorated with a red blanket carelessly thrown over a dimly lit table lamp. We heard the client of another "date," who was obviously on the job, coughing ferociously and my date said to me with not too much concern that "he's gonna die before he cums."

I describe my assignations with hookers in various other parts of the world, including the interviews I had with, and articles I wrote about, Madame Billy and Madame Claude in Paris, and additional research I undertook for a story with some escort girls in Amsterdam. To prevent Luke from feeling like he missed a major part of life, I also describe how the entire business changed when AIDS became prevalent in the 1980s. Then I remind him of the time that we were walking down rue Saint-Denis in Paris after I told Luke how you could determine the state of the French economy by the price of, and demand for, the hookers. When I nonchalantly asked one how much it cost for a trick, she apparently thought I was inquiring on behalf of my then twelve-year-old son and began hitting me with her purse.

As I hear some booming *esplosiones* I tell the Nigerian girls that they should consider switching locations.

"Nobody can really concentrate on sex with all this noise," I explain to them.

"What're they doing out here?" Luke asks.

"It's unlikely they chose this type of life," I say to him. "And unlikely they have much choice about what will come next."

Twelve Mediterranean Labors Conceived by Cunning Circe

The road, with vineyards and lots of horses and cows on the left, continues along the *zona militario*. Our MedTrek towards *Torre di Foce Verde* is now punctuated with improvised ear-shattering explosions. But even the historical *Torre Astura*, formerly an island but now a peninsula, is off limits to MedTrekkers and I'm bothered that there's more litter than usual on this country road. Perhaps the sound of soldiers shooting rapid-fire rounds, which we first hear when we're buying luscious green grapes from a local farmer, scares the litter out of passersby.

We stop for coffee, sandwiches, and olives in Foce Verde before tackling the beach and pleasant promenade on the Strada Lungomare between the Lago di Fogliano and the Lido di Latina. These and other lakes are a favored landing spot for migratory birds and today, a Sunday, there are also plenty of joggers and bikers, but only two MedTrekkers, on the Lungomare Pontino. We are all urged by numerous signs to "Save the Dunes." We descend to the sand dunes down one of the dozens of nice wooden staircases leading to the beach, where the sea has quieted down after the recent storms.

At this stage we're in the lake-filled, 8.5-square-kilometer *Parco Nazionale del Circeo* – Circe's National Park – that was created in 1934 and is now one of UNESCO's protected nature reserves.

At one point, I step on a long garter snake that, as it scurries away, fails to even slightly frighten one of the nearby buffalo responsible for the region's excellent mozzarella cheese. Luke peels some bark from a birch tree to protect his sunburned arms before we cut back down to the sea on the narrow coastal strip between Anzio and Terracina. After a refreshing dip at 5:00 p.m., we reach the jet-set star-struck resort of Sabaudia, a city of almost 20,000 people that is just over 100 walking kilometers (and 91 kilometers by road) from Rome.

"It's very expensive and I could never afford to live here," says a barmaid of German-Spanish origin after charging us €5 for two cokes at a café at the Monaci beach. "I stay in the mountainous back country because this place is becoming the 'Portofino' of the Tyrrhenian Sea."

Luke and I kick off the next day with a charming seven-kilometer sandy beach walk, half barefoot and half shod, during which he takes a shirtless photo of me that's been my Facebook profile picture since the day I friended myself. We're gleefully walking towards the home of Circe on Monte Circeo, whose 541-meter summit looks modestly high at sea level and gets higher and higher as we get closer and closer.

When we reach the foot of Mount Circeo, which was called Aeaea when the bards were singing the tale of Odysseus landing on Circe's island, I tell Luke that we're now on the Ulysses Riviera. Odysseus may have initially landed south of here in Gaeta before he encountered the sorceress Circe, although some Homerphiles believe his encounter with the Cyclops occurred just north of Naples.

Luke immediately points out that Homer was wrong when he called Aeaea an island.

"This obviously isn't an island because it's attached to the land," he exclaims when we approach on the beach.

He's right.

"Homer called it an island but it's undeniably not one today," I agree. "But it still looked like one as we approached by the sea, and I'll bet it looks like one from the sea to the south too. Maybe it was an island back in the day or maybe Homer needed glasses. In fact, a lot of people think that if he existed he was blind which could be another explanation."

Mount Circeo is most certainly now a cape or promontory and Strabo, the renowned geographer born around 64 BC and author of the 17-volume *Geographica*, contended that "Circaeum is a mountain which has the form of an island because it is surrounded by sea and marshes."

Some contend that the Promontory of Circeo looks like Circe's body, or profile, which is why they call the highest peak "Circe's Nose." When I look at it, I often imagine that it is the face and body of a reclining Odysseus.

My friend Maria Rizzi, a photographer from Massachusetts whom I first met in Paris in the 70s, was once married to an Italian count and lived in the shadow of Monte Circeo. She became a believer in its influence.

"The mountain, without doubt, has magical powers and I began to believe in, and was pulled by all of the ancient gods and goddesses," Maria told me. "I became very attracted by the liberty and freedom that they represented before Christianity introduced the idea of guilt. That was the time when it was an honor to be a lover, when mortals were considered god-like themselves. I became convinced that I was the goddess of love in a previous lifetime."

Whatever the geological truth, nobody, especially tourism promoters, wants to let go of the connection to Circe.

As we approach the mountain we can see the five-hundred-year-old Torre Paola, a Roman tower fortification at the western end of the island/promontory, and after studying *il sentiero del promontorio*, a map of multiple webbed rambling paths and trails, we begin a steep climb up a shady but sweat-provoking path to the summit. The arduous hike makes the peak seem much higher than 541 meters.

Along the way we have views back to the Sabaudia lakes, out to the uninhabited volcanic Pontine Islands in the sea, below to the half dozen grottos associated with Circe, and down the coast to Terracina. There are signs around the mountain that advise visitors to "Watch Out For Deer" but none, oddly, saying "Watch Out For Pigs." In fact, the deer sign isn't completely inappropriate because when Odysseus arrived here he almost immediately shot a buck with an arrow.

I'm surprised that the very steep climb gets me breathing heavily and sweating profusely within a few minutes and a stretch of rough rock walking truly tests my dexterity. We get a bit scratched and cut up following some *faux pas* and feel particularly distant from nearby humanity when we run into some Swiss hikers who've run out of water. It's a big mistake to stray from the various hiking paths and almost impossible to make it down through the foliage to the seaside grottos.

Circe's forest, which I'll wind up visiting at various times and seasons during the next year, is almost always dense, dark and witch-crafty. I'm in no hurry to explore the entire island/cape, but it's a perfect time and place to provide more details of the tale of Circe to Luke.

It takes a good look at Book Ten of *The Odyssey*, which is unfortunately entitled *The Grace of the Witch* in the Fitzgerald translation, to get all of the details about Circe, and I spin bits and pieces of the tale to Luke throughout the day.

"When Odysseus and the boys landed on Aeaea it was already known as the island of Circe, who's described in *The Odyssey* as a 'dire beauty and divine,' and they docked in that cove," I say, pointing to a small harbor which Odysseus describes as "a haven for the ship – some god, invisible, conned us in."

"Twenty-two crewmen went out to find Circe's 'woodland hall… and smooth stone house' in the middle of a clearing in a dense forest where Odysseus had seen a wisp of smoke. When they got there, Circe was weaving ambrosial fabric on her loom and singing in a beguiling voice amidst wolves and mountain lions," I continue a bit later, occasionally closing my eyes to transport myself back in time and evoke additional details. "Things looked good at first when Circe gave the men a meal of cheese, barley and amber honey mixed with Pramnian wine.

But unbeknownst to them she also added a pinch of a secret 'drug of evil' and their bodies, voices and heads became just like those of pigs being led to slaughter.

"One sailor, Eurylokhos, who was shrewdly skeptical about Circe and convinced that she did the 'devil's work,' returned to the ship, gave Odysseus the bad news about the crew and told him 'to make sail… and save ourselves from horror while we may.'

"When the mighty warrior went to check things out for himself, he met the messenger god and 'bright pathfinder' Hermês who, as usual, was carrying his golden wand. Hermês told Odysseus how to thwart Circe by imbibing a 'magic plant with a black root and milky flower called a *molü* in the language of the gods.…a great herb with holy force' that would keep his mind and senses clear. Hermês, who lights the way for mortals, 'bent to tie his beautiful sandals that carry him over water and over endless land on a puff of wind' and Odysseus followed instructions and consumed the moly, as it's known in English. When Circe gave him a 'golden cup of honeyed wine' that contained her unholy drug, it didn't faze him a bit. In fact, her reaction was the first time the world ever heard the expression 'Holy Moly.'

"Circe, who'd been warned that Odysseus would appear on her doorstep, knew right away that she'd met the 'great tactician' and, trying another lure, encouraged him to 'put your weapon in the sheath. We two shall mingle and make love upon our bed. So mutual trust may come of play and love.'

"Odysseus winds up sleeping with Circe but only, in one of the quickest bits of dialogue written by Homer, after making her promise not to pull any tricks before they go through the usual bath-and-oil foreplay. After they bed down, he remembers to get his companions freed from the sty. Circe turns them back into men and they all, like I'll do while I'm here, 'feast long on roasts and wine, until a year grew fat.'

"They seem to completely forget that they are sailing home, and it takes a while for Odysseus' men to finally remind their errant leader of his duty: 'Captain, shake off this trance, and think of home— if home indeed awaits us, if we shall ever see your own well-timbered hall on Ithaka' and he finally tells Circe — in her flawless bed of love — that he must depart.

'Not so quick,' she tells Odysseus. 'You shall not stay here longer against your will; but home you may not go unless you take a strange way round and come to the cold homes of Death and pale Persephone.'

"Some readers of *The Odyssey* interpret that as Circe telling the departing Odysseus to 'go to hell.' In fact, she pilots him on his journey into the underworld to hear the prophecy of the blind seer Teiresias and to pour out libations to the unnumbered dead before he returns to Aeaea to learn about upcoming confrontations with the Sirens, Scylla, and Charybdis. By the time Odysseus leaves, Circe has become his mentor and given him advice that saves his life, if not the lives of his crew.

"Without Circe, Odysseus might not have survived and I respect a woman savior with that kind of rep," I tell Luke. "I'll listen carefully to anything she has to say and when I'm done you can come back and join me. By then I'll know the place like the bottom of my feet."

Our final walking stint into San Felice Circeo, about three kilometers from the island's lighthouse, is on a shady, tree-lined path.

When we arrive in town, I illuminate a few coin-sparked candles in the small, ten-seat chapel of Chiesa Santa Maria della Pietà Madonella, which contains a statue of Saint Francis of Assisi, an old vestibule with a crumbly painting of Christ on the ceiling and a replica of Michelangelo's *Pietà*. Then, having made a gesture of goodwill and an appeal for luck in my search for Circe, we have a sandwich and cappuccinos on the town's pleasing main piazza that's blocked to traffic.

San Felice Circeo is built on the site of Circeii, a fortress of the ancient Volsci people that became a Roman colony in 393 BC. We check into the Albergo Pensione Giardino degli Ulivi that has a spectacular view of both the mountainside and Terracina.

It's probably worth mentioning that we didn't check into two other very luxurious living options on the seaside part of the island. Both the Isola di Eea "*relais* bed & brunch" at Quarto Caldo and the inviting Hotel Punta Rosa would have wiped out my annual Circe budget. I wasn't even tempted by the promise, seemingly sincere, at the Isola di Eea that "you can almost see and feel the same things Ulysses did during his stay with Circe."

Circe, of course, is a little more difficult to find today than she was in Odysseus' time, because it's now forbidden to light campfires here and I don't see a wisp of smoke. In fact, I'd be lying if I said Luke and I caught sight of Circe the first day we climbed the surprisingly steep mountain. Luke then returned to London and it took me seven days before the enchantress appeared.

Circe, who resembles Isadora Duncan as she looked when she danced at the Theater of Dionysus in Athens in 1903, is still the same Timothy Leary-like drug dealing seductress she was around 1180 BC. Although she hasn't changed much physically since Odysseus met her, she's matured. For one thing, when we meet while I'm walking near the Prigionieri grotto she doesn't immediately "entice me into her chamber, to her dangerous bed, to take my manhood when she has me stripped…in her flawless bed of love."

Instead she encourages me to carry *The Iliad* and *The Odyssey* with me throughout the island and slowly re-read both books, underlining passages that have to do with heroism, bravery, foolishness, romance, and her.

"I've been instructed by Athêna to help you, and the first thing I want you to do is change your attitude about the walk you're making around the Mediterranean," she says. "You've obviously inherited some traits from both Homer and Odysseus and what you're doing is important to their memories. This is not just a simple hike. It is a legendary quest and you must treat it as such. It's my job to prepare you for what's ahead."

During my first month on the island, Circe and I meet daily near the place where "she set the air a-tingle on lawns and paven courts" to discuss everything about Homer, Odysseus and the gods. She also, in various conversations, interjects thoughts about how – from attitude to experiences, from head/brain to toe/feet – I should pursue the MedTrek as though I myself am Odysseus incarnate.

"You must know both books by heart just like the rhapsodes did," she counsels me. "And in return I'll tell you where each anecdote and vignette in *The Odyssey* actually took place. You'll know, by the time we're done, where the Cyclops lived; where Zeus, "the gatherer of cloud, the lord of storm and lightning" as Homer calls him, was born; how to find the entrance to the underworld, as Hades was frequently called; and the location of the Laestrygonian cannibals. You'll know more about Homer than any mortal walking the earth today."

I tell her that a lot of my perceptions about the characters in Homer's books are forged by Myths and Legends of the Ages, which was published in 1951, and that these childhood lessons and perceptions merged with the more serious and literary versions of Homer I've read.

"These are myths and can be joyous in their various tellings," she says. "But during the next few years you'll get know the mythic reality in a way that very few contemporary men can. You're lucky to have been chosen."

Circe, whom Odysseus calls "the loveliest of all immortals," says she wants to get me in good shape before she gives me any firm instruction about where I'm supposed to be heading and what I'm supposed to be doing on my seaside MedTrek. Each Sunday morning we sit in the lovely piazza in San Felice for coffee before practicing walking meditation to make supplication to the gods for the health of every sentient being.

I'm surprised that Circe is actually interested in walking meditation, and I gradually teach her what I've learned from Thich Nhat Hanh and other practitioners. During the months we're together, I drop seemingly pithy phrases into our conversation that combine to give her an idea what it's all about. "Walking meditation is for your enjoyment. It is not hard labor."...."The practice of walking meditation opens your eyes to the wonders and the suffering of the universe."...."Peace is the walk. Happiness is the walk. Walk for yourself and you walk for everyone."

Again stealing from the pros, I also provide her with some tangible logistical assistance offered by Thich Nhat Hanh in *The Long Road Turns to Joy* and, though I'm just the messenger, she seems really appreciative when, for a solid month, we practice early each morning in the energy of pure air, which I tell her is the best time to enjoy walking meditation.

"When you begin to practice walking meditation, you might feel unbalanced, like a baby learning to walk," I say, continuing to paraphrase from the masters. "Follow your breathing, dwell mindfully on your steps and soon you'll find your balance. Visualize a tiger walking slowly and you will find that your steps become as majestic as his. Walk upright with calm, dignity and joy, as though you are an emperor."

Circe has particular trouble smiling when she walks, and the hardest thing for her to understand is that "smiling as you practice walking meditation will keep your steps calm and peaceful, and give you a deep sense of ease. A smile refreshes your whole being and strengthens your practice. Don't be afraid to smile."

I am very surprised when one day she throws a phrase from Thich Nhat Hanh's book *Be Still and Know* right back at me.

"You know why I don't smile all the time?" she asks. "Because I read that 'if while we practice, we are not aware that the world is suffering, that children are dying of hunger, that social injustice is going on a little bit everywhere, we are not practicing mindfulness. We are just trying to escape.' That's why I don't smile."

By the time I'm ready to leave, she is smiling and what truly amazes me is when she walks, instead of a lotus flower, which appeared after each step the baby Buddha took, a moly herb appears at the place of her every footprint.

"Gosh, the masters would be impressed with you!" I tell her. "I'll bet Thich Nhat Hanh would say something like 'when I see you walking mindfully, I touch the peace, joy, and deep presence of your being.'"

Circe smiles.

Circe gradually gives me little tasks to do around the island to, she says, "prepare you for the twelve serious labors that follow. Think of this as boot camp or spring training before the season of the twelve labors of Hêraklês."

"Your first task, a multi-task actually, is right here and it'll take you a year, just like Athêna prophesied," she says, carrying a long staff in her hand. "And by then you, like the rhapsodes of yore, will be able to recite the entire *Iliad* and *Odyssey* with heart and soul and continue on your journey."

Over the next twelve months, I complete a laundry list of twelve fairly simple but time-consuming things to do around her 'hood while I read Homer. A year, of course, is nothing to an immortal and I'm at the stage of life where, though I'm not immortal, it doesn't seem like much time to me either.

Here's just a partial list of what Circe has me do before she allows me to humbly embark on the Ulysses Riviera towards Naples.

Although it makes me feel more like a novice, a student, a gardener and a map maker rather than a hardy MedTrekker, I set about (1) cleaning and marking the many trails up the mountain; (2) weeding the old pig sty that she no longer uses to keep sailors turned into swine and turning it into a tomato patch; (3) providing decent English translations of the various guidebooks to the Parco Nazionale del Circeo; (4) photographing the seaside grottoes of Presage, Caper, Impish, Prigionieri, Torre Palla and Magi Circe on Mount Circeo; (5) getting a population count of the wild boar; (6) determining the exact number of moly plants on the mountain; (6) adding some adjectives to descriptions of her in every translation of Homer; (7) diverting a stream into a fountain to provide water for hikers; (8) leading guided hikes throughout the island in Italian, French and German; (9) swimming around the entire promontory myself before teaching her how to swim; (10) instructing her maidens how to give a shiatsu massage; (11) bringing her up to speed on the world's religions; and, finally (12) fully digesting her instructions and solid bits of advice about how to proceed on the MedTrek.

After I accomplish all this, Circe informs me of the twelve labors of Hêraklês that will be a pivotal part of my future. Each task, she says, will be the contemporary equivalent of Jason's arduous quest for the golden fleece and will make the above list look like a trip to the mall.

"You've just completed the test tasks and it took you exactly one year," Circe says one morning. "That's not bad."

Then she recites the list of longer labors that will turn my MedTrek into a magical mystery tour of myth, madness and magic. She tells me she thinks that, if the winds blow my way and the gods help me out, I can accomplish them all in five years, once I get the knack of things.

She delivers this enticing list to me in a strange poetic tongue. Her cadence, which somehow seems to mix incomprehensible words from James Joyce's *Ulysses* with verses from T.S. Eliot's *The Wasteland*, is as mysterious and mystifying as it is melodic. I've boiled down the basics and put Circe's twelve labors into contemporary English to, among other things, clarify them in my own head and let you fully understand where we're headed. She insists that I not ask for additional details.

Remember, this is the enchantress who sent Odysseus to the "cold homes of Death and pale Persephone to hear Teiresias tell of time to come." And when he returned from Hades to Mount Circeo, Odysseus was greeted by "handmaids bearing loaves, roast meats and ruby-colored wine" who instructed him how to avoid "being caught by land or water in some black sack of trouble."

She was referring, of course, to his upcoming encounters with the Sirens, the Clashing Rocks that nearly nailed Jason and the Argonauts, the multi-headed Scylla and the tempestuous Charybdis. Her prognosis – "Better to mourn six men than lose them all, and the ship, too." – wasn't completely rosy so I'm somewhat encouraged that she thinks I'll be alive at the end of my quests.

Here's the Herculean shopping list that Circe provides:

1. Consult the Sibyl at Cuma and visit the dead you know and don't know in the shady underworld before hiding a baseball cap at Pompeii that will be unearthed by your grandson's grandson.

2. Establish a base camp above the islands of the Sirens and listen, without putting wax in your ears, to the soothing melodies that seduced and maddened Odysseus, before you find the six-headed monster Scylla, meet Charybdis and become the guiding light of a woman at loose ends.

3. Encounter some thieving gypsies when you least expect to, gain insight into your fellow men and give your foes some tangible.

4. Besides visiting the Cyclops' cave and trying to avoid the Sun God's cattle, find contemporary art in ancient Sicily, and enter the smoky earth on the volcanic mountains of Etna, Stromboli, and Vulcano.

5. Let a marching band lead you to the real cave of Kalypso and, unlike Odysseus who spent seven years with the nymph on the island of Ogygia, see if a contemporary mortal like you can handle her for seven days.

6. Embark on a mysterious ship that will enable you to hear words straight from Homer's mouth and guide you to the Greek island of his birth where you should sit on his rock before finding his actual birthplace. Then island hop to Lesbos, Lemnos, Ithaka and Corfu to encounter many of the characters and places mentioned by Homer.

7. Visit the Oracle of Delphi, who "knew what was, what had been, what would be," and let her lead you to the cave of Zeus' birth, the world's greatest travel writer and the end of an historic footrace in Sparta.

8. Meet with Zeus, the master of cloud, at the cave of his birth on Crete, visit him again at the top of Mount Olympus, and see him once more after you traipse through Troy at the top of Mount Ida in Turkey.

9. You may not choose to sleep with me, Kalypso, Sappho, or even Nausikaa but you must meet them all and absolutely spend a night with Helen of Troy. Do not, however, touch Odysseus' wife Penélopê or your entire odyssey will come to naught.

10. Get some contemporary spiritual guidance by consulting with the monks on Mount Athos. Ask them to pray for your worst enemies, kiss the icon of all icons and climb to the summit of the mountain.

11. Traipse through Thrace before MedTrekking through the killing fields of Gallipoli. Then swim from Europe to Asia across the Hellespont in the wake of Leander and Lord Byron to arrive in Troy to meet Hektor, the son of King Priam who was slain by quick-to-anger Achilles.

12. Make your own homeward journey to your own Ithaka and write a heartfelt and cathartic account about the importance of home and friends.

Circe isn't quite done, though I admit that I'm more excited than anxious about my upcoming trials. What a way to see the world in the 2010s!

"As you know now with certainty, after patiently but fastidiously MedTrekking your first 4,401 kilometers, the goal is the path and the path is the goal," Circe adds. "But between you and me, there's also a personal goal for you, and only you, at the end of this stage of your MedTrek. You will find something more meaningful, more seductive, more productive and more rewarding than a single woman. You will be comforted and no longer an American alien in exile."

Circe knew, of course, that I'd already been to the edge of Algeria when I walked from Antibes in France through Spain and Morocco to Saiida, where Luke and I lost our passports and returned to France. She knew that I then changed directions and MedTrekked down the Italian coast to Rome and Mount Circeo. But more of that is not what she had in mind and she suggests that I change my *modus operandi*.

"There's no reason for you to continue walking every centimeter of the seaside, as you've done up to now," Circe says. "Take some ships, do some sailing, explore some islands, climb some mountains and get SideTrekked to some places of Homeric interest and intrigue. Have some fun for Zeus's sake."

Then, she instructs me, "Now, having completed your 4,500-kilometer warm-up on the Mediterranean, you can, if you choose, go on foot only to the places that are required by the twelve labors, the places Odysseus also visited, before you finish this part of your MedTrek in windy Troy, the site of the Trojan War, or slightly beyond it. Let the winds blow you about a bit and don't be afraid to be buffeted off the path. Start smelling the roses!"

Careening Into Cannibals, the Underworld and Pompeii

"I thought this day I'd see the dead in the underworld. I thought I'd breathed my last!" – *The Iliad*

I couldn't let go of my tried and tested MedTrek MO quite that quickly. Despite Circe's suggestion to deviate from the path and smell the moly, I felt it would be disrespectful and jarring to abandon my stick-to-the-seaside philosophy before arriving at the boot of Italy. That's about 1,000 walking kilometers from here, but once there, after/if I reach Calabria, I might take her advice and change course. After all, this is my project, not hers.

I may begin my off-track walkabout, as she suggests, by

breaking into a sprint around Sicily, the largest island in the Mediterranean and the place where Circe's father Helios, the god of the sun, kept his cattle. But between here and there I'll have enough to keep me amused and busy: the hungry cannibalistic Laestrygonians lived in nearby Formia, the fuming dead in the underworld and the Cyclops are just north of Naples, the seductive singing Sirens are still sitting off the Amalfi Coast and the six-headed monsteress Scylla and whirling Charybdis are on either side of the Strait of Messina.

Homer writes in *The Iliad* that "All princely hearts are capable of changing" and I'm probably no different. I can change. My reluctance to immediately take Circe's advice is, I admit, probably part of my obsessive character that has always made me a bit hesitant to give up anything without a fight, from the one-step-at-a-time-on-every-inch-of-the-seaside MedTrek to cigarettes (I finally quit in 1979) and booze (I finally surrendered and quit in 1985). Life has its cycles and I've been through many – alcoholism, workaholism and spiritualaholism among them – that exhibit my penchant for addictive, compulsive, and excessive behavior.

At one point while reading Homer, I likened my excessive behavior to the way the Trojans fought.

"All things have surfeit – even sleep, and love, and song, and noble dancing – things a man may wish to take his fill of, and far more than war," Meneláos says in *The Iliad*. "But Trojans will not get their fill of fighting."

After MedTrekking this far it's not that easy, for me anyway, to casually abandon the fastidious manner in which I've tackled this project a centimeter at a time, especially after Circe personally confirms that numerous vignettes in Homer's *Odyssey* occurred just down the coast.

Besides, what's the hurry? Unlike tobacco and, in my case, alcohol, walking won't kill me. In fact, the longer this takes, the healthier I'll be.

Luke, who's been somewhat insistent about accompanying me since he saw me tumble off a cliff in Morocco, meets up with me again in Sabaudia so we can take the first steps south of Monte Circeo together.

"Well, what did you learn?" he asks as we leave the Parco Nazionale del Circeo and kick things off with a barefoot 18-kilometer walk on the beach from the port near San Felice de Circeo to Terracina.

"Among many other things, Circe encouraged me to read, reread and memorize *The Iliad* and *The Odyssey* and gave me her interpretation of the events and where they occurred," I tell Luke, who is at this time at graduate school in London, as we set off. "I almost know both books by heart and might soon be ready to perform them from memory just like the rhapsodists did. Hey, you could play Achilles to my Odysseus!

"More importantly, I think you'll be excited about a couple of the things that we'll be seeing between here and Naples and an amusing task that Circe would like you to perform at Pompeii."

I describe how Circe persuaded me to undertake a laundry list of local labors to get into a new MedTrek mindset and explain that I have now to successfully complete twelve tasks, just like Hercules, to add true meaning to my walk.

"They don't look too difficult and some, like sleeping with Helen of Troy and climbing Mount Olympus, should be fun," I say. "One of the first things I've got to do, on the Amalfi coast just after Naples, is find a room that will enable me to observe the islands of the Sirens while listening to them try to seduce me with their singing. That may make people wonder about my mental state."

I talk Luke through the other tasks as we casually head south. As I go through the list, I realize that I now have a meaningful framework and outline to follow for the next few years. So much for *apranihita*, or walking aimlessly.

"I'm going to get to the toe of the boot of Italy before I make any major decisions or diversions," I tell Luke. "Even with Circe's permission it would just throw me off to change the game plan too quickly. And I'm certainly not contemplating a move home."

Then, "knowing the goddess's clear word when he heard it," as Homer wrote in *The Iliad,* "Odysseus broke into a run." And so did I.

Perhaps the most stunning seasonal feature of today's sunny walk on the virginal sand next to the blissfully calm sea is what is missing: there is a complete absence of beach facilities and people. Many Italian rural beaches not only closed down when the season ended on the last weekend of September, but most have also been completely dismantled. Restaurants and terraces have been removed and even solar-powered *doccia calda*, or hot showers, are few and far between. We don't hit a place for a coffee until we've walked eight kilometers.

After we leave Monte Circeo in the sand, we're greeted by tall limestone cliffs that dominate Terracina, which has been a fashionable resort since the Appian Way reached here in 312 BC, during the days of the Roman Republic. Still towering on a hilltop above the seaside town is the vaulted gallery that remains from a multi-columned Temple of Jupiter Anxur erected in the first century BC. Anxur, which means "beardless," was what Jupiter was often called as a youngster and that was the Volscian name for this place before the Romans grabbed it. Jupiter is, of course, the Latin deity who is equivalent to Zeus.

When we arrive in urban Terracina, a few beaches—like the Lido Ulisse, which is decorated with an engraving of Odysseus' boat—still have beckoning umbrellas and multi-colored European flags. We roam through the grounds of the Grand Hotel l'Approdo, which abuts the port on the aptly named Lungomare Circe, and a sign proclaims that we are exactly one hundred kilometers by road from both Rome and Naples.

It's a significantly longer distance in both directions on the seaside but I always enjoy tottering equidistant between two points. It reminds me, as Deng Ming-Dao wrote about the harvest moon, of "equality in the cosmos: light and dark, male and female, heat and frost, hard and soft – all these things are part of an overall equilibrium."

Before verifying that the cathedral in the Piazza del Municipio does indeed contain some pavement from the Roman forum, we have a grilled fish *panini* lunch at one of the many outdoor restaurants on the quiet port. Just a few meters away from us, the fishermen who caught the fish we're eating are repairing their nets and preparing their equipment for an overnight outing.

"You certainly haven't changed the pace of your walk after reflecting about it for over a year," Luke says as we linger over coffee after lunch and obey a sign in English that reads *We pray you to put your trays to this place* (so much for my translation of *piacere* as simply "please" when "pray" sounds so much prettier). "It seems like we're going the same relaxed speed as always."

"Actually I've cut it down a notch – from slow to slowly slow," I reply. "I practiced walking meditation on Monte Circeo, often with Circe, using the tips I stole a decade ago from Thich Nhat Hahn at his Plum Village retreat in France. And I've cultivated a more proper attitude of gratitude as I take a step at a time with no expectation or projection."

We walk slowly slow on the narrow seaside road heading out of Terracina and soon sneak down to the sea through one of many dog-guarded now-closed campsites. There's another ten kilometers of uneventful, unshirted beach walking to Borgo Santa Anastasia, where we cross a unique footbridge designed by a Santiago Calatrava clone.

"This is a miniature version of Calatrava's Sundial Bridge in Redding, which helped make the hometown of my youth a serious northern California tourist destination," I tell Luke. "I wonder if this bridge will propel Borgo Santa Anastasia to similar stardom."

The next morning we find ourselves on the compact sand in front of a string of campgrounds with names like Anastasia and Le Dune, and almost immediately are struck by some unusual sightings that make this day different from every other.

We encounter the first MedTrek police-taped crime scene with one out-of-bounds area where the word *PERDONAMI* (EXCUSE ME) is written in GIGANTIC CAPITAL LETTERS in the sand. I've seen some dead bodies on my walk, including five in one day when the sorceress in Spain accompanied me, but this is my first active-and-under-investigation crime scene. I presume it's the perpetrator who excused himself in BIG LETTERS.

Then we encounter piles and piles of dying, dead and decaying jellyfish and, a few minutes later, piles and piles of dead or dying tiny fish that, Luke suggests, may have been attacked and poisoned by the jellyfish – or vice versa. After this odoriferous discovery, we're treated to an extraordinary acrobatic display by a squadron of NATO jets that could make piles of us.

We pass the Lido Ulisse as we approach the perched seaside village of Sperlonga, an ancient town that was originally a fortress but is now a nearly vertical, picturesque village with narrow terraced streets and colorful, comfortable-looking homes built on a massive rock that sits on a spur of land jutting out into the Tyrrhenian Sea.

"Some people say the name Sperlonga means Long Spur," I tell Luke as we spend an hour tranquilly drinking coffee, eating *paninis* and desserting on banana ice cream and profiteroles at two different outside cafes. "But it's actually derived from the Latin *spelunca* which means grotto."

One guidebook calls Sperlonga "an oasis with a beautiful mixture of myth, history and nature" because it's not only within spitting distance of Circe's home – and from here Aeaea does look like an island – but also just a few kilometers from Formia, the land of the Laestrygonians according to Circe.

Just beyond Sperlonga (we're now 160 kilometers from Rome and 122 from Naples) we drop into the National Archeological Museum, aka the *Museo Archeologico e Grotta di Tiberio*, that features spectacular marble sculptures portraying episodes from the journey of Odysseus.

I stand next to Odysseus's bust and am transfixed before a gigantic marble depiction of him and his men blinding the drunken Cyclops Polyphêmos. Next to that is a four-meter-high marble sculpture of the dramatic attack of the sea-monster Scylla on Odysseus's ship and crew and, nearby, I swoon over a sculpture of sexy Circe with three marble piglets at her feet.

We stroll down to the seaside site of the imperial villa and cavern of Emperor Tiberius, who reigned from AD 14-37 and was even more addicted to Greek mythology than I. He had great affection for Odysseus and it's easy to imagine him relaxing with his collection of memorabilia decorating a cave known as the Odyssean Grotto. The fact that Tiberius narrowly escaped death when the roof collapsed on his sprawling complex that stretched along the seashore adds some spice to the story.

Why his fascination? Not only because Odysseus was an historic personage in this part of Italy, but also because Tiberius, who had spent considerable time traveling or living abroad, including seven years on the island of Rhodes, felt a kinship, in character and temperament, to the Greek hero.

According to a thesis that classics professor Edward Champlin presented at Princeton University, Tiberius "was intensely interested in the deeds and character of the hero Odysseus, to the extent that sometimes he seems almost to have been channeling him."

Tiberius certainly wasn't the only one who had a fixation on Odysseus, Achilles and other Homeric heroes. The list of historic Homerphiles includes Alexander the Great, Julius Caesar, Napoleon, Lawrence of Arabia, Lord Byron, James Joyce, Nikos Kazantzakis and Princess Sisi of Austria.

Joyce, of course, named each chapter in his *Ulysses* after a person or event in Homer's *The Odyssey*. And Plutarch said Alexander the Great so highly regarded *The Iliad* as a handbook of the art of war that he took a copy annotated by Aristotle with him on his campaigns.

"He always kept it under his pillow, together with a dagger," according to Plutarch's *The Parallel Lives*. When Alexander got to Troy, he paid tributes at the tombs of Achilles and Patróklos by anointing their altars with oil and offering sacrifices.

It's intriguing to know that I'm among the latest in a long line of admirers and continuing a channeling process that's occurred through the centuries.

We continue beyond Sperlonga along a seaside that resembles Spain's Costa Brava with numerous smaller "spurs," often adorned with medieval or pre-medieval towers, jutting into the sea and separating long stretches of very inviting sandy beaches. The many strategic watchtowers were used to scope out Saracen pirates long before contemporary tourism started to take off here in the mid-1950s when the coastal road was constructed.

I wade chest-high into the water to get around one promontory while Luke prefers tackling the crumbling rock face. A sight that would have elated both Tiberius and Odysseus as much as it did us is a bronzed and beautiful bikini'd Italian *veline* being photographed for a calendar. At another promontory we're forced from the beach up to the main road and risk our lives, though we're wearing fluorescent vests, walking through a short but dark tunnel.

After Serapo Beach on the northern edge of Gaeta, we spend two hours dashing up, around and down the extraordinary Mount Orlando where we see the mausoleum of Roman general Lucius Munatius Plancus, a friend of Caesar and the founder of Lyon in France. At the lighthouse atop the mountain we have exceptional views of the Mediterranean before we visit the Benedictine-run Spaccata, or Split, Mountain sanctuary, one of the most sacred locations of Christianity. The sanctuary gets its name from a legend that claims the mountain split into three parts at the exact moment that Christ died – and if you doubt that, you can find a Biblical reference in Matthew 27:51 ("And the earth shook, and the rocks were split").

Are you an unbeliever? Watch out! Apparently one Turk who did not believe that the mountain split at the time of Christ's death laid his hand on the rock wall and said, "If this was true, the wall should turn to liquid." According to legend, it did. Or anyway that's one explanation for a very clear handprint embedded in the wall.

We descend 277 windy steps below the sanctuary to the Turks' Grotto while a number of less energetic pilgrims scour a small shop for mementos of the miracles that have occurred here. I'm very impressed by the fact that free climbing is forbidden in the grotto at certain times of the year because some peregrine falcons nest on the grotto walls. Incidentally, it's called Turks' Grotto because Turks used to hide here during the day so they could raid Gaeta and Formia at night.

Luke and I catch the sunset and arrive in the old town of Gaeta on a fragrant pine-scented road at dusk, casually walking down the curvy cobblestone streets past the modern military installation that's completely taken over the sixth-century castle.

My main prop of the day, my emergency whistle, has been coming in handy whenever we run into vicious dogs, but here it generates one of the greatest laughs in MedTrek history when I blow it in a little pizza place where we stop to have an early dinner in Gaeta's old town.

The pizza shack owner/chef, who looks like Italian actor/director Roberto Benigni, cracks up and can't stop laughing after I loudly whistle to get his attention while he's preparing a *tiella*, which is a cross between a pizza and a calzone, stuffed with calamari.

I don't think I've ever made anyone laugh so hard by doing so little. And, while I've tried it with varying degrees of success since then, I doubt that I'll ever make anyone laugh that hard again. At least with a whistle.

Gaeta, one of Italy's most ancient ports immediately identifiable from the sea by its sheer vertical cliffs, boasts all the ingredients of a decent MedTrek base camp: a castle constructed by the Houses of Anjou and Aragon, a cathedral with a dainty 57-meter high Romanesque-Moorish campanile, a welcoming medieval quarter and the inviting Serapo Beach. Plus it's a twin city of, among other places, Cambridge,

Massachusetts, and Mobile, Alabama. The port's name is derived from the Greek *kaiétas*, which means "cave."

We bivouac at the Hotel Gajeta with a number of recently recruited American Navy MPs attached to a NATO base that's been here since 1967. When Luke splits to swim at sunset, I spend an hour with the soldiers analyzing the lyrics of Don McLean's *American Pie*.

The trek south of Gaeta takes us through urban zones, ports, and beaches to nearby Formia. This, if we can believe Circe and more contemporary historians, is where Odysseus lost his fleet to gigantic Laestrygonian cannibals before he arrived at Mount Circeo.

The promenade in Formia (the name comes from the Greek *hormos*, meaning "landing place") stretches from the fourth to the tenth kilometer of our daily MedTrek and is punctuated by more mothers walking more babies than, from my perspective, anywhere on earth – and certainly on the Mediterranean. We enjoy some pleasant urban street walking, even stopping at a McDonald's for a milkshake and at a photo store to transfer the 432 shots that Luke's taken since Rome to a disk. There's a cute little two-year-old girl in the store who is already bilingual in German and Italian and, from Luke's perspective, the prettiest human we see today.

Luke is also impressed that so many Italians post their wedding announcements on telephone poles and he photographs a beautiful bride-to-be who's having her wedding pictures taken on the beach just a few steps away from a pile of the dead fish. I think it's funny that there's a poster advertising the "Itaca High School Musical."

The Formia harbor is so peaceful and calm that I have to use some surplus imagination to visualize Cicero being assassinated in 43 BC on the Appian Way, just outside the town where a tower marks the deathly spot. And a bit more imagination is required to visualize Saint Erasmus, aka Saint Elmo, the patron saint of sailors, being disemboweled here around AD 300 during the persecutions of Diocletian.

But not too much imagination is required for me to believe that Formia could have been the pivotal part of *The Odyssey* where local cannibals wiped out Odysseus' entire fleet, except for his own ship, as he was sailing towards Circe's island.

True or false, I can easily envisage Odysseus's description of "a curious bay with mountain walls of stone to left and right, and reaching far inland, a narrow entrance opening from the sea where cliffs converged as though to touch and close." He put the entire squadron there but curiously, or luckily, left his own black ship moored outside the bay and sent "two picked men and a herald to learn what race of men this land sustained."

The exploratory expedition met a stalwart young girl fetching water, who turned out to be the daughter of Antiphates the Laestrygonian, and she directed the men to her father's lodge. Antiphates, who liked to drink blood, didn't waste much time when he was informed that he had visitors.

"He seized one man and tore him on the spot" and then raised the whole tribe of howling, countless Laestrygonians who "more than men they seemed, gigantic when they gathered on the sky line to shoot great boulders down from slings; and hell's own crashing rose, and crying from the ships, as planks and men were smashed to bit – poor goblets the wild men speared like fish and bore away."

Odysseus sensibly encouraged his own men to leave and "the oarsmen rent the sea in mortal fear and my ship spurted out of range, far out from that deep canyon where the rest were lost."

Though some readers of Homer think the giant cannibals were located in Sicily, Corsica, Greece or even Havana, Cuba, there's additional "proof," or plausibility anyway, that situates them here. Besides Circe's convictions, Pliny the Elder wrote: *oppidum Formiae, Hormiae prius dictae olim, ut existimauere, antiqua Laestrygonum sedes* (the city of Formia, formerly called Hormiae, as they supposed, was once the home of the Laestrygonians), and other historians claim they were based here and spread to Sicily and Sardinia. There's certainly more chance that they were here than in Havana.

"You know, until Circe told me that the giant cannibals were in Formia, I was certain that they were in Bonifacio because of the dramatic limestone cliffs there," I tell Luke, who visited the southern part of Corsica with me a number of times.

One look at the cliffs at the entrance to the 1.5-kilometer natural Bonifacio harbor, located where Corsica's granite interior has given way to Dover-like fossil-filled limestone cliffs, will get anyone thinking that it fits the ticket for the Laestrygonians.

I became convinced of this during a week there when I hiked along the high cliffs to the Pertusato lighthouse, doing periodic push ups while facing Sardinia less than twenty kilometers away, diving into the gorgeous grottoes and swimming among the gargantuan rocks that had fallen or were thrown in chunks from the cliffs above (one is whimsically called the "Grain of Sand"). I also rented a boat and floated underneath Bonifacio's cliffs and into its two largest grottoes. The entrance to one, Saint-Antoine, is shaped like Napoléon's hat (Napoléon was born in the Corsican town of Ajaccio and there's a commemorative sign in front of the house where he lived in Bonifacio's Haute-Ville from January 22 to March 3, 1793) while another, the Sdragonato grotto, has a gap in its "roof" shaped like the map of Corsica, through which brilliant sunshine eerily illuminates the dark cavern.

Laestrygonians or not, it's because of natural sites like this that some Greeks called Corsica *Kallisté*, "the most beautiful," and the French still refer to it as the *Île de Beauté*.

When I left Corsica, I decided it was the site of the Laestrygonian episode but now, I tell Luke, I bow to Circe who places the action in Formia. She had added, perhaps to make me feel better, that the Laestrygonians were a very migratory tribe and almost certainly had an outpost in Corsica.

During my stay with Circe I read a lot of books about Homer to determine how much of what he wrote is real, how much is exaggeration, how much is pure fiction and where, whether fact or fiction, particular scenes occurred. The reality is that in most instances absolutely no one knows for sure, which enables the myth, madness and magic of *The Odyssey* to take off in a million directions.

In addition, no normal person would believe the vast array of literature, not to mention term papers and theses, dedicated to the controversy and speculation surrounding Homer and his works.

My bookcase is lined with esoterically titled tomes – cited in the bibliography at the end of this book – that range from M. I. Finley's *The World of Odysseus*, Robert Bittlestone's *Odysseus Unbound: The Search for Homer's Ithaka*, Eva Brann's *Homeric Moments: Clues to Delight in Reading The Odyssey and The Iliad* and Caroline Alexander's *The War That Killed Achilles: The True Story of Homer's Iliad and the Trojan War*, to *The Greek Islands* by Lawrence Durrell, *The Odyssey: A Modern Sequel* by Nikos Kazantzakis and *No-Man's Lands: One Man's Odyssey Through The Odyssey* by Scott Huler.

I chatted with Scott Huler about the joy of following in Odysseus' path when we had dinner near his home in Raleigh, North Carolina. Huler, a frequent NPR contributor, spent six months traveling around the Mediterranean on the Odysseus trail while his wife June was pregnant with their first son. We shared our mutual passion for *The Iliad* and *The Odyssey* and agreed that, since no one really knows where specific incidents occurred, no one is really right and or really wrong about any premises they concoct. That, plus the unlimited number of assumptions and guesses already on the table, makes this a much more interesting field of study than if we actually did know the facts.

"All of which meant that when I was choosing my Odyssey destinations I had a wide variety of options," Huler concluded about his own trip by plane, bus, train, bike, and foot to various Homeric locations.

Havana here we come.

When we leave Gaeta and Formia, Luke and I encounter many more piles of dead fish before we reach the Garigliano River. If the Laestrygonians were here today, they might consider switching their diet from human flesh to easier-to-find fish. We discuss the cannibals having a field day with the fish when we're invited in for drinks with Antonio and his Polish partner at their recently closed-for-the-winter restaurant. Antonio tells us that the dead fish arrived just after the summer tourists left and claims it is the first time such a visitation has occurred.

One theory, which both Antonio and a fisherman we meet a bit later endorse, is that the fish were killed in the Garigliano by toxic outflow from one or more of the many factories. Another theory is that some type of toxin from an unknown source had entered the sea in Gaeta. When I also see a dead duck and dead seagulls that presumably have expired after eating the infected fish, I'm convinced that the entire ecosystem is being seriously challenged.

On top of that, there's much more litter, an atrocious amount of litter, around campgrounds called Lido Mexico and Camping Arizona than is acceptable, even in garbage-everywhere-is-a-fact-of-life southern Italy. The Lido Topless and Golden Garden camping grounds look like they were named to be intentional jokes. The whole environmental catastrophe is not a pretty sight, though it makes the backdrop of stark mountains, which have few signs of humanity and almost no lights at night, look more inviting than the sea.

An attractive private estate on a promontory after Scauri forces us inland but we don't mind because this has been a distinctly stinky, unattractive beach walk. Fortunately, we find the small Il Rustichello restaurant that serves us decent pasta away from the stench of dead fish. Unfortunately at the end of the day, my socks have the same disgusting odor and when I take a shower I realize that I too smell like a dead fish.

We walk upriver for a few kilometers to Scauri–Minturno where there's a bridge across the perhaps-poisoned Garigliano River. When we cross it, we leave Lazio and enter Italy's Campania region that includes Naples, Pompeii, the Amalfi Coast and Capri and other islands.

There are some spectacular ruins left from Minturnae, which flourished as a commercial center in the Roman Empire and is now twinned with Stamford, Connecticut. But we're still much more interested in the contemporary dead fish drama, and it's the topic of conversation when we run into a pair of men fishing during the two-kilometer walk back down the banks of the Garigliano River to the sea.

"We've seen a lot of dead fish on the coast that people say come from the infected water in this river," I say to them, not wanting to wreck their day but simply to check if they're in denial. "Aren't you worried about catching and eating something that lives in water like this?"

"Absolutely not," sniffs one, abruptly ending the discussion, as he casts his line in Denile.

Although the river might be polluted and the fish poisoned, the streets at the entry to the Campania region are much cleaner than those during the last few kilometers in Lazio. And, while there are fewer dead fish on the sand, there are a lot more dead seagulls. In addition, both Luke and I now have itchy red ankles due to sand fleas that feast on us.

"If the sand fleas ate the fish before biting us then we're dead," I tell Luke, who grimaces. "But don't worry, because I believe in metempsychosis, which in ancient Greek means the transmigration of the soul or its reincarnation after death. Certain Greek philosophers, including Plato and Pythagoras, believed you could be changed into an animal or a tree, for instance. So we'll be okay if we remember that, Dilgo Khyentse Rinpoche says, "Death begins the moment we're born.""

"I'd like to be a redwood tree," Luke says.

Nearing Naples and Reaching Pompeii

Once again, though it's Saturday, the seaside is virtually empty and the beaches vacant. We take a break from walking on the fine sand to stroll through a residential neighborhood with houses that remind me of some of the middle-class vacation homes in France and Spain. Nothing ornate and flashy, which is how Italians generally like their homes, but nothing too trailer-trashy either. And the stark but striking mountains to my left are separated by a string of pine trees.

When we return to the beach, I'm asked where I'm going by one half of a male gay couple.

"To Naples," I reply. *"Vedi Napoli e poi muori."*

He winks, as though he doesn't believe that I actually plan to walk such a great distance to "See Naples and die."

The sky and sea slowly begin to radically change color as grey storm clouds approach us from now-distant Gaeta. In fact, I've never seen the sea's complexion contain quite this striking array of lavender, jade, turquoise, burgundy, cobalt and ebony tints. As the clouds thicken and lightning flashes in the distance, the surface of the sea becomes glass smooth within seconds. A transformation so stunning that it, too, might be called metempsychosis.

The wide sandy beach in Mondragone is perfectly combed, comparatively clean and features showers with running water. But, as we head into town to find a squat for the night on the viale Apollo, I recall what Natasha, the just-married receptionist at the Gajeta Hotel, told us.

"I'd go to China before I'd go to Mondragone," she said. "It's a dump, you'll see. Don't wear your watch."

Natasha got us equally enthused about Naples.

"The people in Naples are very smooth and always win arguments," she added with a soupçon of admiration. "Don't put your wallet in your back pocket. They're the slickest thieves I've ever seen."

We're less than sixty kilometers away from Naples now, but I'm pleased with our sea view room at the sulfur-smelling Sinuessa Terme hotel. And during a stroll in "downtown" Mondragone I find everything a traveler needs, from a Western Union telephone office to a bus station, a football stadium and scores of restaurants. Fat city. And it looks even fatter because Natasha had tempered my expectations and prepared me for Sodom and Gomorrah.

During the night, as the clouds obscure the once-visible lighthouse above Gaeta, we're treated to stupendous thunder, lighting and rainstorms. If Zeus, the lord of lightning, is trying to contact me, I certainly understand the medium, if not the message.

When sometimes skeptical about Zeus and other gods, I remind myself that Odysseus, Achilles and other Homeric heroes never questioned the key role of the deities. Homer insisted, "All men have need of the gods" and added in *The Odyssey* that Zeus, the son of Krónos who "views the whole world most" and "drives the clouds of heaven....can put chaos into the clearest head or bring a lunatic down to earth."

"Our lot from youth to age was given us by Zeus," said Odysseus, who admits in *The Iliad* that Athêna, the goddess with grey eyes, was always beside him "like a coddling mother!"

Even Achilles, the obstinate *über* warrior and principal character in *The Iliad* who towered above most other warriors on the battlefield and was described by Odysseus as "like a god in looks" and "the flower and pride of the Achaeans," obeyed Athêna because, he said, when "immortals speak, a man complies, though his heart burst. Just as well. Honor the gods' will, they may honor ours."

The knowledgeable Athêna frequently soothes me about my future, makes me comfortable in my own skin, and gets me out of a number of seaside scrapes. I've found that taking her advice on my ongoing MedTrek walkabout has made me more self-reliant and increased my confidence. I occasionally feel like the soldier in *The Iliad* who said, "Athêna will never let me tremble."

She's enabled me, as the Taoist philosopher and martial artist Deng Ming-Dao wrote in *365 Tao Daily Meditations*, to "try greater and greater ventures, until we are brave enough to accomplish undertakings far beyond what the average person imagines," though he added that "the higher one's skills, the more precarious one's road."

We take off from the hotel with a brisk four-kilometer walk through the "downtown," Luke on the beach and me on the street to buy us bread, salami and fruit for lunch. While I'm a cautious fan of the town, if the truth be told, it doesn't have a lot to recommend it. And Luke certainly doesn't share my mildly generous opinion of the place. When he joins me he calls it a "shithole filled with short abandoned dogs."

Okay, maybe Mondragone could use some help.

As we pass the pizzeria where we ate last night, more entertained by an apparent coming-out party for a beefy transgendered man/woman than our Scrabble game, I imagine that the Pope will invent a giant vacuum cleaner to pass over Italy and pick up Mondragone and all of the plastic, paper and bottles that cover this part of the coast to return it to its pristine state. I close my eyes. I pray to noisy Zeus. It doesn't happen.

It's a slightly drizzling Sunday, and not surprisingly the beach beyond town, with compacted sand due to the rain, is totally devoid of any trace of humanity, except for two trotting horses accompanied by jockeys giving them a sand-and-surf workout. This is the poorest part of the Italian coast that we've stumbled upon, and a tangible sign that we've transitioned from the richer north to the poorer south. The scrap metal shacks, abandoned homes, and burnt-out structures are not unlike the poorer parts of Spain and much of northern Morocco. The bars and beaches aren't doing any business and we've got the seaside to ourselves when we stop under a tattered thatch parasol to make sandwiches from the ingredients I bought in Mondragone.

Things get even gloomier when we enter the little town, or what we think is the little town, of Castel Volturno on the banks of the Volturno River. A gigantic Turkish rug in the middle of the main street has been swamped by last night's rainstorm and we have to wade through puddle after puddle on the non-existent sidewalk.

Castel Volturno, which was originally settled by the Oscans and the Etruscans who called it *Volturnum*, was apparently an important trading center when it became a Roman colony in 194 BC. By AD 95 the Via Domitiana from Rome reached it and the first large bridge was built over the river.

The town, which had its ups and downs after the fall of the Roman Empire, is now a settlement of a different kind. We realize this when we walk up the banks of the waterfowl-rich river and pass a fenced-in, overtly security-conscious Holiday Inn with a golf course. We next stumble upon a crumbling three-story building teeming with presumably illegal immigrants primarily from West Africa. Once we take a right on the main drag, we pass the Hollywood Diva's Beauty Saloon (sic) and the Bethesda Family Worship Center that advertises church services and Bible studies. Everyone who isn't at the beauty saloon or church seems to congregate in the Tropical Bar where I realize that we aren't in Italy anymore.

Although a sign on the main drag proclaims that we're on the Fontana Riviera Bleu in the *Città dell' Uomo* and the Paradise of

Flowers, where it says there are 316 days of sun each year, I think Luke gets it right when he says, "We're in the middle of Little Africa on the Mediterranean."

Not that most people in the Tropical Bar – including the African hookers and down-and-out lookers – aren't polite and friendly.

I speak to a Nigerian woman who, like everyone else, claims to be in the import/export biz and lets me know that most of her compatriots are here illegally.

"This is a holiday, God's day, and I hope the two of you have said your prayers," another beefy Ghanaian woman says when we meet in a bathroom with no lock on the door.

I tell her that prayers have been a key aspect of my life since I began reading Homer and give her some examples. I mention that Hékabê suggested to King Priam that he "tip wine to Zeus and pray for a safe return from the enemy army" and that once when Odysseus prayed "the mind of Zeus in heaven heard him. He thundered out of bright Olympus down from above the cloudlands in reply – a rousing peal for Odysseus."

Incidentally, thunderbolts and thunder were considered the greatest expression of the Lord of the Heavens, which is why Zeus is sometimes depicted holding a thunderbolt in his right hand and a scepter in his left. To add a touch of humility, he often has a goatskin folded over his shoulder or knee.

"Well, you keep praying!" she says as we listen to thunder in the distance.

Little Africa is, of course, just one example of Italy's controversial and expanding problem of coping with an abundance of legal and illegal immigrants. It's a social situation that is playing out in numerous enclaves and towns like this throughout southern Italy.

There are over four million legal immigrants and many more undocumented ones in the country, which has a population of over 60 million people, and the situation is explosive. Shortly after Luke and I were here, six African immigrants were shot in clashes with the local Mafia-like organization known as the Camorra in Castel Volturno and 400 National Guard troops arrived in Little Africa when violent protests broke out over the deaths.

While there are numerous causes of the ongoing social problem, one culprit is the Mediterranean Sea. With thousands of kilometers of hard-to-patrol coastline, waves of immigrants from North Africa and elsewhere have been able to invade Italy virtually at will. Even numerous fatal accidents at sea have failed to deter them from making Italy their gateway to Europe.

Another reason for the problem, in places from Castel Volturno to the Spanish Steps in Rome, is that the immigrants seem to have little to fear from the authorities.

Two-way international solutions, like a bilateral accord with Tunisia, pledging financial support in exchange for help in preventing would-be immigrants from leaving the country's shores, have failed to stem a tide which one member of the Northern League party, which is known for its tough anti-immigrant stance, says is "of biblical proportions."

And though the immigrants provide an important workforce for Italian agriculture and other businesses, they're frequently considered a threat.

The immigrants' response?

"All we ask is for the chance to work in Europe, not only in Italy, but in Europe," one Senegalese said. "We only want one thing from Italian people: help."

Help is not what I get from the next Italian I meet – and it would have been a lot worse if I were a non-white illegal immigrant.

We're soaked by the time we're forced to cut inland by the broad Giuliano River. Along the way we inadvertently trespass and are verbally assailed by the apparent owner of an alley of gardens that run along the river.

I begin by apologizing but, in typical Neapolitan style, the irate garden owner is so furious that he begins screaming at, and pushing, me. Attempting to be reasonable and diplomatic, I pull out my emergency whistle and blow it as hard as I can. I'm not surprised when it doesn't quite provoke the laughter it did in the pizzeria in Gaeta.

Then I yell "Police, Police" and the irate garden owner pulls his empty wallet (at least it wasn't a knife or gun) out of his back pocket and says, "I'm the police, I'm the police."

I am comforted that Luke is with me because, as Homer wrote in *The Odyssey*, "a man should feel his kin, at least, behind him in any clash when a real fight is coming."

The faux policeman is so upset that we immediately quicken our pace when he reluctantly lets us out his locked front gate. As we cross a nearby bridge and head back down to the sea on the other side of the river, Luke berates me for trying the whistle ploy.

"Why do you insist on pushing these guys?" he asks. "It was our fault really because we were trespassing."

"Why do these guys insist on pushing me?" I reply as we arrive at the Lido Playa Luna, which uses a mixture of English, Spanish and Italian signage that beckons us to "Enjoy Your Life."

I tell Luke that I sometimes feel like the young American

character in the film *Breaking Away* who loves everything Italian until he learns during a cycling race that they cheat and are not very familiar with sportsmanship. I get the same feeling when this irate garden owner policeman in a pastoral setting loses his cool and explodes in an unnecessarily threatening, rather than theatrical, manner.

I'm looking forward to exploring the legendary Greek/Roman ruins in Cuma as I embark on my first Circean task to "consult the Sibyl at Cuma and visit the dead you know and don't know in the shady underworld before hiding a baseball cap at Pompeii that will be unearthed by your grandson's grandson."

To prepare, we have lunch on the beach between Cuma and the sea before climbing the hill to visit the Temple of Jove, which was transformed into a Christian basilica at the end of the fifth century, and to explore the hilltop village founded in the eighth century BC. There's a stunning view from the Temple of Apollo at the top of the town and we pay our respects to the Capitoline Triad (that would be Jupiter, Juno and Minerva) near the remains of the amphitheater.

Cuma was not only the first Greek colony in southern Italy and the linchpin to what later became known as Magna Graecia, or Great Greece. It was also the first true wild west town and the harbinger of a "Go west, young man" attitude as the Minoan Cretans and Aegean Greeks spread their civilization and exercised a wanderlust that sought, among other things, natural resources, wealth, slaves, status, exotica, expansion, consolidation, trade and profit. The philosophy of their expansion was defined by the Greek word *apoikia* that meant "a home away from home."

More importantly, this was also the seat (literally) of the Cumaean Sibyl, a priestess prophet who was an important oracle in the Roman world. In fact, to many, the Cumaean Sibyl was higher on the scale than the Delphic Oracle, whom I'll introduce you to in Greece. Michelangelo included a likeness of her on the ceiling of the Sistine Chapel and others – including Virgil, Ovid, Petronius, Robert Graves and Mary Shelley – wrote about her.

Consulting the semi-divine Sibyl, who was said by Ovid to be over 1,000 years old and still a virgin, was an imperative step before many ancient Romans made any important decisions. Although Cuma began disintegrating when the Romans captured it in 334 BC, the ancient city comes to life for MedTrekkers when the Sibyl, who still pronounces her oracles inside a cave, prophesizes by singing the fates and writing on oak leaves.

Most mortals, of course, accepted fate in those days.

"You know no man dispatches me into the undergloom against

my fate; no mortal, either, can escape his fate, coward or brave man, once he comes to be," Hektor said during the Trojan War.

Luke and I enter her cave, which the Greeks cut out of the rock around 647 BC, to get specific directions to the underworld, the subterranean place of the dead, at the nearby crater of Avernus.

"We're doing the same thing that Aeneas did before he went to visit his father down under and the Sibyl was happy to help him out," I tell Luke. "She should be just as accommodating with us."

"What did she say to him?" Luke asks.

"Virgil wrote her exact words in the *Aeneid*," I reply, handing Luke a copy of the book and letting him read her response for himself. "Apparently it's easier to get into the underworld than to get out, but let's take it one thing at a time."

> *"Trojan, Anchises' son, the descent of Avernus is easy.*
> *All night long, all day, the doors of Hades stand open.*
> *But to retrace the path, to come up to the sweet air of heaven,*
> *that is labor indeed."*

We visit the Sibyl's sanctuary, now one of the most respected remains of the ancient Roman world, by entering a trapezoidal passage cut out of the volcanic tuff stone. As we make our way to the innermost chamber we learn that the Sibyl, according to a sign on the wall, isn't in. But she's thoughtfully left us a collection of writings on some dried autumn oak leaves that sketch clear directions to the nearby entry to the underworld and assure us, as Homer wrote in *The Odyssey*, that we'll easily find "the newly dead drifted together, whispering."

The Sibyl's indirect route leads us first to the smoldering volcanic Campi Flegrei, or Phlegraean Fields (*Phlegraean* is derived from the Greek for scorching or fiery), and our souls/soles heat up as we walk through sulfurous gases, steamy spray, gurgling mud, mystic geothermic forces and teapot-sounding springs in Solfatara.

The *campi*, which inspired Goethe to write, "Here one is amazed by the events of history and nature," are really a gas and, according to the Sibyl's note, "are intended to give you an idea of the temperature and scent of the underworld." Within seconds of arriving in the fields, I know I won't be able to get the witches' chant from *Macbeth* – "Double, double toil and trouble; Fire burn, and cauldron bubble" – out of my head for the rest of the day.

We head to Lake Avernus, which today is about two kilometers in circumference and one of many nearby lakes that fill the crater of an extinct volcano. The name derives from the Greek for "birdless," though you wouldn't know it with all the birds now flying around here.

"The buzz is that things were so hot here that when birds flew over the lake, the heat and fumes killed them and they were literally swallowed up," I say to Luke as we follow the Grotta di Cocceio, an old tunnel for chariots, to the edge of the lake.

I start reading to Luke from Book Eleven of *The Odyssey*, which is entitled *Gathering of Shades* and describes Odysseus's visit to the underworld, because I want him to get some tips from Homer about how we should act down under. Running into deceased relatives, co-workers and friends can be dicey, especially if, as in the case of Odysseus's mother Anticlea, you're being partially or wholly blamed for their death and exile in the underworld.

You probably recall that Anticlea told her son that "only my loneliness for you, Odysseus, for your kind heart and counsel, gentle Odysseus, took my life away" after she gave him news of Ithaka, Penélopê, Telémakhos and his father Laërtês.

Meanwhile Odysseus, who was unable to hug his mom because "she went sifting through my hands, impalpable as shadows are, and wavering like a dream," was primarily seeking a prophecy from the shade of Teirêsias, the prophet of Thebes who appropriately wondered why a live mortal like Odysseus would want to visit a place of death in the first place.

"Why leave the blazing sun, O man of woe, to see the cold dead and the joyless region?" asked Teirêsias before he told Odysseus "anguish lies ahead" on the journey back to Ithaka. He also added, more importantly, that Odysseus would survive the ordeal and that his own death wouldn't come until he was "wearied out with rich old age."

Not the kind of welcome that would make many want to move down under, but still good to know that life won't end tomorrow.

"Better, I say, to break sod as a farm hand for some poor country man, on iron rations, than lord it over all the exhausted dead," Achilles told Odysseus before he came up for air.

I know I won't meet my mother when I descend to the underworld because she's still alive but I doubt that she would have tried to make me feel guilty about being responsible for her own passing. In fact, I think that was a cheap shot by Anticlea, or Homer if he made it up, and in contrast I feel comfortable that some of the people we meet in the underworld will be happy to see me because I played a positive and important role in their entrée to the afterlife.

I created a company called Funeral Script Ink (FSI) in the 1980s after becoming increasingly upset by the lousy, impersonalized funerals some friends of mine were getting in France. I don't think anyone should pass, or descend, uncelebrated after this glorious lifetime on earth and I firmly believe that people should have some control over their funeral rites. FSI enabled me to write funeral scripts, and even produce some funerals, based on the to-be-deceased person's wishes.

I know that many of my past clients, all of whom had great send-offs tailored to their whims before joining the unnumbered dead, will be happy to see me. Although there's one client that never paid me (generally, for obvious reasons, I insist on payment in advance), I decide not to mention the outstanding bill if we meet.

I try to attend and actively participate in celebrations for soon-to-be-deceased friends, like the one where I slightly embarrassed myself by plugging *The Idiot and the Odyssey* while humorously roasting my freshman college roommate on stage. And I carry my own detailed funeral script in my pack when I'm hiking and update it every few years. I want to ensure that people at my funeral will get to remember me as a humble, meditative, quiet, simple, and unassuming sole soul, MedTrekking through "our mysterious world without being a burden to it" (I stole that last bit from Deng Ming-Dao).

I also want to make a little noise on my passing because a bookstore owner gave me the idea of generating some after-death publicity when he said, "If you want to really sell a lot of books, die on the MedTrek."

There are a number of people whom I want to see as we begin our trip to the underworld. One repeated regret in my life is that I occasionally failed to see people who might have been dying sooner than they should. These weren't intentional lapses but were due to logistics or time. I feel bad about not visiting Michael Kolbenschlag, who died of cancer in Los Angeles shortly after he missed my 53rd birthday party, or Stuart Hoffman, who died of complications following surgery and hadn't been able to make it to my 60th birthday party. I also know Luke will be overjoyed to find his great-grandmother Helen Oppegard from Grand Forks, North Dakota. Although I mentioned my grandma quite a bit in my first book, Luke doesn't have much memory of her because they met when he was only five and she died shortly afterwards.

Of course, we're thrown some curve balls by the dead and some ask for favors (like Elpênor, who died at Circe's place, had asked Odysseus for a proper burial on Mount Circeo) or have questions ("Now other souls of mournful dead stood by, each with his troubled questioning," Homer wrote). That, of course, is because a lot of people weren't ready to die when they did and now want me to fill them in on some missing links. Can you blame them? And did you know that some people, even after they pass, are actually concerned about the stock market and the price of gas? In fact, I conduct a poll and estimate that one third of the deceased are concerned about life before death while the remainder are perfectly content to let go and move on.

Others I meet are more serious and give me an illuminating take on their own lives and deaths. I enjoy meeting the Kennedy brothers, Osama bin Laden, and two or three friends that ended their earthly existence by jumping off the Golden Gate Bridge. I make belated amends to some people, give vapor'd embraces to quite a few souls and introduce Luke to a large roster of bygone relatives, including his Uncle Lars. Naturally the most important person I run into is Odysseus, who provides me with a lot of the detailed information you find in this book. He also gives me a forecast about my own death that I'll share a bit further down the road.

After an afternoon visiting the dead, and accomplishing Circe's first task, we pass the appropriately named Fitolife Laboratories during a walk around the lake. On our return to the seaside we stop for drinks at a café in Torregaveta, where we watch a team of rock climbers stretch wiring on the Monte di Procida to prevent slides. We then hike over the mountain and rejoin the Mediterranean at Scoglio di San Martino before proceeding around the Punta di Torre Fuma and strolling from Miliscola to Miseno, which is the name given not just to a lake but also the nearby village, port and promontory.

I surprise Luke by telling him that Circe told me that Lake Miseno was the site of the Styx, the river that the ferryman Charon crossed with the souls of the newly dead en route to the underworld.

"There are lots of myths associated with the Styx," I tell him as I disrobe and take a dip. "It's said that misbehaving gods would lose their voices and go into a coma for nine years if they drank from it, and Achilles became invulnerable, except for that pesky heel, when he was dipped in it."

We continue along the bay and astride the Lake Miseno through Bacoli that features the Tomb of Agrippina the Younger. She was Nero's mother and this is thought to be the place that he interred her after he killed her.

When we think we've arrived in Pozzuoli, which was founded in 530 BC by political exiles from Samos, we're both shouting various loud and amusing pronunciations of Pozzuoli. But a woman corrects us and says, quite patiently, "No, you're in Bacoli."

This precise moment turns out to be one of my most exciting on the MedTrek because I look at my pedometer and see that I've now walked 4,711 kilometers. That's an auspicious number because I've been favoring 4, 7, and 11 as my roulette/horserace/lottery numbers for decades. Luke knows that every locker/safe combination I have is 7-4-11 (he once used that knowledge to empty my locker at the swimming pool in Antibes and leave me clothesless), and I bet on these numbers, sometimes adding 24, on everything, everywhere, every time there's an opportunity. Just by arriving at this number on my pedometer makes me feel that I could end this whole "path is the goal" project today and feel fulfilled.

It's such a key milestone that I suggest to Luke that we return to this exact spot in the morning to resume our walk through Pozzuoli to Naples.

"The numbers will give us the luck we need to get to Naples tomorrow and complete this stage of the MedTrek with another significant urban milestone," I tell him.

Pozzuoli, the birthplace of Sophia Loren, was called Dicaearchia, which means "just government," when it was founded, but got its current name from *puteoli* or small wells. We check into the weathered, faded, paint-peeling and maybe haunted Hotel Terme Puteolane on the Naples side of the Corso Umberto. Our walk the next morning is briefly short-circuited by thunder, lightning and rain, but we amuse ourselves at the colorful fish and fruit market in Baia, which was a fashionable spa many centuries ago, and then in Pozzuoli at the Temple of Serapide (Serapis is thought by some to be a god of traders) and the 20,000-seat Flavian amphitheater that's the third largest in Italy. Somewhere we learn that the geysers at the Solfatara volcanic crater produce a volcanic ash called *pozzolana* used to produce cement.

We're only three kilometers down the path when we pass the gigantic NAPOLI city limit sign that, like GENOA, is the beginning of a 30-or-so-kilometer long city. In the suburb of Dazio we stop in a hole-in-the-wall restaurant across from a high school for an exceptionally tasty €15 deli lunch featuring ratatouille, peppers and chicken, followed by coffee. Then we pass a completely out-of-use-looking factory that, to our pleasant surprise, has been converted into a *Città della Scienza a Bagnoli* where research is conducted in scientific sectors as diverse as evolution, physics, the classical world, and communications.

Unable to make it around a promontory and cliff on the sea, we MedTrek over the Posillipo hill, which French Homeric scholar Victor Bérard claimed to be the home of the Cyclops. Although Circe swore to me that the Cyclopes were in Sicily, there's an Al Ciclope pizzeria/restaurant here, and we have a coffee at the restaurant in Bérard's honor. Just a few minutes later, we get our first view of the stunning Bay of Naples and the Castel dell'Ovo that, I tell Luke, was built by the Angevins in 1271 and has a unique seaside setting near the Santa Lucia port.

"It got its name because Virgil is said to have hidden a magic egg, an *ovus*, in its walls – and breaking the egg would destroy the castle," I mention to Luke as we look beyond the bay to Mount Vesuvius.

As we descend into Naples – which began life as a Greek city named Neapolis before it became a winter haven for the emperors in Rome – we self-weigh and self-pay for a kilo of grapes at a street side fruit stand (much to the glee of the owner who arrives as we leave and salutes our honesty).

Even the usually staid Michelin Green Guide waxes poetic about Naples, and as I relax on the sidewalk near a statue of Poseidon, I read out some particularly lyrical phrases. The guide says the city "is a universe in its own right, imbued with fantasy and fatalism, superstition and splendor....ready to surrender its mysteries to anyone who scratches the surface."

We don't have to scratch too much.

There are armed *carbiniere* wagons at each corner of the American Consulate, another indication of how secure the US has made the world since 9/11, and I use my whistle to call for police assistance when I encounter a crazy-looking guy who claims he's been bitten by a scorpion.

While waiting for the ambulance, I get involved in a long conversation with an attractive young Canadian woman who silently seems to encourage me to admire her legs, thighs, shoulders, and other body parts. This, I think, could be another goddess and, call me naïve, I'm overwhelmed by her beauty, her sympathy for the man bitten by a scorpion and her generally friendly demeanor. I'm sure this is the woman I've been waiting for forever (look, I still feel that every time I get on a plane, and I've taken lots of planes, I'll meet a someone who...) and give Luke a wave to indicate that it's time for a stop. Much to my irritation he walks over, pulls me aside and whispers in my ear.

"It's a guy in drag," says Luke. "It might be time for you to go home for a while."

We reach the Castel dell'Ovo, where a *Bertolucci Images* exhibit is not attracting too many of the overweight cruise ship tourists. While there, we watch the flamboyant butter scene from *Last Tango in Paris* and a taped interview with Maria Schneider discussing how demeaning it was to act with Marlon Brando. Then we walk a bit further down the seaside to the Castel Nuovo that, I mention to Luke, is an almost-spitting image of the castle in Angers, France, because the same architects used by Charles I of Anjou built it here in 1282, though the much-photographed triumphal arch wasn't added until 1467.

We cross the street at the major passenger ship port and, now 335 MedTrekking kilometers from Rome, try to bluff our way aboard the Royal Caribbean cruise ship which, to Luke's surprise but not mine, has substantial security.

My two main memories of this stint in Naples with Luke don't involve the three hours we spent at the Castel dell'Ovo, the scene with the police whistle or even the dazzling transvestite. They have to do with brief interactions with a Neapolitan waiter and an American tourist that you'll soon meet in Pompeii.

First, I out-Naples a Neapolitan *cameriere* when I refuse to pay the bill for a lousy piece of pastry at a café in the glass-vaulted Galleria Umberto I shopping plaza near the San Carlo Opera House.

I'd ordered a pastry that, after the long day's hike, looked delicious and sat at a table to eat it. Naturally, pastries cost more to eat at a table than standing up or taking away. But this one is so stale that I don't eat it and don't pay for it. Instead, I leave a euro tip on the table and walk away.

"Hey, you didn't pay for this!" the *cameriere* shouts as we walk towards the exit to via Roma.

"It's not worth paying for, it's old, it's not edible," I scream. "I wouldn't give it to my dog."

"But you've still got to pay," he says.

"No, no," I reply. "I'm not going to pay."

"*NO?!? Come no, come no?*" he shouts, screaming as I walk away through the Galleria Umberto I, thinking that a bullet or a butter knife will enter my back at any moment. We escape into the anonymity of the via Toledo to discover a city that is much less traffic-congested and threatening than people make out. The fact that I'm not killed makes me feel that the pastry must have, as I thought, been a couple days old.

Today, whenever Luke or I use the word "No," one of us invariably yells "*No?!? Come no?*"

It's become our symbolic association with Naples.

Everyone seems to have a favorite Naples story, usually involving crime or romance, even if they've never been here.

I ran into thoughtful author and provocative essayist Gore Vidal, who lived for decades in Ravello on the nearby Amalfi Coast, shortly after I cheated death in the Galleria Umberto I. We were at a political fund-raiser in Santa Monica, California, and I told Vidal, who was by then confined to a wheel chair, that I thought Neapolitans had mellowed, that the Mafia was now mainly a myth and that there is less of a worry about personal safety.

"You can even get away without paying for a pastry," I enthused.

"No woman I know in Naples is stupid enough to ever wear her real jewelry in public, and no man I know is quite dumb enough to contend the Camorra is extinct," Vidal not-too-diplomatically told me. "Watch your back when you're there or you'll lose more than your shirt."

Gloria Ackley, a former girlfriend from the 1970s in Paris, lived here after she was seduced in Manhattan by a Neapolitan artist with a gold tooth.

"I was 26 and very impressionable when an older Italian man with wavy silvery hair and a sexy gold tooth wooed me with his practiced flattery, flirtation and bohemian fantasies," recalled Gloria, who decades later still insists that gold teeth turn her on. "We moved to Naples, stayed in a sparsely furnished room in a castle on the bay and I learned two things very quickly: that walking by myself without a male companion led to constant harassment and that Neapolitan men are very casual about having sex with other women. I left Giorgio not only because he spent all of my money and cheated on me, but also because he replaced his gold tooth with a white crown."

Vince Tomasso, a former member of the Stanford Classics Department, vividly recalled hearing gunfire outside a downtown restaurant in Naples. He described in detailed bewilderment how many clients causally kept eating their pizzas during the hullaballoo, though others overturned their tables and hid behind them on the floor.

My own Naples story illustrates how callous I was as a journalist.

I took a train here from Rome to visit a high-tech aerospace company shortly after the 1980 Irpinia earthquake that killed 2,735 people. I had a deadline and obviously didn't appreciate the severe impact of the quake, which also destroyed a number of local roads and created numerous detours. Instead I berated a young taxi driver, who got lost taking me to the out-of-town company, until he was in tears. To his credit, when the CEO of the company heard the taxi driver's story he was not very cooperative with me.

Despite numerous changes, Naples still seems to evoke – and perhaps it will always be part of the city's life and lore – vivid stories about never-ending garbage strikes and bodies buried under the sand without, as Homer wrote, "tomb and stone, the trophies of the dead."

I thought the pastry incident with the waiter would be difficult to top until we take the narrow-gauge railway, known as the Circumvesuviana with 138 kilometers of track and 96 stations, to Pompeii the next morning for a quick visit before Luke's departure. In Pompeii, which I've been to a dozen times, I show Luke high spots that include the Forum, the Stabian Baths, the House of the Faun, and the Temples of Apollo and Jupiter.

I've told Luke, and repeat to people hiking with me, that every respectable MedTrekker not only leaves no tracks or traces on the seaside path but also picks up litter during his/her stroll around the Mediterranean Sea, though the latter edict can be a challenge in Italy because there's so much garbage. And if I need to buttress that suggestion with some authority, I quote Deng Ming-Dao that "we should simply walk through our mysterious world without being a burden to it."

But sometimes, as I learn on this visit to Pompeii, it's necessary to leave something behind for archeological, historical, philosophical and/or sociological purposes.

A brash, loud, shrill and not particularly attractive 50ish female American tourist (you know the type), thinking we're stealing stones from Pompeii when we're merely feeling the weight of some lava, rudely accuses us of being thieves.

"They'll arrest you if you steal that!" she screeches, seeming to think that being in Pompeii entitled her to be pompous.

Luke, who rarely gets angry with or takes an immediate dislike to anyone, and I want nothing to do with the bitch and immediately look away.

"We'll show her," Luke declares a minute later. "We'll leave something instead of taking something."

He decides to hide my much-used AIDS WALK LA baseball cap in a niche behind a stone in the labyrinthine Pompeii ruins and takes pictures of the address (#7 REG - VII - INS III), the niche and the stone.

"Will it be there if we return to check in a year or a decade?" he wonders. "Will it become part of the archeological history of Pompeii or be discovered by tourists or the staff?"

Luke bets me a pizza that it will still be hidden here in two hundred years, and I tell him that, according to Circe, it will be found long before that by my "grandson's grandson."

"What, I wonder, will archeologists, historians, philosophers, sociologists and my great-great-grandson think if they discover it?" Luke asks.

"I'll bet that without pictures no one will ever be able to find this particular address in labyrinthine Pompeii where, I'd like to point out, they still spoke Greek when Vesuvius erupted in AD 79," I say as we leave.

The Magical Singing Sirens

"Your hour, you know, has not yet come to die; I have it from the gods who live forever." – *The Iliad*

I resume my walk through Naples *sans* Luke when I catch a 40-minute ferry across the expansive Gulf of Naples to the center of town from my base camp near Sorrento, which the Romans used to call Surrentum. No one on the boat is reading *The Iliad*, *The Odyssey* or *The Idiot and the Odyssey*, but instead everyone seems engrossed by either *Il Giornale* or *Roma* daily newspapers. I'm both looking at the sea and dipping into *25 years of Dharma, Drama and Uncommon Insight*, which seems like a good way to kick off a drizzly April day. One not-too-uncommon insight reminds me to accept what is offered to me with full appreciation and joy.

I'm not sure if Odysseus felt equally appreciative and joyous, but I can easily imagine that he was glad to still be alive on a slightly misty grayish dawn as he sailed in the shadows of the difficult-to-attack steep cliffs (if they were white they'd call this "Italy's Dover") along the shoreline of the Sorrentine Peninsula. The many glam and comfy multihued hotels I see from the ferry weren't here in his day but otherwise, seen from the sea, not much will have changed.

When I reach the exact spot at the passenger port where Luke and I stopped MedTrekking, I immediately take pleasure in my return to the amusing anarchy that is Naples. Even myriad satellite dishes and antennas, the 21st-century equivalent of urban rooftop gardens, atop every apartment building look more anarchic in Naples than elsewhere. They're probably not the reason that UNESCO declared the entire historic town center a World Heritage Site in 1995.

Like the piles of garbage, constant municipal elections, accumulating accusations of Camorra associations and sexy *ragazze Italiane*, generally peaceful urban anarchy is a given in Naples and much of southern Italy. Yet somehow the Naples port seems to function professionally and efficiently without major security precautions, while mothers casually strolling with babies cocooned in carriages to shield them from the spring drizzle underline the feeling of normalcy.

Much of the daily anarchy is more theater than threat, of course. When faced with real anarchy – like my refusal to pay for that dried-out pastry in the Galleria Umberto I – Italians do lots of gesturing and posturing, but generally back down when it comes to push and shove. Ignoring for a moment the existence of the immigrant-filled town that Luke nicknamed "Little Africa" two days' walk north of here, it's a joy to watch everyone being so typically and effortlessly Italian in Naples.

No one, not even dance professionals like Bruno Tonioli or Luca Veggetti, could ever choreograph movements as beautiful as two Italians meeting on the Via Cristoforo Colombo to passionately converse. There is nothing more important to them in the entire world than their current discussion, whether the topic is grocery shopping or genocide. Completely nonchalant and oblivious to everything around them, they calmly continue their animated chat rather than worry about a wandering MedTrekker who asks how to find the Palazzo Cuomo.

A couple of other banal anecdotes this morning characterize the contemporary laid-back local attitude. A concierge at a Best Western Hotel, where I wasn't a guest, was happy to let me squat the Wi-Fi, and when I bought two tangerines at a street-side fruit shop, the owner smiled and gave them to me for free.

Now wearing a baseball cap that reads WIPEOUT, I trudge for ten kilometers along the fenced-off Naples port adorned with tons of containers that completely block access to, and sight of, the sea. Then, almost miraculously, the sun comes out the second I get a decent view of Vesuvius, the 1,350-meter high mountain just east of town that erupted, buried and destroyed Pompeii, Herculaneum and other towns in AD 79. It's because of Vesuvius that there are volcanic references everywhere in and around Naples, from the Ercolano Virtual Archeological Museum, the Vesuvius Hotel, and the Vesuvius Thermal Baths to an ad promoting the *Vulcano Buono* ("Good Volcano") mall with over 160 boutiques, restaurants and bars in Nola, one of the oldest cities in the region known as Nuviana on ancient coins.

As I stroll through Portici, not even bothering to try to imitate the lackadaisical and lingering pace of the Italians I pass, I'm on a once heavily industrialized coast. I pass numerous now-dilapidated factories in Torre del Greco (this Naples suburb, also buried with Pompeii, is known for cameos made from volcanic stone and ornamental tiles that display the town's heraldic symbol), Torre Annunziata (the HQ for the Naples pasta biz, which has been buried a frightening seven times under Vesuvius lava) and Castellammare di Stabia (best known, to me anyway, because author/philosopher Pliny the Elder died here in AD 79 when he OD'd on the volcanic fumes).

I hike inland to the telephone store at the Volcano Buono mall to pick up a SIM card for my cell phone and ask the women behind the counter if I can easily connect to Wi-Fi.

"Don't you realize where you are?" ask Laura, Melania, Marianna and Francesca in surprised unison. "There's no Wi-Fi south of Naples. Forget it."

These twenty-somethings selling high-tech equipment seem to unquestionably accept the concept that the *Mezzogiorno*, where they were born and raised, will forever be a low-tech, old-fashioned region of Europe, with no Wi-Fi. *Mezzogiorno*, which literally means midday, refers to all of southern Italy and has long been blighted by its reputation for poverty and crime.

The quartet also personify the long-existing image of young Italian women who, unlike their French counterparts, act blissfully unaware of men. French women often flirt either blatantly or subtly with every man they meet but Italian women of any age – and I've noticed this everywhere from bakeries to business meetings – seem genetically programmed to look right through any man they meet, or at least any American MedTrekking man they meet, with absolute disinterest. They can also inhale and exhale while speaking nonstop on omnipresent cell phones that appear to have been issued to them at birth.

A few days later I meet four Italian men and women in their late twenties in a bar and tell them about the genetic disposition of younger Italian women who seem resigned to the fact that things are slower and different in the *Mezzogiorno*. The four completely disagree and argue that people work as hard in Naples as they do in Milan. Then one young man, who's been offered a job on Lake Maggiore in the north, tells me that his girlfriend doesn't want to accompany him because "the people in the north are so different from us and think we're retarded."

"I'm going to remain retarded," says his girlfriend.

A lot of the debris on the coast in the gigantic Bay of Naples that stretches from Cuma to Sorrento is due, of course, to the concluding winter season. But I'm not betting any euros that here the beaches will be spic-and-span for the tourist season, as they will be in Saint-Tropez on the French Riviera. Littering and the presence of garbage, which you'll hear quite a bit about as I encounter more of it, is still socially acceptable in the *Mezzogiorno*.

I enter the boat-building town of Castellammare di Stabia, a one-time spa during ancient Roman times which everyone but me calls simply Castellammare. A tagger named Lupo has written *Pense Positivo*, and its translation "Think Positive," on a crumbling out-of-work factory wall near an off-limit military zone. There's not much chance of beach-walking here because there's not much beach. Instead there are breakwaters created from gigantic rocks, steep cliffs and companies like Fincantiria with seaside factories.

I continue MedTrekking towards the jet-set resort of Sorrento along the seaside SS145 (you probably think that SS stands for small streets, or in this case seaside-small streets, but it actually means *strade statali*, or state roads), and pass the Stone Restaurant, which obviously gets its name because it's made of rock. I wash my hands in the sea to remove the sticky remains of my two free tangerines and it's almost at a swimmable temperature.

There's a sign on the Circumvesuviana train track that reads *Perricolo Morto*, or "Danger of Death," and one fishmonger I speak to tells me there are also *molte incidenti* on the SS145, especially at the entrance to the narrow tunnels. I remark that if I had anything to do with assisting pedestrians on this narrow, curvy road I'd put up lots of *Perricolo Morto* signs – and not just at tunnel entrances. There are few sidewalks and I wear my Day-Glo emergency rescue vest throughout the walk.

Another reason the road is especially risky is because many drivers are soaking in the same stunning view as I am – Mount Vesuvius, the vast Bay of Naples, the tall Mount Faito and the animated cliff/ seaside villages – and can't fully concentrate on the SS 145. But I'm walking and they're driving on a bendy and potentially dangerous road that looks like it's a leftover from Graecian times when chariots were the preferred mode of transport for the wealthy.

The word BIKINI is written in big white letters on one cliffy hillside between Monte Faito (the tree-covered mountain gets its name from the Latin *fagus*, or beech tree) and Vico Equesne. When I enter the town of Meta, there are more than 70 B&Bs and hotels listed on a single congested and confusing signpost that attracts every driver looking for a place to stay. Traffic is completely blocked each time someone attempts to decipher the list.

The first thing I notice in Sorrento is a special "Sex on the Beach" cocktail that's offered "all night long" at the Banana Split bar. That doesn't tempt me, but I take time out to lunch with the local newspaper on the terrace of a fashionable restaurant overlooking the port and sea. Then I admire the view from Hotel Royal gardens and decide that I'll put clients here when I lead guided walking tours around the Med. An elevator to the beach seals the sale.

I see one irate pedestrian almost killed by a whirling motorcycle in Sorrento but when he recognizes the driver, they greet each other with a *buon giorno*, offer some cheek kisses and chat as though nothing happened. As I leave town on Amalfi Drive, I pass La Minervetta Hotel on via Capo (Athêna would be shocked by how they've turned her into a totem pole near the entrance) and the Settimo Cielo, or Seventh Heaven, Bar. But after that it's not easy going.

Besides coping with the life-threatening SS145, I make a number of forays down to the sea (the walk to the marina at Puolo, where there's a *BluMare Discochic*, which presumably means a chic discotheque, is actually relaxing) and into the mountains (I follow an arduous trail called the Via del Selva to an Aragon castle in Massa Lubrense that's now the oddly named La Torre One Fire restaurant) while frequently marveling at the island of Capri and the Bay of Naples, which is coated with a layer of brownish smog.

I stroll by a number of orchards with fruit-laden lemon trees, and it takes just a few seconds at a roadside shop to realize that farmers and gardeners don't just make lemonade. There's a lemon *digestif* called *limoncello*, lemon soap, lemon candy and gigantic lemons on sale.

I reach the town of Marciano (and get some odd looks in a *café* when I mention that boxer Rocky Marciano was a family friend) and take a break in Termini, which looks out on the bays of Naples and Salerno. Behind and ahead of me are more cliffs and steep escarpments edging into the sea. I'll see the water constantly during my walk, but won't often be able to touch it.

Then I have an interesting discussion with two retired women from Sweden, who are hiking throughout Europe and limit their daily distance to 20 kilometers (I average 32 a day). They tell me that they were just fined €37 each for not validating their just-purchased bus tickets once they boarded. That's so strict and un-Italian that I'm amazed. And because we're all engrossed in a discussion about the mishap, they miss their next bus.

I continue my ticketless and invalidated walk through Coppetelle and Nerano into the Marina del Cantone, paying my respects at a sanctuary of Athêna on the tip of the cape, without being fined.

The second task Circe gave me ("Establish a base camp above the islands of the Sirens and listen, without putting wax in your ears, to the same soothing melodies that seduced and maddened Odysseus....") explains why I rent a penthouse apartment in melodious Marina del Cantone, or the Singing Marina as I translate it. The hillside crib is particularly isolated and solitary at this time of year and its terrace overlooks the Isola dei Galli – the three islands of Gallo Lungo, La Rotonda and La Castellucia – that many agree were inhabited by the Sirens in *The Odyssey*.

The Sirens are mermaid-like bird women – with the melodic names of Leucosia, Ligeia and Parthenope – who failed to seduce Odysseus because our cunning and crafty hero insisted that his crew bind him to the mast of his ship while he withstood their mind-blowing songs, though some sources say only two Sirens sang while the other played a flute.

Like almost every other venue in *The Odyssey*, the Isola dei Galli (*galla* means afloat while *lo gallo* means cock) is contested by some readers of *The Odyssey*. But that doesn't bother me or many other Homerphiles, including Rudolf Nureyev who once owned Gallo Lungo.

"I suppose some academics concentrate on finding the exact location of events in *The Odyssey* but it's the rich oral tradition of Homer that impresses me much more than the actual locations," said Vince Tomasso, the Stanford-educated classics specialist who proofreads my books to prevent me from making too many factual mistakes about the ancient Greeks and Romans.

Vince also liked one of the many other titles I considered for this book.

"*The Iliad and the Oddity* is brilliant," he explained enthusiastically when we met at Stanford University where he taught in the Classics Department and I mentioned a title that was ultimately discarded.

The current title for this book, in case you're interested, came from a contest on my blog that generated over 500 suggestions from readers that ranged from sophisticated to ridiculous. Many played on a continuation of the brand name, the generally-regarded-as-funny play on *The Iliad and The Odyssey*, while others were completely off the wall.

One reason I like my apartment above The Sirens islands is because the environmentally conscious state of my seaside eagle's nest defies the reputation of the *Mezzogiorno* as a garbage dump.

The intricate instructions left on the small kitchen table make the separation of items for recycling look like a complex mathematical formula designed by Albert Einstein. The procedure is further complicated because there's a different day scheduled for the collection of each genre of refuse in a different type of trash bag. Organic waste in biodegradable bags is collected on Monday, Wednesday, and Friday. Undifferentiated rubbish (which can go in any plastic bag) is picked up on Tuesday and Saturday, multimaterial (sic) rubbish has its day on Thursday in a purple bag, and recycled paper goes on Friday in a brown paper bag. Multimaterial rubbish includes glass, cans, and plastic (but no plastic glasses, dishes, forks, or ear cleaners please) while undifferentiated rubbish includes ear cleaners, razors, pottery, light bulbs, CDs, leather objects, napkins, sanitary towels, and plastic gloves.

No wonder so much garbage winds up rotting on rat-infested street corners in Naples and beyond. No one can understand the instructions. But on my arrival, I rejoice at the effort made to encourage recycling and the separation of garbage.

Circe, using the same words she did when speaking to Odysseus thousands of years ago, went into a lot of detail about how I should approach the Sirens. And, without opening my weathered copy of *The Odyssey,* I recite a few lines from memory when I awake before dawn and look down on the dark sea.

> *"Square in your ship's path are Sirens, crying*
> *beauty to bewitch men coasting by;*
> *woe to the innocent who hears that sound!*
> *He will not see his lady or his children*
> *in joy, crowding about him, home from sea;*
> *The Sirens will sing his mind away*
> *on their sweet meadow lolling."*

My 5:00 a.m. awakening, combined with a tingling sense of anticipation, provoke other iconic Homeric lines – like "the light on the sea rim gladdened Odysseus" – to enter and exit my mind as I sit on the dawn-dark terrace. I let the breeze wash my consciousness during my morning meditation as I not-too-pensively stare at the half moon and vaguely hear the sea's whispering waves lapping the shore two hundred meters below. A bit later I hear some not-too-chirpy birds, watch a very sluggish slug make its way across the terrace and notice shadowy dark clouds that portend a rainy day.

The three Li Galli islands, which have always been a point of reference for sailors, gradually come into focus, and I imagine seeing ghosts of former latter day visitors – Greta Garbo, Roberto Rossellini, Ingrid Bergman, Sophia Loren, and Jacqueline Kennedy. I get into a pleasant MedTrek mindset by almost literally sucking in the view.

I take a photo of the dark dawn and post it on a blog called

Positively Healthy. Blogger and chiropractor Dr. Trudi Pratt is "reporting to you as I hear from Joel, about his journey, how many miles he's walking a day, what he's eating...on his walk around the Mediterranean Sea (you know, the one that includes the coast of countries like France, Italy, Libya, Algeria, Spain, etc.)."

The title of the blog inspires me to photograph, among other things, all the vitamins I take during the MedTrek; visit a nifty seaside restaurant that becomes my new favorite lunch-time eatery on the Amalfi Coast, where I recharged with a seafood risotto after walking 27 kilometers; sample a gigantic multi-flavored (banana, lemon and strawberry) ice cream cone; and write snippets that illustrate my most exciting encounters and track the daily distance I've traveled.

Though observers have made a number of inaccurate assumptions about my mental state during the MedTrek, I want to make it clear that it is here – precisely 4,801 kilometers into my walk around the Mediterranean Sea in an apartment with a stupendous view but no cell service, Wi-Fi or television – that I begin hearing things. It happens at 5:45 a.m. on a soon-to-be-rainy Sunday morning after my two-day 40-mile trek here from Naples through the jet-set resort of Sorrento.

Not only is my mountainside apartment within spitting distance of the Li Galli islands but I swear that The Sirens come alive and make lots of well-I-guess-you-could-call-it-music noises.

What did they sound like?

My first private early morning concert consists of an ongoing repetition of "Ah we'm all wet, ah we'm all wet, ah we'm all wet, ah we'm all wet...." If I had to pick a contemporary reference, I'd say it resembles the refrain from *The Lion Sleeps Tonight*. They don't stop chanting until 7:00 a.m. when they realize, after I run out on the terrace looking like the character in Edvard Munch's painting *The Scream*, that they were getting on my nerves.

An Idiot could make a fortune by putting a video of the singing Sirens on YouTube but I refrain because everyone around here has already tried to make a buck on everything Sirenish. The owners of shops, restaurants and a hotel in Marina del Cantone like to call their village the Sirenussae, or The Sirens. The Syrenbus in Sorrento claims to be "Pleasure on Wheels," and a lot of tiled portrayals of the place, like those on a wall in the nearby village of Amalfi, make the Sirens resemble Darryl Hannah in *Splash*.

I decide to keep my siren-sounds to myself.

Once I lure myself away from their somewhat irritating refrain, I take off on one of the best, if not the only, close-to-the-sea walks on the Amalfi Coast. I leave my temporary hillside home and carefully step down 150 concrete stairs until I turn left at the pebbly beach. Then I pass the Hotel Restaurant Le Sirene in the Marina and almost immediately hit the Alta Via dei Monti Lattari path that is marked by reassuring red-over-white slashes.

For the next eight hours, from various angles and altitudes with spectacular views of the Gulf of Naples and the Gulf of Salerno from Sant' Agata sui Due Golfi and other spots, the Isole dei Galli are constantly in my sights, though deceptively differing in appearance depending on the *bella vista*. Sometimes they appear to be three distinct islands, sometimes two, sometimes one, sometimes close to shore, sometimes distant, sometimes big, sometimes small. Despite hours of observation I never see the Sirens during daylight, though on two occasions I silently recite Circe's words to Odysseus:

> *"There are bones of dead men rotting in a pile beside them*
> *and flayed skins shrivel around the spot.*
> *Steer wide; keep well to seaward; plug your oarsmen's ears*
> *with beeswax kneaded soft; none of the rest should hear that song.*
> *But if you wish to listen, let the men tie you in the lugger, hand and foot,*
> *back to the mast, lashed to the mast,*
> *so you may hear those harpies' thrilling voices;*
> *shout as you will, begging to be untied,*
> *your crew must only twist more line around you*
> *and keep their stroke up, till the singers fade."*

A Meander Along the Amalfi Cliffs

It increasingly rains cats and dogs (or *piovere a dirotto/catinelle* as I translate a phrase that, proud of myself, I mention to every Italian I meet during the day) as I make my way to Positano. In fact, I'm drenched not long after I start my walk on what turns out to be a remarkably scenic but very wet, very steep, very slippery and very slow-going 30-kilometer slog.

Even totally soaked I enjoy the remarkable terrain – a mix of steep mountain paths, orchards and terraced vineyards. There are only a few agriculture workers out and most of them are perplexed, as they plow their olive groves and build stone walls to retain the crumbling earth, to see an Idiot arrive in Torca, where I stop for two coffees, a loaf of bread and two bananas. However other hikers, including one German couple doing the walk for the fifth year in a row, understand my motivation and tell me the weather is always like this in April. An American walker, who chats with me about Illinois politics, also understands the call of the wet wild and keeps me from feeling like a complete fool as we both get wetter and wetter during the steep, slippery and slow-going march.

Again, I'm wearing my Day-Glo vest. Not just to be found quickly if I slip off a cliff but also because I hear gunshots and don't want to be nailed by a Dick Cheney-like hunter. I do, however, have a retort if someone Cheney-like should mistake me for a deer: "Shot Happens." And if that doesn't work I'll quote Lao Tsu: "Racing and hunting madden the mind."

Despite the weather, I'm glowing with an out-on-a-MedTrek "Ahh omm" feeling as I admire the raging sea, the firm terra under my feet and the blossoming spring vegetation. I smile when I recall my friend Cassie's story of being drenched on her MedCrawl from Italy through the south of France. She and a girlfriend stopped at a laundromat near Monaco to get their wet clothes dry – and wore just their panties and hid themselves with their umbrellas as they awaited the end of the drying cycle. Alas, as you might imagine, there are no laundromats here.

After 14 kilometers on the blazed trail I walk another 16 kilometers on the coastal road to reach Positano and quickly decide that the Amalfi Coast should be called the Amalfi Cliffs. It's a gorgeous bit of the planet, sure, but completely vertical, massively rocked and horribly overshrubbed.

Another thought that occurs to me as I continue on the Amalfi Cliffs road concerns Joey Amalfitano, because the coast is called the Costiera Amalfitana. I resolve to find out what happened to the utility infielder who played for the San Francisco Giants in the 1950s and 1960s. It turns out that Amalfitano, who's a member of the Italian American Sports Hall of Fame and came from San Pedro, California, became a major league manager and coach.

It's almost immediately apparent that the road is the only path if I want to stay very close to the sea, though I hope to take occasional forks into the hills to visit hilltop villages like Ravello. At one point I get out of the rain at a bus stop and admire a trick that the Italian locals have down pat. When there are too many people waiting for a bus in the rain, the Italians walk around the bus and enter from the rear door (theoretically a no no) while the foreigners remain politely lined up at the front.

As I approach Positano, I gaze in a stupor at the vertical mountains and the gorges/cliffs that steeply cascade into the sea. Despite the Italian penchant for sorting apartment garbage, I'm disturbed to see some *sauvage* dumping, including two cars and a refrigerator, in one gigantic gorge along the way. In contrast to the wild littering, just before Positano, on a nearly vertical slope, are twenty bathtubs spaced on the terraces to collect rainwater to be used, presumably, for irrigation.

I walk down a few hundred steps into Positano, which artist Paul Klee called "the only place in the world designed on a vertical axis," and wonder where Picasso, Cocteau and Steinbeck lived when they were here. As I pass numerous boutiques I recall the Positano fashion trend during the 1950s when every member of the jet set looking for *La Dolce Vita* came here to buy sandals and brightly colored clothes.

I'm as wet as I've ever been on a MedTrek, and this is the longest I've ever hiked in constant rain. To rebound, I choose a nice mix of Italian specialties in a *salumeria* and, while they're being heated, talk to a fellow my age about my walk. He tells me that there are lots of paths in the mountains paralleling the coast and doesn't seem to understand my MO of staying as close to the water as possible. If, unlike me, you don't feel compelled to stay close to the sea, take his advice and climb the hills to enjoy the views on the "Path of the Gods" up above.

After critiquing my hiking method, my new pal diagnoses my command of Italian when he hears me make the salesgirl smile and blush when I say that *"lei è la piu bella regazza Italiana da Positano."* That's an expression I tend to use frequently in whatever town I happen to be in because Italian women seem pleased to hear that "you're the prettiest Italian chick in ...... (insert the name of the town you're in)."

He tells me he's a barber then asks me where I learned to speak Italian and, though it may sound like a compliment, seems to imply that I had one hell of a lousy teacher, though many women, like the salesgirl, often compliment my attempts to communicate.

Okay, face it, my Italian could use some work.

I never get that bewildered Samuel Beckett stare in Italy that I got in Paris when I asked the author in French, at a red light, if he was waiting for Godot. Instead Italians frequently look at me with candor and say, "I don't understand a word you said." They're not angry, embarrassed, impatient, condescending, or hostile; they just honestly didn't understand a word I said.

I take my deli-bought lunch down to the sea and eat under the drizzle on the black beach at Positano, where I replace my wet hiking shoes and socks with a dry pair of tennis shoes and socks. Then, looking a bit like a zombie, I visit the posh Buca di Bacco hotel/resto/club complex on the *Spiaggia Grande*, or the Big Beach. I drop in just to see the wine cellar (the place gets its name from the Italian words *buca*, or hole, and *Bacco* for the Greek god of wine) that was the site of romantic dinners and focus of social life for Richard Burton, Elizabeth Taylor, and almost everyone else who stayed here.

Did I mention that Circe also told me that I should emulate Odysseus and take to the water?

"You can't love Odysseus if you don't love to sail and visit islands," she told me.

Okay, maybe it's Circe's advice; maybe I want to see The Sirens islands from a few different vantage points; or maybe it's just the persistent April showers. In any case I decide to ferry to the islands of Capri and Ischia in the Bay of Naples during the next couple of days. Circe didn't specifically mention them, but I figure Odysseus might have frequented both islands.

"The end of your path will be beyond Troy, but you'll find many treasures well before then," Circe counseled. "Don't leave any stone unturned and remember that the path is the goal. And quit this ridiculous habit of not counting the kilometers you walk when you're on an island. This is research – it all counts."

Actually, don't tell Circe, but I didn't count the many kilometers I walked on and around Monte Circeo. But so much of *The Odyssey* occurs on islands that from this point, I expect to visit a number of them, both large (like Sicily, where I'll find the Cyclops and the Sun God, and Crete, where Zeus was born) and small (like Gozo, the home of Kalypso, and Ithaka, the home of Odysseus, in Greece) and will start counting.

One reason that I'm interested in Ischia and Capri is that there's some buzz that one of them might have been Circe's island, though you'd think she would have confided in me if this were true.

It's that possibility that sends me out on the 9:30 a.m. boat from Sorrento to Ischia which, when known as Pithekoussai, was among the first Greek settlements in the west around 770 BC. Once on board I meet Tonio, the hairdresser who says he happened to see me posturing in Positano. We chat during the ride, and I'm particularly intrigued that he goes to Ischia once a week to relax in one of the island's three main thermal baths (a fourth, the Military Thermal Bathing Establishment in a royal palace of the Bourbon kings, is only for military staff).

"The water comes out at so many different degrees that one visit isn't enough for anyone," he tells me.

Call me an Idiot, but I ignore the baths and go on a Circean search that takes me to an intriguing castle, an interesting bookstore, an inviting garden of aromatic Mediterranean trees and plants (where there are lots of Mediterranean cats and pigeons but no paths named after Circe) and the highest peak on the island.

I spend a few hours exploring the Aragonese Castle that was built in 474 BC by Hieron I of Syracuse before it progressively fell into the hands of the Romans, Visigoths, Vandals, Ostrogoths, Arabs, Normans, Swabians and Angevins. While there are a number of surprises – including displays of medieval weaponry (hey, a catapult!) and male/female chastity belts – and decent views from the belvedere and watchtowers, I'm particularly enchanted with the Nun's Cemetery located beneath the church.

Most nuns found themselves at the Convent of Our Lady of Consolation because they were the firstborn daughters of noble families and were frequently sent to the nunnery to ensure that the family inheritance passed on to the firstborn male. But what's much more interesting is how they left the convent. The way the nuns disposed of the remains of their sisters proved that it took more than chastity to live a good life.

The deceased sisters were placed on stone thrones with a bowl underneath, which resembles a large toilet, to collect their draining body fluids. Then, to illustrate that the heart of the body is spirit and everything else is waste, they were left to slowly decompose until their skeletal bones were tossed in an ossuary (a polite word, if there ever was one, for a pile of bones) after the decaying process was complete.

Here's the kicker: when the nuns went down to regularly pray and meditate daily for their dead sisters – and perhaps reflect on the concept of death – many got sick and died themselves due to the rotting conditions. All this while the first-born male was collecting the family inheritance and living a life of leisure.

I pass a restaurant called Ciccio, which I figure could be the local spelling for Circe, before entering the enticing Imagaenaria bookstore on Via Giovanni da Procida. I'm somewhat dismayed that the owner, who shows me books in Italian from the early 1900s that link Ischia with the Homeric tales, tells me that "every island on the Mediterranean claims Ulysses was there. We're nothing special." He also dismisses the theory that Ischia is Skhería, the last island Odysseus visited and home of the Phaiákians, or Phaeacians.

Although the view from the top of Mount Epomeo is negligible (I almost hesitate to admit this after the long walk up) due to the clouds, fog and generally lousy weather, I pass a number of (literally) hole-in-the-mountain caves that would have fit perfectly with Circe's lifestyle. So there may be merit in theories espoused by some academics – like Mauricio Obregón in *Ulysses Airborne* and the title of a musical piece called *Ischia, Island of Circe* by Mark Eliot Jacobs – that Circe was here.

And if she wasn't, I realize during my walkabout who had been. I recognize that many scenes from *The Talented Mr. Ripley* starring Matt Damon and Jude Law were shot on Ischia.

Given the choice, if I were Circe, I would have lived on the nearby island of Capri. I love the hike up to the top of Mount Solaro that has one of the best island views of the entire Mediterranean – north towards Cuma, south past The Sirens to Salerno, east towards Naples and west over the sea.

Although I feel a little embarrassed about my new cap with CAPRI written in flashy gold lettering (I gave my WIPEOUT cap to Tonio), which makes me look like a real *touristico* as I head from the Marina Grande port up the Via Monte Solaro, I sniff and sneer at people taking the buses, funicular and chair lift.

None of those transport modes is suitable for The Idiot. I march straight up the very steep steps and equally steep trail to the top of the 587-meter hill. I pass one Italian woman luxuriating in a chaise longue in the sun and say "tough life" in English when she glances up at me. When she looks as though she doesn't understand I say *'una vita difficile'* – a phrase I picked up when I saw a Dino Risi film with that title in the 1960s – and she laughs.

I spend an hour (I'm in no hurry and consider the day out here one of caprice) savoring the views from every perspective and slowly sip a latte macchiato at the peak. As I walk back down through the middle of a gaping overflowing-with-glowing-green-growth gorge, I again get that satisfying and contented "ahh omm" MedTrek feeling.

But what happens when I descend into Capri town, go into the Taschen Bookstore at the Capri Tiberio Palace Hotel, and ask for the latest buzz on Omero, as the Italians pronounce Homer's name?

"This is probably one of the few islands on the Med where, except for The Sirens nearby, there's nothing to do with Homer," exclaims the bookseller.

I have a coffee in the Jacky Bar, a contemporary recreation of the Cotton Club and 60s Cuba, where I overhear one tour operator talking to another about the beauty found in almost every region of Italy.

"I love Tuscany and the lakes and almost everywhere else in Italy, but when a place isn't on the sea, well, then it absolutely will never please me as much as Capri," says one woman.

Everyone else – from Emperors Augustus and Tiberius to a member of the Krupp family, Le Corbusier, Churchill, and Eisenhower – who spent some time here seems to agree with her. Indeed, the sales pitch for some of the cliffside villas would have screamed "location, location, location" and "belvedere, belvedere, belvedere" even three thousand years ago.

Tiberius, who lived here during the last eleven years of his life, continued the Odysseus theme from his digs in Sperlonga at his eight-story Villa Jovis, or Jupiter's Villa, that sits over 333 meters above the sea. From his east-facing dining room on the top floor, Tiberias could see Circe's Mountain, the entrance to the underworld, the Temple of Minerva on the Sorrentine Peninsula, and The Sirens Islands. I, however, am much more interested in the Salto di Tiberio, or Tiberius' Leap, the cliff over which the Odysseus-loving emperor apparently threw his enemies.

I also check out the Tragara (from the ancient Greek *tragarilon* which means, amusingly, "goat pen") Hotel, and get a look at the three oddly-shaped Faraglioni islets. Then I dip into the exotic garden, the small port and, of course, scurry by all those shops on the Via Le Botteghe selling Capri sandals (a trend I heard about when I was growing up in California during the era of Capri pants that date from the year of my birth), lemon chocolates (I can't pass a shop selling lemon chocolate without tasting/buying some and admit I've become a – and this is the appropriate word – sucker for anything lemon), and the usual contemporary designer luxury goods. I even, for the first time on this outing, stop, sit in the sun and have a salad and some authentic Capri water just to soak it all in.

I'd been to the Blue Grotto during a trip to Capri in the early 80s and, though the swim in the sky-reflecting water was exceptional, the visit was most memorable because it was one of the few times I got called on my expense account by the head office of a magazine in New York.

I'd been traveling throughout Europe, writing a report about *téléinformatique*, a word that was à la mode for about a week and meant telecomputing before the Internet existed. My business partner John Keeney and I spent a weekend in Capri, and the bill for the scuba dive into the Blue Grotto was questioned by the suits in New York – not the hotel, not the lavish meals, not anything else, just the scuba dive. Maybe because I forgot to add that I was actually diving to investigate an underwater fiber optic cable, which was partially true. I let it go.

Keeney recalls that we actually made a very serious dive in the cerulean waters of the aptly named Blue Grotto, a color so impossibly intense that it stuns the eyes and the soul. We wanted to go elsewhere too, to find the underwater cable and other treats, and sought a knowledgeable dive guide. Our local choice was a broad-shouldered Italian with curly hair and a strong handshake who spoke nearly perfect English with an Italo-Bronx accent after years in New York.

"Yes, I am the best diver on my island home," Giovanni admits when we locate him. "I've been an instructor for eighteen years and have logged thousands of hours underwater. But cave diving and tunnel diving? For you? I can tell you, my friends, that is a dangerous business. I had a Navy SEAL officer here a few months ago and he became so very upset in such dark place that we had to give up and return. There are many kilometers of tunnels under Capri, a whole world of tunnels and caves, but let's start with a short one to try you out."

Equipped with wetsuits and lights, we descend down gnarled grey walls of stone, surprised by a school of silver fish that speed by at about 20 feet. We'd already dived to this depth with snorkels to pry prickly black urchins off the rocks with our knives, going for three or four in one descent, a contest between us. That was off a breakwater in the port made of huge hunks of granite, strewn with different seaweeds with sharp bright shades of reds and greens. It was like spring underwater, clear and gorgeous, and in an hour we had our bounty and enough take for the two of us to have an urchin, bread and wine feast on the beach.

I was daydreaming amidst my exhaled bubbles, a bit mesmerized by my amplified breathing at a depth of about 40 feet, when Giovanni signaled a small opening in an outcrop of rock. Turning on our wide flashlight beams, we followed him into a narrow aperture with just room enough to extend both arms. By the time we had finned our way for about 60 meters, the tunnel was so tight that our tanks were scraping the "ceiling" and our bellies were grating the "floor."

Abruptly the light in Keeney's hand, behind me, went out. Well, I thought, I hope he's not claustrophobic and I'm not surprised this experience scared a Navy SEAL. I felt a tremor of concern, allayed only by the competence of our leader who certainly wasn't going to let anyone die during a test outing. Or so I hoped.

As tunnels go, though, this was a thorough test, I told myself as we arrived at an elbow curve, tank grating sharply above me, a slightly sickening noise. Keeney grabbed my fin, wiggling it up and down. I took that as a good sign, and in any case I couldn't do anything because it was impossible to move backwards. After another 20 meters, the tunnel began to widen and we surfaced in an open pool. When we surfaced, a light wind combined with the adrenaline made us feel like heroes of some kind.

"Pretty dark at your end?" I said to Keeney.

"No worse than Puget Sound at 120 feet and no way as cold – see I'm not even shaking!" he responded merrily.

Giovanni gave us both a wry smile.

"You passed the easy exercise," he said. "Tomorrow we'll go up a notch. Maybe double tank 500 meters to find a big, dark cavern at the end."

"Unfortunately I've got to go look at a fiber optic cable tomorrow," I replied. "Maybe the next day."

By the end of my MedTrekking day, I have nooked and crannied some 21 kilometers on Capri, which is only six kilometers long and three wide, as I explored various lookouts and out-looks. I still think Circe should have bought property here.

I'm put right back in Odyssey mode when I leave Positano

eating a bar of orange "chocolate" and pass La Sirenneuse Hotel, the Poseidon Hotel, the Tritone Hotel and the Luna Hotel where a plaque says that Henrik Ibsen and Richard Wagner once stayed.

It's a Sunday morning, and when I arrive on the main road – which makes the highway through Big Sur in California look like a super freeway (a writer in *The Los Angeles Times* actually compared the two and wrote "like Big Sur, the Amalfi Coast is a place of savage beauty, all truculence and temerity") – a bicycle race has completely stopped all traffic. I'm able to casually walk on the edge of slightly rain-slippery SS163 road towards Amalfi as cyclists from the opposite direction whiz by.

It's a pleasure to have a car-less few hours on the usually busy road. I can actually walk far enough from the edge of the road to avoid tumbling off the cliff and enjoy the never-ending rock formations in the Lattari Mountains and the belvederes, basilicas, cliffs, heavy-duty scrub vegetation (which might prevent me, and possibly even a car, from rolling too far down the cliff), smooth-surfaced sea and everything else on both sides of me. I even notice that the ceramic kilometer markers have lemons painted on the tiles.

The Amalfi Cliffs/Coast put some parts of the French Riviera, Spain's Costa Brava, and even the northern Moroccan coast to shame – which is why, since 1997, almost every city, monument, and structure here has been classified a World Heritage Site by UNESCO. There's a sign at Furore indicating that it, and perhaps the gorge in which it sits, is one of the prettiest cities in Italy, and the terraced vineyards and lemon orchards are – and you know I hate this expression because Richard Nixon used it to describe the Great Wall of China – "picture postcard perfect."

This beats walking in heavy traffic with subconscious thoughts that a car might hit me, though if I get hit by a bicycle instead any thoughts/fantasies/woes/projections that I'm entertaining would be put in their proper unimportant perspective.

I stop for a cappuccino and two marmalade croissants in Praiano, where I counsel the bartenderess to take the day off because of her terrible cough after she tells me "this is the real heart of the Amalfi Coast." I chat with a number of fruit sellers on the roadside and they try to convince me that their produce is about half as expensive as that at a village fruit store. I even talk to some tourists when I arrive, after 13 kilometers, in touristy, arcaded, colorful, sloping Amalfi.

Amalfi's Piazza Duomo is the place for a gigantic multi-flavored (banana, lemon and strawberry) ice cream cone, an absolute dietary/physical/spiritual/mental necessity after the seaside, cliffside hike.

Founded in 840, Amalfi is Italy's oldest republic and was a major shipping hub for both cargo and crusaders a thousand years ago. I can sense its mix of an Oriental and Romanesque past as I wander aimlessly into little squares and alleys off Via Genova and Via dei Mercanit.

Shortly after Amalfi, at a place called Atrani, I get led astray. I head five kilometers off the narrow seaside track up an even narrower road through the Dragon Valley to palace-and-villa-filled Ravello, where Gore Vidal lived for decades. I'll be the first to agree that the views from the car-less town onto the Mediterranean and the Gulf of Salerno merit the three stars the Michelin Green Guide gives the place ("The site, suspended between sea and sky, is unforgettable," it waxes). I even concur with the guide's comment that "the aristocratic restraint of Ravello has, over the centuries, beguiled artists, musicians and writers" like André Gide, Virginia Woolf, D.H. Lawrence (another literary hero of mine, he wrote part of *Lady Chatterley's Lover* here), Graham Greene, Henrik Ibsen, John Huston (he shot *Beat the Devil* here), Greta Garbo and Joan Miró.

Polemicist Vidal, who died in 2012, was an expatriate mentor for me. I loved the way he'd come back to the US exuding the *savoir faire*, worldly self-assurance and a *je ne sais quoi* that his years abroad added to his natural vanity. He'd return to New York and take on William F. Buckley, Norman Mailer and anyone else who threw a verbal or physical punch his way. I'm excited about seeing where he wrote his many caustic but thoughtful essays and historical novels like *Burr*, still one of my favorites.

Vidal doesn't live here anymore when I visit. He left Ravello because a bad knee made it difficult for him to negotiate the town's narrow, steep cobblestone streets and steps, and Howard Austen, his long-time partner, was ill.

Vidal and Austen had lived here from 1972, when he bought his cliffside villa *La Rondinaia* (The Swallow's Nest) on six acres for $272,000, until 2006 when he sold his home to a local hotelier for over $17 million. Guests at his terraced, multi-level white-stucco complex, which was constructed in the late 19th century by the daughter of Lord Grimthorpe who owned the nearby Villa Cimbrone, included everyone from Princess Margaret, Rudolf Nureyev, Paul Newman, Tennessee Williams, Graham Greene, Sting, Susan Sarandon and Brad Pitt to Hilary and Chelsea Clinton, who left a photo with the note "Thanks for letting us trespass."

I drop into the town's 11th-century Duomo, sit on a bench for a while and think of the now-deceased Vidal and Austen before visiting the 13th-century Villa Rufolo, which was the inspiration for Klingsor's magic garden in Wagner's *Parsifal*.

Although he's no longer here, I can feel Vidal in Ravello as much as I felt Tiberius in Capri, both of them, as Chuang Tzu described, "ambling about in the Garden of Perpetual Harmony one fine day."

"A slice of the moon" and Thieving Gypsies

With the skies still comparatively clear, I tumble down a chapel-filled path to Minori. Once I reach the seaside road, I continue to Maiori, which quickly becomes my new favorite town on the Amalfi Cliffs. Why? Because it has the only serious promenade on the entire "coast" that, late in the afternoon, is choc-a-bloc with strollers, and it's near the very intriguing *Le Torre de Normanni Ristorante* that occupies the top floor of a weathered medieval tower perched on a rock on the water.

When I continue towards Erchie, Cetara and *Vietri sul Mare*, I pass the Hotel Pandora and it starts raining again. I struggle to pass two aging Italian women without umbrellas who tell me, "It's great weather, fresh and cleansing." I don't argue. Ahead I can not only see Salerno, with tankers in the port and a flat coast beyond it, but also get a tantalizing view back on the cliffs, the coast, Li Galli islands, the promontory near my mountain squat, Capri and a captivating, flaming red sunset.

Erchie is an appealing little port with an attractive little beach on each side of an alluring little medieval tower that's among the last villages of the Amalfi Cliffs before I enter the much-bigger-than-I-expected port city of Salerno. It's only 13-kilometers from Erchie to Salerno, and I plan to move my gear to a new base camp further south in Agropoli because I know Odysseus and Circe would love that town's great Greek name.

There are two other villages on the way and I expect to enjoy Cetara, the first one, because of its name. I meander through so many little villages that at the end of any particular day, and certainly at the end of a month-long outing, the names blur, and I often just say Et Cetara, Et Cetara. Now, at least, that's where I am.

Cetara (pronounced Chet-ara) has one of the Med's sweetest municipal slogans written on the tile at the city limits. It says the town is *una falce de luna, une dolce fiordo di costeria, una delecta sinuosita tra monte et mara, uno fazzoletto dei case blanche* (I let my fluffy poetic self emerge and translate this as "a slice of the moon, a sweet sliver of coast, a delicate curve between mountain and sea, a handkerchief of white houses"). I learn when I buy some fruit for lunch that I'm about to leave the lemon capital of Italy for the fig capital of Italy. The fruit vendor gives me some dry figs to sample, and, because figs are one of my favorite fruits and the figs on the trees aren't quite ripe, I buy a pound for the road and have an all-fruit lunch on the town's large-rocked breakwater, which looks onto a ship loading loads of lemons.

The next town, Vietri sul Mare, which I translate as Windows on the Sea, is just that, and it now moves into first place for having the longest beachside promenade on the Amalfi Cliffs. There's so much space here that they've even put a football stadium on the coast. Vietri sul Mare is also a window on the *autostrada* that runs just above it and features an attractively sloping Duomo and a stupendous ceramics shop.

I'm surprised by the size (there are thousands of cars and thousands of containers waiting to be loaded for somewhere), security (razor wire and serious guards) and seeming efficiency of the Salerno port compared to Naples, which must stay in business because it's controlled by the Camorra. Equally surprising is the shady, tree-lined seaside Lungomare Trieste promenade – a rarity, but ever so practical, on the hot Mediterranean shoreline. There are not only palm trees, plane trees, and tamarinds in Salerno, which is sometimes referred to as the City of Socrates, but also a seeming representation of the world's best shade trees. Shade's not what I need on a rainy day but I do let the trees serve as umbrellas as I sprint to the bus station.

I get the Samuel Becket/Mad Magazine "what me worry" stare from one bus driver who pulls out and away without opening the door to let me ask him where he's going. Then I have a friendly conversation with another driver who lived in Boston for 33 years and is now dreaming of moving to California. I don't have a chance to ask my quasi-American friend why drivers on the Amalfi Coast always look at each other with such scorn when they cause a traffic jam. I've noticed that the drivers of the SITA local buses never seem to cut the tourist bus drivers any slack. They give each other the Samuel Becket/Mad Magazine stare.

I kick off the next day with a few polite conversations in order to find the distant train station, a two-kilometer walk from my apartment near the Agropoli port, to catch a train back to Salerno and resume MedTrekking. With forty minutes to kill before the 8:45 a.m. train (though none of the four clocks in the station have the same time), I get into a conversation with the head of the station brigade known as the Police Ferroviaria and a couple of his buddies. We discuss the pros and cons of trains versus buses, the amount of time it will take me to walk from Salerno to Agropoli and the weather (everyone is predicting sun for the weekend), and I pepper them with questions about a few other things. Then the police capo shouts:

"*Basta domanda!*" or "Enough questions, Idiot!"

I'm tempted to say "*Come basta domanda?*" but I'm not quite yet feeling my morning oats, so I simply shrug and walk to the train platform. Doesn't this guy realize that I don't often get a chance to talk to informed people about key logistical tidbits regarding the Mediterranean? Shouldn't he feel privileged that I'm seeking information and advice from him?

I kill a few more minutes chatting with a Norwegian woman who's been here a week taking day hikes with her husband along the Amalfi Cliffs and in Cilento National Park and Vallo di Diano further south. She wonders if I always hike alone, and I mention that René, a French friend who was going to join me today, cancelled at the last minute – and that many of my friends just can't grasp the concept behind my type of hiking.

"When I mention how far we walk to people in Oslo, they think I'm crazy," she agrees.

I return by train to Salerno, and I relish – after all the ups, downs, steps and climbing on the Amalfi Cliffs – a flat walk-on-the-beach day in the direction of the one-time Greek settlement, and now historic ruins, at Paestum, where there are temples dedicated to Poseidon (the town was called Poseidona in 600 BC), Zeus, Hêra and Apollo.

It's also, after all that rain, a joy to have a sunny day, and I change from jeans to shorts before I buy a *ravioli ricotta* at 11:00 a.m. to eat on a seaside bench. Despite the garbage laws concerning recycling, the beaches here are filthy and there are tons of refuse around a garbage can that has nothing in it. In addition, many of the one-time factories, cafés like the Bora Bora Bar and swimming establishments are in a ramshackle, dilapidated state.

To be fair, there is a newish McDonald's, a Carrefour, and an Isola Ecologica in Arechi where cosmetic efforts are underway to prepare the beaches for the upcoming summer season. But it's only the *Lido di Carabiniere*, the private beach for the cops and military, which has clean sand.

After 15 kilometers, I'm hiking shoeless on the sand and enjoying the touch of MedWater on my bare feet. I stop at one entrepreneurial café that offers a cappuccino and a croissant (or *cornetto*, as the Italians call their sugar-coated breakfast treat) for a reasonable €1.30 and applaud the owner. I'm impressed with a pizzeria named Guilio Cesare and the nearby Hotel Olimpico, though I'm wondering why there isn't a memorial commemorating the 1943 US beach landing here in World War II, especially since tomorrow, April 25, is the anniversary of the 1945 fall of Mussolini's Italian Sociality Republic. While there are some well-tended war cemeteries a few kilometers inland, I'd love to see a memorial on the beach.

The most amusing moment of the day occurs when a hooker

standing on the nearby seaside road noisily clears her throat, spits, and then catches me catching a glance of her spitting. She's very tall, not unattractive, and pretty well dressed (well, for a hooker along this stretch of beach), but I think she's a bit embarrassed and maybe expects me to yell something demeaning like "Spitters are Quitters," (I chuckle as I imagine myself spitting out the probably hookerly incorrect phrase in Italian) or at least inquire how much she charges for a trick. Instead I walk past in silence and just nod.

After managing to saunter 34 mostly barefoot kilometers from Salerno towards Agropoli, I'm tired of exercising the muscles of my feet in the soft sand and need a break from the sun. I decide to stroll through a very dense pine forest parallel to the beach. It includes an exercise trail with "stations" to do push ups, stretches and other gymnastics, though it too is infiltrated with garbage.

My desire to get some shade on terra firma turns out to be a big mistake and a vivid reminder that I should always stay as close to the water as possible.

I walk past a small tribe – three cars, one caravan, ten people – of Gitans, or Romani as they're called in Italy, and three of the young gypsies, who look like they're well into a bottle of kerosene or whatever foul-smelling liquid it is that they're drinking, start cackling at me. In return, I squawk back with my patented Tule Lake goose call – the one I demonstrated for you when I walked through Spain – and they all cackle, good naturedly it seems, back at me as we bond in typical nomadic fashion.

I continue walking, without a care in the world, until their screeching gets closer and it slowly dawns on me that I've just put myself alone in the middle of the woods with a trio of taunting thieves who want me for more than my goose call.

"Domadoro, domadoro, domadoro," the three shout in a well-practiced chorus that would have made the Sirens pay some attention. "Give me the gold, give me the gold, give me the gold."

I notice that they are looking very thirstily at the solid gold band on my right wrist, the gold link bracelet on my left wrist, and the gold chain with a white-and-yellow gold yin/yang locket around my neck.

When walking through cities like Naples (where anything goes when it comes to ripping people off), I religiously take off two of these flashy ornamental lures, which would obviously attract any big fish. But I didn't even think of removing them in this rural stretch for two reasons: (1) I have this theory, about to be proved wrong, that people are afraid of a guy walking alone which is why I haven't encountered any type of serious aggressive situation during the first 4,933 kilometers of my MedTrek and (2) Circe, during the time I spent a year with her north of

Naples, actually told me to "wear your gold, exhibit your wealth; that will give you stature among the men you meet. They will realize you have armies and hesitate to attack you."

Turns out we're both wrong and that Circe certainly lives in a different world. Then I remember her forecast that I would "encounter some thieving gypsies when you least expect to, gain insight into how to evaluate your fellow men, and give your foes some tangible lessons when it comes to robbing MedTrekkers." Well here I am. She set me up.

When I finally realize what's happening, I veer off the forest path, cut a quick beeline through the trees towards the beach and yell a bilingual "I'm coming, guys, I'm coming. *Viene amici, viene!*"

"I've got some friends with guns over the embankment so you better not follow me or you'll be in big trouble," I tell the chorusing Gitans in a ridiculously low caste accent that mixes Italian/French and that I imagine might impress them.

Unfortunately, this ruse doesn't stop them for long, and when I reach the edge of the water, I have no choice but to confront them. They know, much to my chagrin, that they've found a solo peripatetic jewelry store with no friends or guns. So do I. Despite the danger, I immediately have a flashback to what my friend Henrietta Dax told me a decade ago: "Every time I see you, you're wearing more gold – you look like a walking jewelry store!"

"Domadoro, domadoro, DOMADORO," they spit at me again in unison, not bothering to hide the rocks they each hold in each hand. They stare, fixated, at my right wrist.

That's the wrinkle.

The gold band on my right wrist, unlike the chain around my neck and bracelet on my left wrist, can't be unclasped. It's a permanent fixture. It's been on my wrist since I had it made in 1969 when I turned 21 and gold was still worth $32 an ounce.

Guy Cheng, the jeweler in Vermont who designed and made the piece, perfectly complied with my request that "I want to wear something that won't come off until I die."

"It can't come off without a major effort with a chain saw," he told me.

Indeed the band has been on my wrist for almost forty years and has seen everything – two marriages, two children, two different centuries, drunkenness, sobriety, youth, middle age, thousands of workouts in hundreds of pools and thousands of kilometers on hiking paths. I don't want to lose it. Or my right hand.

I get the feeling that these guys won't settle for just a token offering – a bit of gold, some money, my weathered backpack – but would prefer (and what robber, gypsy or otherwise, wouldn't?) to take everything I have. Of course, to get the bracelet they will either have to cut off my hand and/or maybe knock me off. That just doesn't seem like an acceptable solution and when one of them grabs, and breaks, the chain around my neck, I know it's now or never.

I first think of quoting the iconic phrase from Lao Tsu who suggested that I "give up ingenuity, renounce profit, and bandits and thieves will disappear."

Then I imagine myself as Bruce Lee-sur-Mer. I visualize myself taking out the one on the left with a solid punch and a balls kick; the guy next to him I knock out with an elbow to the temple employing the reverse energy, wind up and thrust I learned during many years practicing aikido; I'd get the third Roma with a paralyzing three-finger jab to the throat.

Fortunately I have a better idea.

"*Attenzione!*" I yell as I point behind them. "*Polizia!*"

The trio, in a perfectly choreographed movement, look over their right shoulders in unison to see the non-existent squad of policemen, and I take off running down the beach (I know, I know, you're supposed to comply with a robber's requests but out here, in the middle of nowhere, I have no idea how they might deal with someone who'd seen their faces, knew the location of their campsite and was worth more than his weight in gold). Hoping that the fictional police trick and the kerosene they have consumed will slow them down, I am running faster than I have since we had to sprint the 220 for time in the eighth grade at Sequoia School.

I'm 60ish, they're 20-somethings, and I know I'll be really cooked if they catch me. I see a few thrown stones bounce off the sand at my side but keep sprinting and don't turn around. When, very winded, I do look to see how close they are, I see the three of them were standing like they don't know what happened. It doesn't look like they are going to come after me, presumably because they are drunk, fatigued or worried that someone might be on the beach and see them. Then, a few seconds later, I realize they're looking for the necklace chain and pendant that their leader had broken. Unbeknownst to them, or me at the time, the white-and-gold yin/yang pendant and chain are stuck inside my sweaty shirt.

"Who was that gray-haired guy?" I imagine they ask themselves. "How did we let him get away and how can we not let this happen again?!?"

There are, of course, between eight and twelve million gypsies scattered around Europe and one of the things they do best is rob and scam. I don't quibble with that professional choice but I think it's time to give them some help.

Here are my five helpful hints to would-be gypsy robbers on a beach south of Salerno:

1. Don't mix kerosene and thievery.

2. If a guy wears glasses, like I do, grab them to disorient your potential victim.

3. If a guy doesn't wear glasses, grab his backpack, which usually has something of value in it. Then, when your mark is completely distracted and thinks you're going for the glasses or backpack, move in for the jewelry.

4. Give your mark a break. Tell him that you only want cash and won't hurt him if he hands it over. I might have gone for that.

5. Don't rob MedTrekkers wearing sweaty T-shirts.

I have a few more suggestions for thieves that I'm going to dispense in a booklet that I'll try to sell to gypsy gangs in various European cities.

The next morning there is a story on Italian TV and in the newspapers about someone who had been killed and was found in a sandy grave on a beach near Naples. I'm happy to report that it wasn't me.

I walk very quickly for another few hundred meters and turn up the first access road, warning the first three people I see that I'd been accosted by gypsies and urging them to leave the forested area, which happens to be called Foce Sele (after the nearby Sele River) in the commune of Eboli. The last person I warn, who is sitting in her car near the main road, is a hooker.

"I've been working in this same spot for twenty years," she says (and looks like it) with a self-assured air that kind of irritates me, "and I've never been attacked. And I've got something for them if they try," she adds, holding up a canister of mace.

Hmmm. Mace. Maybe I should add that to the arsenal in my backpack.

"Say, can I take a look at your bracelet?" she smiles, and I, thinking she might also be contemplating a robbery or perhaps even be in cahoots with the gypsies, walk away and quicken my pace.

Though technically nothing has been stolen, I consider reporting the incident to the police and will be happy to press charges against the singing gypsy cretins. But after an hour walking and admiring the setting sun, I let it go (little do I know then that I'll be afraid to approach anyone, much less cackle at them, for a few weeks). In fact, I begin wondering if the gypsies built that sports path, and put the garbage around it, to make it look authentically Italian as a ruse to entice hikers like me into their lair. And I also wonder if they would have come after me at all if I weren't wearing the Capri baseball cap with gold lettering that accentuated the jewelry store look. Anyway, the cops will just call me an Idiot for being a walking jewelry store in a dark forest.

By the time I reach a fisherman who offers to take me to a bus stop to catch a ride back to my base camp in Agropoli, I don't even bother telling him the story. Instead, we talk about fishing and his Bulgarian wife. I do describe the incident to the Camorra-like character running the apartments where I'm renting a room, but when I'm done, realizing that this is such a minor affair in the global scope of things, I nonchalantly say, "Don't worry about it. No reason to go get those guys. It's just a minor offense. I don't want to bother your men with it. But I'll tell people that one of the longest, flattest stretches of beach south of Naples is a natural magnet for gypsies."

The next day is devoted to wanderment, wonderment and limited ambitions after yesterday's excitement. All I want to do is to slowly hike on the Lido Kennedy and the SS18 to and through the well-preserved and intriguing ruins of Paestum, or Poseidonia, as I still prefer to call it. A slow, relaxed day.

It's an easy ten kilometers along the sea to the Lido delle Sirene at Paestum, where I have a latte macchiato and croissant near the beach before walking a few extra kilometers inland (at Circe's request, I'm now counting kilometers to all Greek historic sites) to explore the fascinating ruins.

On the way, I further prepare myself for a great Greek day when I pass the Nausikaa Café, the Mithos Café (which has a logo of a centaur), the Kalypso/Minerva/Helios Hotels, the Ulisse/Poseidonia/ Athêna/Zeus campgrounds, the Hêraklês Village, and the Tempio de Venere and Giulio Cesare pizzerias. I feel, when I arrive at ancient Paestum where they promote the environment with the slogan "Keep clean is quality of the life," that I'm ahead of the game because a sign says it's 51 kilometers by road to Salerno and I only walked 44 on the beach.

I spend a fascinating few hours at Paestum not only because I'm enchanted by the well-preserved Doric colonnades at the Basilica, which is dedicated to Hêra, and the Temple of Neptune (which, though it should rightly be called the Temple of Poseidon, is now thought to have been constructed for Apollo) but also because I actually run into Athêna at the Temple of Athêna.

For someone at least a few thousand years old, Athêna is looking pretty good against a backdrop of Doric columns and Corinthian vases. She gives me one of her knowing owlish winks when I approach.

When I thank her for saving me from seductive Sirens and thieving gypsies, the goddess passes the buck and says simply, "It's Circe who's constructed this part of your MedTrek but from my perspective, it looks like an introduction to fear and fun."

This is not, apparently, a moment when Athêna will be providing me with any tangible guidance. But as usual, her soft voice and soothing words calm me down, and I am absolutely entranced as I stare at her before she sends me on my way with renewed determination and optimism.

She counsels me, "After you visit the intriguing museum here that depicts many of Odysseus' encounters on ceramics, go with the slow flow of the sea and wind."

Caught between a Rock and a Hard Place

"Odysseus's dilemma led to the Latin expression *Incidis in Scyllam, cupiens vitare Charybdim*, or 'You fall prey to Scylla in trying to avoid Charybdis.' In contemporary lingo, my hero was caught between a rock and a hard place. We all know the feeling." – *The Idiot and the Odyssey: Walking the Mediterranean*

My Athêna-inspired slow flow and leisurely pace, after a revitalizing grilled chicken and fresh spinach lunch on the Paestum Lido, involves steps on beaches, rocks and a bit of road leading into Agropoli.

I take the next day off to hand-wash my laundry, explore the town and spread the saga about my encounters with the Sirens, the gypsy boys and Athêna to anyone who will listen. I conscientiously study a map of the coastally mountainous *Parco Nazionale del Cilento e Vallo Diano*, the Cilento National Park and Diano's Valley nature reserve founded in 1991, where I'll head tomorrow.

I'm so relaxed that I even make a pyramid out of the vitamins I'm taking for my joints, muscles, heart, blood and general wellbeing. The mix includes fish oil, Glucosamine Chrondrotin complex, magnesium, niacin, Vitamins C & E, Coenzyme Q-10, Alpha Lipoic acid and baby aspirin. Although I frequently refuel on well water, fresh fruits, garden vegetables, pasta, pastries/bread, fish, veal, olive oil and ice cream, I credit the vitamins with keeping me MedTrekking without picking up even a cold.

Haze White, a New Zealander I met on the path, frequently reminds me how amused she was when I proudly showed off the copious variety of supplements that I carry around with me.

"I thought of you because I've just started taking a single multivitamin every day," she emailed. "And you had dozens of containers with vitamins I didn't know existed. I thought you were an addict."

I wish I could get by with one multivitamin. But for years, whether I'm on a walkabout for a week or seventy-five days, I painstakingly count out the precise number of necessary tablets before I hit the road. I'm not sure if that precision is a sign of good health or mental illness, but, though I'm occasionally injured, I don't seem to get sick while MedTrekking. The expression, "If one is sick of sickness, then one is not sick," frequently buzzes through my mind.

There certainly weren't many vitamins taken during the Trojan War when things were a bit more basic.

"That man stayed with victualing and wine can fight his enemies all day," Odysseus told Achilles in Homer's *Iliad*. "His heart is bold and happy in his chest, his legs hold out until both sides break off the battle."

Wish they'd bottled that!

The next morning I'm eager to get on the path at the crack of a dawn that, as Homer described it, rises "up from the couch of her reclining...with fresh light in her arms for gods and men." I'm excited because in 23 kilometers I'll cross the 5,000 kilometerstone on my MedTrek shortly after entering the lushly vegetated Cilento National Park.

After an easy start on a dirt road that begins right outside my door, I find myself leaping and jumping from large boulder to large boulder along the sea for two hours at a snail-like three-kilometer/hour pace. There's an easier road up the hill, which gets high marks on bestbikingroads.com, but I want to stay close to the water as I round the Point Tresino to Santa Maria di Castellabate.

These first bounding steps are part of a four-star hike punctuated by the green terrain (even the backs of the lizards are becoming bright green to blend with the spring foliage), lots of wind (I get another free sand dermabrasion treatment) and stupendous views of the whacking, whipping sea. I hike through a number of agreeable seaside and hillside villages; make one very steep climb up a nearly vertical cliff; and almost forget to observe the 5,000-kilometer mark between Point Licosa and Ogliastro Marina because I'm counting the olive and fig trees.

One thing I learned at the museum in Paestum is that grapes and figs were considered very good omens by the Greeks because their many seeds enable them to mass produce (whereas with an olive you just get the pits). And it was the branch of a fig tree that Odysseus grabbed, shortly after his men went down with his ship, to save himself from being gobbled by the whirlpool Charybdis a few hundred kilometers south of here.

I sit down in front of the raging sea during the afternoon and wonder how much water in the sea today was in it when I started the MedTrek a decade ago. I thank all of the gods for their help in enabling me to keep walking when so many other people can't. In fact, I'm dedicating every step I take on this outing to Henry Levinson, my freshman roommate at Stanford who has multiple sclerosis. When I appeared a few weeks ago at a tribute to him at the University of North Carolina, I told H, as his college friends still call him, that I'd be prancing along the Italian coast on his behalf.

H was the first guy I met in my dorm when my parents dropped me at Wilbur Hall at Stanford University in September 1966. We were opposites in many ways – he was dark, unathletic, Jewish, privately schooled and had a car – but we became close friends and he helped influence me to drop pre-med and concentrate on religious studies (I became the dorm authority on Paul Tillich) and creative writing.

After Stanford and a doctorate at Princeton, H taught courses in American religious thought, modern Judaism, and the philosophy of religion at Stanford and Harvard; wrote three very serious books; and ended his career as head of the Department of Religious Studies at the University of North Carolina Greensboro.

But forget all that. At the roast in his honor I thanked him for introducing me to theologian Martin Buber and his book *I and Thou*. It proved to be the most successful dating advice of my college career.

In brief, Buber, who died in 1965, felt relationships give meaning to life and ultimately lead man to God. A shared I/Thou relationship, rather than a selfish and impersonal I/It relationship, is profound and without bounds. The tip enabled me to create, or preach about creating, intimate I/Thou relationships, and that was music to the ears and heart of any co-ed during the late 1960s.

This frequently led to deep all-night-long cuddly discussions on the San Gregorio beach with a blanket and a bottle of wine before having very slow and extremely meaningful sex. The intense spiritual and physical aspects of those relationships, especially during the 60s period of free love, frequently carried us to heaven, if not God.

I wasn't always too good at this. I had a girlfriend on the east coast when I was at Stanford, and we stared at each other's photographs every night at 9:00 p.m. in an effort to provoke a long-distance, simultaneous, cosmic orgasm. Though it went well, and I wrote a paper that got me an A about this type of extraordinary transcontinental connection, I realized after a week that we hadn't taken the three-hour time difference into account.

H called me once when I was living in the south of France to say he was seriously considering suicide. He didn't take that step and his strength in coping with MS, which progressively made him unable to do much of anything, is inspiring.

"What's the secret of your fortitude?" I asked him once, expecting him to thank Yahweh, Zeus, God, Martin Buber or some other higher power.

"Alcohol!" he said without hesitation.

On one visit, H showed me a draft of his autobiography and, though much more didactic than personal, I was particularly struck by a rare revealing paragraph involving a night with a co-ed in 1967. It was so moving that I immediately contacted the woman involved and suggested they speak. Remarkably, she had equally starry memories of the night in question and their telephone conversation brought H back to life.

"That was better than alcohol," he smiled.

Speaking of alcohol, I'm also dedicating my every step to Malcolm MacPherson, a journalist friend who had a massive coronary earlier in the year.

I stayed with Malcolm, who was working with *Newsweek* at the time, at his place on the fringe of the Nairobi Game Park, where his Labrador puppy was snatched by chimpanzees from the terrace of his spacious house. We were hard partiers in the early 1970s and something Malcolm said made me think that maybe I had a problem with booze.

"You're not an alcoholic unless you drink straight vodka from morning to night," he told me late one evening.

"But that's what we've been doing," I replied.

Just before Montecorice, where there's a trying-to-be-chic residential development called La Dolce Vita, I witness an impressive display of wind and kite surfing. I recall how I used to travel to remote parts of the world to windsurf and that one of the more fortuitous or karmic incidents of my life occurred while windsurfing in the mid-80s. I was on a board at Cedar Beach on Lake Champlain in Vermont when my wedding ring fell off. Miraculously it landed on, and remained on, the windsurfing board in the middle of the lake and I was able to retrieve it.

When I walk to the end of the wind surfing beach I'm unable to hike around the point on the seaside. Instead of backtracking I choose to climb a steep, nearly vertical hill that is fortunately planted with pine trees and not too much thick shrubbery. I'm able to get a handhold to scamper to the road above but more than just a few times during the 15-minute uphill ordeal (wearing gloves and often on my hands and knees), I wonder if I still have the strength/agility to handle the climb, much less today's challenging wind and waves.

Fortunately, I'm not wearing a wedding ring.

The next bit of the walk, due to the inaccessible and unwalkable seaside, takes place on the SR 267 (signs inform me that this used to be a *Strada Statale*, or state road, but it's now a *Strada Regionale*, or regional road). The lack of cars and dramatic views are reminiscent of my walk on the GI 682, a stretch of two-lane blacktop road on Spain's Costa Brava that's so picturesque it's been declared a "European Monument" by the European Union.

At dusk, a teenager picks me up hitching in the center of Pioppi (which is not pronounced Popeye) and gives me a lift to a distant inland train station to enable me to get back to Agropoli. We discuss his fascination with cars, his skill at hunting for mushrooms (and identifying which are poisonous), how glad he is not to be walking as far as I do in any kind of weather, and his infatuation with everything American, especially the movie *Fast and Furious*.

"This part of Italy is really quite *terzo mondo* because there are no buses or taxis and the Internet is slow," he says. "Just the opposite of the U.S."

"Yeah, but everyone is relaxed and less stressed here," I reply, using the word *agio*, the best Italian word I know for 'comfortable in your own skin.' "You'd be disenchanted quickly by the speed of the United States."

The teen adamantly refuses to take the €10 I offer for the ride (hey, it was pouring at the end of the day, and he saved me a lot of time and trouble) because he didn't want me, and everyone I meet, to think that Italian teenagers pick up MedTrekkers just to make a euro. I tell him he saved my life (well, my day anyway), and that it is a small price to pay. He, like any good Catholic kid, crosses himself before reluctantly taking the bill.

The long day's walk is the right mix of MedTrekking magic, but I would urge anyone following me not to do it in one 48-kilometer stretch. Instead, stop after 41-kilometers in Acciaroli and take a break at the all-glass, triple-decker seaside Mediterraneo restaurant.

The next day takes me from Pioppi through the Marina di Casal Velino, past the ruins of Velia (which some Phocaean Greek refugees founded in 535 BC and called Elea) into the Marina di Ascea.

There's been so much thunder and rain that every river is swollen and the sea has become murky and multicolored – brownish murk near shore, greenish murk a little further out, a clear bluish color beyond that. Today a tumultuous, turbulent, thrashing and wavy tempest seems to be testing the breakwaters with all its force. Even the locals are stupefied and one shopkeeper I speak to says "Neptune is getting nasty."

"Is it always like this?" I ask a woman negotiating the puddles in Castellamare di Velia as I pick up a few confused snails to prevent them from getting squashed while attempting to cross the road.

"*Assolutamente no!*" she replies as I walk by an incongruously named Marrakech bar. "This is craaaaaaaaaaaaaaaaazy."

Almost every house around here has an *Affittasi*, or "For Rent," sign, but there's no one sampling the market today.

I admire the weather from a spitting distance at first, but then find myself in the eye of the storm when, after getting out of the rain by checking email at an Internet Point (one of the few in Italy that hasn't asked me for an ID, a precaution that's part of the security system implemented by the Italians after 9/11), I climb around a headland and embark on a steep, stunning, view-filled walk along a narrow, crumbling path for the next five hours. Not for the weak-hearted, this long, rigorous climb becomes an up-and-down brush/bush walk but, because of the tempest, enables me to observe the sea at its most emotional.

It takes me a ridiculous amount of time to make the walk but it would be worse driving – roads here are forced to divert inland to make the connection between the different villages. But the train, when it is running, goes through long tunnels that make it a breeze to get from A to P (Ascea to Pisciotta).

I discover when I return to Agropoli that I have the biggest blister in MedTrek history on the bottom of my left foot, due, I surmise, to the boulder jumping/climbing or just walking during the last few days. For some obscure reason I start thinking about young Italian girls and their penchant for wildly colored tennis shoes.

I invited Cassie, who hiked with me in Spain and Morocco, back for a birthday round of MedTrekking in a rental car that she'll use to chauffeur me when she's not walking. Now this is the way for a hiker to travel to and from the path!

"It's remarkable that you MedTrekked this far in just two days,"

Cassie says during the 90-minute drive from Agropoli to Pisciotta.

I mentally move into MedTrek companion mode, and when we descend on a muddy path to a boulder-congested beach I unquestionably follow Cassie's sensible suggestion to return to the road. After passing a very modern and solar-paneled soccer field right on the sea, we reach sandy Pisciotta beach on the *Baia del Silenzio* and continue to the majestic Palinuro promontory, which gets its name from the Aeneas' helmsman Palinurus.

The quick, two-hour, ten-kilometer beach/road walk, made even more pleasurable with Cassie's Ziploc bags of tasty treats, ends with a pizza-and-pastry lunch. Throughout southern Italy things are absolutely dead during lunch, between 1:00 and 4:00 p.m., and we see almost no one on foot or in a car as we go to the tip, top and bottom of the Palinuro cape on village roads, a trail and a path.

"This has been divine," says Cassie, who will drive ahead to Marina di Camerota to secure our next seaside squat as I continue MedTrekking.

I stick to the road (I can't get to the beach because of the steep escarpments on the Palinuro cape) for a few kilometers to cross two wide rivers and then take a trail into the mountains on a casual walk that affords constant glimpses of the sea and wondrous views of the mountains in the Cilento National Park (the slogan of this and many other national parks in Italy is *qui la natura è protetta*, or "where nature is protected").

I admire the budding yellow primrose flowers, relish the nearly perfect path through pine forests on the mountainside and am surprised that the crescendo sea sound paradoxically seems louder and closer on the crest than it does on the beach. The sea sounds on the Med always amaze me because they're so different from the louder noises on the Pacific, Atlantic and Indian Oceans.

When I'm caught in a dazzling thunder, lightning and rain storm, I figure Zeus is obviously irritated at someone (could it be me?), especially when one of his lightning bolts hits a nearby communication tower at the top of the hill.

As I descend to Marina di Camerota, I catch a vibrant rainbow on the sea and crack a smile when I see an advertisement for the Cyclopes Discothèque, pass a bar called Alcatraz, and walk by the America Hotel. With these attractions, who could refuse to stay in Camerota, which was founded in the sixth century BC and got its name either from the Greek word *kamaroma*, which means arch or vault, or the beautiful Kamaratòn, who spurned her lover Palinurus and was turned into a rock by Venus, the goddess of love.

Cassie has checked into a third floor room at the seaside Albergo

Tirreno, and when I arrive, soaked, I'm pleased that all I can see out the window is the sea, which was a brilliant array of blue throughout the day but has now reverted to its multicolored stormy gray-green hues. Does Poseidon control this coloration? Do the gods have anything to do with such a pleasing pastiche?

The next morning I'm among the first sentient beings to hit the only local bar that is open before sunrise. I have a *latte macchiato*, which literally means *marked milk* because the steamed "pure" white milk gets "stained" by the addition of espresso, but I'm not sure if it's actually strong enough to enable me to speak excellent Italian because the bartender fails, after my concise explanation, to grasp the reasons I'm making the MedTrek. When I ask if he's understood me, he replies simply *Più o meno*, or "more or less." It's not the last time I'll get that response, but usually I become much more fluent and convincing after my morning Joe.

I decide not to follow the muddy, wet paths and raging rivers today but instead to take the windy mountain road through Lentiscosa and enjoy the exquisite high-altitude views of the sea. The entire walk is a moving panorama of mountains to my left and steep canyons/caverns/gorges leading to the sea on my right, along with a few perched villages and a stunning church/monastery atop a hill between San Giovanni and Scario. Because it's the May 1st Labor Day holiday there are few cars, and the main sounds are the bells on the goats and the omnipresent barking dogs. I have another one of those "ahh omm, this is perfect" feelings that, after 5,000 kilometers, I realize can surprise me anywhere anytime.

Cassie catches up with me in the car after my first 16 kilometers, and we meet in San Giovanni a Piro, where the owner/chef at La Pergola restaurant has prepared tasty €5 ravioli with baby asparagus tips.

During lunch Cassie admits that she's made a logistical mistake by offering to be my chauffeur.

"That is the most gorgeous road in the world," she tells me. "If you'd told me it was that pretty, I would have walked it."

And then she expounds, over lunch on the eve of her 54th birthday, about her own MedTrek philosophy that inspired her, using the name Carlo Z. Roberts, to create a successful company called The Blue Walk that leads more relaxed hikes on the French Riviera.

"I adore beach walks, coastal trails and urban strolls," Cassie explains. "And, although I've loved MedTrekking with you, climbing up boulders, swimming in the Med and leaping like a gazelle from rock to rock is a bit much for most people. So my lighter version is just a few hours walking along the Med each morning with afternoons free in a different Riviera town each day."

But I must be doing something right, because Cassie suggests that her clients read *The Idiot and the Odyssey* and regularly hires me to be a guest guide on her walks between the Italian border and the Esterel.

Cassie drives ahead to Sapri (yes, Sapri with an S, not Capri with a C) and books into a room with a sea view at the Locanda del Trecento while I continue another 25 kilometers along the sea and stony beaches/ promenades through Scario (which isn't all that scary), Policastro Bussentino (the bay here is called Bay of Policastro, which gets me thinking about Fidel and Cuba), Capitello and Villammare. The promenade in Villammare is choc-a-bloc with locals when I arrive at five o'clock, and a Workers of the World Unite May Day parade turns the town into a festive mode.

I spend a few minutes admiring the *Torre Petrosa*, an Aragon tower built between 1556 and 1596, as my mind works overtime determining the cause/effect behind a pack of five uneaten Mon Cheri chocolates I find on the sidewalk. Tossing out empty cigarette packs irritates me, but I understand the rationale of someone wanting to ditch the residue of a product that could kill them. Why anyone would throw still-wrapped chocolate on the street always stumps me? So I eat them while I walk into Sapri.

Sapri, at the southern end of the Cilento Park, has a number of statues, plaques, memorials, and monuments in memory of Carlo Pisacane because this is where he and his three hundred men battled with the Bourbons in 1857. It didn't turn out too well. "They were three hundred, they were young, strong and dead!" wrote poet Luigi Mercantini in *La Spigolatrice di Sapri*. Yet that futile battle, which is re-enacted here every August, led to an anti-Bourbon movement and the unification of Italy.

After a traditional Italian breakfast (coffee, *cornetti*, yoghurt, *biscotti*, juice), Cassie and I take off from the hotel and cross the bridge that leads out of town. There's a manicured path on the Mediterranean seaside for three kilometers just below the ever-continuing SS18 road. We look back on the mountainous Cilento Park and the trail I hiked yesterday.

The walk beyond the Golf of Sapri on the Bay of Policastro through Aquafredda di Maratea to Maratea itself is a real beauty – right up there with the Costa Brava, the Amalfi Coast and northern Morocco. It includes the yin-and-yang contrast between the sheer rock faces on our left (all kept together with spider wire to prevent rock falls) and the expansive sea with its rock formations, grottos and shimmering aquamarine-and-turquoise colored coves to our right. There are a few beaches but, like the Amalfi Cliffs, the most sensible way to explore the seaside here is by boat. At the 225.8-kilometer mark on the SS18 we leave the *Compartimento di Napoli* and enter the *Compartimento di Potenza*.

The curve around the next bend leading into Maratea reveals the top-of-the 623-meter-high *Monte San Biagio*, on which sits a 22-meter-high Statue of the Redeemer, not far from the basilica of San Biagio. The concrete-and-white marble statue, which has been here since 1965, immediately evokes comparisons with the Christ the Redeemer statue, which is 38 meters high and sits on a 700-meter-high peak, on Corcovado Mountain in Rio de Janeiro.

I climbed to the one in Rio decades ago and immediately note the differences in the positions of the arms and hands. The bearded and serious Corcovado Christ appears as a perfect cross with palms faced forward towards the sea. The younger and more-friendly looking Maratea Redeemer that I'm looking at now has upraised arms, the palms face upward, and looks towards the mountains.

The next day kicks off with a compliment from the night porter at the hotel as he serves me (now that he knows I'm hiking around the Med) another copious Italian breakfast.

"You look fantastic, like Richard Gere," he says. "You're in great shape and must be my age. About 42, right?"

"60," I say.

He collapses. I laugh.

Cassie is heading back to Rome and expresses concern about being gassed and robbed on the 0211 (that would be just after 2:00 a.m.) train from Sicily that I suggested she take. I warn her, after hearing how certain she is that she'll be attacked, about the danger of expectations and projection. But to no avail.

We've discussed the improbability of her being gassed and robbed, though that actually happened to her and two companions on an Italian train in the 1970s. I assure her that ploy ended in the 80s after almost a decade during which people **were** kept asleep with gas and robbed during the night throughout the European train network. But when I see the immigrant express that she's taking to Rome I fear that she might be right. Heck, I even feel bad letting her get on the train and into a compartment with three guys from Senegal.

I'm relieved when I finally get a call from her telling me that, though she didn't sleep a wink or even close her eyes, it was an uneventful trip.

"I felt like I was going off in a refugee train, never to be seen again, and I had to look brave, because I didn't want them to smell the fear," Cassie told me later. "I should have driven here in the rental car instead of turning it back in."

I return to Maratea and immediately march five steep kilometers straight up the hill to pay my respects to Christ the Redeemer. It's a blissful walk and at one point I share the path with a bunch of young Italian mothers who are taking their chatty eight-to-ten year-old children up the hill to get a close look at the statue.

"Ah, you're from California!" one mother says in order to explain my mad romp around their sea to her kids.

Once I've visited the Redeemer, I decide to stay above the road, sea and tunnels as long as I can. I follow a muddy cow path and then hit a mountain road that traverses the hills high above the coast and gives me great views of Christ, Sapri and the mountains. That sweet road is too good to last, of course, and I spend ninety minutes negotiating an arduous, rocky get-cut-up-at-every-opportunity bush and bramble scramble that finally takes me to a communication tower at the top of a peak. A forest service road leads me on a walk downhill across the Lao River, which is a big kayaking/rafting destination, and onto the lengthy promenade through *Praja a Mare*. The train station, due to the ongoing closure and combining of stations in this part of Italy, is called Praja-Ajeta-Tortora. Just a few years ago there were individual stations in each of the three villages.

An "ahh omm" Moment in San Nicola Arcella

After the mountains, it's a relief to continue my walk on the Tortora/Praja promenade and feast on some pastries for lunch. But the main sight to see in Praja, the first town I run into in Calabria, is the *Isola di Dino*, a gigantic island that is just a few meters off the shore. Dino Island, which is three-kilometers long and surrounded by crystal-clear water, is perhaps the closest island to the shore on the whole Med and slightly resembles Monte Circeo. Before leaving town I drop into the Cave Sanctuary to see the sacred statue of Maria the Virgin, Praja's protector.

Then I find myself smack in the middle of the second annual MotoRaduno motorcycle convention, which explains why I'd been hearing motorcycle varooooms when I was walking in the mountains this morning, and trot through a horse riding school until I reach a visibly decent path that is blocked by a tall locked gate. I nimbly climb over it and fifteen minutes later arrive at an expansive empty beach. I cross it, thinking that I'll probably have to backtrack because the cliffs are too steep for me to climb, and then find a narrow tunnel that leads to a larger, turquoise-colored cove.

Bingo. I have another glorious MedTrekking "ahh omm"

moment when I stumble upon one of the best surprises of the entire trek on a sandy beach with an arched rock that leads into the sea.

I take a dip (who could resist?), admire the view through the rock formation and then begin climbing up a set of stairs when I run into some Italians coming down the steps.

"Just where am I?" I ask.

After expressing surprise and admiration that I've walked from Maratea, a father-son-grandson trio tell me that I'm on the hidden, but not private, beach at San Nicola Arcella.

"This is the way out and every pebble on this beach is worth a fortune during the summer because it's so crowded," says the grandfather.

At the top of the steps I explore the closed San Nicola train station and think of sprinting through a tunnel to save some time. But the passage looks very dark and very long, so I begin my first road trudge of the day on the SS18 to Scalea. I make good time and when I get to the main drag and the nice-looking part of town, I ask a hooker where to find the train station.

"I'm not from here. I don't know," she says with exasperation when she realizes that I'm not a customer.

Then I thank Christ the Redeemer in Maratea for the fantastic walk, the marvelous beach discovery and catch a train back to my base camp in Sapri.

I'm in a packed carriage sitting contentedly happy after a 37-kilometer day, when a man quickly rises from his seat and instructs his family of ten teenagers to move, with their masses of luggage, to another carriage.

"Okay, okay," I say to myself. "I know after a day like this that I smell but, gosh, isn't that a bit much?"

"Why did they leave?" I ask someone sitting next to them.

"The old man said it was too hot, and when the capo decides to moves everyone obeys."

A beefy man immediately moves from his nearby seat and sits next to me. He asks me all sorts of questions and naturally I explain the MedTrek and where I've been. Before I know it, he is very gently moving his finger over the numerous red scratches on my legs.

"You should wear long stockings, you know," he says. "You're probably the only boy in Calabria wearing shorts."

"Actually the correct phrase is that 'you should have worn long stockings,'" I reply. "It's too late now."

"But just for me would you please wear long stockings today?" he continues.

"Today should be okay," I tell him. "My wife and I are just walking by the sea."

"Your wife? Where's your wife?"

"She's two carriages ahead," I tell him. "We never travel in the same train compartment in case there's an accident."

It's rare that men hit on me and I never seem to be on any guy's gaydar. In fact, the only time a guy tried to seriously pick me up, at Elaine's in New York in 1971, he was seriously drunk. And even in that state he was *compos mentis* enough to add, "I'm not sure this will work out because I'm usually very picky."

My lack of attraction to my own sex is something that I've come to accept, and it hasn't prevented me from having lots of gay friends, being friendly with gay relatives and painting my toenails a rainbow color to support gay pride every June. And when, once in a very blue moon, a gay guy does come on to me, I try not to blush or brush him off. Nor do I wish to encourage him.

It can be a delicate situation, and I play it by ear. Sometimes I'll mention that I'm a member of a gay and lesbian masters swim team in West Hollywood; at other times I'll describe my somewhat undiluted heterosexuality. Or occasionally I'll be completely off the wall and feign that my wife and I never travel in the same railway carriage, just like many couples don't fly together. That remark both calms and slightly irritates my neighbor on the train. When I get off, I even pretend to wave to my non-existent wife so my new friend won't think I'm a complete homophobe.

Incidentally, I used to take pride in not buying tickets on Italian trains because they so rarely checked. Now, though, I'm so indebted to trains for getting me from A to B when they say they will that I insist on buying a ticket and am not even upset when the conductor doesn't ask to see it – a real sign of maturity.

I'm anticipating a day of flat, uneventful walking and a casual dip in the sea after yesterday's mountain trekking and train conversation left me scratched and reflective. That might not be possible.

"We're usually swimming on the first of May, but all the rain this year will keep us out of the water until June," predicts a bartender in Scalea.

Everywhere I've been, people are preparing the restaurants, beaches, and bathing areas for the crowds, but the weather and the crowds just haven't responded.

I return to the beach through a you-can-get-anything-you-want flea market and relish the coarse pebbled sand and listen to the gentle lapping of the waves. I look forward to an uneventful day on pebbles, bike/walking paths, and the roadside, and after 12.5 kilometers, I lie down on the small stones and actually fall asleep.

There is some excitement during my walk to Diamante. Right next to a flock of baaing sheep is the rusty hulk of a wrecked double-decker London bus that has been converted into a rural pub. It is adorned with a statuette of Christ, presumably to deter any would-be robbers from committing a sin. Doesn't take too much to get me excited.

Diamante, which touts its murals as a tourist attraction, is a real jewel/gem of a place when it appears at the end of a long stretch of sand. I stop for a coffee at a bar that has the sexiest server with the shortest skirt in Calabria. It's obvious that a lot of guys are dropping by for coffee just to look at her butt and just as obvious that she won't give any of them the satisfaction of a smile, though she did seem much friendlier to everyone when they were about to leave. Before I depart I notice a jewelry store called "Ancora," or anchor, and a still-closed hotel called Poseidon.

A bit later in Belvedere Marittimo – a nice little normal town with bars and a promenade, a new port financed by European Union funds, and a restaurant called *Il Povero Pesce*, or the poor fish which, of course, they all are once they've wound up there – I experience that refreshing start-of-the-day feeling that I get on every MedTrek morning after the first few klicks, as I occasionally call kilometers. Once again, when I notice breakwaters being constructed, it occurs to me that the sea must be rising if there are new breakwaters everywhere.

I continue on the beach/road/path/breakwaters through numerous developments just itching to come alive with the summer season – though on May 5 it's still around the corner. I recall that a woman on the train the other day told me that the weather this April resembled December. These places also resemble December, which is why this is a great season to hike. But I appreciate the fact that this will all change in a few weeks, and the urban residential development with its streets named after flowers – Viale delle Roses...Mimose...Petunie – will be in full bloom.

I pass a gigantic pool at the *Hotel delle Stelle* in Sangineto and realize that I haven't had a swimming workout on this outing. Then I see a Chattanooga Pizzeria and begin to reflect on the global economy. There are local touches, like the graffito that says *Napoli Regna* and a shepherd who's got his "Baaaaaaaaa" imitation down so well that he must have been a sheep in an earlier life.

I drop into the "Day and Night" restaurant on Capo Bonifati for an ice cream, and the complete nonchalantness of the bar tender, who makes me a coffee and gives me an ice cream, makes me realize that, in this lifetime anyway, I can't even fake being an Italian. Maybe, though, I am nonchalant enough to be an Italian saint, I think when I see a statue of *San Francisco di Paola* who has *lungomares* named after him in Bonifati and Cittàdella del Capo.

Seeking Light at the End of Tunnels

It's an appropriate day to dedicate my hike to Richard Tobiasson, a polio-struck grade school friend who was hit by a train in Redding, California, over fifty years ago, because I spend most of the next 39 kilometers walking between the railway tracks and the sea.

Unlike the trains, which speed through tunnels along this coast, I've got to cope with obstructions like the Capo Andrea. While the train buzzes through a 1.2-kilometer tunnel, I spend two hours moving slowly on the rocks, in the water, and up and down self-made paths to get around the stunning cape. I have shoes on for 45 percent of the day, sandals for another 45 percent and go barefoot for the remaining 10 percent. To get around the cape, I have to switch from sandals to shoes/socks three different times.

Only an Idiot would, at any age, hazard a walk through railway tunnels. But I'm forced up to the tracks by a lack of beach, and when there's no way around or over two promontories due to the terrain, I decide to go underground. I realize that the tunnels are short (I can see the light at the other end) and that there are walkways with recesses every 20 meters to duck into if a train comes. I'm somewhat confident because it's lunchtime and I presume that not many trains – though, of course, it only takes one – will be running. Who could resist?

Not that I don't think about the odds a bit, which gets me thinking about Richard for the first time in years, except when I drive near the stretch of railway tracks where he was killed at the age of nine in the 1950s.

His family lived near the tracks, and I lived a mile away down on the Sacramento River. We were in the same grade, and I admired how Richard tried everything, even baseball, despite wearing clumsy leg braces and using crutches. I've always wondered, but will never know, if he was playing chicken with the train, got his brace caught in a track or just wanted to end it all on the day he was killed.

Anyway, when I walk into that first tunnel today, I think of Richard and dedicate my perhaps foolish efforts to his memory, though not before recalling the time when, seven years after his death, I was almost killed by a train while seeking hidden treasure (no, not the Golden Fleece, but a pot of "gold" hidden by a radio station). I was following the clues when I asked my mother to let me out of the car on Highway 99, waited for a train to pass and crossed the tracks – only to be nearly hit by a train coming from the other direction. The next day I found the "gold" on the other side of town, got my picture in the paper and was declared to be a "human bloodhound" during a radio interview.

Not that I'm quite that stupid today. When I enter a 1.2-kilometer tunnel and can see nothing but darkness, I retreat. And I'm very relieved that I did when I hear a very fast train crash by just a few moments later. I make it around the cape through Marina di Cetraro, which is the first place I've seen that advertises its boat trips to Stromboli, and along the pebbled and sandy beaches and palm-tree decorated promenades of Acquappesa and Intavolata (of course, I think of John Travolta) to Guardia Piemontese Lido where I find the family-run €35-a-night Hotel Zilema.

When I check in, the son of the owner gets very enthused about the MedTrek and gives me the history of *Magna Graecia,* or Great Greece, which is the name of the coastal areas in southern Italy and Sicily colonized by the Greeks; colonization that he says was "inspired by curiosity, trade, and banishment that brought geniuses like Pythagoras to Italy."

The fishmonger makes his daily call at the Zilema Hotel the next morning around 8:00 a.m. and the capo of the hotel family greets him with a loud "Ho" when they see each other (one reason I like Italians is that, like me, they use the "Ho" expression very frequently).

While he's inspecting the catch, I ask what lies ahead.

"Di monte, di palude e di mare, di mare, di palude e di monte," he says as he selects and buys some squid, which I'll be eating for dinner when I return this evening.

"Mountains, marshes and sea, sea, marshes and mountains," I translate to myself.

I anticipate another day of seaside walking between the ties of the railroad and the tides of the sea. Indeed, that's what I find the moment I cross the street from the Zilema and turn left.

As I walk towards the Marina di Fuscaldo, I'm in meditative MedTrek mode due to the cadence and seductive Siren-like sound of the waves lapping the pebbled/graveled/sandy beach. The soothing effect of the sea is complemented by the densely treed mountains, the now Day-Glo phosphorescent green color of the geckos, and the cloud cover over the mountaintops.

I meet the saint of the day, of the whole region actually, when I near Paola, where San Francesco of Paola was born in 1416. I first see a statue of him, then the *lungomare* named after him, then another statue, then a street named after him. JFK probably has more streets named after him than any individual in history, but in these parts, in his *casa natale* of Paola, it's strictly San Francesco. He obviously has an impact on me because within a few minutes of seeing the first statue I am carrying, like he does, a wooden staff to negotiate the sand and measure the depth of the rivers when I make crossings.

When I reach Paola, I'm surprised that despite, or because of San Francesco, there seems to be more snogging/fornicating on the beach and in cars parked on the beach at noon on a Wednesday in May than in any other place on the Med. I shouldn't be too surprised because even when they're not fornicating, Italians get the European Award for the most numerous displays of intimate affection in public.

Although I'm not impressed with the town itself, I make a rare foray east of the railway tracks to climb some steep steps to the *centro storico* where, it's said, San Francesco gave a sermon. Then I climb further away from the sea to visit the sanctuary and basilica/college/church complex named after him.

Francesco's big pitch, it doesn't take long to learn, was *CHARITAS*, or charity. The word is written more often in Paola than any graffiti tag and, naturally, compels me to leave a few more coins than usual when lighting a candle at the sanctuary and making offers at various saintly contribution containers. The sanctuary not only has an expansive view of the Mediterranean, but the river running through it creates a meditative singing sound that rivals that of the Sirens and would bring a smile to even the most serious monk.

A city that does have much more charm than Paola is San Lucido, just a few kilometers further along the coast. It's not just a storybook perched village. It's a storybook perched village with 360 degrees of stunning views due to a circular road around its perimeter. Every hillside village should adopt this sensible road network. The other great thing about San Lucido: the double-scooped gelato I got for €1 (cheaper than nearby Sapri).

This is a sandal day from start to finish, which is fortunate because there are numerous rivers and creeks to cross – and the seawater bathes the scratches on my legs to promote healing. Despite some clouds, I'm sure spring is edging towards summer, because at one point the sand is too warm to walk on barefoot and there are some thonged Italian twenty-somethings out working on their tans.

I hope to make it to the station in Amantea for a train back to my Guardia base camp, but everyone – and I mean everyone – tells me it's further than I think. They're right. I continue on the seaside and pass out-of-order railway stations in Torremezzo di Falconara Albanese, where not a soul seems to be stirring during the afternoon on the *molto longo lungomare*, and *Fiumefreddo*, which of course means that the river I just crossed is obviously cold. Although these train stations offer almost no passenger service, they are quite eerily brought to life by a recorded voice that unfailingly announces that a train is about to pass on Binario 1 or Binario 3 that will NOT be stopping. As dusk, then dark arrives, I'm still a long way from Amantea.

My feet are sore the next day, but I remain upbeat as I walk further south, towards Scilla (yes, the seaside village of the Scylla and Charybdis fame) and Sicily. Just a few more 30-kilometer days, I tell myself, and I'll be at the locale of another dramatic scene from *The Odyssey* and another pleasant stopping point on Circe's magical Mediterranean mystery tour.

"Go on, go on," I tell myself. "You don't need a day off."

So I go on, noticing that the town of Longobardi seems to be an area devoted exclusively to artisanal research. There's one laboratory conducting research on pasta and another concentrating on *liquori*. The town's also just put in a very nifty close-to-the-sea wooden bridge that enables me to cross a river without getting my feet wet and observe fishermen in a few boats not too far offshore pulling in their nets.

That gets me thinking about my own fishing career that, when I was I kid, was an avid pursuit. I fished everywhere near my home in northern California – Shasta Lake, the Sacramento River, Olney Creek, Rising River, Trinity River, the Pacific Ocean –and always enjoyed repeating the phrase I learned from my stepfather:

> *"Fishy, fishy in the brook,*
> *Joel catch 'em on the hook,*
> *Mommy fry 'em in the pan,*
> *Daddy eat 'em like a man."*

I've got a lot of friends – like Christian Fryer in Colorado, Charlie Price in California, and Vincent Meade in Paris – who swear by the reflective and relaxing aspects of "catch and release" fishing. But I've given up the sport with the same enthusiasm that I quit golf. I haven't put a hook, line or sinker in the water during my entire journey around the Med.

Why?

The last time I went fishing was in 1987 at the fashionable Gleneagles resort in Scotland, where we hired a gillie to be our guide because we thought he knew where the fish were biting. After four hours, my father, two brothers and I didn't catch, or see, anything resembling a fish.

"Never seen anything like this before," the gillie lamented in a tone that implied he'd seen this before.

Then, when we were back at the dock, I saw a beautiful trout skimming along just under the surface. I put my fly on top of the water, leading the fish by an inch or two, and walked along the dock hoping to catch or snag the only fish in the lake. I looked at that fish with complete concentration, and just as I expected the trout to strike the dock ended and I fell in the water.

By the time we returned to the Gleneagles Hotel, which is about as far as you can get from a humble MedTrek squat, the story of my misstep got around town and seemed to be far more important and humorous than the fact that we didn't catch any fish.

I haven't baited a hook or cast a fly since.

I'd been told by a post office employee I spoke to at a café that Belmonte Colabro "has the prettiest women in Calabria." That's not all we talked about, of course. I learned that he's my age, makes only €1,300 a month (but has a job and healthcare for life), used to live in Sardinia, likes wearing spiffy tennis shoes and just got fined €33 for overtaking another car in a tunnel on the SS18.

When I walk on the seaside approaching the perched village of Belmonte Colabro at 10:00 a.m., which is well before fornicating/sun tanning time on any beach anywhere in Italy, there's not a soul, male or female, around. Is the town's reputation for beautiful women an urban legend? Who knows? I'm not going to hang around until three when the prettiest women in Calabria, if indeed they're here, will be out tanning. Instead I head out of town past the Villa La Vagabonda and the prettiest thing I see are two batches of puppies all with identical patches on their left eyes.

After I've gone ten kilometers, there's a sign at a seaside train station that reads simply _M T_ . I presume, consulting my map, that this is AMANTEA with a few letters missing and verify that when I have a coffee at the station and get in a conversation with the older and younger women working the bar.

"What do you think of this part of Calabria?" the older one asks me.

"I think it's got the prettiest women in Calabria," I say, which brings a smile to the younger server.

"But what do you think of the countryside, the mountains, the sea, the soul of the people?" sniffs the older woman.

"I think they're all as beautiful as the women," I reply.

She sniffs a little more. The younger one smiles a little more.

I leave to visit Amantea's attractive hillside _centro storico_ and drop into a _producto tipico_ store on the way out of town to refuel with a delicious cacao cake. It's thirty more kilometers to Lemezia, much touted as the most important town around because it's got an airport and Julia

Roberts landed there when she shot parts of *Eat Pray Love* here.

The two African guys walking on the beach parallel to me are kicking a makeshift soccer ball back and forth and immediately get my attention. Thieves, I think to myself. Just like those gypsies. So, admitting that I'm a possible racial profiler, I walk closer to the railroad track than the sea and figure that I'll sprint to the road if I'm the victim of another attack. I've been paranoid like this, whether the guys are white or black, since I was held up two weeks ago.

It turns out that this duo is heading to the Circus Lidia Togni a few kilometers out of town that, like a big top of yore, has been effectively using old school advertising and publicity. There are posters with cabaret dancers, posters with tigers, posters with clowns, and discount coupons being given away at every red light and street corner.

Once I decide that I've made the Africans a threat that they're not, I stroll through the circus grounds past an elephant, a camel, some ponies, some identical horses and dozens of circus employee caravans with satellite dishes. It's so enticing that I consider coming to the show tonight.

I arrive in Campora by walking on the beach through the comfortable-enough looking Village Trevi complex that has all sorts of accommodations and luxuries. When I get to the entrance/exit at the other end, I realize I could use some of these luxuries, especially a facial and a foot massage.

I get back to my sea-view room in Guardia, ask around and learn that there's a beauty salon and a woman named Sabrina who can give me a facial and a pedicure.

I find the place but it turns out that Sabrina got married last Saturday and, her mother tells me, isn't going to be working for a week. She tells me to find Romy, who works out of her apartment in the center of town and, without an appointment, I get a splendid €25 facial as we discuss life in this part of Italy.

I mention to Romy that on the way to her place I passed by the local church on via Aldo Moro with a crowd spilling onto the street at five o'clock on a weekday afternoon.

"Catholicism must be alive and well," I said to myself as I entered the church.

It turned out that there was a mass for a young boy who was killed by a speeding car on the local lungomare. I'll walk for him tomorrow – and for all the crazy Italian drivers who treat the SS18 like their private Formula One racetrack.

"We're really still a very simple, and very poor, people down here," Romy tells me during the facial.

The next day I set up a new base camp down the coast. There's no easy train/bus service to get me anywhere because the trip involves two different Italian provinces. I don't know if I've mentioned this, but one problem that mankind hasn't quite resolved is how to marry different transport systems when going from country to country, state to state, county to county or province to province. They all prefer to stop the buses at the border.

I try to hitchhike, which can be a little more complex with all my gear rather than just a small backpack.

"They'll never pick someone like you up," a guy twice my age stops his car to tell me. "They're afraid of you."

"But look at me – trusty silvery hair, clean clothes to kick off the day, a small backpack, a striking resemblance to Richard Gere – what's not to trust?" I ask him. "And this is Italy's wild west!"

"You're in southern Italy, you're a man, and you're alone," he replies as two *caribinieri* stop to take a look at my ID and get the low down on my plans.

"There's not much public transport around here," I tell them.

"*Che poco,*" admits one cop.

"*Che poco o che niente?*" I retort.

"*Che niente,*" he admits.

They laugh it off and let me loose, but when a couple with two dogs and lots of luggage gets picked up before I do, I give in, stash my gear at a local bar, tell them I'll be back that night and go for a little walk on the beach to wash my mind of my impermanent dilemma. Nothing better than a stroll to resolve a problem and convince myself that, as Deng Ming-Dao said, "whether we remain ash or become the phoenix is up to us."

The 26-kilometer walk from Campora San Giovanni to Lamezia (or actually a coastal suburb of Lamezia called Borgo della Marinella, because Lamezia and its train station are a four-kilometer walk inland from the coast) also stymies me. My boots are on their last steps, it seams (sic), and so much sand is coming in through the many holes that it's becoming impractical to walk with much efficiency on the beach.

There's a hooker working the border between the Cosenza and Catanzaro provinces at the roaring Savuto River, but she doesn't seem to care about my transport dilemma. In fact, I learn very quickly that I can talk transport to bus drivers and sex to whores in my primitive Italian, but I can't talk transport and sex too well to either at the same time.

So I toss all these transport problems to the waves and enjoy myself as I head towards Falerna Marina wearing sandals and thinking about life beyond the many dilapidated buildings on the coast.

Speaking of sex, though, I keep seeing a red-on-yellow ad for SEXY SHOP in Amantea and, based on other roadside ads, have to admit that this an eye-catching color scheme for an ad for SEXY SHOP or anything else.

Then I walk by the "Old America Hotel" and, right next to it, a restaurant called "Ocean," which offers "steaks and more." Neither of them is open even though June is just a few weeks away, and I remind myself that Ocean is a key character throughout Homer. It's the personification of a stream that surrounds the known world and is the source of all bodies of water, including the Mediterranean.

I see two Arab men on bikes and, like with the Africans yesterday, imagine they're also going to ambush me. I'm obviously somewhat paranoid, because I got the same feeling a bit earlier today when I ran into, or walked by anyway, a group of white skinheads, all wearing tight black Ts looking like they were straight out of *Fight Club*. Turns out, though, that once again my fear is just a hangover from the gypsy encounter, and I remain unrobbed and untouched by either group.

I finally set up a base camp on Capo Suvero where there's a hillside hotel, not surprisingly called the Hotel Capo Suvero, hovering above the sea with a low price, and working Wi-Fi.

I am now on the *Golfo di Sant'Eufemia* that continues for a couple days' walk to Capo Vaticano. I spend a few minutes kicking an orange ball used as a flotation marker for fishing nets and also see an airplane, the first since Naples, making a landing in Lamezia. As I enter the commune of Gizzeria, I hit the marshy and lakey part of the Calabria coast that, as the SS18 and train tracks distance themselves, is a dream walk. I'm lost in a mindless reverie (the MedTrek has, as Homer wrote in *The Iliad*, "won my mind to mindlessness") until I hit the Hang Loose Beach (like many places and brands today, it's known solely by its initials, HLB). A wind surfing instructor tells me that this particular spot is as windy as Tarifa in Spain and has the "best kite surfing on the Mediterranean."

I walk beneath the kite surfers towards the most inner part of the gulf and am informed by an old couple, whom I intentionally interrupt in mid-argument, that I've arrived at Gizzeria Lido, that there might be a bus to the distant Lamezia station but they don't know when it will come and *basta, basta* before I let them resume arguing.

A few kilometers further I arrive at the out-of-place, luxuriously styled Ashley Hotel in Marinella, where Pasqualino the concierge tells me that a room goes for €120 and a cab to the train station costs fifteen. I'm sure the room is nice and the cab fare's a deal, but Pasqualino's hood isn't in my price range. So I catch a bus (the building across from the bus stop has PARADISO written on it so maybe that's where I've wound up) and then train north to spend a few hours retrieving my stuff and getting it moved to the Hotel Capo Suvero.

The big event of this little trip is that I get rid of my holey hiking boots that have almost disintegrated. Although I first plan to leave them on the train to create of a bit of where-did-that-American-man-go-mystery, I wind up, primarily because they smell so bad, putting them in a trash bin at a train station. I'm taking a break from MedTrekking in a few days and figure I can make it to Reggio Calabria wearing my worn tennis shoes.

Along the way, the sun transfixes me as it prepares to set on a sea that tonight looks like an infinity pool (we're talking real infinity here). And when it finally goes down, I sense that it's winking at me. Or maybe at the full moon that will appear an hour later.

Although the sun and the moon are mentioned frequently in Homer, did you know that there's also a reference that could indicate a solar eclipse?

"The sun has been obliterated from the sky, and an unlucky darkness invades the world," the seer Theoclymenus told the suitors in *The Odyssey*.

What turns out to be a 27-kilometer sand walk (and if you add this to the sand of the past few days, you've got a lot of kilometers of sand walking) on May 9 starts off with a nice prognostication by a tall, dark, but not particularly handsome Italian man who accompanies me for a few kilometers.

"This is the first day of spring," he says as we take off along a just-being-built promenade in Marinella next to the regional command station of the *Calabria Guardia di Finanza*. "It's the first day I've felt like winter might be over."

Indeed, there's not a cloud in the sky, the sea is calm and it almost feels warm before 9:00 a.m., just like summer is supposed to on the Med. I see the faint outline of a bridge in the distance and ask the not particularly handsome Italian man if I'm seeing things – or if I've just found a shortcut across the Golfo di Sant'Eufemia and gotten a spring break.

"No, I don't see any bridge," he says, looking at me with newfound suspicion.

Well, I do. And I figure it's one way I can trick Odysseus, who sailed down this same coast after spending a year with Circe and didn't tell his crew that Scylla and Charybdis were just ahead.

My walking friend leaves me after two kilometers, and I basically spend the next 13 kilometers trying to find the most solid place to saunter on the soft sand and occasionally pebbly/gravelly beaches. I ford three different rivers by delicately feeling my way with a wooden staff across the sand bar where the rivers meet the sea.

The river crossings turn out to be a time-consuming activity and the sand makes it even slower going. Not that I'm particularly concerned. There are a few Saturday fisherman and a few joggers, but Italy in general hasn't heard that the sun is out and spring is here. It turns out that my "bridge" is an out-of-use 250-meter docking facility for cancerous petroleum products that extends far enough out onto the gulf so that it looks like a bridge.

At noon, a bit worn out from sand walking and river crossing, I stop and have a filling spaghetti *marinara/pescatore*, with nice fresh seafood and a few pieces of bread for a rare MedTrek sit-down lunch. I spend an hour just eating and chilling and talking to the waitress and her owner-mom in the otherwise empty restaurant.

The waitress tells me that there's a big river ahead that's impossible to cross. I reach it after passing two beaches with *chaises longues*, umbrellas and sunbathing facilities (and some sailboats for rent), but few sunbathers. This turns out to be the easiest and shallowest of the four rivers I cross. I figure that July and August must be the key months for these resorts, perhaps as important as Christmas is to retailers, because it's still slim pickings in May.

Counting Steps and Compiling Statistics in Calabria

I'm still seeing potential gypsy thieves behind every pine tree when I again enter a forest to both get off the sand and attempt to get over my fears of walking through a forest. When I ask a caretaker at one of the beach facilities about the depth of the next river, I'm actually worried that he'll follow me and hold me up. A bit later when I see three Italians chatting around a car in the forest, I turn around and take another path. I'm even suspicious of some of the fishermen. About the only sentient beings I meet during the day who don't worry me from a thieving perspective are four buffalo, a dead sea turtle, and one nun testing the water in her habit. I'm getting tired of looking over my shoulder and have got to overcome this paranoia.

When the sand ends, I walk on streets, big boulders, and breakwaters (at this point any break from the sand is a relief) to get through Pizzo (the signs spell the name with the O in the shape of the sun, though I imagine it as a big pizza surrounded by triangular pizza slices). Just before Pizzo, a characteristic hilltop village with a very active and bustling main piazza whose motto is *"Città per la Pace,"* or City of Peace, I enter the Piedigrotta grotto/church/sanctuary adorned with religious figures carved out of stone and votive offerings left by pilgrims.

But forget all that! I'll always remember Piedigrotta because I caught a Catholic nun bathing in the sea and took a series of photos called Sister Act One, Two and Three.

Beyond Pizzo, I head quickly to Vibo Marina, which turns out to be a thriving port, certainly the biggest pleasure/trade port since Salerno, and an aero naval base.

I try to hitch back to my base camp but this time it's a Libyan at the bus stop that tells me not to bother.

"Calabria men are too macho to pick up hitchhikers," he laments.

As I walk three kilometers to the train station, I notice that all these "macho and sado" guys also have crosses hanging from their mirrors. There's absolutely no reason for me to think that "Love Thy Neighbor" has anything to do with "Love Thy Hitchhiker."

The regional train back to my base camp only has two passenger carriages, and its slow pace lets me appreciate the agricultural activity (olives, onions, and oranges just to stick with the os), *autostrada*, oddly named train stations (Filadefia is one, Eccellente another), and densely shrubbed hillsides just a few kilometers from the coast.

I take the next day, Mother's Day, off and monitor my current progress by making a list of important and completely ridiculous statistics. I scrawl this tally on a napkin during a lunch of spaghetti with squid and a nice piece of swordfish with two scampi.

Total kilometers walked since April 17: **622**
Total kilometers walked around the Mediterranean to date: **5,357**
Most kilometers walked in one day on this outing: **48 (on April 27)**
Amount of time spent sunbathing: **7 minutes (on April 25 and May 9)**
Most memorable encounter: **Being attacked by gypsies on April 24.**
Second most memorable encounter: **Running into Athêna in Paestum.**
Best music: **The Sirens singing to me in Marina del Cantone.**
Rivers forded: **18**
Best unobstructed Med view from balcony: **Marina de Camarota**
Fish caught: **0**
Fish seen caught: **4**
Pastas eaten for lunch: **2**
Pastas eaten for dinner: **22**
Number of baptism dinners attended: **1**
Favorite gelato flavor: **Nocciatello**
Best non-gelato dessert: **Profiteroles in Sapri**
Average cost for a room: **€31**
Hitchhikers besides me seen on the road: **5**

I try to make the walk from Vibo Marina to Tropea as sandless as possible. Whenever there's an alternative to the soft-sanded beach I take it. After I hit the morning market in Vibo Marina (even I, after years in the south of France, am amazed at the two dozen different types of olives on sale), I MedTrek on rocks, dirt paths, trails, a little-used local train track, and even a bit of road at the end of the day.

Just after Briatico I walk above the cliffs through a fragrant field full of flowers, thorns, thistles and everything else that buds and blooms in spring. I look down on, without a doubt, the sweetest beaches and cleanest sea, punctuated by rock formations both underneath and above the water level, that I've seen in quite a while.

Although it's warm enough to be the first day of summer (even an Italian looking for shellfish tells me that it's *molto caldo* – and he, like everyone else, seems to have forgotten the lousy weather of just a few days ago), May is still a very transitional month. Most of the hotels, campsites and villages on the coast haven't been cleaned up, much less opened (in contrast to Spain where they seem to spend the entire winter getting them ready for the season), and there's been minimal beach cleanup. That's fine with me because they usually have paved paths and shady walks, and no one disturbs me when I take them.

I recall Lao Tsu pointed out that "stillness and tranquility set things in order in the universe."

I ignore the barge and rock work underway on a new road and carefully jump from boulder to boulder (occasionally wishing I had my hiking boots instead of less sturdy tennis shoes) on a very rocky coast near Marina di Zambrone.

The highpoint of the day is a skinny dipping session in the clear, cool water when, dripping with sweat after walking a few kilometers on seaside rocks, I arrive at the iconic rock formation that's on the cover of most Calabria guidebooks. I strip down, jump in, and relish the fresh, cold change-of-season Mediterranean water.

Soon as tired of boulders as I am of sand, I take the steps up to the German-filled Rocca di Tropea Hotel and hike on the road until I can cut down to the Tropea port, past restaurants and pubs called Poseidon, Circe and Ulisse to find a €42 room that includes breakfast and dinner at a price that will double in August.

Tropea, incidentally, is the St. Tropez of the Calabria Riviera (which, thank god, they don't call the Calabria Riviera). It's perched, animated, bustling, exciting, and is particularly well-known for its red onions, known as the cipolla di Tropea. Yet I'm surprised by the *gelateria* that makes red onion flavored ice cream and has other flavors based on squid ink and *nduja*, the local spicy salami.

The local Calabrians, perhaps because they're at the foot of the boot of Italy, are especially appreciative of my footloose feat.

"Bravo," says the owner of Le Roccette Mare hotel on the beach beneath the San Leonardo rock in Tropea where I'm installed for a few days. "*Complimenti*," adds the waiter.

It's always satisfying to take off at dawn from the place I'm staying on the beach. I lock the door, sniff the air, and march down to the water under the eye of the still-sleeping cliffside town of Tropea. I'm inspired to take off at 6:00 a.m., which has an obvious downside because most Italian hotels don't serve breakfast until eight.

I have to walk six kilometers on the clean and cool *lungomare*, past lots of camping sites and diving centers, before I run into an open bar across from the hospital. There I get one, then two and then three cups of strong espresso with a dab of milk. I also receive a cautionary warning that it's impossible to walk on the seaside before or after Capo Vaticano due to the coastal rocks and large mountains/promontories/cliffs/ *scoglio*/escarpments/*rocce*/you name it. *Scoglio*, incidentally, doesn't just mean reef or rock in Italian but also, very appropriately, stumbling block.

That's why I'm sucking up the coffee. I'll need stimuli to keep me going on what promises, due to the nature of the coast and the cliffs, to be an up-and-down day at best. In fact, it's worse than that. It's a walk-on-the-sand-until-you-reach-a-mountain/ promontory/cliff/*scoglio*/ escarpment/*rocce*/you name it that you can't surmount without getting killed. Then-climb-up-to-a-trail-to-get-you-over/ around-the-obstacle-then-when-you-think-you're-in-the-clear-cut-back-down-to-the-beach and go through the whole process again and again and again for 44 kilometers.

The positive payoff is stupendous views from the top of Capo Vaticano, from above the beach in Coccorino and on the steep road down to Joppolo (someone obviously had a fun time naming these places). Not everyone is so creative, but they do have a sense of humor. One café is called *Il Tempio di Nettuno* and as I head down to the Santa Maria di Ricadi beach, I see a hotel called Heaven and a pizzeria called Paradiso.

I'm sure I see Odysseus at the helm of one of the boats on the glass-smooth sea and the water takes on all sorts of different hues, including red and purple, due to the many underwater rocks and position of the sun. Whenever I'm directly above the sea, I look down at the seaside and wonder if I could have made it on foot. But today I admit that it doesn't look good. I mean, it looks good but it doesn't look good.

I also walk through lots of fields with lots of wild flowers after taking a coastal path that passes both a medieval tower and a modern communications tower beyond Joppolo. I enter a 456-meter train tunnel because, beyond the patches of wildflowers, there's thick foliage with thorns both up the hill and down the hill that would have cut me to shreds. Who could resist an open thornless train tunnel in the middle of all this? Except for the tunnel, the terrain adds a lot of kilometers to the walk. When I reach a desolate looking Nicotera (the Lido El Morocco and the Sayonara Club are peopleless), I've gone 34 kilometers compared to 27 or so it would have been on the road.

There's a sign in San Domenica that says "leave it clean, find it clean" that nobody on the garbage-strewn coast seems to have read. It encourages me, however, to pick up a lot of garbage and throw it in the bin in front of a lot of bewildered German tourists.

A campsite called the Forum Erculis promises "bungalows right on the beach, total shade and abundant water" but actually provides a very rocky nudist beach with a lovely waterfall, a crumbling hillside and a sign: *"Non Guardoni,"* which I translate as "You're on your own" or "No voyeurs."

After getting a *nocciatello gelato* in Nicotera, I avoid the beach run to San Ferdinando di Puglia by walking for an hour on a hard sand path through the middle of a 50-meter wide pine forest, which is distinguished by the fact that most trees are tilted at 45 degree angles due to the constant breeze from the sea. On one side there are uninhabited holiday resorts and on the other an uninhabited beach.

Again, I'm working on my post-gypsy paranoid therapy and tell myself that the shade is worth $1 million even if I do get attacked again.

San Ferdinando di Puglia turns out to be a huge and completely unexpected modern port a few kilometers before Gioia Tauro. When I get there, a young mother folding her laundry in the street in front of her house offers me a drink of water, and we discuss some recent violence in nearby Rosarno, a town of 16,000. That's another spot in southern Italy that's had violence related to some 2,500 primarily African immigrants who are responsible for picking most, if not all, of the fruit in citrus groves throughout the Calabria region.

Two days of riots here in January 2010, triggered by a minor shooting incident involving a Togolese, were among the worst the country has seen, and commentators said the situation was exacerbated by low pay, the overall economic downturn, race, and organized crime. Scores of police and rock-throwing rioters were injured, cars were torched and over 1,200 immigrants were put in detention centers while their makeshift tin shanties on the fringe of town were destroyed by bulldozers.

The incident sparked controversy that led to a discussion of the Italian economy, human rights violations, the abuse of low-cost foreign labor by residents of the town, and the role of the Calabrian Mafia – which is called the *'Ndrangheta* and controls much of agriculture, public works, prostitution and other parts of the economy – in inciting the violence.

Even Pope Benedict XVI pitched in and reminded his flock in the Catholic nation that "an immigrant is a human being, different in origin, culture, and tradition, but he is a person to respect, with rights and duties."

Though some local Italians welcome the workers, others have become hostilely xenophobic after the riots. One Italian protester held a sign that read "Twenty years of cohabitation isn't racism."

I have, as I acknowledge sore muscles from yesterday's up-and-down 44-kilometer trek, no great expectations today. I simply want to get around the gigantic Port of Gioia Tauro, which a bus driver insists is the second largest port in Europe after Amsterdam, without getting scraped, scratched or sliced up. That'll also get me back to the coastal railroad track system and permit me to move my base camp to Scilla, the site of the legendary confrontation between Scylla and Odysseus in *The Odyssey*.

One of the shortest days walking in MedTrek history, only 12 kilometers, couldn't have gone smoother. I kick off, aided by a loaf of bread and two bananas, on the long promenade in San Ferdinando and soon wind up next to the unassailable double-fenced, barbed wire-topped, heavy security around a port that, until I saw it from a distance in Nicotara yesterday, I didn't even know existed.

It isn't a difficult hike since I have no incentive to try to break into the place, and there are no short cuts to take as I follow the inland route from sandy beach to sandy beach. I walk out of town on a back street and discover a firm that specializes in import/export to Canada. It's on viale Nievo near the city limit, not far from the *Campo Sportivo Comunale Rocco Gambardella*, should you ever want to expand your business.

This, the main thoroughfare between San Ferdinando and Gioia Tauro, is one of the sleepiest streets I've been on during the past three weeks (which could be due to the rather quick change in temperatures to summer-like heat). And I'm still a couple of days ahead of the Circus Lidia Togni that, I now see, is on its "Evolution Tour."

It is typical of contemporary MedTrekking that at one point, despite all the security at the sophisticated port, I walk next to a herd of sheep for half a kilometer and am able to perfect how to walk at a sheep's pace. I'm also impressed that, in the midday heat, there are more joggers than I've seen anywhere in Italy at any one time. Now that I think about it, I probably should have reported a guy on the beach who was taking photos of the place with a zoom lens (he had to be a terrorist), but it's too late for that now.

Gioia Tauro, which sounds so majestic, presents a double face. There are some up-market shops (and even a Disneyland Fantasy Store and a Disneyland Bar that I'm sure contribute meagerly to the profits at Disney's California HQ) and a fairly modern railway station that seems to represent the economic boom due to the port. At the same time, some of the neighborhoods remind me that Calabria is still one of the poorest regions in Europe.

When I take the first bus back to Tropea to get my gear, I'm joined by a dozen clad-in-black women who all get off at the cemetery a few kilometers out of town. Turns out they go there everyday to visit their departed loved one(s). I like that.

I have a new hiking companion who's come from Australia to get a taste of MedTrekking. The first day, based on what I've seen, will enable her to get her feet wet because there's a large river that we may not be able to ford just 1.5-kilometers from our starting point in Gioia Tauro. There are also enough steep mountainsides and varied terrain to test her mettle.

Judy Barnett bought a copy of my first book in Launceston, Tasmania, and found it a source of inspiration for more adventures in her own life, following a divorce. We corresponded after my book tour in Australia and, bingo, here she is during the last week of my trek from Naples to Sicily.

She's armed with a heart rate monitor (her heart rate, which she says is already high in anticipation of her first day of MedTrekking, reaches 163 when we climb the steep steps to the top of Mount Santa Elia) and calorie counter (our 41-kilometer day, which features a mix of almost every type of MedTrek step imaginable – beach-walking, river-fording, rock-climbing, boulder-stepping, mountain-climbing, train-track-walking, wildflower-field-stepping and road-hiking but no tunnels – "consumed" 2,692 calories). Judy performs remarkably well and concludes that "MedTrekking exceeds my expectations."

The day strolling down the Costa Viola (or purple coast, which gets its name from the color of the water) from Gioia Tauro begins on a seaside promenade but only twenty minutes later we arrive at a wide and deep-looking river that we cross on a sandbar.

Then we MedTrek on a garbagy and pebbly beach into Taureana where fishermen are repairing their nets and playing cards in the shadow of the Hotel Miami, while a mother-daughter team on the sidewalk tries to sell me *spatola*, a deep-water scabbard fish that looks rather menacing but is extremely tasty and easy to prepare because it doesn't have scales.

Getting beyond Taureana requires serious rock climbing that takes us around a promontory until, stymied by the depth of the water, we climb steps through a housing development guarded by a proud German shepherd dog, which seems to have become an Italian household staple since World War II. Judy doesn't flinch as we sidle through a locked but partly opened gate to reach the SS18.

Some remarkably creative tiles, illustrating amphorae and the insignias of the Province of Reggio Calabria, decorate the roadside into the marina in Palmi, where a friendly travel agent in the main piazza assures us that it's possible to climb to 579-meter high Monte Santa Elia and then "*scendere, scendere, scendere*" to Bagnara Calabra and Scilla.

The steep climb up a series of seemingly never-ending stairs to the top of the Santa Elia Mountain does indeed reward us with stupendous views back towards Gioia Tauro and Capo Vaticano, and ahead towards Scilla and Sicily. But the *scendere* part proves a bit more problematic as we descend on a mix of back roads, trails, dirt paths, ivy-shrouded pine trees, farmland and fields full of spring wildflowers. I claim I'm Dusty Springfield as we walk through one farmer's tilled earth and begin the very long labyrinthine descent into Bagnara.

During the descent I provide Judy with a brief description of the benefits of walking meditation.

"The empty path welcomes you," I tell her explaining that I was taught this by Thich Nhat Hanh. "When we walk, we know we are walking. With each peaceful step you take, all beings, near and far, will benefit. If you can make one peaceful step, then peace is possible. And in making decisions, you will find that you are more calm and clear, with more insight and compassion."

We continue on the seaside, between train track and tide, on boulders, breakwaters, railway tracks and the SS18 to Favazzina. I'll always remember this village because a 78-year-old café owner bets me a free drink if I can prove that I'm over forty. He pays off when, with some amazement, he sees my driver's license.

When we walk into Scilla at the northern part of the Straits of Messina, the first thing we see in the waterfront part of town called Chianalea is a tiled representation of Scylla taking down three of Odysseus' men with, in the background, a swordfish (swordfish are verrry big here!).

"My favorite part of the day was the rock climbing and mounting those endless stairs to the top of Monte Santa Elia," says Judy, whose average heart rate was 104. "My worst moments were losing my sock in a sewer and negotiating the rocks on the beach."

Scilla, of course, is the location of the Scylla part of the dramatic

131

Scylla and Charybdis scenes in *The Odyssey*. Judy and I contemplate how Odysseus, arriving today, might react to the train, the dramatic and dizzying *autostrada* bridges, the houses, the people, the garbage. We walk on a recently redone sidewalk in Chianalea, under the rock that housed Scylla that's now known as Ulysses' Cliff. When we come out of the tunnel, which also features a newly redone grotto with religious icons, we're on the *Spiaggia delle Sirene* and I'm ready to stay in the presence of Odysseus, Scylla and Charybdis.

After Circe described the Sirens during our chat on Monte Circeo, she told me about Scylla (her descriptive name is thought to be derived from either the Greek word *skyllaros* for hermit crab and/or the word *skylax* for puppy) and the choice she'd given Odysseus on his homeward journey.

"One of the two courses you may take, and you yourself must weigh them," Circe said. The first included the Clashing Rocks, or Drifters, that "not even birds can pass by" because, like cymbals, they come together quickly and crush anything between them. That's why their "boiling surf, under high fiery winds, carries tossing wreckage of ships and men."

She mentioned Jason and his Argonauts who, helped by Hêra, did get by the rocks before adding that "a second course lies between headlands" with "a sharp mountain piercing the sky, with storm cloud round the peak" that "no mortal man could scale."

This, of course, is "the den of Scylla, where she yaps abominably, a newborn whelp's cry, though she is huge and monstrous. God or man, no one could look on her in joy."

Except me. I'm spending a week in town to see as much of Scylla as I can and to verify, as Homer wrote in *The Odyssey*, that "her legs – and there are twelve – are like great tentacles, unjointed, and upon her serpent necks are borne six heads like nightmares of ferocity, with triple serried rows of fangs and deep gullets of black death."

Those are jaws that snatched six of Odysseus' crew and devoured them because Circe told Odysseus that it's smarter to lose six men to Scylla than his entire ship to Charybdis across the strait.

I don't want to expose Judy to Scylla right away, especially after her first 41-kilometer MedTrek, so we have a pizza on the port in front of my base camp bivouac at the Palazzo Kratalis Hotel, where my gigantic room, just a few meters from the Mermaid's beach and the bell tower of the nearby church, looks onto Ulysses' Cliff and Scylla's cave.

The ten-room hotel in an 18th-century building, once the stables for a noble family, is a few steps, and a few euros, up from my normal MedTrekking squat. But Judy is writing an article about my exploit and I want her to sample a nice room with a good view.

During dinner I tell Judy that Scylla, the daughter of Phorkys and a goddess named Ceto (or Triton and Lamia according to the Greek poet Stesichorus), was once a beautiful nymph but, according to Ovid, had been transformed into a sea monsteress by Circe. Circe blamed Scylla for preventing the sea god Glaucus from falling in love with her and poisoned the waters where Scylla bathed.

"It was her vengeance to get back at Circe that accounted for her hostility towards Odysseus," I explain. "And her association with the equally dangerous whirlpool Charybdis across the strait led to the idiom that, in contemporary lingo, means you're caught between a rock and a hard place."

After dinner we walk through town, talking about the allure of Greek myths before spending much of the evening watching ships plow through the dark up and down channel in the Strait of Messina. The next morning we take a hike to the top of the village and visit the castle (one myth says Odysseus built a temple in homage to Athêna on the hilltop site), where we look onto the Aspromonte Mountains and catch a view of the Aeolian Islands. As we're looking at the sea I tell Judy that there's a mountainous rock as high as the one we're standing on just under the water. Known to scuba divers as Montagna, or Mountain, it rises 20-25 meters above the floor of the sea and teems with underwater life.

That afternoon we dawdle in San Giorgio, Scylla's old town, where I meet a luthier and take a tour of his workroom before we investigate a *passerella*, one of the boats with ladder-like poles used to catch swordfish.

During each of the next four nights I leave the hotel at midnight and take the three-minute walk to the seaside below the cave. I can't climb up to it, of course, but I am hoping that Scylla will make an appearance and that I might see how "she sways her heads in air, outside her horrid cleft, hunting the sea around that promontory for dolphins, dogfish or what bigger game thundering Amphitritê feeds in thousands."

I am wondering if now, almost three thousand years after her conversion from beauty into beast, she "takes, from every ship, one man for every gullet" and imagine myself sitting with her as a sentry watching ships approaching and leaving the Strait of Messina. More important, Circe, who herself has mellowed during the past 3,000 years, wants me to give Scylla a present on her behalf.

When we finally meet at around 3:00 a.m. on the fourth night, Scylla is obviously suspicious of anything, or anyone, having to do with Circe.

"That bitch pretty much wrecked my life when she turned me into the creature that I am now," Scylla says. "I should do to you what I did to Odysseus' crew and thousands of other sailors."

"But I'm not a sailor, and I've come on foot with a present that'll change your life again," I say in contemporary Italian as I hand a small vial with a green liquid that Circe concocted to one of Scylla's twelve tentacles.

"Do you think this is *Alice in Wonderland*?" Scylla asks. "Well, you're wrong. This is real life."

"Drink it," I suggest softly as I remove the cap. "It can't make real life any worse."

Scylla takes the shot and is gradually transformed into a lovely naiad, a nymph of the Mediterranean Sea.

"Your inspirational and prophetic powers have returned and you can again be worshipped in association with divinities of fertility and growth," I tell her.

She thanks me and then spills the beans on a number of myths, providing her own interpretation of history.

"First of all, it's not my fault that Glaucus fell in love with me and not Circe," Scylla says as we recline on a chaise longue on The Sirens Beach. "And I don't know why today I'm relegated to the phrase 'Scylla and Charybdis' whenever anyone is looking for an example of 'between a rock and a hard place.' It's not like we're related or anything and a lot of people have sailed through the strait and avoided both of us."

It would have been an easy and civilized 27-kilometer urban seaside walk from Scilla to Reggio Calabria – and a smooth and fitting end to the 774-kilometer MedTrek outing that began in Naples – had it not been drizzling, then raining, then pouring.

Judy and I wind our way along the coast, getting a great view back to Scylla's cave and an equally stunning perspective of the Straits of Messina and Sicily. An intriguing aspect of the walk is the proximity of Sicily and all the ship traffic going across and up and down the strait. Judy is threatening to boycott all Italian beaches because of the surfeit of garbage but I convince her to keep going.

We get out of the rain in Cannitello by snuggling under a palm umbrella before spending an hour chatting at a Catona café with a bunch of Italian weathermen, who convince us that the rain will never end and suggest we toss in the towel. I pass the time with Judy by citing some rain-oriented wisdom from my daily readings, beginning with a short poem by Deng Ming-Dao:

"Rain scatters plum petals;
Weeping stains the earth.

One can only take shelter
And wait for clearing."

We arrive at the Catona train station just as a train is pulling out so, despite the ongoing rain, we switch gears and decide to continue towards Reggio Calabria. Smart move. The rain slows to a drizzle and then to nothing.

Reggio, incidentally, has a palm-lined promenade next to an expansive seaside promenade and is, by Calabria standards, remarkably clean – both streets and beaches. We not only make it to the very sleepy and slumbering port but also visit the stunning Riace bronze sculptures of two naked Greek warriors at the National Museum, which specializes in the treasures of the Magna Graecia.

This stage of the MedTrek, which started with me sleeping for a week with the Sirens in Marina del Cantone and ends with me spending four nights within spitting distance of Scylla's cave, is a record-long outing.

In one month, with five days off, I go 774 kilometers (at an average of 30.96 kilometers per day), make it to the boot of Italy and become, as Circe predicted I would, the guiding light of a woman at loose ends. Now I'll prepare myself for Sicily, where a few incidents in *The Odyssey* are thought to have occurred.

I also continue a tradition I began during the first 4,401-kilometer stint of the MedTrek and send out a sixth email update to family and friends.

MedTrek Milestone #6

I just MedTrekked over 1,100 kilometers from Rome to Reggio Calabria in southern Italy and survived a year with Circe, my visit to the shadows of the underworld, the allure of the seductive Sirens, a robbery by gypsies, and a flirtation with the one-time monster Scylla. In doing so, I completed the first three labors given to me by Circe and have already been given a remarkable insight into the reality of some of the more dramatic scenes in Homer's poems – and myself, of course.

I'm now 5,509 kilometers into my amusing romp around the sea and am mentally healthy and physically well after all the walking meditation and wonderment produced by the MedTrek. Although struck with a slight bout of PMTWS (Post MedTrek Withdrawal Syndrome) after walking the entire length of Italy and bidding farewell to Judy Barnett, I'll soon cross the Strait of Messina and spend eight weeks MedTrekking around Sicily, the largest island in the Mediterranean. There I'll continue with Circe's twelve tasks.

The Idiot and the Odyssey II

PART TWO

STROLLING AROUND SICILY AND
STUMBLING ONTO KALYPSO

A Healthy Breath of Aeolian Winds
Seeking a Blind Drunk Cyclops
Making Out with Kalypso on Malta
Pursuing the Sun God and Finding Cyclops

A Healthy Breath of Aeolian Winds

"You will find the scene of the wanderings of Odysseus
when you find the
cobbler who sewed up the bag of the winds." –
Eratosthenes

The next morning I take advantage of one of the best travel deals in Europe: the €2 round-trip ferry from Villa San Giovanni on mainland Italy to Messina, the third biggest city on Sicily.

Homer called Sicily, which is the largest island in the Mediterranean, *Thrinákia*, or "triangle," because of its shape. Odysseus, who "could have no mortal rival as an orator" because his "words came driving on the air as thick and fast as winter snowflakes," said the seductive island "is not a bad place at all...men could reap a full harvest." A few centuries later, the Greek poet Pindar agreed that "Sicily the rich was the pride of the blossoming earth."

The island was so central to early sea trade and the development of Greek colonies that it became the star of Magna Graecia. In the fifth century BC it was known as the breadbasket of Rome and was more prosperous and important than many of its mainland counterparts because of the production and export of wheat, grapes, and olives. Even today there's nothing more sensual than smelling, seeing, touching and almost tasting the rich ruby-colored earth that's made Sicily so agriculturally rich for the last three thousand years.

The bustling seaside town of Syracuse, or *Siracusa* as it's called locally, on Sicily's eastern coast was the powerhouse of the Greek presence and by 415 BC was so influential that Athens sent a fleet of fighters to put the upstarts in their place. But the celebrated Battle of Syracuse ended with the underdog locals overwhelming the invading Athenians.

As I board the ferry for the brief three-kilometer crossing, I'm reminded that every recent Italian government has stated its intentions to build a bridge linking Sicily to the mainland, despite threats by Mafia clans to derail or sink the project. The latest word is that a suspension bridge is expected to cost over €6 billion and be completed by 2017. Don't count on it.

Until then, if *then* ever arrives, ferries will continue to flourish and I'll continue to regard Sicily as the equivalent of the Wild West. In fact, I'm not sure if I want or would appreciate faster methods of arrival from the mainland.

I MedTrekked 1,097 kilometers and, counting my time with Circe, spent well over a year to get here from Rome and I'm astonished, and slightly humbled, when I consider that the Eurostar train now makes the same trip from Rome's Termini Station to Villa San Giovanni in a little over six hours. Although it stops in Naples, Lamezia, Gian Tauro and a few other spots, the speedy train goes much too fast for passengers to even make out the names of most of the seaside stations that I visited during the MedTrek, not to mention the various spots where I swam, slept or ate. A bridge would have a similar impact on the short trip across the strait.

I'm urging a boycott.

The anticipation of launching my circumnavigation of Sicily doesn't stop me from spending half a day exploring Messina, which was founded as a Greek colony called Zancle in the eighth century BC, and I visit at a ferry-slow pace.

I casually drop by the Duomo, which was rebuilt after the devastating 1908 earthquake, and pleasantly linger at a café table near the Orione fountain to watch the mechanical figurines on the ornamental astronomical clock in the bell tower do their daily midday dance. I have an overpriced coffee in the ornate Galleria before climbing the Caperrina hill for stupendous panoramic views from the aptly named Montalto church.

After a leisurely afternoon and a 10:00 p.m. pizza on the Piazza 25 Aprile, I spend the night at the port-side Jolly Hotel in a third-floor room that looks onto the sickle-shaped Zancle harbor (*zancle* is Greek for scythe), the Strait of Messina and Scylla's cave across the strait. Once again I'm transfixed by ship traffic in the deep, dark night. And, just before dawn, I arise to watch well-lit vessels as they continue to enter and leave the port. At daybreak I gaze meditatively on the towering statue of the Virgin Mary with an inscription that reads: *Vos et ipsam civitatem benedicimus*, or "We bless you and your city." The quote is said have been made by Mary, yes the Virgin Mary.

I've been an early riser since the time I used to awaken at 5:00 a.m. to deliver the morning edition of the *San Francisco Chronicle* by bicycle in my Northern California neighborhood. Now I'm regularly up, always without an alarm, an hour or more before sunrise, which enables me to read and meditate before I put myself on the path or otherwise kick off my day. My early dawn starts give me a particularly fresh outlook wherever I happen to be.

This morning I have to decide whether to head south towards chic and crowded Taormina, where Odysseus's crew purportedly slaughtered the Cattle of the Sun God, or north towards Capo Peloro to embark on a counterclockwise circuit around the island. Do I want to keep the sea on my left (south) or on my right (north)?

I decide to take the right path and go north before heading west towards Palermo, the seaport founded by the Phoenicians in the eighth century BC and now the island's capital city. Once there, I'll continue my counterclockwise circumnavigation around Sicily that, if I can believe the maps, is about 1,100 kilometers in circumference.

Why go counterclockwise, which of course symbolizes walking back in time?

One reason is my desire, at the outset of my Messina-to-Messina trek, to call on Charybdis, the whirlpoolish monsters that almost sunk Odysseus's raft, and thus conclude my second Circean labor. I'm excited about making my way along the Sicilian seaside to the exact spot where "Charybdis lurks below to swallow down the dark sea tide" and to see if it's true that "three times from dawn to dusk she spews it up and sucks it down again three times, a whirling maelstrom."

I also want to survey, from a distance, the mountainous and steep Calabria countryside that I just MedTrekked on the Italian mainland and I am eager to get to Milazzo to catch a boat to the seven volcanic Aeolian Islands where Aeolus, the king of the winds, gave Odysseus a bag of wind that was intended to help him sail home to Ithaka.

All of the speculation about what did or did not happen in *The Odyssey*, which may or may not have been "written" by a blind poet named Homer, is best summed up in the much-quoted statement of a Greek mathematician, poet, athlete, and geographer who assessed the situation hundreds of years after Homer's time.

"You will find the scene of the wanderings of Odysseus when you find the cobbler who sewed up the bag of the winds," joked Eratosthenes in his three-volume work *Geographica*. Eratosthenes lived between 276-195 BC, was head of the library at Alexandria and was probably the first person to use the word "geography."

And he gives me one goal in Sicily. Find the cobbler.

This is also the direction the Romans took in 264 BC when they launched the Punic War against the Carthaginians and the Sicilian Greeks. Lastly, I want to save, as a finale, Mount Etna and Taormina, where the Greeks founded a colony in 358 BC and my daughter Sonia was conceived in December 1981. I'm hoping Sonia will join me for a celebratory walk when I get there in a couple of months.

Seeking the Cobbler

I'm often asked, since the gypsy incident, whether I feel safe walking on the Mediterranean. In response, I contend that most of the security problems I've had have been either accidents or the result of something I did or caused myself.

Still, I'm somewhat reassured to learn that Italian police have captured the No. 2 leader of Sicily's Cosa Nostra Mafia in Trapani, in northwest Sicily, for crimes that included the murder of a rival's nine-year-old son, whose body was thrown into a vat of acid. I feel much more at ease with the legendary "Mimmo the Veterinarian," as he was nicknamed, off the streets. But if you think I'm going to write his surname, which happens to be Raccuglia, you're crazy.

Also, in the interest of security and to appease my mother, I'm carrying a SPOT satellite communicator and personal tracker that enables me to transmit my location and send a distress signal to friends, social networks and emergency responders. In addition, the pocket unit will faithfully record the exact site of the cobbler's shop, the Cyclops' cave and other discoveries.

After watching the sun rise over Italy and gradually sneak into my Jolly room, I feast on a copious breakfast and walk across the street to the seaside. I pass the dock where my ferry landed and wonder why I didn't consider swimming across the strait or walking on the ferry. After all, when I took a ferry from Spain to Morocco I strolled around the ship and kept on my feet during the entire crossing. I didn't feel compelled to MedTrek on this ferry because my destination is an island, not part of the Mediterranean perimeter. And I didn't swim because the boat/ship/ferry traffic, as well as Homer's stories of fatal pitfalls like Scylla and Charybdis, scared me off.

I head north along the port and the strait of Messina on a

bustling, buzzing and busy morning. After just a few kilometers, I approach Sicily's *Riviera del Nord*, or Riviera North, and am particularly inspired when a sign indicates that I'm in a suburb called *Comtemplazione*, or Contemplation. When I reach the Hotel Paradis, I decide this is one of most aptly named, meditative and paradisiacal little towns on the Med.

I pass the *Villa dello Stretto* (many things here, including a campground, are named *dello Stretto* due to their proximity to the Strait), which is a pretty rhythmical and contemplative name in itself. Later, near Ganzirri, a signpost indicates that this is also the *Littorale de Pace*, or the Riviera of Peace. When I find a two-liter bottle of water for sale in a store for only 20 cents, about as cheap as you can get, I know I like the price of peace.

I continue to be overwhelmed with optimistic vibes when I stumble upon dozens of shops and street-side vendors selling a colorful array of competitively priced fruits and vegetables – including peaches, watermelons, tomatoes, oranges, potatoes and grapes – that are overflowing from boxes and crates. I buy some tomatoes, grapes, peaches, an orange and, for lunch, a piece of smoked fish sold by one of the many fishmongers. As I suck on and savor the orange, I consider myself pretty lucky because many of these fruits and vegetables weren't available to Odysseus when he was returning to Ithaka. And I'm glad that every village, whatever the size, has a local fishmonger, *pescheria* or an outdoor fish market.

Although Homer occasionally mentions pears, pomegranates, apples and figs, the main foodstuffs in classical Greece were olives, wheat, wine, fish and meat. In fact, at one point in Sparta it was frowned upon to cook anything other than meat, and vegetables basically consisted of cabbage, onions, lentils, beans and peas. Many of the foods we take for granted, like tomatoes and potatoes, weren't introduced to the Mediterranean until much later.

Signs inform me that I'm entering the *Capo Peloro* Natural Park (once again "where nature is protected"), the name given to the tip of northeastern Sicily that juts out into the strait. *Capo Peloro* features some tranquil saltwater lagoons, but its most distinguishing feature is the 232-meter (760 feet) high electric tower near Torre Faro, where another sign informs me that I'm 261 kilometers away from Palermo.

I stare up at one of the tallest electric poles in the world (with its counterpart across the strait these are, not unsurprisingly, known as the Pylons of Messina) and would swallow my gum if I were chewing any. What are the pylons for? Actually they haven't carried any electricity across the strait since 1994, when power transmission went underwater.

"They're now protected as historical monuments," a security guard tells me. "And they're used for weather measurements, telecommunications and high altitude rescue training."

"Do you suppose they'd let me shimmy or tightrope across the strait on the high wires?" I ask.

"What kind of Idiot are you?" he responds.

I've only walked 12 kilometers, but I'm at the exact place where Charybdis took it out on Odysseus for eating the Cattle of the Sun God in *The Odyssey* . Will I also get swept away?

Homer writes that "a good bowshot" is the distance between Scylla and Charybdis, but I don't think Odysseus, or even Achilles, could shoot an arrow across the three-kilometer gap. Homer also contends that "a great wild fig, a shaggy mass of leaves," grows on the tongue of land here but, and you've got to trust me on this, there's no longer any sign of a fig tree. As for Charybdis being "the dire gorge of the salt sea tide" with a "yawning mouth" who "shot spume" that "soared to the landside heights and fell like rain" making "all the sea like a cauldron seething over intense fire, when the mixture suddenly heaves and rises"? Well that doesn't happen on my watch. Instead, I spend two hours meditatively gazing onto the mirror-smooth Strait of Messina at the presumed location of Charybdis. There's isn't even any wind riffling the water.

Still, I can picture Odysseus winding up alone here after his crew perished and his ship was sunk. That happened when Zeus, after learning the men had eaten the "silken beef of Helios," decided to throw "down one white-hot bolt, and make splinters of their ship in the wine-dark sea." Incidentally, although I don't see a cow today, I'm reminded that every bovine in contemporary Sicily is possibly an offspring of the Cattle of the Sun God, Helios's herd that Circe had told Odysseus to avoid eating.

I can imagine Odysseus watching his crew bobbing "like seabirds on the waves" and sadly realizing that, for them, there was "no sweet day of return; the god had turned his face from them." I can envisage Odysseus himself being saved when "the whirlpool drank the tide" and being caught on to a great fig tree "like a bat under a bough" where he then "clung grimly" until, finally, the mast and keel "at last reared from the sea."

Odysseus, then completely alone, got back on his makeshift raft and "rowed hard with my hand to pass by Scylla." Then for "nine days I drifted in the open sea before I made shore, buoyed up by the gods upon Ogygia Isle," the island where "the dangerous nymph Kalypso lives and sings there in her beauty."

Bet he wished he had a SPOT locator with him.

As I ponder Odysseus' predicament I recollect that somewhere nearby is the Marsili seamount, a massive, invisible (because it's underwater) and active volcano between Sicily and Naples that has the potential to collapse, or maybe even erupt, and create a tsunami that would make Charybdis seem like a tempest in a teapot. Scientists predict that its seismic waves could flood large portions of the coast I've walked, am walking and, the gods willing, will be walking.

The summit of Marsili, which was discovered in the early 1960s, is now about 500 meters below the surface of the sea. It's a walloping 70 kilometers by 30 kilometers in area, rises some 3,000 meters above the sea bed and volcanologists keep a close eye on it, though they say water pressure will probably keep it from ever totally blowing its stack.

Perhaps it was Marsili that created a Charybdis effect when Odysseus was here.

Marsili isn't the only subterranean volcano near Sicily. To the south, between Sicily and Tunisia, is a volcanic island that was first seen in 10 BC and last rose above the sea in July 1831. Seven hundred meters in diameter, the volcano spouted for a while, but by January 1832 it was eight meters underwater.

At that time there was speculation that it might be part of a subterranean mountain range stretching from Sicily to Tunisia and four nations rushed to claim the short-lived island. The British named it Graham Island; the Italians called it Ferdinandea, in honor of King Ferdinand II; the French came up with Julia because it appeared in July; and the Spanish also made a claim. Bets are that if it appears again, the Italians will have the best territorial rights.

Until then, the four countries are trying not to make waves about it.

The beaches are sand, and I do a lot of barefoot/sandals walking today, despite the comfort of my new Vasque hiking shoes. Although I've lost track of how many pairs of lightweight hiking shoes I've worn on the MedTrek, I like to switch brands. I've tried Adidas, Mephisto, Merrell, Nike, Quechua, Scarpa and Vasque, along with virtually every kind of lightweight tennis shoes as a second pair.

After I hike 36 kilometers and am just past a little village called Rodia, I use my SPOT satellite locator for the first time. At the push of a button, it will let people know via the GEOS satellite network that I'm not dead – and where I'm not dead.

The SPOT is especially practical when there's no email or spotty cell phone coverage and is especially helpful if there's ever a real emergency. My latest high-tech hiking tool has a "Help" button to contact emergency assistance in every country through the GEOS International Emergency Response Center.

My mother gave the SPOT to me as a birthday present after the incident with the gypsies, but I'd have to be in very serious trouble, like the guy who lost his arm in *127 Hours*, to push the button. There were some hikers who pushed the panic button in the Grand Canyon because they were thirsty and the last thing anyone needs is an unnecessary call for help from a thirsty MedTrekker.

The Italians aren't out in particular force on this weekday, but there are enough of them, including kids who probably should be in school, to ensure the presence of a lifeguard on almost every beach. After I send the SPOT message, I get in the water and let myself be beaten/crashed/crushed on the pebbles by the waves in a natural version of *thalassotherapy*. My brief dip illustrates why there are lifeguards. This sea, even without a threatening Charybdis, could suck a little kid down in no time.

From the water I can see the Santa Elia Mountain that Judy and I climbed above Palmi, as well as the volcanic Aeolian Islands, though right now I can only identify the distinctive crater of Stromboli. Some pillboxes remaining from World War II on the nearby shore also intrigue me. I thumbed through a book about WWII battles in Sicily at a Messina bookstore and considered producing a tome with photographs of every remaining pillbox on the Mediterranean. Gun shelters aren't the only abandoned structures here. I run into a number of derelict buildings that have recently served as well-attended party venues, if the stacks of empty beer bottles are to be believed. I won't bother photographing those.

When I arrive in Villafranca Tirrena, 41 seaside kilometers from Messina and 180 kilometers east of Palermo, I celebrate with a melon/pistachio *gelato* and five glasses of cold local water. Everyone in the bar seems amused when I ask for the *acqua* Villafranca rather than bottled mineral water.

"Why are you so thirsty?" asks the mini-skirted barmaid as she scoops the ice cream.

"I've just walked here on the beach from Messina!" I reply as I ask her to please fill my canteen.

"You're not just thirsty, you're stupid!" she smiles.

What a perceptive comment to inaugurate my hike around Sicily.

She shows me a bit more respect when I provide a summation of the day:

"My day hike out here was a piece of *panettone*," I recount in flowery Italian. "I was able to walk barefoot a good deal of the way, investigate some World War II pillboxes, and take a refreshing dip at the pebbled beach in Rodia before I met a beautiful mini-skirted barmaid in Villafranca."

"Can I offer you a coffee?" she smiles.

Stirring up a Sulfurous Stink on Stromboli and Vulcano

It doesn't take long to realize that vivid seaside displays of an embarrassing amount of garbage are as prevalent on Sicily as on the mainland.

To protest this disgusting habit, I'm wearing a black baseball cap with "Environmental Defense" inscribed in white. That universal message usually doesn't risk offending anyone, though it could here if Sicilians think I'm bitching about the voluminous quantity of garbage that I'm sure is one reason for many *Divieto di Balanare* (Swimming Forbidden) signs.

I've got to determine why Italians are among the trashiest people on earth, or certainly the trashiest in the developed (a misnomer if there ever was one) world. There are so many comments and contradictions about this situation that I may start a blog devoted solely to garbage and dead fish on the Italian seaside. Until then, here are some Idiotic questions and observations.

Why are there blossoming stacks of garbage everywhere in Italy? Even when trash collectors aren't on strike? Even when it's May, and there aren't many tourists to blame? Why is the norm piles upon heaps upon full trash bins of smelly rat-infested garbage? Mountains of garbage everywhere. Even on the beach. How can one of the most aesthetic countries on earth be one of the trashiest? Why don't health authorities and doctors realize the negative impact of trash, including discarded needles, mounting outside a hospital in Agropoli?

Italian homes, or the houses and apartments of the well-off, anyway, are usually equipped with top-of-the-line marble finishing, shiny floors, sparkling everything else, and either starkly contemporary or authentic vintage furniture. Do the owners think their homes look better surrounded by garbage?

Is the Mafia failing to organize its garbage-collecting troops in an effort to prove something? If that's the case, is this mess a success? If the Mafia was really in control of garbage, as many people contend, would there be all this savage dumping? Does the Mafia no longer exist?

Is tossing garbage anywhere, and pointedly ignoring waste receptacles, a genetic trait? Is this the way Italians declare their personal independence and irritate authority? Is it a "sociocultural" thing, as twenty-something Alessandra tried to convince me one morning? It's ironic that the country, as I illustrated during my stay with the Sirens, has one of the most comprehensive recycling plans in Europe. Why hasn't it caught on? Is it too complicated? Or, wait, has garbage become the latest form of creative expression? Is every litterbug an artist?

If so, we've got a lot of Michelangelos and Leonardos coming our way.

This line of reasoning enables me now to applaud the vast amount of garbage because it contrasts with Italy's natural beauty and helps me to appreciate the yin-and-yang effect of MedTrekking. The ugliness accentuates the beauty. And it certainly speaks voluminous volumes about the evolution of the southern Italian and the *Mezzogiorno* mentality.

After Villafranca Tirrena, I have to make a choice that's perhaps more important than the flavor of ice cream. When I arrive in Milazzo should I catch a boat out to the Aeolian Islands, where Aeolus, the son of Hippotes and guardian of the winds, gave Odysseus that famous bag of wind that led to the expression "windbag"? Or should I postpone the excursion until I've trekked around the entire island?

Militating against the voyage is an email I received from the mayor of Palermo, the island's capital city, offering to name a small beach *L'idiota e l'odissea* ("The Idiot and the Odyssey") when I reach town. The offer probably won't be rescinded if I spend a week on the islands, but it might be smart to strike before the mayor changes his mind.

I'm pondering my choice when I arrive in Spadafora, where a new beachfront is being installed with European Union funding (who knew that was still around?). Lots of drinking fountains (a rarity anywhere on the Med) are being installed and there's a bustling morning market with a pair of shoes going for €8 and men's suits for €40.

From a distance I don't like the look of the power plant and oil refinery between here and Milazzo, but when I finally reach the eyesore, I'm slightly impressed. Unlike in France, Spain and other parts of Italy, where access to the water is frequently restricted by filth-oozing industry, it's possible to walk between the plant and the sea on bridges over two canals that empty water and whatever-kind-of waste there is from the plant into the sea. And the nearby Giammoro industrial zone has a surprising waft of sweet perfume coming from one plant.

When I have lunch – a surprisingly tasty vegetarian panini served by two carefree women at an AGIP gas station at the entrance to Milazzo – the wind is blasting with enough force to blow Odysseus back to Troy via Ithaka in a day. It prompts me to ferry to the islands because I figure these are the same strong winds that King Aeolus, the Lord of the Winds, put in a sack for Odysseus.

Both the Carthaginians and the Greeks also proceeded towards the Aeolian Islands soon after they arrived in Sicily, though they wanted to take over the main island of Lipari. With its location at the center of the Mediterranean and only 30 kilometers from Sicily, this first became a boomtown on the Med when obsidian, a rock of naturally occurring volcanic glass, was discovered on the island and became valuable during the Stone and Bronze Ages because of its sharp cutting edge and durability.

My hydrofoil, appropriately named Kalypso, breaks down in the Mediterranean Sea en route to volcanic Stromboli, after successfully stopping and starting at the Aeolian Islands of Vulcano, Lipari, and Salina. Acknowledging yet another obvious omen, I scrap Stromboli and instead get a room in Lipari, where the damaged boat docks. This'll be my base camp for exploration of the seven islands during the next week.

There's debate, of course, about which island was Odysseus' base camp, but the general consensus is that he too stayed on Lipari, though it was undoubtedly not named that in his day. All Odysseus tells us is that "We made our landfall on Aiolia Island, domain of Aiolos Hippotadês, the wind king dear to the gods who never die – an isle adrift upon the sea, ringed round with brazen ramparts on a sheer cliffside."

Though there are ramparts and a sheer cliffside in Lipari, most tourists on my boat couldn't care less about whether this is the island of Odysseus, the Greeks, or obsidian. They're primarily here to tan and/or tone their skin in mud pools at one of the several spa hot spots.

My room in Lipari is in Maria Villini's boarding house at Vico Salina 27, right on the main drag, and includes use of a fridge, cutlery, and a dining table on the top floor terrace. Maria is another *bella ragazza* Siciliana and, at 50, one of the best-looking *nonas* (yes, grandmothers) on the island. She meets my limping ferry at the dock when it arrives, and I feel like a character in *Mamma Maria*, as they call *Mamma Mia* here. Within five minutes I've met all the tour touts, the owners of the "best" restaurants and any important people between the ferry and my room.

Incidentally, Odysseus was a bit more upscale during his stay when he spent a month "lodged in the town and palace, while Aiolos played host to me...to hear the tale of Troy."

The next morning I explore Lipari's vast Aeolian Archeological Museum, housed in a hilltop castle, and I'm blown away (an apt synonym for "overwhelmed" on the windy island of Aeolus) by the quantity and quality of historical artifacts and remnants. The various buildings located in the castle complex contain scores of thematic and chronologically organized rooms that provide vivid testimony of the expansive historical time-line and successive civilizations that inhabited the islands. Displays range from simple-but-utilitarian prehistoric tools (there's a room dedicated to obsidian) to vases and other ornate leftovers of the Neolithic Period, Bronze Age, Greeks, Romans, and the Middle Ages.

I consider my lengthy visit to the museum, especially when I return for a second time a few days later, as one of the educational highlights of the MedTrek. If you come here, go there! Seriously, where else are you going to find more than a thousand theatrical masks made at the request of myriad playwrights? Or necropolises that illustrate burial techniques throughout the ages? Not to mention amphorae and other tangible vestiges of history.

I again realize, as I frequently do in museums, that if I were the first man on earth, I'd have trouble coming up with many of the innovations and inventions on show – making the basic obsidian blades would stump me, not to mention the ornate *kraters*, amphorae, coins and jewelry. And forget inventing the wheel or lever. Heck, I'd be so baffled if I traveled three thousand or more years back in time that I might not even be able to figure out how to procreate.

I never really look for, much less buy, souvenirs while MedTrekking. But I'm very impressed with the miniature masks made by Giovanni Spada and sold on via Vittorio Emanuele in Lipari. The reproductions are based on masks in a museum that, Giovanni tells me, "is the most important museum in the world for masks and the third most important in Europe, after the Louvre and the British Museum, when it comes to Greek history." Who knew?

Speaking of history, the Greeks apparently still have an affection for these Italian islands. One of the financial vehicles that led to Greece's economic collapse was called Aeolos, after the god and his bag of wind.

My €60 boat trip to the islands of Panarea and Stromboli includes stops for two dips in the Med and a walk around Panarea, the smallest of the Aeolian Islands with a distinctive black lava coastline. I meet Toby Lorenzen, a college professor from Massachusetts who hikes in Europe during summer breaks, and I vaingloriously explain what a seasoned and weathered traveler I am. After establishing my *bona fides*, I tell Toby that I made a dramatic concession to swiftly and legally make it to the summit of Stromboli. For the first time ever on my MedTrek, I booked a group tour and a guide.

"I went from a solo, seasoned, weathered, and experienced MedTrekker and adventurer to a group tourist," I tell Toby.

Then I shock myself and amuse Toby when, acting like I own the place, I order a *latte macchiato nelle bichierre grande* at a bar on Panarea that costs a whopping €5. I get scammed like a novice traveler. After that, I'm stung by a jellyfish while swimming among algae, anemones, crustaceans and mollusks amid *formiche,* or rocks, that have caused innumerable shipwrecks since antiquity. Although I try to explain to Toby that jellyfish are attracted to me due to my medically documented abnormally high level of testosterone, I get stung like a novice diver.

As we chat, I realize that Toby and I have completely different trekking habits. He books ahead, I don't; he rarely interacts with people, I do; he's reluctant to try out his Italian, I'm not. It's fun to discuss and contrast the differences. Yet I'll never forget that I'm the one who got socked for a €5 coffee, bitten by a jellyfish and turned into a naïve tourist. No wonder some people call me The Idiot.

To climb the volcano of Stromboli, there are only eight in our group (four solo Americans and two couples, one from Italy and one from France). With our destination emitting blaring explosions and blazing eruptions every twenty minutes, we meet up with Franco Snozogni, who's a guide here in the summer and in the Alps in the winter.

Franco joins us in the port of San Vincenzo and shows-and-tells us about everything, from absinthe and caper plants to Stromboli's 2002 eruption and the phenomenon of the Sciara del Fuoco, the crater's lava face.

Franco supplies face masks to help us avoid severe sulfur inhalation and helmets to protect us from debris before we slowly march three hours up to the 900-meter summit (another 2,000 meters of Stromboli is under the sea). We all marvel at the fluffy hanging clouds, a startlingly splendorous sunset and the constant smoke, steam, explosive noises, incandescent brimstone and burning magma emanating from Stromboli's most active vent. When darkness falls, we are mesmerized by the most enchanting ongoing natural fireworks show on earth.

Joining a group was a smart move. There are not only signs threatening a €500 fine for anyone hiking without a guide above 400 meters, but I see numerous officers from Italy's Guardia di Finanza, as well as rangers, patrolling the potentially dangerous mountain. They look for errant solo MedTrekkers among the 200-300 daily visitors making the early evening climb up the mountain that was featured in the 1950 Roberto Rossellini film.

It can be cold, windy and sulfur-smelling atop steamy Stromboli – and everyone without gloves regrets leaving them behind. But as Franco-in-speed-mode leads us down a dark, steep and slippery path of black sand back to the port of San Vincenzo, Toby and I agree that the guide, group tour, evening full of endless explosions, exultant eruptions and lots of satisfied human noises, a jellyfish sting, and even a €5 coffee isn't a bad way to spend a day. And I just love the way Franco pronounces *Strombolicchio*, the tiny island off Stromboli's shore.

The next morning I pick up a map of Lipari trails and seriously study it over a *caffè* at the Ulyxes Café on the Via Vittorio Emanuele.

There are 11 different walks, differentiated by colors, which vary in length from six hours to less than an hour, and I select a 27-kilometer six-hour "black" path that goes around almost the entire island.

I head counterclockwise (why change a good thing?) from Lipari on Canneto's popular pebbly beaches, past the pumice mine and obsidian quarry in Capo Rossa and into Portobello, where nothing much seems to be mushrooming. I stop for another coffee in Aquacalde, where the remains of a collapsed commercial conveyor belt extend into the water, and feast on local cookies made with fig marmalade in Punta di Legno Nero before continuing into Quattropani and Pianoconte.

It's a lazy day but, and this is what the map fails to convey, a visually exciting outing. At various points I have impressive views of each of the other six Aeolian Islands, as well the coast of northwest Sicily. Not to mention all the up-close rich colors of the earth, vegetation, fruits, vegetables, spring flowers, sea, sky and sun. As I gaily traipse around the island, I learn that pumice is a major export used to make cosmetics and stonewashed jeans and I'm so jaunty that I put a red flower behind one ear and a white one behind the other.

Towards the end of the daylong hike, I enter a purple-flowered alley that veers neatly downhill to the center of Lipari. As I'm cruising and whistling down this narrow path, I see an octogenarian sitting on a rock and enthusiastically say *buon giorno*. Presumably noticing that I'm a foreigner saying *buon giorno* after 5:00 p.m., which is *buona sera* time, he starts laughing and choking and trying not to laugh and choke. I'm afraid he's going to die.

The next day Toby and I take a ferry to the island of Vulcano and climb to the rim of its crater. Vulcano is not too high (390 meters); has an intriguing history (Vulcan, the god of fire, aka Hêphaistos, worked here); gave us the word volcanology; affords great views (of Sicily, Stromboli, Lipari and other islands) and is comparatively safe (there hasn't been an eruption since 1890).

It's only a twenty-minute ferry ride from Lipari and if you want a comparatively easy volcano to climb, the bowl-shaped *Crater della Fossa* on Vulcano is the place to go. Be forewarned that a €3 "contribution" is required to make the climb, investigate numerous *fumaroles* (fumaroles, from the Latin *fumus* or smoke, are volcanic gas and steam vents opening in the earth) and possibly OD on smoky sulfurous vapors.

If you scramble, as we did, down the pathless backside of the crater, you'll see some intriguing graves-to-be that I told Toby were prepared for visitors who don't make the €3 contribution and choose to wind up very much "under the volcano" (Malcolm Lowry's book of that name is a favorite of mine).

When you return to sea level, don't skip the sulfurous and therapeutic mud thermal baths that help heal all the bruises and cuts you incurred going up, in and under the volcano. They also make you smell like a sulfurous mud bath for a week and destroy your swimsuit, if not your entire hiking wardrobe.

Like an Idiot, I dove heedlessly into the soothing and smelly baths at the Laghetto di Fanghi despite the fact that everyone told me I'd stink afterwards. I gleefully posed for a picture wearing my red hiking cap with an equally mud-covered Laura Poff, an equally unsuspecting American exchange student from the University of Connecticut who also had been bitten by jellyfish and was staying with a Sicilian family.

I later learn that Laura had to wash her flashy multicolored bikini ten times to eliminate the smell.

"When I got back home to Milazzo, my host family was like 'Laura! You went swimming in the mud baths didn't you!'" Laura emailed me. "Apparently they really neglected to warn me that the smell would stay in my hair for up to a month, so I've increased my showers to two a day to speed up the process. Good luck with your scents and jellyfish stings!"

I not only tossed away the swimming suit that I wore in the baths but, a few days later and after several washes, also ditched my T-shirts, shorts, socks and underwear. My first three showers with scented soap didn't make a dent in the stench and I'm positive Odysseus didn't smell this bad after he met Nausikaa and was "gently bathed, anointed with sweet oil, and dressed afresh in tunics and new cloaks with fleecy linings."

On the ferry back to Lipari I explain to Toby that I frequently give away caps to people I like during the MedTrek. I mention that when Odysseus left the islands, Aiolos "stinted nothing, adding a bull's hide sewn from neck to tail into a mighty bag, bottling storm winds; for Zeus had long ago made Aiolos warden of winds, to rouse or calm at will."

"Unfortunately, while Odysseus slept on the job," I continue, "his crew, thinking the bag was filled with gold and silver, untied it and 'every wind roared into hurricane; the ships went pitching with many cries' and Odysseus was blown back to Aiolos where, understandably, the king wanted to have nothing more to do with him because 'your voyage here was cursed by heaven.'"

Before I left Vulcano I gave my smelly baseball cap to Luciana, the attractive 60ish woman who sells tickets at the entrance to the thermal baths. I did so because, when she sold me tokens for the after-bath showers, she joked that she'd join me for €1,000.

Luciana ferries to work at the baths every day from Lipari. I have dinner with her in Lipari the next night and, as she amusingly shows off her seasoned and weathered red baseball cap, she tells me that her family has been on the island for generations and that most of her female ancestors were seamstresses.

"It's a noble profession, and I presume you're aware that weaving and looms play an important role in Greek myths and the works of Ovid," says Luciana, surprising me by noting that Athêna was the "weaver goddess and turned pretentious Arachne into a spider." Luciana, or whatever goddesses she is channeling, then describes in detail how Penélopê tricked the suitors by weaving a shroud during the day and unraveling it at night. And how Circe, Kalypso and Helen of Troy were all weavers and the spindle used to be a symbol of security.

"And I presume you know the story of Ariadne, the wife of Dionysus who spun the thread that enabled Theseus to get to the center of the labyrinth and back again," she adds.

I don't suppose you can help me solve the riddle of the cobbler and the wind bag, can you?" I ask as she orders *cannoli*, the Sicilian treat once considered a symbol of fertility, for dessert.

"There was no cobbler because the bag was closed with shining silver wire by Aeolus himself," she says. "Come with me and I'll show it to you, in a secret room in the museum, where they've hidden it from prying spies."

Seeking a Blind-Drunk Cyclops

"Some god protected him and saved him." – *The Iliad*

Odysseus' run-in with Cyclops, a son of Poseidon called Polyphêmos, is one of the best-known scenes in literature. Many scholars and historians, though not Eratosthenes who was skeptical about most things Homeric, concur that their encounter occurred in Sicily, though there are ongoing disputes about the actual location of the cave where the Cyclops was blinded before wildly launching gargantuan stones at Odysseus' ship.

One of my preoccupations in Sicily, and the fourth of the twelve labors that I'm attempting to accomplish for Circe, is to locate the correct cave. Some say it's on the slopes of Mount Etna in the east, others insist it's near Trapani in the west, and a very few claim it could be in the nearby Grotta di Polifemo, or "Polyphêmos' Cave," near Milazzo in the north.

I start my Cyclopean quest after I ferry from Lipari to Milazzo, which is capped by an expansive fort built on the same site as an ancient Greek acropolis and a tenth-century Arab citadel. While I perch on one of the fortress's dizzying parapets, I gaze onto the remains of a Roman burial ground, iconic Spanish walls, medieval towers, the Aeolian Islands and the Baia del Tono, which gets its name from its erstwhile role in the thriving tuna industry. Incidentally, it was also at this fort that representatives of Sicily's five regions met in 1295 to form a parliament.

As I descend to the pebbled beach, the afternoon sun transforms the entire city, which is laid out in a grid pattern, into a sparkling diamond. Somehow I manage to get completely soaked crossing a creek the size of my bathtub while I amble away from Milazzo on a long strip of sand towards the purported Cyclops' cave. Once near the Grotta di Polifemo, I sprint up the hillside to the cave with the gusto of Odysseus who, Homer says in *The Odyssey*, "climbed, then, briskly to the cave."

After just a few seconds I can't believe this cave is even a serious contender, because there isn't room for the sizable flock of the Cyclops' sheep. Nor can I imagine that even three thousand years ago there were, as Homer writes, "tall trunks of pine and rugged towering oak trees" on the steep-slanted hill. Other cave candidates – with space for trees, ample pasture land, a larger interior, a big slab to close the cave and the proper terrain for the Cyclops "to break the hilltop and heave it"– are sure to be more plausible.

I dismiss this contender cave and continue around the bay to arrive at the beach near Barcellona (yes, it has two "l"s), where I stroll through a seaside park and meet an English woman named Barbara who's been married to a Sicilian named Marco for fifteen years. While we sit and chat in the well-equipped beachside playground, Barbara tells me that I'm the only native English speaker she's seen in months and that she's thinking about going back to Liverpool for the first time in a decade.

"I want my 100 percent Sicilian kids to see where I came from and experience the English culture," she tells me. "It's so completely different from this that it'll either be a complete turn off or they'll love it."

Somehow this prompts a discussion about men and machismo in Sicily, where I have yet to see any male look at me with anything resembling even a disingenuous smile. Once she gets going, Barbara tells me a couple of things about Sicilian males: a Sicilian man is not embarrassed to be living with his mother after 30; a Sicilian man will never be seen putting anything in a garbage can; a Sicilian man will flaunt his ability to discard waste anywhere but in a garbage can.

I concoct the idea of compiling a list of the macho traits of Sicilian men as I observe them during my jaunt around the island.

As I continue on a clay-earthed lane for walkers and a paved lane for cyclists, I decide to quickly strip to my swimsuit and jump under one of the many showers on the adjacent beach. A sign in Terme Vigiliatore says "Warning: Bathing Service Without Saving" (I'm not sure if the translation written in Arabic is any clearer) which encourages me to jump in and test the water. As I look back to and beyond the beach, Sicily's mountainous topography illustrates that I have some cliffy terrain ahead of me.

Back on dry land, I tool along at a five kilometer/hour pace to Tonarella, which is billed as "the city of the immaculate conception," though I'm not sure if that means that this is where *the* immaculate conception took place or if the city itself is the result of an immaculate conception. I enter a tiny delicatessen to buy an its-never-tasted-so-good tuna-and-tomato sandwich, which I eat at a bench on a seaside promenade named after Sicilian author and Nobel Prize winner Salvatore Quasimodo who died in 2001.

When I arrive in Portarosa, the first thing I see is a sprawling private resort complex packed with cars that is off limits for uninvited MedTrekkers. I pass the *Residence Via di Calipso*, pleased to see a name that evokes something Greek, and approach the steep and daunting Cape Marinello on the *Golfo di Patti*. It's unclear if I'll wind up going around, over, or under the church-crowned, cacti-covered cape, though a fisherman, who says that the towering *Santa Maria di Tindari* is one of the *bella*-est churches in Sicily, claims "you can walk all around the entire capo on the sand."

Thirty minutes later – after a magical seaside stroll under a not-too-crumbly escarpment through a nature reserve full of lakes, flora, fauna, caves, echoes and stunning uphill views of *bella*-est *Santa Maria* – I'm stymied by the sea's considerable waves and insurmountable cliffs. The fisherman is wrong. I turn around and retrace my steps after exploring a bird-and-plant-filled tidal pool called *Laghetti di Marinello*.

What's my next move? Will I make the arduous climb up the pathless hill to visit the church, in a perched village founded for refugees from Sparta in 396 BC and the more recently built Sanctuary of Tindari, which houses a Byzantine Black Virgin? Will I use my flashlight to point the way through a 2.136-kilometer-long dark railway tunnel? Will I scurry through the equally long and forbidden-for-pedestrians tunnel on the *autostrada*?

Tired of getting scratched and cut, I scrap the climb up the harsh hillside. Instead I boldly enter the very dark train tunnel but chicken out and retreat after 200 meters when there is no light visible at either end. I then don my orange Day-Glo safety vest and proceed quickly and carefully through the *autostrada* tunnel. Unfortunately there are cops at the other end (who knew that someone actually monitors the tunnel cameras?). They ask to see my passport and harshly remind me that it's completely illegal and incredibly stupid to walk through the tunnel. After looking like they know an Idiot when they see one, they direct me to a skimpy path that returns to the sea.

I wind up the MedTrekking day in Patti, where I admire some

third century Roman ruins located directly under the suspended *autostrada* that were discovered during construction. It's dusk and just the right time for a cappuccino at a hotel on the sea complemented by cream-filled, you guessed it, Patti-cakes.

The next morning I'm on the cliff-hanging SS 113 (the SS here stands for the *Settentrionale Sicula,* the seaside road) on the mountainous coast from Patti to Capo d'Orlando. Fortunately there aren't many cars on a somnolent Sunday, though there are dozens of bouquets of both fresh and wilted flowers indicating the places where people have been killed on the road. Some fatalities might have occurred during the annual car rally that brings a buzz to the Costa Saracena as it careens through the villages of Brolo, Piraino, Gioiosa Marea, Nose, Ficarra and San Giorgio. But the most noise I hear today is produced by a brass band that greets me on arrival in San Giorgio, where many signs in English correctly identify the village as Saint George.

The MedTrek between Saint George and Gioiosa Marea reminds me, as I look down onto a rocky shore with clean coves and pebble beaches, of Spain's Costa Brava. It soon becomes the scene of one of the most dramatic moments of my MedTrek when the narrow tarmac stretch along the coast is closed for three kilometers and traffic is diverted up and over the mountain. I scale the barricade with a "No Trespassing" sign and relish having the closed-to-traffic road all to myself.

I soon realize the reason for the sign. This is not one of the usual "not-really-under-construction" construction projects and at one point the road has completely crumbled into the sea. There's a 20-foot gap with an impassible vertical cliff and a steep drop to death on the rocky seaside. No way up, no way down, no way across. Fortunately I feel spry enough to work my way up to the iron spider-web cables that keep the remainder of the cliff above from completely falling apart and toppling into the sea. I put on my gloves, humbly pray to the gods and gingerly edge my way across with my legs dangling into the abyss. Although I'm aware of the obvious stupidity of attempting a feat that would have challenged Philippe Petit, the French high wire walker, I am tremendously satisfied when I reach the other side.

There's a lot of partying at a gigantic resort called Capo Calava, but most villages, like Brolo with its private medieval family castle, are calm on a Sunday afternoon. The pay-to-drive *autostrada* now gets most of the traffic between Messina and Palermo, and these little seaside villages are somewhat isolated except for locals.

I make myself a cheese, tomato and fresh tuna sandwich on the rocks below the 16th-century Torre delle Ciatole just before Gliaca di

Piràino, which was purportedly home of Cyclops Pyracmon. This is such a delicious spot that I post a blog photo with the title *Sexy Spot for a Sixty-Second Snooze on a Sunny Sunday in Sicily* and take a five-minute nap before MedTrekking another 15 kilometers to Capo d'Orlando, which was originally called Agathyrsus until Charlemagne changed the name to honor Orlando, one of his heroic paladins. My serene saunter continues past a 17th-century sanctuary and ends with a gelato on the comparatively lively beach front in Capo d'Orlando.

Road signs along the coast point to either Palermo or Messina, but I know I'm still closer to Messina because most license plates still have ME (Messina), rather than a PA (Palermo), on them. I don't realize that Sicilians have a verbal abbreviation for ME, or Messina, until I overhear a conversation.

"I'll get to Mess in an hour," a man said to someone at the other end of his cell phone.

And I'm sure he's not referring to mass.

Even in slightly remote places like Sant'Agata di Militello, Italians are still fanatical about wearing branded clothes – and don't even get me started about their attitude towards shoes. The Sicilian seaside is a continual fashion show, and one not-so-macho guy I meet has *Fashion Marky*, yes *Fashion Marky*, inscribed on his flashy new sweatshirt.

Fashion Marky is the stereotype of what a young Sicilian guy should be – gelled-back hair, gigantic sunglasses, spiffy white pants, brand names on every accessory and article of clothing, a few tats and, oddly, a pregnant and very normal looking partner.

I too, want to be part of the designer-name game and set out on today's 38-kilometer MedTrek from chic Capo d'Orlando through sweet Acquedolci to sunset-on-the-seaside Caronia wearing my *Trust Me...I'm an Alcoholic* T-shirt.

This doesn't only show off my brand consciousness but also illustrates how a multiplicity of meanings can be associated with just a few words. I try to explain to Fashion Marky, in my constantly improving Italian with a Sicilian twang, that the phrase *Trust Me...I'm an Alcoholic* can mean that "you can trust me because I drink a lot" or "I personally know that I have a problem with alcohol" or "I'm a drunk and anything I tell you is questionable."

Fashion Marky, though his eyes are hidden by his shades and his hair is seemingly Botoxed to avoid the display of too much emotion, looks like he isn't buying any of it. He refuses a trade when I suggest swapping my sweaty T for his brand new sweats. No one else makes an offer for my shirt during the day and, between us, I don't think many people understand even one of its multiple meanings.

Like the number of pairs of shoes I've worn on the MedTrek, I have trouble remembering the wide variety of T-shirts I've sported. Friends keep giving me new ones with clever slogans to help differentiate me from the Italian fashionistas. One of my favorites, proffered by Gloria Ackley in Manhattan, says "Shhh" with a logo of the New York Public Library. Gloria gave me one T that reads "I AM A MAN," which was a slogan popular during civil rights demonstrations in the 1960s, and another splendid Che Guevara shirt that she brought back from Cuba. Many other Ts are equally meaningful with slogans like "Raven Lunatic," "Increase the Peace," "Practice Non Violence" and "Adopt-A-Minefield" though some have confusing and somewhat meaningless phrases (to an Italian audience anyway) like "Sleestak," who was the green humanoid on the 70s show *Land of the Lost*.

Almost all the shirts I wear on the MedTrek have either English or nonsensical logos – and all my baseball caps also have something written on them. This isn't just because of my fastidious sense of fashion but also because it "announces" me – assisted by my brightly colored shorts – as a definite foreigner, which I think is to my benefit.

For the record, many of these shirts were part of the swag in goody bags that I got when I was covering the biz and writing a column in Hollywood. Tomorrow I'll wear my favorite that says *EVEN BIGGER GIANT F**KING ROBOTS ARE COMING*. That'll wake 'em up.

I leave *Capo d'Orlando* with especially spry steps after investigating an inspiring mosaic on the promenade that commemorates "the naval battle of *Capo d'Orlando* on July 4, 1299" and I'm pleased that Americans aren't the only ones who think July 4 is important. Acquedolci across the bay looks like an easy 20-25 kilometer stroll, and I stay on the seaside promenade after the Santa Rose campground and a hotel called *Capo Nettuno* (or Neptune, the Roman version of Poseidon).

The beaches are an irregular mix of pebbles and sand and there are proliferating bamboo fields as I breeze past *Marina di Torrenova* where the view to my left includes lemon orchards, impressive elevated *autostrada* bridges, and lovely-looking (from a distance anyway) hilltop villages. I continue into *Sant'Agata di Militello* where the *Circo Bizzarro Avangard* is taking up space on the lungomare. I'm shocked at the comatose state of the animals lazing around the big top and they get me thinking about Homer's use of animal analogies during battle scenes in *The Iliad*.

At one point, Homer writes, the Trojans surround Odysseus "as tawny jackals from the hills will ring an antlered deer, gone heavy with his wound." Hektor, the son of Priam, defeats Patróklos like "a lion in his pride bringing down a tireless boar" and one cool soldier "steadily waited, like a mountain boar who knows his power, facing a noisy hunt in a lonely place: his backbone bristles rise; both eyes are fiery; gnashing his tusks he waits in fury to drive back dogs and men."

Meanwhile Achilles pursued Hektor "the way a hound will harry a deer's fawn he has started from its bed" and promised that "dogs and birds will have you, every scrap." He told Hektor before they came to blows that "as between men and lions there is no concord between wolves and sheep."

I order a vegetarian *panini* at a street-side café to avoid offending any animals.

The amble into Acquedolci produces two unexpected bonuses. Just out of town one of those remarkable suspended bridges is closed and I have a tranquil four-kilometer walk across the view-rich overpass above *Torre di Lauro* all to myself. As I relish the privacy and the view, I say to each of the eight highway workmen *"Quelle bella strada privata –* Stratte-McClure *Privata!"* They agree, though I'm not sure they have any clue that I'm naming their private road after myself.

The walk is so enjoyable that I'm not even bothered when I learn the railway station in *Torre di Lauro*, like many in Sicily, is decommissioned. When I reach *Marina di Caronia*, I enjoy one of the brightest and roundest sunsets I've ever seen and recall that Sicily is where Helios, the sun god, kept his cattle.

Encountering a Restaurant Romance

I catch a train at a small station the next morning. There's no automatic ticket machine, the local tobacco shop where tickets are always sold is four kilometers away and closed today, and the *capo di trenno,* or conductor, of a train stopped at the station tells me that "No matter what excuse you've got it will cost you €50 if you ride without a ticket." But when he sees I'm a hiker he calls the *capi di tutti treni,* the conductor of all the trains, and gets me a special dispensation to pay for a ticket on the train without a fine.

I now pay fares so religiously, after a couple of close calls, that I'm reluctant to get on a train without a ticket – and this in a country where everyone used to sneak on trains. Incidentally, one reason that Sicilian trains are on time or late is because there's only one track and a great deal of precision is required to start and stop the trains according to schedule. The *capo di trenno* on the train tells me Sicily is a *"bella paese"* and encourages me to hike *"piano, piano,"* or slowly slowly.

That's unquestionably my mode when I head out of Caronia on a back-and-forth day between the *spiaggia* and the *strada*. I find myself on a rocky beach strewn with driftwood, on a road paralleling the train tracks, in a lovely scented orchard of lemon trees and crossing train bridges and cheating death on the SS 113, aka the E90.

The day takes a serendipitously romantic twist when I arrive in San Stefano di Camastra on the *Lungomare delle Nereidi.*

There are five ristorantes/pizzerias/trattorias in San Stefano, but the only place you'll ever catch me eating in this town during this lifetime is the Manueliana restaurant.

This isn't because the owners, Manuel and Eliana, refuse to take any of my euros for the tasty tuna tagliatelle they serve me at lunch as I regale them with a few anecdotes from *The Idiot and the Odyssey* and describe my ongoing walk around Sicily.

"I haven't even driven around Sicily in a car," confesses Eliana. "I would never let anyone who's walking around my island pay for lunch in my restaurant!"

Nor is it because Eliana compliments me on my Italian and Manuel cracks up when I mention a few of the reasons that I think Sicilian males are the most macho on earth. It's because thirtyish Eliana spins one of the sweetest love stories to come out of Italy since the era of Romeo and Juliet. She and Manuel are living proof that youthful romance blossoms on the Sicilian seaside.

"Manuel and I took snapshots of each other when he came here on vacation from Northern Italy with his parents in August 1990," Eliana says as I begin to slowly consume my first liter of water after walking 13 kilometers on the rocky coast from Caronia. "I was only ten at the time, and he was thirteen. I forgot all about him until I saw the photos a decade later and realized that something in my heart told me I needed to see him again."

It took Eliana a while to track Manuel down, but when she located him they spent two years courting by telephone until Eliana, who was born in San Stefano and had never left Sicily, made the trip to Lombardy.

"I hated northern Italy because the people are cold and the weather is colder," Eliana continues. "But I loved Manuel, and after two years together we decided to return here, where the weather is hot and the people are hotter, to get married. Now a love story that began twenty years ago with a forgotten photo has given us a daughter and a lovely family restaurant where I can buy you lunch."

Don't blink, even if you're slowly walking through San Stefano, or you might miss the lovers, their story, their daughter, and Manueliana at Via Marina 15.

I leave Manueliana impressed with the delights of young love and pass the *Hotel La PlaYa* (sic) *Blanca* and a vacation residence called

Noah's Arc Village, with lots of pairs of sheep and other animals, on the beach going out of town. After examining the gigantic *Window on the Sea: Monument to a Dead Poet* sculpture by Tano Festa, I exhaust myself jumping from boulder to boulder on the breakwater on the outskirts of San Stefano. When I don't do much better walking on the slow-going rocky coastline or the congested SS 113, I toss in the towel in Castel di Tusa after only 25 kilometers because I like its USA-sounding name. I spend an hour on the marina enjoying a coffee and learning about Antonio Presti.

Presti is the local artist responsible for commissioning the *Window on the Sea* and a number of other gigantic artworks on display in the nearby countryside, including *The Pyramid of the 38th Parallel* by Mauro Staccioli. Since 2010, *The Pyramid* has towered on a mountain above Castel di Tusa as part of Presti's innovative program called *La Fiumara d'Arte*, or The River of Art.

Presti says his project, which he launched in 1982 and initiated in 1986 with the *Window*, is Europe's "largest outdoor gallery." He won't get much argument, because it stretches from the sea to the Nebrodi Mountain and now features over a dozen gigantic artworks.

Presti also runs the unique *Atelier sul Mar*, or Art Hotel, complex on the marina in Castel di Tusa where half of the forty sea-view and art-filled rooms were capriciously decorated by a variety of designers and artists during the 1990s. In one room, called *La Bocca della Verita,* the bed features a "mouth of truth" headboard by Mario Ceroli, influenced by a work of the same name at the Basilica di Santa Maria in Cosmedin in Rome. Other rooms are named *Linea d'Ombra* (Shadow Line) by Michele Canzoneri, *Su Barca Di Carta Mi Imbarco* (I'm Boarding on a Paper Boat) by Maria Lai, *Hammam* by Sistej Xhafa, and *La Stanza del Mare Negato* by Frabrizio Plessi that, of course, negates the presence and view of the sea outside the window.

Pressing on to Palermo

It's 226 kilometers from Messina to Greek-created Cefalù with its dominating fortified Rock that includes a well-known Temple of Diana. But what do I find when I have a late lunch on a terrace above the Mediterranean at the Bar del Faro on my arrival into town? A table of six Germans with mountain bikes, a French family of four, and two Americans on their way back to Milan. That's because Cefalù is the must-see hot spot of Northern Sicily.

Not that I let other foreigners turn me off. I establish a base camp here in a small studio about thirty-nine steps from Cefalù's 12th-century Norman Cathedral and its vibrant Italian-and-tourist-filled piazza. Located off a tilted cobblestone street between the cacti-covered and heavily fortified Rock and the Sea, this is a good place to launch my MedTrek to prestigious Palermo, Sicily's capital about 75 kilometers down the coast.

It is a speedy walk (28 kilometers in six hours) here from Castel di Tusa because I intentionally spend most of the time on the two-lane asphalt just above the sea. I probably walk only five kilometers on non-asphalt all day but don't mind, because the day before consisted of jumping, dodging and slipping on all kinds of pebbles, stones, and rocks on the jagged coastline.

I get in some upper body exercise after I spring for a two-liter bottle of water and spend an hour doing bicep pumps. I pass the *Scoglio* camping site and notice that it promises *"No Discotheca – No Animazione"* but rather "shade, sea, and quiet for everyone." An attractive allure. The cruise through *Finale di Pollina* on the *Costa di Turchina* features greenery everywhere – flowers, plants, bushes, weeds are all rich spring green – and quite a few of the long, black, Sicilian serpents known as a *biaccio*.

The road MedTrek is especially relaxing because between 9:00 a.m. and 4:00 p.m. there aren't many cars, though I'm excited when a Fiat model called *Ulisses* passes by. One reason for the scarcity of vehicles is that the centers of most main towns – like Tusa, Pollina, and Castelbuono – are on hilltops a few kilometers back from their smaller coastal marina counterparts. I cross from Messina (ME) province into Palermo (PA) province, and at the Babata Beach I'm warned that "Bathing is not sure for lack of special lifesaving service!"

Cefalù, incidentally, gets its name from the Greek *kephale*, which is what its first inhabitants called the place in the fourth century BC. It means, depending on who you ask, either head, cape, extremity, point or promontory, and it's capped by a 270-meter high Rock, which locals typically call *La Rocca*. The Rock is topped with a castle built in the 11th century and a belt of *"mura megalitiche,"* or megalithic walls, that illustrate Cefalù's once-important geographical and military location. As if that's not enough, the impressive gold-colored Norman Cathedral built in the 12th century (at least, construction actually began in 1131) is considered a fine example of Byzantine, Arab, and Norman architecture, and there are all sorts of archeological remnants from various eras at the Mandralisca Museum.

I take the next day off to enjoy the town, do my laundry (a breeze at a semi-self service where I get my very smelly clothes washed, dried and folded for €12), visit the museum and hike up to the Temple of Diana and *La Toppa Rocca*, as I call the summit.

The second person I think of while I spend two hours in the museum (the first, of course, is its creator Enrico Pirajno, the explorer/

naturalist Baron of Mandralisca born here in 1809) is Aaron Paul, the Harvard curator who could have explained the details on the numerous ceramic bowls, chalices, craters, cups, vases and oil lamps originating in Lipari, and other parts of Sicily, in the 6th-4th centuries BC.

Sure, I'm able to identify a tuna salesman on one fourth-century BC *krater* (a *krater* is a classic mixing bowl for wine), but the figures on many of the other *kylixes* (a *kylix* is a cup), amphorae and *kothons* (a *kothon* is container for oil or perfume), while aesthetically pleasing, require more knowledge than I possess. And I have a number of questions about figures and inscriptions on other bowls, coins, craters, cups, oil lamps, and vases. Aaron could swiftly and expertly describe the themes, myths, inscriptions, gods, muses, satyrs, centaurs, and ordinary people depicted on these rich remnants of the past, though I'm not sure how he would react to the museum's stuffed birds, porcupines and other animals.

I met Aaron, an art historian who mainly works at Harvard University's Center for Hellenic Studies in Washington, D.C., when he was lecturing on a cruise to lesser-known Greek islands. A specialist in Greek vase painting and the go-to guy when it comes to Greek and Etruscan art, Aaron considers these vases "windows into antiquity and a visual language that depicts many of the fascinating aspects of Greek life." He took an extensive trip throughout Sicily (though not on foot) a few years ago to select pieces for a major exhibit in the U.S.

"Vases were designed for social conversation, and vase painting is a fascinating and revealing mirror of the psyche of the times," Aaron told me during breakfast as our ship floated by the island of Ikaria. "Incidentally, some academics studying Greek vases call themselves potheads.

I send Aaron a "wish you were here" email with the subject line *Experienced Pothead Needed ASAP in Cefalù*.

After being stumped by ceramics at the Mandralisca Museum, I spend two hours hiking up, and back down, La Rocca di Cefalù. I drop in on the fifth-century BC Temple of Diana, investigate cisterns used by the Greeks in 400 BC, and look at the terrain I'll be walking tomorrow from the top of the *castello*, where there are breathtaking views of the Cefalù cathedral and the town's red-tiled rooftops.

It isn't a difficult hike up the Rock, and people of all ages and nationalities slowly but surely make the climb. But one American kid, who couldn't have been over 25, called his parents in the U.S. from the top to tell them "it was a scary hike, it took me hours, Peter flaked out, but I kept on going, I've never been this high though I don't know how high it is, and I'm still sweating like a pig – but I've got two bars so I

wanted to call and let you know I'm alive."
That'll keep them talking at home.

Cefalù has both old-fashioned and contemporary touches. A tailor on one narrow street off the main Corso Ruggero sews a patch on my tattered Levis, a mobile fishmonger weighs each fish sale with a portable scale, and a fruit seller appears outside my door just before lunchtime with tangerines and strawberries. Everything closes from one to four each afternoon and the only place I can get cell reception, due to the thick walls in my rented studio, is at the top of the cathedral steps. Every second retail outlet seems to sell *gelato*, garbage is left in plastic bags in front of each house for collection every morning, and late each night, I get a Wi-Fi connection at a chic and high-end restaurant and art gallery called *La Galleria*. Another Cefalù highpoint is the 40,000-hectare Madonie Park, which is considered one of Sicily's best hiking and biking getaways.

I am most impressed by Cefalù, though, after taking off early one morning and forgetting to lock the door of my tiny apartment. I return at 10:00 p.m. to find the street-side door wide open. Perhaps the wind blew it open or maybe a Mafia don opened it to show me who controlled the neighborhood. Whatever the case, I was prepared to enter 27 via Francavilla to find my possessions ransacked and cleaned out. Remarkably not a thing – not my computer, not my passport – had been touched.

After carefully locking the door the next morning and bounding through the *Piazza del Duomo* down to the sea, I pay homage and thanks to the anti-theft gods at the lovely little 16th-century *Chiesa dell'Itria*. The full moon is still high in the western sky as I scurry along the seafront that abuts the town's beach. It's just me, a few fishermen, a few joggers, a German photographer, and an urban walker or two as I pass the ultra-modern Monacoish Cefalù Sea Palace Hotel, a dilapidated Club Med and the chic Calanica exclusive resort.

My senses are titillated by pine and birch scents and the cooing of doves, pigeons and quail as I pass inviting seaside villas on a small road between the train tracks and the sea. I walk down a number of dead-end lanes to find clusters of secluded hotels and homes, like the *Baia del Capitano* and the ornate stone arabesque house at the *Baia dei 7 Emiri*. Ignoring a *Locals Only* sign written in English in large white letters, I head down to a tiny beach. A sign near the Carlton Riviera Hotel in *Capo Plaia* indicates Palermo is 69 kilometers away.

Both the *Territorio di Lascari* and the *Lungomare Compofelice di Roccella* are a breeze on a beach walk that enables me to avoid not only a few villages but also serious construction underway on a new high-speed railway. Passing the *Torre Rocella*, I wind up on the *Gorgo Lungo* until I get through *Compofelice*. Crammed vacation villages, with names like 101 Pines, contrast with the archeologically rich *Plaia di Himira* where numerous artifacts from the Punic, Greek and Roman eras have been excavated.

There are no shops to buy water, and I'm grateful when an older man at the Residence Acacia invites me into his home, offers me a 2-liter bottle of water and refuses any *soldi*, or payment, adding that "nothing opens around here until June when the schools let out." I promise that I'll make a donation on his behalf at the next church I pass, which makes him smile.

The wide Imera River forces a long detour inland underneath the *autostrada* and prompts a serendipitous stop at the ruins of the *Temple della Vittoria*, built around 480 BC to honor a victory by the Greeks over the Carthaginians.

When I refuel at a little road stop near *Buonfornello*, I've got my eye on a tall electric power station furnace and, beyond it, the hillside town of *Termini Imerese*. But I'm not sure how far away it is. A truck driver insists it's 20 kilometers, the *café* owner says it's 12, and a cyclist tells me it's ten. Fortunately the cyclist is right. He also confirms that I wouldn't have been able to ford the "fast and dangerous Imera river," warns me not to walk under a railroad barricade just as a train zips by (*grazie*, good advice!), and tells me the sea is dangerously polluted and there are *Divieto di Balneazione* (Don't' Swim) signs everywhere. When I tell him I've hiked 40 kilometers by foot today, he apologizes that he's only done 40 kilometers on his bike.

I hike through a nondescript industrial zone and ask myself who chooses to locate their company in such a depressing place. If I've convinced you how dirty the Italian seaside is just because of home-made garbage, think what it looks like when you add industrial waste and the ENEL electricity tower.

Termini Imerese, which gets its name from its scalding and sulfurous thermal waters, has hilltop views in every direction from the appropriately named via Belvedere on the expansive terrace behind the 17th-century Duomo. I arrive there after negotiating a pleasant maze of alleys and steps through the old town where I have a breakfast consisting of two *cornetti* and three bracing cups of coffee to celebrate May Day.

Walking down the hill towards Palermo, I briefly take a step back in time and march through fields where horses are pulling carts and families are tending their crops. The first half of the day is spent walking on a pebbly beach and noticing that Sicilian women are as overweight as their American counterparts before enjoying a carb-heavy *cannelloni* lunch. I manage to soak my shoes in some deceptive marshes near Trabia and change into dry shoes and socks after walking on a rarely-seen-in-Sicily sidewalk to an inviting bench at the San Nicolo Marina. Then I work my way past the agora and frescoed villas among the ruins at hilly Solunto, which the Carthaginians founded in 4 BC, and around Cape Zaffercano to the extended fringes of Palermo.

Sicilians use their May 1 Labor Day celebrations to inaugurate the seaside summer season. Every beach is choc-a-bloc with smoky and scented barbecuers picnicking on lamb to blaring music. Teenagers have taken over their parents' beach homes, gypsies circle their trailers *à la* wagon train, and extended families meet at congested coastal parking lots. I have enough lamb offered to me at the different parties to forget about dinner and think that these folks could teach Americans a lot about how to celebrate the 4th of July.

The final multi-kilometer trudge into Palermo at the western end of the long town takes me through suburbettes with descriptive names like *Bandita* and *Settecannoli*. At one point I climb over a fence to get to the main road and meet perhaps the only person in Palermo who isn't in party mode.

"Do you want to get shot?" he barks, pointing a pistol through the broken window.

"*Perdoname, Scusa, Perdoname*, I'm lost and need to get back to the main road," I plead. "Please don't shoot me. It'll just cause trouble."

"You're trespassing and I can shoot you if I feel like it," he barks again.

"But it's Labor Day," I say. "No one shoots anyone on Labor Day."

I hear a resounding "BANG!" But, fortunately, he is only shutting the window.

Although I try to take it easy after yesterday's 41-kilometer outing, I walk 43 kilometers before I call it a day. I'm eager to reach Palermo's ornate central train station that opened at Piazza Giulio Cesare, or the Julius Caesar Square, in 1886. In dramatic contrast to the tiny, oft-closed railway stations that I've encountered, this gem evokes an old-school European city station. There are even cops making sure that no illicit Africans get on the *Treno Notte*, or night train, to Rome, the one that I called the African Express when Cassie picked it up in Sapri.

In case you want to follow in my footsteps, the 315-kilometer MedTrek from Messina to Palermo, minus the excursion to the Aeolian Islands, took me nine hiking days.

Palermo was founded by the Phoenicians in 734 BC (they called it Ziz, or "flower"), then taken over by the Greeks (they called it

Panormus, from the Greek for port) and later conquered by the Arabs in the ninth century when it became an important Islamic center (they called it Bal'harm). It became one of Europe's greatest cities in 1072 when the Normans took control and called it Palermo.

Neither the Normans, represented by Charles of Anjou, nor anyone else had an easy time if they mispronounced the name of the city or any other Italian word. At one point in history, any Frenchman who couldn't pronounce *Cicero* correctly was killed. Glad they don't test my Italian like that today or you might not be reading this.

During a day off I enjoy a walking exploration of a historically rich city that survived bombing raids during World War II and a severe earthquake in 1968. I take a bus south of the town to photograph *Monreale* (Mount Royal, or Monte Reale, was its first name), where the splendid, mosaic-filled Church of *Santa Maria La Nuova* has a fountain-filled courtyard inside the cloisters with delicately carved and carefully sculpted figures on the wooden columns. Pigeons and other birds always seem to haphazardly get in my photographs, like one coming in for a landing on a fountain with a circular bowl crested with animals.

At the Capuchin Catacombs just outside the city gates, I drop in to check out thousands of mummified bodies, including 8,000 Capuchin friars, virgins and children. This sanitized and naturally air conditioned version of the afterlife is nothing like my visit to the daunting and haunting shades in Homer's underworld. These mummies have a more comfortable and cooler resting place.

The catacombs, which contain corpses dating back to the 16th century, are an amazing must-see because, among other things, the dead are also divided into sections – women, children, priests, professionals, military – and many bodies are dressed in the attire that signifies their lifetime trade.

I violate the *"No Foto*/No Film" and "Sacred Place to Respect" signs to get some shots for a brochure. Don't get me wrong, I seriously respect sacred places and don't like to disturb the deceased. But could you resist taking a shot of this "No Smoking" sign amid the mummified cadavers?

After this contemporary underworld it's time to visit the nearby tomb of Giuseppe Tomasi di Lampedus, who wrote *The Leopard*, to get some fresh cemetery air. Then I take a two-hour tour of the qanats (one of my favorite Scrabble words, it means "a system of underground tunnels and wells in the Middle East") and check out the shops on *Corso Vittorio Emanuele* and *Via Maqueda*.

My last touristic stop is the Palatine Chapel in the Palace of the Norman Kings. French writer Guy de Maupassant called this "the most surprising religious jewel ever dreamt of by man" and the chamber of the Sicilian Parliament now occupies what were once Royal Apartments.

I hate to sound like a guidebook but the royal chapel, built by Roger II between 1132-1143, is "a prime example of Byzantine-Arab-Norman artistry exemplified by its mosaics, gold, wood-carved ceiling, and inlaid marble floors and walls." What really excites me are the detailed frescoes depicting six of the Twelve Labors of Hêraklês, including the slaying of the multi-headed Hydra of Lerna and the taming of the three-headed dog Cerberus. And a totally relaxed one-headed cat napping at the chapel's exit.

There are now lots of Bangladeshis in Palermo, mostly selling Kleenex at traffic lights and taking euros for attending parking lots. I'm gratified that one of the longest running street jobs in Italy – an oft suspicious-looking man charges you to park in an otherwise free parking place, and you pay him because you think your car will be damaged if you don't – is still alive and well in Sicily. But I'm slightly surprised that it's no longer an Italian-only occupation.

After my touristic Sunday, I return to the Palermo train station, just off via Abramo Lincoln, to find out if there might be a "Lost and Found" office. Maybe the tiny Olympus tape recorder I left on a train the other day has been turned in. There is a "Lost and Found." But everyone I ask for directions gives me a smiling shoulder shrug indicating I'll never see my trusty recorder again.

When I finally find the "Lost and Found," the young woman attendant smiles in sympathy, checks to confirm that nobody has turned in my recorder and then asks "*Lei piace Italia?*" ("Do you like Italy?").

"*Me piace Sicilia!*" ("I like Sicily!)

"*Ecco, bravo!*" ("That's cool!") she replies with a big smile.

I walk down Lincoln Boulevard and along *Foro Umberto 1* to the pleasure port and *cala*, or ancient harbor, and take a detour to *La Vucciria* Market to buy a *sfincione*. I eat the delicious if messy early lunch (the flat baked dough is topped with anchovies, onions, breadcrumbs, herbs and tomatoes) on a seaside bench. Then I continue along the via Francesco Cripi and around the port of Palermo – where ships and ferries are departing for Naples, Genoa, Livorno and other ports on the mainland – in the shadow of *Monte Pellegrino*, a mountain dominated by the *Church of Santa di San Rosalia* and a government-run *Castillo Ultveggio*.

My late morning MedTrek is brightened by dozens of florists-in-a-row at the Palermo cemetery. Then I traipse through the delightful little towns of Arenella, Vergine Maria and villa-rich Addaura to arrive at the two-kilometer sandy beach of Mondello, a terrific place if you're in the mood for a *passeggiata* in the early evening, and approach with awe the "floating" Charleston Restaurant Bathing Facility, the best on-the-water restaurant that I've seen in 6,457 kilometers.

Created in the late 1920s, a 2007 renovation has made the Charleston better than ever. I'm so excited that I can't resist taking photos from several angles as I walk by.

The next thing I run into is an excellently disguised German pillbox from World War II. I stumble onto it when I spend four hours tackling the steep, glorious, almost inaccessible *Capo Gallo* and the *Capo Gallo* Nature Reserve. It's not as fashionable as the Charleston but the Nazi remembrance blends right in with the rocky coast.

I wisely decide to backtrack after six kilometers because the grotto and the vertical Mount Gallo are too dicey and dizzying to tackle without equipment. But until my turnaround, this was a four-star walk on a sunny, breezy morning that included a nifty nudist zone with no nudists, though there is a sign on a large rock at the *Zona Nudista* that says "*Rispetiamos,*" or "Respect Us," just before the rocky coast and cliffs make things totally unmanageable.

Occasionally it can be a bit perturbing when, after hours of arduous climbing/trekking, I encounter an obstacle that forces me to humbly backtrack, patiently retrace my steps and cautiously attempt to find a new route around a difficult part of the Mediterranean Sea. But today I simply turn around and silently pray to the numerous gods and goddesses in Greek mythology.

Myths are not, of course, too much in vogue these days. But in Homer's time every Greek believed that the entire world, from pre-history to history, could be explained by myths, though that began to wane in the wake of the fall of Rome in AD 496. Heck, when I retreat, awestruck by the steep, scary scenery, from the inaccessible cliffs of 586-meter high Mount Gallo, I'm one of the rare guys on the block praying to Zeus, who thunders in high heaven.

I take the higher road over the mountain and find myself on a wooden walkway leading into delightfully named Sferracavallo, a colorful village featuring local fishermen selling local fish.

I haven't yet bought a notebook to replace my lost Olympus and start scribbling on an abandoned Marlboro pack, a practical ruse that enables me to pick up litter at the same time as I record my movements. I can't help noting that the name of the cigarette pales in comparison to the larger "*il fumo uccide*" ("Smoking is Suicide") warning on one side of the pack and the "*Proteggi I bambini: non fare loro respirare il tuo fumo*" ("Protect children: don't let them breathe your smoke") on the other. Not that the font size seemed to impact the omnipresent smoking in Sicily.

The next seaside village I reach is Isola delle Feminine, or Women's Island. Everyone I chat with seems to have an explanation about the solitary tower on the small island not far offshore. A female police officer in the small town – which is twinned with Pittsburg, California, and has a Piazza Pittsburg – tells me the tower symbolizes and honors all women. A fisherman says it was once a jail for women. A young barmaid says she hopes the crumbling structure stands for the liberation of women.

The best bet? Your final choice?

Apparently there was a women's only prison on the small island in the 16th century.

It's an overcast day that feels like rain (which almost certainly will not arrive because I'm carrying both a poncho and an umbrella) and I'm so mellow that I spend some time between *Isola delle Femmine* and *Capaci* watching teams of African laborers construct cafés and clean beaches in preparation for the summer season. Though now very distant from the physical site of the gypsy incident, I'm still wary and my mind concocts all kinds of robbery situations. None of which, of course, occur.

I follow the beach, the shore and the promenade to the seaside village of Carini where many houses have boats "docked" on their terraces for the winter. As I round the cape, I change from Levis into worn and torn shorts, and find a nice path through the sprouting daisies to *Torre Muzza*.

The airplanes buzzing overhead are quite symbolic because many believe Daedalus, who founded Carini and called it Hyccara in memory of his son Icarus. Icarus, you may recall, tried to escape from Crete wearing wings that his father sculpted from feathers and wax. Although Daedalus, who had built the labyrinth in Knossos and was imprisoned by King Minos for revealing its secrets, warned his son not to fly too close to the sun or the sea, Icarus crash-landed when the heat melted the wax.

That's not the only tragedy associated with Carini. The Baronessa di Carini was killed by her father in 1563 for having an affair with one man while engaged to another, and the episode is the subject of numerous poems, ballads and parental instructions.

I continue on the very narrow and nearly carless *via Cristoforo Colombo* on the seaside to the Palermo airport on the *Punta Raisa/Cinisi* and once there behave like a kid in a candy store. I have a coffee and become pals-y with the waiter who fills my water bottle, then chat up the women at two different tourist offices and try to book a seat on Alitalia for my flight to Rome in five weeks. I tell some visiting American students where to rent a car, and detail my every step since Messina to some taxi drivers who say *Complimenti*, and seem to mean it, when I tell them about my walk. I quote Thich Nhat Hanh – "I always leave for the airport an extra hour early, so I can practice walking meditation there" – to one unamused traveler who just misses his plane.

I bet I talk to more people in that airport in ninety minutes than I've talked to during the past two weeks – and in about six different languages.

The reason I take time to make all this small talk is because I'm trapped. I can't go west past the airport without crossing razor wire-topped fences, as well as a runway or two, and it's obvious that I'll have to backtrack for five or six kilometers to reach the road to bypass the airport. So I chill and chat.

I tell the visiting students that the name of the Falcone-Borsellino Airport honors an anti-Mafia judge (Falcone) and another citizen (Borsellino) killed by the Mafia. I tell a woman from California that I saw some houses with "Buscemi" and "Pacino" on the post boxes when I was walking here which, I guessed, "means that Steve and Al have vacation houses sensibly placed near the Palermo airport." I tell another couple that I'm walking to Trapani, which was founded by the Elymians as the port for the nearby hilltop city of Erice, known as Eryx during Homer's time, because there was a Cyclops sighting there recently and, "as a Homer scholar, I'm being sent to check it out."

I tell an older couple from Rome that southern Italy is very trashy and that the people are so used to seeing garbage piles that they don't hesitate to litter and compare the garbage situation here to the dictatorship in Burma.

"The Burmese know there's surveillance, censorship, house arrest and political prisoners but they no longer see it because, after fifty years of dictatorship, it's become the norm," I said. "And in Italy, garbage has become the norm."

Then I notice a cop who seems to be wondering, "Why is this sweaty, smelly backpacker with a red baseball cap disturbing everyone in the airport?"

I'll bet he would have arrested me if I'd stayed there another hour.

My Psychoanalysis of Sicilian Men

One reason that I've walkesd over 6,500 kilometers around the Mediterranean Sea is to make contact with local communities and spend time getting to know the people, places and history.

Sometimes, though, I go a bit too far trying to illustrate how much I think I know. I especially felt I might be in some trouble when I heard that there was some criticism of my blog item *Why Are Sicilian Guys The Most Macho Men On Earth?* In case you're not up to speed, here's my list of reasons that Sicilian men exude more machismo than any other group of grown men anywhere on earth.

Why Sicilian guys are the most macho men on earth:

They know *The Godfather* is ALL about them.

They are never the first ones to say *Ciao.*

They don't talk, they pontificate.

They think a sneer is a smile.

They are real Marlboro men who completely ignore the gigantic *il fumo uccide* message on cigarette packs.

They know that the diamond goes only in the left ear.

They refuse to help little Asian women unload big boxes off trains.

They've got a different intimidating wink for every conceivable circumstance.

They wear black, and only black, unless they go cycling.

They snidely snicker when they learn that an American is attempting to walk around their island.

They don't even slightly snicker when they learn that an American is
compiling a list of why Sicilian guys are the most macho men on earth.

They know that they never have to say they're sorry.

They love the songs that they think Carly (*You're So Vain*) Simon and Shania (*That Don't Impress Me Much*) Twain sing about them.

They respond to every question, even one about the weather, with "Why d'ya wanna know?"

They look like they're chewing gum even when they aren't.

Their right hand seems to be glued to their crotch.

They consider it against the law to smile at a foreign male.

They're not at all embarrassed, like many Roman men seem to be, to still be living with their mothers at thirty.

They all claim to have absurdly high testosterone levels.

They all wear the same annoying brand of very dark sunglasses.

They look like they belong to a tribe of James Dean wannabes.

They won't drive a car at anything less than its maximum speed.

They always win, against me anyway, at chicken on the narrow roads.

They know that at 33 they'll marry someone like mamma, have kids and become goodfellas.

Pamela Navarra, whose family owns the Cerri Hotel where I stay in *Golfo del Casetellammare*, thinks I'm more right than wrong about macho men.

"My ex-boyfriend was a Sicilian macho man to the core and you've nailed his personality and character," says thirty-something Pamela, who's now dating a non-macho Sicilian man three years her senior. "My ex always pontificated, never said he was sorry, drove too fast and thought everything was about him. And he was SO proud that he still lived with his mamma.

"But you made some mistakes. Some younger Sicilian guys have actually quit smoking and many Sicilian women also ask 'Why d'ya wanna know?' in response to a question. It's not just a macho trait. Also, we Sicilians have always felt discriminated against by other Italians. Consequently, all of us, even macho men, always help other people, especially little Asian women on trains. The guys you saw were probably from Milan."

Is my hardly comprehensive list too tame? Some foreign women actually like these guys.

"I love the macho aspects of Sicilian men because it makes me feel very desired," says Marisa, an American friend of mine once married to a Sicilian, as we feast on a *couscous pesce*, the local fish dish, on the port in Castellammare. "But Sicilian men have no control over the maternal pull and my only competition during a marriage otherwise blessed by the gods was mommy dearest. When I asked him to choose between me and his mother he decided, in a decision that he now regrets, to take his mother."

And what will happen if my list gets in the hands of some Sicilian macho men? Will I be dead?

"Just tell them that the list applies to other Sicilian macho men but not to them," Pamela advised. "They're all so arrogant that they'll believe you!"

When I take the train from Castellammare back to Terrasini to resume the MedTrek, I am concentrating, as always, on the lay of the land I'll be walking. Then I get involved in a discussion between the conductor and an English couple heading to Palermo who haven't been in Sicily long enough to know that you can't buy a ticket on the train.

I become the intermediary between the frustrated conductor and the calm but confused English tourists. Despite the conductor's consternation and threats of a €50 fine, I help work out a typical Sicilian conclusion. The couple will get off at the stop near the airport, where there are frequent trains into Palermo, and buy two tickets for the next train. Everyone is happy.

After walking through Terrasini station I enter the Riserva Natural Capo Roma. Like many natural parks in Italy, this is a WWF project and stretches along a beautiful expanse of coast with rocky red cliffs that prevent access to the sea. My walk between the striking mountains and the soothing sea takes me on forest paths, paved narrow streets and residential dirt roads. I make a couple forays to the actual seaside through a labyrinth of fenced residential areas, but every blind alley winds up at a cliffside dead end. Fortunately, one Italian couple I speak to tells me they'll look the other way when I jump over their neighbor's fence to avoid BackTrekking.

At another dead end a striking black South African woman, who tells me that she and her Sicilian husband buy and sell property in Milan, gives me directions back to the omnipresent SS 113 where there's a billboard featuring an ad for *GRECOMOBILI*, or Greek furniture. It's good to see the Greeks, now Europe's poor man out, getting credit for some high-end furniture, I think as I continue past hotels with unoriginal names like *Perla de Mare*, *Citta del Mare* and Hotel Riviera into Trapetto.

I finally descend to a series of sandy beaches, with names like Lido Surfers Paradise and Lido Eden, and when I arrive in Balestrate the sun is setting over *Capo San Vito* beyond *Castellammare del Golfo*. Van Morrison's song There'll Be Days Like This (when everything goes right) plays through my head as I slowly sip a bottle of bubbly water and silently feast on a *spaghetti alla marinara* (shrimps, clams and mussels) at a little hole-in-the-wall seaside restaurant.

Van Morrison doesn't appear the next day. I'm innocently misled about a bus departure time when Alessandra, one of the *tre ragazze Siciliane* working at Pamela's hotel, misreads the schedule ("*O mio Dio!*" she apologizes sweetly). However, what's an hour during one outing on a 20-year project? There'll be days like that, too.

I resume MedTrekking in Balestrate and figure the town is named after my stepfather, Paul Stratte. I assume that *Bale* means "Paul" in this part of Sicily and that my dad adopted the name Paul B. Stratte when he left the old country for the US. He wanted to be Norwegian instead of Italian, I conclude when I pass the Lido Peter Pan (now, really!) and the *Camping Nausikaa* to walk into *Castellammare del Golfo*, once the port for the ancient cities of Segesta and Erice.

I leave Castellammare on the *via Quintino Sella* and the *via Porta Fraginesi* and hike to the Belvedere above town, where I'm rewarded not only with a splendid view of the gulf but also a truck selling ice cream. Then I head past sun bathers and medieval towers in Guidaloca, the old tuna fishery in *La Tonnara* and a B&B called Grace's Place right next to *Villa Paradiso* in Scopello and pay a €3 fee to enter the Zingaro Nature Reserve (Zingaro, from the Greek "*Athinganoi*," means "gypsy").

It's worth paying the fee to have well-tended and well-marked paths with a detailed hiking map that points out various trails, cliffs, beaches, picnic areas and museums that merit a visit because they highlight purely local tools, artifacts and remnants. A number of swimming holes, like *Cala Capreria*, also make the entry fee a bargain.

That's not all European walkers get for their €3 in Sicily's first nature reserve. The charge enables me to hike seven kilometers along cliffside paths that provide dazzling views of the Gulf of Castellammare, the stunning mountain peaks, some 16th-century watchtowers, old tuna factories, scores of animals (tortoises love this place) and 700 (no, I didn't count) types of vegetation.

Many settlements here date from the Neolithic and Mesolithic epochs and I find at least two hillside caves and grottoes where the Cyclopes may have lived. Investigating the *Grotta dell'Uzzo* and the *Grotte di Mastro Peppe Siino*, I mentally agree with a ranger who calls this the "pearl of Sicily." And I'm sure that every sheep I see is a distant offspring of the ones Odysseus used to sneak his men out of this cave once he blinded Polyphêmos.

Odysseus may have arrived here after he encountered the Lotus Eaters, who many suspect were located on the island of Djerba off Tunisia. In Book Nine of *The Odyssey,* Homer has Odysseus describe the Cyclopes as "giants, louts, without a law to bless them" who "neither plow, nor sow by hand, nor till the ground." Adding that they "have no muster and no meeting, no consultation or old tribal ways, but each one dwells in his own mountain cave dealing out rough justice to wife and child, indifferent to what others do," he's got nothing good to say about them.

One reason the caves here fit the bill is because of the surrounding countryside and their size. It's easy to imagine "a ponderous doorway slab of solid rock" that "two dozen four-wheeled wagons, with heaving wagon teams, could not have stirred" being used to close the cave. Also the nearby terrain is an ideal place for the Cyclops "to pasture his fat sheep."

Strabo contends in his *Geographica* that Homer "borrowed his idea of the one-eyed Cyclopes from the history of Scythia, which was in what's now the Caucasus north of the Black Sea, where the Arimaspians were a one-eyed people with a single eye in the middle of their forehead." But wherever they're from and wherever the incident took place, the story about the circle-eyed giant is one of the key dramatic elements of *The Odyssey.*

As I approach the cave and look at the sea, I pull out my tattered copy of the book, close my eyes and visualize the entire incident occurring right here. But this isn't the first or last possible cave candidate and you'll get more information about the Cyclops as we continue our MedTrek around the island.

The 12-kilometer hike beyond the Zingaro Park to the seaside resort of San Vito is an uphill haul on a little-traveled and very windy road. A sensible person would have called it a day and lounged around the pool at the Calampiso Club, not far from the reserve's northern entrance, but I climb to the top of the mountain and get a bird's eye view of the San Vito while appreciating the startling and stark beauty of the undulating Sicilian mountains. Imagining Odysseus sailing along the coast below, I spend hours scrambling down the mountain, finally arriving in the little town of Macari where I hustle water from some construction workers. I've now walked from coast to coast across northern Sicily and clock the seaside stroll at 448 kilometers.

This is the land of B&Bs and I spot one called Karma in

Castelluzzo on a road that Pamela at the Hotel Cerri correctly warns me is "*molto brutto*." Avoid it. However, if you do wind up in Castelluzzo, go to the Loria grocery store and have Loria make you a great salami and cheese "American sandwich on Sicilian bread."

I aim next for the Egadi Island of Favignana because this is where, according to author Scott Huler, "Odysseus and his men feasted on goats before the Cyclops feasted on them."

In his informative book *No-Man's Lands*, Huler describes his visit to the purported Cyclops's cave at the end of *Via del Cyclope* just north of Trapani in Crocefissello. He says the cave "serves still as an animal pen" with "plenty of space for Odysseus and his dozen men to hide" and concludes that he "had found the very cave long identified with the Cyclops Polyphêmos." Homer translator and British essayist Samuel Butler came to the same conclusion.

But when I visit the cave, I have to agree with Huler's conclusion that "I can scarcely describe my disappointment." After he spent two hours there, Huler asked himself "What the hell was I doing, sweating in a cave full of goat shit north of Trapani, Sicily?"

Personally I wouldn't put much money on this being the cave that housed Polyphêmos because it totally lacks the "feel" of a true Homeric location. That said, I have to admit that a fertile imagination is frequently required to pinpoint any single cave or other Homeric venue with even subjective certitude. I'm surprised that, just before he left the cave, Huler insisted he felt the presence of Odysseus.

"The hair stood up on the back of my neck," he wrote when he heard some goats and sheep passing outside. "It felt magical to be wakened from my reverie in the cave by sheep among the crags...I had left home to see what Odysseus saw and feel what he felt and, if even for a tiny moment, I did."

No matter where the real cave is, or what it looks like, this hair-on-the-back-of-the-neck feeling is what my MedTrek and Huler's pursuit are all about. And as the old journalistic adage goes, "Never let the truth stand in the way of a good hair-on-the-back-of-the-neck story."

The Michelin guide contends that the bay of Cala Rotonda on Favignana is where "Odysseus was washed up after doing battle with Cyclops." Homer wrote that Odysseus and his crew approached the fertile island "where grain would grow chin high by harvest time," docked in a bay on a foggy night, slept on the beach and feasted on wild goats for breakfast. Then he took twelve of his best fighters and a goatskin full of sweet liquor and sailed towards the Cyclops' cave.

Odysseus says that it was on Favignana that "Heaven gave us game a-plenty...we made our feast on meat galore and wine," sailed to Sicily and climbed up to the Cyclops' cave to discover "a drying rack that sagged with cheeses, pens crowded with lambs and kids....and vessels full of whey."

Before ferrying to the island of Favignana I explore the elevated village of Erice, where the first restaurant I see on the 751-meter high plateau is called *Ulisse*. It's said that on a clear day it's possible to see Tunisia, which is more than 100 miles away, but my eyes don't make the connection. I look down, backward and forward onto what's been MedTrekked and what will be.

Erice, which has more than 60 churches and monasteries, is so famous that it's even got a UNESCO clubhouse, as well as a B&B called Ashram but way too many TV and communication towers to qualify as a UNESCO Heritage Site. Lots of historical figures – including Eryx the king of the Elymi, Hêraklês, and Aeneas, who buried his father here, to name a few – are associated with Erice. Hêraklês stopped off here on his way back to Greece and killed the Elymian king near a temple where, according to the Michelin Green Guidebook, "the Phoenicians worshipped Astarte, the Greeks venerated Aphrodité, and the Romans celebrated Venus."

I drop in to venerate and celebrate them all. Then I explore the Chiesa Matrice, the cobblestone lanes, and the truly spectacular 12th-century *Castello di Venere*, or Venus' Castle, that has long been a landmark for sailors off the coast and MedTrekkers on it.

For additional inspiration I visit Segesta, which Thucydides presumed to have been founded by the Elymi after the Trojan War. Because of its mountain-surrounded location, Segesta features some of the best-preserved monuments of its era anywhere on earth and is one of my favorite archeological sites. Each time I visit I'm absolutely floored by the well-preserved state of the 36-columned Doric temple, as well as the theater, agora, church and other ruins. Both up close and from afar, this is one of the most delicious nuggets of antiquity.

There's a cable car from Erice to Trapani, a medieval-looking town that has a unique and pleasant Arab/Spanish Mediterranean feel, but I walk down the mountain to catch the half-hour hydrofoil ride to Favignana. The largest of the Egadi Islands, known as Aegates, or Islands of the Goats, to Greeks in Homer's day, Favignana is named after a local wind called the *favonio*. The island is shaped like a butterfly (hence its nickname *La Farfalla*) and the treaty ending the First Punic War in 241 BC was signed here.

Upon arrival, I immediately climb to the castle atop the 300-meter high Monte San Caterina, once a Saracen lookout, to situate myself. Although it's a comfortable walk up to San Caterina, I come down quite roughly on the pathless backside of the mountain and am not only cut to shreds by shrubs but also fall off a centuries-old rock wall and gash my shin.

Fortunately I have my first aid kit. Once bandaged and patched up with "New Skin," the antiseptic liquid bandage I use for scrapes and cuts that is made by a company called Medtech (Medtech, MedTrek, get it?), I scramble down the hill to the rhythmically named *Grotta degli Innamorati*, or Lovers' Grotto. Limping onto the beach at *Pozzo dell'Aqua*, I speak to an 80-something father who is watching his son snorkel for octopi, and then wend my way along a flat, unpaved road to the lighthouse at Punta Sottile from where I can see Marettimo, another Egadi island.

A MedTrek Milestone and a Date With a Dancing Satyr

My epiphany of the day comes when, after sniffing my way past a tourist-oriented *Villaggio Approdo di Ulisse* and continuing on sharp, stark rock, I arrive at the natural port of Cala Rotonda. It was here that Odysseus and his crew moored and feasted on a herd of goats before their showdown with Polyphêmos. One local tells me that Homer's hero hosted a mid-afternoon snack session that gave us the expression "goatea."

After I bask in the sun, knowing that I have just achieved a significant historical milestone on the MedTrek, I swim amongst the jellyfish in the port and enjoy a vegetarian pizza and *poplette di tonno* before returning to Trapani.

The moment I MedTrek into *Mazara del Vallo*, which looks delightfully North African with women wearing headscarves, I sense that the weather is changing and this is going to be a very hot day. Three windmills on the hillside are spinning like whirling dervishes on speed, and I can feel the *sirocco* wind preparing to blow lots of hot air, and probably lots of red sand, in from North Africa.

My urban objective here is the two-room *Museo del Satiro* in the former Sant'Egidio Church. I want to get up close and personal with the alabaster eyes of the dashing *Dancing Satyr*, an alluring 2,350-year-old seven-foot high bronze statue that is the highlight of the museum. The *Dancing Satyr*, which gets its name from its flowing locks and flapping goat ears (it's missing arms and a leg), was found by local fishermen at a depth of 480 meters in the Sicilian Canal southwest of here in March 1998. Some experts believe it could be the work of Praxiteles, one of the hottest Attic sculptors in the fourth century BC.

Little did I know that the *Dancing Satyr*, which steals the show from a display that includes a few other amphorae and artifacts, has more physical security than the Mona Lisa. There are six, yes six, very humorless guards patrolling the tiny museum and throughout my half-hour visit – and I am the only paying visitor – one security officer sticks to me like a mollusk on a cold-hearted bronze statue at the bottom of the Sicilian Canal.

There are twelve signs indicating that photographs aren't permitted and very visible security cameras in every corner, cranny and nook. I politely ask for permission to take a photo of the statue's alabaster eyes for you, but am told to contact the *Sopraintentenza di Trapani*. I'd hoped my request would simply encourage the guards to let me take a quick snap before MedTrekking out of town. No such luck. After an animated chat with the somber security officials about my ongoing walking adventure, and a few more pleasant guard-accompanied minutes in the captivating presence of the seductive *Dancing Satyr*, I leave the museum and take a photo of static dancers adorning the doorway across the street.

I head south on the wide *Lungomare Mezinni*, a promenader's delight, on a sunny, incessantly *sirocco*-windy day and cross streets – like *via Salerno* and *via Reggio Calabria* – named after Italian towns on the mainland. It's an easy beach walk to Granitola where I devour a large plate of pasta on an outdoor sea-viewing terrace and the café owner insists I can easily make it to Selinunte in a of couple hours.

The next towns, like the *Dune di Pozzitello*, *Tre Fonte* and *Triscina* are pleasantly dead. Everything – and most of everything is low-income holiday homes – is shut tight and the beaches, with the exception of a few surfers and two couples making out, are deserted.

I continue down the seaside for 33 kilometers until I arrive at the back door (no ticket office here!) of the expansive ruins at Selinunte, which was founded in the seventh century BC by folks from Megara Hyblaea on the east coast. Entering the sprawling architectural park, I begin singing *She Came in Through the Bathroom Window*, substituting "backdoor" for "bathroom."

I dismiss a temple dedicated to Hêra because it was reconstructed in 1957 but spend an hour wandering aimlessly amidst the stoned ruins. These are in various states of decay due to destructive attacks by Hannibal, as well as a few earthquakes, but I am in such a good mood at the end of the day that I do a little dancing satyr jig on the sand. No photo of that either.

I indulge in one of the laziest and longest seafood lunches of the MedTrek on the terrace of the *Sabbia d'Oro* restaurant near the stunningly white *Scala dei Turchi* cliffs, where the *scale*, or steps, make it easy to reach the water. At *Capo Bianco*, with its white-sanded beach and Eraclea Minoa ruins, I visit the house where playwright Luigi Pirandello was born in the town of *Il Caos* (and presumably born into chaos) and admire the fifth-century BC Greek *krater* that once held the Nobel Prize winner's ashes.

Not far from *Il Caos*, I find myself in the middle of a heated debate and chaotic culture clash at the Valley of the Temples (as every visitor learns within sixty seconds, the valley is actually a ridge) in the gigantic Agrigento archeological site.

An exhibit called *Contemporary Art for the Temple of Zeus* prominently displays paintings and sculptures by more than forty international artists amid temples, gardens, a villa, a necropolis and other ruins dating from 580 BC. The goal of the exhibit is to use the proceeds to further restore the Temple of Zeus. And perhaps cause a heated hullabaloo as visitors sample modern sculptures on display at the Temple of Concordia, the Temple of Hêraklês, the Villa Aurea garden and other sites. Museum employees at the site, that was at its prime during the era of Theron from 488-472 BC, tell me that half the visitors like the temporary new look and half don't. I'll let the pictures tell the story and you can decide how you feel.

I begin to enjoy the artistic juxtaposition, however sacrilegious, on a second visit just before continuing south from the Hotel Costazzurra in Agrigento's seaside suburb of San Leone. I leave on *via Nettuno* towards the "Free Beaches" and run into some street cleaners wearing the same Day-Glo orange vest as me. I tell them I like the sign near their clean-up job reading "*Agrigento e Tu...pulite e piu bella*" ("Agrigento and you: cleaner and prettier").

As the beach changes from sand to pebbles, I'm so enchanted by some pleasing stone-churning verses made by the waves that I'm encouraged to cross the river at San Leone barefoot with my pack held high above my head. A few kilometers later I'm walking under cliffs with perhaps the slipperiest, slidiest and slimiest grey (or any other color) clay on earth – or anywhere else. And when it's dry, it looks like rock but crumbles. A tricky surface for any walker.

Before I reach the Punta Bianca, where the seaside cliffs are a vibrant white, I discover a trunk-sized object covered with makeshift packing. A real treasure? The pot at the end of my rainbow? Not quite. After finally removing all the twine and tape and wrapping, I find a Styrofoam box filled with empty but capped plastic bottles. This was a raft presumably used by someone from North Africa trying to enter Sicily and the European Union. If only plastic could talk!

I continue along somewhat savage and thoroughly uninhabited beaches and hillsides, where I see two foxes, until I arrive at the *Castello di Montechiaro* in *Marina di Palma*. The owner of the closed Hotel Gattopardo opens his empty hotel/bar and sells me a few bottles of much-needed mineral water. Then I have coffee on the beach with a

Dutch couple, whose three kids are playing in the water, and I'm told that their nine-year-old son is a Greek myths fanatic and reads them constantly.

"Hey, that's how I started on this adventure at the age of nine," I tell them.

We also discuss Sicilian driving which has a unique flare.

"They have their system and somehow don't kill each other," says the father. "But I've only seen one driving school since I've been here."

I'm not overly thrilled with all of the seaside industry in Gela but am particularly impressed with the new port and seaside promenade in *Marina di Regusa* and the beaches in Donnalucata and Sempieti – as well as a number of marshy nature reserves near the sea. The most memorable event of the day, though, is my very short and very severe €10 haircut in Pozzallo, which I have time for just before buying a €100 round-trip ferry ticket to Malta.

I want to spend some time with Kalypso, whose name means "conceal" or "hide" in Greek, on the island of Gozo and accomplish Circe's fifth task.

Making Out with Kalypso on Malta

"A friend's persuasion is an excellent thing." – *The Iliad*

I take a brief break from my Sicilian Cyclops search to seek another legendary cave and, this time, a potentially seductive cavewoman.

It's a 100-kilometer ferry ride from Pozzallo to Valletta, the capital of the densely populated island of Malta and its two smaller sister islands of Gozo and Comino. This three-strong strategically situated archipelago was ruled by the Phoenicians, Greeks, Romans, Arabs, Normans, Aragonese, Habsburg Spain, Knights of Saint John, the French and the British before gaining its independence in 1964. During the crossing, I catch bits of *The Maltese Falcon,* starring Humphrey Bogart and Mary Astor, that's showing on the ship's video screens.

The next morning, after an evening's exploration of the enchanting walled hilltop city of Valletta, with its baroque buildings and neoclassical architecture, I leave the seaside suburb of Sliema to catch another ferry to Gozo. I am following Circe's instruction to spend a week with the fabled sea goddess Kalypso on the island that was known as Ogygia in Homer's day.

"Let a marching band lead you to the real of cave of Kalypso," Circe instructed, "and, unlike Odysseus who spent seven years with the nymph on the island of Ogygia, see if a contemporary mortal like you can handle seven days with her."

Another rough assignment.

Malta is, compared to Sicily, a tiny island in the Mediterranean Sea. And everyone on Malta considers nearby Gozo, which is one-ninth the size of Malta, with an area only slightly more than 60 square kilometers, a really minute Mediterranean island, though Comino is even smaller with only four inhabitants. So it can't be too difficult to find Kalypso who, in a dramatic and emotional episode in the fifth book of *The Odyssey* that translator Robert Fitzgerald entitled *Sweet Nymph and Open Sea*, kept Odysseus in her clutches and her cave for seven years where "he cannot stir, cannot fare homeward, for no ship is left him."

A week isn't very long in the presence of a sexually enticing goddess, and I certainly don't want to waste too much time finding her. Immediately after disembarking in the main harbor of Mgarr, I begin asking almost everyone I meet, from the ferry captain to the teenage receptionist at the tourist office, a basic question: "Has anyone here seen, or slept with, a beautiful and immortal nymph named Kalypso, who kept the wily Greek warrior Odysseus in her sea-hollowed cave for seven years?"

This type of direct why-beat-around-the-cave inquiry, incidentally, was partially influenced by my exposure to foreign correspondent Edward Behr. The diminutive and bespectacled Behr was covering a siege at Stanleyville in the eastern Congo in 1964 and the distinctive way in which he questioned survivors made a telling and amusing title to his later memoir: *Anyone Here Been Raped and Speak English?* His book is an amusing depiction of how journalists occasionally create some of their scoops.

If this direct method doesn't actually enable me to find "Atlas' guileful daughter," a "softly-braided nymph," I'm sure the overtly inquisitive approach will enable me to run into someone who claims to have slept with her or, at the very least, some women named after her.

I meet a contemporary Kalypso just after stepping off the Gozo Channel Line ferry. Rita Meilak, the goddess-like concierge at the Grand Hotel overlooking the port, immediately upgrades my online-booked room to a suite with a terrace and panoramic sea view when she discovers that I'm on Gozo on a serious mission. No wonder Odysseus, who was offered immortality as well as free room and board and panoramic sea view, stayed here seven years! The natives are friendly.

But Rita, who was born in Gozo, worked in New York in the 1980s and has two sons, firmly denies that she's Kalypso, or even a Kalypsophile.

"The real Kalypso was beautiful and thin, always wore a flowing white gown, had seductively long hair and had a permanent halo around her head," the short-haired Rita, wearing a sober black dress, tells me as I prepare to launch my 61-kilometer walkabout around the island. "Nobody here makes a big deal about her today. The government doesn't use her in publicity campaigns and I'll bet most people never think about her."

Rita claims, to my astonishment, that today no one in Gozo is named Kalypso. There's a Kalypso Hotel, Kalypso Antiques, a Kalypso Street, a Kalypso Diving School and a few houses named Kalypso. There is even an animated movie for kids called *The Enchanted Kingdom of Kalypso* being screened at a weekend festival when I'm here. But not one person that Rita knows bears her name.

"I haven't even heard of a pet being called Kalypso," says Rita who, like most Gozitans I meet, speaks enchanting Maltese, her country's Arabic-rich language that includes numerous English and Italian words.

I've enjoyed pronouncing and spelling the name Kalypso since I first became aware of her at the age of nine and am certainly not alone. A friend in France, TV and radio commentator Richard Barnes, likes the name so much that he named his daughter Kalypso, although he spelled it Calypso.

"The story of Kalypso and Odysseus was the first real love story ever written," says New Zealander Barnes. "Kalypso as a name evokes romantic, enigmatic and interesting thoughts. It has such a beautiful ring to it."

I thought it was a universally popular name. After all, Jacques-Yves Cousteau named his research ship after Kalypso, John Denver wrote a song called *Kalypso* and there's a goddess in *Pirates of the Caribbean* called Kalypso. But apparently not on Gozo, where I had imagined that there'd be dozens of women named Kalypso and that I could at least buy one of them a cup of nectar during my tranquil Sunday morning MedTrek.

To ensure that I'm not being misled, and that Zeus and Rita are not conspiring to keep Kalypso away from me, I walk for an hour to visit the Mnarja Band Club, a social group named after an important Maltese festival, in the little village of In-Nadur. None of the 26 men at the club bar and tables, where coffee goes for forty cents and members seem to hold more cards than instruments, admit to ever having met or kissed a woman named Kalypso. After I note the absence of women, I'm told the wives are at home cooking lunch but sometimes come out at night.

There is consensus among club members that the nearby official site of Kalypso Cave above the sandy Ramla Bay is a hoax and not the actual residence of Homer's seductress.

"Don't waste your time looking for Kalypso, or even someone named after her, in that hillside hole in the ground that the tourist people tell you is her cave," scoffs the oldest member of the Mnarja Band Club. "She certainly didn't spend any time there."

I apparently look so despondent that another band member comes to my rescue.

"You should go sit in the real cave for a while and your imagination will enable you to envision Kalypso and Odysseus living together on our mythical and magical island," enthuses the youngest member of the Mnarja Band Club as he sketches, on a slightly used napkin, directions to a cave above another part of Ramla Bay. "Don't worry, you'll find her."

I leave the card-playing band and walk a few kilometers down to sandy Ramla Bay. Then, using the napkin as my map to an unburied treasure, I turn right along the sea and climb a hill on a path that takes me through some slanting vegetable gardens and shrubbery. Once I enter a large hole-in-the-wall, I spend two hours in Kalypso's "real" cave soaking up the ideal location, "feeling" the presence of the earlier tenants and enjoying a mesmerizing view of the turquoise-colored sea. While consuming the atmosphere in the half-dark cave, I admire the lack of décor, try out the nifty backdoor entrance and attempt to make some psychic contact.

It is certainly not difficult to imagine that "divine Kalypso, the mistress of the isle," would have been at home in this spacious cavern almost large enough to house the Cyclops and his sheep. I can see her as "upon her hearthstone a great fire blazing scented the farthest shores with cedar smoke and smoke of thyme, and singing high and lovely in her sweet voice, before her loom a-weaving, she passed her gold shuttle to and fro.... Even a god who found this place would gaze, and feel his heart beat with delight."

As my godless heart beats with delight, I walk to the edge of the cave where, in Odysseus' day, "a deep wood grew outside, with summer leaves of alder and black poplar, pungent cypress....and four springs, bubbling up near one another shallow and clear."

I spend a few days here and on the second night, when I conclude my evening meditation, Kalypso makes her first appearance and asks "Why are you calmly and contentedly sitting in a trance with your legs crossed when the last man I had staying here was constantly fretting, homesick and plotting how to get away from me?"

She was referring, of course, to Odysseus who became a bit skittish after his first two years with her.

I'm amazed that even now, millennia later, Kalypso still wonders why Odysseus preferred his mortal wife to her. But I'm sympathetic as she peppers me with questions.

"Can I be less desirable than Penelope? Less interesting? Less beautiful? Can any mortal woman compare with a goddess in grace and form?" Kalypso asks me, using the exact words from Homer's *Odyssey*. "Wouldn't you rather sleep with me than some mere mortal?"

Kalypso undeniably needs reassurance and companionship rather than another guy hitting on her. During the next few days I give her a short course on sitting meditation that channels, combines and plagiarizes some of the wisdom of Deng Ming-Dao, Lao Tsu and myself. If she's at all adept, I know she'll certainly benefit from some exposure to a calming practice.

"Our spiritual problems don't substantially differ from those of our ancestors and we each are the battleground for good and evil," I tell her. "The depth and solitude of meditation can help us learn everything without thinking about anything."

Then, continuing my channeling, I explain the process.

"When I sit down to meditate, a smile comes to my lips and a feeling of joy permeates my body," I continue, looking at the sea beyond the shadow of her sensuous body in the entrance of the cave. "I try not to cling to forms like sound, smell, taste, image, touch and sleep, and basically do nothing. I don't do this out of habit or ritual, but because it's the best way I know to adore my gods and express the wonder of being on this earth. And in my daily action I try to do no harm and do nothing that will haunt me later."

"And what, exactly, is the point of all this?" Kalypso asks before we get started.

"I've had people tell me that it provides improved digestion, better bowel movements, increased sexual vigor along with enhanced control, greater vitality, improved circulation, increased appetite, stabilized emotions, calmer mind, understanding of deep spiritual truths, and total absorption in a blissful state of being," I say, quoting Deng Ming-Dao. "It will enable you, whether trapped in the wilderness or dealing with a social gathering requiring etiquette and grace, to be able to cope with aplomb and ease. Give it four more days and it'll help you let go of Odysseus."

"Sign me up," she says, as we began to practice sitting meditation.

The waters and deep woods no longer surround the real cave, though there are still "beds of violets and tender parsley," and one morning, while gazing down at the barren seaside and the easily accessible hole-in-the-ground that for years has duped tourists as the

"Calypso Cave," I decide to revisit it.

I stroll over, stay in it for an hour, and enjoy the pleasant-enough view of the surrounding seaside from the faux cave. But I quickly agree with the boys at the Mnarja Band Club that a sea goddess wouldn't have chosen it as her lair for any significant period of time. Visitors shimmy through a very narrow entrance and have a very restricting window-sized view of the sea from inside the main room, which is very, very dark. The only good thing that can be said about it is that the promoters aren't charging an entrance fee.

With my imagination on high beam, I leave the faux cave and continue my walking adventure on Kalypso Street and head towards the village of Xaghra, home to the spectacular Ġgantija megaliths. I almost immediately begin to sense the presence of Kalypso and Odysseus everywhere on the island.

Gozo, which has less than 30,000 inhabitants, might be small, but for a MedTrekker it's still soundly mythical, seductively magical and startlingly monumental. Especially when I'm armed with a box of Maltesers chocolates and a bottle of San Pellegrino, the pilgrim's water that guarantees hiking endurance.

I enjoy a rocky, windy, wavy, cliffy, sunny, gods-kissed walkabout, and there's enough of a path along most of the stark rocky shore and the dramatic cliffs (Kalypso told me that when Odysseus was here, he gave the cliffs a rating of 12 on a scale of 10) to make the place intriguing.

Not that an English gentleman, who's a proud member of the Wirt Ghawdex Association on volunteer duty at the Mgarr ix-Xini 17th-century coastal tower, completely agrees with my positive assessment. When I mention the local government's "Eco-Gozo – A Better Gozo" program that Giovanna Debono, the Maltese Government's Minister for Gozo, claims will make this "an eco-island by 2020....to protect the Gozitan lifestyle, the island's environment, resources, culture and identity," the volunteer greeter gets livid.

"I call her the Minister of Dreams," says the seventyish gentleman, who very politely points out different paths all over the island and says his goal is to see a blazed and marked coastal path around the entire perimeter. "Everyone here is basically apathetic and no one appreciates what they've got."

He then explains that his association, founded in 1981, exists to foster the knowledge and safeguarding of the natural, archaeological, historical and anthropological patrimony of the islands of Gozo and Comino.

"I don't see anything about Kalypso or her cave in the document, and that's all I really care about," I tell him. "But you'd be amazed how much cleaner this place is than nearby Sicily. I actually saw someone stop his car, get out and put a cigarette in a trash bin on a country road earlier this morning. I think that kind of thing might be against the law in Italy."

Once I start seriously walking, I encounter visions of Kalypso and Odysseus almost everywhere. I imagine them having a swell time together as I stroll along the stony seaside and on the cliffside paths, through terraced fields and into little villages with names like Xlendi, Nadur and Sannat, where I find a makeshift band singing *No Woman, No Cry* at the top of their voices in a pub. I tell them that I've been leading Kalypso in a meditative chant of *No Man, No Cry*.

Odysseus actually whispers to me at one extraordinarily windy point of my MedTrek that he is still very impressed with the cliffs, hills, natural harbors, wind, waves and other natural elements in Ogygia. The island, he tells me, reminds him of the northern half of his kingdom in Ithaka and that resemblance is one reason he yearned to get home to his wife and son Telémakhos when he was here, though he acknowledges that Kalypso was "immortal and most beautiful."

Whether he was Kalypso's prisoner and/or a slightly reluctant lover during a stay that began when he washed up on the shore after losing his ship and crew has, until now, caused much speculation among Homeric scholars.

The facts as told to me by Circe were these: Kalypso admittedly fell hard for Odysseus and "clung to him in her sea-hollowed caves – a nymph, immortal and most beautiful, who craved him for her own." She offered to make him her immortal husband and bless him with eternal youth. They were beyond doubt lovers during his seven-year stay, Homer says, although Odysseus "fought shy of her and her desire, he lay with her each night, for she compelled him." According to the Greek poet Hesiod they had two kids, Nausithous and Nausinous. Or, if you choose to believe the scholar Apollodorus, just one son named Latinus.

At the same time, a frequently homesick Odysseus often "sat apart, as a thousand times before, and racked his own heart groaning, with eyes wet scanning the bare horizon of the sea."

He claims that being with Kalypso wasn't all that much fun.

"Do you know what it's like to be with someone who's absolutely besotted and obsessed with you, despite the fact that you're already married and want to get back to your wife, home, and son?" he asks me when we speak on "that island in thralldom to the nymph." "Each day I longed for home, longed for the sight of home."

"I know what it's like to have your cake, eat it too, and think you can get away with it," I agree, looking at Odysseus who listens to my words as though he has no clue what a cake has to do with anything. "But I'm not quite sure if I would be discontent with what you had here. In fact, I think you willingly stayed longer than required just to test the waters."

Whatever their day-to-day relationship, Kalypso wasn't pleased when Zeus sent Hermês, the messenger of the gods, to "make it known that we, whose will is not subject to error, order Odysseus home." That irritated her so much that she uttered, or at least muttered, the famous lines "Oh you vile gods, in jealousy supernal! You hate it when we choose to lie with men—immortal flesh by some dear mortal side."

Not that all goddesses like sleeping with us normal guys.

"I endured a mortal warrior's bed many a time, without desire," complained Achilles' mother Thetis, the loveliest of goddesses.

And we also find fault with them.

"My word, how mortals take the gods to task!" Zeus complained in *The Odyssey*. "All their afflictions come from us, we hear. And what of their own failings? Greed and folly double the suffering in the lot of man."

So what's the point of being a mortal?

"We mortals realize that we have only a very short time to make an achievement, to prove that our existence was worthwhile, and so we strive harder," according to Deng Ming-Dao. "An immortal can never conceive of such effort. Maturity only comes from the threat of mortality. Success only comes from the threat of failure."

But Kalypso wanted a man and, unlike Hermês, did not mind that she might "compromise an immortal's dignity – to be received with guests of mortal station."

After all, she told me, "It was I who saved him – saw him straddle his own keel board, the one man left afloat when Zeus rent wide his ship with chain lightning and overturned him in the wine-dark sea. Then all his troops were lost, his good companies, but wind and current washed him here to me. I fed him, loved him, sang that he should not die nor grow old, ever, in all the days to come."

Fortunately she bowed to Zeus's mandate and helped Odysseus build a boat, gave him food and wine and supplies for the trip back to Ithaka, and supplied "a following wind to help you homeward without harm – provided the gods who rule wide heaven wish it so." She made it clear before he left that "if you could see it all, before you go – all the adversity you face at sea – you would stay here, and guard this house, and be immortal."

He chose not to. Instead the gods let him depart with "no company, gods or men, only a raft that he must lash together."

What would you have done?

I like to think that, despite Odysseus's frequent homesick tears and constant moaning about being trapped on Gozo, he and Kalypso had some good times together until the gods broke them apart in a separation that led to the expressions "seven-year ditch," "seven-year witch" and "seven-year bitch."

He certainly had a number of things to keep him busy as he wandered the island. Maybe, like islanders today, he gathered wild-growing fennel, peas, figs, capers and salt as he walked through Ogygia. He must have wandered to every extreme of the island, from what's now the harbor at Mgarr to the site of the looming lighthouse near Saint Dimitri, and visited the prehistoric Ġgantija temples.

Rita says the Neolithic Ġgantija temples, which are dedicated to the Great Earth Mother and a pilgrimage site in ancient Malta, are much more of a draw for tourists than Kalypso could ever be. That's understandable because one of these two round prehistoric temples containing statues of goddesses is considered the oldest stone structure in the world, centuries older than Stonehenge and the Pyramids. And I have to admit that they are more impressive than the fake Kalypso cave.

Incidentally, between you and me, Odysseus probably wouldn't be too impressed with today's downtown Victoria, the biggest city named in honor of that queen's Diamond Jubilee that locals prefer to call Rabat, unless he wants to get a Big Mac and look at a few classical buildings.

Almost everything here, where they drive on the left-hand side of the road, is earth and sandstone colored, from the gradations of the stones themselves to the numerous stone-built churches. Occasionally a white cliff will stand out. The words to describe Gozo's beauty, and beautiful it is, are all seemingly negative adjectives like stark, treeless, barren, windblown.

One thing I learned during my urban walkabout on the island is that, as in other parts of Malta, almost every house has a name as well as a number. It didn't take me long to realize that I preferred traditional, even conservative names, like "Miracle of Love" or "Shelter of the Earth" and "Promised Land" to things like "Woodpecker," "Jawbone," and "Bee Hive."

Beyond Kalypso's real and promoted caves, I continue along the wave-crashing sea to Marsaforn, a spectacular seaside town buffeted by waves of turquoise water and filled with pubs and restaurants, where I stop for a pasta salad lunch and two scoops of ice cream.

A completely meditative walk along the Qbajjar Promenade passes the saltpans and goes to the Gordan Lighthouse, around the San Dimitri Point and along the stunning cliffs to San Lawrenz, a rock formation known as the Azure Window, and the Inland Sea at Dwejra

Point.

It is at the Azure Window at sunset after a long day's hike that I am approached by a beautiful, long-haired and slim woman in a flowing white gown and a narrow white headband. The setting sun, or maybe my fatigue, makes it look like she has a golden crown floating just above her head. And she immediately peppers me with questions that would have made Edward Behr proud.

OMG, I think to myself. It's been over 3,000 years and Kalypso, despite our meditation, continues to be baffled by Odysseus' reaction to her. No wonder Circe asked me to spend seven days here. The goddess still needs some TLC after all this time. I suggest that she walk with me.

"Come along and we'll walk and talk," I say as we turn back towards the Azure Window.

"Was Odysseus really that hot a guy?" I ask. "I mean, after all, he was a mere mortal and, despite your powerful lures and allure, couldn't he find a way to get off the island during those seven years if he really wanted to?"

Homer doesn't even intimate that he attempted a serious escape. Why not? After all, this is the guy who came up with the ploy of the Trojan Horse, tricked the Cyclops and went on to defeat over one hundred suitors making a play for his wife.

And that's what we talk about as we stroll around Dwerja Bay and let the sun slowly set.

"Watch Helios and imagine what a nice job he has piloting the sun," Kalypso says as we walk hand-in-hand. "Look how smooth the sea is and imagine how peaceful Poseidon is when he's not irritated. But me, I'm still tortured. Of course, Odysseus could have left because, face it, I'm not just some damsel in distress. He obviously felt something towards me and then, like many men since then, he got bored."

I may not have found someone who slept with her, discovered a Kalypso cult, or even found someone on Gozo with the same name. But my visit to what some members of the Mnarja Band Club consider Kalypso's real cave and my discussion with Kalypso herself make this SideTrek a worthwhile break from my ongoing circumnavigation of Sicily.

And I hear from the guy selling ice cream at Ramla Beach that when he was a kid his father had a dog called Kalypso.

The memory of Behr's book, the questions I asked about Kalypso, and the questions Kalypso asked me get me thinking about my own journalistic career outside the United States after I covered Woodstock in 1969.

After I earned a masters degree from the Columbia School of

Journalism with a thesis that described the atmosphere at Elaine's restaurant, the closest thing New York had to a literary salon in the early 1970s, I returned to Paris where I'd lived for six months. This time, armed with a diploma, I wasn't just going to sit around cafés, play pinball, drink *pastis*, go to daily horse races, and fall in love. I was going to be a journalist.

Moving to Paris to be a budding journalist is like moving to Hollywood to be a budding actor. I went into the UPI office and offered to blow the stack off the truth behind Jim Morrison's death in the Marais district. I got a job writing guidebooks to Paris and Rome. I joined my friend Harry Stein in the creation of Continental Features Syndicate to sell low-priced stories to a wide number of media outlets. And I was a waiter at Joe Allen until I was fired for hitting a customer, though it was more of a shove.

Besides being mostly out of work, I was by then fed up with the constant gray skies and winter cold in Paris and in January 1973 decided to drive to Cape Town when a woman I met on the sidewalk told me it was summer there. I drove down with my girlfriend Henrietta Dax, a Franco-British-American woman whose parents lived in Maryland. I made an insignificant amount of money writing Continental Features Syndicate stories from Eastern Europe, the Middle East and Africa as we tooled our way in my red Simca through Budapest, Istanbul, Damascus and Amman, to the port of Aqaba, Jordan. There – ah those were the days – we caught a Polish cargo ship that took us to Port Sudan and then dumped us in Ethiopia.

I still have some of the stories I wrote at the time from Ethiopian monasteries and Kenyan meat markets. There was one article from the Danakil Desert and another from the mountain range where we went in search of the elusive walia ibex.

Although I ran into Edward Behr, my career got serious in Nairobi when I met Peter Younghusband, the doyen of African journalists and author of the delightful *Every Meal a Banquet, Every Night a Honeymoon: Unforgettable African Experiences*. He invited me to Cape Town and showed me how to sell the same story to newspapers on different continents and taught me to use my imagination when writing expense accounts.

The sea is so rough when I try to leave Malta that my ferry back to Pozzallo is cancelled. A friend blames this on Kalypso and says that she's trying to get me, in a contemporary version of *The Odyssey*, to stay there. If so, she's connived with other gods, including Poseidon, to turn the sea into a double-double-toil-and-trouble bubbling cauldron.

I don't learn of my predicament until I leave a delightful Italian restaurant on the waterfront, where I'd spent an hour drinking a liter of water, eating a pizza, hanging out on the Wi-Fi and getting a *complimenti* from the place's Sicilian owner on my Italian and cross-island MedTrekking.

When I get to the ferry and learn of the cancellation, I'm told to spend the night in Valletta and come back in the morning. Delays like this don't upset me, and I gamely walk along the harbor and up numerous stairs into the old town of lovely sandstone-colored and sandcastle-looking Valletta, which was built after the Knights of Saint John repelled the Turkish invaders in 1565 and has been a UNESCO World Heritage Site since 1980.

At the British Hotel I get a room that has five beds and looks onto the Grand Harbor. I tell the owner, Dave, to send any other stranded passengers to make use of the available beds at no charge and then spend a few hours walking through the walled citadel on Republic Street, by the palace and down to the Saint Elmo Fort.

At the end of the evening after walking back on Strait Street, I'm having a coffee in the square in front of Saint John's Cathedral when all of a sudden, for the first time in a week, I get a thought that doesn't have anything to do with Odysseus or Kalypso.

It occurs to me that Valletta, with the official name of The Most Humble City of Valletta, should be the seat of Mediterranean heads of state and governments participating in the "Barcelona Process," aka the Euro-Mediterranean Partnership. This organization, which officially began in 1995 and welcomed Malta into its ranks when it joined the European Union in 2004, is supposed to ignite regional cooperation among the countries situated around the Mediterranean. But other problems have kept its 43 members, which include the 27 European countries and sixteen partner countries on the sea's southern rim, from making much headway on its goals of creating an area of peace and security in a free-trade area.

I still think that the goal of developing, modernizing and integrating the southern Mediterranean countries with their northern counterparts should be a priority for Europe. And Malta, stuck between the two and almost in the center of the Mediterranean Sea, is the place to get it going. Bringing them all here on a full-mooned night and letting Kalypso at them might provide just the spark they need to begin seriously discussing economic inequalities and attempt to resolve some immigration problems, improve security, and create a region that could have over 800 million inhabitants by 2050 and be a major competitor with China and the US.

As I walk down to the ferry with two Polish women at 3:45 a.m. it turns out that Dave told them the same thing about their room with five beds – and they, like me, had offered to let other stranded travelers sleep "with them" and split the cost. I try to make them feel better with a little chatter about the Euro-Mediterranean Partnership, but they prefer to hear about my experiences with Kalypso.

I spin the story of my time on Gozo during our ferry ride back to Sicily and mention that once he left, Odysseus, after great adversity at sea "choking, unmarked and lonely," called Kalypso "a lovely goddess and a dangerous one."

"No one, no god or man, consorts with her but supernatural power brought me there to be her solitary guest" and "the enchantress in her beauty fed and caressed me, promised I should be immortal, youthful, all the days to come; but in my heart I never gave consent though seven years detained."

Gosh, she seemed so nice during my week here.

Pursuing the Sun God and Finding Cyclops

"Dawn in her yellow robe rose in the east out of the flowing Ocean, bearing light for deathless gods and mortal men." – *The Iliad*

"The anger of a god is cruel anger." – Aeneas in *The Iliad*

I head to the dramatic and scenic *Fort di Capo Passero* at Sicily's most southeastern tip to launch my northward MedTrek to Messina. The verdant setting is a welcome change after the rocky, barren and moonlike surfaces on Gozo and a queasy return ferry ride that had 80 percent of the passengers vomiting and the other 20 percent, including me, close to it. If nothing else, that trip enabled me to sympathize with Odysseus' bouts of queasiness in *The Odyssey* and made me wonder if Circe's so smart when she instructs me to take to the water.

The first thing I see after leaving the Hotel Vittorio in *Portopalo di Capo Passero*, where I check in and drop off my laundry, is an abandoned castle. Sure, the place will need some work to make it palatial again, but it's got great potential, and I imagine renovating it, moving in and making it the editorial headquarters of my *Follow the Idiot* blog. From the top terrace, I can see fishing boats returning to the local quay and locate, due to the color of the water, the exact spot where the tuna-rich Ionian Sea meets the Sicilian Canal.

The initial nine kilometers of the day's hike, fueled by some still-warm-from-the-oven olive bread, are alongside a clear and calm sea that dramatically contrasts with the conditions on my ferry crossing. Stone paths, paved walks, manmade seawalls, sandy beaches and a bit of rocky road take me to Marzamemi (another village name that trills romantically off my tongue) where I hook up with *Le Vie Dell'Estremo Sud*, The Paths of the Extreme South that pass once-prospering tuna factories, salt works, and a few chic boutiques selling tuna-related products and other local specialties.

Things are even more serene in the pristine and peaceful 574-hectare *Riservea Naturale di Vendicari*, or the Vendicari Nature Reserve, created in 1984 for migratory birds, sand-loving vegetation and slow-walking humans. There are some locals on the clearly indicated pathways and seven sunbathers have trekked a few kilometers to reach the relatively secluded Calomische Beach. A lot of my walk is barefoot, which is fortuitous because my Vasque hiking shoes are on their last legs (an appropriate phrase) after the rigorous volcanic stone walking in Gozo.

Although I could conceivably ford the Tellaro River, I choose to walk inland along its banks to visit the renowned Roman mosaics at the *Villa Romana del Tellaro*. Between you and me, they're not worth the €6 entry fee, though I did sneak three photographs of geometric floor-al designs. After glimpsing the excavations at Eloro, which was founded in the seventh century BC as Helorus, I reach the beach in Avola where, after walking 35 kilometers, my reward is a *panino* and an ice cream that, as it turns out, are my dinner.

The inland city of Noto is a Baroque beauty set amid olive groves and almond trees on a plateau overlooking the Asinaro Valley. With an hour to spare here, I take photos of the cathedral, theater and other monuments, as well as a nun and the colorful sneakers on a mother and her two daughters, on the Corso Vittorio Emanuel.

The old Noto was about ten kilometers from this new Noto, which was constructed in 1693 after an earthquake destroyed the old town. The rebuilding enabled the town planners to create an ornate and airy city center with numerous piazzas, churches, palazzos, gateways, balconies and, more recently, bus stops. Apparently this was considered a safer site, but it's indicative of earthquake preparedness that homes for the nobles were still built on higher ground than those for the clergy, whose residences are above those of ordinary folk.

To return to my hotel on the coast, I take a bus that drops me five kilometers from Portopalo, where a woman and her four-year-old daughter, Vera, immediately pick me up hitching just before dark. Naturally, we discuss how macho Sicilian men don't stop to pick up hitchhikers.

The next day I am heading to Syracuse, Augusta and Florida. No, I'm not back in the USA. But as I continue my walking adventure up Sicily's eastern coast, I MedTrek through the Sicilian towns that might have been responsible for the names of their American counterparts.

My first stop is Syracuse and its mythically named island of Ortygia. Established by Greeks in the eighth century BC, Syracuse became the powerhouse and pride of Greek colonies in Magna Graecia and gained historical prominence when its armies defeated troops from Athens led by the renowned generals Alcibiades and Nicias between 415-413 BC.

My two-day, 54-kilometer MedTrek into Syracuse includes a long lunch in Fontone Bianche, a sun tanning stopover in Arenella and a delicious walk around the sharp-rocked lava of *Capo Murro di Porco*, which I translate as The Pig Wall Cape. I'm amazed that I don't get arrested after breaking/sneaking into two places to get you some exclusive photos.

Along the way, I pass the hospital in Avola and am pleased to see a nearby bus stop. If I get hurt, I'll know where to come and how to get there. At one point the path takes me along a narrow, cliffhanging walk and when I cut slightly inland because of the impassible coast, a farmer nonchalantly unlocks his gate to let me through his fields.

"The path is dangerous and if you follow your own nose you'll go two kilometers and have to BackTrek," he warns me as he sketches a map in the dirt to show me where to go. Where did he learn the word BackTrek, I wonder?

Upon arriving in Cassibile I'm surprised to see, in the shaded parking lot near the beach, a handwritten flyer tacked to a tree apologizing for the amount they charge guests for parking. After lunch on the sparkling white beaches in Fontane Bianche, I continue with some dodgy rock walking to *Capo Ognina*, enter the commune of Syracuse and arrive at the gargantuan Arenella Resort, located ten kilometers out of town.

Strolling into Syracuse I notice that many people seem to be wondering why I constantly have my hand down my pants. Indeed this gesture could easily be misinterpreted and, if I didn't mention it already, I want you to know that my odd-appearing behavior is due to an inguinal hernia incurred in Mondello a few weeks ago when I sprinted for a car while hitchhiking. (A sprint is frequently necessary before the driver looks in the rearview mirror and changes his mind about picking me up which, I have to confess, happens from time to time.) The hernia will require surgery, but until there is time for that, I have to keep pushing it back in with my hand. Fortunately most men, even non-macho men, in Sicily have their hands down their pants so, until now, I haven't felt too conspicuous.

The walk from Arenella around the *Capo Murro di Porco*, where I lunch on two delicious spinach-and-ham-filled calzones purchased in a hole-in-the-wall mini-market, is like a step-by-step ballet on a bombed and pockmarked moon surface because of the lava rock. The surreal approach to Syracuse includes a visit to *La Rosa sul Mare* hotel before I pass the stark and austere *Punta del Pero* lighthouse on the cape, which is part of a much-publicized marine reserve called Plemmirio. The walk puts me into mellow meditation mode and when I arrive at the sweet and alluring bay on the Sicilian Canal, I gleefully take a wake-up dip in the chilly water.

My meditative day ends abruptly a couple kilometers after that, at the tip of what locals call the Isola, though it's not an island. Any further walking along the sea isn't possible due to cliffs and private property, especially the multi-starred and gated Grand Hotel Minareto, completed in 2008, whose rooms look like they might even be worth the €200-plus price.

I manage to sneak into the hotel to tour the cliffside pool, sumptuous residences and luxurious facilities and take some photographs of Ortygia, the island abutting Syracuse that seduced the Greeks when they arrived from Corinth around 2,800 years ago. Walking around the grounds as though I own them (the guests probably presume I'm a gardener with a backpack), I think it's remarkable I don't get arrested more often. After all, I am trespassing.

The second I have that thought, I eat my words. As I try to sneak out of the imposing seaside luxury resort that prevented me from hiking along the sea, I'm nailed by the resident Sherlock Holmes who is suspicious of my tattered and gradually disintegrating hiking shoes, smelly backpack, scruffy shorts and sweaty baseball cap.

"You don't look like a guest," he says with an obvious frown as he surveys me as though he's a fashion critic for *Vogue* or a cop who'd just busted Al Capone.

"I can't tell a lie," I reply, trying to smile. "I'm just passing through."

I talk myself out of a trespassing charge but have to agree to return to stay in one of their more expensive rooms when I transition from MedTrek mode to business traveler mode in a few weeks. Not a bad punishment for trespassing, I think to myself as I'm allowed to snap a few more shots of the hotel and Ortygia across the aptly-named, horseshoe-shaped *Porto Grande* bay.

My plan is to walk into town on the beach, but as I work my way around the seemingly never-ending *Porto Grande* I decide to pay my respects to the Greek gods at the sixth-century BC Temple of Olympian Zeus. I hike a kilometer inland to be met, much to my amazement and consternation, by a locked gate. I climb over and break in, to what I imagine is the thunderously silent applause of the gods, to see and photograph what little is left of the temple.

I traipse through a briar patch to theoretically take a short cut into Syracuse but have to follow the paved Via Elorina to cross four rivers, including the Ciane (a papyrus-filled waterway that gets its name from the nymph who tried to stop Hades from abducting Persephone). The freshwater was obviously an additional allure of the place to the Greeks.

It takes a couple hours to round the *Porto Grande* and I'm relieved to finally cross the *Ponte Nuovo* bridge onto the frozen-in-time island of Ortygia. Once there, I spend hours casually exploring the narrow streets, numerous churches and old, less-old and not-so-old ruins before stepping off the island into bustling contemporary Syracuse.

I haven't been to Syracuse, the birthplace of Archimedes in 287 BC, since 1981. It was while taking a bath here that the great mathematician came up with his principle that a body immersed in a liquid is subject to a force equal to the weight of the volume of the liquid that has been displaced. When Syracuse fell to the Romans in 212 BC, Archimedes was working on another mathematical theory during the attack. It's said that he was so focused that he seemed oblivious and unbothered when he was killed by a Roman soldier.

Syracuse is still the type of town that would have enchanted Homer, Odysseus and Zeus and I dedicate the day to this trio. That night I walk through the Arkadina part of town to attend a performance in the city's Neapolis (Neapolis means "new town," but a new town it's not) and thank a policewoman for stopping traffic when I cross the street.

"*Grazie molto* to you and your colleagues for not arresting me today!" I say with a smile. "Your presence makes me feel very secure on your lovely island."

On the way to the fifth-century BC Greek theater, where the seats are still as stone hard as they were millennia ago, I visit the *Orecchio di Dionisio*, or Dionysius's Ear, and make sure that the ear-shaped cave named by Caravaggio in the 17th century echoes as well as it did when I was here thirty years ago. I don't leave town until I stroll through the gigantic San Giovanni catacombs carved out of limestone.

Once underground, I recall a line from *The Odyssey*: "All mortals meet this judgment when they die….dreamlike the soul flies, insubstantial."

The next day takes me even further back in time. On the MedTrek to Augusta, I plan to drop in on Thapsos, which thrived during the Middle Bronze Age in the 15th-13th centuries BC. That settlement and culture on the Magnisi peninsula make Homer, Odysseus, and, especially the UniCredit Bank next to the San Paolo Church and Temple of Apollo on Ortygia, look very, very young. And with luck there will be someone at the gate to enable me to pay the usual €6 entrance fee instead of again trespassing to get a taste of history.

I head to the sea in Syracuse on the via Catania and walk along the port and through a parking lot with a lot of camping recreational vehicles from Germany until a fence blocks my entry to a nicely tended private beach. Naturally, because I don't think any beach should restrict a MedTrekker from walking around the sea, I "negotiate" my way in and get a few high-nosed sniffs from the fat, female tanners on *chaises longues*. I expect to get a tongue lashing from the owner of the Musciara Syracuse Resort, but the woman I meet is such a sweet *bella ragazza Siciliana* that we wind up chatting about the pretentious, fat, female tanners.

Near a memorial to Italy's *Caduti in Africa*, or the Fallen in Africa, I encounter the real *treat du jour*. A wide tailored path, blazed along a former train track, hugs the sea above the cliffs for the next eight kilometers. This is one of the best MedTrekking trails I've encountered and lots of people – bikers, joggers, walkers, young mothers with baby carriages – are using it. I urge you not to leave Syracuse without at least admiring this nifty seaside trail. It's a well-tended path that should be duplicated everywhere on the Mediterranean Sea where there's an out-of-commission train track.

It's easy to meditatively walk around *Capo Santa Panagia* but my serene path ends at a continuous industrial zone that runs from the tanker-filled Port of Syracuse to the tanker-filled Port of Augusta. This non-stop patch of petrochemical plants, oil refineries, docks and everything else associated with an industrial zone is the exact opposite of the lovely blazed path that brought me here. Avoid it! Anyone with any sense should turn around when they get here.

The Idiot, of course, does not. In fact, I accept this as another yin-and-yang, beauty and beastly, example of MedTrekking.

I cut up to the SS road through the Targia train station and immediately see a poem in English written in BIG BLUE letters on the tarmac between the station and the SS. A segment reads: "I have to struggle so I put my arms around you and I hope you won't hurt me as if I was in the woods with you and I hope that you will do no wrong."

There's no author's credit.

At a gas station I grab a quick *panino* and cappuccino for lunch and, after major discussions with everyone in the café, plan to continue along the main road as far as the turnoff for ancient Thapsos, which has ruins from Mycenaean and Maltese settlements.

Then a real miracle (by my MedTrekking standards anyway) occurs. I see a Decathlon, my favorite French-based sporting goods store, at the roundabout near a closed Holiday Inn Express in *Marina di Melilli*. The hotel has shut down due to lack of business (this is the *autostrada* exit for Syracuse, Augusta and other points, and the owner mistakenly thought he had a ready market of industrial zone tourists), but Decathlon is buzzing.

I've needed new hiking shoes since the destructive workout mine got in Gozo, so I MedTrek right into Decathlon, have a quick consultation with Marlena (yeah, another *bella ragazza Siciliana*) about what I like in a hiking shoe (lightweight, quick-to-dry, good sole/soul), and am quickly out the door with a new pair to continue my march north and climb of Mount Etna.

My old soles remain behind, on display in the window as an example of when it's time to change shoes and move on.

A few kilometers from Decathlon I take the turn to Thapsos and begin my walk out to the Magnisi peninsula. Again I meet a locked gate, an out-of-control field of weeds, and no explanation why the ruin is refusing paying customers. Everything, including the oval huts and cemetery with hundreds of rock-hewn tombs, is overgrown and forgotten.

I wave down two cars, the only two cars to be seen out here, and four guys immediately jump out of each vehicle like I've got a major price on my head for trespassing. They look like gangbangers but calm down when they realize I'm just an English-speaking, California-based idiot. While agreeing that "Yes, this is Thapsos," they don't seem to have any idea why it's closed until the head gang member says "It's Schwarzenegger's fault" and everyone else laughs.

I don't see any reason to argue, or laugh, but before I have time to open my mouth another gangbanger suggests that if I walk on the beach I'll see some of the old tombs and burial chambers. A third, much to my surprise gives me a plasticized card with a photograph of San Michele Arcangelo from the Palazzolo Acreide with a prayer on it. It's still on my refrigerator. Not bad guys at all.

I continue for a few kilometers between the sea and a salt-smelly Saline Reserve in Priolo Gargallo but am ultimately forced back to the very dangerous main road until there's a turn off for another archeological site. Renowned Megara Hyblaea, which is overshadowed by chimneys from the oil and petrochemical plants at the Augusta port, features layers of life from different civilizations, including the Megarians who settled it in the late eighth century BC. They created a grid of streets and same-sized houses on same-sized city blocks that, some historians now claim, indicated a tendency towards democracy.

The origins of Megara Hyblaea were described by Thucydides and the city was destroyed first by Gelon, who is still known as the tyrant of Gela and Syracuse, in 483 BC and then by the Romans in 213 BC. Excavated in 1891, this archeological gem is not really closed (there's a custodian who unlocks the gate for me and gives me a free ticket because he thinks I'm over 65!) but is in obvious overgrown disarray. The custodian apologizes for the lamentable state and two French archeologists surveying the site agree that its dilapidated condition is an embarrassment to both the past and present civilizations.

"It's a problem of 'No money, no people,'" one tells me.

"It's in such neglect that I'm amazed that you were even able to find it," the second adds. "They've let it go to pot."

And who are "they?"

The buck apparently starts and stops with the Sicilian regional political authorities that treat these archeological treasures like rat-infested Italian garbage dumps. I decide to launch a war against the regional authorities for ruining ruins like Thapsos and Megara Hyblaea.

A father/son farmer team (the son being about my age, the father in his late 80s) gives me a lift from the ruins to the main road.

"You're very courageous to be walking around Sicily by yourself," the father says. "I'd never have the guts to do it."

When he mentions that he's lived here all his life, I wonder how the invasion of industry and increased port activity must have changed things, despite adding employment.

"It's much less busy now than it used to be because a lot of companies went out of business," he says. "But I think everyone agrees that it hasn't all been positive for us."

As it gets dark, I worry that I'll be sleeping between ruined ruins until a talkative commercial agent named Paolo Ficara gives me a lift to Syracuse and joins me for drinks with his girlfriend on Ortygia later that night.

The life-threatening walk between the combined commercial ports of Syracuse (which, in fact, is beyond the Syracuse limits and officially in the town of Melilli) and Augusta would test any MedTrekker's mettle and patience. In fact, it almost throws my yin-yang beauty/beasty theory out the window. I'm so tired of the over-industrialization, and all of its products and by-products, that I take the next day off to visit the Belvedere and Castello Eurialo in the hills behind the Decathlon store (the Greeks would love that reference). Looking down on the industrial complex that I traipsed through yesterday from the Walls of Dionysius, which once extended across the Epipolae plateau and formed an impressive fortress that protected Ortygia, I feel like a real Idiot having bothered to walk through such a depressing blot of coast.

The next day I return to the Magnisi peninsula to see if Thapsos is perhaps open on a Saturday morning. It's still locked up tight.

In Augusta, I investigate a billowing military hangar that looks like a cathedral before continuing down the *Corso Principe Umberto*, the main drag of the old town, to the end of the peninsula, which has been taken over by the Marine Commando. Then I cross the modern bridge, walk out to the lighthouse at the *Capo Santa Cruce* and rejoice to finally arrive in colorful and quaint little seaside villages like Brucoli and Agnone. Looking ahead, the sands of the Catania beaches are visible and, a bit further, the base and cloud-surrounded summit of 3,350-meter high Mount Etna, Europe's tallest and most active volcano. There are already lots of advertisements touting Etnapolis, a commercial center with 120 stores.

My last 15 kilometers into Catania are barefoot on the sand and as I approach, all sorts of strange things start happening.

First, a *bella ragazza Siciliana* is fighting with her much bigger macho Sicilian boyfriend. They're hitting each other really hard, they're screaming, they're rolling in the sand, they really seem to be upset. I know I'll have to do something if they're still at it when I go by (I also know that when you interfere in a fight like this you often get the blame for having started the thing), and I'm wondering what approach to take.

Fortunately they break it up just as I arrive. The *bella ragazza Siciliana* tells the Sicilian macho guy to fuck off and as she stamps down the beach past me I give her a knowing nod that says, in any language, "Good for you and I'm pretty sure I would have had the balls to come to your assistance if things got much worse."

She smiles, her bright blue eyes contrasting with her suntanned olive skin, and seems to understand my gesture. She purposefully strides down the beach and never looks back. That guy, and I don't even look at the guy, is history.

Next I'm attacked by two dogs that actually force me into the sea up to my waist. The dogs' fat owner looks at me like it's my fault that they're barking, growling and trying to kill me. "Jesus!" I scream as I look back at him, "Do something to stop this!" He doesn't. He just rolls over. Okay, I'll give him the benefit of doubt. Maybe he's a fat, deaf dog owner.

Fortunately I'm carrying a big stick, mainly as a deterrent for moments just like this. The large dog attacks again when I move from the water back to the sand. When his fangs are a few inches from me, I whack him hard on the head. He runs back to his fat, maybe deaf owner who now looks at me like it's really all my fault. The guy just doesn't get it.

As I walk towards Catania a gigantic Grimaldi Lines ship is leaving the harbor and the planes departing from Catania airport look larger with every step I take past well-tended, sand-groomed beaches with names like America, Souvenir, Graziella and Marine Militari (*Divieto Acesso*, or No Entry, to that one). Despite dog and people fights, this is the most developed and the longest concentrated stretch of beachfront in Sicily.

These are such fantastic beaches, with such an array of relaxed bodies on them, that I check into the Miramare Hotel and make it my base camp for a few days. It's just across the street from the beach, though from my south-facing window I see the sea to the left and airport runways to the right. Yin-yang forever!

Early the next morning the sand at the America and Souvenir beaches is being raked with small ATVs, and the staff is preparing to entertain an ever-increasing number of beach bodies as summer approaches. There are tanning lounges and massage parlors, volleyball courts and soccer fields, unabashed lovers (Sicilians too, love almost doing it in public), no visible lovers' spats, obedient dogs on leashes, tourists, bars, restaurants, and guys selling ice cream and water.

During a leisurely pasta and salad lunch I again wonder why people here, or at least the bodies on the beach today, are so seemingly healthier than in the United States. It's got to be the Mediterranean diet that we all know has such a positive impact on cholesterol, triglycerides, blood pressure and blood sugar. I always tighten up and drop a few pounds while I'm MedTrekking, due primarily to all the walking. But I suspect that my overall health improves just because, by both choice and dining options, my intake is rich in fruits and vegetables, olives and ambrosia olive oil, low-fat dairy products and fish to create antioxidant and anti-inflammatory effects.

The next morning at breakfast, pleased about how healthy I look and feel after a couple weeks of sun, I have some of the best and butteriest *cornetti* and cakes of the MedTrek. Then I walk through and beyond Catania for some rockin' and rollin' on the *Riviera dei Ciclopi*, or the Cyclopes' Coast.

The shadow of Mount Etna becomes more and more impressive as I go north through a town where many of the buildings are constructed with black lava from the volcano. Known as Katane when the Greeks founded it in the late eighth century BC, Catania has regularly been hit by lava flows and earthquakes. Like Noto, it's largely been rebuilt in a pleasant Baroque style with elegant fountains (yes, also from lava), a sulfur refinery that's now a concert and exhibition hall, a spacious park at the Villa Bellini and chic shops on the Via Etna.

I walked 6,869 kilometers to reach the *Riviera dei Ciclopi* for an intentionally slow Sunday stroll.

And why take it easy?

First, to savor the moment that I set my eyes on The Rocks of the Cyclops, the sharp black lava boulders that many believe Polyphêmos blindly threw at Odysseus as the Greek warrior sailed away after their confrontation in the cave on the slopes of Mount Etna. Then to very carefully check out these protruding ebony gems mentioned in *The Odyssey*.

I walk by the Lido Aurora American Bar, the Azzurro Lido and Lido Arcobaleno before reaching the Catania port where the customs officials wave The Idiot, and everyone else, through for a two-kilometer stroll to the exit on the other side. Heading towards Aci Castello I pass another "A" Lido, the Lido Aldebaran, and try to contain my excitement by meditatively observing the calm Mediterranean Sea with scores of Sicilian sunbathers on my right, and beaming Mount Etna and beckoning African sunglass peddlers on my left. I pretend not to have any expectations.

I get my first view of The Rocks from the top of the Norman Castle, which like everything else around here is built of black lava. I immediately determine that the left-handed Cyclops didn't have a great throwing arm. He obviously needed a bit more oomph to toss The Rocks beyond the little Island of Lachea and actually nail Odysseus' ship. Fortunately he didn't hit any of the up-market villas just beyond Aci Castello.

When I arrive in Aci Trezza, which is the quasi-official hub of the Cyclops' Coast, I casually but carefully investigate The Rocks. I photograph the *Faraglioni dei Ciclopi* (that sounds a lot more impressive than "The Rocks of the Cyclopes") from different angles, swim around them, watch sunbathers interact with them and keep an eye on them while feasting on a roast chicken and salad lunch at the fishing boat-filled port in Aci Trezza. As I slowly eat, I can't get a poem called *Morning Sea* written by the Greek poet Constantine Cavafy out of my mind.

> *"Let me stand here. Let me also look at nature a while.*
> *The shore of the morning sea and the cloudless*
> *sky brilliant blue and yellow*

> *all illuminated lovely and large.*
> *Let me stand here. Let me delude myself that I see these things*
> *(I really did see them a moment when I first stopped);*
> *and not that here too I see my fantasies,*
> *my memories, my visions of sensual delight."*

After successfully reciting the entire poem, I go down to the beach and reread the passage in *The Odyssey* about the encounter between Odysseus and Polyphêmos. You'll recall that Odysseus stupidly goes into the Cyclops' "cavern yawning above the water" with twelve of his best fighters and a "goatskin full of sweet liquor...brandy, pure and fiery." He enters the cave when "Cyclops had gone afield, to pasture his fat sheep," and decides to stay to "see the caveman, what he had to offer."

The one-eyed Cyclops returns with his herd, closes the cave with "a slab of solid rock" and, after milking his ewes, discovers Odysseus and his crew.

"Are you wandering rogues, who cast your lives like dice, and ravage other folk by sea?" he asks.

The Cyclops is not at all impressed that, as Homer writes, they're "from Troy, Akhaians, blown off course by shifting gales on the Great South Sea." He calls Odysseus "a ninny" before "he clutched at my companions and caught two in his hands like squirming puppies to beat their brains out, spattering the floor. Then he dismembered them and made his meal, gaping and crunching like a mountain lion."

Odysseus realizes that they'd never get out of the cave without the Cyclops' help moving the heavy stone door. After the Cyclops feasts on a few more crewmen, Odysseus says, "Cyclops, try some wine. Here's liquor to wash down your scraps of men." They get him drunk, blind the Cyclops with a blazing spike that they ram "deep in his crater eye" (this, incidentally, created the expression "blind drunk") and escape when Odysseus ties each of his men to the underbelly of a sheep. He prevents the Cyclops from spreading the alarm by saying his name was "Nobody: mother, father and friends, everyone calls me Nobody."

But Odysseus stretched it a bit when he went down to the coast and, rather than silently and stealthily heading out to sea, screams back, and taunts Polyphêmos.

"How do you like the beating that we gave you, you damned cannibal? Eater of guests under your roof!" Odysseus asks. "Zeus and the gods have paid you!"

That's when "the blind thing in his doubled fury broke a hilltop in his hands and heaved it" but it "struck and sank whelmed in a spuming geyser." Odysseus taunts him again by giving his real name, and the

Cyclops then "laid hands upon a bigger stone and wheeled around, titanic for the cast, to let it fly in the black-prowed vessel's track. But it fell short, just aft the steering oar."

It's difficult, I would imagine, for any blind person to pitch with any accuracy, and newly-blinded Polyphêmos should be excused for his lousy throws. One of my blog readers said he obviously had "tunnel vision," and I think that's to be expected.

The rocks certainly didn't reach Odysseus, but they did land at an appropriate place to give some credibility to the buzz that the true cave is located on Mount Etna.

Judge for yourself.

After half a day looking at a few rocks, and thinking a lot about them, I take a final photograph from Cape Mulini as I leave them in the dusk.

Mounting Etna and MedTrekking to Messina

I'm ready to spend the next few days – using some elaborate algorithms provided by the mathematics and physics departments at University of Palermo – climbing up, over, around, and in Mount Etna and then trying to pinpoint the exact spot from which Polyphêmos threw The Rocks. I also plan to visit the nearby Cyclope Commercial Center, a big mall, to see if there are any clues there.

Once I round the Cape Mulini I stay on the beach/cliffs/coast until I arrive in Acireale, where there's a statue of Acis and Galatea, and where I sit on a bench in the Piazzo Duomo tranquilly eating a *cono* of banana *gelato* before exploring the town.

The Rocks and sunbathers, and there are a lot of both, aren't the only things on my mind at the end of my 30-kilometer seaside MedTrekking day in Acireale. I actually recall why the names of all the towns around here (the three I've mentioned plus Aci Bonaccorsi, Aci Catena, Aci Platani, Aci San Filippo, Aci Santa Lucia and Aci Sant'Antonio) begin with "Aci." It's because I'm in the Aci River Valley that gets its name from the river spirit Acis. Acis was in love with a sea nymph named Galatea and was knocked dead by a boulder tossed by a rival suitor, the Cyclops Polyphêmos that we know so well. Galatea turned Acis' blood into the Acis River.

Meanwhile the nearby *Cyclope Centro Commerciale* has, to my surprise, a somewhat amusing logo. There is an eye in the O in CYCLOPE. Guess they hadn't heard that Polyphêmos had been blinded by Odysseus. But I'm very impressed by the automatic electronic scanner/checkout eye when I buy some potato chips, cookies and a Coke Zero to celebrate my visit. That eye is sharper than the Cyclops'.

Heading out of town I pass the *Faro Santa Anna*, see lots of isolated lava beaches, walk on an interesting mix of paths/roads/fields, and find myself in *La Timpa* nature reserve, a 256-hectare park that's six kilometers long and is meant to protect the environment between Mount Etna and the coast. Along the way I encounter my second Italian lovers' spat and am glad I don't have anyone in my life to argue with like that. I pass a puppet theater (puppets are big here) and the *Terme di Santa Venera*, the faux classical baths dating back only to 1873.

The next highlight of the day's MedTrek is the MACIMED, or *La Mobilita Cicotouristica nelle Isole de Mediterraneo*. This well-marked seaside 12.67-kilometer bike path enables me to verify that my pedometer still functions correctly and leads to a contented walk that concludes in Recanati on the outskirts of Giardini Naxos, in the shadow of Mount Etna and Taormina.

There are some other educational highpoints. The locals like to consider *Marina di Riposto* an international port, the river in Fiumefreddo not all that cold or deep, and the best-named beach to be Simpsons' Lido, which features a welcome sign decorated with the cartoon's characters.

Giardini Naxos is one of the first/oldest Greek settlements in Sicily. One myth is that an irritated Neptune grounded a ship here when its crew got distracted while making a sacrifice to him. One sailor, Theocles, lived to tell the tale and persuaded some of his countrymen to colonize the place between 743 and 735 BC.

I take off from my sea view room at the Villa Linda only to find that the Hilton has put a fence around its beach to block all MedTrekkers. It's too early in the morning for a spat so I walk around it, knowing that there's a lot of beach between Cape Schiso to the south and Cape Taormina to the north, both formed by lava flows from Mount Etna. It's also too early to visit the Naxos archeological zone, which I want to see after my frustrating visits to ruined ruins near Augusta, though I plan to avoid an amusement park called Naxoslandia.

I head out on the lava-floored seaside promenade and immediately notice that Giardini Naxos has complemented its Neolithic, Bronze Age, Greek and Roman archeological treasures by commissioning sculptures with historic connotations and modern twists for its palm-lined beachfront on the Mediterranean Sea.

One prominent piece is artist Turi Azzolina's take on Theocles and another is Azzolina's vision of a city father called *Mito di Naxos* with his flowing locks and long beard. Though it's unlikely that many of these creations will have the staying power of the remnants on display at the Naxos archeological site, they look particularly intriguing as the theme song from *Saturday Night Fever* blares from a pub.

Naxos art has inspired aesthetic competition in other seaside villages as well. *Santa Teresa di Riva* has gone extremely modern while Roccalumera has chosen something less aggressive.

Sometimes a MedTrek photo and a followtheidiot.com blog item benefit academics. Leigh Lieberman, a graduate student in the Department of Art and Archeology at Princeton, was intrigued by my photo of Theocles.

"I was wondering if you had any more pictures of the sculpture that I'd be able to use in an informal presentation for my peers?" she wrote. "I'm talking about how the Greek colonists in the area connect with their past and I think the modern sculptures in the area make a really interesting point of comparison."

Based on my unofficial survey, however, most people don't come to Giardini Naxos for the art or artifacts. They simply want to sun on beaches in the shadow of hilltop Taormina, which is where my base camp will be next week when I MedTrek up, on, around and in Mount Etna looking for the Cyclops' cave.

Taormina gets nearer with every step, but I leave the beach and hit the SS14 two-lane blacktop to get around the Capo Sant'Andrea, a rocky cape with lots of grottos being visited by lots of boats. Beyond is the bay of Mazzaro and the little Isola Bella which is, like so many other spots on this coast, part of a nature reserve. It's hot and I want to swim, but the wind and the threat of jellyfish stymie me, and instead I admire the *télépherique* to Taormina that enables people to reach the chic resort without getting caught in the continual traffic snarl.

I keep sand walking on the long Spisone and Mazzeo beaches to Letojanni, where I drop into a *salumeria* for a fresh mozzarella/tomato sandwich, banana and cold water. As I lunch on the beach I can, for the first time, see the toe of the boot of Italy across what will soon officially become the Strait of Messina.

I'm about to round another rocky cape, the *Capo Sant'Alessio*, when I see a staircase where two men are doing stonework. Walking up the steps, I politely ask if I can trespass.

"Please, please, be our guest," one replies. "This is a little known shortcut."

When he learns that I'm walking around Sicily and connects that with my choice of these particular steps up the hill he says, "You've got the right instinct."

"I better have the right instinct after walking almost 7,000 kilometers," I reply. "Or I'll be in a lot of trouble."

I catch a bus back to Giardini Naxos to tour the ruins. On the bus, I watch a bunch of school kids who make this to-school-and-back run above the sea every day and take its beauty for granted. My kids did the same thing in the south of France. They took it for granted until they saw the rest of the world and realized how special it is.

The next morning I move my base camp from the seaside Giardini Naxos to the hilltop Taormina, which still clings to the edge of Mount Taura where a Greek colony was founded in 403 BC. This is the first time I've returned to the crowded and expensive village since my daughter Sonia was conceived in the Timeo Hotel here in 1981. But I manage to find a spacious apartment to rent for a week – the Villa Galante off via David Herbert Lawrence with a view of Calabria and the Strait of Messina – and invite a few friends to join me as I explore nearby Mount Etna and continue the MedTrek to Messina.

I spend the first afternoon and evening re-familiarizing myself with the place. I re-visit the Timeo Hotel (one reason that I'm not staying there this time is because rooms now start at €595 for a double), climb to the top seats in the Greek theater and enjoy remarkable views of the seaside that I walked or will walk.

My daughter isn't able to join me here but I'm sentimental enough that when I get back to Taormina I take a look at the lengthy diary I've been keeping since 1982 about Sonia and Luke, who was conceived in Paris and born in the south of France.

Paris, 18 September 1982, 6:00 p.m.
Dear Sonia,

I have no idea when you'll be able to read this but the thought that you – today a three-day-old baby squirming in the Clinique Sainte Isabelle in Neuilly (where, you'll be pleased to know, this noon I changed your diapers and dressed you in pale pink attire) – someday will, is what inspires this chronicle of your life. At the moment I plan to send it to you when you turn 18, in the distant-sounding year of 2000, and even now anticipate you watching it unfold on the computer monitor.

Today I'm using an Apple III, one of the early personal computers, and when you get this disk I doubt whether that company will be around (though I do have some stock in it). I am sure that most of your education will have been computer-supplied so you won't have any problem manipulating the text.

Your birth was nothing short of incroyable (I also assume you'll be bilingual). Your mother and I had been waiting, anticipating, conjecturing and finally getting impatient for nine months. We had all sorts of premonitions that you'd be a girl, premonitions with no foundation of course, because your mother refused to let the ecographist reveal your sex.

To start with, you were conceived in Taormina, Sicily, in Room 19 at the Timeo Hotel (there has been endless debate about this contention but, myth or not, I suggest you don't ask any questions) where we stayed for a few days in early January. Room 19 is a corner room, with one window looking onto the Mediterranean Sea and the other onto Mount Etna, Europe's largest active volcano. The latter view, towards the female volcano, led me to predict your femininity and for a time, in February and March, I wanted to call you Etna. (Unfortunately, the name doesn't work in French. I'd previously wanted to call my first daughter Petra, after the hidden city in Jordan which was, when I visited it, a masterpiece of nature, but that means "fart" in French and would have been worse than Etna. Sonia, however, is derived from Sophia, Greek for "wise"....

Then I flash forward to the first paragraph I wrote when Luke was born on the Mediterranean Sea in the Clinique Californie in Cannes.

Cannes, 24 December, 1984, 3:00 p.m.
Luke, you were born at 11:30 this morning on a wintry day that follows three of sun. You are now wrapped warmly in room 32 at the Clinique Californie, a room decorated with a lovely bouquet of flowers which I ordered while waiting for your arrival, a room overlooking the Mediterranean and the islands off Cannes.

You came out of the womb with the speed of light which, now that I think of it, is another good reason to call you Luke (from lux, which means "light" in Latin), and, according to your mother, you're now sleeping as quietly as the gospel writer and physician Luke described in the New Testament. (If, it turns out, you don't like the name Luke, just think what it would have been like to be called Jesus, or Christ, or Noel, had you been born tomorrow!)

I emailed this bundle of hundreds of thousands of words to the kids when they turned 21 to provide them with a diary of how they got where they are. It's not just about them but contains correspondence, articles, thoughts, musings and other documents of varying degrees of interest and relevance. I've read it from time to time and it's a fabulous record of life before and during the MedTrek era.

I return to the theater early the next morning, before even the garbage collectors have made their rounds, and I'm inspired by a mouth-watering dawn view of the cone of Mount Etna from the best seats. As I continue with an unhustling dawn walk through town, I pay homage to the statue of an angel who is half-cow in honor of the Sun God Helios and the land of the cattle.

These are, of course, not just any cattle. For one thing, Homer tells us "these fat cattle never die," and for another they have two

213

"sweetly braided nymphs" as cowherds.

The angel atop the statue in the Piazza Duomo is the patron of Taormina and the episode from *The Odyssey* continues to play an important role in local legend and folklore.

Incidentally, it seems clear that there were 350 bovines ("fifty head in every herd, and their herds are seven," wrote Homer) back in the day, and I've seen a dozen of their offspring/descendants – and actually stepped in some of their cow paddies on a seaside path near Fiumefreddo (just so I could write that I did so).

But don't think that number is actually correct. Archimedes came up with his well-known "cattle problem" that requested, "If thou art diligent and wise, O stranger, compute the number of cattle of the Sun, who once upon a time grazed on the fields of the Thrinacian isle of Sicily."

His formula was so complicated that Voltaire said that there was "more imagination in the head of Archimedes than in that of Homer." Hint: the correct answer contains 206,545 digits.

I'm not worried about the number of cattle as the sun rises, but rather how to get to the top of Mount Etna, one of the top draws in Sicily.

I know that there is a €100-plus Disneyland-like "ride" that takes moderately adventurous tourists close to the top from the Rifugio Sapienza on the south side of the mountain. It involves a ride in a cable car and in a heavy-duty jeep up to 2,700-meters. Then there's a guided group walk to the 3,323-meter (10,902 feet) summit. That expensive, somewhat challenging route is recommended/sold to everyone wanting to legally get to the central crater.

I prefer a less-congested and less-legal approach to reach not only the summit but also pinpoint the cave where Polyphêmos lived when he tossed those rocks at a departing Odysseus. I embark on an adventurous backdoor MedTrekking path that, albeit illegal until the month of July when the snow melts and guides are available, makes me feel that I actually earn the stupendous views from Etna's cold, windy, smoky, and sulfurous summit on a June afternoon.

This route doesn't only end with a wondrous lookout from the largest island in the Mediterranean Sea and a close glimpse inside its smoky, sulfur-smelling, bellowing crater at Hêphaistos/Vulcan, the Greek god of fire and metalwork. There are also forests and surprising sights on the way. Plus the chance that Etna could erupt, as it has more than 200 times during the last 3,500 years, and send lava down the path on my side of the hill. It's no surprise that the name Etna comes from either the Greek for "I light up" or the Phoenician for "furnace."

Here's the 31-kilometer roundtrip that The Idiot suggests you make from the north side of Etna:

Once you get to the trailhead at Piano Provenzana, which was badly damaged by a 2002 eruption that created more than twenty new craters, follow the dirt track up Mount Etna towards the observatory. Just before you arrive, take the path off to the right and spend a few hours gingerly traversing up and around the mountain through the snow.

In a few hours you'll see the Disney crowd heading to the top of a mountain. You can join them by following one of the guided tours up to the crater, though not too closely because the guides don't like MedTrekkers coming through the back door and you'd run the risk of being hassled or arrested.

Then savor the sights (don't take a deep breath because the sulfur is toxic) and remember that it's an hour quicker to get down the mountain than it was to get up.

Incidentally, one of the most comical sights provoked by a companion on the MedTrek occurs at the beginning of my hike towards the summit. I have a friend (I respect her desire not to have her real name mentioned in conjunction with this anecdote, so we'll call her Sarah Jessica Parker) visiting from Manhattan.

SJP's tiny pink pack is decorated with evil eye trinkets, her brand new white Italian tennis shoes are adorned with colorful beads, and she's wearing white Capri pants, a pink T-shirt, and a straw hat that makes her look like *Sex and the City Comes to the Wilds*.

"You look like Sarah Jessica Parker," I chortle, good-naturedly I think, when I see her outfit.

"Hey, I'm a city girl and this is what I wear when I walk in Central Park," she replies. "Besides, there's no way that I can climb that mountain."

She's right and sensibly turns back after 45 minutes on a perfectly walkable, albeit steep, trail. Later that morning, she takes a €47 two-hour bus tour to the observatory near the summit.

I've just passed a home destroyed by the 2002 eruption when two local forestry workers, taking some earth-moving equipment up the mountain, tell me that it's *molto pericoloso* to hike up to the crater in the snow. They don't even wave to me when, an hour later, I've clearly ignored their advice and pass them clearing snow on the dirt track. A few footprints in the snow as I traverse the mountain assure me that I'm on the right path, but I'll be the first to admit that my airy Quechua MedTrek shoes aren't, and they aren't even supposed to be, snow-worthy. Don't tell Sarah Jessica, but they're not much better than her designer tennies.

It's warm enough to be wearing shorts, but my feet get very wet and very cold and when I traverse the mountain I get a stern look from a guide leading a slow bunch of people up to the rim of the crater. Though bending the rules doesn't bother me too much, I'd be the first or second to admit that it's stupid to make this journey alone. I'll feel pretty dumb if I take a fall or collapse due to frostbite.

It takes me only four hours of fairly rapid MedTrekking to reach the rocking/smoking crater where I zap a SPOT from the rim of the volcano while I eat some lunch, admire the stupendous views, inhale too much sulfur and talk to a few people who've taken the Disney tour.

An hour later, my shoes and legs blackened by lava dust, I head back across the snow, which is now melting, and descend with soggy shoes and socks in hope of finding Sarah Jessica alive. As I approach the earth-and-snow-removing team I meet a German climber who's been trying to get to the volcano since mid-morning but failed to find the right path. It's now mid-afternoon and he's extremely frustrated and a bit scared. I convince him that the snow conditions aren't right for him to continue and he's obviously relieved to walk down with me. Gosh, him being on the trail alone is even stupider than me hiking solo.

When we get to the trailhead, we find SJP lounging with a book and tea in a small café. I look back up at the hill – bare, lava scarred, dusty, snowy (though the snow at this time of year is speckled with black) – and she's amazed at my feet and feat.

"Definitely not the place for tennis shoes and a pink pack," Sarah Jessica Parker says when she sees me. "But at least mine are still clean and dry."

The next day, pleased that the climb up Etna was so uneventful, I begin searching for Polyphêmos' actual cave on the southeastern side of Mount Etna. It's somewhere among the mountain's 231 grottos, and, based on my study of the trajectory of the rocks and other inside information, including the secret algorithm, I have a rough idea where it's located.

To kick things off, SJP takes me on a 100-plus mile drive around Mount Etna on a foggy day through Zafferana (honey), Trecastagni (chestnuts), Bronte (pistachios), Linguaglossa (roast chicken), Adrano (*penne alle* pistachios), and back to Taormina through the high hill village of Castiglione di Sicilia and along the Alcantara Gorge. We're relaxed enough on this day off to have a creamy pistachio penne in Bronte before, the next morning, I look for the possible vicinity of the cave.

It still takes me hours, even with the detailed and revolutionary algorithmic directions supplied by researchers at the University of Palermo, to locate the reputed cave of the Cyclops on the southeastern slope of Mount Etna.

That was the good news.

The bad news is that the previously undiscovered cave, unbeknownst to anyone until today, has been tightly plugged by a lava "cork" presumably formed during a 24-day eruption in 2001. You're getting this scoop at the same time as the academics at U of P, but don't let them know that the MedTrekker told you.

It will take me time, of course, to organize financing and a skilled team of archeologists to unseal and explore this key historical treasure. I plan to return for an extensive investigation after I complete my twelve labors.

On the last night of SJP's visit, we eat at a restaurant with the best view and the best food I've had on the trip. Called simply Ristorante Pizzeria Taormina, it's just across from the celeb-rich Mocambo Café and looks down on the Giardini Naxos which, on this night, has a five-masted sailing ship docked in the bay. I have a delicious seafood salad accompanied by a pistachio pizza and some grilled tuna, but what is particularly memorable is that this is the first restaurant I've come across on the Med that demands a down payment (€20) simply to secure a reservation.

My MedTrek to Santa Margherita, on the southern outskirts of Messina, occurs on a delightful breezy day and features lots of beach walking and a roasted chicken for lunch. It's close enough to Messina to assure me that I'll soon be sleeping again at the Jolly Hotel.

In Sant'Alessio I pass the Kennedy Hotel, which has a KH insignia on its seaside back door, and buy some new Ts at the outdoor clothes market in *Santa Teresa di Riva*. As I try them on, I notice an old Italian woman in black holding onto the rail, her daughter at her side, looking intently at the sea. I try to imagine her thoughts and images of bygone moments involving the Mediterranean. Was her husband a fisherman? Did she, like so many Italians today, lay with him on the sand?

I get a *complimenti* from a young barmaid at the Odissea bar in Furci who says, "I don't know anyone around here who's walked that far!" and my promenade continues through Roccalumera, Nizza di Sicilia, Ali' Terme, Itala, and Scaletta.

I'm able to see the boot of Italy quite clearly throughout the day and soon approach ferries coming across the Strait of Messina from Villa San Giovanni. For the first time in Sicily I have some oil residue on my own boots from globs on the beach. Yes, the last few kilometers into Messina were toxic and positively not swimmable, as a number of signs pointed out. Polluted smelly streams emptying into the Med and tossed garbage slowly being burned to a crisp.

After reaching the Piazza Duomo I celebrate with a bottle of fizzy San Benedetto *"Frizzante"* water and a Buongusto pizza, complete with spinach and salmon, at the Dolce Vita restaurant. Palestinian waiter Ahmed Amer takes a few celebratory photos of me in front of the cathedral and the Fontana di Orione, and I light an electric candle inside the church in gratitude for my safe journey around the Mediterranean Sea's largest island.

A few weeks later Ahmed and I exchange a couple of emails.

Me to him: Ahmed, you were a prince of a man to meet during the last steps of my circumnavigation of Sicily! And your appreciation/ awe/amazement of my Mediterranean walking adventure was very heartening to hear, see, and feel when I MedTrekked into the Piazza Duomo in Messina. Keep those ice cubes coming, and Follow the Idiot to Ramallah! Ever omward, Joel

Him to me: HEYYYY MAANN...WONDERFUL TO SEE U ALIVE :=) ...I STILL HERE COME BACK WHEN EVER U WANT TO EAT PIZZA AGAIN GAS WATER AND ALOT OF ICE :@) THE ORIONE FONTANA IS WAITING. ANYWAY HAVE FUN.

MedTrek Milestone #7

Anyone who might want to Follow the Idiot and MedTrek around Sicily should go to the Piazza Duomo in Messina and flip a euro coin. If it's heads, MedTrek 448-kilometers to *Capo San Vito* in northwestern Sicily and continue counterclockwise. If it's tails, MedTrek 260-kilometers to *Portopalo di Capo Passero*, the furthest point to the southeast, and continue clockwise. If the coin lands on its side, catch the ferry to Malta and meander for 61-kilometers around Gozo.

I check back in with Manuelina on my way to Palermo for my flight to Rome (Incidentally Alitalia calls its business class Club Ulisse Elite, and their in-flight magazine is *Ulisse*) and plan to take a picture of the couple. Unfortunately it's their day off. So I spend my last night at Pamela's Cerri Hotel in *Castellammare del Golfo*, do my best to avoid Macho Sicilian Men, and plan to stay in Rome for a few days to cope with the usual PMTWS (Post MedTrek Withdrawal Syndrome) after a delightful seven-week Mediterranean walking adventure in Sicily and Malta.

This has been a remarkable locale to "sense" what Odysseus and his crew felt when they encountered Charybdis and the Cyclops and to experience a scintillating slice of Mediterranean history on the sea's largest island. Walking around an island completely changes the MO of the MedTrek because I really don't "get" anywhere or make it any further around the sea. But islands are where it was at during much of history and should not be missed! In fact, I'm looking forward to visiting scores more!

PART THREE

SWITCHING GEARS IN MAGNA GRAECIA

Circe Sends Me Island Hopping
Finding Homer on Chios
Liberating Lesbos and Lemnos
Hanging Out with Odysseus on Ithaka
Searching for Nausikaa on Corfu

Circe Sends Me Island Hopping

"So far as my experience goes, travelers generally exaggerate the difficulties of the way." - *Henry David Thoreau*

"Hear me, goddess: come, bless me with speed." – Odysseus, *The Iliad*

I begin the next segment of the MedTrek on a ridiculously luxurious cruise from Messina to Athens. Then I continue on the *Corinthian II* while it calls at various Greek islands before I finally disembark on Chios, the isle off the Turkish coast where many Greeks contend Homer was born.

Circe told me to "take some ships, do some sailing, and explore some islands." But I'm not sure this opulent voyage is what she had in mind when she said "Embark on a mysterious ship that will enable you to hear words straight from Homer's mouth and guide you to the Greek island of his birth."

Would she have been shocked, or pleased, with the way I talked my way onto a combination of two back-to-back Mediterranean cruises sponsored by the Columbia Alumni Travel Study Program and the Stanford/Harvard Alumni Associations?

Not that it's all play. During five days and nights, besides discussing *The Idiot and the Odyssey* during two onboard presentations, I interview the accompanying professors – Elena Tzelepis from Columbia, Shelley Wachsmann from Texas A&M, Marsh McCall from Stanford, and Aaron J. Paul from Harvard – and chat with many passengers.

The trip brochure for *The Journey of Odysseus* fueled my imagination: "Homer's epic account of Odysseus' journey home after the fall of Troy is more than just a poem for the *literati* – it is a beacon to the adventurer…the ultimate journey. The islands Odysseus visited, the caverns he explored and the mountain peaks he climbed are among the most magical places in the Mediterranean."

Who could resist a few days off the MedTrekking path and on the water, especially when Circe recommended it?

I'm back at the Jolly Hotel in Messina the night before I sail and awake just as the *Corinthian II* arrives in port with passengers who embarked in Istanbul and have visited Troy, Delos, Pylos, Valletta, Trapani and Pompeii. When I arrive at the ship at noon I'm almost the only passenger onboard. Everyone else, except a bloated and red-faced blowhard named Jack who remains glued to the bar throughout the voyage, is either visiting Taormina or taking a walking tour of Messina.

The all-suite *Corinthian II* has 57 cabins and the most expensive, the deluxe penthouse suites with private balconies, cost a cool $17,790 for single occupancy on a ten-night cruise – not including airfare. I learn the ship was built in 1992, refurbished in 2005, and has way too much food and "complimentary" wine available in the "well-appointed" (their words are as good as any other description) dining room or al fresco on the sun deck. If I tire of in-cabin luxuries like air conditioning and fancily packaged toiletries, I can get online for an extortionist rate in the library.

Anchors aweigh.

The first part of the cruise, from Messina to Athens, is highlighted by a participatory reading of selections from *The Odyssey* led by Dr. Kathryn Hohlwein, a retired 80-something year-old professor from Sacramento who founded *The Readers of Homer.* Kathryn and her partner-in-rhyme, Emmy-winning actor/producer Yannis Simonides, have led similar Homeric readings from the Getty Museum in Malibu and the 92nd Street Y in New York to the Bibliotheca Alexandrina in Egypt and the Rock of Homer on Chios.

One of the more delightful aspects of the onboard, open-to-all reading is that every participant brings something unique – a different language, a singing voice, a knowledge of ancient Greek, a dramatic style – to the rendition of rhapsodies from Robert Fagles' translation of *The Odyssey*. Their desire to participate is heightened by daily shore visits to some of the actual and mythical venues described in the epic that's been translated into almost 200 languages.

Jean Davison, a retired college professor from Vermont, reads brilliantly in ancient Greek. Virginia Chen from Stockton, California, enthralls everyone when she professionally sings the lines from the book. Puck, a 30-something movie producer who got her name from *A Midsummer Night's Dream,* performs with youthful thespian flourish. Although it's happened at other readings, no one at this particular event reads in Swahili.

During dinner, I ask Kathryn Hohlwein if *The Odyssey* is one of the five books she'd take to a proverbial desert island.

"I know it by heart," she says. "I wouldn't have to take the book to an island. It's all in my head."

Not that Kathryn, or anyone else shipwrecked on an island for decades, would be able to absorb or grasp everything intended by Homer in his oral narratives.

"*The Odyssey* is open to so many possible interpretations that no one would get bored or saturated no matter how much time they had alone on an island," enthuses Elena Tzelepis, a professor in Columbia University's Classics Department.

Elena, who has a PhD in philosophy from the New School for Social Research in New York, says she constantly revisits ancient Greek philosophy and literature to attempt to make it more relevant to today's world. Her approach is illustrated by the titles of her onboard lectures. One is called "Homer: The Historical and Socio-cultural Context of the Epics" and another "*Odyssey*: A Poetic Narrative of the Human Adventure."

"As a philosopher I try to make sense of the influence of Homer and myths as a valuable way of thinking," Elena says as we sail towards the island of Ithaka.

Her third lecture is entitled "Penélopê: The Feminine Act of Weaving Beyond Confinement."

"Homer's works provoke and challenge people," she says, "and feminism, in its various forms, has produced new and important questions and interpretations about Homer's text. Women are certainly the seducers in *The Odyssey*, and we can learn a great deal from rich feminine characters like Circe, Nausikaa and Kalypso.

"Most women reading *The Odyssey* also appreciate the malleable, adaptable aspect of Odysseus, who is both heroic and violent, a king and beggar, and revered or treated badly," Elena continues. "He's very ambiguous – sometimes seductive, sometimes manipulative – and I like him because, unlike many men, he was willing to be metamorphosed."

"Is interest in Homer dwindling or increasing?" I ask.

"More people seem to have a desire to relate to the texts as they make their own journeys, because Homer's epics enable us to come up with theories about both life and death," she says. "Personally, I don't look for didactic lessons or instructions but enjoy the text, because it allows me to engage with myth without giving me ready-made conclusions."

I somewhat pretentiously quote Glaukos, whose father Hippolokhos sent him to Troy and commanded him "to act always with valor, always to be most noble, never to shame the line of my progenitors," from *The Iliad*. I want to illustrate to Elena and Kathryn one of the many philosophic thoughts I've plucked from Homer's works: "Very like leaves upon this earth are the generations of men. Old leaves, cast on the ground by wind, young leaves the greening forest bears when spring comes in. So mortals pass; one generation flowers even as another dies away."

Then I go to bed.

Shelley Wachsmann, a professor of Biblical Archeology at the Institute of Nautical Archeology at Texas A&M University, has been teaching courses in ancient seafaring and biblical archeology since 1990. He recently directed a joint Greek-Canadian expedition in search of fleets lost during the Persian War in the fifth century BC, and his onboard presentations included "Homer and the Phoenicians," "Sailing the Wine Dark Sea: Ships and Seafaring in the Time of Odysseus," "The Palace of Nestor at Pylos and Greek Colonization: Why are we going to Sicily to look at Greek Temples?" and "The Bow of Odysseus."

How did he wind up here?

"My parents bought me a child's version of *The Odyssey* with a lot of pictures, and it's the first book I remember reading after Dick and Jane and Spot," Wachsmann recalls as we sit on the deck of the *Corinthian II*. "Although I didn't grasp all of the Homeric themes, the book was a prime changer in my life and one of the reasons I chose to become an archeologist."

Wachsmann went to Israel in 1976 and worked for 13 years in nautical archeology as an inspector of underwater antiquities.

"I worked in a wet suit," he smiles as he describes the various shipwrecks of Saint Paul on the deep, wide, and unpredictable Mediterranean. "And there was no shortage of spots to study to enrich our understanding of Biblical descriptions because there's probably a shipwreck, or the remains of a wrecked ship's cargo, every 100 meters along the Israeli Mediterranean coast."

"One big question I have is whether Homer was writing about a period that may have occurred half a millennium earlier and arrived to him in an oral tradition, or telling the stories from the perspective of his own time and experience," Wachsmann wondered, noting that *The Odyssey* contains all of the themes and archetypes described by Joseph Campbell in *The Hero With A Thousand Faces*. "When talking about a bow or a ship, was Homer describing his current period or the old days? Would it be like you writing about the discovery of America today? If you're relating to his epics as great literature it doesn't really matter, but as a source for history and archeology, it requires rigorous evaluation."

"Except that we know that Columbus discovered America, and we don't know if the Trojan War ever happened or Homer ever existed," I reply before I return to my cabin to watch snippets of a sappy 203-minute long version of *The Odyssey*.

Each night I climb to the top deck for some solo sailing meditation and let the SPOT broadcast my location at sea. My satellite positioning during the next few days unquestionably illustrates that traveling by ship is much speedier than traveling by foot. Although I go through MedTrek withdrawal after a few days at sea, I do enjoy getting off in various ports for a short time to get a taste of where I'll be walking during the next few years.

Our first stop involves a quickie mini-bus tour of Ithaka, which is the agreed location of Odysseus' palace. I photograph a bust of Odysseus in Stavros (it means "*cross*") at a site overlooking three bays near the Polyphêmos restaurant, have a coffee on the seaside in Kioni, and admire the Cyclopean Walls at Alkomena.

Ithaka, which was severely damaged during a 1953 earthquake, certainly looks like Odysseus' home, especially with a rainbow sunrise as we enter the port of Vathi. I'm tempted to jump ship and spend two weeks walking around the island to explore the field of Odysseus's father Laërtês, the palace, the cave of the nymphs and other attractions from *The Odyssey*.

There's no time on this type of outing, but don't worry. I'll soon be back to thoroughly explore Ithaka. I'm particularly intrigued and inspired by a plaque in the harbor that quotes Lord Byron during his visit in August 1823: "If this island belonged to me, I would bury all my books here and never go away."

There are thousands of islands in the Mediterranean Sea, many formed when the land that was a bridge between Asia Minor and Europe "sunk." Although you'll get a different answer from everyone you ask about the precise number of Greek islands, I've chosen to accept the Wikipedia figure that there are over 6,000 islands and islets, that 227 are inhabited, and that only 78 have more than one hundred people living on them. Many of the unpopulated, mountainous islands are not MedTrekkable because they are primarily volcanic with stark, steep crags and, of course, no paths.

Circe suggested I visit two dozen different islands – including Chios, Corfu, Crete, Ithaka, Kos, Lesbos, Lemnos and Rhodes – and MedTrek on or around them. They're grouped in a number of geographical clusters. Ithaka and other islands west of the Greek mainland are known as the Ionian Islands, while those in the center of the Aegean Sea are the Cyclades and the Dodecanese are between Crete and Turkey.

To reach Athens we pass under the dramatic Rio-Antirio Bridge, traverse the Corinthian Gulf and float through the romantic Corinth Canal that links the Ionian and Aegean Seas. I'm so keen on getting a good look at the bridge that I abandon the reading of *The Odyssey* for a few minutes.

This narrow waterway was first proposed by Periander when he was the tyrant of ancient Corinth in the second half of the seventh century BC, but he unimaginatively opted for a paved slipway, or *diolkos*, that forced sailors to drag their ships from sea to sea on rollers until the 13th century. Alexander the Great and Caligula also toyed with the idea of a canal, but it was Nero who began digging in AD 67 and personally struck the first blow using a gold pickaxe.

The dramatic channel, cut through solid rock, wasn't completed until 1893 and is over six kilometers long and 23 meters wide with vertical sides rising 90 meters above the water. One thing it did, from my perspective, is turn the Peloponnese into an island.

Passengers on the *Corinthian II* are intrigued by Homer and actively discuss the author, his books, and books about him during the cruise. Lion Miles, a retired pilot from Stockbridge, Massachusetts, gives me excerpts from a book called *Ulysses Airborne* that features another round of guesses about where events in *The Odyssey* occurred. Sheila Gorsky, a union organizer in New York, presents me with me her copy of the Fagles translation of *The Odyssey,* and Homer scholar Froma Zeitlin, a Radcliffe classics major and professor at Princeton, provides me with the outline of her lecture *Homer, Odyssey: Survival and Homecoming.*

What I love about Professor Zeitlin's comprehensive overview – with themes like *"Elements of Folktale and Myth," "Mythological Landscapes"* and *"Divine Intervention" –* is that you, me, or my mother could use the same outline, and we'd each give a completely different lecture concerning eternal questions surrounding the quest and the journey, the return of the hero, disguise and recognition, and a woman's wit. That's why you'll find a million theses when you Google "Homer" and why my onboard chat about *The Idiot and the Odyssey* fits in so nicely with a crowd that appreciates the all-encompassing nature and myriad possibilities of the text.

My cruise companions have other interests beyond Homer, of course. Oskar Siven wants the lowdown on gay beaches. Yannis Simonides describes the thrill of sailing past Stromboli at 3:00 a.m. Dr. Tom Stair brought his adult children on the cruise to bond on the open sea. Carla from New Jersey talked about her sheep farm during the rainbow/sunrise over Ithaka.

Elderhostel, a tour company that specializes educational travel for seniors, also has a group onboard. I room for two nights in a staff cabin with Geoffrey Morgan, an avid bird and dolphin watcher from Wales who snores like a cross between an owl with a sore throat and a dolphin with a cold.

Not everyone likes the lectures.

"Most people don't know Homer or *The Odyssey* and we never got the big picture," complains one 80-something Elderhostel guest. "And the topics are much too arcane. I mean, really, an hour about the bow in *The Odyssey*?"

I was the only passenger to stay on the ship in Athens for a second cruise called *Undiscovered Greece: Unspoiled Islands, Pristine Villages, and Remote Ancient Sites*. Before we sail, I visit the comparatively new Acropolis Museum, which sits in the shadow of the rocky Acropolis promontory that reigned over classical Athens, and take a quick tour to see what happened to all the sites and athletic venues that were spruced up for the 2004 Olympics. I use the Internet at the Hotel Grand Bretagne in Constitution Square before joining Stanford Professor Marsh McCall, Harvard art historian Aaron Paul, and a dozen other guests on an excursion to the Sanctuary of Artemis in Brauron and the Temple of Poseidon at the end of the Sounion peninsula, where I couldn't find the rumored graffiti tag that Lord Byron is said to have left on one of the marble columns.

This is not the first time I have visited Athens. That was in June 1968 with Congressman-to-be Buzz Hamburg who was studying with me at a Stanford campus in Vienna. Impacted by the assassinations of Martin Luther King and Robert Kennedy during an era when we vigorously protested the war in Vietnam, we both dropped out of school and made a road trip to Yugoslavia and Greece before returning to the United States.

In Athens we slept, for a pittance, on the top floor terrace of a cheap hotel in the Plaka, the historical district known as the "neighborhood of the gods" in the shadow of the Acropolis. I got food poisoning and was delirious when taken down the hotel's tiny, windy staircase on a stretcher to an ambulance. Once I regained a semblance of health in a local hospital where I was put in a large ward with thirty beds, not only did I see two patients die but I also contracted hepatitis from the dirty needles they used to feed me intravenously.

I've been back to Athens numerous times since, including two working/vacationing trips in 1984. It was on one of these visits, while zipping around the Mediterranean to write a section called *"Mediterranean Destinations"* for *Time*, that I first officially indicated in print that I would walk around the Mediterranean Sea. My author description in the *Time* article informed readers that I planned "to hike the perimeter of the Mediterranean by 2001."

Little did I know.

Learned Lectures, Roaming Rhodes and Calling at Kos

Classics professor Marsh McCall has made over two dozen of these trips and is considered a Stanford star when it comes to entertaining alumni in the Mediterranean.

"The ancient world has been my life for more than 50 years and continues to fascinate me," McCall says as we saunter around Brauron and discuss Artemis, the goddess of nature and the protector of women in childbirth. "What makes these voyages so intensely rewarding is being able to read from the great literature of antiquity at sites evoked in the books."

"There's also pleasure teaching older people, who bring experience to the table, versus eager college freshmen," McCall continues a few days later while we look at ancient manuscripts in a cliff-hanging cathedral on the island of Amorgos and he translates the scrawl into contemporary English. "The knowledge of ancient texts enables us to cope with questions we all ask at the later stages of life and a mature audience brings insights to the party."

Harvard-trained curator and art historian Aaron Paul, an associate of the Material Culture Program at Harvard University's Center for Hellenic Studies in Washington, DC, specializes in Greek art, particularly vase painting, and had recently curated an exhibition called *"Greek and Etruscan Encounters: Contact and Change in Ancient Italy."*

Paul gives his take about performing on ships while we enjoy a lunch of *moussaka* at the Poseidon temple.

"One aspect of giving these lectures is undeniably theatrical and I'm asked back because I give good theater," he boasts.

I look forward to seeing whether he can make "*In the Realm of Dionysus: The Art of Wine and Ancient Greek Pottery,*" "*The Human Animal in Greek Art: Centaurs, Satyrs, Gorgons*" and "*The Royal Tombs of Vergina: Masterworks 'in situ'*" theatrical enough for some of the less-interested passengers.

Every lecturer has a different approach to the electric and/or eclectic crowd on the ship.

Professor McCall gives effusive, demonstrative, ear-splitting performances that frequently involve polling the audience on hot topics like "fate versus free will" or a "just universe versus unjust universe" (the crowd is almost equally split on both issues) while exploring themes like "*Sophocles: Oedipus Rex*" and "*The Heroism of Achilles*".

Seventy-something McCall claims during one cocktail chat that politically "I'm much further left than you," meaning me, after I describe myself as a fiscally conservative communist. The former chairman of the Stanford Classics Department is also smart enough not to speak to me on the record and lets his lectures do the talking.

McCall begins one lecture by alluding to a round of traditional Greek dancing on board ship the previous night and insists that the audience scream in unison "Why should I dance?" in Greek. Then he hands out Daniel Nussbaum's story of *Oedipus the King (Of The Road)* told by 154 vanity California license plates. Incidentally, my latest California vanity license plate reads MEDTREK, only because the Department of Motor Vehicles said IDIOT was unavailable.

Here are snippets of McCall's talk, captured on my new Olympus recorder:

"*The Iliad* and *The Odyssey*, which are the bibles of ancient Greek culture, are so extraordinary partly because we don't know much about their origin," McCall begins "We don't even know where Homer, the single most revered cultural hero in the history of the Greek people, was born, if he was blind or if he even existed. Though we know Virgil wrote *The Aeneid*, there's no way to know if Homer actually wrote or even dictated *The Iliad* and *The Odyssey*, which were the innovative rap music of the day and changed each time they were performed. It takes about 24 hours to recite *The Iliad*, usually at a multi-day gathering or pan-Hellenic festival. That improvisational skill was lost when printing began and the 12,000 verses of *The Iliad* and the 15,000 verses of *The Odyssey* were finally written down.

"We get stories from the likes of Sophocles and Homer transcribed by dogged, loyal, unimaginative scribes who have been told by their monastic masters to 'Don't change a thing' to the text they're copying," he continues.

At one point McCall reads Richard Lattimore's translation of the first seven verses of *The Iliad* and has his onboard audience pronounce τιμή or *timē* (teem-aya), the Greek word for "honor." Within three tries, everyone in the room is screaming *timē* as though chanting for the Stanford football team during the Rose Bowl.

"If an heroic person like Achilles is insulted or provoked he must maintain *timē*," McCall goes on. "It's very close to the way super sports stars behave in our contemporary American society. The *timē* code is to react because 'he didn't give me no respect.' The heroes of *The Iliad* live for fame, for a sense of immortality, for their sense of *moira*, or allotted destiny, that will survive after the war. It's a warrior code society."

Honor and glory are certainly themes that preoccupied Homer's characters. I recall that King Priam said in *The Iliad* that "everything done to a young man killed in war becomes his glory," while Achilles went into battle like a fierce lion, "flashed to right and left like a wild god, trampling the men he killed, and black earth ran with blood" and "brought the Trojans harrowing grief" with "his great heart bent on winning glory."

Gods and men continue to underline the importance of these two key themes in Homer's works.

"You must no longer hang back, but attack, for honor's sake, as every one of you is a first-rate soldier," Poseidon told the Akhaian soldiers when he came to arouse their spirits.

"I take my place in the front rank for action and for honor whenever battle's joined," said a very cool Meríonês.

"You perished, but your name will never die," Agamémnon consoled Achilles. "It lives to keep all men in mind of honor."

Naturally soldiers who didn't respect the code were often verbally assaulted by warriors like Achilles and Odysseus.

"You spellbinder! You sack of wind!" Odysseus said to Thersítês in *The Iliad*. "I say there is no soldier worse than you…You sicken me!"

The *Corinthian II* sets sail from Athens to Amorgos, a geographic stepping-stone and crossroads between eastern and western civilization, and we dock at 7:00 a.m. on a cloudy day in the horseshoe-shaped port of Katapola on the island where Luc Besson filmed *The Big Blue* in 1988.

Cruise director Peter Graham, who first went to sea as an entertainer and has been to Antarctica more than a hundred times, calls Amorgos "dramatically rugged." He says it's been inhabited since 3300 BC, and lists its main cities as Minoa, Arkesini, Chora and Egiali. He tells us the Cycladic population migrated inland to the mountains during the eighth-century Islamic invasions and he makes the climb up 330 cobbled steps to the 11th-century Byzantine Monastery of the Virgin Khozoviotissa sound like a slog up Everest.

Half of the 80 passengers are too scared to attempt the ascent, and a few others are so intimidated by the dress code (no shorts for men and women, no sleeveless tops) that they spend the day in Chora, the generic name given to the capital town on each of the Cyclades. Not me, though, because I know that the vertical Greek Orthodox monastery, which is 40 meters wide and 5 meters in depth, is one of the favored pilgrimage destinations in the Aegean.

It turns out to be an easy walk up to the monastery dedicated to the Virgin and I get the feeling that I'm receiving comfort from millions of present and past prayers said here. I light a candle amid crosses, chalices, icons, water bowls, and myrrh containers before softly murmuring my usual daily prayer, which I've modified a bit since it was conveyed to me decades ago by Sogyal Rinpoche who wrote *The Tibetan Book of Living and Dying.*

"By the power and truth of this practice.
May all sentient beings enjoy happiness and the causes of happiness,
May they be free from suffering and the causes of suffering,
May they find the great happiness that is devoid of suffering,
And may they dwell in the blissful equanimity that is free from anger,
aggression, anxiety, arrogance, and assholes."

As Deng Ming-Dao wrote: "When people visit a holy place, some say that the spirits of that place speak to them. Others remember the exotic pageantry. When it comes to sacred sites, it's better to be a pilgrim than a tourist. Go with a humble attitude, and let you heart be moved by what you experience. Then you receive the true treasure of the shrine."

There are only two monks here now and, though there were a hundred in the monastery's heyday, there have never been more than six during the past twenty years. We're greeted by a bearded abbot who looks the part with his *epimanikia* (cap), purple gown/skirt and black jacket as he hands out Greek/Turkish delights with *raki*, the anise-flavored spirit.

Besides the images of the icons, there are photos of past abbots/ monks and manuscripts dating from the 10th to 18th centuries with the name of the scribe who copied the codex or relative material, like priest Kallistos of Mount Galesion, who copied one in 1298.

"Each monastery has its own manner of venerating and adorning its icons," explains Stella, our Greek guide. "This monastery also influenced Bauhaus architects like Corbusier, who used the design to create a similar church in France. The ex-votos, including a watch and sunglasses, are left to indicate the sincerity of the people who have come with specific wishes that were fulfilled."

The Stanford/Harvard group has its own character, though Ellen Fox who just turned 70 claims it's full of "old geezers." Miho Kawagoe is a freelance Japanese journalist who specializes in cruises; Will Grossman has been Miho's doctor for 25 years and is traveling with his Korean wife Sonny; Francie Johnston is a art-major-turned-lawyer from Menlo Park who wears bright skirts ("If I can't wear them here, when can I wear them?"); Stephen Fay, along with his South African-born wife Prue, was a journalist for the *London Sunday Times;* and the eight members of the Osborne family from Carmel Valley all seem to be former hippies. I join Ellen Fox, and Dr. Richard Mazze and his wife Dr. Sheila Cohen for dinner and will see them again when we return to California.

Many are upset that Fox (not Ellen, but the TV) is the only channel broadcasting on the ship. Aaron Paul's friend Bonita Cobb from Saint Petersburg, Florida, admits she did some arm twisting to negotiate the price of the tour. Janet Sebenius tells me about her son's efforts to promote the Abraham Path in the Middle East and Bill Gifford's mother suggests I buy her son's book *Ledyard: In Search of the First American Explorer*. Patricia Taylor, married to Stanford grad Ronald, who started DeVry University, grabs a copy of my book from the library to devour – and, she tells me later, steal.

Aaron Paul uses slides for his onboard theatrical assignment and waxes enthusiastic about everything ceramic.

"Greek vases are windows into antiquity and produce a visual language that depicts many of the fascinating aspects of Greek life, including the social quality of the people," says Paul the Pothead. "Ancient vases and literature compliment each other, and I love the field because we've found only a tenth of one percent of what's there."

I catch a video of *Troy* starring Brad Pitt as we sail to Chios and early the next morning chat with Aaron over breakfast as the *Corinthian II* floats by Ikaria.

"Homer provided entertainment for the people and a bard often came into a town for 24 days to entertain the locals by enacting a different book from *The Iliad* or *The Odyssey*," Paul explains. "Brad Pitt's portrayal continues to embellish that iconic story, and he was a perfect Achilles. His blonde highlights and classic face form the image I've always had in mind when I picture Achilles in Troy tugging at the heartstrings of men and women as the top hero. Incidentally, *The Iliad* was the more popular of Homer's two books because people were more interested in blood and guts than in a chick flick like *The Odyssey* in which Odysseus goes back to his wife and son."

Although they didn't have Brad Pitt or feature films, Paul contends that the ancients Greeks saw heroes and warriors in action on vases.

"We can identify two warriors battling on a Greek vase as early as the eighth century BC and the representation illustrates that the common people were aware of Homer," Paul explains. "Seventh-century BC vases have inscriptions identifying the characters, and in the fifth century BC we begin to see scenes of everyday life as philosophers start to question and make fun of gods."

The most popular figures on vases were Aphroditê (the goddess of love), her sometime husband Arês (war), Hêra ("the ultimate bitch," says Paul), Dionysus (the god of the grape harvest), Zeus and Poseidon. The Muses, the satyrs, the centaurs and Athêna are minor characters on vases and, he says, "the icing on the cake." A theme frequently evoked on vases, and the most tear-jerking scene in *The Iliad*, is Priam coming to Achilles to beg for the body of his dead son Hektor.

"Vases depict heroic moments and mirror the psyche of the times," says Paul, who enjoys the study of antiquity because "it's investigative reporting, and there are many questions that will never be answered. When a distraught Achilles weeps over the body of Hektor, it's very emotional and a major statement on the futility of war."

The psyche of the times frequently included alcohol, according to Paul, and "vase painting depicts intoxication in antiquity, including people vomiting red wine."

"Many vases were containers for wine and when people ask me how the Greeks were able to drink out of the saucer-shaped *kylixes*, or cups, my frequent response is 'very carefully,'" Paul jokes.

Wine is, of course, frequently mentioned by Homer, and its virtues are debated by Hektor and his mother in *The Iliad*.

"Wine will restore a man when he is weary as you are, fighting to defend your own," insists Hecuba.

But Hektor isn't so sure.

"No, my dear mother, ladle me no wine," he replies. "You'd make my nerve go slack: I'd lose my edge."

"Incidentally," Paul concludes, as the ship nears Chios, "Dionysus, the god of wine, says that after three craters, the judicious go home. After the fourth crater anger begins. After the fifth, fisticuffs."

Squalls and bad weather change our next destination from Karpathos to Nissiros, a little-visited island in the Dodecanese archipelago, where it's rumored that there are 900 people and 44,000 pigs. I feel, like Odysseus, being blown about by Poseidon as we arrive at this contemporary version of Circe's island.

Situated between Kos and Tilos, Nissiros is a circular volcanic island that got its current shape in 1422 when a violent explosion blew the top off the 4,593-foot peak and left a huge caldera. Greece's only active volcano has several water-filled mini-craters, including the still-active Stefanos crater, and a number of sulfur-smelling hot springs. The rumor is that a giant is sleeping underneath the volcano and every time he turns there's an earthquake. People in the capital city of Mandraki don't seem too concerned.

The highlight of our visit – and we didn't see one pig – occurs when our Greek guide Ellie breaks into a refrain from Sophocles' *Electra* at the bottom of the crater amid gurgling holes emitting lots of steam.

"The passage says 'O light of the sky and you wind that covers the whole earth, how many times you've heard me crying and shouting at the crack of dawn,'" Ellie explains after the eight of us who followed her to the bottom of the crater applaud.

The rim village of Nikia, with brightly painted houses and *choklakia* pebble mosaics, has a tiny volcanology museum. But I'm content to light a candle at the church, admire the local priest sitting in the main square, and grab views of the volcano below from different angles. Lots of the men in the city, who left after one of the many earthquakes, have returned from sojourns in the U.S. and speak excellent English. One, wearing a New York Mets cap, laments that his home team is having a bad season.

Greeks from islands in the Aegean can never resist dropping an historical tidbit into the conversation. Some mention, for example, that ships from their island were sent to the Trojan War. And, indeed, in Book Two of *The Iliad* numerous islands are listed when Homer writes "Let me name only captains of contingents and number all the ships." It turns out, because of Homer's attention to detail, that almost every man has an island.

There's something alluring about almost every Aegean island.

It's not difficult to MedTrek around tiny and barren Delos, the ruins-filled birthplace of Apollo and Artemis and a sacred site to ancient Greeks, because its area is less than five square kilometers.

I go ashore at Kos because a doctor friend in Paris wants a photograph of the site where Hippocrates, the father of modern medicine, was born around 460 BC. My friend will be discussing the Hippocratic Oath with politicos in Washington, DC, and wants to show his audience a contemporary shot of the Asklepieion.

Fortunately the ancient healing temple sacred to the god Asklepius is just a few kilometers from the port and I enthusiastically MedTrek there, bound up the many steps to the upper terrace and take photographs of what Hippocrates would see today.

Continuing on the little-traveled road up Dikaios Mountain to the tourist-and-shop-filled town of Zia, I enjoy a strong coffee at the Oromedon Taverna, owned by a Greek who lived in New York for 11 years. Before leaving the island, I spend a leisurely morning in Kos town and get some shots of the Hippocratic oath being sold in various languages.

We stop at Rhodes, the largest island in the Dodecanese archipelago, where my visit involves a diving board and a peacock.

Said to have the best climate in the Mediterranean, the "island of roses," as it's called, features an animated old town and coasts over-populated with swank hotels. It was a leading maritime power more than 2,300 years ago and a bastion of Christianity from 1306 to 1522. The Knights of Saint John of Jerusalem ran the place and constructed an array of enticing and enchanting Provençal Gothic-style citadels, fortresses and churches. Almost everyone who comes here wonders if they might have time travelled to Avignon, France, by mistake.

The Colossus, the gigantic circa-300 BC statue that once symbolized the island's power, is no longer at the entrance of the Mandraki port, but there are more recent remnants of the Turks, Italians, and Greeks who controlled Rhodes after the Knights were ousted by Suleimaniye the Magnificent.

The diving board I mentioned? Fortunately the Italians, who ran Rhodes from 1911-43, left behind a permanent in-the-sea diving platform that, trust me, is a one-of-a-kind marvel on the Med.

And the peacocks? I don't climb the Filerimos Mountain just to check out the ancient temple of Athêna Polias next to the Monastery of Our Lady on the top of the hill. A friend back in Boulder, Colorado, told me to say hello to the peacocks that have taken over the area.

I learn from a concessionaire that the peacocks have only been on Mount Filerimos for a decade.

"A guy drove up and asked me and my wife if he could leave a peacock and a peahen in the park," he recalls. "We had nothing to do with it and told him we didn't see why not. Now there are hundreds and they drive us crazy."

Having attained those two goals, I return to the Mandraki port to visit the medieval section of Rhodes and explore the citadel, the Palace of the Grand Masters, colorful courtyards, cobblestone streets, a gigantic moat, and an eerie eye drawn on a tree trunk.

When I later MedTrek the northwest and northeast coastlines of Rhodes during a three-day stopover, the over-riding impression I gain –

from the cruise ships in the harbor to the hotels on much of the coast – is of the elaborate tourism infrastructure. Although there are some rustic touches, Sheratonization is the most memorable aspect. Hotels with names like Eden Roc, Paradiso and Illusion with multiple pools and dance/game animators are a pan-Rhodes thing.

Of course, Sheratonization does have some benefits. It's now much easier to walk on the sand on many beaches.

The next stop is Symi, about 45 kilometers north of Rhodes. The harbor, considered one of the most alluring in Greece, features an 1884 clock tower and, not far past it, the Bay of Nos beach. I climb 375 steps to the neoclassical mansions at the top of the hillside and imagine Symi after it attained its greatest prominence under the Ottoman Empire, when shipbuilding and sponge diving made it more affluent than Rhodes. A plaque at the *Restaurant les Katerinettes* commemorates the signing of the official surrender of the Dodecanese island to Allied forces on May 8, 1945.

But I'm especially intrigued because Symi gave birth to one of Poseidon's sons and this son named the island after her. The island is also said to be the birthplace of the three Graces and home to King Nireus who, next to Achilles, is considered "the most beautiful man who came beneath Ilion."

Whoever thought that obviously hadn't seen Brad Pitt in *Troy*.

Finding Homer on Chios

"You'll know more about Homer than any mortal
walking the Mediterranean." – *Circe*.

Enough boating about. It's time to undertake Circe's sixth task. When the *Corinthian II* arrives at the island of Chios I'm anxious to "sit on Homer's Rock before finding his actual birthplace."

First, though, I join the Stanford and Harvard alumni groups on a tour of the Greek Orthodox monastery of *Nea Moni* (New Monastery). The stunning monastery, founded in 1042 by Emperor Constantine IX Moonachie, is about ten kilometers from Chios Town. It's built on the spot where three hermits found an icon of the Virgin hidden in a wooded vale and, though I'm not quite sure of their minute-by-minute thought process, they predicted that Constantine would accede to the throne.

Still surrounded by a fortress wall, *Nea Moni* is considered one of the most important and most ornate ecclesiastical buildings in Greece. Restored in the 1980s, it now houses only one very old nun and the skeletons and bones of some of the thousands killed here in 1822 in retribution for a rebellion against the Turkish rulers. The chapel is still used for weekly services, but the buzz is that when the nun is no more, the monastery will become a refuge for monks.

My erstwhile shipmates also visit the sprawling Argentikon Estate, an old mansion with wonderfully maintained gardens that's become a boutique hotel in Kambos on the plain south of town. Built as a summer residence by the Argenti family in the 16th century, this prime example of medieval Genovese architecture is now, says a brochure, a "gracious estate for the distinguished and most demanding clientele" who pay more than €2,000 a night for a five-room suite.

I learn three surprising things about Chios from our guides before I abandon my ship and shipmates.

1. Chios – which has been severely impacted by wars, massacres, refugees, and an 1881 earthquake – prospered not only from shipping but also, since medieval times, from wealth generated by the trade in mastic gum and resin.

2. Christopher Columbus was in Chios for 18 months in 1472 and, by the time he left, was able to sign his name in Greek.

3. The Dutch ambassador to Chios saw lalades, or wild tulips, here and encouraged their introduction to Holland in the 1500s.

Who knew?

More importantly, despite serious challenges from the nearby city of İzmir in Turkey, Chios has a serious claim as Homer's possible eighth-century BC birthplace. Initially settled during the Neolithic period, the island was colonized by Ionians from Asia Minor and the port became a convenient place for ships to stop en route to Thessaloniki, Crete, Rhodes, Cyprus and what was Constantinople until 1453 when it fell to the Turks and became Istanbul. A series of the island's rulers – which included Venetians, Genoese, and Turks – constructed long protective breakwaters that make it an easy place for modern ships like the *Corinthian II* to dock.

As I look out the window of my €30 per night room at the port-side Amalia hotel onto the Turkish coast five miles away, I decide not to waste any time. My first objective while MedTrekking around Chios is to quietly sit and meditate on Homer's Stone, known as the *Daskalopetra* or "Rock of the Teacher," near the seaside town of Vrontados. Then I'll pursue leads to different places where Homer might have been born on this wildly beautiful volcanic island known for luscious green valleys concealed amidst dramatic rocky crags.

Cruising on a luxurious ship with the constant attention of a staff from the Philippines was an intriguing break from my usual rough-and-roll traveling style. But after five nights, countless meals, group tours and interesting lectures, I'm admittedly looking forward to downshifting into MedTrekking mode. I'm so itching to go the next morning that I awaken when it's still dark. There's a delightfully cool breeze at 6:00 a.m. as I sit on my tiny terrace and meditate while trying not to focus on the flashing green-and-red beacons in the port or, beyond them, the lights on the shores of Turkey.

I have a coffee at a nearby café (well not coffee really, but Nescafé, which is the preferred morning beverage of many more Greeks than you'd ever imagine) before marching off at the break of daylight under overcast skies.

Incidentally, Greece has got to be one of the biggest markets for Nescafé in the world, and a foam-topped *frappé* made with Nescafé is the iced drink of choice here. Greece is also one of the most expensive places in Europe to drink coffee. Not because of the economy, taxes or the price of coffee beans but because the Greeks sit for hours nursing a single cup of coffee and cafés factor the sit-down time into the charge.

"Italians gulp coffee down and get on with the day but Greeks can nurse a cup of coffee for a week, and this social aspect of having a coffee explains our high prices," says Peter Argyris, the South African owner of the Dodoni café in Ithaka, who charges €1 for a standard Greek coffee. "The fact that nobody buys a second cup but keeps their seat for hours, makes prices high for regular coffee drinkers like you. And Nescafé is laughing all the way to the bank."

I'm not a Nescafé or *frappé* kinda guy and prefer to wake up brewing my own rich coffee instead of paying the highest prices in Europe to have the right to stay in the café all day and chat with my pals without getting a second cup.

Unlike in France, Spain and Italy, where I can talk my way around town and out of trouble, I have just a few Greek words at my command, including *Kalimera* (good day), *Yasou* or *Yasas* (hello), *Parakalo* (please), *Endaxi* (okay), *Efharisto poli* (thank you very much), *Kalispera* (good evening) and *Kalinikta* (good night). That's enough to get me as much morning coffee as I need and a warm spinach-filled roll while I watch television news that, except for the occasional foreign item, is really all Greek to me. As I head north along the port, I learn that it's not only the Greek language that will confuse me here. The word **SEVERIOUSLY** is written near the entrance to the port to warn people about the danger of trespassing.

I don't bother testing the veracity of the sign but remind myself that one advantage of not speaking or reading Greek is that I can pretend not to understand when I'm told not to trespass – and give a positive and innocent thumbs up if confronted.

I meander through the back streets of Chios Town, noticing that there are more parrots and parakeets kept on the front terraces here than in any other European city, and stroll through a cemetery with inordinately narrow and tall tombstones in a neighborhood that's seen better days (in fact, it once had Greek, Turkish, and Jewish mansions). I manage to get boxed in when I walk along high medieval ramparts that presumably survived the 1881 earthquake and, for a MedTrekker, are as impenetrable and solid as when they were initially built by the Genoese rulers in the 14th century. I'm forced to BackTrek and sense that I've finally reached the outskirts of town when I see three windmills that would make any Dutchman proud, though all they inspire me to do is come up with the refrain that "the answer my friend is not blowing in the windmill."

I walk intently and purposefully along the beach – presuming that the dramatic, craggy volcanic mountains that dominate the island are probably responsible for the pebbly seacoast – because I can't wait to reach Homer's Stone. When I arrive, after a nine-kilometer walk, I approach it with the reverence of a pantheistic pilgrim simultaneously reaching Mecca, Jerusalem and Rome.

Homer's Stone is a sight to behold and revere. A large slab of stone with a protruding hump that, I like to think, Homer either stood or sat upon as he addressed a crowd of admirers and poetry-writing buddies with the goat-filled, stark and steep mountainside as backdrop.

As the only visitor, I sit quietly on the top of the stone, in a Tim Tebow position, and, recalling that Kathryn Hohlwein led a *Readers of Homer* performance here, dramatically utter a few refrains from Homer's *Iliad* and *Odyssey*. "Friends," I shout as if I'm Aías during the Trojan War, "respect yourselves as men, respect each other in the moil of battle! Men with a sense of shame survive more often than they perish. Those who run have neither fighting power nor any honor."

After an hour, just before leaving, I say a prayer for all deceased actors and adventurers, like Patrick Swayze. I'd spent a few days with Swayze when he was emceeing the World Music Awards in Monaco in 1994 and was impressed with his adventurer get-go willingness to try everything, from piloting a high-speed boat in the Monaco harbor to jumping on a horse almost every day with his wife Lisa Nieme. Why am I thinking of him today? Because he too should have been cast in *Troy*.

I also reflect on the fact that today is my daughter Sonia's 27th birthday and feel at peace as I hear the sound of the stone's silence and history. I'm content just to be sitting here and am reminded of what Thich Nhat Hanh felt when he visited the mountain where the Buddha taught and wrote: "I walked on the same paths he did. I stood on the earth where he stood. I sat on the same boulder he sat on. Watching the brilliant red sunset, I knew the Buddha and I were watching the sun at the same time." Ahh omm.

As I leave, I whisper *efharisto poli* to Homer for giving us epics that have inspired my own odyssey and impacted western civilization. I'm ready to take Thich Nhat Hanh's suggestion that to continue to have peace, I can begin by walking peacefully. "Everything depends on your steps."

Not everyone agrees that Homer was born on Chios or used Homer's Stone as a podium. "But that's the legend, and I'm not going to contradict it," says a man setting up a sound system in the adjacent parking lot as I leave the site.

A bit later in the day I encounter an Athens environmental worker and tell him I find Greece to be one of the most conscientious battery recyclers in the world, that even in Chios there are containers for used batteries on almost every street corner. Then I ask him about Homer's Stone and the environmentalist, who was educated in Edinburgh, adds his two cents: "It's really not Homer's Stone, though it was dedicated to a goddess (Hêra's mother Rhea, he thinks), but they call it that just for the sake of the legend. And Greeks love their legends."

So do I.

After getting rocked by Homer's Stone I continue along the seaside, occasionally walking on the road because of the inaccessibility of the steep and rocky coast. I frequently glance at the Turkish mainland until I reach the monastery of *Panagia Myrtidiotissa*. Naturally all I can see when I look at the sign is one part of the word – *idiot* – and wonder if the Orthodox Greek Church is trying to tell me something.

I pass the village of Isidoros, where, despite plentiful graffiti scrawled on every street sign that makes them nearly impossible to read, the town's name gets me thinking of Isadora Duncan and her horrible death in Nice in 1927. Isadora was a passenger in an Amilcar, and her long flowing silk scarf, draped around her neck, became tangled around the open-spoked wheels and rear axle, breaking her neck and killing her instantly.

When I reach Lagkada, which has a number of fish farms just off the coast, I take a picture of a "Photographs are Prohibited" sign written in Greek and English. I have a simple *moussaka* lunch at a port-side café before continuing out of town on a path into the mountains where I serendipitously stumble upon the most important find of the entire MedTrek. I'll tell you about this discovery in a while.

The steep road heading north is punctuated by a few flat spots where, ever conscious of the necessity of upper bodywork while MedTrekking, I briefly stop to do planks and pushups above the sparkling blue sea.

One of the pleasantly surprising things about Chios, I learn on my first day off the ship, is that a number of people, even including a mother/daughter team, casually stop and ask me if I'd like a ride. Hospitality is a key theme in *The Odyssey* and I notice, or imagine anyway, a genetic willingness to welcome a stranger that, I think, is perhaps proof that this was indeed Homer's island.

Naturally I refuse all the offers of rides while MedTrekking and end the day in Nagos by climbing up the steep stone steps from the beach to a Greek Orthodox church at the tip of a promontory. As I approach the chapel, a group of young soldiers emerge from their military post. Once they accept my explanation that I'm not a Turkish terrorist intending to put their radar system out of action, they're intrigued by my contention that "Circe sent me here to chase the scent of Homer." I don't think they'd heard that one before.

One soldier, a very handsome 31-year-old from Athens, speaks excellent English and explains that he's doing his military service after an education and career in the United Kingdom. I quote Agamémnon in *The Iliad*, who counsels that even royalty "must do service, too. That is the way the Lord Zeus burdened us when we were born." The soldier seems bemused.

As the SPOT beams my location to friends and family, we discuss the Turkish threat (or lack of it) to Greece, U.S. military forays in Iraq/Afghanistan, how well-equipped U.S. soldiers are compared to Greeks (my soldier friend insists that U.S. soldiers get three pairs of well-made boots while Greek soldiers only get one pair of mediocre quality), the weather in England versus Greece (no contest), and the lack of a path around northern Chios.

He refills my canteen with water from a spring, takes me on a tour of the church, and says "I hope I look like you and hike like you when I'm in my 60s."

I hitch a few kilometers back to town with a Greek shepherd and then get a long ride with a Dutch couple who are not convinced that Chios is the origin of their country's fascination with tulips.

That night I have a chat with Manolis Psoras, the nephew of the owner of the Amalia Hotel, about how Greek boys learn to work the omnipresent worry beads carried by every Greek man. Manolis says most boys start carrying beads at 15 and describes the various types and means of caressing, fingering, and manipulating them. He gives me a set and demonstrates some moves that stump my clumsy fingers when I attempt to duplicate them.

Somewhat comforted by a Hellenic Coast Guard ship docked below my window, I go to bed with *Middlesex*, the Pulitzer Prize-winning novel by Jeffrey Eugenides that depicts the journey of one Greek family to America.

I mention the handsome army officer to a 24-year-old travel agent named Elena when I book a ferry to Lesbos, where I've got a date with Sappho, urging her to get out there quick. But a few days later, when I pick up the ticket, she says "couldn't you just give me his telephone number and email?"

What happened to romance?

I discover a reason to head south the next morning while enjoying a lamb dinner at an outside table on the port.

It's Mast, a refreshing sparkling Greek elixir made from *mastica*, the natural resin of *pistacia lentiscus*, or the Chia, a lentisk tree found only in the southern part of Chios, where there are 1.5 million trees and fortified villages are called *mastichóhora*. *Mastica* is not only used in this invigorating beverage but also in pharmaceuticals, perfumes, cosmetics, bakery goods, and sweets, as well as for cooking and caulking (the buzz is that Christopher Columbus realized the importance of mastic for ship repair when he was here). The resin is the root of our word "masticate" and the trees, which live up to 200 years and grow to a height of about two meters, produce income for 2,000 farmers. Indeed, income from mastic products sold at numerous shops in Chios Town is the economic backbone of this bustling, cosmopolitan metropolis with 65,000 inhabitants.

I walk south of Chios Town along the sea, past an up-market hotel called The Graecian Castle, and alongside the airport into a supermarket where I buy bread, cheese, bananas, and another two cans of Mast for lunch.

Southern Chios appears to be more affluent than the north, and I regularly see signs for tourist resorts like the Sea View Village and Sun Village. I pass the local electric power plant and, on the hilltop across from it, in true MedTrek yin/yang style, a monastery. A left turn to Karmas keeps me along the sea for twenty-something kilometers, and as I walk, I study a page with the Greek alphabet that I'm attempting to learn.

First, I try to match the letters with my vague recollection of the names of college fraternities. I know the Greek letters for Phi Kappa Sigma – ΦΚΣ – because I pledged it for two days while at Stanford. But there was such an uproar about the discriminatory selection process used by fraternities that I withdrew and boycotted any further relationship with the Greek alphabet until now, though I do remember that I used to make jokes about Sigma Phi Nothing (ΣΦ0). I try to make sense of words that I see on the road but the only one that is clearly identifiable is

EYPΩ, or EURO.

Today learning Greek is not the only thing on my mind. The island is speckled with dozens of restored Eastern Orthodox churches and scores of miniature church replicas on the roadside that look like colorful dollhouses. The tiny chapelettes, some built to commemorate the site of a fatal accident, have little windows and little doors that open and are decorated inside with little candles, little matches and little icons. Forget the Greek alphabet. I spend the next few hours on my way through little villages like Megas Liminoas making up stories – about horrid automobile accidents or religious revelations – behind each miniature chapel.

During the afternoon I see enough mastic bushes to believe that there really could be 1.5 million of the resin-producing lentisk trees. I'm so intrigued by the omnipresent verdant plant that I constantly nibble, smell, rub, bite, and chew the sticky leaves. Some hunters, dressed in bright red shirts, are baffled when I try to explain my mastic-fascination, or mastication, even though I show them an empty can of Mast to try to get the point across.

When I return to Chios Town that evening I beeline to the Mastic Spa, where everything on sale contains mastic. A sign claims "mastic is a legendary and mysterious elixir which seeps from the mastic tree, known since antiquity for its medicinal properties and therapeutic benefits for the skin." A blurb on a pack of mastic chewing gum calls it "a unique product with many beneficial qualities and wide-ranging uses since antiquity." A brochure contends that "scientific research shows that Chios Mastica has anti-microbial, anti-inflammatory, and healing activity. It contributes to a healthy gastrointestinal system and has beneficial effects for both oral hygiene and skin care."

Combine that with a little MedTrekking, some meditation, and exposure to the gods and I'm home free.

During my stay in Chios I meet enough people who swear by the health-provoking effects of mastic, which has gradually gotten a fairly decent reputation in other parts of Greece and a few foreign cities, that I think this could be more than a commercial stunt. I take a photo of a Mast can cuddled in a real mastic bush in case I decide to market it in the U.S. This, I figure, could be the next Vitamin C.

Naturally I tell everyone I meet about my positive reaction to Mast, which reminds me of the taste of pine resin that I occasionally used to chew as a kid.

Hitching back to Chios Town, I get picked up by two different shipping engineers – one on a tanker, one on a large cruise ship, both unmarried and chillin' in Chios between lucrative contracts – and try to convince them that they can make more money marketing Mast than they can working on ships. That's a tough argument because they make enough after a few months on a ship to live work-free for the rest of the year. They both encourage me to go for the big bucks.

The walk along the beach, and through little villages like Anakoin, where the main courses at restaurants go for about €5, is very rocky, cliffy, and hot. More than once the mastic bushes help me along the way because of the spider web of paths that lead to masses of mastic groves planted on every arable square inch of southern Chios. Marvelous mastic has come to the miraculous aid of meandering MedTrekkers.

After passing through Esconia, I notice a gorgeous stone house on the edge of town, with an isolated view of the sea, that, I say to myself, I could actually live in. It even has its own water treatment plant. But when I stroll on the shore below a sign says "No Swimming In This Area" that tarnishes my fascination with the place. Or is this a fabrication by the homeowners to keep people like me away?

I continue, more slowly than usual, for hours of pebbly, rocky, and stumbly beach slogging and am relieved when a fisherman tells me that it's only *dekha,* or ten, kilometers to my destination. When I arrive in Komi, I'm on a sandy, lifeguarded, and restaurant-filled seaside, and, after my 35-kilometer hike through mastic country, I strip and plunge into the clear and refreshing seawater to stretch my muscles.

I spend the night a bit inland in Pyrgi where I investigate and admire the well-known painted geometric designs, produced using a technique known as *xista* or *skalistra,* that adorn almost every house in town.

My Most Important MedTrek Discovery

The next morning I hitch a ride on a tractor back to Komi and, well rested, am ready to sprint around the southern coast of Chios with the speed and fluidity of a fleet-footed Hermês. Just after Emporio I energetically walk on a fabled black-and-grey-pebbled beach, known as Mavros Gialos, where "camping and nudism are prohibited." Four very energetic stray dogs trot along with me, first on the sand and then as I climb on sharp rocks and boulders, up a hill that, after nine kilometers, leads to a trail down to the bottom of a long ravine and on to one of the most pacific and perfect bays I've encountered on the MedTrek.

It's so peaceful, and I'm so tired after three 35-kilometer days in a row, that I go horizontal on the pebbles with my feet uphill, let the warm rocks soak into my back and hamstring muscles, and fall into a deep sleep for twenty minutes. The turquoise water is so clear that the distant bottom looks magnified when I go for a quick skinny dip on my *beach du jour.*

Then my day hits a wall. Although there are mastic groves, and although there are trails to the mastic groves, there's no uniform trail up and down the scrubby difficult-to-negotiate rock-and-shrub-covered hills. The views are spectacular, but I can't get anywhere without shrubs slicing my legs and rocks slicing my shoes to shreds. I accidentally leave my tape recorder on when I trudge up one hill and when I play the segment I hear myself huffing, puffing and blowing like the three little pigs in unison. Realizing, gulp, that I'll soon run out of water, I stoically attempt to forget my thirst and admire the medieval defense towers, or what's left of them; the gorgeous bays that pop out around every corner; and the intriguing rock formations.

It's soon apparent that there aren't any other hikers out here because of the challenging terrain. The one farmer who has a menagerie – including roosters, goats, dogs, and a jackass – in the middle of nowhere is nowhere to be found and the only signs of other humans are shotgun shell casings left on the ground by hunters. There's no running water that I can find.

I finally emerge – bloody, exhausted, dehydrated, and sweaty – from the bush onto a one-lane paved road and try to flag down the only car that comes by. This gesture generally produces results here because of the Chivalrous and Courteous Civil Code of Chios that encourages local drivers to stop for obviously stranded MedTrekkers. (Chios is pronounced Hios, without a C, but I won't let that bother my alliteration). Unfortunately this approaching vehicle is a rental car containing tourists who look at me like I'm Jack the Stripper.

My main worry now, though, is water. I have none. During the next 75-minutes I check out not only every plastic container on the roadside (Note to self: no one, on Chios anyway, throws away half-empty plastic water bottles), but also stop at a little church and check every nook and cranny for holy water before I recite my usual prayer asking for happiness for all sentient beings – and a drop of water or two.

I recall how the Greeks frequently prayed during the Trojan War.

Lord Nestor, for example, "stretching his hands out to the sky of stars" prayed: "Father Zeus, if someone long ago in Argos of the grain fields offered up fat haunches of a cow or sheep in fire and begged you for a safe return from Troy, winning your promise and your nod, remember now, Olympian! Defend us against this pitiless day! Do not allow Akhaians to be crushed this way by Trojans!"

Achilles "made offering to no god but Zeus" and "looking up toward heaven, he prayed and poured his offering out, and Zeus who played in thunder heard his prayer."

Even skeptics show respect for religion, and perhaps even a

particular deity, when they run out of water. Right now, I certainly admire the pantheon of Greek gods as I recall how they helped or harmed Odysseus and other participants in *The Iliad* and *The Odyssey*. I figure that, whatever the god or situation, if I live a good life, do no harm, and behave correctly, I'll be able to get through most incidents without skirmishing. The gods, or God, may or may not play a role, but it's smart to play it safe, especially when I'm thirsty.

I reach the main road at 3:00 p.m. and my water prayers are answered when a car comes by and the driver, a mason from Albania, picks me up. He understands my parched whimper and stops for water at the first opportunity. I buy him a Mast and nod enthusiastically, saying "*Ne, ne*" ("Yes, yes" in Greek), every time he says "America good... Liberty good...Democracy good....Albania good."

A few days later I'm enjoying the relatively easy 35-kilometer walk up the west coast of Chios that, in terms of sights and ease, is the best stretch of trail-and-road seaside walking on the island.

The first six kilometers out of Limenas, a port that is being vastly expanded by ongoing construction, is on a road that veers inland to curve around the coastal mountains to Lithi. After I pass my first of many medieval towers of the day, I speak to the Greek wife of an Australian restaurant owner (the menu is in impeccable English) in the village of Irinia. She tells me not to follow the road inland and points to a dirt path on the seaside.

"My husband rides his motorcycle to the Lithi market on that every day," she says. "It goes right along the sea and you probably won't see a soul."

She's right. The path is a hiker's delight, and when I enter Lithi, a hillside village painted completely white, I've shaved five kilometers off the 20-kilometer road distance. This encourages me to celebrate with an ice cream bar at one of the three outdoor restaurants on the town's tiny port. Then I scramble up a bramble-filled hillside and let the watchtowers point the way on a narrow and curvy road for the next 20 kilometers. There are delectable swimming bays, like Elinta, with translucent, turquoise water around almost every curve, and pine forests have replaced the mastic trees.

It isn't my intention, the next day, to walk 35 kilometers across the entire island of Chios to visit Volissos and Pityous, two towns on the west coast that each claim to be Homer's birthplace. But I do. Although the Michelin Green guide tends to favor Volissos, I approach the duality issue with a completely neutral perspective.

After leaving Chios Town, I hike up and across the steep, stark, arid, austere, and uninhabited interior towards the two villages. It's a beautiful and serene trek, and I realize that the island's rugged interior must have influenced Homer as much as the surrounding sea.

There are very few cars on the main road, which winds uphill beyond Chios Town in a steep serpentine switchback fashion, and I see only goats, splendid views, and an occasional hillside village along the way. When I reach one plateau, after about ten kilometers, there are lots of cypress trees, a soccer field, and an outstanding six-lane swimming pool in the Aepos complex. The wide top of the mountain resembles a lunar-like rockscape.

For some reason I think of Helen, the Greek housekeeper in my Junipero dormitory during my freshmen year at Stanford. We took a collection and flew her back to Athens for a visit as a Christmas present. Then my thoughts randomly turn to my half-Greek artist friend Elisa Brainos, who had 26 pairs of tennis shoes when we met in 1984 and supplied me with signed pieces of her Grecoesque artwork.

I dip into one valley and see the sign for Pityous, a contender for the birthplace of Homer, that is four kilometers north of the main Chios-Volissos road, although there's no billboard proclaiming "Come Visit Homer's Birthplace." I munch on delicious blackberries, mulberries, and grapes while admiring rock terraces with lots of olive trees and buzzing beehives as I walk slightly uphill towards Pityous (the name is derived from the word for "pine" or "pine-covered").

Just before I enter the village, I can see the sea to the north and imagine that a village at this elevation might please the gods if they had anything to do with Homer's birth.

Pityous is pastoral and bucolic, though when I visit a finely restored medieval tower and Byzantine church I learn that "there is no evidence that the present village of Pityous was inhabited in ancient times, but there were some settlements scattered around it."

This piteous description, presumably written with the approval of the city fathers, is not a good sign for Homerphiles, because any town worth its municipal taxes would, I think, tout itself as the bard's birthplace. The village baker, who once lived in Indiana and insists on giving me some warm bread, jokes "I'm not going to be the one to deny that Homer was born here."

Then I have a coffee with a 64-year-old seaman, who spent three years in Australia and six in Canada. He tells me "No one is really insisting that Homer was born here, but we tend to all agree that he lived and taught here for a while as a fugitive after something nasty occurred at Homer's Stone."

Well, that's a nice twist and illustrates that, wherever he was born, everyone wants a piece of Homer.

Continuing the ascent and descent to Volissos I'm pleasantly waylaid for an hour in the one-restaurant hillside town of Katavasi, where I have a delicious and filling goat, chicken, and lettuce lunch with two 1.5-liter bottles of water. I should, of course, have had just the goat or just the chicken but the fat Greek cook – who says he once worked at the Waldorf Astoria in New York – entices me to order both dishes for what he claims is a remarkable "locals-only" price of €15.

I hoof it another nine kilometers to Volissos and near the entrance to town see a handsome horse, the first and only horse I've seen on the island. I'm reminded that Homer has Telémakhos tell Nestor – whom Homer calls "the Pylians' orator, eloquent and clear" – that Ithaka is not an island for horses. Nor, apparently, is Chios.

You'd think there would be a one-upmanship competition between Volissos and Pityous concerning which town is the true birthplace of Homer and that they would try to outdo each other with gimmicky names/places/light shows/promotions to attract tourists. But I'm pleasantly disappointed. Not only because this gives additional credibility to my earlier discovery of Homer's real birthplace, but also because I'm tired of seeing all of the Homeric names and references dotting virtually every beach on the Mediterranean, where there's often an unabashed exploitation of every Greek god and Homeric hero at every corner.

I find it refreshing that there are no signs or bright lights here proclaiming that Volissos is "Homer's Birthplace." In addition, there are no restaurants named after Zeus, Poseidon, or Athêna, and the only visual reminder I have of Homer is an amphora at the entrance to a private home decorated with a battle scene from *The Iliad* with warriors "lunging like wolves." Presumably people come here because of a Juji Bar, a Neukadia Beach Bar, and a Taverna Zincos tucked amid olive groves, fig trees, and fields of watermelons.

There is, however, some joking about Homer being born here.

"That's his house!" smiles the local shopkeeper in the main *agora*, vaguely pointing towards the medieval hilltop with a great view of the southern part of the island.

"You walked all that way looking for Homer? That would be a great place for a Homer museum!" laughed a German woman as she pointed to one of the many empty shops.

The only promotional effort for anything in Volissos is for a hiking path to a water mill that is billed as "an old road that permits the communication between the nine water mills in the valley" and a bust of a local official, who lived from 1906 to 1996, in the *agora*.

How could you expect Homer to compete with that?

So where was Homer born?

The most important discovery of my entire MedTrek occurred a few days ago in a remote olive-and-fruit-tree-filled valley that resembles a Garden of Eden on this rocky island. I'm convinced I've found the remains of a fieldstone house that, despite numerous modernizations during the past 2,600 years, is where Homer was born.

Why am I sure this is the right place? Primarily because there's an uncanny resemblance between my Chios find and Homer's description of the swineherd Eumaios' cabin on Ithaka. The setting of my discovery eerily resembles the passage in which Odysseus was brought to the swineherd's door in a remote clearing "from the cove through wooded ground, taking a stony trail into the high hills." Besides the site itself, I'm convinced that Homer used details of his birthplace when he described Eumaios' "fieldstone hut timbered with wild pear wood" in *The Odyssey.*

I'll invite some archeologist friends to confirm my suspicions that this is Homer's birthplace. Watch this space.

♀

Liberating Lesbos and Lemnos

"Remembering her solely as a lesbian icon reveals only one aspect of her multifaceted personality." – Nancy Freedman, author of *Sappho: The Tenth Muse*

"The Olympian (Zeus) is difficult to oppose." – Hêphaistos in *The Iliad*

I take a snapshot (what a lovely, passé noun that is) of Chios as it fades in the ferry's wake and realize, from this perspective, how large the island – with 1.5 million mastic trees and at least three possible Homeric birthplaces – actually is. Then, as I catch sight of Lesbos, the third largest island in Greece after Crete and Euboea, I realize how comparatively small Chios is. Perspective, perspective.

I'm glad that Circe didn't request that I MedTrek around the entire 320-kilometer circumference of Lesbos because it looks, with the exception of some coastal villages, like one massive mound of rocky, bouldery, scrub and shrub. In many places, as I survey the shore with binoculars from the bow of the ferry, I can't make out any paths, tracks, or roads. In addition, I smashed my big toe while negotiating a staircase on the ferry (Memo to self: don't wear sandals on a 4:00 a.m. ferry) and it is now a bloody pulp that resembles a nearly decapitated over-ripe strawberry. I'm not sure how much I'll be able to walk with hiking shoes, or even if I can fit the swollen appendage into a shoe at all.

Fortunately I'm here, again at Circe's behest, simply to seek out the poetess Sappho ("You may not choose to sleep with me, Kalypso, Sappho, or even Nausikaa but you must meet them all...") who was born in the town of Eressos, which has been the site of an all-female get together during the past fortnight.

This visit is also part of Circe's sixth task to "island hop to Lesbos, Lemnos, Ithaka and Corfu to encounter many of the characters and places mentioned by Homer." I may also climb the local 1,000-meter high Mt. Olympus (it's not the one associated with the gods), enter the island's celebrated petrified forest, visit a distillery to study production of the most highly touted *ouzo* in Greece and dip into one or two of the numerous spas and thermal baths.

As the ferry enters the port of Mytilene on the island's Turkey-facing east coast, I recall that Meneláos and Nestor landed in Lesbos on their comparatively uneventful return home from the Trojan War to the Peloponnese. And that Odysseus was once, according to *The Odyssey*, in a wrestling match with Philomeleides here and easily smashed the island's champion.

Lesbos is named after the patron god of the island and, just FYI, its 90,000 inhabitants are not called Lesbians. However, the origin and meaning of the word "lesbian" derives from Sappho's free-spirited presence here, and her poems that contain emotionally powerful content aimed at women are generally interpreted as an expression of homosexual love.

As we dock in Mytilene in mid-morning, I see a statue just below the *kastro*, or fortress, on a promontory looking over the harbor and initially presume it must be Sappho. But I'm wrong. The Statue of Liberty-like creation, while perhaps an apt expression of Sappho's liberating philosophy, is a bronze imitation of Eiffel's statue on Liberty Island sculpted by Georgios Iakovidis and dedicated to the heroes of the 1912-1913 Balkan War. I'm glad that, when I saw it, I didn't scream "Hey, look at that statue of Sappho!" to everyone on the ferry. That gaff would certainly have amused one of my New York blog readers with the online tag "Ferry Godmother."

I limp into the Sappho (the Greeks pronounce it Sap-PHO not SAF-fo) Hotel (who could stay anywhere else?) on the port just after a gay French couple take the keys to the last room with a sea view. I silently settle for a room with a mountain view, though the seaside is visible if I contort myself with a fully craned neck around the corner of the building. I need a place, any place, to clean, bandage, and ice my sliced toe and give it a day off.

I relax during the afternoon and review online maps of Lesbos during a dinner spent watching Greece beat Slovenia in a European basketball tournament. A post from "Ferry Godmother" expresses hope that "you find a true Lesbian to trek with you on your Sapphonic mystery tour." She quotes two phrases from Sappho – "I begin with words of air, yet they are good to hear..." and "In gold sandals dawn like a thief fell upon me" – to inspire me.

Sappho, one of the great Greek lyrists and the best-known female lyricist of the ancient world, was so distinguished that Plato later called her "the tenth muse." Born here in the late seventh century BC, when the island was considered an Aegean cultural center, aristocratic Sappho married a wealthy merchant with whom she may have had a daughter named Cleis. She studied the arts, wrote poetry in the Aeolic dialect, and traveled extensively throughout Greece while running a school for girls, which she called a *moisopolon domos*, devoted to the praise of the Muses.

Sappho was in the *avant-garde* of a wave of Greek poets who wrote about love – and loss – from a personal, sensual, rhythmic and homoerotic perspective. Her lyric poetry was often performed to the accompaniment of a lyre, and she gradually developed her own unique meter. Her poems of sensuous adoration, most of which were later destroyed by the Christian church, and her overtly-evoked, passionate love of women, made her synonymous with Female, with a capital F.

Nancy Freedman, in her book *Sappho: The Tenth Muse,* called her "the toast of kings for her verse" and also "a shrewd businesswoman, an educator, an advocate of women's equality, and a rebel who was banished from her island home."

Paradoxically, Sappho left Lesbos to find a man, and that man, it's said, led to her suicide in western Greece. Don't worry, I'll take you there, and let you know what I think of the cliff called Sappho's Leap. Tragically, author Lawrence Durrell named his daughter Sappho, and, in 1985, she committed suicide by hanging.

The next morning I'm called an "arrogant American" by the owner of the Sappho Hotel when I point out, after much testing and frustration, that his Wi-Fi doesn't work. Much to my surprise, I immediately agree with him because, though the Wi-Fi doesn't work, he's right. I am being an "arrogant American."

Sometimes – despite all of my meditation and ongoing attempts to practice humility in my every social interaction as I traipse around the Mediterranean through countries that lack, often for the better, many conveniences found in the United States – I do embody American arrogance and convey an it's-all-about-me attitude. I find myself right up there with some of my countrymen who have an Ugly American image because they shout loud to make themselves understood, regularly complain about the lack of modern conveniences, and are convinced that life is our way or the highway.

I recall that one of my sisters-in-law, while visiting my home in the south of France in the early 1990s on her first trip outside the United States, recognized that "they do a lot of things different than we do." Her tone implied that "we" do it better than the French, who have their own manner of dealing with everything, which, to my way of thinking, is frequently much more palatable, rational and sensible than the excessive, ostentatious, entitled, and extreme style preferred by Americans.

One payback after living abroad for over three decades is that familiarity with various national differences creates awareness, and a respect for, or at least a tolerance of, another culture. Normally I adapt to local behavior and habits. That's why it's rare that I speak in a tone of voice that today gets me called an "arrogant American."

Vive la difference!

I head down to the square near the Central Café, where last night I ate a Greek salad and Super Kalcone pizza, to take a snapshot (don't worry, I'll soon get tired of this outdated phrase) of a statue of Sappho holding a lyre in her left hand. I caption it *Write on Sappho!* because graffiti covers it from head to toe.

I also decide, and I must be in a very reflective mood due to my swollen toe or accused arrogance, that while on Lesbos I will ponder my own sexuality and the virtues and vices of monogamy and fidelity.

I walk 13-kilometers in, around, and out of Mytilene before I accept that the only way I'll get to the Sappho's birthplace and attend the last day of the annual International Eressos Women's Festival, which promises attendees "two full weeks with activities by women for women," is to take a bus through the forested island to distant Eressos on the western side.

The hardly subversive, non-profit festival, which is actually held a few kilometers from Eressos in the beach resort of Skala Eresou, "celebrates the history, culture, achievements and diversity of women." A website proclaims that "all women are welcome, included, and celebrated here, regardless of their race, age, interests, or sexuality, whether they are newcomers to this beautiful island, or have made

Lesbos their holiday place many times before."

As a male MedTrekker, I've never taken a long bus ride to reach an all-women festival. Fortunately my lack of knowledge about local buses, and even the exact location of Eressos, prompts an outburst of assistance from every Greek, both arrogant and non-arrogant, I encounter.

First, a hard-helmeted man controlling traffic at a construction site outside town stops six buses to determine the right one for me to get on. Once aboard I sit in the only empty seat, next to the overweight local village idiot, while everyone in the bus amicably tries to help me, the foreign village idiot, negotiate the numerous bus changes required to cross Lesbos.

On the second bus, I sit next to a Greek who lives in Reading, Pennsylvania, and frequently returns to visit his mother, now 93 and living in a retirement home at the Leimonos monastery that, he says, resembles an American college campus. As we roll along, he helpfully points out the Museum of Industrial Olive Oil Production and the Silver Bay Hotel on the Kolpos Geras Bay.

My companion, Michael, who's my age with a wife and two kids in their 20s back in Reading, tells me that there are over 11 million olive trees on Lesbos and, before he disembarks, gives me his take on U.S. politics.

"An alcoholic president got us into a stupid war and wrecked the economy for decades to come," says Michael, who only attended school until the fourth grade, left Lesbos for Athens when he was fifteen and worked on tankers before marrying a woman from his village. "And, because of him, America has become polarized and completely dysfunctional. It makes our Greek politicians, who've driven this country into the ground, look only mediocre rather than completely stupid."

I get him off the subject by talking about *Middlesex* and mention that the prize-winning book is about a "move from the mythic innocence of Greece to the promised, and more mythic, American dream."

"It's a theme similar to your own odyssey," I remark.

A bit later, on the third bus, the crowds have dwindled and there are only six of us left after passengers disembark in villages like Skalochorion and Antissa. Catching the fourth, and last, bus involves a half-hour wait for kids to get out of the local school and we continue to Eressos to the delightfully rocking tune of contemporary Greek hits to which everyone but me sings along.

This time my seat mate is a visiting-for-the-summer Greek who lives in Newburyport, Maine, but is originally from Skala Eresou, the beach community where the women's festival has been held since 2000.

"The lesbians are great, but there are fewer of them at the festival this year," he shouts over the blare of the music. "Every year Joanna at the Sappho Travel agency in town says it won't be held again, but every year it takes place."

As we approach Eressos, scrub mountains and Arizona-like mesas have replaced the island's forests. I get off the bus in the square when I see the *Café d'Amour*, the Love Café, and figure this must be where the action starts. But it, and the Gusto Café, are shut down for the season and it's clear that I've made a mistake. Sappho might have been born here (though there are no signs or proclamations indicating that) but her devotees are all down by the sea.

Before walking out of town I pick up a brochure that proclaims "The International Eressos Women's Festival in Skala Eressos is an opportunity to join in events, to make new friends, to network and meet women with exciting new ideas, learn new skills, share your own talents, and have a lot of simple fun with a taste of Greek culture."

During a relaxing four-kilometer stroll to the seaside village, I pass an intriguing field of abandoned art and am almost run down by a phalanx of female cyclists, or "dikes on bikes" as they call themselves.

When I reach Skala Eresou, the program for the almost-concluded festival is plastered all over town with enticing activities that include snorkeling trips, daily walks, barbecues, bike rides, boat excursions, breathing workshops, massage therapy, Greek dance lessons, women-only sunset cruises, a "Rediscover the Truth of Nature" seminar, a swim-to-the-rock-in-the-bay race, a "Developing the Psychic Self in Five Days" seminar, and a "clean up the beach" event.

The narrow beachfront features a dozen bars and restaurants with seductive names like Café Passione, Zorba the Buddha, The Tenth Muse, and Aubergine. A few visitors are savoring the sun and swimming in the smooth-surfaced water while others are lolling on windsurfers and sailboats to pass the time until happy hour begins at every bar. The festival closing party at the Belle Vue tonight is called "Too Many DJs – DJ Sophia, DJ Kassandra, DJ Ladyproof, and DJs Party Fox and Mish Mash." Might give that one a miss.

It's all very casual in a village where many businesses – Sappho Travel, Sappho Real Estate (which has a picture of a supposed Sappho as its logo) and Sappho Garden of the Arts – have adopted the Sappho moniker.

"We're perfectly happy with the crowd this year, and the festival is now established as our traditional end-of-the-summer-season hurrah," said a male baker where I buy ingredients for lunch after scoping out the many apartments, houses, hotels, and places for rent with names like Aeolian Village and Helitropos Studios.

"The International Eressos Women's Festival is a life-changing experience," concludes a pitch on the website. "No woman will leave Skala Eressos without knowing more about herself and the impact of women in the world around them."

The omnipresent salute to female introspection and accomplishment encourages a bit of reflection about myself and the impact of women on me. Let me begin by saying that compared to the Greeks of Homer's day I'm one tame dude.

"Most of the Greeks at that time were notorious philanderers and the extent of their dalliances with nymphs, mortals, and assorted goddesses is described in a remarkable recent publication called *A Genealogical Chart of Greek Mythology*," wrote Robert Bittlestone in *Odysseus Unbound*, referring to a tome written by Harold and Jon O. Newman.

Okay, I may have had some traits in common with the bygone Greeks at earlier and more inebriated stages of my life. Not only have I been married twice but before, during and after my first marriage I, well, philandered and dallianced. During my second pre-marital relationship and subsequent marriage, however, I was completely faithful for seven years. What did I learn? That fidelity alone is not the key to a successful partnership.

In retrospect, I rebounded too quickly to marry my beautiful and witty second wife. I certainly went against my therapist's advice that "You need an ex-hippie with a chipped tooth, not another superwoman." Now, as Madonna said on David Letterman, "I'd rather be hit by a train and get my teeth knocked out" than get married again.

Call me gutless, but I'm currently enjoying a period of liberation after thirty generally pleasant years with wives, jobs, kids, houses, gardens, dogs, cats, pools, and other trappings that emerge during the decades-long child-raising and money-earning phase of life. Today I tell every woman I encounter that I'm not interested in a committed, long-term, monogamous relationship or marriage. They all go along with it for about a week.

Many friends who know about my alcoholism claim that I have the same predicament with women that I did with booze.

"You can't ever seem to put women down for very long," said my friend Alison, with whom I have a long, non-sexual friendship. "Like the liquor bottles you used to hide in different closets, there always seem to be nine women in nine different countries and you maintain these long-distance relationships by cutting and pasting similar emails."

I agree there's some similarity between my obsession, compulsion and addiction with alcohol and my desire for women. But I told Alison that I recently learned this behavior was not solely due to my alcoholic temperament.

"I've been diagnosed with abnormally high testosterone which my doctor considers a key part of my lust, both wander and otherwise," I said, describing the social obligations and responsibilities that come with such an affliction. I said this when Alison and I met in the garden of a monastery on the French Riviera, adding: "I feel validated and get off on brief but amorous love affairs, great sex, good friendships, separate houses, and a dual exploration of similar interests."

I've talked to lovers, friends, and therapists about both my desire for women and lack of desire for any one woman. The fact is that, as simplistic as it may seem, right now I'm content with the "love the one you're with" philosophy, and enjoy making the woman currently in my presence feel like she is the most important person in the universe.

Sometimes I even borrow a line from Homer – "My lady, never a man in the wide world should have a fault to find with you" – to help me along.

When things head sideways or south, as they frequently do in our impermanent world, I recite what Deng Ming-Dao said in one of his *365 Tao Daily Meditations*: "The pursuit of love and compassion is not without pain and confusion."

Not that I couldn't do better.

"I would make love with you as many times a day as you wish if you'd simply talk to me a little more and display just a bit more intimacy," said one patient partner.

"That's okay," I replied. "Once a day is enough."

Fortunately, many women of my age practice a similar philosophy.

"I like the fact that I can be single and intimate at this phase of life without any obligations," said Sandy Stewart, whom I've known since we were kids.

A good friend I lived with decades ago in Paris recently wrote: "I just want to express my appreciation for our lively and colorful ongoing relationship. I haven't discussed Homer's birthplace and the merits of mastic, or shared quotes from Cavafy and Sappho with anyone in a long time - if ever. It's all very stimulating and great fun."

My 90-something-year-old mother tells me I'm making a big mistake not finding the next "right" woman and contends that I'll be really lonely when I get to be 85. I respond that I might find a wife at 86.

I hitchhike out of Eressos and get a short lift from a female Austrian couple who have been coming to Lesbos twice a year for the past decade. They extol the virtues of the remote island and their enjoyment of, and solidarity with, the annual festival. There's no reason they should be even remotely interested in my thoughts about relationships, but I do mention that I've been thinking about Martin Buber, who was born in Vienna, and tell them that I used to enjoy "I/Thou" relationships in my late teens and that I try to practice that intimacy in my every dalliance today.

"We try to have an 'I/Thou' relationship with each other, but it can be as difficult between two women as it is between heterosexuals," one assures me. "It's rare that both people in a relationship are at the same place at the same time unless they're very young, very mature, or very old."

"Well, I'm getting older," I reply.

One reason they picked me up, they tell me, is because they've found that Greeks on Lesbos often ignore hitchhikers because "people are scared that you might be an Albanian." That's not the first time I've heard this rationale for lousy hitchhiking results, but it's true that the pick-up-a-hitchhiker ethos is less prevalent here than on Chios.

"With all of the Albanians living in Greece isn't it time to get over negative national profiling?" I ask.

The two Austrians, slightly impressed that I still speak a bit of German after studying in Vienna for a while in the late 60s, agree that I don't look too Albanian and claim that they are one hundred percent against any type of profiling.

When they drop me on a back road, I hike for four kilometers through the delightful desert-like hills under a clear sky. My next lift is from a trio of Albanian masons who are returning home after breaking rocks all day.

As I sit in the back of an it's-seen-better-days pickup and stare at the azure sky and russet mesas, I have a sudden alarming feeling that my life is in their hands and that this could be an eventful trip. We could have an accident, they could rob me, or maybe even swap passports and turn me into an Albanian. Although there's perhaps some rationale to these politically incorrect thoughts, as well as my lingering fears of any threesome following the gypsy incident, the odds are that they will do nothing to me and that this encounter, like most on the MedTrek and elsewhere, will be uneventful.

My next thought is that I owe them, in a real if minor way, my life and my thanks for keeping me alive, in the same way that Odysseus was indebted to his various saviors. Nausikaa in *The Odyssey* and Hêphaistos in *The Iliad* refer to this type of debt as *zoagria*, or "the price of a life," and those who benefit from such kindness, especially in the days of the ancient Greeks, don't forget their benefactors.

When I jump out of the truck I profusely thank my Albanian saviors in a mélange of Greek and sign language, gratefully shake their hands, and clasp my palms together and bow as though we're a quartet of Thai monks.

Within five minutes, a Turkish couple stop and invite me into the air-conditioned Audi that they've brought across on a ferry for a short vacation. Mazhar and Oya Yazar live in Istanbul, where he's in paint production and she's a chemistry teacher. Their daughter went to Stanford, is doing her PhD in Santa Cruz and they were recently in the U.S. for her marriage. They take me to Kalloni, enabling me to incur even more *zoagria*, and we talk about national profiling and specifically what the "good old" Europeans to the west (that would be the French, Dutch, British, and Germans) think about the "not quite so good old" Europeans to the east (that would include Albanians, Greeks, and Turks).

Many Turks, of course, were *Gästarbiters*, or guest workers, in Germany and it's a relationship that was not always considered mutually beneficial. It's one reason that under current conditions, Mazhar doesn't think there's any reason for Turkey to join the potpourri of nations in a European Union.

"We won't be in the European Union by 2023, because they keep telling us that we're too big, with 70 million people and lots of ambitious entrepreneurs, for them to swallow," says Mazhar, who doesn't consider Turkey historically part of Europe. "All they want to do is have us let their big companies come in and buy up our small ones for nothing so they can dominate the market. But they still don't think we're good enough for them."

When they drop me off, it's late in the day so I spring for a quickly negotiated €20 cab ride back to the statue of Sappho in Mytilene. Although that's a bargain for the 45-kilometer lift, I always feel like I've violated the MedTrek credo by taking a cab. But I'll put it on my expense account as part of my sociological investigation into Lesbos.

"I don't consider Skala Eresou and that whole gay conference as part of my island," says the beefy driver as we speed along at 140-kilometers-an-hour over the island's narrow and windy roads. "It's a whole different world out there and far from those of us who live and work here."

Although I only MedTrekked 23 kilometers today, the discombobulated combo of buses (4), hitchhiking pickups (3), and a taxi make for a long day.

When I return to Mytilene, I drop in for a cappuccino at the Panellinion café and restaurant, which is decorated in a *fin de siècle* décor and features homemade, honeyed desserts. I read a history of the island that claims Lesbos was a Thessalian who came to the island and married Methymna. It adds that many of the village names, including Eressos, derive from the offspring of the Pelasgians' King Macar.

The next morning, as Circe instructed, I book a ticket on a 3:40 a.m. ferry to Lemnos the following day before getting a shave from a barber who insists on speaking to me in a perplexing mix of German and Italian that, much to his amazement, I not only understand but also seem to be able to speak. The barber is so titillated by my linguistic skill that he telephones a friend who rushes to the barbershop and speaks to me in the same mongrel manner. When I finally get away from this brain-frying experience, I walk by the town's historic Ottoman bath and head north for ten kilometers.

I pass an ancient Hellenic *agora* and meet an archeologist who tells me that the site dates from 4000 BC. After some discussion, we determine that he means 400 BC. I walk past the not-so-old ruins and along the windy seashore past a Lidl supermarket and distribution warehouses for multinational brands like Gillette, Duracell, Komatsu, Listerine, and Bonne Maman.

There are some workers on the road wearing orange Day-Glo vests while they pick up litter and, since I haven't worn mine for a while, I take my glowing orange protect-me-from-getting-hit-by-a-car vest out of my pack, put it on with great flourish and wish them all *"Kalimera,"* as though I were an orange-vested god descended from Mount Olympus. They love it.

I arrive in the little village of Panagiota and hook up with two-dozen cats quietly watching the local fishermen mend their nets in the shadow of the silver-domed Greek Orthodox Church.

A little further north is Pamfila, where, after admiring some saddled mules and noticing that most of the houses have solar water heating units on the roof, I enter the gigantic and ornate Saint Barbara church for a few moments of reflection under a colossal chandelier and a gargantuan eye looking down on me intently from the ceiling.

Surrounded by a loud ticking clock, lots of chalices and scores of saintly paintings, I recall that I saw a woman yesterday stop to kiss paintings and icons of a saint. And I've noticed that most Greek men cross themselves when they pass churches, airports, and intersections. I leave as the bells toll 11:00 a.m. and on the bus back to Mytilene, decide that since I walked ten kilometers north of Mytilene before noon I'll walk ten kilometers south after noon.

I head south past half a dozen fish restaurants and through the freighter port where a group of Romas have set up home in the parking lot. Then I arrive in a pleasure boat port along a fine-villa'd road, where a United Colors of Benetton ad says simply "BEAUTY." My intended ten-kilometer hike, with Turkey constantly on my left, turns into a 16-kilometer romp, and after passing the airport I arrive at the end of the well-forested cape where I can make out Chios in the distance and the

Kolpos Geras Bay just below me. I watch a dozen boats trolling near a fish farm site and, when I get back to town, I stop at a café to indulge in enough honey-flavored *baklava* to call it dinner and desert before my 2:30 a.m. wakeup call.

And what happened to Sappho?

She allegedly jumped to her death when Phaon rejected her love in Nidri, in western Greece. Stick with me and we'll soon visit Sappho's Leap.

Heaven on Earth on Lemnos

I catch the 3:40 a.m. ferry from Lesbos to Lemnos after squatting the Wi-Fi at the Central Café during my walk to the port at 2:45 a.m. It's obviously too dark to see anything once onboard, so I sit in the lounge, sip a strong Greek coffee and study a blonde Greek woman who, hands down, is the most attractive woman I've ever seen anywhere in the world at 3:53 a.m. Maybe it's a result of some genes passed down from her foremothers and fathers?

Lemnos, my destination this morning, is the volcanic island where the women killed off the men until Jason and his Argonauts arrived to repopulate it. The island is also where Zeus, in a moment of fury, tossed Hêphaistos, the god of metalworking, from the top of Mount Olympus (the real one on mainland Greece that is home to the gods). Hêphaistos was rescued by Achilles' mother Thetis who, he claims, "was my savior, after the long fall and fractures that I had to bear."

As a lame god Hêphaistos, also known as Vulcan, continued metalworking at forges on an island full of volcanoes and made armor for Achilles and Agamémnon ("Before them now rose Agamémnon, holding the staff Hêphaistos fashioned once," Homer said in *The Iliad*).

I get my first overview of Lemnos, which is a popular destination for Bulgarian surfers, when I climb to the *kastro* that I can see from my room at the Hotel Lemnos, which is run by a Greek who lived in New Jersey. From the castle that many – including the Venetians, the Genoese and the Turks – have inhabited since it was originally a temple to Artemis, I have an exceptional panorama of the capital, Myrina. It is a municipality that appears remarkably bustling considering that it has a population of only 7,000. The herds of deer roaming the fortress grounds are a nice touch, but garbage, non-existent paths, and lack of signage should prompt a contribution from the country's pay-to-see-the-monuments program.

There's certainly nothing wrong with the bays, coves, and sandy beaches just north of town. The first beaches – the *Romeikos Gialos*, or Greek beach, and the *Riha Nera*, the low-tide beach – look pretty decent. But the many British tourists (there are more English-speaking tourists here than in Chios or Lesbos and many of them are biking, walking, or windsurfing enthusiasts) prefer the better-known *Ormos Kaspaka*, or Kaspaka Bay, near the Portomyrina Palace hotel. There are wild cacti just off the road but some up-market villas have luscious green gardens with palms. To my left, across the sea, is the faint but inspiring silhouette of Mount Athos on mainland Greece.

Last night's equinox denoted the end of the summer season, and there are only a few swimmers, and not one open restaurant, visible when I arrive at Agios Ioannis. By the time I reach Garbounolaka, as the church on the hilltop (and there are churches on many hilltops here) is called, the road has turned to gravel. I leave the tourists in the dust and am alone as I walk to the end of the promontory and up a mountain with a clear overview of the arid, stark volcanic island which is inhabited by only 17,000 people.

Except for bleating goats, I have only one encounter. I meet a farmer and his mother (at least I hope it's his mother) who don't appear to understand when I tell them that living between Mount Athos and Asia Minor -- with this wondrous sky, mountains, sun, air, and sea – must be heaven on earth. At the tip of the promontory is a military base and numerous signs indicate that I've entered through the back door and am walking on "prohibited ground," where not only photographs but also videotapes are banned.

I casually saunter down the military-only road divided by one continuous yellow line (this, I learn, means it's a private military road that can also be used by the local farmers) past four noisy geese-squawking wind turbines. I'm saved from possible imprisonment and certain embarrassment when an officer in dashing paratrooper garb and a spiffy red MG (certainly out of character for this island) picks me up.

"Try not to get in any trouble," he tells me when he drops me off the moment we get off the base.

My goal is to reach Ifestia, where Hêphaistos landed when Zeus tossed him off Mount Olympus. I'm also looking for traces of Jason, who arrived here with the Argonauts when they were in search of the Golden Fleece; the 2800 BC ruins in Polilchni; and the Kabeiroi, the mysterious gods of the underworld said to be the offspring of Hêphaistos. They're regularly venerated here with popular nocturnal festivities in *Kavario-Holi*, the Sanctuary of the Kabeiroi.

I hoof it out of Myrina towards Kontopouli, where there's a five-kilometer dirt road to Ifestia, and my spirits brighten immediately when I see perhaps the best-named store in Greece – "Captain Hook – The Best Fishing Stories" (it turns out that it's actually "The Best Fishing Stores" but I prefer my misread version). I notice that all the words on a restaurant's fast-food menu are in Greek except for "Hot Dog" and remind myself to check with the Ministry of Culture in Athens to determine if hot dog is impossible to translate.

It's fortunate that I'm not in any hurry because "relax" is the most-used word in Lemnos. The key card for my hotel says this is "the island for your most relaxing holiday," and everyone uses the word relax to replace "boring" or "there's nothing to do here." Even a young Bulgarian teaching kite surfing to visiting foreigners says "I spend my time here relaxing, not clubbing." The mood of the island matches my belief that ferries – much slower than cars or trains – are the right and relaxed mode of transport for anyone visiting the Greek islands. The spirit is the pace, the pace is the spirit.

I stop for a coffee at Zapatas, erroneously assuming that someone running a pit stop with a Spanish name would speak Spanish. In fact, it turns out that the Greek owner had some type of fascination for General Emiliano Zapata, the Mexican revolutionary. I meet a 51-year-old ironmonger, a contemporary Hêphaistos, on the way to his workshop. Discovering that I'm a foreign visitor, he buys me some pastries, and points out the church atop the 799-meter high *Profitis Ilias* Mountain. Prophet Elijah is the name frequently given throughout Greece to the highest mountain peak, or the chapel on the highest mountain peak, and denotes the country's association with the Biblical prophet.

Just past the airport, which is 22 kilometers from town, I pass the base for the Hellenic Air Force's 130 Combat Group that flies regular sorties above the Aegean. When I hike into Ifestia, located on another promontory jutting into the sea, I notice that financing for rehabilitation of the site was provided by the "European Union Support Framework 2000-2006," although we're long past 2006.

The Ifestia archeological site is very (I know you're starting to hate this word) relaxed, and I laze on a hillside bench above the Hellenistic/Roman theater before taking a quick look at the *agora* below. I reflect on Hêphaistos' probable landing spot and recall his own description of the event to Hêra in *The Iliad*.

"Zeus caught me around one foot and flung me into the sky from our tremendous terrace (on Mount Olympus)," Hêphaistos said. "I soared all day! Just as the sun dropped down I dropped down, too, on Lemnos – nearly dead. The island people nursed a fallen god."

I visualize Hêphaistos, the island's protector god, making Ifestia the principal city, and later the seat of a Byzantine see, until a landslide knocked it out of commission.

A German woman, who's also particularly relaxed, interrupts my thoughts. "I've become as relaxed and hospitable as the Greeks after only ten years here," she jokes when she and a friend offer me a room that night at their place in Kontias.

I walk around the bay to a gigantic abandoned resort, which the locals refer to as Ghost Ville, before being the last visitor of the day at the *Kavario-Holi* museum that, among other things, memorializes the Kabeiroi. I visit a temple (which forms a triangle with Delphi and the Acropolis, according to the German woman) before scurrying down to the sea to examine a cave where, again according to the German woman, an injured crewman on the Argo was left by Jason and cared for by the women on the island.

Jason and his crew are credited with impregnating many Lemnos women after the ladies killed all the local men. What caused this slaughter? Apparently Aphroditê, upset that the women of the island aided Hêphaistos, caused them to have such a foul stench that their husbands deserted them. Or, goes another version, the women were upset that their Lemnian men brought back female captives after they raided Thrace on the mainland. Typical of women scorned, for whatever reason, they killed any men they could find.

The husband of one of the museum workers gives me a lift back to Kontopouli, and I walk another six kilometers on the road through lovely fields with rolled hay, medieval defense towers, farmers driving old-school tractors, barking dogs, and more trees than yesterday.

Dogs, of course, seem always to have been part of farm life in Greece. Odysseus runs into them when he returns to Ithaka, dressed by Athêna as a beggar "in rags you'd hate to see some other mortal wear."

As he approaches the swineherd's farmstead, "those snarling dogs spotted Odysseus, charged him fast – a shatter of barks."

By this time, I've started mooing at every cow and barking at every dog I see before I get a lift to the airport with a calamari fisherman ("*Kalimera*, calamari," I joke to myself). Then I ride into Myrina with a 70-year-old local called Chris who lived in Australia for over thirty years and whose son is now a priest. He crosses himself, his three fingers held tightly together to represent the trinity, as we enter town past the biggest church on the island.

The next day I head south of Myrina along the port to Plati Beach where richer vacationers are staying at the Afroditi Villa Hotel or the Lemnos Village Resort Hotel. They're enjoying the string of beaches and bays that include Thanos, the long beach along Konias, and the Agios Pavlos Bay.

What strikes me on this brisk morning walk, before I catch an early afternoon ferry to Thessaloniki, is the dichotomy between the expanding tourism trade and the rural, chicken-clucking, dog-barking, rooster-crowing, pig-stying farm life that still occupies most of the population. They co-exist on the lovely dirt road and the little hillside village of Thanos seems immune to the pools and *chaises longues* down below.

I meet a young man and his mother, who's particularly impressed that I say *"Efharisto poli, Kyria,"* when I get out of the car. I knew, incidentally, that *Kyria* means "Lady" because I frequently meditate to the soothing *Kyrie* (which means "Lord") by Robert Gass and the renowned chorale *On Wings of Song.*

I spend my last hour in Lemnos at a beachside Wi-Fi café where I simultaneously hear the waves, kiss the sand, and see Mount Athos across the sea as the sun sets.

I really do love the relaxed speed, or the non-speed really, of ferries. Even the *Lissos,* one of the Anek Line's new up-market ships with dozens of restaurants and lounges, goes slowly enough to enable me to retrace almost every step I made when I marched around northern Lemnos. Two hours after we leave Myrina, the ferry approaches Mount Athos and we sail by the monastic promontory that is the center of Greek Orthodoxy and the easternmost of the three Chalcidice peninsulas.

Athos has been off-limits to females, except cats, since 1060, and no one, male or female, is allowed in without permission. That's one of the reasons I'm heading to Thessaloniki, Greece's second largest city and port, which was founded in 315 BC and gets its name from the half-sister of Alexander the Great who also happened to be the wife of Kassander, a Macedonian general. I plan to visit the Pilgrim's Bureau of the Holy Executive of The Holy Mount Athos at 109 Egnatia Street and obtain permission to spend time with the monks and climb to the top of the Holy Mountain.

Athos seems to be a refuge of religious sincerity and drama. There was an item in the newspaper about a rogue bunch of priests at one of the monasteries under the control of Mt. Athos being sentenced for creating a schism. Apparently the priests are upset with Greek Orthodox leaders who want to cozy up to the Catholics.

From the looks of it, I'm the only passenger gazing intently in the direction of the holy land as the ship sails towards Sithonia and Kassandra, the two promontories west of the Holy Mountain. When the ship cuts north along the Kassandra peninsula only a few people get out their binoculars to look at Nea Skioni and other villages.

On the other side of the ship to the west I can see the snow-glare of Mount Olympus, perhaps the most mythical mountain in the world, standing alone and majestic across the slightly rippling Mediterranean. The ferry passengers don't abandon their books, conversations, cell phones, cigarettes, or coffee to glimpse at either mountain while I have a feeling of contentment as I float between Athos and Olympus, both of which I'll be climbing.

Thessaloniki, despite the ongoing construction of an expanded subway system, is a delightful place to land. Not just because its cafes, markets, churches, museums, and generally bustling joviality typify a Mediterranean port but also because the city constantly reflects its Hellenistic, Byzantine and Ottoman past.

I have a coffee in the main seaside square of Platia Aristotelous and continue along the seafront to the *Lefkos Pirgos*, or White Tower, before I check into the simple and spartan Nea Metropolis hotel. The next morning at dawn, long before the Pilgrim's Office opens, I embark on a free-wheeling, light-a-candle-at-every-stop tour of Greek Orthodox churches and services. My romp takes me first to the Panagia Chalkeon, where a small candle costs 50 cents, but by the time I get to Gios Athanasios, Panagia Acheiropoietos (the name means "not made by human hand"), and Gia Sofia, the Church of the Holy Wisdom, I'm buying the tall €5 candles.

I walk through the Kendriki Market and visit Agios Dimitrios, the site of the tomb of the town's patron saint, before going to the Pilgrim's Bureau where I meet Christos Lilos and am told there won't be any problem spending a week on the Holy Mountain if I apply precisely six months, and not a day earlier or later, before the date of entry. And that's exactly what I do.

After a few weeks on islands, I'm so keen about the buzz in Thessaloniki – its lovely boardwalk, incessant café life, the inviting and omnipresent mouthwatering array of *mezedes*, fabulous markets, gigantic squares, adorned churches, chic shops, and sexy chicks – that I briefly consider bivouacking here to write this book.

My early morning religious odyssey also gets me enthused about spending more time listening to the sermons and chants, and generally prepping on the Greek Orthodox religion, before I visit Athos.

But the real reason I might move here is because I discover one of the best bakeries in Greece. Beginning at daybreak I go there a few times a day for a cup of strong coffee and a just-out-of-the-oven *bougatsa crema*, a delicious (that word is so inadequate), cinnamon-and-vanilla-scented, cream-filled, mouth-watering phyllo pastry.

Seeking Sappho's Suicide Spot

After a few days of urban debauchery, I reluctantly head from the Nea Metropolis to the bus station outside town and embark on a five-hour bus ride across northern Greece with the speed of Hermês. By the time I travel through historical Ioannina and mountainous Iperios to arrive in Lefkada, or Leukas, on the west coast, I calculate that Odysseus would have saved 9.8 years if he'd taken this route back from Troy to Ithaka, where I'm now heading.

Although it's linked to the mainland by a narrow strip of land and a bridge built in 1987, I choose to consider Lefkada an island but don't waste much time in the capital before I take a bus to Nidri, the island's main resort. It's pouring, and I hang out at Angelo's, a port-side café where I cool my heels and talk to Angelo for two hours about his career on a tanker. He tells me that there are no boats heading to Ithaka from here until April and suggests I bus further down the coast to Vassiliki, where there may be some active ferries. The theatrics involved when I catch the 8:00 p.m. bus from Nirdi to Vassiliki, the site of Sappho's suicide and just a few nautical miles away from Ithaka, are comical.

Five different people tell me that the bus to Vassiliki will stop across from Borsalino Travel on the main road through Nidri. To be sure I go into Borsalino Travel and introduce myself to Nikos, who another five people told me was the man to see about the new ferry schedule for the winter (they call late September "winter" here).

"I better call the bus company to make sure they're stopping on this road and not the big road," says Nikos.

He calls the bus company and says "*Nae, nae, nae!*" before he tells me: "Wait, they'll call back in one minute."

The phone rings 58 seconds later.

"*Nae, nae, nae!*" Nikos says on his cell.

"They've changed plans," he smiles. "They'll pick you up on the big road in twenty minutes."

"Sure?" I ask.

"As sure as any Greek can be about the bus service," he smiles.

He explains how to get to the stop on the big road (it is dark now), and I follow his instructions. A few minutes later, as I find myself the only pedestrian on a tiny road leading to the big road, a police car with the siren blazing and light flashing pulls up in front of me like I am at the top of the country's most wanted list.

"The bus company called Nikos," says the nonchalant cop in decent English. "They're not going to take the main road."

"Why?" I laugh.

"They're carrying posters for a political rally that have to be dropped off at a bar," he says. "Let us take you back."

So, with siren blazing and light flashing, I am driven back to the Borsalino Travel where two more policemen and Nikos greet me.

"We weren't going to let the bus go by without you, and we'll stay here until you get on," Nikos explains. "But don't be upset if there's no boat tomorrow. It's going to be windy."

He was right. The dark, eerie night I spent in Vassiliki was the windiest (the shutters and boats combined to make a clatter that would have scared ghosts), wettest (the rain pelted the terrace and walls of my room in a building that is spitting distance from two docked ferries being buffeted in the port), noisiest (the thunder shook the building and made everything tremble, including me) and darkest (the electricity was out, and I welcomed the bright sparks of lightning) of the MedTrek.

All the adjectives and descriptions in *The Odyssey* about the state of the sea hit me, and I relished being on comparatively dry land during what Homer called "a howling, demonic gale, shrouding over in thunderheads the earth and sea at once."

It is the kind of thundery, lightningy, hard-rain-falling almost-impossible-to-get-to-sleep night that used to make Humphrey, our American Cocker, tremble and flee into a closet to hide himself from the expressions of nature. When he got up, there'd be a wet spot on the floor because the climatic conditions literally scared the piss out of him. Here on Vassiliki I was glad there was a toilet down the hall.

That wasn't the only drama. Earlier that night, before the storm hit, I went to use the Wi-Fi at the Yacht Bar on the port and had a polite exchange with the blonde Estonian waitress about a visit I made to Tallinn and a story I reported there in the 1990s.

When I send my SPOT, I put the unit on a chair that I move six inches into the street to ensure a good signal. Then I meet my first Greek asshole, who was either the owner and/or the waitress's boyfriend. He grabs the SPOT off the chair and puts it in the middle of the road (gently, I suppose he could have smashed it) and goes into a rant.

"Everything is supposed to be perfect in a restaurant and you can't move things around," he screeches. "Go sit at a table by the water. Go sit somewhere else inside. You don't just move chairs like you own them……"

This went on until I left the Estonian, who I hope doesn't have anything personal going on with this guy, a €10 tip.

It reminded me of an incident in Constitution Square in Athens in 1968, probably just before the generals took over the country, when I put my feet up on a chair in one of those cushy outdoor terrace cafés. The waiter came over, put a pillow under my feet, asked me if I was comfortable – and then screeched, jerked the pillow away and threw me out.

I am the first potential passenger to ask the ferryman if there's going to be any action and a boat to Ithaka. No luck, he says as the wind and drizzle continue. Although the sea is still rough and the wind is still howling, the sun comes out at noon and I decide to seek Sappho's supposed suicide spot at the seaside tip of the mountainous island.

Vassiliki is more touristic than I thought, I realize when passing the Kalypso Luxury Studios and the Odeon, Xenia, and Odysseus Hotels. I'm particularly amused when I see a sign for the Odysseas (sic) Watersports Club.

An uncompleted road stretches along the hillside opposite my ferryboat dock hotel, and, though I make a logistical mistake and wind up having an uphill scramble through brambles (I should have taken, as I do on the way back, an uphill trail that I missed going through an olive grove), it's a nice stroll on a mainly tarmac'd road to the lighthouse.

Nearing the famous Lefkada Leap (aka Sappho's Leap, which is also the title of Erica Jong's 2004 book about the poet) located at the headland of Lefkada Island in the Ionian Sea, I immediately try to buttress my theory that poet Sappho did not have the temperament to commit suicide by jumping to her death here.

I take snapshots from a variety of perspectives and confirm my conclusion that Sappho wasn't the type of woman to jump 72 meters into the churning sea from what was once a Temple to Apollo because (1) she was not caught on the sophisticated surveillance cameras at the lighthouse, (2) she would have been, as I was, cut to shreds by the brambles trying to get to the take-off point, and (3) no matter how handsome Phaon was, a poet like her (Sylvia Plath, maybe, but not Sappho) would not end her life for a guy.

From the butts on the ground it's evident that the last person who contemplated jumping smoked a few cigarettes before leaping into the sea. I admire the force of the rocking swells, the froth of the breaking waves, and the thunderous noise as they bash the austere and beautiful rock formations. I'm not sure I could jump into that without a smoke first either.

I meet a Greek lawyer from Athens, who's here to supervise tomorrow's elections, and we discuss the did-she-or-did-she-not Sappho suicide. Then I take the road and downhill path back to Vassiliki, where I have late afternoon *moussaka* made by a Greek born in Melbourne, and we discuss the Greek luncheons I had there with some Aussie foreign correspondents while promoting *The Idiot and the Odyssey*. Two hours after I return to my €25 a night room, following my 30-kilometer round trip MedTrek, I'm invited to the nearby Vagelara's restaurant owned by the young couple on the floor below and dine on fresh grilled calamari.

When I awaken the next morning, the first Sunday in October, I admire from the balcony of my port-side, third-story room, the West Ferry that will take me to Ithaka. Before leaving I spend fifteen minutes talking to the French couple in the room next to me and give them the scoop about how to get to Sappho's Leap. Then, not wanting to leave town with a bad reputation, I head to the Yacht Bar and apologize to the owner for our altercation.

Once there I get a post from the "Ferry Godmother" who writes that she's "....just thinking (now that you're on your way 'home' to Ithaka), that you've been island-hopping independently for about three weeks now."

It turns out that she's worried about how I've been eating.

"As much as I love calamari and yoghurt, the Greek cuisine can get VERY repetitive – your thoughts must wander now and then to a scoop of Cherry Garcia ice cream."

And she gives me a bit of support: "Your perseverance, patience, and cheerfulness – not to mention endless energy – in the face of storms, ferry, and monastery schedules, slippery slopes, dead goats and other demons are admirable indeed. P.S. Maybe you could swim to Ithaka."

Maybe I could.

Hanging Out with Odysseus on Ithaka

"As you set out for Ithaka hope that your road is a long one, full of adventure, full of discovery." – Constantine P. Cavafy, author of *Ithaka*

Although it looks like I could swim to Ithaka when I stand at the top of Sappho's Leap, I'm still hoping, weather permitting, to catch a 2:00 p.m. ferry. Because the wind and sea conditions continue to be variable, I won't know if I'll be heading to Odysseus' home at 2:00 p.m. until 1:59 p.m.

Fortunately Vassiliki is a pleasant and not-too-touristic seaside village and port that's about as close to Ithaka on the Greek mainland as anyone can get. It's not a bad place to be stuck, even if I do have to constantly eat fresh grilled calamari (I'm usually a gyro/lamb/*moussaka*/fish and Greek salad fanatic).

I've also got Fagles' translation of *The Odyssey*, which is considerably different from my translation by Robert Fitzgerald, and during the morning I carefully reread every section that takes place in Ithaka. I particularly relish descriptive passages that portray the stark countryside, the suitor-squatted palace, the lovely weaving Penélopê, the coming-of-age Telémakhos, and the bloody finale when Odysseus confronts the scummy suitors. What were the suitors really like? "Never were mortal men like these for bullying and brainless arrogance," says Telémakhos.

Among my favorite passages that Athêna speaks to Odysseus in *The Odyssey* are these: "Patience, iron patience, you must show; so give it out to neither man nor woman that you are back from wandering"..."And I foresee your vast floor stained with blood, spattered with brains of this or that tall suitor who fed upon your cattle"..."Cold earth instead will take in her embrace a man or two of those who fed so long on what is his."

Then, of course, there's the dramatic description of the reunion between Odysseus and Penélopê, the wife he hasn't seen for twenty years.

"Think what difficulty the gods gave: they denied us life together in our prime and flowering years, kept us from crossing into age together"..."She could not close her eyes till all was told"..."So they came into that bed so steadfast, loved of old, opening glad arms to one another."

This literary indulgence makes for a mellow and lazy morning while I enjoy my third gargantuan latte at the Yacht Café, where the owner claims our late-night tiff was his fault and offers my first coffee on his house. The view of the now mirror-smooth sea from my port-side table is serene, and there's a soupçon – and not much more than a soupçon – of excitement in the air because another Greek election is being held today.

I'm in slow mode but subconsciously looking forward to the ferry to close-but-yet-so-far-away Ithaka, where I'll explore Odysseus' 'hood by MedTrekking on a few well-tended walking paths through a challenging countryside with enchanting vistas amid scores of Homeric connections, museums, and archaeological sites.

No worries, no drama. One island at a time.

It's an almost uneventful two-hour ferry ride past the island of Skorpios – the private domain of the Onassis clan where Aristotle married Jacqueline Kennedy in 1968 after she openly declared "If they're killing Kennedys, then my children are targets...I want to get out of this country" – via the island of Cephalonia to the port of Frikes on western Ithaka.

The trip becomes slightly dramatic when my ferry almost crashes into a classic-looking sailboat with a captain attired in pretentious seafaring regalia (you know the type, spiffy white pants and a sparkling blue cap adorned with a yacht club insignia) who jarringly resembles Richard Branson. The Branson-like captain of a catamaran with a crew of eight plays chicken with the ferry as it pulls into port during a quick stop at Friskardo on Cephalonia, which academics like Robert Bittlestone believe is the actual Ithaka of yore.

I have to admit that, though I like Branson, I side with the ferry captain as the risk-taking entrepreneur swerves away from the path of the ferry, then moves back into it, prompting all sorts of hoots from the ferry's horn and swearing from the irritated pilot. Then the Branson lookalike, with that patented I'm-one-of-the-richest-men-in-the-world-but-still-a-hippie-at-heart smile, nonchalantly waves to us as he heads out of the harbor with the air that he's done us all a favor by making a cameo appearance.

My first view of Ithaka as we approach the eastern side of the island illustrates why, due to the island's harsh terrain, Telémakhos refused to accept a gift of horses from Nestor. The steeply mountainous and bramble-filled steep interior will be difficult to negotiate on foot, much more so on horseback. Homer's description – "the winding beaten paths, the cover where ships can ride, the steep rock face of the cliffs, and the tall, leafy trees" – seems appropriate even from the sea. That's why, of course, Ithaka's three main towns – Frikes, Kioni, and Vathi (aka Ithaki) – are on the west coast facing the Greek mainland. I also get a glimpse of the small flat island of Daskalio between Ithaka and Cephalonia where the suitors may have laid in ambush for Telémakhos after his trip to the Peloponnese.

The first thing I see after disembarking in Frikes is a poster advertising *Homer's Walk*, then I drop into Kiki's market to learn that the best place to stay is at the Aristotelis Apartments run by a man named Telly. I walk five minutes up the street and Telly shows me the largest and best equipped €30 room I've encountered on the MedTrek. The two-story apartment features a double bed and kitchen downstairs, two single bedrooms upstairs, a terrace looking onto the port and sea, and a bathroom that is probably larger and more luxurious than the one on Richard Branson's sailboat. I return to Kiki's to stock up on milk, cereal, bananas, coffee, and other supplies.

Naturally there's almost as much controversy about the existence of Homer and the veracity of *The Odyssey* in contemporary Ithaka as anywhere else. But Constantine P. Cavafy's poem *Ithaka*, written between 1894 and 1910, contends it doesn't matter what I find on arrival and paraphrases my own *raison d'etre* for the MedTrek: the goal is the path, the path is the goal. I reread parts of the iconic poem as the sun rises after my morning meditation.

"Always keep Ithaka in your mind.
To arrive there is your ultimate goal.
But do not hurry the voyage at all.

It is better to let it last for many years;
and to anchor at the island when you are old,
rich with all you have gained on the way,
not expecting that Ithaka will offer you riches.

Ithaka has given you the beautiful voyage.
Without her you would have never set out on the road.
She has nothing more to give you..."

The poem's message is an excellent complement to my daily readings from four different books before I meditate for 24 minutes with soft Buddhist chanting in the background. I allow oft-simplistic phrases that I read year after year, like this sample of Deng Ming-Dao's *Tao Daily Mediations,* to gradually penetrate and permeate my mind, body and soul before each sunrise.

"Contemplate in the morning
Pull weeds in the afternoon
The joys and labor of a single day
Are part of the whole journey."

It's just before 6:00 a.m. when I awaken in Frikes to the pre-dawn wake-up crows and calls of a distant cock, which on Ithaka is considered a symbol of Odysseus. After my meditation, as dogs start barking and donkeys braying while fishermen make their way to the sea under a vivid full moon, I feel like I'm Hercule Poirot on a mysterious island.

Will I, armed with marked up maps, solve the puzzle, find some artifacts, and prove that this is definitely where Odysseus reigned?

I expect to have a great time trying. As I sit in the dark at the table on my terrace I'm again, as I was when I visited the Sirens and stayed in Scilla, bubbling with excitement and enthusiasm.

By the time I'm ready to hit the road, just before the 7:30 sunrise, I have studied the local maps, reviewed the myths, and am armed with my camera and SPOT. I head north of Frikes, where one beachside restaurant is named *Telémakhos,* along a dirt path, or perhaps a carved out road-to-be, that runs along the mesmerizing coast. The sunrise approaching from mainland Greece illuminates other islands in the sea as well as Ithaka's many medieval hilltop defense towers and windmills.

"This is a great place to let my imagination go berserk," I joyously murmur to myself as I arrive at a little locked church at Marmakas and begin taking more photos (41) than on any other single day of the MedTrek.

There are a number of individuals and associations hyping walkabout options around Ithaka, which a guide named Katrina calls a "verdant stunning island with panoramic views and rare indigenous flora and fauna rich in mythology, culture, and living history."

The Michelin Green Guide gives "Ithaka on Foot" a rare two-star rating and contends that "the island is ideal for keen walkers." A brochure published by the municipal government in the main city of Vathi adds that "there are 360 degree views of blue sea dotted with islands of all shapes, the mountains of the mainland, and the steep slopes, green valleys, magnificent coastline, and picturesque villages of Ithaka."

Other flyers and websites extol the dozens of beaches, marine adventures, snorkeling at Polis Bay, and the Pelikata Archaeological Museum with "tangible, tactile insights and artifacts into ancient and modern Ithaka."

As a newcomer, I find surprises around every rocky twist and turn.

Who knew about a naturally carved Hêraklês Rock near Anoghi? Or was aware that Ithaka was first inhabited by Neolithic tribes between 10,000 and 6,000 BC, long before the Mycenaean civilization that saw Odysseus prosper here? Or that Lord Byron was here during the Greek War of Independence in 1823 and that Heinrich Schliemann, the excavator of Mycenae and Troy who single-handedly put those "lost" cities back on the map, came to dig in July 1868?

There are well over a dozen Homeric sites on every you've-got-to-see-this-in-Ithaka-before-you-leave list, and compelling fables and folklore about almost every nook and cranny on the island. There's so much speculation that many places associated with Odysseus are found in duplicate or triplicate. There are at least three sites claiming to be Odysseus' palace, a few contenders for the cave where his treasures were deposited upon his return from Troy, and a couple of suggested locations of his father Laërtês' farm.

Ithaka is a delightful archeological jigsaw puzzle that I plan to slowly investigate with wonderment and merriment.

There are only 3,000-something permanent inhabitants on Ithaka, and they are far outnumbered by the ubiquitous goats. I toss each of the many goats I encounter my "the goat is the path" line as I gleefully dance beyond Frikes to the jingle, or cacophony, of their bells. There are a few half-completed houses here because, as elsewhere in Greece, homeowners like to complete a house over time as they get the money. Saving water is also *de rigueur* and every house has a water reservoir, called a *sterna*, on the roof. It's apparent from the number of trees that olives are the main crop.

I reach Aphales Bay and, as I head uphill, pleasantly surprise myself at nearby Kalamos when I "discover" the well-known School of Homer Archeological site and dig. Most of the excavations are either covered or locked, precautions that I respect, but two are open, and I'm fascinated with one that has tagged the different strata of soil built upon through the ages.

The dig is swamped and damp because of the recent storms, but these ruins on the Pelikata Ridge fit the many descriptions of Odysseus' palace and, in my mind's eye, I picture the entire layout, including the hall filled with desperate suitors and Odysseus' bedroom with the trunk of a massive olive tree.

After a few hours probing the School of Homer dig and imagining the palace of the past, I climb to the abandoned village of Exogi, which thrived during the era of piracy but hit bad times when the population moved down to the coast. On the way I barely restrain myself from taking a loaf of bread that a mobile baker has left hanging for a customer in a plastic bag from a tree limb. At the top of Kalivia hill there's a handwritten description in the Pernarakia church: "There high up in the beautiful Village of Exogi it stands amidst North and South winds. I watch the ships and as a mother I send dreams, kisses and caresses. People come and go like water but they always love you. Exogi, in my soul you have stayed, like fire in time."

It doesn't take me long to realize that the Michelin is correct about the plentiful paths on Ithaka. There are lots of different blazed trail markers – common ones are yellow-on-blue signage with directions in Greek and white-on-blue panels with directions in English, as well as various red/yellow/blue paint marks on stones and trees – indicating the path to Polis Bay, which got that name (*polis* means city) because there was a city and port there in 1000 BC.

I select my personal *beach du jour, building site du jour,* and *glade du jour* on the way to the *landing du jour,* which is considered by many as the place the Phaeacians dumped a sleeping Odysseus when they returned him to Ithaka. The bay contains the Cave of the Nymphs, or Naiades as Homer called them, where, upon arrival, Odysseus and Athêna hid his "shining pile" of treasures – including tripods, cauldrons, cloaks, gold, bronze, and clothing given to him by the Phaeacians.

Excavations of this Cave of Loizos by British archeologists between 1930-35 turned up 13 bronze tripod cauldrons, the exact number the Phaeacians gave to Odysseus as one of their many gifts, and other remnants of his fabled treasure chest. The cave, where an *ex-voto* was found inscribed with "my vow to Odysseus," was perhaps the first place of pan-Hellenic worship and venerations of Odysseus are said to date to the ninth century BC. One archeologist contends that the cave, which collapsed during a 1953 earthquake that destroyed many homes and buildings throughout the island, is one of the most important discoveries in Greek history. A photo on a seaside plaque shows British archeologist Sylvia Benton at the dig in the early 1930s.

From the port I can see the mouth of the cave, which Athêna shut with a stone once the treasures were hidden, from the port and allow my imagination to take me on a colorful journey into the earth that reminds me of the scene when Harrison Ford acquires the ark in *Raiders of the Lost Ark.*

The bay is also considered another possible location of Odysseus' palace which is now, say some explorers, submerged.

I scamper from the seaside to the village of Stavros, where I got a snapshot of a busted Odysseus when I was here with the Stanford group, and grab some grapes and bread at the local market. As I munch on them on a park bench in the town square, I recite lines I recall from Odysseus' homecoming.

"I am at home, for I am he. I bore adversities, but in the twentieth year I am ashore in my own land"…"Now shrugging off his rags the wiliest fighter of the islands leapt and stood on the broad door sill, his own bow in his hand"…"Let me test my fingers and my pull to see if any of the old-time kick is there, or if thin fare and roving took it out of me."

The locals look at me like I've found Odysseus but completely lost myself.

I step into the nearby Pelikata Archeological Museum run by the personable South Africa-born Fotini Couveras, who started working here with her husband in 1965 and has been its main "keeper" since 1985. Like thousands of visitors each year, I admire some of the artifacts discovered at both Polis Bay and the School of Homer in a building renovated in 1992.

Although it's theoretically against the law for Fotini to give me a tour (legally she's not a guide), she proudly shows me a variety of the museum's artifacts: the cauldrons that Odysseus was given by the Phaeacians; a small triangular shaped piece of pottery indicating, she says, that Odysseus was venerated in the cave at Polis Bay; fifth-century funeral vases with images of Athêna, Odysseus, and Telémakhos; and Mycenaean cups, clay vessels and toys illustrating that Ithaka was settled well before the era of Odysseus.

Fotini explains that many archeologists believe Pelikata Ridge was the site of Odysseus' palace due to a passage in *The Odyssey* indicating that from the palace it's possible to see the three bays of Polis,

Frikes and Alphales. She acknowledges that others think the palace may have been in Polis Bay or near Aetos in the southern part of the island. The possible options don't keep her awake at night.

"As long as the current digs and research prove that *The Odyssey* all happened on Ithaka I'm not too concerned about the specific locations," Fotini tells me. "I can't walk too far anymore so please think of me during your exploration."

I'm so enchanted by her little museum that I write in the registration book: "Mesmerized by this wonderful museum on this delightful island as I MedTrek from Odysseus's palace to Laërtês' farm with Athêna, Telémakhos, and the rest of the gang."

I head towards Kioni the next morning feeling spry and fit after yesterday's 47-kilometer, 12-hour MedTrekking day. I pass one beach congested with pleasure boat sailors heading en masse into the €2 showers and another where a bearded gentleman taking a dip eerily resembles Odysseus. I approach the respected warrior, who laughs when I ask if he's Odysseus.

"Why must you lie, being the man you are, and all for nothing?" I reply, quoting the words the swineherd Eumaios asked Odysseus.

I kick stones out of the middle of the narrow seaside road and pick up litter (again, cigarette packs are the main culprit) as I watch a cruise ship glide through the unruffled sea.

When I arrive in Kioni, I enter a café called *Mentor: The Turquoise Eye of the Cyclops* and read a flyer plastered on the wall that contends "the best way to explore the island is to rent a boat." Another poster, presumably targeting the British boating crowd or passengers on the *Escapade* from Nice, promotes a *Feelings* class that starts in the water at 9:30 a.m. That's fifteen minutes from now and, though it's always good to soak feelings, I'm too anxious to keep hiking to bother with it.

Another tract issued by the PhilHomeric Association of Ithaka explains why Ithaka is unquestionably the island of Odysseus. The lengthy elucidation cites descriptions in *The Odyssey* and says, "Ithaka is easily seen to be an island. It is narrow and long, there is a sea passage between it and Cephalonia, there are places that enabled Telémakhos to see three bays from the palace courtyard, it is rugged, it is unsuited for horses and it has royal springs."

It goes on to proclaim, in an effort to debunk an argument made by many Ithakaphobes, that the ongoing debate about the island's geographic location is due to a misreading of the original text. It concludes with the assertion that coins with Odysseus's image have been found on the island and that "a visit to 31 places that you've just got to see will convince you that this is the setting of Homer's *Odyssey*."

Already a believer that Ithaka is Ithaka, I "sense" some of the spots evoked throughout *The Odyssey* when I take off from Kioni on the ancient uphill path to Anogi on the slopes of Mount Neritos. Like Exogi, Anogi has seen better days, though Fotini Couveras at the museum insists that almost every family on the island can trace their roots back to one of these two villages.

I sit atop the stone of Hêraklês to admire views of mainland Greece, the sea, the coast, the islands, and the sky. The stupendous vista continues as I proceed to the Katharon Monastery, site of the first Christian church on the island built in 1700, and one of the purported sites of Laërtês' farm and field. I recall that Heinrich Schliemann read lines 205 to 412 from the 24th book of *The Odyssey* on this very spot while simultaneously translating the text into the local dialect. He describes the reaction of his audience.

"Their excitement was boundless as they listened to the account in the musical language of Homer, in the language of their glorious forbears of three thousand years ago, of the terrible sufferings which King Laërtês had endured on that very spot where we were gathered, and to the description of his great joy when he found again, after twenty years' separation, his beloved son Odysseus whom he had held for dead," Schliemann recounted in his 1869 doctoral dissertation *Ithaka, der Peloponnese und Troja* (*Ithaka, the Peloponnese and Troy*). "The eyes of all were swimming with tears, and when I had concluded my reading, men women and children all came up to me and embraced me with the words: 'You have given us great joy, we thank you a thousand times.' I was carried in triumph to the city where they all competed to give of their hospitality in abundance."

The view from the monastery of that city in the southern part of Ithaka is as much a visual treat as the narrow cliff-hanging road that winds down to the eastern coast.

When I return to Frikes, I tell Peter Argyris, the South African owner of the Dodoni café, that he's related to Fotini Couveras.

"Greece is all one big family," Argyris agrees as I proceed to relate the theme of *Middlesex* in which bad genes are passed down through a brother/sister marriage. "But this isn't *Deliverance Two*."

I stop by Kiki's to buy dinner and the salesgirl isn't completely pleased that the tourist season is almost over. "This means that now I've got to pick olives, and that's much harder than dealing with customers," she says.

Seeking the Cave of the Nymphs

When I leave Frikes the next morning at 6:55, to move my base camp to Vathi, I run into Haze ("It's short for Hazel") White from Perth at the bus stop. She's been visiting different parts of Greece every other year for ten years and is currently sampling islands in the Ionian Sea. Like me, she's doing it on a budget, and within five minutes we're talking like a couple of hippies on the road on Crete in the 1960s. How did you get from Corfu to Frikes? Where did you stay in Corfu? How much are you paying here? What's been good? What's been bad?

We're having such a good time that when we get to Vathi, the "capital" of Ithaka which is also called Ithaki (the Greek word for "precipitous"), we hang out together at a café in the main square. Haze, who's in her mid-fifties, has been offered a sailboat ride by a 23-year-old sailor from Port Aetos near Vathi to Cephalonia. We discuss his true motivation while she accompanies me to rent a €30 room at Adriana Angelios' boarding house. Coincidentally I'm just two doors down from both the world headquarters of the PhilHomeric Society and City Hall, where I learn about the location of another purported Cave of the Nymphs and am told that I'll find the swineherd Eumaios "near Raven's Rock and the well of Arethousa."

At this end of the island they contend that Phorkys Bay, where they claim a sleeping Odysseus was put ashore when he returned to Ithaka, is actually the Bay of Dexia just outside Vathi. There, they assure me, I'll find the real Cave of the Nymphs. The Fountain of Arethousa and the Raven Rock are just south of Vathi and not, as others claim, near Kalamos and Afales Bay in the north.

I try to get a few more clues to the actual locations by visiting the Ithaka Archeological Museum which is filled with treasures found at Pisa Aetos. A poster informs me that the 11th International Symposium on *The Odyssey*, hosted by the Center for Odyssean Studies, took place here a month ago with the theme *Myths, Text, Images: Homeric Epics and Ancient Greek Art*.

I show Haze the plaque in the harbor that commemorates Lord Byron's visit in August 1823 and tell her that Byron visited the Cave of Eumaios and hosted a dinner party for friends on tablecloths.

During the day, after I describe my book/divorce/life, Haze spins some good travel yarns of her own, especially about being a single woman on the go.

"The hotel owner in Corfu asked me before breakfast one morning if I'd slept with anyone in my room that night," she says. "Naturally I was taken aback but said 'Why?' He said "Because if you did you'll have to pay more money.' I told his wife, who's English, how inappropriate that remark was, and all of a sudden he treated me with some respect. I'll bet you don't get that kind of crap!"

We have a Greek salad lunch together ("I think you'll have four marriages and four divorces," she predicts) before Haze (yes, she's heard all the white and purple haze jokes) walks one symbolic kilometer out of town with me. After she leaves, I continue in a clockwise direction along the Bay of Dexia up the hill past the Venetian Cannon at the Loutras Fort until I reach a big villa with "Private" scrawled on the gate. I wonder if this type of signage would have irritated Odysseus or if, as king, he might have sided with the upper class when it comes to fences. While they may have some agricultural or social purpose, such obstacles force MedTrekkers to walk through lots of brambles and bushes.

I reach Skinos Bay and briefly join a few octogenarian Greek women, who are having a ball as they causally swim with flippers, in the water. Then I head down the island on a path that is sometimes well tended and shady, sometimes wild, thorny and brushy. I walk along a long, sandy beach and find myself in an unblemished cove where I celebrate the 6,000-kilometer mark on my MedTrek with a leisurely skinny dip in the clear and cleansing water before laying down on the warm pebbles to dry.

Once that significant commemoration is concluded, I continue past another bay and cut uphill through almost-ready-to-be-picked olive trees to finally dead-end at some small farms teeming with dogs, sheep, goats, and chickens. I amuse myself by bleating back at the bell-chiming goats, convinced that I've got the bleat down as well as I had the Tule Lake goose call mastered when I met the gypsies. You never know when something like this will come in handy.

I gradually wind my way back to Vathi, getting occasional whiffs of early autumn garden fires, and conclude that there is an ongoing war between southern and northern Ithakans when it comes to who "owns" Odysseus. Fiotini makes a point of telling me that the Pelikata Archaeological Museum is financed by North Ithakan money. And the authorities in Vathi attempt to claim that everything Odyssean happened on their part of the island. Whether he existed or not, whether he was ever on Ithaka, Odysseus is easily the island's best-known celebrity.

The probable path around southern Ithaka often looks deceptively easy on a map.

I thought my next day out would be a simple sprint up to the purported Cave of the Nymphs followed by a saunter on an across-the-mountain path to the supposed Castle of Odysseus in the ancient city of Alaikmenai and a stroll on the slopes of Mt. Stefano to the Taxiarchos monastery.

Hah! Maps don't show overgrown paths and instead of an effortless day I have, well, another cut-opening (and cut-reopening) scramble through prickly bushes and conclude that the paths in northern Ithaka are much better maintained than these in the south. And, though this is a truism most people learn at the age of two, I'm again reminded of the fact that a somewhat clear path going up the mountain doesn't mean there will be a somewhat clear path going across or down the other side of the mountain.

I ignore the sign indicating that the Cave of the Nymphs is "closed" and march up a hillside road between olive groves and goat farms to investigate. I find a deep, dark, dank, bat-filled cave that, based on the faint letters on the "Keep Out" sign, has been out of action for a while. I manage to get inside, throw a rock down to ascertain the depth (too deep to fool around in without lights and ropes, and a serious danger zone for any kids at play) and come away flummoxed.

Why would the Odysseus-touting south let an obvious tourist gem go to rot? And what's it doing high on a hill instead of on the seaside? I mean, this is supposed to be the seaside Cave of the Nymphs, one of the coolest venues in *The Odyssey*, but the closed entry looks like a shack in Appalachia with a hangover. Is everyone now convinced that the cave in Polis Bay is the right one?

Ah, the joy of conjecture, I say to myself as I ruminate about the caves.

As I continue, I meet a non-English speaking Greek on a moped, show him my map, and ask if he thinks I should go to Piso Aetos directly over the mountain or on the road. I think he indicates the road and that is probably why I choose to go over the mountain. At first I'm pleased with my decision, especially when I arrive at a small, isolated, and unlocked hillside chapel where I light (glad that I always carry a lighter) two candles on behalf of the just-deceased aunt of a friend.

After that it takes me an excruciating hour to struggle downhill through the brush to the road where I see signs indicating the route of a past Ithaka Marathon, which was billed as "I Walked In Odysseas (sic) Footsteps."

I am getting continually cut up as I wander through thick, thorny brush, and after only ten kilometers I am very tired of it.

I take the road to Piso Aetos, briefly drop into the ancient city of Alaikmenai (which has been taken over by a goat herder) and spend another hour investigating a trail along the mountain to the monastery. Bah humbug! If there ever was a real trail here, it's now completely overgrown. As I hike back to Vathi I run into a Greek gardening outside his villa and ask him about the lack of a path and the sad state of the

Cave of the Nymphs.

"The politicians claim they have the money to clean the paths but either the people in charge never get it or get it and don't clean the paths. Typical government corruption!" he barks. "And if the paths in the north are better tended than the ones in the south, then I think you've got to conclude that there's more corruption in the south.

"And you know why the Cave of the Nymphs is in such disrepair?" he continues. "It's Washington's fault. The US government gave a lot of money to a university professor pre-Obama and he dynamited the cave to see if there was a connecting tunnel between Phorkys Bay and the hillside entry. Now it's completely out of commission. If that guy ever shows up here again, he'll be killed."

"So I gather you're here for the sun, sea, sand and sky and not the paths or the politics," I reply.

"Actually the sun, sea, sand, and sky are just as nice on Long Island in New York where I live," said the man, who is proud that at 74 he is an active gardener. "I'm only here because my mother is 100 and when she's no longer here then I'm no longer here. And I don't know why you're walking here anyway. Odysseus was a king. He never walked."

I continue along Phorkys Bay to Vathi and figure it would have taken quite a bit of dynamite to make the connection between the cave and the coast. Whoever came up with that scheme should be banished.

When I reach town, I decide to get a haircut and shave when the barbershop reopens at 5:00 p.m. On the way I see a bust of Odysseus on the port, a statue of him near the main square, a drawing of his head on a rock leading to a villa and a mural on the wall of a café.

"Do you think Odysseus actually lived in southern Ithaka?" asks the barber as I get in the chair.

"Absolutely," I smile, though I might have disagreed with that contention if he'd asked me when I got out of the chair.

I have one section of Ithaka left to MedTrek and think, or hope anyway, that I've left the easiest, and perhaps the most interesting, for last. I head directly south on the uphill road out of Vathi, the one that passes the hospital and school, with four objectives: (1) not to incur one more cut on my already sliced up legs that look like an ad for a defective razor blade; (2) visit the well of Arethousa and, if possible, drink from it; (3) reach the Marathias Plateau to see where Eumaios may have herded his swine; and (4) find out if the ravens are still flying at Raven's Rock.

There's a refreshing autumnal chill in the air as I walk on an olive treed, vine-yarded road, pass a few holiday homes with swimming pools and don't see a single car. The only sound is, as usual, goat bells. The road stretches to the end of the island, and blazed paths lead up, down and across to each of my destinations.

I get my first pleasant surprise of the day when, after five kilometers, I see a sign for Rize's Cave. I walk fifteen minutes uphill on a clear path and am rewarded with not only a cool cave but also a cool topless cave. I enter the tiny opening to find, high above me, a slice of nice blue sky visible through a large slit in the rock roof.

A few kilometers later, I march downhill towards the sea to the alleged well of Arethousa located midway between the sea cove and a rock ravine. The well contains not only water but also a black plastic bucket that enables me to sample the water, though a bat flies into my face when I throw it into the spring. That doesn't stop me from tasting the "dark still water" that could have been drunk by Odysseus and almost certainly watered Eumaios's stock as they rooted nearby for acorns.

The electrifying thrill of this unique experience sends chills up and down my back as I stare at tiny Perapigadia Island and two sailboats anchored near the bay where I celebrated the 6,000-kilometer mark.

A paved road continues to a large, comparatively flat area that may have been the best place to raise pigs in all of Ithaka back in the day – and, from the odors, even today. There's a sign for Eumaios' Cave, and I'm reminded that Athêna told Odysseus: "You'll find him posted beside his swine, grubbing round by Ravens Rock and the spring called Arethousa."

I walk as far as I can go down a dirt path and a number of big birds are flying above Ravens Rock. I'm not actually sure that these are ravens, but for the sake of this story, I'll pretend they are.

I SPOT from here, looking out over the smooth sea towards Cephalonia, and then march back to Vathi where a couple take a photo of me posing in front of a statue of either Zeus or Poseidon. Although it may take archeologists a few more decades to indisputably ascertain that Ithaka is the setting for Homer's *Odyssey*, I'm already a contented believer.

Searching for Nausikaa on Corfu

"The grey-eyed goddess Athêna made her tarry, so that Odysseus might behold her beauty and win her guidance to the town." – *The Odyssey*

I'm heading to the island of Skhería, Odysseus' last stop on his return from Troy and the finale of Circe's sixth task requiring me to "island hop to Lesbos, Lemnos, Ithaka, and Corfu to encounter many of the characters and places mentioned by Homer."

The fabled land of the ship-designing Phaeacians who, much to their regret, gave Odysseus a lift to Ithaka, is also known as Kerkyra, Corcyra, and Corfu. It's located north of Ithaka off the west coast of Greece and Albania, but there's no direct ferry. Most travelers from Odysseus' island to Corfu take, as irrational as it might sound, a ferry four hours south to Patras on mainland Greece and then, after a four-hour layover, another ferry six hours north to Corfu. This convoluted 15-hour solution is, to me, unacceptable, and I embark on a shorter, if more circuitous escapade using a combination of ferries, buses and thumbing.

The transport logistics and route are somewhat problematic, but as a seasoned MedTrekker I'm in no hurry. After my recent scramble around Ithaka, I could use a few days off before exploring Skhería to find Nausikaa, the lovely young daughter of King Alkínoös and Queen Arêtê whose name means "the burner of ships."

Nausikaa, "so fine in mould and feature that she seemed a goddess," ran into Odysseus on a beach (Athêna was responsible for that), had him bathed and cleaned up, and led him to her father's enchanting, garden-surrounded palace. The sumptuous feast that followed produced the story-telling that makes up much of *The Odyssey* and illustrates the importance of welcoming strangers, providing refuge, giving gifts, and other commendable social traits of Odysseus' era.

My idiotic routing to Skhería is a bit quicker and cheaper than taking 15 hours and paying €50 to ferry via Patras. Not much, though. It takes me 13.5 hours and costs €34 to catch a quick ferry from Ithaka to the town of Astakos, which means "lobster," on the mainland. Then I catch a bus to Mitikas, get eight hitchhiking rides of various distance to just past Parga, grab another bus to Igoumenitsa, and board the ferry from there to Corfu.

The multi-machined odyssey occurs on a beautiful day on a stunning part of the Greek coast, and I generously thank the eight drivers who pick me up – and many others who don't. The lifts are provided by a Greek Canadian raised in Toronto; a Greek delivery man learning three words of English a day (he tells me how complicated it will be for me to learn Greek "because there are multiple words for every object and action"); an Albanian carpenter who takes me into Vonitsa because "the U.S. and Albania are brothers"; a Greek businessman going for a Saturday afternoon swim; a just-married Greek utility meter reader who has "nothing to do" for two hours and offers to drive me to the Preveza before recounting, as we whiz past early Christian basilicas, that he's out to beat his father's 240 km/h speed record; a Flemish-speaking Belgian who takes me two kilometers; a German-speaking Greek working for Vodafone; and a 42-year-old Greek teacher and football coach.

Each of the drivers is intrigued by my MedTrekking exploits and, though I should obviously be speaking a little more Greek than I do, all of them tolerate my attempts to communicate in English, French, German, and Italian. Another seven cars, including one with a young mother and her baby, stop to see if I need any help. This makes the coastal odyssey much more educational and enjoyable than riding on two ferries, especially one going the wrong way.

My mode of travel is particularly instructive because the friendliness shown to me – an anonymous backpack-carrying wayfarer –

is illustrative of a characteristic of contemporary Greeks that is often lost sight of in the midst of the economic mess the country is enduring.

My last two saviors are going to spend the weekend with their parents, and the final lift deposits me at a bus stop 38 kilometers from the ferry-filled port of Igoumenitsa. It's a star-lit crossing to Corfu, which the Michelin guide calls "the most charming of the Ionian Islands: luxuriant gardens, rocky bays, large sandy beaches, history and a mild climate."

I set up a base camp in a hotel near the ferry dock in Corfu Town and am checked in by a receptionist who had just spent three years studying in Chicago. She gives me the lowdown on the local action and, after our chat, I decide to follow the curvature of Garitsa Bay past Corfu's Ancient Citadel to the gun emplacement in Kanoni. Then I'll visit Mouse Island (aka Pondikonissi), which is thought by some to be the petrified ship that the Earthshaker Poseidon turned to stone after the Phaeacians upset him by returning Odysseus to Ithaka.

I kick off my Sunday morning walkabout by MedTrekking through Corfu's old town with its decrepit and aging Neapolitan and Italianesque buildings. There are so many architectural and other visible foreign influences -- Venetian (Italian was once the official language), British, Russian, Turkish, French (Napoleon considered Corfu the key to the Adriatic), and Austrian – that I have to remind myself that I'm in Greece.

A taxi driver directs me to the only open bakery in *Palea Poli*, as locals call the old town, and I stumble around a few alleys to discover, among other things, a Mastic Spa and a Dragonfly Tattoo and Piercing Shop. I stroll through the Spianada Square, which was once used to drill soldiers and is still the site of Corfu's cricket pitch, with its spreading shade trees and an arcaded terrace known as the "Liston," inspired by the rue de Rivoli in Paris. Then I visit a delightful little park dedicated to fraternal authors Gerald and Lawrence Durrell, who lived on Corfu from 1935-1939.

The dedications in the park call the Durrell brothers *Philhellenes*, which means they were major lovers of Greece, and there's a bronze bust of each with a quote. Lawrence's (1912-1990) reads "Greece is the country that offers you the discovery of yourself...." while Gerald's (1925-1995) begins "Corfu, the garden of the gods...."

Though I found Lawrence Durrell too ponderous to read when I was younger, I thoroughly enjoyed Gerald Durrell's numerous books, with titles like *My Family and Other Animals* that hilariously recount his time here.

"You used to read Gerald and I used to read Lawrence," recounted Henrietta Dax, who lived with me in Paris during the '70s and now runs a bookstore in Cape Town. "There's a big difference between the two."

She's right. And I admittedly enjoyed Gerald's playful humor over Lawrence's profound ponderings, though I recall that Henrietta also liked Gerald's description of Corfu in *How To Shoot An Amateur Naturalist*.

"The island lies like a strange, misshapen dagger in the blue lonian Sea, midway along the Greek and Albanian coastlines," he wrote. "In the past, it has fallen into the hands of a dozen different nations, from all of which it has absorbed what it found good and rejected the rest, thus keeping its individuality. Unlike so many parts of Greece, it is green and lush, for when it was part of the Venetian empire they used it as their oil store, planting thousands of olive trees, so that now the bulk of the island is shaded by these carunculated giants with their wigs of silvery-green leaves."

I look back on the *Paleo Frourio*, or the Ancient Citadel, and see a ferry approaching from the mainland before, just for fun, I check out the Corfu Palace Hotel where The European College for Tourism Studies is located. Next I take the self-guided Archeological Tour of Byzantine Monuments of Palaiopolis, which was the site of the town of Kerkyra in ancient Roman and Byzantine periods. The tour is described as "a pilot project restoring and accentuating local monuments and linking them in a network of archeological sites."

I drop into Sunday services in the Agios Spiradonas (Saint Spiridon was the island's patron saint in the fourth century AD) and the Agios Ioannis (Saint John) churches before arriving at the Temple of Artemis on the Odos Stratia. This was a place of worship in the early sixth century BC and had what is considered to be one of the earliest stone pediments with relief decoration in Greece. I stop to admire *Mon Repos*, a villa designed in 1824 that sits on the site of the ancient acropolis of Corcyra and, in 1921, was the birthplace of Prince Philip, the Duke of Edinburgh. A villa near *Mon Repos* is called *Mon Plaisir* and for some reason it reminds that I called my garden-rich villa in the south of France *19 Pines, Some Palm and a Bonsai*.

Passing the Nausika (sic) Restaurant (I'm on Nausikas Street after all), I arrive in Kanoni, where I find the island's single runway airport and walk, as though I'm a privileged guest, into the Corfu Holiday Palace Hotel. But I obviously lack a bit of confidence because I don't take the "For Guests Only" elevator down to the beach.

I have to admit that I'm immediately skeptical that Mouse Island, which is just offshore, was created by Poseidon when he turned the Phaeacians boat into stone. It's way too Disneyesque (kids are taken out for free by one boat company) and too petite to be taken seriously.

Nonetheless I do light two candles at the nearby Monastery of Vlaherna for any sailors that might have been lost in that incident and examine T-shirts with sketches from *The Odyssey*. A local tour guide informs me that a more appropriate candidate for the rock-ing ship is Kolovri Rock in the Bay of Paleokastritsa.

As I cross the footpath on a levy across Lake Halikiopoulos, I'm amused by signs that warn "Don't Fall In" and "Crossing By Pedestrians Is Done at their own Risk." In fact, the major risk here would be getting hit by one of the arriving airplanes that swoop just overhead.

In Perama, I seek out the strawberry-pink villa where Gerald Durrell lived and recall that he wrote "The warm air was thick with the scent of a hundred dying flowers, and full of the gentle, soothing whisper and murmur of insects." Then I stop for a coffee at the hillside Nisos Paradise café, where owner Georgios and I discuss the end of the tourist season, the predicted rainstorm, the facts about Mouse Island and the relaxed situation in Greek cafés ("We're relaxed because of what we see when we drink," he says, pointing at the sea below).

"The reason it's called 'mythology' is because you can say anything you like and no one can prove you wrong," said Georgios. "Mouse Island's a good story, a good fairytale. Who cares if it's true?"

Continuing onto Benitses Beach, I'm not all that impressed with the on-a-cheap-holiday-tour British and Dutch lazing on the beach, but I do enjoy the classic rock music at Connection. Over another coffee, I decide to MedTrek as far south as possible during the remainder of the afternoon and leave town along a row of bars and beach sites that are in the last throes of the season. No one cares that I walk amid the pools or disturb a few sunbathers before the free Greek Nights party at the Golden Beach bar in Moraitika.

"This is the last hour of the last day of the summer season," says the barman at Marbella Beach in Agios Ioannis. "You can do anything you want."

Strolling along the beach, amid all the soon-to-be-shut hotels, I reach Mesongi and then head inland to Linea and across the island to Saint Georgios, which features one of Corfu's best sandy beaches. On the way I enjoy the olive groves, autumn smells, cool afternoon yard fires, a group of English-speaking bicycle riders, and the sea on the western side of Corfu. What do I eat on a walkabout like this? Corfu nuts for lunch and a Corfu fig pie for tea (without the tea).

There is a loud, bright, and hard thunder-lightning-and-rain storm during the night, and a coffee and an apple pie at the ferry terminal are breakfast before I head to Paleokastritsa to gaze at the real Stoned Ship created when Zeus told Poseidon to "strike her into a rock that looks like a racing vessel, just offshore." Even more exciting, today I may find the beach where Odysseus – who spent twenty days "in the winedark sea, on the ever-lunging swell, under gale winds, getting away from the Island of Ogygia" before he got here – met Nausikaa "of the white arms" and was led to her parents' palace.

By the time I arrive in seaside Paleokastritsa, the heavens are really opening up. I spend an hour kicking back at the Xenia bar drinking coffee from an all-you-can-drink-for-€2 urn while the few other customers attempt to predict the weather and the hiking conditions.

"This isn't a day to try the path up to Lakones and Angelokastro," warns one hippie-ish waitress. "You'll slip and break something on that wet rock goat trail."

I chat with a Glaswegian about her mountain hiking background and know she's one of my tribe when she asks "Where's your base camp then?" and begins asking me about the equipment I carry. Then, attempting to show that I'm a MedTrekker for all seasons, I ignore everyone and slog up the hill behind Paleokastritsa.

A billboard says there are fifteen beaches (one of them, presumably, is where Odysseus met Nausikaa) and six caves in the Liapades Bay (some, it says, you can only reach by boat). But I leave them behind – as well as the Yellow Submarine boat trips, Moody Blues bar, Golden Fox Restaurant, Arianna Pool Bar, Odysseus Hotel, and shops pushing other local big sellers like olive oil and cumquats – to ascend to Angelokastro, a very precariously and strategically placed impregnable 13th-century Byzantine hilltop fortress.

The rain really never stops during the blustery, windy day. I get soaked one hour and partially dry the next – three different times. Taking the wet-dry-wet-dry-wet-dry-wet cycle in my stride, I climb through oak woods, olive groves, cypress forests, and the villages of Lakones and Makrades.

Although abandoned during the 19th century when such castles failed to serve much purpose, Angelokastro has been preserved with the aid of a European Union program for Stoned Ship viewing. Indeed, from the rampart I see the Stoned Ship and spend half an hour admiring it in spite of the admittedly storm-clouded view.

As I SPOT from the fort, I wonder exactly how a very good-looking John McManus, memorialized by a chunk of marble that reads "In memory of John McManus, aged 41 years, who tragically lost his life 26/6/93 – Happy Loving Memories," ended his life. I then sit quietly and read a bit from *The Odyssey* about the ship turning to stone.

"When all who watch upon the wall have caught sight of the ship, let her be turned to stone – an island like a ship, just off the bay," Homer wrote. "Mortals may gape at that for generations."

Poseidon accomplished the task "at one blow of his palm" and the Phaeacians looking on wondered "Who in thunder has anchored, moored that ship in the seaway?"

King Alkínoös, however, knew the ship-to-stone transformation was on the cards.

"This present doom upon the ship – on me – my father prophesied in the old time. If we gave safe conveyance to all passengers we should incur Poseidon's wrath."

Chalk up another group of seamen lost because of Odysseus.

On my descent I survey kitsch souvenirs at the "Tourist Shop Machos – All Kinds of Souvenirs." I observe that every restaurant has signs and menus in German, stop at the Taverna Sunset in Krini that bills itself as "sunset on heaven's garden," and notice a little shop called "Quo Vadis," a question that I've been answering since it was posed by Frere Jean-Pierre at the Lerins Abbey on the second day of my MedTrek over a decade ago.

I drop into Colombo's in Makrades for *moussaka, baklava* and a Greek coffee (€11) to recharge my batteries for the walk downhill. While eating, I begin to imagine a castaway Odysseus following Nausikaa's maidens to King Alkínoös' palace.

I relive their initial meeting when Odysseus was "debating inwardly what he should do: embrace this beauty's knees in supplication? Or stand apart, and, using honeyed speech, inquire the way to town and beg some clothing."

Naturally he goes for the honeyed speech approach and uses a well-practiced line that I occasionally borrow: "Never have I laid eyes on equal beauty in man or woman. I am hushed indeed."

Nausikaa falls for it, and quickly realizes that Odysseus "looks like one of heaven's people. I wish my husband could be fine as he and glad to stay forever on Skhería."

And that encounter led to the expression "a match made in heaven," though Odysseus and Nausikaa didn't become a match.

I follow the path they may have taken to the town and palace, and let my imagination continue to run wild with myth and legend as I enjoy a delightful up-and-down-the-hill frolic in the rain. In particular, I think of honeyed speech and the pride taken by Homer in his characters' command of language. Although often at the mercy of different translators, Homer offers honeyed speech aplenty in his *Iliad* and *Odyssey*.

"In looks a man may be a shade, a specter, and yet be master of speech so crowned with beauty that people gaze at him with pleasure," Homer writes in *The Odyssey*.

Hektor, in *The Iliad*, is obviously impressed with Achilles's vocabulary on the battlefield in Troy when he says that his adversary has "turned into a word-thrower, hoping to make me lose my fighting heart and head in fear of you."

Sometimes, though, honeyed speech can cloud the conversation.

"You speak with art but your intent is honest," King Alkínoös told Odysseus during the long recount of his travels.

Then I think about what could have transpired between Nausikaa and the man who "looks like one of heaven's people."

Walking towards Paleokastritsa, I hope to find the woman from Glasgow who seemed like part of my tribe when we had coffee many hours ago and may think I'm from heaven.

But instead when I arrive on the outskirts of town, I enter a shop with "handmade souvenirs – traditional oil, wine, honey, herbs, homemade marmalade – supplied by the AgroTourism Cooperation of the Women of Paleokastritsa." I spend the rest of the day there attempting to verify that Nausikaa, once she realized her future didn't lie with Odysseus, founded the co-op and spent decades waiting, unrewarded, for a suitor whose honeyed speech impressed her.

Meeting a Homerophile at the Achilleion

The next morning a serious wind just before dawn clears the rain-threatening cloudy sky and inspires me to MedTrek to Achilleio, south of Corfu Town, to see a project created by one of the world's most ardent Homerphiles.

Everyone – the lovely woman at the bakery on the port who sells me a *bougatsa crema*, the Patras Travel rep who books me a private cabin on a ferry to Italy, the Lithuanian waitress at breakfast who gives me a free cup of coffee, the man out for an early morning walk – has the same reaction when I tell them I'm walking to Achilleio.

"But that's twelve kilometers away!" they each exclaim using the same words, though the ferry ticket seller concludes with "then turn right at the psychiatric ward."

In fact, it's only nine kilometers to Achilleio and the Achilleion, Corfu's neoclassical equivalent of Versailles. After I endure the first five kilometers of urban drudgery and jumble (illegally parked cars, a few dead cats, the airport, radio and TV towers, lots of pet shops, supermarkets and vegetable stands selling loads of garlic and onions, truck and bus traffic, and a travel company called Achilles Tours), it's a pleasant walk to the hillside where Empress Elisabeth of Austria designed and built a Pompeii-influenced neoclassical villa in 1890. Dedicated to *The Iliad* hero Achilles, the Achilleion is adorned with a panorama of statues, sculptures, busts, paintings, and frescoes in his honor.

I would have been happy to walk a lot further to feast my eyes on this gem fastidiously created by an empress who played down her celebrity, despised the formality of Hapsburg court life and came to vibrant life herself once she got out of Vienna. Dressed completely in black after the suicide death of her son Rudolf at Mayerling in 1889, Empress Elisabeth watched her diet, wrote poetry, adored Heinrich Heine, and coped with an inherited neurosis that afflicted other members of her clan, notably her cousin Ludwig II of Bavaria.

Sisi, as she was known, was perhaps a greater fan of Homer than me. Born in 1837, she took a tour of Homeric sites, and even dressed *incognito* to get into forbidden Troy in defiance of her husband's wishes. There's an interesting parallel, I think, with Sisi's masquerade and Odysseus' frequent efforts to disguise himself. I not only identify with her but also am so intrigued by her infatuation that I learn as much about her as I can, including the fact that she was stabbed and killed by a mad Italian in Geneva in 1898.

"Achilles was her idol, she admired his strength and divine beauty, and she adored the perfect world of Homer," said the audiotape at the Achilleion adding, "It is worth noticing the small size of her waist, about which so much has been written and said."

Sisi's infatuation with Achilles and the creation of the Achilleion make me look like a fair-weather Homerophile. She's not alone, of course. Zeus-fostered Achilles was considered the greatest of all Greek warriors and, said Odysseus, "the flower and pride of the Akhaians."

The second I enter the villa, an ethereal Athêna, who this time appears in the shape of a statuette on a hearth, gives me one of her knowing owlish winks and points me in the direction of the large statues in the villa garden which, planted with Mediterranean flowers and trees, look onto northern Corfu, Greece, and Albania. I'm impressed that an obviously blind Homer (and an all-seeing Shakespeare) are among busts of twelve wise men Sisi chose to display. I marvel at larger statues that include *The Dying Achilles,* created by the German sculptor Ernst Herter in 1884.

I'm not sure Sisi would have been pleased that in 1907 her villa was bought by Kaiser Wilhelm II, who claimed that Achilles was the "leader and inspiration" of his Prussian forces. However, she might have appreciated the gigantic sculpture of *Achilles the Victor* that the Kaiser commissioned. It weighs 4.5 tons, stands 11.5 meters high, and was lighted, in another sign of Prussian humility, so that it could be seen from the Kaiser's yacht.

I'm so thrilled with what Sisi left behind that I take smiling and satisfied steps the rest of the day as I walk to the Cliff of Aerostrato in Sinarades on the western side of the island. My day ends at the hilltop village of Pelekas, which was known as the Kaiser's throne because Wilhelm II went there frequently to admire the view.

The Love Canal has such a malevolent connotation in the United States (located in Niagara Falls, in the state of New York, it was a dumping spot for toxic waste) that when I hear there's a *Canal d'Amour* in Sidari (the tourist hot spot in northern Corfu that has two stars in the Michelin Green guide) I've just got to see it. I'm even keener when I read on a blog that there "seemed to be a slight odor in the air." Who could resist? I may be on the cusp of a major ecological/environmental scoop.

When I arrive in Sidari it's clear this town is the focal point of English tourism on Corfu. Want a cheap English breakfast, a pub to buy a pint, football on Sky television, the latest London papers, or a chance to snog with a plump British bird on vacation? This is the spot.

The names of the bars – 1 For The Road, Shaker's, Black Horse, Mojo Music, Paradise Cocktail, Three Little Pigs, The Fruit Press, The Aquarius, The Falcon, The Madison, The Sea Breeze, The Kalypso – make the party atmosphere apparent even in the early morning. And the barrage of bargains, including a full English breakfast for only €2.50, indicate that the party will be affordable.

Despite a cool and windy autumn morning, the British are out in their swimsuits ready to tan, or booking tours at one of the many travel agencies, or visiting Corfu Medicare, a medical facility where "English is spoken and no appointment is necessary." The inordinate tourist buzz feels like Torremolinos has been transported from Spain to Greece.

The *Canal d'Amour*, created by the unique rock formations and constant sea action, doesn't smell when I visit. In fact, it's worth an outing to Sidari to see the water rushing through eroding sandstone cliffs and to walk on paths to coves, caves, caverns and swimming holes. Albania, just a few kilometers away, is an attractive backdrop.

I run into the same young German couple with two daughters that I saw at the Angelokastro and the Achilleion.

"Where will you be tomorrow?" asks the father, as though he'll make a point of going somewhere else.

After walking five kilometers around town and on the beaches, I go to the sedate village of Kassiopi, where I get unintentionally wet negotiating rocks and waves on the seaside. Then I weave my way on the bewitching beaches and bays, and along the high *corniche* road, past Alicinous's House, Nausikaa's House, the Dionysius Camping Village in Daphnilas, and the Nautillus Hotel in Barbati.

While the views of Albania are wondrous, the high point of the day is a visit to author Lawrence Durrell's former house on the pebbled seaside in Kalami. The sprawling white house is where Durrell wrote

Prospero's Cell with its evocative description of the house and its views on Albania. That book and two others, *The Greek Islands* and *The Dark Labyrinth*, are on sale at the White House Restaurant that, thank the gods, does not have any dishes named after its former owner.

A simple plaque indicates that Lawrence and his wife Nancy lived here before World War II, and a brochure informs me that the Prospero Apartment and the Villa White House can be rented by aspiring writers who might enjoy creating literature on the same dining room table used by Durrell.

One of my favorite books about Greece, Henry Miller's *The Colossus of Maroussi*, includes interesting anecdotes about Durrell, and I would have loved to be along when the duo had their "on the road" experience in different parts of Greece just before World War II.

I send a SPOT from the White House terrace before continuing along a corniche sandwiched by a towering mountain on my right (with the Pantokrator monastery amid the radio towers at the top) and olive trees, the sea, and views of Corfu Town, Greece and Albania on my left. My steps end at a nice strip of beach on a very calm bay in Ypsos-Pirgi, where the Temple Bar, like much of the rest of the town, is closed for the winter.

The next day I return to Igoumenitsa by ferry to see the most cut-throat and visible security of any port on the Med – rolls, not strands but rolls, of razor wire around the perimeter – and continue by overnight ferry to Bari, Italy. From there I take a train to Rome, book a room at the aptly named Il Stromboli hotel near the Termini station and send out an email update.

MedTrek Milestone #8

A full month of MedTrekking gets me another 657 kilometers "around" islands in the Med, and I'm now at the 6,166-kilometer mark. As you see, I followed Circe's directions and visited various islands which, unlike walking around the sea itself, has a randomness that contradicts my natural inclination to meditatively speed, if that's not a contradiction, from A to B on the mainland coast. Its been a good test of my flexibility.

After finishing my steps around Corfu, an island that Gerald Durrell called "the garden of the gods," I visited Amelia at the Oxygen Spa downtown for a necessary pore-cleansing mastic facial following my six-week stint of travel and MedTrekking. She was pleased to hear that I'd now completed six of my twelve labors and am heading to Crete, the Peloponnese, Mount Olympus, and Mount Athos to continue the game.

The Idiot and the Odyssey II

PART FOUR

GETTING GREASED WITH THE GODS

Ode on a Cretan Urn
Confronting the Colossal Cretan Cave Conundrum
Greeting Zeus on Mount Olympus
Prancing about the Peloponnese
Sleeping with Helen of Troy
Monking Around on Mount Athos

Ode on a Cretan Urn

"'Crete,' I murmured. 'Crete...' and my heart beat fast." –
Zorba the Greek, Nikos Kazantzakis

I didn't decide by myself to head to Crete, Greece's largest island in the southern Aegean, to MedTrek for two months. First I went to pay tribute to, and get some guidance from, the iconic Oracle at Delphi. Circe told me the renowned seer would inform me how to approach the Peloponnese and circumnavigate Europe's southernmost isle of Crete.

Circe's seventh labor embodies the physical and spiritual direction that she suggested I obtain from time to time. "Visit the Oracle of Delphi – who 'knew what was, what had been, what would be' – and let her lead you to the cave of Zeus' birth, the world's greatest travel writer, and the end of an historic footrace in Sparta." Not everyone likes the advice that they get from soothsayers like the Delphic Oracle: "You visionary of hell, never have I had fair play in your forecasts," Agamémnon complained in *The Iliad* when he was displeased with another clairvoyant's prediction – but I plan to listen and obey.

I stop in the picturesque village of Arachova, perched on the flank of Mount Parnonas, the home of Apollo and the nine Muses, on my way to consult the Oracle. When I reach Delphi, I'm flabbergasted that some ornate hand-carved walking sticks in a shop cost €60, but not surprised to see hotels named Apollo, Oracle, Zeus, Kouros, and Sybilla near restaurants called Dionysus and Vesuvio.

I start my outing in Delphi, which is seven kilometers from the Mediterranean as the birds fly, carefully carrying a €4.50 glass of fresh orange juice as I stroll through the Sanctuary of Athêna Pronaia just after sunrise. Pilgrims traditionally pay a visit here before seeking advice from the eminent Oracle, who speaks the will of the Apollo.

I promised Athêna and Apollo, the god of prophecy and healing, that I would learn both ancient and modern Greek before my arrival in Delphi. That didn't quite work out, so I practice my multilingual introductory spiel in Athêna's sanctuary before I humbly stroll up Delphi's Sacred Way to the Temple of Apollo, located at the exact spot that Zeus and his gang considered the center of their flat earth.

As I approach, I formulate questions posed by 27 well-meaning friends who want a response from the Oracle, who's also been known in the fortune-telling biz during the last few millennia as the Pythia or the Delphic Sibyl. Their questions are mostly about personal or political issues. Would a female pal fall in love, or even make love as, Odysseus said, "men and women by their nature do," anytime soon? Would Greece resolve its debt problem? Would Sarah Palin (this one from my right-wing mother) ever win the presidency? Would China get out of Tibet?

I'm not sure that the Oracle, who is shrouded by vapors and slightly resembles Vanessa Redgrave in her early 60s, even has a clue about current affairs, romantic or otherwise. However, I told my inquiring pals that I'd try to get them some answers before dealing with my own logistical conundrum.

It turns out, according to a priest who "translates" messages conveyed by the Oracle's trance-induced utterances and paroxysms, that Pythia/Sibyl doesn't really make predictions about love, elections, or football games. Instead she prefers to simply give advice, either coherently clear or irritatingly ambiguous, from atop a rock where she's been holding court since her inner sanctum in Apollo's sanctuary was destroyed by an earthquake centuries ago. The priest warns me, and every other visitor, that taking photos of the Oracle will produce very bad omens. In fact, there's not a single representation of her, in stone or bronze or paint or photo, in the worth-visiting museum nearby.

I'm hardly the first to seek out the Oracle's guidance. According to Strabo, ten percent of the men from the Greek city of Chalcis, which was in the midst of a serious drought, came to offer themselves as a sacrifice in 730 BC in an effort to reduce the population. Instead, the Oracle sent them to found the colony of Rhegion, which means "break away," that we know today as Reggio Calabria on the toe of Italy. Pretty sensible resolution, I think.

At first, all I can mutter during my séance with the world's most reputed psychic is "Good Morning" and "Thanks for seeing me!" in Greek and six other languages. The Oracle doesn't seem at all bothered by my lack of decent Greek. She also dismisses my questions about Tibet and romance and doesn't waste more than a minute considering my primary query.

"The Idiot might personally prefer to proceed to the nearby Peloponnese Peninsula and calmly walk counterclockwise towards Athens until his appointment to climb Mount Olympus and visit the monks at Holy Mount Athos," she informs me with slightly somber seriousness. "But before that The Idiot should visit the birthplace of the father of all gods in the caves of Crete."

One reason she directs me first to Crete is because the buzz, from authorities like Hesiod and Homer, is that Zeus was born on the fifth largest island in the Mediterranean (after Sicily, Sardinia, Cyprus, and Corsica), which was also the birthplace of Minoan culture and home to Europe's first real civilization. I haven't been to Crete since 1982 and look forward to again visiting the Palace of Knossos and discovering the cave where Zeus was born.

My next question for the Oracle, who is far too intimidating to invite out for a bonding *chai*, is if I should quit MedTrekking and get a day job.

"Should you give up your MedTrek?" she chuckles. "That's like asking whether I should stop being an oracle. Our mid-life projects stimulate, intrigue, and define us. We should both keep at them while we're physically, emotionally, and spiritually able to. Illness or death will let you know when it's time to stop, though I'm here for eternity."

Then, as suggested in the book *Twenty-Four Hours a Day*, I tell her that this morning I "pray that I may not ask to see the distant scene. I pray that one step may be enough for me."

After our chat, I have a vigorous four-hour romp around the Oracle's hillside home before meandering through the museum adjacent to the luxuriant archeological site. There I admire a stone frieze of the gods, which originally decorated a building in the area, which was sculpted around the same time that Homer wrote *The Iliad*. I am also transfixed by the bronze statue of the proud and erect Charioteer of Delphi.

This may sound vainglorious, but I may be the only visitor who realizes that I have something very much in common with the Charioteer, a life-size relic cast around in 478 BC and taken to the 474 BC Olympic Games to commemorate a victory.

What is it? The noble appearance? The victor's headband? The colored eyes?

Nope. Feet.

My feet, after walking more than 7,000 kilometers around the Mediterranean Sea, look exactly like the Charioteer's.

A good friend, Gayle Guest, compares our feet when she sees a photo of the Charioteer and suggests a surprising premise: "I think your feet represent Homer's books. Your left foot is *The Iliad* and depicts your journey to Troy and your right foot represents the journey home and spiritual growth in *The Odyssey*. The ten toes symbolize both the ten-year war and the ten-year journey home."

I get a last snapshot of Oracleville before heading downhill to Patras to catch a ferry to Crete. As I leave, I feel that the Oracle embodies a conclusion arrived at by Lao Tsu: "Those who know do not talk. Those who talk do not know."

Zorba the Greek author Nikos Kazantzakis best defined the more-than-mere-physical beauty of Crete's landscape when he called it a *palimpsest*, a lovely word often defined as "rewritten manuscript." This was due, Kazantzakis said, to the fact that the land, like a parchment that has been scraped clean and used again, bore "twelve successive historical inscriptions: contemporary; the period of 1821; the Turkish yoke; the Frankish sway; the Byzantine; the Romans; the Hellenistic epoch; the Classic; the Dorian middle ages; the Mycenaean; the Aegean; and the Stone Age."

I don't need an Oracle to make my first move in Hêraklion, which is named after Hêraklês and became the capital of Crete in 1971. Hêraklês arrived here, on one of his own twelve labors, to deal with the Cretan bull that was ravaging the land. My eighth task, to "meet with Zeus, the master of cloud, at the cave of his birth on Crete," is less challenging than that.

When the rain stops at 8:30 a.m., I decide to head west around the island to the village of Fodele, the birthplace of the Spanish Renaissance artist El Greco in 1541. Then I continue towards the seaside villages of Bali (I've visited the other Bali, in Indonesia, and thought this might have a similar allure), Rethymno, and Chania, the animated crescent-shaped port below the snow-covered peak of Lefká Óri, or the White Mountains.

Why kick off my MedTrek around Crete by heading counterclockwise, which seems to be my MO, for over 600 kilometers rather than go the other way?

I plan to meet Walter Lassally, the Academy Award-winning director of photography on *Zorba the Greek,* near Chania. I also want to simply MedTrek for a couple of weeks before ardently pursuing Zeus, and this directional choice will give me a chance to hike the fabled

Samariá Gorge before the tourist season officially begins. And I don't have an appointment to see Canadian archeologist Sandy MacGillivray in Palaikastro at the eastern tip of the island until mid-May.

My first day on the Cretan path starts at the Dominican Monastery of Ayios Petros near the Hêraklion port and ends thirty kilometers away at Fodele Beach, just a few kilometers from El Greco's birthplace.

In between, I have a stupendous cloud-shrouded view of Zeus' supposed profile lying quietly under Mount Gioúhtas, where some Cretans believe he's entombed; learn that the seacoast is rocky, steep, pathless, and wild (*Michelin Green Guide* writers were obviously on drugs when they wrote that "there is a marked route around the island"); confirm that the goat/sheep population hasn't been impacted by Greece's economic woes; and am soaked from hair to toenail by mid-April rain.

Zeus' purported mountain tomb, incidentally, led to a negative rumor about the people of Crete. Callimachus, the third-century BC poet and scholar, wrote in his *Hymn to Zeus* that "Cretans always lie" because they constructed a tomb for Zeus who is immortal. An immortal, Callimachus pointed out, doesn't need a tomb.

Before leaving Hêraklion, I see one of Crete's famously large eagles and the massive bird evokes another line that Kazantzakis wrote in *Zorba*: "How beautiful Crete is...Ah! If only I were an eagle, to admire the whole of Crete from an airy height..."

Eagles are one of the many birds that deliver good and bad omens throughout Homer's epics, which are speckled with sentences like "And Zeus that instant launched above the field the most portentous of all birds, an eagle, pinning in his talons a tender fawn." That particular eagle took the fawn to the altar of Zeus in Troy and, as a result, the Greeks "flung themselves again upon the Trojans with joy renewed in battle."

Indeed, "joy of action," rather than the "clammy dread," is what inspired Greek troops during that war. Homer wrote that "an eagle beating upward, in its claws a huge snake, red as blood, live and jerking" was an ill-fated portent for the Trojan troops when "the snake fell in the mass of troops."

Some Trojans didn't pay eagles much heed.

"You would have me put my faith in birds, whose spreading wings I neither track nor care for, whether to the right hand sunward they fly or to the left hand, westward into darkness?" Hektor said at Troy. "No, I say, rely on the will of Zeus who rules all mortals and immortals. One and only one portent is best: defend our fatherland."

I recall, looking at the eagle, another line from my *365 Tao Daily Meditations*: "When birds fly too high, they sing out of tune."

My counterclockwise choice doesn't mean I'm not equally excited about running into Zeus and his cavernous birthplace(s); visiting Knossos and King Minos' labyrinth (the story of the Minotaur and the labyrinth is one of my favorites); and climbing Mount Ida and discovering other remnants of Minoan civilization. I'm fairly sure these natural and man-made treasures on Crete aren't going anywhere.

Don't get the idea that the coast between Fodele Beach and Bali (pronounced Baa-LEE) is sandy. My first twenty kilometers are rough, rugged, steep and slippery. I MedTrek on the seaside, on country roads through villages like Sises (Note to self: bakeries in little towns like Sises tend to run out of bread before noon), and on the national road when it's the only option (Warning to self: Cretan drivers treat the shoulder of the road, which is the only place to walk, as the middle of the road).

The seaside terrain often "forces" me onto springing-to-life hillsides and into fruit-rich fields and orchards, where I encounter omnipresent Greek Orthodox chapels of various sizes and refuel with oranges that I pluck off trees.

I also discover some novel, to me anyway, agricultural advances that might date from the ancient Minoan culture that thrived on Crete during the Bronze Age that began in the 27th century BC. How, you might wonder, do the Cretans keep tree limbs growing correctly when they're battered by the many different types of vicious Mediterranean winds? What's the real reason that goats stay in their pens on Crete? The pictures tell the story.

Crete's Bali features a few small, sandy beaches, but no one, except an Idiot, would expect it to resemble its Indonesian counterpart. Still, it's a gem on the northern coast and looks alluring as I approach.

I send my SPOT tracking position from the Bali port while I explain my MedTrek project to Georges, the owner of the Akrogialli Taverna who says he saw me walking near Hêraklion earlier in the day. He's so impressed that I hoofed it all the way here that he plies me with free coffees to keep me going.

During our wide-ranging conversation, after I explain my fascination with Odysseus' homeward journey, Georges reminds me that Cretan warrior Idomeneus and his followers not only escaped death in Troy but also made it expeditiously home after the Trojan War. Who knew?

Rain keeps me in Hêraklion the next day so I decide to knock about Knossos and mingle with King Minos, one of Zeus' sons, before continuing west. I also visit the morning market on Odós 1866 to pick up some yoghurt, honey, and figs and laze about the Platía Eleftherías, Liberty Square, and the Platía Venizélou to do some afternoon people watching. Then at sunset, which can be witnessed from the terrace of my sixth-floor room above the port, I walk out to the Venetian Fortress at the entrance to the harbor.

I learn something new each time I visit Knossos, which Homer called "the chief city of King Minos, whom great Zeus took into his confidence every nine years" and other Minoan palaces at Phaistos, Mália, and Zakros. For example, I didn't know that during the Trojan War the "Kretans, all who came from Knossos…all from that island of a hundred cities served under Idomeneus, the great spearman."

"Follow the weathered Royal Road," I sing to myself as I approach the grounds of Knossos, which was initially explored by Sir Arthur Evans in 1894. There's no shortage of history here. Homer refers to Knossos in *The Iliad* when he describes the finely crafted shield that Hêphaistos made for Achilles, "in which the famed lame-one wrought a *chorós* like the one that Daedalus fashioned for Ariadne of the beautiful tresses in broad Knossos."

After calmly strolling up the weathered cobblestones of the Royal Road into Knossos, I pick up other delicious tidbits while I traipse around the ancient site and not-so-sacred grounds of what was once the greatest city in the Mediterranean. That's really no surprise because this spot was home to Neolithic man long before the first palace appeared around 2000 BC, before the era of King Minos began in 1700 BC. Today I discover the origin of the word "Wow," investigate the world's first urban garbage dump and compost heap, and tell a French tour group that the frescoes at Knossos are reproduction.

My imagination is stimulated by envisioning the labyrinth that Daedalus designed here to hold the Minotaur, the monster with a bull's head and a man's body to whom King Minos fed his enemies. Knossos is also where Theseus seduced Minos' daughter Ariadne and was able to find his way out of the labyrinth after slaying the Minotaur when Ariadne gave him a *mitos*, or ball of thread, that he unwound to guide himself. I've always enjoyed the definition of *mitos* as a lifeline created by the Fates at birth that we each unravel as we age to avoid being forever lost in the labyrinth of life.

Sandy MacGillivray, an archeologist whom you'll meet when we explore his dig in eastern Crete, is among many who still have a lot of questions about Knossos.

"The hard truth is that well over one century after Sir Arthur

Evans declared that he had found the Palace of Minos at Knossos, we still do not know what he really found," says Sandy, who wrote a book called *Minotaur: Sir Arthur Evans and the Archeology of the Minoan Myth.* "There is still no direct evidence of the existence of a monarchy, let alone a legendary King Minos or the Daedalian Labyrinth where Theseus slew the Minotaur. Why have we not found any evidence of royal burials? Why is Minoan art void of political propaganda?

"I don't disparage Sir Arthur Evans in my book, but rather I criticize the discipline of archeology," Sandy explains as we discuss various academic interpretations of Knossos from Strabo through Victor Bérard. "Academics never agree and that's one of the reasons there's seemingly so little progress. Socrates thought King Minos existed but *minos* is often the translation of 'first king' or 'man' rather than a particular individual. I tend to think of Knossos and other Minoan palaces as elaborate festival halls, great sanctuaries, and lively places where the community gathered to celebrate on their many festival days."

I pick up more novel information about the site during a visit to the Archaeological Museum in downtown Hêraklion.

I learn that the Minoans' domestic produce included cattle, sheep, pigs, and goats and that they cultivated wheat, barley, chickpeas, grapes, figs, olives, and poppies. I discover that the snake goddess was a sovereign figure in the Minoan pantheon and that snakes are symbols of fertility. I agree with Sir Arthur Evans that *La Parisienne* (he named it that because of the "malicious charm of her expression") is the sexiest fresco found during the New Palace period.

Although I don't make much progress trying to decipher the symbols inscribed on the Phaistos Disk, I marvel at a marble statue of Zeus Serapis depicted as the Lord of the Underworld with the three-headed hound Cerberus at his side. And I can see why warriors at Troy felt so protected wearing a boar's tusk helmet.

My imagination goes wild when I look at cups and bowls from the palatial buildings that, I figure, indicate heavy-duty partying, and coins that show the Minotaur on one side and a labyrinthine swastika with a star or sun motif on the other.

The sign I receive from an ode on a Cretan urn is particularly apropos for my walk. It reads simply "With each step, a breeze will rise." As I enjoy the message that seemingly endorses my perambulations, I recall that Thich Nhat Hanh once told me "the breeze is the peace and joy that blow away the heart of sorrow."

How was I able to so astutely gather all this information in just a few hours? Because I was wearing the *comme il faut faux* military pants that are the *de rigueur* mode for Greek men, which enabled me to mingle with King Minos and Zeus without looking like another tourist.

The terrain beyond the hill behind Bali is comparatively flat. I proceed along the rocky, scrubby, and sandy sheep-and-goat populated coast with constant views of a snow-capped peak. I walk through villages like Panamos, along the beach, through sheep-grazing fields and into a few massive resort hotels. At the still-empty Creta Panorama Hotel, a circular labyrinth walk takes me through luscious and well-tended grounds. I see a few people get in the water for the first plunge of spring and can't believe there will ever be enough tourists to empty the rent-a-car agencies of their inventory, especially when the price of gas exceeds $10 a gallon. Yet despite my skepticism every house seems to rent cars on the side.

It's a 31-kilometer MedTrekking day into Rethymno, and I'm invited to join a big Greek Easter dinner at the Rethymno Beach complex. Instead I choose to relax at sunset on a chaise longue on the beach with a homemade dinner – cheese, two Easter eggs, two rolls, a banana, and an orange. I'm impressed that there are another two chocolate Easter eggs on my pillow when I bed down in a modestly priced hotel.

Easter becomes a bit more exciting for me the next night, when I'm asked by the hotel concierge to present photographs of my 60-kilometer Easter parade walk between Skepasti and Georgioupolis to a group of touring Greeks in their 80s.

Who could say no?

I also photographed a lot of random sights on my Easter weekend walk. These included Sri Lankans playing Easter cricket, a patch of my own private Astroturf for sunbathing and lots of Greek beach barbecues with ladies dancing. And I learn that one reason the buses run so efficiently is because their biggest advertisers are ferry companies, like Minoan Lines and Anek, who pride themselves on maintaining a strict schedule.

I wisely avoid Highway 90, the dangerous seaside national road, on Easter Monday by crossing the river in Georgioupolis and heading straight up the mountain on little-traveled two-lane blacktop.

My first treat is a very crowded church service – with chanting, singing, praying, and merry-making by an overflow crowd – at a small hillside chapel in Argyromouri. The rest of the day is a mindless, meditative and sometimes uphill, meander through little towns like Vamos, where I have a Greek coffee at a café with some British habitués who live there, until I reach the sea at Kelyves, where I have six pieces of honeyed *baklava* for lunch. Kelyves is a somewhat downtrodden seaside resort, but that may be explained by the lack of a real beach and waves that thrash against a manmade breakwater.

I continue on the seaside Old Road through Kalima until I arrive in Souda, which is where ferries from Piraeus to Chania dock. There's a bus line to and from Chania, which is only six kilometers away as the cars drive, but much further for a MedTrekker who hikes across the sparse Akrotiri Peninsula, where two monasteries and numerous archeological treasures can be found. My walkabout on the arid, windswept, vacant, and vast peninsula takes me through lots of little villages, all of which seem to start with K or C, like Kalathas, Kalorrouma, Koumares and Chorafakia.

Lunching With Walter the Greek

The highpoint of the day is a Mediterranean seaside lunch with *Zorba the Greek* Academy Award-winner Walter Lassally in the village of Stavros, where the film was shot half a century ago. I immediately baptize the 84-year-old, Berlin-born, British-raised cinematographer Walter the Greek because I realize that he's a contemporary symbol of the independence, passion, spirit, and wile embodied by Anthony Quinn's portrayal of Zorba.

Lassally, who "retired" to the seaside village in the 1990s, loves the place so much that he bequeathed his Oscar to Christiana's Restaurant. The much-handled statuette was on permanent display on the bar for years until it was destroyed in a fire at the restaurant in 2012.

Comparatively sleepy Stavros has been spared the onslaught of tourist resorts, large hotels, and supermarkets. There is one public telephone, and Lassally frequently has lunch at either Christiana's or Maleka's Taverna.

"When we shot Zorba there were no roads, no electricity, no water, and no trees — and not too much has changed," Lassally says while drinking a glass of honeyed *retsina* on the sandy beach at Maleka's. "I've been around the world and never found a place to live that's better than this spot on Crete. It's easy, relaxed, and I like the volatile attitude of the mountain people."

As director of photography, who shot a dozen films in Greece and scores of others throughout the world, Lassally was best known for his work on *Tom Jones* before tackling *Zorba*. Today, perhaps subconsciously influenced by the verve and vitality of both movies, he's living life to the fullest and seems to embody Zorba's assertion that "a man needs a little madness, or else he never dares cut the rope and be free."

In his mid-80s, the multilingual Lassally (he speaks German,

English, Greek, and French) is learning Polish, his mother's native tongue; is preparing to shoot a documentary about the 1866 Cretan revolution; is organizing a pan-Balkan film festival; and takes his two dogs on daily walks. During lunch, our conversation ranges from his thoughts about the director's cut of *Heat and Dust*, the not-for-the-good changes in the Hollywood system, the ongoing collapse of the Greek economy, and the jealous nature of Greek women when it comes to Zorba's philosophy that "me - I live as though I might die tomorrow."

"Nobody around here thinks he's Zorba the Greek," Lassally insists as we walk on the beach where he filmed the hilarious hillside logging accident and Zorba's dance, which is called the *sirtaki* and is an iconic cliché of a Greek night out. "But we're all fascinated by his story."

Lassally describes some of the social restrictions in Stavros ("I can never have a conversation with two women at once around here because they all detest each other") and his fascination with the *I Ching*.

"I wrote a book called *Thirty Years With the I Ching,* but I couldn't get a publisher, so now it's called *Forty Years With The I Ching,*" he jokes before he describes the bitter enmity that has existed for generations among some of the larger families in the area. "The Cretans are very tough and usually have rows over land, but once there was a murder here over deck chairs on the beach."

He thinks that a long-lasting feud may have been responsible for the torching of Christiana's, though he is philosophic about the tragedy.

"The fire was almost certainly started deliberately, probably as a result of one of those tribal fights that unfortunately are only too common here, and I look upon it as the end of an epoch," Walter says. "The Oscar had a good life. There are thousands of photos of it with me and with the mountain that the film made famous."

As I leave Stavros and Walter behind, I recall another line from *Zorba the Greek*: "On this Cretan coast I was experiencing happiness and knew I was happy."

A Whole Lot of Kissing Going On

The buzzing and busy port of Chania with its Venetian harbor, iconic lighthouse, and crescent-shaped seaside promenade is one of the most pleasantly active social spots on the Mediterranean. But due to an impending storm it has a dark, foreboding, and mystical appearance when I hit town after the lunch in Stavros.

Chania has been completely revamped since its Ottoman and Venetian days and manages, from my perspective, to out-Saint-Tropez Saint-Tropez. There are dozens of port-side restaurants with barkers beckoning passersby and chic jewelry stores along an immaculate port, so clean it could be mistaken for a Disneyland attraction.

Why do I get an early evening haircut in Chania after my day with Walter? I'm preparing myself for an anticipated onslaught of some serious snogging in Kissamos, a town down the road with a name that overwhelms me with romantic fantasies because they are going to call it Kissalot for a day. The barber, who says he's a former chess champion of Greece, is so involved in a computer chess game that he gruffly says, "Sit down" and gives me the most unpleasant welcome I've ever had in a barber shop.

"I can't be human and play chess at the same time," he half apologizes. "The shop's not supposed to be open tonight (it's 7:00 p.m. on a Wednesday), but I was too engrossed to close the door."

He doesn't have a clue what I'm talking about when I mention the possible orgy in Kissalot.

I check into the €30-a-night Ideon Hotel just outside the city walls and start my next MedTrekking day on a flat seaside with lots of packed sand, lots of urban streets (with scores of mini-markets, cafes and tourist shops), a former WWII German military base, and a few luxury hotels.

I amble through a half dozen little seaside villages – Stalos, Agia Marina, Platanias, and Gerani – that all feature a resort-and-beach-waiting-for-the-season-to-arrive wistfulness. The style of hotels and lodgings ranges from the fairly spectacular for individual high-end travelers, to the spectacularly downtrodden for low-end package tours. I have a conversation with a lovely Danish girl – she actually quotes a line from *The Iliad* claiming that she is "a traveler like yourself, well-made, well-spoken, clearheaded, too" – at one hotel and buy some excellent olive bread at a bakery.

But the skies open – and don't close – around 2:00 p.m. and I wind up soaked and well short of my intended destination of Kissamos. The Zeus-is-pissed outbursts and downpours force even an otherwise self-sufficient MedTrekker to frequently run for cover during the intermittent deluges. It's any port in a storm when the god of thunder unleashes a fury of striking lightning, cracking thunder and driving rain.

Though my quick-dry gear is already soaked, numerous people help me get out of the rain. A Romanian gardener lets me into his shed, the English receptionist at the singles-only Hotel Mistral in Maleme offers me shelter from the storm, I climb into an old pillbox in a bunker at a former World War II German air base, and the monks give me cover at a Greek Orthodox monastery.

When the sun returns the next morning, I leave the Gonia Monastery and spend a glorious day traversing the Rodopos Peninsula between the villages of Kolymbari, where they're building a gigantic hotel, and Kissamos amid nearly vertical hillside olive groves, well-balanced grazing goats, nectar-seeking buzzing bees, and exhilarating views of the multicolored (brown from the rain, grey from the clouds, blue in spots) sea. Kissamos is temporarily changing its name to Kissalot in honor of a royal wedding in London and, according to local buzz, will become the kissing capital of the world for a day.

Along the way I meet a Canadian couple (she's of Greek heritage) who have come to baptize their young, blond-haired son. "Holy Moly," she says when she learns how far I've walked. I tell her about Circe and the origin of the "Holy Moly" expression, and she explains that "the baptism will be a big shebang, but no one can understand how/ why my Greek son has such blond curly hair."

When I return to the beach I'm taunted by some joy riders in a red truck. I probably don't help my cause when I pretend to be a matador as they try to run me down. As I near Kissalot I put on orange hiking shorts and a bright blue shirt for the occasion. In retrospect, I fantasized too much about the possibilities and potential of arriving in the kissing capital of the world.

I enter Kissamos (*amos*, as in Kissamos, means "thick sand") late in the afternoon expecting to have scantily clad, lithe Greek maidens throw rose petals in my path and smother me with kisses. But an arrogant 12-year-old Cretan kid on a moped informs me that the snogging stopped the second the wedding ended in London. I am hours late and to my dismay, and that of my romantic imagination, there's no kissing at all and I don't see a single lithe Greek maiden.

"You should have been here at noon!" the kid chortles.

I rush to the Kissalot city hall and appeal to the mayor, who looks all puckered out, but am abruptly (a bit too abruptly, I thought) told that Kissalot is finished. I'm back in good old Kissamos.

"You should have been here at noon!" the mayor guffawed.

I'm so distraught at my bad timing that I walk to the end of the beach, reflect on the many injustices in the world and decide I need a break from rain-provoking Zeus and temporary Kissalot.

Gorging on a Gorgeous Gorge

I take a day off and do nothing except enjoy an overflowing mixed-grill, mixed-seafood combo that I have the chef concoct at the Monastiri Taverna in a Venetian building on the port in Chania. It's just the right meal after almost 300 kilometers of Cretan MedTrekking and afterwards I relax for an hour at my table on the waterside terrace, observing people promenade. At the end of a day off, there's nothing sweeter than watching dusk turn to dark on a fine port like this one. The air, the smell, the lights, the strollers, and young couples add a warm and fuzzy feeling to an array of other Mediterranean sentiments.

The next morning I check out gorge-ous Crete and hike down and through the Samariá Gorge – the island's most famous, most touristic, most iconic and most *must-see* natural site. It's the first day the trail has opened this spring and I'm among the first on the path.

Do you want some comparatively easy MedTrekking amid the usually savage landscape and rocky Mediterranean seaside in southwestern Crete's White Mountains? Then walk the island's equivalent of the Grand Canyon and follow the blazed E4 hiking trail north or south along the coast.

The 1,250-meter (4,100-foot) descent through the Samariá Gorge is 13 kilometers long, but it's a downhill walk in the (national) park and an exceptional deal for the €5 entrance fee. There's a constant supply of spring water, WCs, trashcans, picnic tables, shaded rest areas, some wooden steps, and park rangers.

There are, however, signs warning hikers to "Walk Quickly" to avoid falling rocks, steel netting to protect hikers from falling rocks, and a chapel en route if all else fails. The path through pine and plane trees is generally in excellent shape, though some hikers have trouble crossing the wood-slatted bridges on the river running between sheer rock walls that rise to over 2,000 meters. There's one very cool passage through the walls that's only about ten feet wide and I make the walk from Xilóskalo on the Omalós Plateau, at 1,050 meters, to Agia Rouméli on the edge of the Libyan Sea in under four hours.

Most gorge-goers take a late afternoon ferry back to Sfakiá, and civilization, when they reach the sea. But I am so smitten by the well-marked E4 yellow-and-black marked hiking path, a MedTrekker's dream, that I hike it for three days. It follows the contours of the coast, is well marked, passes beaches and chapels, and certainly makes it unnecessary, as the Green Michelin suggests, to take a boat trip to see the mountainous coastline. As I walk I recall another paragraph in *Zorba the Greek*, which, before it became the celebrated film, was a novel by a Greek author and philosopher Nikos Kazantzakis:

"I climbed a hill and looked around. An austere countryside of granite and very hard limestone. Dark carob and silvery olive trees, figs and vines. In the sheltered hollows, orange groves, lemon trees and medlar plants; near the shore, kitchen gardens. To the south, an expanse of sea, still angry and roaring as it came rushing from Africa to bite into the coast of Crete. Nearby a low, sandy islet flushing rosy pink under the first rays of the sun."

I head west to visit Elafonissos (it's considered a two-star attraction by the *Michelin Green Guide* because the peninsula features pink sand, rolling caramel-colored dunes, and clear turquoise-tinted water), Paleochora and Sougia.   Then I return and go east towards Loutro, which is accessible by foot or ferry, and Sfakiá.

Loutro – where there are sheep and chicken being barbecued on every smoky and smelly grill – is so rarely visited by tourists that I find a room for €10, an internet/satellite connection with a parrot guarding the Wi-Fi, and meet almost everyone in town within an hour.

"I love docking each night in a place I can only get to by boat," the ferry captain says about the place he's chosen to live when we meet in a bar.

The next morning a café owner offers me a hardy Greek coffee at 6:30, an hour before his usual opening time. He refuses to let me pay, and I lamely leave a pile of coins on the table.

Although I only meet a few other people on the E4, there's no shortage of goats (I still get a kick out of every goat I talk to), and when I arrive in Sfakiá I'm pleased to encounter Despina Fountulaki at her Café Dispensa. She makes me a stiff filter coffee with a dash of milk (again free, again I tip) and takes my picture because, she says, "you look so sexy and gorge-ous for someone who's walked so far."

Confronting the Colossal Cretan Cave Conundrum

"Zeus gives men more excellence or less as he desires, being omnipotent." – *The Iliad*

I often meditate at dusk on a tiny terrace outside my sixth floor room at the Irini Hotel in Hêraklion. But one day at sunset I, instead, make a pilgrimage to Nikos Kazantzakis's tomb on the highest point of the Venetian fortification on the fringe of the city. Kazantzakis was born here in 1883, but the Orthodox Church, which he taunted in his books and in person, wouldn't allow him to be buried in a cemetery. He probably wouldn't have minded. An inscription on the cross at his grave is taken from his book *The Odyssey: A Modern Sequel*. It reads, "I hope for nothing. I fear nothing. I am free."

When I arrive at the tomb I take out my weathered copy of *Zorba the Greek* and, after a moment of silence, read one of my favorite paragraphs written by the popular Cretan who embraced Buddhism.

"I looked at Zorba in the light of the moon and admired the jauntiness and simplicity with which he adapted himself to the world around him, the way his body and soul formed one harmonious whole, and all things – women, bread, water, meat, sleep – blended happily with his flesh and became Zorba. I had never seen such a friendly accord between a man and the universe."

Then I opened *The Odyssey: A Modern Sequel* and read the first and last sentences of the book that takes up where Homer's *Odyssey* ended.

"And when in his wide courtyards Odysseus had cut down the insolent youths, he hung on high his sated bow and strode to the warm bath to cleanse his bloodstained body." Then, 774 pages later, "Forward, my lads, sail on, for Death's breeze blows in a fair wind!"

Sitting near Kazantzakis's entombed body, I for some reason recall New York Mayor John Lindsay telling a television interviewer back in the 1960s that he was thinking of giving up politics to join some hippies living in the caves on Crete. That, I thought, would be a very Zorba-like and Buddhistic thing for a politician to do.

Lindsay obtained his cave information from an August 1968 *Life* magazine article and photo spread about the hippie-inhabited caves in Mátala in southern Crete. The caves were such a rage at that time that Joni Mitchell mentioned them in her song *Carey* and it became very important to your hippiedom status whether YOU were a Cretan caveman or cavewoman pre-*Life* or post-*Life*.

Decades later, I still find Lindsay's comment surprisingly off the wall but now believe every contemporary politician, indeed every contemporary human being, could benefit from some meditative downtime in a Cretan cave. The next morning I head to Mátala, which is where Zeus once swam ashore in the form of a bull with the beautiful maiden Europa (yes, Europe's named after her) on his back, to explore holes-in-the-wall that are thought to originally have been tombs, chapels, and/or dwellings for troglodytes.

I discover that the Mátala caves and the town's beaches, a hippie allure forty years ago, are now major tourist draws with the usual pros and cons associated with such development. But the "Red Beach," just FYI, is for nudists only. The caves and beaches are still in excellent shape (the sand "floor" in one cave I checked out is as neatly raked as a Zen monastery) but no one, not even a certified hippie or MedTrekker, is allowed to sleep in them.

It's worth pointing out, I learn on my MedTrek, that Mátala and nearby Kommos have more than caves in their legendary history. They were both ports for the nearby Minoan hilltop city of Phaistos, which flourished in the Messara valley from 1900 to 1450 BC.

Phaistos, where archeologists have unearthed ruins from the

Neolithic period circa 3000 BC, is thought to have been the palace of King Rhadamanthys, the brother of King Minos, as well as the birthplace of Epimenides, a soothsayer considered one of the seven wise men of the ancient world. Although destroyed by earthquakes in 1700 BC and 1400 BC, Phaistos was rebuilt and its warriors participated in the Trojan War.

Incidentally, it's here that my trusty Nonac camera took its 9,999th snapshot and immediately   – after I photographed the royal courts, the great staircases, the theater, the storerooms and the famous disk of Phaistos – went berserk, became blurry, and died. I attribute its death to a sign from Epimenides and decide that all of the photos I take from now until I arrive at Troy will be with my iPhone.

Between you and me, apart from the natural setting and panoramic views, I don't think Phaistos deserves its three-star *Michelin Green Guide* billing. I walk down a paved road to the ruins of the Royal Minoan Villa of Agia Triada about three kilometers away, then traverse olive groves and run into a hillside of colored beehives on the way to the seaside. To remind myself that I used to be hippie, I swim nude and sunbathe on a large stretch of sand on the beach near Kalamaki. Then I decide to go looking for a real cave.

I walked 8,089 kilometers around the Mediterranean to reach the birthplace of Baby Zeus, the king of all gods. Finding the cave of his birth is the eighth of my twelve labors ("Meet with Zeus, the master of cloud, at the cave of his birth on Crete…" said Circe). Typically I owe thanks to Athêna for directing me to the correct location.

"Zeus was not born, as many think, at the Dictaean cave on the Lassithi Plateau, but rather on the north side of Mount Ida, Crete's highest mountain," grey-eyed Athêna confided to me when she appeared during my descent at the Samariá Gorge. "Look for the big birds when you are inside the Idéo Ándro (Idean Cave)."

Athêna also confirmed this wouldn't be my last encounter with the lord of storm and lightning. She told me she'd arrange for me to meet Zeus at the top of Mount Olympus and again in Troy, where he called the shots during the Trojan War.

"He can be difficult but he'll definitely see you," Athêna said. "He wants to clear up a number of misconceptions that have evolved during the past 3,000 years."

Before I head to Idéo Ándro on the 2,456-meter (8,057 feet) high Mount Ida, Athêna suggested I pay a quick visit to "the island of Atlantis," now thought by some to be the Cyclades island of Santorini. I presume she sends me there to appreciate the size of the *caldera*, a cauldron-like volcanic feature, which was the result of an earthquake and eruption in the late 17th century that contributed to the end of the Minoan civilization. Now that was an explosion that proved that Zeus doesn't play around.

I take a day to speedily catamaran from Hêraklion to Santorini, which has been inhabited since 3000 BC and is also still called Thera, after a Spartan invader. Like Corsica, it is also nicknamed Kallisté, or the "most beautiful" island, and inspired Jules Verne to write *Mysterious Island.*

I'm shocked at the number of cruise-ship-delivered tourists on Santorini, which is also known as the island of love and fire. There are 30,000-50,000 people arriving each day, many of them newlyweds not at all interested in Zeus or the island's past. They flock to Santorini because it's difficult to beat the setting of the erstwhile sunken city of Atlantis. What was a big round island until it blew its stack and became a crescent, is now considered the most romantic island with the most popular sunset on the Mediterranean, especially when seen from the castle ruins at Oia. The unique blue color of the trim of the houses built from lava and pumice is enhanced by the sky and the cerulean sea. The whitewash sun-struck walls reflect the heat and look like snow on the cliff as the catamaran approaches.

Today on Santorini there is more wine than water, more churches (365) than houses, and more donkeys than people – if you don't count the aforementioned tourists, who account for 97 percent of the economy. I'm pleased to learn that the company operating the cable car – which replaced most of those donkeys that used to carry visitors and luggage from the sea-level port to the elevated villages – has to give the donkeys (or maybe their owners) 20 percent of its annual income to compensate them for lost business. And I'm delighted that the Bronze Age ruins at Akrotiri reopened in 2012 after being closed for seven years.

"I sent you here to remind you of my father's powers before you personally seek him out," Athêna, in the guise of a lovely dark-haired waitress, informs me as I eat a honey bunny (yoghurt, honey, walnuts, banana) in the town of Fira. "All credit and all blame, large and small, goes to him and the other gods. Now go to the cave."

There are only a dozen people – and no one selling tickets – when I arrive at the Idéo Ándro on barren and rocky Mount Ida. Although there's an unfinished welcome center, a closed *taverna,* and an almost completely empty parking lot at the site of the Idéo Ándro cave, which is easily accessible on Crete's E4 hiking trail, there's really no infrastructure for tourists.

During the last two-kilometers of the climb up a rocky path, I explain to an Austrian couple, the only other visitors walking up to the cave, what Zeus was doing here in the first place.

"Zeus' mother Rhea brought him to this cave because his father Krónos, who was a descendant of the earth (Gaia) and the sky (Ouranos), had an irritating habit of devouring their children to prevent them from ever challenging him. So when Zeus was born he was suckled here by a goat named Amalthea and fed by a bee called Melissa.

"A sleepless dog watched the entrance, pigeons brought ambrosia from the ocean, an eagle carried nectar to the baby boy, and a sow also got credit for nursing Baby Zeus with her milk," I continued. "This cave has attracted pilgrims throughout the ages, and the latest digs have uncovered objects dating from the Neolithic period."

"As he aged, Zeus bestowed rewards on these animals," I went on, taking advantage of my now breathless audience. "The pig became sacred on Crete, the Horn of Amalthea was equated with happiness and abundance, the eagle became Zeus' permanent symbol, dogs were removed from the class of edible animals, and pigeons became symbols of purity. There's even a bush, which the locals call Dictamos, that Zeus endowed with miraculous healing qualities that Hippocrates said made childbirth easier for women."

"But how does anyone know that this is the right cave?" the Austrians ask in unison.

I lead them down some stairs to the bottom of a voluminous bat-filled cave and ask them to look up through the gaping entrance.

As they do a giant bird flies over, just as Athêna said it would.

Leaving the cave, I walk a bit further up the hill and as I look down at the valley below, recall another phrase from *Zorba the Greek*: "To my mind, this Cretan countryside resembled good prose, carefully ordered, sober, free from superfluous ornament, powerful and restrained...But between the severe lines one could discern an unexpected sensitiveness and tenderness; in the sheltered hollows the lemon and orange trees perfumed the air, and from the vastness of the sea emanated an inexhaustible poetry."

As I head down the mountain I admire the stark but poetic countryside with its gigantic vultures, sacred pigs, happy goats, pure pigeons, inedible dogs, and farmers who now drive ubiquitous four-wheel drive pickups. Why I wonder, if this is actually where Zeus was born, are there so few visitors?

"The Dictaean Cave has done a better job of promotion than we have," I'm told by a Greek café owner in Anogeia, about 20 kilometers from the Idéo Ándro. "This would never happen in the U.S. if Zeus had been born there. We're sitting on a gold mine and ignoring it."

He's right because the Idéo Ándro, which was excavated by Italian archeologists at the end of the 19th century and found to contain bronze shields and other artifacts from the ninth century BC, is a stark contrast with the Dictaean Cave at the Lassithi Plateau where I'll arrive in a few MedTrekking days.

Why, if Athêna and I were convinced that Zeus was born in the Idean Cave, would I bother to seek out a second purported birthplace? Is it even necessary to explore the Dictaean Cave and become enmeshed in what's known locally as the Colossal Cretan Cave Conundrum?

Quite frankly, I want to cover myself, especially after learning from a hotel concierge in Hêraklion (I'm continually amazed at how much the "average" Greek in the street knows about history and mythology) that the two caves are equidistant from Knossos, forming a perfect triangle.

"Both caves must be important," he insists.

The concierge, who might be a god in disguise for all I know, figures Zeus was born at Ida and raised at Dikti. He mentions that a tribe of Kouretes (Crete, or Kriti, gets its name from them), who were well-mannered giant spirits, played drums and danced around the caves to keep Krónos from hearing Baby Zeus's cry.

Although the usually trustworthy goddess Athêna insisted Zeus was born on Mount Ida, I have to acknowledge that there's popular, academic, and archeological contention that the "king of all gods, men and the world" spent time in a crib in the Diktéo Ándro, or Dictaean Cave, on the Lassithi Plateau on Mount Dikti.

Tourists obviously feel that way too.

The more accessible Dictaean Cave, which I reach on a Sunday morning on the E4 hiking path, attracts tour buses and offers donkey rides up (€15) and down (€20) a one-kilometer stone walk from the parking lot (€2 per car) to the cave (€4 per visit). Nearby are Zeus handicrafts shops, Zeus ceramic shops, the Zeus Hotel, and numerous restaurants and tavernas, each with outside stoves ablaze to roast lamb.

"The only people who don't believe that Zeus was born here are those who want to make money off the cave at Mount Ida," says Petros Zervakis, the guardian at the Dictaean Cave for thirty years and owner of the Petros Taverna, where I have a little lamb (€8.50) for lunch.

"Academics, archeologists, and historians have documented finds, including votive offerings and artifacts, that indicate this is Zeus' birthplace, and the cave has long been a shrine and the source of cult worship and pilgrimages," added Zervakis, who at age 70 still leads guided overnight tours (€200) up Mount Dikti every summer weekend.

The east-facing Dictaean Cave at an altitude of 1,025 meters, is deeper than the Idean, has fewer bats, contains a pool of water, and features stalagmites (one large one is known as the Mantle of Zeus) and stalactites that visitors can reach by navigating down a slippery staircase with a solid banister.

Zervakis points out a photograph of his grandfather in the cave in 1899 and suggests I read *The Dictaean Cave* (€6.50) by Georgios I. Panagiotakis to get the facts. I duly buy a copy. The book contends that Crete, which was certainly in the vanguard of Greek religion and divine worship, is the only place Zeus could have been born. It quotes one archeologist: "Only in this grandeur, of harmony and aesthetic peace, was it possible for the greatest of the gods to be born." It goes on to describe the "feeling of the divine, in the depth of the mountain, that arouses and unites the powers of living nature as a continuous offer to the divine visitor." It explains that King Minos came to the cave every nine years to get a new set of instructions from Zeus and report on life down below.

There's also a probability, acknowledges Zervakis before I leave, that Zeus inhabited both caves.

"You won't get much argument from anyone educated in Greece if you contend that Zeus was born at the Dictaean Cave and raised at the Idean Cave," agrees Zervakis, describing the various images of Zeus on Cretan coins.

I MedTrek east of Hêraklion along a tempestuous, wavy, color-changing sea in wind so strong that my ears ring. The morning's pleasant stroll on an urban promenade alongside the port gradually takes me through a garbage dump, then over pathless rocks, and finally along a fence topped with barbed wire that marks the boundary of the airport. Planes, with corporate names like Condor and Germania, buzz directly over my head as I negotiate the lava rock and admire the growingly ferocious waves.

The day gets interesting when I'm stopped by military cops for casually walking between the sea, the airport and, unbeknownst to me, a sprawling military base. The military cops agree with me when I indicate that there are no signs or fences in the direction I've come. Still, they seriously shadow me, after taking my passport details, as I continue along the fence. "Is my MedTrekking the action of a spy/terrorist assigned to get the lowdown on the Hêraklion Airport?" I ask myself as I finally head down to an accessible beach.

After the town of Vathianos Campos, I continue on a sea-and-sand-sprayed walk along dirt paths, one-way streets, and seaside promenades through villages like Gouves, where I take a photograph of the raging, tormented, and even ugly sea as it wipes out beach umbrellas. Further along, in popular Hersonissos, are shops, restaurants, pubs, hotels, jewelry stores, car rental companies, and everything else a MedTrekker, or any tourist, might conceivably need on a windy day.

Both locals and tourists are dressed like Eskimos today, in

contrast to yesterday's sunny semi-nudity, but I'm so delighted by the climatic conditions that I keep going for forty kilometers.

My 13th MedTrekking day on Crete kicks off in Stalis as I wend my way along the seaside, through a long string of popular-with-tourists buzzing-on-Saturday-morning resorts. A cemetery, a 1450 BC crypt, and a chapel appear in my path before I reach the ruins in Mália, where I traipse around the third-largest Minoan palace on Crete, discovered in 1921 and excavated by French archeologists. Then I plot my route across the Spinaloska peninsula in an effort to get to Ágios Nikólaos, which is named after the Greek patron saint of sailors, fishermen, ships, and sailing.

I walk on beaches, thoroughfares, little roads and paths on a panoramic route that takes me through seaside Milatos, over a range of scenic mountains and along a peninsula with oasis-like green valleys, lovely villages, and no traffic except herds of sheep.

I stop to have two *souvlakis* and a piece of cake for lunch near Neapolis and discover an unpaved road that leads to the end of the peninsula with views of the Bay of Elounda and Spinalónga Island. The Venetians built a 16th-century fortress on Spinalónga, the Turks took it over in 1715, and from 1904 to 1958 the island was a leper colony.

When I get to the Bay of Elounda, which I last visited when my wife and I brought our 18-month old daughter Sonia here to learn Greek in 1984, I try to find the hotel where we stayed. It was The Elounda Something – Bay or Beach or Mare or Village – but there's now a row of exclusive resorts on the seaside with guards and gates. And they all look the same.

What a change a couple of decades makes. Thirty years ago I would only stay in Leading Hotels of the World or *Relais & Chateau*-like luxury hotels. Now that's all there is here, and it's exactly where I don't want to stay when I'm in MedTrek mode.

I encounter a Polish woman and her two-ish daughter who can't find their hotel, don't have any money with them, and have been misadvised about its possible location by a bus driver. I watch them pass in front of one of the chic hotels and the snooty guard treats them like homeless scum until I step in, chastise him, and force him to call them a cab.

"Have you completely forgotten how to treat normal people?" I berate him. "When I stayed here in 1984 the Greeks still knew how to be hospitable. Now you act more arrogant than the French or Germans."

He tries to backtrack and offers me a tour of the place but, with equal arrogance, I abruptly dismiss him and continue to Ágios Nikólaos, where I check into the simple Lato Hotel. My view of the port from my €28-a-night base camp through palm trees, beaches and great greenery is hard to beat.

I have a *soumada*, a non-alcoholic drink made from almonds, with a beer-chugging 19-year-old Australian backpacker around the Lato pool. We discuss the MedTrek, I describe my days as a teen traveler, and I encourage him to stay on the road. Later that night I meet a Greek woman from Melbourne summering here "because I know this place is good for my soul." She's teaching Pilates at the swish hotels on Elounda Bay "because I know this place is also good for my pocketbook."

Resisting Temptation at the Panorama Taverna

The pouring rain slightly subsides as I set out from Ágios Nikólaos wearing a fleece jacket and a baseball cap while carrying a limp umbrella. That doesn't prevent me from getting completely soaked as I edge around the attractive port and arrive at Lake Voulismeni, which was once known as Artemis' Pool, in the middle of town. Then I head east for five kilometers on a combination of promenades, beaches with tongue-twisting names like Kitroplatia, roads, and sidewalks, including a nice split-rock sidewalk adjacent to Highway 90.

I mindlessly leave my lifeless umbrella on a rock where I stop to change socks, and am still drenched and soggy when I arrive at the Panorama Taverna on the outskirts of Istron, which the locals prefer to call Kalo Chora, or "beautiful country."

Actually, I don't choose the Panorama Taverna, it chooses me. The young Romanian woman standing on the main road in front of the restaurant pleasantly smiles, pleasantly takes my hand, pleasantly leads me to an outdoor table, and pleasantly sits down next to me. The lady is, of course, a Romanian call girl attempting to lure clients inside, a common occurrence at almost every Greek restaurant in every Greek port, but a slight oddity out on a rural road when there are no other nearby establishments.

The stout owner introduces himself and, without missing a beat, tells me he's a renowned "sex machine." The three of us amuse each other with lurid sexual tales as I down a giant gyro accompanied by a heavily garlic-scented *tzatziki*. That's followed by a Greek coffee adorned with yoghurt, cherries, a cookie, a piece of chocolate, and a flower.

I figure this presentation is part of the usual price scam and will be reflected in the bill, but I see the owner wink at the call girl, and the whole lunch costs only €4. The owner pegs me either as a knowledgeable traveler or a fellow scammer. I appreciate his gesture and let him continue to boast.

"Don't brag about walking around Crete, because I do more walking than you do every day in this restaurant between April to November," he tells me, adding as we enjoy the view onto the Mirambelou Bay and its rocky coast, that he's had five wives.

After I leave the Romanian call girl and oversexed restaurant owner, I wind up walking on an abandoned seaside road into Gourniá, a Minoan settlement dating from 1700 BC that was primarily excavated by American archeologists. Walking onto the barren and windswept beaches of Pahia Amos, I'm confronted with a wave of black clouds that portend more rain as they gurgle above the tall range of mountains. So this afternoon, in case you wonder what I do during rainy downtime instead of MedTrekking, I answer questions posed by blog readers that merit short, crisp answers with a sentence, a photo, and a caption.

1. Do you interact with other tourists?
Actually, I do. For example, I took a photograph of a contemporary French hippie chick taking a photograph of the once hippie-inhabited caves at Mátala.

2. Why are there so many miniature chapels on the road?
One reason is to commemorate lives lost in automobile accidents.

3. How are the Cretans trying to improve driving habits?
They shoot delinquent drivers.

4. Where is Nikos Kazantzakis burried
In a grave on the fortified walls in Hêraklion.

5. Do Cretans still fish?
There are fresh fish in every market and old school fishermen in every port.

6. What do you eat when you MedTrek?
I'm usually a Greek salad and gyros kinda guy, but occasionally, after a long outing, I'll have a mixed-seafood, mixed-grill combo.

7. Do you notice the sad state of the Greek economy when you walk?
Some projects, like this new road on Crete, are at a standstill.

8. You mentioned that Zeus was fed by a bee named Melissa. Are there beehives on Crete?

Yes, and they come in all colors because Cretan bees are not colorblind.

9.How often do you see Minoan Ruins?
Very frequently. Today I walked to, through and above Gourniá, a Minoan settlement east of Ágios Nikólaos dating from 1700 BC.

10. What kind of view do you get from a €28 Room on Crete?
Here's the view from the Lato Hotel, my abode in Ágios Nikólaos. For some reason, and this happens only on Crete, I try to keep my room price (averaging just over €34) roughly equivalent to the kilometers I walk each day (averaging 31.27 kilometers after eighteen MedTrekking days).

11. Does Crete have sandy beaches?
Actually Greece's largest island features many more bouldery, cliffy, gravelly, mountainy, rocky, pebbly and stony (you get the idea) patches of seaside than strips of fine sand. In fact, there are probably more archeological sites on Crete than sandy beaches.

The next day I encounter only one brief rain shower, a pleasant surprise after yesterday's constant soaking. After 12 kilometers I divert off the road down toward the seaside village of Mohlos and spend the afternoon hiking in a valley with no cars, great paths, and some of the best cliffs on the Mediterranean.
I realize how lucky I am when I stop for a coffee at the Panorama Café in Postano and look back, 35 kilometers back, at Ágios Nikólaos with a magnificent view across the vast rocky Mirambellou Bay. I have a splendidly simple lunch (*moussaka*, Greek salad, and yoghurt with honey for €12) in tiny Mohlos at the Wi-Fi-equipped Kavouria restaurant, and become Facebook friends with owner Spiros Galanakis.
I leave feeling elated by the satisfying meal and stark terrain, and head cross-country for 15 kilometers amid chapel-decorated hilltops in the shadow of the impassible cliffs that line the bay and through olive fields ("Every Greek man owns an olive tree," I was told the night before by the bartender at The Blue Marine hotel. "I also have vines and a pick-up truck to complete the picture."). There's a quarry at the western end of the valley, but even it has a reforestation program underway between the different levels of gouged out rocks. There are lots of Minoan-touched areas, including a ravine where stones were extracted to construct Gourniá, and numerous shops sell homemade oil, vinegar, thyme, honey, and *raki*.

I ignore the main road up the hill to Sfakiá and explore a number of paths and small roads that finally lead me to Turloti and Myrsini, where I've been told there's a commune established. Walking through town looking for evidence of alternative lifestyles and contemporary hippies, I find instead some nicely restored homes, a very clean town, and just a few gracefully aging hippies.

I take off on a trail above the town wandering through everything from olives and grasses to vines, lettuce, and all else that grows green. It feels, despite the wind, like the first day of spring. Birds are actually chirping, plants are odoriferous, flowers are looking Day-Glo fluorescent, goats and sheep are looking happy to be goats and sheep. The view back towards Ágios Nikólaos and Mochlos Bay is stupendous, and I take an Adios Ágios Nikólaos shot to commemorate the beauty.

The little-traveled walk is through mountains and gorges, and I spend half the day on different tracks, unused secondary roads, and other untraffick'd ways and byways. When I see a hunched-over Greek woman in black negotiating the road I don't feel quite so alone.

Passing two small towns – Ekso Mouliana and Mesa Mouliana – and a number of gorges, including the Richtis Gorge, I simply suck in the breathtaking scenery until finally rounding the proverbial bend at the top of the last hill and see Sitía. I stop for a cheese-croissanty sandwichy lunch in Scopi and then head downhill to the port where, with the wind at my back, I book myself into the Itanos Hotel.

The next day on my Ierápetra walkabout I head 15 kilometers east to the Kakkos Bay hotel to file a report and some photos for my friend Eve Siegel per her request:

"Kakkos Bay is the name of the resort outside Ierápetra off whatever the main road is," she emailed me. "About 17 years ago, we went to see the place, which was a cliff of white bungalows going down to the sea. Bill said, 'That's where I want to have my 50th birthday!' So we did, in July 1996, inviting friends from Sweden, England, & the States for a four-day event of welcoming new arrivals, eating meals together, swimming at the rocky beach, & having an early-morning champagne breakfast & toast. Is it still there?"

"It is!" I wrote in an e-mail accompanied with shots of the place.

To get back to town, I stick out my thumb to hitch while sitting nonchalantly on a bus stop bench. The first car, with a young she's-Swiss-working-with-Swatch-and-he's-Dutch-working-with-Johnson & Johnson couple living in Bern, stops, and the Dutchman tells me this is the first time he's ever picked up a hitchhiker. Once they learn about the MedTrek they pepper me with questions about walking, life, my career as a journalist, and The Idiot.

My base camp in Sitía looks out over the harbor, and after

shooting the rising sun, I take off along the sandy beach, where I swam and sunned after my arrival from Ágios Nikólaos yesterday afternoon. Walking on the old road, the new road, and various paths, I pass the Minoan villages and archeological sites of Petras and Tripolitis, followed by the more modern town of Analoukas.

I stumble on a ghost town hotel called Dionissos that has the longest man-made swimming pool (160 m) that I've seen on the Med. Both pool and hotel sit on hillsides and face the sea, a commonality between the Minoans and Cretans I figure. Two caretakers are trying to get the complex in shape for the season, but it will be an uphill battle.

Sandy Drops a Bombshell in Palaikastro

I continue over the mountain on various paths in the vague direction of Vaï and drop into the Toploú Monastery (*toploú* is Turkish for cannon), which was founded by the Venetians in the 14th century as Our Lady of the Cape.

My cross-country traversal takes me past noisy wind turbines, and I wind up at Vaï where I stumble upon what is said to be the only natural palm grove in Europe and a remarkable stretch of white sandy beach. Just down the road is the Itanos archeological site, but it appears everyone's opted for the beach.

I lose an hour and a half as I arduously work my way around a promontory at the south end of Kouremenos Bay. Shoes off, shoes on, shoes off, shoes on. I could have simply walked over the ridge in fifteen minutes, but I'm still in time for my scheduled ruinous lunch with Joseph Alexander "Sandy" MacGillivray, my archeologist friend based in nearby Palaikastro.

I hope that Sandy, whom you met briefly at Knossos, might help me resolve the "Colossal Cretan Cave Conundrum" and other Cretan mythological/historical issues while we dine on fresh fish prepared by Olga at the Kakavia Fish Tavern in Chiona Bay near his ongoing excavations at Roussolakkos, a Minoan town that includes a sanctuary of Dictaean Zeus.

Sandy, born in Montreal in 1953, studied at Edinburgh University and first came to Crete as an archeologist in 1983. He's now co-director of Palaikastro excavations, financed primarily by the British School of Archeology at Athens and grants from various foundations/institutes/benefactors.

We start lunch with double-baked bread, aka puppy bread, served with olive oil, oregano, Sitía feta cheese, and local tomatoes. This is followed by Olga's patented fish soup, and the meal ends with homemade halva. Sandy drops a bombshell during dessert, right after Olga gives me some just-baked biscuits for my descent tomorrow down the Valley of

Death gorge, which got its name because the many caves were used as graves by ancient Minoans. It's a stormy and thundering afternoon that we both agree is atmospherically charged because Zeus is trying to tell us something.

"The municipal government actually wanted to change the name of the gorge to the 'Valley of Life' to make it more attractive to tourists," says the bearded MacGillivray with a laugh. "But the change never occurred. Incidentally, keep your eyes open because you might find the real cave of Zeus there."

"WHAT!?!" I exclaim. "I've already publicly claimed to find the cave where Zeus was born and/or raised on Crete – twice. Once on Mount Ida in a blog snippet called *The View From Zeus' Crib*, another time on Mount Dikti in an item entitled *The Colossal Cretan Cave Conundrum*. And now you're telling me...."

Sandy – who had been casually making references to Pythagoras, Socrates, Strabo, the Anatolian migration, Linear A tablets, and competition between academic archeologists – quickly convinces me, and who am I to argue, that the actual Zeus cave still hasn't been discovered.

"The real cave would contain lots of post-Minoan material and, according to a variety of sources, including Pythagoras who spent time there, it is located here in eastern Crete," Sandy adds nonchalantly, noting that recent progress concerning the Minoan civilization is being made due to DNA studies and quantum physics. "I'm trying to find speleologists to conduct a serious search, but of course we don't know if the cave was buried by Christians, who destroyed all of the temples in AD 395, or an earthquake. Anyone could find it or it may never be found."

There is no shortage of cave candidates. One count contends that 389 of the 3,058 caves on Crete bear the names of saints – and there are churches in 120 of them.

"I'm on the case beginning tomorrow," I promise.

Our discussion continues as Sandy drives his 1979 BMW to the nearby archeological dig and describes how his ever-changing team of volunteers, usually operating with an annual budget $50,000-200,000 per year, has made and processed thousands of finds, including the Palaikastro Kouros, a youthful male figure dating from 1500 BC that's carved from hippopotamus ivory, is clothed in gold and has eyes of rock crystal and a serpentine head.

Fragments of the culturally valuable and historically significant statuette were found in the late 1980s by Seán Hemingway, Ernest's grandson, who returns to the dig at Palaikastro almost every summer.

You'll meet him when I take you to The Metropolitan Museum of Art in New York,

"Shway (as Sandy calls Seán) found the statuette in hundreds of pieces right here," said MacGillivray as he kneels down in the dig. "The Palaikastro Kouros, which is about 18 inches high, is now the main attraction at the Archeological Museum in Sitía."

"If Seán can find something of that size, I can find the Zeus cave," I proclaim, while Sandy makes us late afternoon tea at the stone dig house owned by the monks at the nearby Toploú Monastery.

The patient and practiced archeologist tries to be encouraging as he moves amid boxes labeled "Shell," "Marine Organism," and "Fish Bones" near an old olive press that dominates the structure.

"Every time I take a walk in the hills around here, I literally stumble upon something ancient," says Sandy, who taught at Columbia University in New York for a decade, still practices cliff jumping and now lives with his wife and two kids in Athens. "You may get lucky because we estimate that 90 percent of Minoan sites on Crete have yet to be discovered."

After my lunch and discussion with Sandy, I am particularly careful while MedTrekking through the notorious Gorge of Death to conscientiously check out every cave, cranny, crevice and shadow. This is obviously not because I have suddenly developed an interest in bats, bones or dead body parts, nor because Deng Ming-Dao's adage that "death is the opposite of time" kept echoing through my mind. It is solely because I'm determined to find the real cave of Zeus.

That objective keeps me in the gorge for hours and I manage to do a thorough investigation and get some good photographs of my latest cave candidate for Baby Zeus' birthplace. I am so excited that I virtually ignore the fourth royal Minoan "palace" in Kato Zakros before briefly visiting the Pelekita Cave on the long hike back to Palaikastro. Naturally, I have the presence of mind to skinny dip at a bay called Skinias before I shoot up and over the ravine-and-gorge-filled hills to the Sanctuary Peak. It is in the chapel there that I learn where to go next.

"Forget where Zeus was born," intones Athêna, who (and you've got to take my word about this) takes the shape of a brightly burning candle that I light both in prayer and to illuminate the dark interior of the austere, whitewashed mountain shelter. "You should go to Mount Olympus to meet my father."

"But the Oracle told me to go to the 'Peloponnese Peninsula and calmly walk counterclockwise towards Athens until my appointment to climb Mount Olympus,'" I whispered, hoping no one will enter and hear me talking to my latest flame.

"Oh, please!" Athêna replies. "Circe and Sibyl are just messengers doing my bidding. They knew you'd be receiving instructions directly from me from time to time. Loosen up and listen up!"

As the candle miraculously dims, then extinguishes, I notice that the smoke fleetingly takes the form of Zeus sitting on his throne atop Mount Olympus.

Greeting Zeus on Mount Olympus

"Dawn in her saffron robe came spreading light on all the world, and Zeus who plays in thunder gathered the gods on peaked Olympus' height." – *The Iliad*

"Feels like I'm knocking on heaven's door." – Bob Dylan

I follow Athêna's advice and arrive in Thessaloniki in northern Greece to attempt to accomplish one of the most enticing of the twelve labors prescribed by Circe: the climb up above the clouds to the peak of iconic and mysterious Mount Olympus to meet Zeus and the other eleven Olympians.

When I reach the village of Litóhoro, known as the City of Gods, at the sea-facing foot of the mountain, majestic Olympus is shrouded in fog and cloud – as any gods-rearing mountain should be from time to time. I can't see the mountain through the trees. In fact, I can't even see the trees. Despite the weather, I head to the Prionia trailhead, about a four-hour walk above Litóhoro, to get the lowdown on climbing conditions from hikers returning from their march madness. Once there, I hole up in a still-open "utterly captivating little restaurant," as the Fodor guide describes it (in words I hope never to use), and chat with returning mountaineers.

The assessment, as you would expect in such obviously poor conditions, isn't too cheerful: it's too cold/icy/dicey/foggy to get to the Mitikas peak, which is also known as the throne of Zeus. Most hikers aren't making it past a well-equipped refuge a few hours up the trail. Despite this pessimistic assessment, I decide to return the next morning, give it a shot and proceed or retreat according to the fickle weather and the will of the gods.

The rest of the early autumn afternoon is spent visiting the just-being-restored Dionysus Monastery and the ruins and museum at nearby Dion at the foot of Mount Olympus.

An amusing – well, call it embarrassing – thing happens to me on the way to the monastery. I want to buy something from a small street-side shop to support flagging Greek commerce and choose what I think are licorice candies. Instead, as I bite into them, I discover that I've purchased small chunks of charcoal used to light a chalice or incense. I spit out the granular chalky faux bonbon, remind myself that I really must learn to read Greek, and leave the uneaten remains at a church entrance to be used by someone smart enough to know not to put it in their mouth.

Dion is best known for an athletic and theater festival, called the Olympics Games of Dion, which Archelaos hosted here in the fifth century BC in honor of the nine Muses. The Muses, incidentally, were Zeus' daughters and provided the inspiration for arts and sciences in a city that then was the symbol of ancient and powerful Macedonia.

The word on the street is that this riverside harbor could have been inhabited as early as the tenth century BC and that much later, during the Roman era, it was home to more than 15,000 inhabitants. One definite fan of the spot was Alexander the Great who built the fortifications here in the fourth century BC. His Macedonian successors maintained the sanctuaries to Zeus, Demeter, Artemis, and other gods until things went downhill (as they always tend to in our impermanent world) in the fourth century AD when Ostrogoths sacked the place.

Excavations to explore Dion didn't begin in earnest until the 1970s and, since then, dozens of streets and warehouses, public baths, latrines and private houses have been unearthed. My favorite spot is the villa of Dionysos, uncovered in 1987, which features a mosaic showing the god of wine and festivity in a chariot flanked by centaurs and propelled by panthers. The villa and other remaining vestiges of the past, from sanctuaries and *odeons* to the Temple of Olympian Zeus, seem especially dramatic – holy even – due to the proximity of towering Mount Olympus.

My visit to the intriguing three-story museum, filled with

mosaics and statues, illustrates the bounty of the fruitful underground exploration. Again, I'm humbled by its contents, realizing that even today I couldn't come up with many of the innovations the Greeks did – not their alphabet and certainly not their plumbing, heating and toilet network, and burial *stellae*.

Early that evening I scout out Litóhoro and within half an hour meet a young local woman named Stella who confesses that she has never climbed Mount Olympus "because I'm scared." Not of the gods, and whatever they might mete out when confronted on the summit, but of heights. As I aimlessly wander about the mountainside town I run into three German women in their early 20s who, discouraged by a few days of bad weather, are catching a bus to Delphi "as part of our see-all-of-Greece-while-we're-young tour." They had spent six hours carrying their heavy backpacks from Litóhoro to the Prionia trailhead and trudged straight back downhill when they realized they'd be hampered by bad weather.

After dining on a freshly grilled chicken on the terrace of a local *taverna*, I return to the Guests of Zeus Hotel, whose logo features a sketch of Zeus holding three thunderbolts. I mentally recount tales I've known since childhood about the "home of the gods." Among other things, I recite each of the gods' names – Zeus, Hêra, Apollo, Athêna, Hestia, Poseidon, Hades, Artemis, Hermês, Arês, Aphroditê, Hêphaistos – and their particular "job."

I'll be the first to admit that I don't know if there's a heaven, hell, purgatory, reincarnation, a continuation of life, a big nothing, or something somewhere in between after we die. I convinced myself long ago that we already live in heaven on earth and no longer engage in too much projection, or have any expectations, about what comes next. But I do know that mountaintops like this provide a knock on heaven's door and that tomorrow I'll hopefully meet some gods of my understanding.

There is nothing to see beyond the path at my feet on the way up Olympus the next morning. The heavy fog at 7:00 a.m. obscures any view of what might lay ahead and above. But I sense I am somewhere special and, though I can't see beyond my foggy glasses, I enthusiastically start the climb inspired by the energy seemingly emanating from the mountain.

As I take the path through the low-altitude forests towards a massif of crystalline schist, I notice a few signs informing me that I'm on the E 64 trail en route to the refuge run by the local Alpine Club. My first friendly encounter of the day on the low-visibility ascent is not another climber but a sleek yellow-on-black spotted salamander that I name Aristotle (scientific name: *aristotless platonica rex*), who inspires me, as he slowly crawls with his webbed feet up a grass bank, to march on.

As I continue the visibility-impaired hike up the hill, I recall many of the myths/stories/truths associated with Mount Olympus until I run into a young English man reading *The Iliad* under a leafy Holm Oak tree to stay out of the rain.

"What passage are you reading?" I ask.

"Hêra took pains to follow his command: from Ida's crests she flashed to high Olympus quick as a thought in a man's mind..." he read from a section entitled *The Lord of Storm*.

As we chat, a German hiker arrives and the three of us discuss the possibility of making it to the top. We aren't too encouraged because there is absolutely no sign, as the three of us simultaneously look towards what we think is the top of the mountain, of "the many-ridged Olympus" where the Olympian gods live or, depending on your personal take, lived.

I recall that Suzanne Stohl, a friend in Palm Beach, Florida, cautioned me in an email this morning not to take the bad weather too seriously.

"Definitely don't swear at Zeus, he is all powerful!!" she wrote. "He can steal your wife and do all kinds of things, remember? Just don't forget that bad weather is temporary."

When I finally arrive at the refuge, I decide to wait two hours to determine how impermanent the storm is. I'm not alone because the rain, fog, hail and generally inclement weather force every other gods-seeking climber inside.

The ruggedly handsome young mountain woman pleasantly greeting guests at the cozy, fire-warmed refuge, an especially welcome spot for every hiker heading up or down Mount Olympus on such a dour day, is beyond doubt a goddess in disguise. The multilingual Anastasia says she wants to be called Ana as she greets each guest with the same cordial welcome that Nausikaa gave Odysseus when he arrived drenched and distraught on the beach in Skhería. We discuss the climatic conditions, and she indicates that most hikers have opted to head downhill at the first break in the rain.

Ana, who reminds me of a Laura Ashley-clad hippie posing for a David Hamilton photograph circa 1972, counsels me, with the experience of someone who realizes that some stubborn mountain climbers often won't hear or listen to her warning not to try to make it to the summit. She makes this point not only because of the inclement weather and poor visibility, but also because the path is slippery and dangerous. She invites me to dry my soaked gear near the fire and agrees with my plan to wait two hours before I decide whether to head up or down.

"I'm glad to see that you're not impatient. It's now or never for so many people who make it here," she says, asking me if I'd like a cappuccino (at a bargain €2), bread with coffee or tea (€4) or maybe even a room for the night (€12).

"I'll enjoy the break, the warmth, the coffee, and the bread," I reply, silently swooning.

Many climbers sensibly choose to arrive at the refuge, which remains open until mid-October, and spend the night before tackling the summit at daybreak. If the bad weather continues, I'll sleep here and try summiting tomorrow. In the meantime, I slowly sip cappuccino after cappuccino while chatting with some of the 16 kids from a private international school in Thessaloniki who had spent the night, hiked an hour uphill this morning, were forced to return to the refuge and are now waiting to descend to Prionia. They seem much happier to be back in the refuge than disappointed by their frustrated attempt to climb the mountain.

As we all sit around the fireplaces watching our wet and muddy clothes dry, we discuss (they spoke excellent English) the gods, marijuana, U.S. healthcare and Homer. One Spanish student tells me how impressed he is that Greece had always been such a religious country and mentions that no Greek until 1913 would ever have dared to climb Mount Olympus.

"They weren't scared of the mountain but of the gods at the top," he says.

He's right. Officially this mountain was not climbed for the first time until 1913 and, in a storm anyway, it still seems more virginal than vanquished.

As time passes, everyone – Latvians, Romanians, Bulgarians, and every other nationality – is trying to predict the weather. Most hikers who attempted to climb the mountain earlier are returning with tales of low (or no) visibility, intense fog and no view of the top of the mountain even near the top of the mountain. I am the only American in the place, and they ask me what I'm doing in Greece.

"I'm here because I'm interested in Homer," I tell one Greek.

"Homer Simpson?" he smiles.

"Homer Run?" adds a young wisecracker from London.

"No, Homer, Omeros, the man who wrote about Odysseus," I reply.

The weather slightly improves and I decide to head uphill. Although fewer than ten people attempt the ascent this afternoon, refreshed and ready I gradually make my way up the mountain. As I progress, I begin to appreciate the grandeur of Olympus, which since

1938 has been part of a splendidly clean national park that now includes 25 percent of all Greek flora, thirty-two species of mammals, and 108 species of birds.

I make it without any problem to Skolio peak, where I sign the visitor register in honor of recently deceased Phyllis Guest, my friend Gayle's mother whom I knew for more than fifty years. Then I blissfully sit for an hour on the stark and windy summit above the clouds at what the Greeks felt, eons ago, was the top of the world. Karmically, the sky above me gradually clears, the clouds below begin to disperse, and I continue to the Mitikas peak where, if I'm lucky, the gods won't be crazy.

Mount Olympus (the name in classical Greek means "the luminous one") is not only the highest peak in Greece but, at 2,917-meters (9,570-feet), it's the tallest mountain in a chain that runs north into Bulgaria and south into Turkey. The weather continues to improve at the snow-craggy summit, and I can begin to make out the eastern slopes of the mountain as they edge into the Thermaikos Gulf in the Aegean Sea.

As I meditatively sit with eyes half closed, it's easy for me to visualize the gods meeting with far-seeing Zeus, to discuss the status of the Trojan War.

"They all made their way to the hall of Zeus, lord of the clouds of heaven, taking their chairs in sunlit courts, laid out with all Hêphaistos' art in polished stone," wrote Homer about one gathering, noting that each god had an individual throne. I envisage their arrival at the palatial setting, where Zeus' "home and all his treasures are for ever," and it's clear that the gods have already taken different sides in the conflict at Troy, supporting either the Trojans or the Akhaians, as the Greeks were known.

It's apparent that Zeus, as he sits with ease upon the ridge with an ample view of the world below and beyond, encourages the gods to "go into action, side with men of Troy or with Akhaians, as each has a mind to." Right here where I'm sitting, to paraphrase Bob Dylan, "the line it was drawn, the curse it was cast" and, writes Homer, "the gods in bliss roused the contenders, hurled them into war and broke in massive strife among themselves" as they set the city of Troy atremble.

It isn't too difficult to identify the supporters for each side.

"Hêra, Athêna, Poseidon, girdler of the earth, and Hermês, most sharp-witted of them all; Hêphaistos, proud and brawny but with tottery shanks: these were the seaborne Akhaians' partisans," according to Homer. "For the Trojans, Arês in a flashing helm, beside him long-haired Phoibos, Artemis, Lêto and Xánthos, and the smiling goddess Aphroditê."

The gods, perhaps unaware of my presence, bicker among themselves, and I listen in. Athêna seems particularly upset that her brothers and sisters are going too far to influence the conflict. She takes Arês to task.

"Arês, bane of all mankind, crusted with blood, breacher of city walls, why not allow the Trojans and Akhaians to fight alone?" Athêna suggests. "Let them contend – why not? – for glory Zeus may hold out to the winner, while we keep clear of combat – and his rage."

Others openly express their opinions.

"No need for senseless anger," says Poseidon. "Why should we be quick to embroil ourselves as adversaries of the other, being far more powerful than they are? Let me make war."

Athêna, I thought, was hoping Zeus would step in to resolve the situation, and she clearly wanted additional guidance about the direction and outcome of the war. She had told me once that her father not only could see everything from his perch on Mount Olympus but also that his decisions were final. I awaited his judgment.

"O Father of us all and king of kings, enlighten me. What is your secret will?" Athêna asks as she sits comfortably amidst sparkling bronze, gold, amber, silver, and ivory furniture. "War and battle, worse and more of it, or can you not impose a pact on both?"

The three Fates, nine Muses and many others, including the "silvery-footed" Thetis, a sea nymph and Achilles' mother who called the Ocean home, are in attendance. I happen to see Thetis arrive and recall what Homer wrote in *The Iliad*: "Thetis had kept in mind her mission for her son, and, rising like a dawn mist from the sea into a cloud soared aloft in heaven to high Olympus. Zeus with massive brows she found apart, on the chief crest enthroned."

Athêna stands near me, and what we overhear almost makes her shout in protest. But perhaps more on that if we ever get to Troy.

During my reverie my baseball cap, with "Environmental Defense" written on it, blows off my head and literally flies off the top of Mount Olympus. When I meet Zeus I'll tell him that I left it as a token veneration for the gods, or at least a token gift for a fellow hiker who needs a baseball cap. Then I grab a tiny stone for Judy Fox, a friend who wanted something from the top of Mount Olympus for the altar at her home in Chico, California, and put it in my backpack just as Zeus appears.

The god of gods isn't smiling as he approaches me.

"Never litter and never steal," he says in a stern, paternal, and frustrated tone. "I suggest we postpone our discussion about my childhood on Crete, and my *Weltanschauung*, and thoughts about immortality, until you get to Mount Ida in Turkey. The topics interest me, even you interest me, but at the moment I need to deal with this squabbling over the Trojan War."

I consider mentioning that many mortals are upset with his support of Troy in the conflict and I'm ready to relate that I heard Meneláos say, "O Father Zeus, incomparable they say you are among all gods and men for wisdom; yet this battle comes from you. How strange that you should favor the offenders – favor the Trojans in their insolence ever insatiable for war!"

But sensing Zeus' current mood I think it might be smarter to keep my mouth shut and not to overstay my welcome.

As I begin my descent I start thinking about all-powerful and all-wise Zeus because, after all, he wasn't particularly polite and cuddly with me today. I remember that poet Robert Graves characterized him as "strong, brave, stupid, noisy, violent and conceited."

Until now, and I don't want to rush to judgment, I thought of Zeus as a benevolent and kind god, especially compared to his cruel father Krónos. I still think it a good thing that Zeus and the other Olympians defeated Krónos and the Titans. And that since then Zeus was considered the leader and lord of men, the foundation of things divine and human, the judge of the universe and the overseer of everything.

I'm not his only fan.

"Zeus is ether, Zeus is the Earth, Zeus is the sky who sat in his golden chair, as underfoot the mighty mountain of Olympus quaked," wrote the dramatist Aeschylus. And Homer calls "O Zeus beyond the storm cloud, dwelling in high air," the "undying" and the "ruler of gods and men" who pours "wondrous riches" upon them.

In fact, Zeus and the other Olympian gods were revered by almost everyone in ancient Greece.

"In the pantheism of the ancient Greeks, gods are everywhere and a force in everything, which is why there are gods for wine and metallurgy," archeologist Sandy MacGillivray told me on Crete. "Everything depended upon them."

These days Zeus is brought up in the strangest contexts. Look how Louann Brizendine introduced him as a leading member of "The Cast of Neurohormone Characters" in her book *The Male Brain*:

"Testosterone – Zeus. King of the male hormones, he is dominant, aggressive and all-powerful. Focused and goal-oriented, he feverishly builds all that is male, including the compulsion to outrank other males in the pecking order. He drives the masculine sweat glands to produce the come-hither smell of manhood – androstenedione. He activates the sex and aggression circuits, and he's single-minded in his dogged pursuit of his desired mate. Prized for his confidence and bravery, he can be a convincing seducer, but when he's irritable, he can be the grouchiest of bears."

Well, that explains it. He's having a grouchy bear day due to the minor irritation about the course of the decade-long Trojan War. I'll cut him some slack.

Why am I so flexible? Did I mention that I feel a kinship with Zeus, or at least some of Zeus' traits, as I sit near his throne?

I stop at the refuge to spend the night and enjoy a mountain man's dinner of bean soup and bread. As I sop up the sauce, I have a contented "Ahh omm, I did it!" end-of-the-day feeling and when another hiker asks me about the mountains in California, I reply that they may be taller, but the gods aren't there.

The next day in Litóhoro, where I arrive around 3:00 p.m., I have a haircut simply, as I told the barber, "to be cut near the gods at Mount Olympus." Naturally I thought of Samson, who lost his strength when he lost his locks.

That afternoon I email Gayle Guest a photograph of my dedication to her mother in the guest book atop Mount Olympus and almost immediately receive a response for my meager gesture: "Thank you for your great thoughtfulness. I know my mother would be thrilled (is thrilled) that you wrote that note and dedicated your climb to the top of Mount Olympus to her!"

Lex Hames, a friend who attended Stanford with me and has joined me on climbs in the Andes and the Himalayas, saw my SPOT signal from the summit and writes: "I'm sure you must be feeling some awesome vibes and a godly presence   I'm being serious, not kidding at all – up on top of Mount Olympus. I know, when I was in Greece, it seemed more filled with a godly presence (or the presence of many gods) than any place I'd ever been.   They seemed imminent – right there, just hidden behind a cloud or a rock or a temple column, about to step out. It must be wild to be on top of the sacred mountain."

I sent him a note back with a few words of Homer: "Never a tremor of wind, or a splash of rain, no errant snowflake comes to stain that heaven, so calm, so vaporless, the world of light."

A Greek/American couple staying at the Guests of Zeus Hotel spend most of the day sitting in front of the hotel watching village life move by. That evening I join them, and Larry tells me about his youth here: climbing, gathering firewood, just scraping by during World War II, how much more snow there used to be when he was a kid.

"I never thought once, with all the climbing I did to gather wood, of going up that mountain for fun," he says.

And for some reason, right then, I realize that it was Homer who created the motivation for foreigners like myself to climb this particular mountain.

As I leave Larry, I ask him to translate an email I have just received from a friend in New York: "Συγχαρητήρια!!!!"

"Congratulations!!!!" he smiles.

During the next few days I circumnavigate Mount Olympus – through the villages of Tirnavos, Elassona, Agio Dimitrios, Foteina, Katerini, and back to Dion – to see what the mountain looks like from every side. Olympus is often so completely veiled in black cloud and I feel such a sense of dread and darkness that the three photographs I take are completely black. The gods must be playing with me, or with my iPhone.

At the end of the afternoon the weather again clears and the mountain sparkles as the sun sets and the moon rises. The transition is so impressive that I bow in reverence, and the next morning the crystal-clear peaks of Mount Olympus are gleaming and glistening in their glory. I feel like the gods are giving me a generous and encouraging farewell smile.

It's such a nice day that I'm inspired to climb the mountain again and see if Zeus is ready for a powwow. I recite a line from *The Iliad* that "pure Dawn had reached Olympus' mighty side, heralding day for Zeus and all the gods…" and grab my backpack.

Prancing About The Peloponnese

"A god moved him – who knows? – or his own heart sent him to learn, at Pylos, if his father roams the wide world still, or what befell him." – Medon in *The Odyssey*

The Oracle at Delphi didn't just tell me to make my way to Crete to discover the birthplace of Zeus. She also gave me specific instructions about my circumnavigation of the Peloponnese, the rugged mountainous peninsula that has technically been an island since the Corinth Canal breached its link with mainland Greece in 1893.

The Peloponnese, known for its tortuous terrain and craggy peaks, is where the early books of *The Odyssey*, called the *Telemachia*, occurred after Telémakhos left Ithaka to seek information about his father. I was instructed by Circe to meet a number of Homeric characters, including King Nestor and Helen of Troy (Circe actually wants me to sleep with Helen which seems a bit far fetched), and check in on Sir Patrick Leigh Fermor, considered the world's best living travel writer. Another tough assignment.

"It would be smart to stay at the Tzaki Hotel in Rio on your first night," said the Oracle, referring to a small community in the northwestern Peloponnese. "They've got glorious sunsets and, yes, Wi-

Fi."

Nothing better than a practical and romantic soothsayer just a few kilometers from Rio as the eagle flies.

Still unable to fly (though that may happen soon), I cross the world's longest multi-span cable-stayed bridge that links the Peloponnese with mainland Greece to get to Rio. You may recall that when I cruised under the 2.9-kilometer (9,449 feet) Charilaos Trikoupis Bridge (aka the Rio-Antirio Bridge) that stretches over the Gulf of Corinth, I abandoned a group reading of *The Odyssey* on the *Corinthian II* to admire the pleasing aesthetic structure.

You can imagine my excitement, therefore, when I physically cross the bridge from Antirion in western Greece to Rio. It's an event right up there with meeting the Oracle at Delphi and listening to the Sirens sing. Odysseus certainly would have felt the same way if he had encountered it.

I have a severe reality check when I realize that the one-way car toll to cross the bridge, which opened in August 2004, is now up to €12.90. That makes it, for non-MedTrekkers, €25.80 for a roundtrip, though you get a slight break if you make the return journey in less than three hours. Yikes!

Perhaps the cost is a small price to pay for the practical result of man-made architectural beauty. Maybe the income from the bridge is being used to pay down Greece's onerous debt. Possibly it's worth that amount to have speedy access to the Peloponnese, which previously required taking a ferry. Or does the price seem high because I'm used to the $6.00 round-trip fare across the Golden Gate Bridge in San Francisco?

Seriously how many people, tourists or locals, can afford it?

I learn (every Greek in the Peloponnese seems to know this) that the toll revenue is being used almost exclusively to pay off Vinci, the French company that led the French-Greek consortium that built the bridge, which was largely financed by the European Union, for a whopping €630,000,000. The Greeks, it turns out, get less than €1 from every toll. No wonder they're broke.

I kick off my Peloponnese MedTrek with a 33-kilometer stroll from Rio through Patras, Greece's third biggest city and the largest port on the west coast. I'm a little unnerved by gangs of Albanians and gypsies roaming Patras, the modern capital of the Peloponnese that features ferries to almost everywhere. I jam my wrist with the gold bracelet into my jacket pocket to make it look like my hand has been amputated before I climb a hill to get a view of the Achaean plain, the Gulf of Patras and the islands of Ithaka, Cephalonia, and Zakynthos. As I look over the city, I recall that the Turks burned Patras to the ground in 1821.

Most of the post-Patras walk on my first day is on the beach, or the road next to the beach, and through seaside resorts and villages like Tsoukaleika and Kaminia. In Paralia Kato Achaia, I meet a French-Canadian-Greek teacher and we discuss the bridge, the mood of the country due to its seemingly never-ending debt crisis, ("Everyone is nervous and negative," he says), Greek politics, and Greek idiosyncrasies ("They always look like they're ready to kill each other when they scream loudly during an argument," he says, "but it's all theater because we're a dramatic people."). The next morning at the Tzaki Hotel an American-Albanian-Greek man traveling with his Greek mother describes their emotional trip "home" to visit his recently deceased dad's relatives in Tirana.

As military jets practice maneuvers overhead, I edge around fertile Cape Araxos on a 30-kilometer outing replete with rural treats – figs, grapes, and watermelon all ripe for picking – produced by that so-good-looking-I-could-eat-it red earth. I'm surprised to see signs forbidding photos, and two very serious fences preventing entry, at the Wall of the Dymeans archeological excavation near Kalogriá.

What's with the heavy-duty security? Does the Greek government know more about this Cyclopean construction from the Mycenaean period than meets my eye? It's called Cyclopean because only a Cyclops was strong enough to move rocks and build a wall 200 meters long, 50 meters wide and 33 meters high – so one is likely to steal it. Are nuclear weapons hidden underneath the *kastro*, or fortress? Are they planning to do something odd with the ruins of the ancient city of Dyme? Maybe open a Dyme store?

I forget about Dyme a few minutes later when I pass a stone chapel situated in the middle of a purple-tinted marshland surrounded by all genres of respectful waterfowl. Due to its location, hue, surroundings, or my state of mind, its beauty blows my hiking shoes off my feet.

I walk barefoot on the beach until I end the day slightly inland in Metochi, where I witness, and participate in, a remarkable little operetta that I'll call *The Lady in the Bright Blue Smock*.

The stout, squat, stern, and sturdy octogenarian star of *The Lady in the Bright Blue Smock* runs a mini-market near the bus stop that is full of Greek tweens buying after-school candy, drinks, cookies, and ice cream. While it didn't seem odd to me that I'd like to know the time of the bus to Patras, she looks at me as though I've asked her a personal and insulting question. She screamingly berates me in front of everyone inside and outside the shop until the police arrive and question me. My late afternoon saunter turns into a segment of *Twilight Zone*.

The most surreal thing on the Mediterranean between Metochi and Kilini is a €3 million port complex in Lechaina Beach built with those, once seemingly endless, European Union funds. The construction of the port involved some serious, almost Cyclopean, rock moving, but only a few dozen small fishing boats are using the berths. This is almost certainly the most expensive dock with the fewest boats on the Mediterranean.

There are a dozen cabanas and a few fly-by-night restaurants in Lechaina Beach, though none are open as I walk through the village. I must have looked famished because a man takes me by the hand and leads me into a house where two elderly ladies attired in traditional black dresses are at the stove. They want €9 to serve me lunch but I somewhat politely bid them ἀποχαιρετισμός, or *adieu*, and hit the beach. My most selfless act of the day occurs when I toss a washed-up, six-inch long fish back into the surf. He looks a lot happier with me than the ladies in black dresses.

Miniature Greek Orthodox churches, chapels, and shrines are still a drachma a dozen in the Peloponnese. So there is nothing unusual about MedTrekking past a candle-filled shrine south of Lechaina in the middle of a sandy beach. When I arrive in Kylini, I spot two shrines on the same rural street corner.

The views of Ithaka and Kefalonia throughout the day inspire me to take a ferry to the island of Zakynthos where Shipwreck Bay, which the Michelin Guide contends is "probably Greece's most famous natural landmark," is reputed to have the best beach, and cleanest water, in the Mediterranean.

I board an 8:15 a.m. ferry that leaves from the harbor just outside my €35-a-night base camp at the Ionion Hotel in Kylini. It's September 9, and as we embark on the sunny, smooth, and serene sea I dedicate the day's outing to my brother Lars, whose birthday it would have been had he not lost his life in a firefighting accident in 2001.

I described Lars' job flying air tankers and fighting forest fires as "funner than stepping on pollywogs or tadpoles" at his memorial service, and my eulogy concluded with the phrase "the fire is out but our memories of you are ablaze." This may sound odd, but I keep thinking I'll stumble on a pollywog today that could be my reincarnated brother. For those who don't know, polliwogs are young frogs with just a tail and a tadpoles are young frogs with both a tail and legs.

Lars would have laughed at this thought because he always had a sick sense of humor, even about the weight he gained and his terrible back problem. "It's not my back that's the problem, it's my front," he'd say. Not that his weight slowed him down. Lars once climbed up an outside drainpipe to get through an open window and unlock my fifth floor apartment on Île Saint-Louis in Paris.

Another time the two of us rented a plane in Brittany and had a minor mechanical problem in flight (in fact, the door came off). The nearest airstrip was a military base near Rouen but the control tower adamantly insisted we not land. Lars, pretending not to understand the French-accented English, put the plane down and, typically, where another pilot might have been arrested or shot, became great buddies with the controller on the ground.

After the short ferry ride, I spend an hour walking along the Zakynthos harbor and get the lowdown on the island from an extraordinarily helpful young woman at a seaside travel agency. She knows I'm hiking and am not a serious customer, but she pleasantly stops what she's doing, shows me the route to Shipwreck Bay on a detailed map, describes the dizzying viewing platform above the inaccessible-by-land bay, and tells me how long it will be to walk.

"Most tourists view and visit Shipwreck Bay by boat or take a €50 air-conditioned taxi to see it from above," she says when I tell her I still plan to walk. "You must be incredibly patient."

I leave Zakynthos Town through the villages of Tsilivi, Marineika, Gerakari, Katastari, Orthonies, Anafonitria, and Agios Georgiou on a jaunt that reconfirms my MedTrekking Theory of Aesthetic Appreciation. The MTAA dictates that the level of appreciation of a destination increases in the eye of the beholder in proportion to the distance, time and struggle involved in MedTrekking to it (AA = D + T + S).

Consequently my patient, 35-kilometer stroll from Zakynthos Town (contemporary habitués call the place Zante but the Venetians, who ran Zakynthos from 1489 to 1797, named it the "Flower of the Levant") along the coast and over the limestone peaks to Shipwreck Bay results in massive aesthetic appreciation.

Odysseus almost certainly saw Zakynthos on his passage to Troy, as did Telémakhos when he floated by two decades later. They undoubtedly noticed Shipwreck Bay and admired the towering white limestone cliffs. But they categorically did not see the shipwreck or a Russian tourist admiring it. The wreck dates from less than four decades ago when the *Panayotis* was beached here (before the shipwreck, the bay was called Agios Georgios after a nearby village).

A day later I drop into the 13th-century Chlemoutsi medieval fort about eight kilometers from Kylini. Built by the Franks who called it Clermont, the chateau is a remarkably intact vestige of the Crusades and

French occupation of the Peloponnese. I light a candle at the 12th century Vlacherna Monastery and take a thermal bath in Louta Kilinis before hiking on sandy and hotel-filled Golden Beach.

I take the afternoon off and celebrate with a long lingering lunch, a two-hour nap, and a quick dip in the sea enjoying dinner (warm red beets, grilled octopi with spinach) while reading *The New Yorker* on my Kindle. See, I can relax.

The next morning I continue down the sandy and swimmable Peloponnese coast to rhythmically named Katakolo, where I cut inland through the rolling hills (actually Mount Kronion and the Alfiós Valley) to ancient Olympia, site of the first Olympic Games almost 2,800 years ago.

Nikos Kazantzakis's book *Travels in Greece* prompted me to make the SideTrek to Olympia. He wrote that "in all Greece there is no landscape more inspiring, none that so gently and perseveringly invites peace and reconciliation. The ancients chose it with unerring eye, so that every four years all the clans of Greece might gather here, to sport and fraternize."

At Olympia, where the Games were held quadrennially for six days beginning in the eighth century BC, I meander for two hours in a spot that Homer said is "blessed by Zeus and spacious." The site, once a Sanctuary of Zeus with a statue that was considered one of the wonders of the ancient world, seems particularly spacious when there are no naked Greek athletes practicing in the stadium (which could hold 45,000 people), gymnasium and other areas.

The Olympic flame is still ignited here for every Olympiad and I'm inspired by the locale to do a few dozen pushups, sit-ups, planks, bends and stretches. Then I seek out the sacred olive tree from which the winners' wreathes were cut with a gold scythe and take a photograph of *Hermês of Paxiteles*, the iconic statue dating from the fourth century BC that shows the messenger god holding the infant Dionysus, in the Olympia Museum.

While lunching on breast of chicken and spinach at a local *taverna*, I tell an American woman at the next table that Greek athletes used to eat lambs' testicles to get a jolt of testosterone to increase their strength.

"I'm not sure that chicken will do the trick," she winks with a smile.

The port town of Katakolo exists primarily to service multi-level cruise ships with thousands of passengers who tour Olympia and drop hundreds of euros in scores of curio shops. Not that Katakolo should be dismissed. At the exceptionally offbeat Museum of Greek Technology I see "100 operating reconstructions of mechanisms and inventions from

Greek Antiquity," including the first robot, the first alarm clock and the first odometer. But this place subsists almost solely on cruise-ship tourism. The second the ships split, everything except the bars shut down. After all, what do locals want with pornographic Greek statuettes or outdated calendars with cats on them?

After a 15-kilometer walk beyond Katakolo on hard, packed sand (so hard and packed that even cars are driving on it) due to the furious rain, I notice that something is missing. There are no hotels or infrastructure on the marshy beaches and rolling sand dunes. And the nearby fire-scarred mountains are still recovering from blazes that raged throughout the Peloponnese in 2007.

There are always some remarkably surreal sightings in isolated coastal areas like this. I chuckle, partly in amazement, at a very fat lady (think Little Lotta from the 1950-1972 comic strip) sitting on the sand at the edge of the sea and pulling up her billowing bathing suit to get just the right amount of wave action at just the right anatomical spot. I wonder who stuck a tall tree limb firmly in the sand with a hangman's noose around it and left a toppled stool underneath (as though the hanging had just taken place and the body had disappeared). And why does one uninhabited lean-to fly a Che Guevara flag? Whatever the reasons, it is delightful to see some completely naked lovers in action under a skimpy umbrella while a few older couples timidly attack the waves as I body surf nude in Neochiro. One man with a horrifically mangled leg reminds me how fortunate I am to be able to MedTrek though this wonderland.

The next day all of the elements – sun, sea, sand, light, temperature – are in alignment, and I kick off my sandals the second I hit the seaside. I maintain my usual five-kilometer-per-hour pace during the entire 28-kilometer beach walk into Kyparissia, my new base camp that was known as Arkadia in the Middle Ages.

Again I walk on mostly empty beaches (the Greeks tend to end their summer earlier than the Italians and it's been "low" season since August 20). I know I've achieved Zen mode when I see and appreciate a beautiful nude body and it turns out to be a guy, the first of man-y on this stretch of beach. There are some campers near Kyparissia, which obviously got its name from its many cypresses (though I tell my brother Kip that it's named after him). One circled corral of pan-European recreational vehicles symbolizes contemporary Europe on the move. Labeled FR-D-NL-P-A-and-B, they are from France, Germany, Netherlands, Poland, Austria, and Belgium.

I go to bed with rock music emanating from one of the disco

clubs on the beach and wake up to Greek Orthodox bells and chants cascading down from the church up the hill in the main part of town. Across from my room in the Ionian Sea are the Strofades Islands, home of the Harpies that were monsters represented as birds with women's faces.

Ten kilometers south of Kyparissia, I stumble upon one of the oddest faux castles on the entire Mediterranean. The pretentious structure, known as the Faux Nestor Palace, certainly did not belong to Lord Nestor, and it is even too surreal to belong to Lord Disney.

Aubergines, tomatoes, potatoes, watermelon, olives, you name it, grow and thrive in the rich soil next to the beach. My daily lunch often consists of three sun-warmed tomatoes, two purloined figs, and a stolen watermelon. As I walk on a rural road (the National Road is a few more kilometers inland) for the last six klicks into Marathopolis, I chat with a couple of cyclists.

"Is it harder to walk or cycle?" one asks, leading to a debate that goes nowhere.

I get a lift back to Kyparissia with a Greek from Sydney named Sam Roussis whose company, Ariston Hellas, exports extra virgin olive oil to the US and other markets. Driving a brand new Audi, Sam mentions that the annual harvest is just a month away. He also tells me that he married an American from Hartford, Connecticut, and that they have one daughter and a house in Marathopolis, which he calls simply Maratho. Then he gives me the local news.

"The coast south of here is one of the last undeveloped stretches in Greece, but a shipping magnate is putting in a multi-million dollar development that you'll see when you walk towards Pylos," he says. "Everyone is trying to get a piece of the action here now."

The first 12 kilometers from Marathopolis towards Pylos are arduous and slow because of razor-sharp rocks that challenge my hiking, balance, sanity, and shoes. I'm always relieved when I survive a long stretch like this without falling and getting cut or scraped. When I finally reach a sandy beach after 15 kilometers, I celebrate by eating a freshly picked watermelon.

I continue into Romanos-Costa Navarino, where the chic resort that Sam told me about is located, and pick up a brochure that describes "crystal clear waters and captivating views of the Ionian Sea...a beacon of sophistication that blends the rich history of the region of Messinia with the contemporary amenities of Novarino Dunes."

The three-kilometer long sandy beach and the Romanos resort itself are setting an up-market pace for local tourism. "Pristine coastline, virgin lagoons, extensive olive groves, waterfalls, and endless golden sandy beaches define this land as much as its intriguing history," boasts the brochure and it goes on, "Traditional Greek design with contemporary touches sets the tone in each space, where the sparkling blue of the Mediterranean is the preferred hue."

More importantly, this is where Telémakhos is purported to have landed when he arrived to meet Lord Nestor of Gerênia. He was greeted by citizens of Pylos gathered on the seashore to offer a sacrifice of black bulls to Poseidon, the "blue-maned god who makes the islands tremble."

It's easy to visualize Telémakhos following Athêna to Lord Nestor's fresco-adorned *megaron,* or royal residence. As they approached the palace, Athêna counseled Odysseus' son: "Not the least shyness, now. You came across the open sea for this – to find out where the great earth hides your father and what the doom was that he came upon. Go to old Nestor, master charioteer, so we may broach the storehouse of his mind. Ask him with courtesy, and in his wisdom he will tell you history and no lies."

A nervous Telémakhos wasn't used to serious conversations with noble adults, but Athêna assured him that "reason and heart will give you words."

"I want news of my father, Odysseus, known for his great heart, and I will comb the wide world for it," Telémakhos says to Nestor. "Tell me of his death, sir, if perhaps you have witnessed it, or have heard some wanderer tell the tale."

First excavated in 1939, Nestor's breezy (especially today when there are no walls) two-story palace in the Englianos hills – about 17 kilometers north of the current location of Pylos and six kilometers from the beach where he landed – is one of best-preserved ruins I've run into.

Thoroughly explored in the 1950s by American archeologist Carl Blegen, the discovery of clay tablets and other artifacts confirm that Pylos was an important political, administrative, economic, military, religious, and financial center in ancient Greece. The nearby Archeological Museum in the village of Chora features numerous palace treasures – including discoveries from Mycenaean *tholos* tombs, ritual vases, pounds of gold jewelry, amphorae, arrowheads, *kylikes*, *kraters*, friezes, tripod vessels, chimney pipes, and loom weights. I even discover a surviving photograph of how the palace looked in Nestor's day that enables my imagination to pleasantly wonder and wander during a leisurely afternoon there.

It's no surprise that many archeologists agree that this is Lord Nestor's palace, and Pausanias, known as the "Greek Baedeker," wrote that Odysseus dedicated a temple to Athêna here.

The *megaron*, with aged and gnarled olive trees in the garden, affords a spectacular view over the distant Bay of Navarino and Sphakteria Island. It comes alive for me the second I enter the same gates that Telémakhos passed through.

Walking around the palace grounds I envisage Lord Nestor, scepter in hand on a throne just to the right of the hearth, gabbing with Telémakhos. I get a look at everything, including two archive rooms, the headquarters of the palace guard, the inviting bathroom, the guest rooms, the waiting room, the court, the observation tower, the pantry, the oil and wine storage facilities, the fresco-decorated halls, the queen's apartments, and the portico.

Then, in my mind's eye, I see Telémakhos submerged in the bathtub as the lovely Polycaste, Nestor's youngest daughter, washes him and anoints him with oil.

Athêna and Telémakhos, who arrived just before dinner, were led to soft lambskins on the floor, given wine in golden cups and asked to "pray to the gods on whom all men depend." Athêna led the prayer to Poseidon: "Earthshaker, listen and be well disposed. Grant your petitioners everything they ask."

Lord Nestor, who made it back from Troy without any of the delays encountered by Odysseus, tells Telémakhos that Aías, Achilles, Patróklos, and his son Antilokhus were killed during the decade-long war when "the hand of heaven was against us" and "Zeus was hatching mischief."

And though he has kind words about Odysseus ("He had no rivals, your father, at the tricks of war"), he has no news.

"I urge you to call on Meneláos, he being but lately home from distant parts in the wide world," Nestor said after the ritual feast as he offered to have his sons take Telémakhos overland to Sparta to meet the man who, he says using one of the most popular expressions of the day, will "tell you history and no lies."

I too will visit Meneláos, but I don't go overland to get to Sparta. Instead I leave Lord Nestor's and soon find myself on a stretch of packed red earth that is the foundation for a new national road linking Pylos with Patras. I presume that, like everything else around here, its construction is due to the new resort.

During the day I meet a barman who thinks I'm crazy, an English teacher who wishes me luck, an electrician who isn't surprised that I don't have a wife, a hunter with a big shotgun on the front seat of his car, an English expatriate, and a campsite director who gives me a discount on some delectable Greek desserts because of all the walking I'd been doing.

The barman quickly becomes my favorite friend when he makes me a seriously decent espresso coffee with milk, though he cannot fathom why anyone would walk around the Mediterranean. "You actually have time to walk that much?" he laughs. "You're still young enough to keep working. You're an idiot."

The English teacher tells me about her high school students from small villages who are getting their first introduction to English. I volunteer to come and talk to her class but she says "They won't understand a thing." I think she's referring to their feeble command of English but she might be criticizing my accent.

The electrician is concerned about his future because his two-year contract with the luxury hotel is soon to expire. I describe the MedTrek and he asks me if I'm married. We both crack up when I say "MedTrekking isn't for married men."

The hunter offers me a ride that I would have refused even if I hadn't seen the 12-gauge shotgun on the front seat, and I get some tips about the path towards Spacteria Island and Pylos from Nigel, an Englishman who lives in Gialova.

My last social encounter of the day, at 29 kilometers, is with the owner of the very full Erodios Campsite near Gialova. I'm famished so I select a kilogram of Greek desserts. I mention that I'd been by The Romanos ("Privacy reigns in 321 exquisitely appointed sea view suites with 121 individual infinity pools" the brochure continues), and he says: "They let you in?"

Before I get to Pylos, I walk through a new golf course being built by, of course, The Romanos. Gigantic earthmovers have been leveling fairways and creating sand traps, but they've stopped when I pass and have my best score ever on a golf course. Zero.

I MedTrek into the main *Platia Trion Navarhon*, or Three Admirals' Square, in the picturesque, pleasant, protected and strategically key port of Pylos and settle into a new base camp on the port.

That night I meet an English couple from Yorkshire and a young Greek primary school teacher. The Englishman, a former RAF officer who is rabidly anti-immigration and very old school English, says, for no particular reason, "*Inshallah*" to the dark-skinned young Greek, presuming from his olive skin that he's an Arab. The Greek jokingly dismisses the intended slur with an "Ah, you must be Jewish" response. I have a coffee with the teacher and discuss everything from hippiedom and journalism to MedTrekking and the new resort.

I end my walk down the west coast of the Peloponnese with a fortifying day of MedTrekking. Two forts, in fact. One built by the Turks in the 16th century in Pylos and another 13th century citadel in Methoni, which is called "the eye of Venice" due to its strategic position on southwestern tip. After a 290-kilometer MedTrek from the bridge in Rio I sit atop the Bourdzi Tower, once a key watchtower in the eastern

Mediterranean, and wonder what I'll find on Sapiendza Island just offshore.

Inshallah.

During the next few days I MedTrek from Methoni through Koroni into olive-rich Kalamata, the capital of the Peloponnese that also has fabulous figs and a daily bus to Tirana. The city is eerily clean and modern because it was totally rebuilt after an earthquake in 1986.

I head inland to visit the ruins at ancient Messini (Messene was once its queen) and spend two hours investigating the rich archeological site – from residences with mosaic floors to the well-preserved theater, a stadium with a grass center, burial tombs, and other attractions. The city was also rebuilt by the Theban general Epaminondas in 369 BC after his victory over the Spartans, and when I arrive at the Arkadia (it's pronounced Ar-KAH-dia not Arcade-ia) Gate I marvel at the Great Wall of Messini that once surrounded it.

To get an overview, I climb to the top of 800-meter Mount Ithome, once the site of the sanctuary of Zeus Ithomatas and later the 17th-century Monastery of Panagia Voulkanou. From the top of the mountain, which was the center of resistance during the Second Messenian War in the seventh century BC and the focus of a Helot revolt in 463 BC, I see another temple dedicated to Apollo on a mountain top about 35 kilometers away. A forest ranger tells me that locals believe the temples help prevent forest fires, though that didn't seem to be the case in 2007.

Seeking Celebrated Sir Patrick

I'm now heading to Kardamili and the home of Patrick Leigh Fermor, often described as "the world's greatest living travel writer," on the Mani Peninsula. The Mani is the place where, in the 17th century, the inhabitants were described as "famous as pirates by sea and pestilent robbers by land." Kardamili was one of the seven cities offered to Achilles by Agamémnon if he would get back into action during the Trojan War and in 1821 the Greek war of independence began on this rugged peninsula.

When I arrive in Kardamili, about 35 kilometers south of Kalamata, I install myself in a €30 B&B close to the seaside and the owner's thirty-something daughter immediately invites me to a family dinner party. I put on my light cotton white pants and a collared shirt for the first time on this outing. Naturally someone spills red wine on the white pants the second I arrive at the party, which lasted four hours and was conducted with typical Greek gusto. So much for trying to be chic in the Peloponnese.

The next morning I enjoy a mouth-watering, 25-kilometer

panoramic mountain MedTrek in the Taygetos range above Kardamili. It affords extraordinary views of the Messennian Gulf and a string of beaches, including Kalamitsi and Neo Proastio.

Kardamili has one of the best-marked local trail networks in the Peloponnese due, I'm told, to the large number of hike-loving Dutch and German tourists. My stroll takes me up the Viros Gorge to the villages of Petrovouni, Aghia Sofia, Tseria, Exochori, and Prasito. I relish the towering walls and bouldering path; meditate to the morning chants of the priest at Aghia Sofia; have a much-needed coffee at a new hotel in Exochori; and cut myself to shreds coming down a hillside near Prasito.

I pass numerous Byzantine churches, including the tiny chapel near Exochori where Sir Patrick scattered the ashes of author and fellow travel writer, Bruce Chatwin in 1989. It's then and there that I decide to call my MedTrek around the Mani Peninsula a Mani Pedi.

I linger and loiter the next day. The lingering is in Kardamili, where I have coffee at two different cafés, slowly eat two bananas, sample a sesame biscuit at the market and investigate the old town. The loitering is around Sir Patrick Leigh Fermor's house just a few kilometers out of town.

I know it's the right house when I see an envelope with "Sir" in the address sticking out of the postbox and "190" scrawled on the front gate. There's a formidable six-feet high stone wall around the property, yet a quiet passerby can hear conversations through the open grey shutters and admire olives ripening in the terraced grove amid towering cypresses. I walk along the stone wall and reach the beach where Sir Patrick took his a daily swims when he was younger. There's a sign on the steps up to his home marked "Private."

Let me be clear about one thing: I did not establish a base camp in Kardamili to inconvenience Sir Patrick, or Paddy as his friends call him. After all, the English World War II commando and knighted author is 95. He deserves to be left in peace in the cat-filled stone home he designed and built on the Kalamitsi beach following his arrival here in 1962. I let him enjoy the "mad splendor," as he called it once, of his home knowing that, as Priam told Achilles, "he stands upon the fearful doorstep of old age" and, as Antílokhos said in *The Iliad*, that "the immortals honor the older men as much as ever."

The evening before, however, I did offer to Elpida, Sir Patrick's long-time housekeeper and assistant (her name means "Hope"), to drop in and cheer up the man who walked from London to Constantinople as a teenager, swam the Hellespont in his 60s in homage to Lord Byron, and has a tattoo of a double-tailed mermaid on his shoulder.

"If he's up for it, I'll show him my legs and tell him some

amusing walking adventure stories to pep him up," I tell her.

I figure Sir Patrick will laugh if he gets a look at all of the recent cuts and scratches I got while MedTrekking. And I thought a few of my patented MedTrek anecdotes – my fall in Morocco, my encounter with thieving gypsies in Italy, my nights at a nudist camp in France, my adoration of *ragazze Siciliane*, the time I lost my passport and money in the Mediterranean – would bring a smile to his face.

Or maybe he'd like to go for a swim or see some pictures of my 90-year-old mother, though I'm not sure if the war hero and linguist whose wife Joan died in 2003, would hit it off with mom.

I give Elpida another call from the front gate but she nixes my visit, informing me that "Sir Patrick has the flu." I'm no longer working for gossip-rich *People Magazine*, when I wouldn't have left town without an interview or some kind of scoop, and I doubt that I could add much to William Dalrymple's excellent 2008 profile of Leigh Fermor

So I politely thank Elpida, tell her to wish Sir Patrick a speedy recovery and leave her my number just in case he has a change of heart.

During my visit I read Fermor's book *Mani* that was written in 1958 about this Peloponnesian promontory. I particularly enjoy his infatuation with classical antiquity; his digressive, eclectic, erudite, literary, and seemingly serendipitous writing style; and his frequent breaks from the narrative to ruminate about art, cuisine, history or some personal matter. The last of a generation of warrior–travel writers, Sir Patrick died within a year of my visit at the age of ninety-six and is buried in Dumbleton in the English countryside.

He was a fastidious writer, and it always took numerous rewrites before he was pleased with his work. In 1933, at the age of 18, he began his enterprising and inspiring footloose journey to Istanbul with a copy of Horace's Odes in his rucksack. His first book about it, *A Time of Gifts*, wasn't published until 1977 while the second, *Between the Woods and the Water*, appeared in 1986. A third book, which will take him through the Balkans and into Turkey, is presumably among the pile of papers I see while peering over the wall into his study.

When Fermor wrote about his visit to three great monasteries in *A Time to Keep Silence* in 1953, he said the retreat gave him an opportunity to write because "the troubled waters of the mind grow still and clear."

I'm sorry that I so nearly missed meeting him.

If Kardamili has the feel of a we're-in-shape-let's-head-for-the-hills hiking community, Stoupa to the south feels like it attracts a lay-on-the-beach-and-turn-beet-red British crowd. To my surprise, there's an excellent path from Stoupa down the coast to Ágios Nikólaos. I continue on rocky beaches beyond Agios Demetrios, pass a seaside house with a pool so tempting that I almost dive in, and have a Greek salad and buy three liters of water in Trachia.

That's because the waiter tells me that I'm facing rough terrain – a gorge, snakes that bite, thistles, cliffs, no trails, impassible landscape. He lays it on thick. I'm glad I have lots of water when I find myself on the true rough and rugged Mani Peninsula. I'm not sure that even Sir Patrick in his prime would have enjoyed the last six thistle-biting, cliff-hanging, rock-cutting, briar-bashing, pathless kilometers of this day.

After a longer-than-expected ten-hour MedTrek, I emerge in a village called Chotasia and head an hour uphill to the main road where I'm picked up by the first car going to Kardamili. The German driver from Stuttgart has just read *Mani,* and we discuss it during the 45-minute drive. I point out Sir Patrick's home as we drive by Kalamitsi and show the backpacking German some photos I took the other day of nearby Messini. That night I enjoy an end-of-the-day fruit salad and ice cream at the seaside bar to the tune of *When You Wish Upon A Star.*

On my way down the coast I indulge in a 1.2-kilometer boat ride in the dark Diros Caves, which has an underground river and numerous stalactite-and-stalagmite-filled chambers, before arriving in the small fishing village of Gerolimenas. There I seek out the village's first stone building, mentioned by Sir Patrick in *Mani,* and discover that the historic structure has been converted into the luxurious-by-any-standards Kyrimai Hotel, a lavish refuge amid the harsh reality of the inhospitable terrain of the challenging countryside.

"Inhospitable," incidentally, is everyone's favorite adjective to describe the uneven terrain and hostile topography of the southwestern coast of the Mani Peninsula. The beautiful region is so stark, barren, rocky, cliffy, windswept, arid and remote that six new words are being invented in contemporary Greek each year to more colorfully describe it.

The hospitable Kyrimai Hotel sits on the water and against the cliffs in the virtually unpopulated, untouristed middle of nowhere. The manager gives me a serious discount when he learns I'm a MedTrekker. I welcome a bit of luxury and don't leave the next morning until after breakfast is served at 8:30. No one, especially a MedTrekker, could pass up a meal like this to kick off the day.

The 30-kilometer MedTrek assault to and beyond the southernmost spot in the Peloponnese occurs on a cloudy, windy, and comparatively cool day and is mostly on a carless tarmac road instead of the pathless seaside. Always in sight of the sea, the road keeps me looking cool, calm, and collected instead of sweaty, smelly and scratched.

I stroll on empty cobblestone sidewalks amid the mostly vacant stone towers in Vathia, the hilltop village that the green Michelin Guide says "is the most impressive of the tower communities which are characteristic of the Mani." However, Vathia contains just a few of the 853 tower homes on the Mani peninsula, and the rule of thumb is that the more powerful and wealthy the owner, the higher the tower.

I slow my pace and stop for a leisurely lunch in Port Cagio, which means "Quail Port" (it presumably gets its name after the bird that everyone around here is trying to shoot at dawn and dusk), and unhurriedly visit an isolated hillside Byzantine church on the way to the Sanctuary and Death Oracle of Poseidon Tainarios on Cape Matapan. This has long been considered by some Greeks to be the entrance to Hades and is now filled with contemporary votive offerings that include notes, postcards, unsmoked cigarettes and lots of coins.

When I arrive at the Akrotirio Tenaro lighthouse, which is near one of the deepest spots in the Mediterranean and the place where the Ionian and Aegean Seas meet, I'm at the southernmost point of continental Greece. I spend a dawdling hour watching cargo and cruise ships round the cape, leave a baseball cap as an offering in the sanctuary, and wonder what it will be like to try to sleep with Helen of Troy.

Sleeping with Helen of Troy

Dueling for a Haunted Lady – the title of Book Three in
The Iliad
"The immortal gods had never willed it." – *The Iliad*

My next challenge in the Peloponnese involves, as Circe requested, finding the bed where Paris spent his first night with Helen before taking her home to Troy. And, Circe insisted much to my surprise, "Sleep with her!"

Despite that seductive allure I have to admit that, not used to luxury on the MedTrek, I have trouble pulling myself away from the cornucopia of comforts at the Kyrimai Hotel in Gerolimenas. I sleep, I eat, I blog, I swim, and I tan until the early afternoon. All very tranquil and Zenny.

But then I embark on a long but easy meander, interrupted by only an occasional mule in the road, through tower-dominated hilltop villages and into colorfully decorated Byzantine chapels, across the Mani Peninsula to Kokala. From there, I spend a few days following the seaside walk through Chalikia Vatta, where I order a gigantic €5 Greek salad for lunch and entertain four very intrigued school kids who've never seen a MedTrekker, to Githio.

This is where, I've been told, I'll find the bed where Paris first had Helen.

Most Greeks are well enough versed in the classics to know that Paris, the besotted Trojan prince, slept with Helen, the unfaithful Queen of Sparta, on the minute island of Kranai before whisking her to Troy more than 3,200 years ago. Their fateful frolic and reckless spree led to the long-running Trojan War. Had that night not occurred, had Helen not engaged in a torrid extramarital affair, we would not have Homer's *Iliad* and *Odyssey.*

The incident has had such an impact on Greek history that many contemporary lovers in the Peloponnese use their first romantic date to visit the tiny island, which is also called Marathonissi and is now connected to the mainland with a causeway. Indeed, local couples consider a night spent on the island a requisite rite of passage in the evolution of their relationship.

After a couple weeks on the stark and solitary Mani Peninsula, I don't hesitate to get in on the amorous action. As part of my MedTrekking research, I decide to camp for a night in exactly the same spot – though not in exactly the same bed – that led to the Trojan War.

Although Kranai is small, it requires a somewhat lengthy investigation and time-consuming process of elimination to determine precisely where the ancient couple actually bedded down. No fool, I immediately discard structures that didn't exist on their momentous night together under a full blue moon circa 1195 BC. That eliminates a Byzantine chapel, the Tzanetaki Tower and museum, and the lighthouse.

There is no guidebook specifically identifying the whereabouts of what was perhaps the most tragic liaison in history. But after I spend two hours in the museum, the curator takes a few minutes off work to accompany me towards the lighthouse at the tip of the island. There, he points to a stunted column carved out of stone.

"That, some archeologists claim, is the precise site of the Trojan encampment before Prince Paris and Queen Helen sailed to the nearby island of Kythera and then on to Troy," he told me. "That is where they slept and this is where their spirits appear once in a blue moon."

As soon as I locate the stunted column, I set up my own camp and, slightly excited, look forward to sleeping with the fabled Helen of Troy if she appears. Not, alas, in a four-poster bed with silk sheets, fluffy pillows, and inspiring incense but in my lightweight sleeping bag strategically positioned on matted grass.

It turns out not to be ideal conditions for making the earth move, but around midnight Helen, who still resembles the golden-arrowed goddess Artemis (think Megan Fox of *Transformers*), appears in all her splendor at the foot of my sleeping bag. Unfortunately, the full moon was not too visible because of torrential rain and noisy thunderstorms, which I blame on Zeus.

It doesn't surprise me that Helen's a bit hesitant at first, because her last little frolic here paved the way for serious retribution by the Greeks when they arrived in Troy. A lot of people took Helen's abduction and seduction very personally, especially her husband Meneláos. Homer records that Meneláos "burned to avenge the struggles and the groans of Helen" and was so unhappy with the young Paris that he proclaimed, "I'll cut him to bits, adulterous dog!"

Meneláos told everyone who would listen, including his brother Agamémnon and Zeus himself, that Paris would pay for his profound imprudence.

"O Zeus aloft, grant I shall make the man who wronged me first pay for it now!" Meneláos said. "Let him be humbled, brought down at my hands, and hearts in those born after us will shrink from treachery to a host who offers love."

Hektor called his brother Paris "a woman-crazed seducer."

"You bad-luck charm!" Hektor said scornfully. "Paris, the great lover, a gallant sight! You should have had no seed and die unmarried. Would to god you had…My heart aches in me when I hear our men, who have such toil of battle on your account, talk of you with contempt."

The women of Troy also took a hit because of their prince's amorous folly.

"Let no man press for our return before he beds down with some Trojan wife, to avenge the struggles and the groans of Helen," instructed Lord Nestor of Gerênia.

It's Agamémnon, who leads the Akhaian troops to Troy, who best comprehends the historical impact of Helen's infidelity. He told Odysseus "the day of faithful wives is gone forever."

And my night with Helen? Was it an island romance that would perhaps lead to a faithful marriage? The best one-night stand of my life? Memorable from a historical perspective?

Forget it!

Much to my dismay and surprise, Helen wants to have a profound historical, philosophical and existential discussion. About the agony of her misguided affair with Paris ("I acted so disgracefully"); about how the whole melodrama was due to a wretched curse by the scheming goddess Aphroditê ("I was sorry for the blindness Aphroditê brought me....I repented the mad day Aphrodité drew me away from my dear fatherland, forsaking all – child, bridal bed, and husband"); about how tough it is being known as the woman who launched a thousand ships and started a decade-long war ("all because of me and my mad passion for Trojan Paris"); and about how she admired Odysseus when he "threw some rags on and, like a household slave, slipped into Troy among his enemies" before she " bathed him and rubbed him with oil."

I'm the ideal listener and let Helen completely control our nocturnal discourse. In fact, I only make one comment, and certainly not a single pass, throughout the entire stormy and sleepless night.

"I'm not quite sure if blaming this whole thing on Aphrodité's curse will get you off the hook these days," I tell her as the clouds clear and a somewhat rosy-fingered dawn approaches.

Then, trying to calm her down, I mention that not everyone put the full blame on her. Even Priam, the king of Troy and the father of Paris and Hektor, passed the buck up the mountain.

"You are not to blame," Priam said. "I hold the gods to blame for bringing on this war against the Akhaians, to our sorrow."

But Helen, presumably after a few centuries of therapy, still refuses to take the easy way out and seems ready to accept responsibility for her actions. Repeating a comment she made to her father-in-law thousands of years ago, she says: "Painful death would have been sweeter for me on that day I joined your son, and left my bridal chamber." Helen undeniably still has some personal issues to resolve before she can truly move on. It's clear that she worries about everything from her self-worth to an ability to have a sane and lasting relationship. In fact, she's sometimes upset that she exists at all.

"Brother dear – dear to a whore, a nightmare of a woman!" she exclaimed to her brother-in-law Hektor. "That day my mother gave me to the world I wish a hurricane blast had torn me away to wild mountains, or into tumbling sea to be washed under by a breaking wave, before these evil days could come!"

"God, that I might have died sooner!" she says to me in an exasperated tone.

I try to make Helen feel better by reminding her that she wasn't the only woman who caused a great deal of grief during the Homeric era. Achilles, I tell her, refused to fight in the Trojan War because Agamémnon took away his concubine Briséis. And that action was another reason that the war dragged on.

But the two warriors let it go much quicker than Helen has.

"Agamémnon, was it better for us in any way, when we were sore at heart, to waste ourselves in strife over a girl?" Achilles asked. "By heaven, I drop my anger now. No need to smolder in my heart forever!....Let us recover the joy of battle soon....Slaughter and blood are what I crave, and groans of anguished men."

As she prepares to depart just after sunrise, I fully expect long-robed Helen, still a goddess among women, to give me "an anodyne, mild magic of forgetfulness" that would make me "incapable of tears" for a day. That's what she gave to Telémakhos.

But she doesn't want to leave before reminding me of what she said to Paris when she greeted him with downcast eyes after he returned from the battlefield in Troy. She says she was basically urging him to kill himself.

"Home from the war?" she asked Paris with disdain. "You should have perished there, brought down by that strong soldier, once my husband. You used to say you were the better man, more skillful with your hands, your spear. So why not challenge him to fight again?"

Then she told Paris precisely why that would be a stupid idea.

"I wouldn't if I were you," she continued. "No, don't go back to war against the tawny-headed man of war like a rash fool. You'd crumple under his lance."

Paris' response to Helen's disdainful remark is typical of a young male who's gotten in over his groin.

"Let us drop war now, you and I, and give ourselves to pleasure in our bed," Paris suggested. "My soul was never so possessed by longing, not even when I took you first aboard off Lakedaimôn, the sweet land, and sailed in the long ships....Greater desire now lifts me like a tide."

Helen, and I know this still bothers her, fell for it.

Although my main goal in Githio was to spend a night with Helen of Troy, during a daylong walkabout north and south of town I can't help noticing the garbage stacked on the street at both ends of town. The smelly scene would make the littering Italians green with envy and is due, says my Greek acquaintance Anna Patrikakou who I met at a hotel in town, to the fact that "there's no local disposal facility, and the subcontractor is not doing his job."

During the day I also notice a shipwrecked fishing boat rusting on a beach about six kilometers to the north (which Anna thinks is beautiful); and, nearby, a completely deteriorated out-of-use resort complex (that Anna says is very old) with rotting buildings named after Hermês, Poseidon, Athêna, and other gods.

Don't think my liaison with Helen was a one-night stand. We will hook up again a few days later when I arrive in Sparta, part of King

Meneláos' kingdom during the Mycenaean epoch and Greece's most powerful city from the eighth to the fourth centuries BC. It is here that I witness the end of an historic footrace and check in on Telémakhos, Meneláos, and other members of the Homeric gang.

This time I find Helen lying next to her husband, King Meneláos, in the Menelaion, their stone sanctuary in a secluded high-up-on-a-hillside olive grove overlooking Sparta, the Spartan plain, the Eurotas River and the Taygetos Mountains. Amazingly they got back together after the Trojan War because, despite everything, the king royally accepted the Aphroditê rationalization.

I find the well-hidden and not-too-publicized monument at the top of a rocky path that meanders between two olive groves. It consists of a serene and solemn mound of rocks and earth, but has a view fit for a dead king and queen.

It was to Sparta, which Homer calls the "land of many ravines," that Telémakhos came after he left Nestor's palace. He visited Meneláos and Helen, who greeted him with great hospitality, in their splendid and massive palace with a high-arched roof, to get "history and no lies" about his father. Meneláos described his arduous eight-year return home from Troy through Egypt, Cyprus, Phoenicia, Ethiopia, and Libya (all of these return-to-Greece-from-Troy stories are known as *nostoi)*, and Helen provided Telémakhos with details about his father's heroics during the war.

"You must be the boy he left behind when he took ship for Troy," she said. "Aphroditê's curse was already wearing off when last I saw your father. What a man! I'll never forget his daring and his guile. He had beaten himself black and blue and dressed up in a beggar's rags to sneak into Troy. But I recognized him when he spoke to me there in the house of Paris. I bathed him and gave him a fresh robe, and he made his escape, killing many a Trojan on his way. I rejoiced, for I missed my home and the blameless husband I had forsaken."

Her husband broke in and made an allusion to the Trojan horse.

"And remember, my dear, how you suspected that we were hiding inside the wooden horse?" the fair-haired Meneláos recalled. "Odysseus was in command. It was everything he could do to keep us quiet when you started calling out to us, imitating the voice of each man's wife."

Then King Meneláos informs Telémakhos that his dad is still alive, though marooned on an island. He quotes immortal Proteus of Egypt, who was known as an Ancient of the Salt Sea: "I saw him weeping, weeping on an island. The nymph Kalypso has him in her hall."

I am so enchanted by their ancient tomb that I tell Helen I hope to return at sunset to meditate with her and help her let go of the past. If she'll simply exit from her grave for an hour, I offer to give her one of the massages that I perfected during a year of practice in the mid-90s.

"It helps me create a non-sexual intimacy with women and will totally relax you," I say. "It will bring you back to earth and remake you as the stoic Spartan you were bred to be."

I proceed towards Sparta and, before I return to massage Helen, also plan to visit Mystras, the hillside capital of the Byzantine Despotate of the Morea in the 14th and 15th centuries, located on a steep spur of Mount Taygetos. Tomorrow I want a bit more altitude and hope to make it to the top of Profitis Ilias, the highest peak of the Taygetos.

I walk into the town and wonder why the roads are blocked and there are policemen at every corner. It turns out that I'm near the finish line of the Spartathlon, a 246-kilometer (152.85-mile) run from Athens to Sparta. There were 450 competitors when the race began in Athens almost 24 hours ago and the 120 still running will soon arrive. Apparently Zeus wasn't happy with them either because bad weather and thunderstorms dramatically narrowed the field on the overnight jog. But each arriving competitor gets an olive wreath at the statue of Leonidas, a Spartan king. An Italian finishes first in just over 23 (yes, twenty-three) hours.

I'm told by a hotel concierge that the Spartathlon traces the footsteps of Pheidippides, the Athenian messenger sent to Sparta by commanding generals in 490 BC in order to get some help in the Battle of Marathon against the Persians. According to Herodotus, Pheidippides arrived in Sparta the day after he departed. So the Open International Spartathlon Race, which has started at the foot of the Acropolis since 1983, goes through Corinth and up to the top of Mount Parthenio to replicate the ancient run.

An event like the Spartathlon fits my image of Sparta, where inordinate bravery, patriotism and respect for the law were the code for warriors dressed with plumed helmets. Spartans constantly trained for combat, didn't have day jobs, were especially austere and fearless, and practiced the Pyrrhic war dance while sustaining themselves with a somewhat famous black broth made from pork stewed in blood.

"As for the brave man, his face never changes, and no great fear is in him, when he moves into position for an ambuscade," Homer wrote. "His prayer is all for combat, hand to hand, and sharp, and soon."

Cowards, of course, were frowned upon in Sparta.

"Cowards are men who leave the front in war," said Odysseus. "The man who will be worth respect in battle holds on, whether he's hit or hits another."

The most impressive aspect of Sparta though, without a doubt, is my end-of-the-afternoon climb to the citadel in Mystras. I calmly march up on a cobblestone path that weaves through a conglomeration of Byzantine churches, monasteries, houses, palaces, an active nunnery (though there are only five nuns), and the remains of the town that became known as the "pearl of Morea."

From the citadel I have a view of the Spartan plain with its thousands of olive trees, try to pick out the Menelaion on the other side of the Eurotas River and admire the sunset-lit city of Sparta below.

The next day, I climb Mount Taygetos to get an even better view. I hike on a well-marked forestry path that passes a closed refuge before becoming a rocky, shaley mountainside trail to the fogged-in, 2,404-meter summit. Because of the cloudy and rainy conditions near the top, there are only a few other hikers and the windy, cold weather reminds me of the slog up Mount Olympus.

Near the summit I realize that the true reason for my climb is to encounter 62-year-old solicitor Paul Causton from Bournemouth, England. Paul made it up to the top just before I arrive at the crest and he tells me that there's absolutely no view, though there is a roofless chapel containing some icons and candles.

We walk down together and have a pleasurable chat because of his exposure to the Greek classics at university and a number of hiking trips he's made throughout Greece. He's one of the few tourists I meet who speaks even an inkling of Greek and he's just gotten a master's degree in modern history from a university in London. This is his third attempt to climb Mount Taygetos (weather hampered him during the other two occasions) and I'm impressed when he gives a liter of water to some stranded Germans waiting at the refuge.

"I offer this in the interest of peaceful European co-existence," he says jokingly.

We have a delightful descent discussing Sir Patrick Leigh Fermor (Paul had read all of his books, as well as many by Eric Newby and Bill Bryson), Greek literature (he had studied *The Odyssey* and was very familiar with Greek history and myths), his Greek hikes (including in a gorge near the Albanian border and up Mount Parnassos in the neighborhood of the Delphic Oracle), Stalin and the Spartathlon. The most surprising revelation occurs when Paul sings Phil Harris's *The Darktown Poker Club* and *Woodman Spare that Tree* in comic American English.

"I'd never do it if I thought anyone could hear me," Paul says as I listen closely.

I leave Sparta, cross the Parnonas Mountains to the sea and head north to Nauplion, which the ancients say was founded by Poseidon's grandson Nauplios. It was also the first capital of modern Greece from 1829 to 1834.

Walking past the Bourdzi Island, where Napoleon's public executioner once lived, I find myself on a glamorous seaside path that curves around the Acronauplia Citadel ("Walking into Nauplion is a piece of baklava," I says to myself). I climb scores of steps to reach the highest point of the Venetian Palamedes Fort to enjoy the views of the town, the bay, the plain, and the coastline.

I spend the evening in the most attractive old town in the Argolid – the region dominated by the nearby city of Argos – which has cobblestone streets, chic stores, scores of cafés, and a restaurant called "Helen's Place."

The next day I head to the "strong founded citadel" of Mycenae, which Homer called "rich in gold." The home of Agamémnon, the commander of the Achaean troops during the Trojan War, is larger than Pylos and I consider it one of the least-ruined ruins on earth. It was so acclaimed that it gives its name to the Mycenaen period of Greek history. Entering through the Lion Gate and its 20-foot thick Cyclopean Walls, I investigate the beehive-shaped *tholos* tombs that were filled with golden treasures when Heinrich Schliemann uncovered them in 1876. Then I perch myself atop enticing Mycenae and imagine Agamémnon looking onto the fish-breeding Mediterranean in the distance just before he was killed by his wife Clytemnestra and her lover Aegisthus.

What intrigues me most about the Greek palaces in Mycenae, Delfi, Messini and Pylos is the choice of a strategic location that combines defense with a great view. But even that couldn't keep a king from getting killed in his own home.

A few mornings later I'm among the first visitors at Epidauros and manage to catch the spectacular theater at sunrise. The 14,000 seats are hard and I'm not sure I appreciate the mismatched restoration occurring at other parts of the archeological site.

But the former Sanctuary of Asclepius, who was the god of medicine, is an excellent venue for Kathryn Hohlwein's production of *The Readers of Homer.* The works of Aeschylus and Sophocles comes to life here and I am impressed with the sound effects of the venue. When an actor dropped a euro coin on the center stage, I hear it clink from a distant seat in the top row of the theater. That'll do.

During a week in non-MedTrek mode, I publicly transport myself from the Peloponnese to the center of Greek Orthodox monasticism at Mount Athos in Macedonia. I move north slowly with stopovers in Athens, Volos, Meteora, Mount Olympus, Thessaloniki, and the Chalkidiki Peninsula. I'll be completely out of touch for a week as, computerlessly, I meander amidst the monks and monasteries on the Holy Mountain.

The first thing I do in Athens is compare the Herodes Attikos Theater near the Acropolis with Epidauros to see which is the better venue for Kathryn's performance of *The Odyssey*. I meet Athêna twice on this stay in Athens – once at the temple to Erectheus on the Acropolis that contains a shrine to her and again at the Acropolis Museum. She agrees that Epidauros, due to its setting, would be the apt choice. Then she encourages me to find out what normal Greeks think about the monks before I visit the Holy Mountain. She even gives me an article from *Vanity Fair* to read that blames the Vatopaidi monastery on Mount Athos for Greece's financial collapse.

"In a perfectly corrupt society, it had somehow been identified as the soul of corruption," wrote author Michael Lewis.

On the way north, I MedTrek through the Pelion Mountains that are the mythological home of the Centaurs – the wild half-man, half-horse creatures – and visit the glam hillside town of Makrinits, where I light four candles in the little Greek Orthodox chapel. The candles are for Derry Hall and Chris Munnion, two friends from decades ago who both died recently; for, at the request of her aunt, a young baby who died last week; and for all other sentient beings.

I walk down the hill to Volos, where Jason and the Argonauts left on their odyssey to retrieve the Golden Fleece. There's a replica of their ship, the *Argo*, in the port. I have an ice cream with a very pregnant Natasha Pope, a friend of my daughter Sonia who lived with us for a year in the south of France when she was a teenager, and her Greek tanker captain husband, Thanasos Moschos.

Thanasos tells me that Volos was called Iolkos until 1911 when the name changed and a new harbor was built after the end of Turkish rule. Then he discusses Mount Athos.

"The Orthodox church is becoming like the French Foreign Legion and attracts a wide variety of men," says Thanasos. "It's initially the great escape for many, though it frequently turns out to be the right solution for some."

A bit further north I visit Meteora (the word means "things suspended in the air") and the more-lovely-than-promised 14th century monasteries that rise from the plain of Thessaly. I hike into the Varlaam and Megalo Meteoro monasteries, all equipped with libraries containing ancient tomes.

Unlike men-only Mount Athos, these monasteries allow female visitors and masses of tourists. I learn that many monks, frustrated with a touristic onslaught that upsets their monastic tranquility, are retreating to Mount Athos.

To get into an even godlier mood before reaching the Holy Mountain, I spend another night at the Guests of Zeus Hotel in Litóhoro and make an offering to the gods atop Mount Olympus. During a walk around town the next morning, I meet a woman in her garden, comment on the brilliant day and mention my upcoming trip to Mount Athos.

"Go for the magic of the mountain, not for the monks," she tells me. "Incidentally, if you want to hit it off with any Greek, tell them you're going to Mount Athos and will pray for them. They'll love you forever."

To get to the Holy Mountain I meander and hike through the rugged pine forests and vineyards, and along the rocky seaside and sand beaches on the Sithonia promontory. It's the first time I've seen Athos up close since passing it on the ferry from Lemnos, and I relish the view while enjoying a sandwich lunch at a beach café.

I ask the waiter if he thinks I'll be able to see him from the summit of Mount Athos.

"The most you can see from the top of Mount Athos is what you feel," he said, adding that he "likes eating too much to become a monk."

"Well, when I get there I'll look to this very spot and pray for you," I said.

He didn't charge me for the sandwich.

Monking Around on Mount Athos

"Where is the wisdom now that made you famous in the old days?" – Hékabê, *The Iliad*

I arrive in Ouranópoli, the seaside town on the edge of Holy Mount Athos, at mid-morning in early October. *Ágio Óros*, as the Greeks refer to the Holy Mountain, has been considered the holiest place on earth by the Eastern Orthodox Church since AD 963. Less than a hundred kilometers from Thessaloniki, it's the easternmost of the three promontories on the Chalkidiki Peninsula and is separated from the mainland by an almost impenetrable forest and a long security fence.

I didn't make advance reservations at different monasteries during my five-day sojourn, as the Holy Executive of the Holy Mount Athos Pilgrim's Bureau in Thessaloniki sensibly suggested when I applied for my entry permit six months ago. As a MedTrekking nomad, I simply presume that I'll be accepted as a peripatetic monk without any questions and generously be given a room as I traverse trails marked by grey-and-white stones between heathers, thorn bushes, and sweet-smelling herbs. I immediately buy a detailed map to determine whether it's possible to MedTrek to all twenty monasteries during the short period that I'm allowed to visit the mythic, male-only peninsula. Am I going to be welcomed or homeless in this Holy Land?

The monasteries on Mount Athos can be viewed from the sea on tour boats out of Ouranópoli that cruise a hundred meters offshore, but only 120 Orthodox and ten non-Orthodox males (I am one of these) are allowed in each day. That's not a lot of visitors (about 90 percent of the pilgrims are Greek) on a peninsula ten kilometers wide, 45-kilometers long and punctuated by a 2,027-meter high Holy Mountain towering above the Aegean.

My basic plan is to quietly explore the fully functioning quasi-autonomous state, with its own capital city, that operates under a charter granted by the Byzantine emperor at Constantinople over 1,040 years ago. I plan to visit and light a candle in each monastery chapel, talk to a variety of monks and sleep in a different bed each night as I explore the fairytale-like Byzantine land of ornate monasteries, cliff-top hiking trails, cupolas, chimneys, towers, crosses, icons and dense, hilly, and rugged forests of chestnut, oak and pine trees.

The night before ferrying into Mount Athos I stay in a hotel in Ouranópoli that is billed as having "comfortable rooms if a little monastic, ideal if preparing for life on Mount Athos." After chatting with the locally born Macedonian hotel owner about Mount Athos – and getting his assessment of everything from paths and roads to Byzantine-style brickwork and vertical gardens – I have a *moussaka* and beet salad at a restaurant on the port.

The next morning, like other short-term visitors, I take my passport and €30 to the Pilgrim's Office in Ouranópoli to pick up a special permit that allows me to enter the Holy Mountain to be housed with, fed by and pray alongside charitable monks.

As I get my permit I hear a distinctive American voice.

"Ah, you're American too!" says a Greek Orthodox monk who looks just like any other Greek Orthodox monk with long black vestments, a shaggy beard, a monk's cap and prayer beads.

I've just met Father Sava, a former Catholic from New Orleans who became interested in the Orthodox Church when he read Dostoevsky's *The Idiot* in high school.

Before he has a chance to speak, I start thinking about the diversity of beards on Orthodox monks and flashback to a long conversation I had while strolling in Madrid in 1990 with *Time Magazine's* Marc Weinberger, though we were talking about the diversity of breasts, not beards. Marc outrageously contended that "all women's breasts are the same" and I immediately rebutted that "every woman's breasts are different and unique."

We walked into a bar and there was a poster (the only poster of its kind that I've ever seen) showing dozens of different shapes of women's breasts. The variation was extraordinary and I now feel the same way about the unique shape, color, and consistency of every individual monk's beard. Each is different and unique.

Father Sava, who is in his early fifties, is delighted to chat with another American and as we have a coffee near the ferry dock he describes in detail how he attended "a monastic boot camp" – the St. Gregory Palamas monastery in Hayesville, Ohio – for sixteen months in 1999 and 2000. He came to the Vatopediou monastery on Mount Athos a year later and was told by Father Ephraim, the abbot, to go to the Manastirea Oasa in Romania. He's been there ever since and is on a two-week visit to the Holy Mountain.

"I was formerly a banker and traded mutual funds and my only regret is that I didn't become a monk much earlier, because this is a very sane and healthy lifestyle," says Father Sava, who's had no physical contact with his parents since he joined the priesthood. "I never had a desire to be a village priest, and my day-to-day life is primarily work, study, and prayer. Paying my first visit to Athos in four years is part of my spiritual program."

We continue our conversation on the ferry where we meet an English Anglican priest with his son, son-in-law-to-be, and a nephew. The priest was first here in 1965 and this is the third visit he's made with his son. Father Sava describes to us all how the Orthodox church, which he calls a "hospital for souls," is "a religion of the heart" concerned with an individual's relationship to God and an inner spiritual peace attained with the assistance of chants, incense, candles and kissing quite a few religious icons.

My watch stops working (I swear this is true) the second that I board the ferry in Ouranópoli that will chug along a rocky, wooded, but otherwise barren coastline. I disembark at Zografou, the first stop, with one other monk while most other passengers and pilgrims continue to the main port of Daphni.

It's less than an hour's walk from the ferry dock to the Zografou Monastery where a Bulgarian worker is mixing cement amidst a crane, some scaffolding, a new bell tower and lots of ongoing reconstruction. He says "*Da da*," and only "*Da da*," when I ask the time in English. Like many monasteries, this one is primarily inhabited by monks from a particular country, in this case Bulgaria.

Not knowing the time didn't bother me too much, and it's confusing anyway. That's because many monasteries have clocks showing both Greek and Byzantine time, which starts at sunset. In fact, Greek or Byzantine time doesn't really matter when the wake-up call is at 3:00 a.m. and dates are calculated according to the Julian calendar.

I return to the seaside on a different path, take a left and meet six of the 40 monks at the Dohiariou monastery, who are building a stone wall on the trail. They invite me to join them for a quick lunch (food is sustenance here, not pleasure, they explain) consisting of bread, olives, and *moustalevria*, a fabulous organic grape must pudding.

"This must seem like animal food to an American," says one monk.

"This is what most Americans should be eating," I reply.

While we sit and eat on the under-construction wall, each monk tells me a "before being a monk" story (one was a Metallica fan, one once knew a girl at UCLA), then asks me questions and makes some pertinent observations.

"Are you Orthodox?" "Where are you from?" "Are you baptized?" "Who pays you to walk?" "You need new shoes!" "I don't want to be pushy, but Orthodoxy is the only way." "Have you been to the Orthodox monastery in Platina, California?"

One monk, who is here for a few weeks to take a break from his priestly obligations in Volos, is soaking olives. He asks me: "Have you yet experienced the miracle?"

"I'm waiting," I reply.

Young monks are common around Mount Athos today, where I estimate the average age to be about 40, and many arrivals are well-informed and street savvy. The wall-building monks, for example, initially don't want to be photographed because they're worried about the Internet. I convince them the photo may never appear online.

The younger monks are an important part of the overall population of the Holy Mountain, which currently numbers 1,700 monks and is larger today than at the end of the monastery's first millennium in 1963. Then there were only 700 monks and there was sacrilegious chatter in Athens about turning the monasteries, many of which were in complete ruin, into luxury hotels due to financial problems.

Today there are cranes, scaffolding, earth-moving equipment, dock enlargements, new roads, and teams of Albanian, Russian, Serbian, Romanian, Bulgarian and other imported workers almost everywhere. There may never again be 30,000 monks at 30 monasteries, as there were in the 1500s, or even 9,000, as there were just before World War I, but growth is so rampant that Mount Athos looks like the beneficiary of the Obama Stimulus Package, European Union funds, Greek government allocations, and hefty charitable donations combined.

I figure it's a safe bet that all of the current building and improvements, as well as the number of young monks, will help ensure that Mount Athos is around for another thousand years.

"The world is going through a period of disenchantment and that's led to an increased desire for a serious spiritual life," Father Sava told me. "Neither materialism, philosophy, or science has provided all the answers. An increasing number of people think Mount Athos is the answer."

But don't think everything goes smoothly in paradisiacal Mount Athos.

Absolutely *nyet*.

I continue walking along the coast to arrive at the Russian Panteleimonos monastery in the late afternoon and immediately seek the head hotel monk, whose office is officially open only from 11:30 a.m. to 1:30 p.m. Each monastery is run by its own superior, or abbot, in charge of the novices and monks. Each also has a monk in charge of guests who usually greets new arrivals like me with a drink and pleasantly chats with them about the status of their visit, the state of their soul, and the advantages of the monastic life.

Not here.

I obviously show up late, according to the clocks showing both Greek and Byzantine time, with no reservation. I obey a sign that says "No Photos, No Smoking, No Yelling" as I explore the ornate, icon-filled, frescoed buildings and walk through a five-story guest house with hundreds of rooms. I find a gigantic and almost completely empty dormitory on the fifth floor and can't believe there will be a problem with accommodation. But there's no sign of the guesthouse monk.

As I wander around the grounds, I meet a twenty-something Russian pilgrim who speaks some English and is absolutely beaming. He's just flown in from Moscow to thank God for enabling his wife to get pregnant. He invites me to join him at the early evening services, which are announced by a monk beating on a piece of wood with a mallet, and afterwards we have dinner together. He explains that following his first visit, exactly a year ago, he met his wife, got married and they're expecting a baby in two months.

"The miracle happened," he says.

At dusk the happy-go-lucky father-to-be introduces me to the stern hotel monk, who looks a bit like Nikita Khrushchev and seems to think he's the president of Hilton Hotels. Nikita takes one look at me and, without taking off his shoe, yells an abrupt "*Nyet*" in a tone and expression that I haven't heard or seen since Khrushchev waved or slammed his shoe on the table at the United Nations General Assembly meeting in 1960.

"I think he's upset because you don't have a reservation," says my now recoiling Russian pal.

"Is it because I'm not Russian, not Orthodox, and an American?"

I ask, pretty sure that I won't be given a room.

Indeed, it's strongly suggested that I leave but instead, after feigning departure, I sneak into the dorm on the fifth floor of the guesthouse. I find a vacant bed but after a few minutes have second thoughts and decide I don't want to stay on the sly. I skedaddle down the road, catch a great sunset and arrive at the main port in Daphni in the dark. The owner of the only small hotel informs me that there are no rooms. He tells me I can crash in my sleeping bag on a hard bench in the basically abandoned customs hall.

Before I hit the hay (actually the cement bench) the cashier at an icon-and-incense shop says no one really likes the Russians. Two days later I meet a German who had the same experience as me but waited seven hours until the hotel monk in Panteleimonos finally relented.

Is there a message in the fact that I'm spending my first night on Mount Athos in exile on a cement bench?

Although every man may have a unique beard on Mount Athos, there are no female breasts, and while there are still occasional protestations, no one expects females to ever be allowed on the promontory. That's the way it's been for over a thousand years.

The ban is officially due to the Orthodox Church's desire to honor the Virgin Mary and their contention that Christ gave the peninsula to his mother as her private garden. All other women are excluded in order to more properly respect Mary, though there have been a few exceptions. Mount Athos granted sanctuary to refugees, including women and girls, during the Greek Civil War, and in the 1930s a Greek beauty queen dressed up as a man and sneaked in.

The exclusion of women is, naturally, controversial outside the confines of Mount Athos. The European Parliament has endorsed a report containing a paragraph that suggests this is a violation of women's rights. The Greek government has responded that the special status of Mount Athos was recognized in conjunction with the treaty when Greece joined the European Union in the first place. Nobody expects much to change.

While I'll let the authorities battle about women, I'm delighted by the unique, pristine and nearly virginal ecosystem due to a lack of female sheep, goats, pigs and other domesticated animals – except cats.

After a night sleeping on a concrete bench, I have two strong coffees and a delicious hot roll at the café when it opens at 8:00 a.m. Then I casually walk on a path and road to Simonos Petras monastery, where I attend mid-morning services. Non-Orthodox pilgrims like myself are sometimes segregated from the monks during church services and at one point I'm very politely asked by a monk to step into an outer section.

I don't take it personally.

Simonos Petras, with four stories of wooden balconies reminiscent of mountain monasteries in Tibet and the Himalayas, rises on an outcrop of rock above the sea like Shangri-la-sur-Mer. Founded by Saint Simon in the 13th century, its steep towers and terraces were initially required to protect the monks from pirates.

Although I don't pay too much attention to food when I'm in a spiritual environment, I'll always remember the copious and scrumptious lunch here. Served in an ornate dining room, the meal includes spaghetti, coleslaw, quiche, bread, cheese, pears, wine, and fruit and vegetables from the well-tended terraced gardens.

After lunch I take a leisurely walk around the monastery and am only slightly skeptical about the authenticity of an icon identified as "Mary Magdalene's left hand." Relics like this play an important role in Orthodox tradition and the monastery has many that are reverentially kissed, touched or venerated by visitors. I spend an hour in the library with thousands of ancient manuscripts before walking downhill through the nearly vertical garden to the seaside trail.

If the host monk at the Russian monastery was Khrushchev, the one at San Grigoriou is Mother Teresa. As soon as I enter his office at 2:00 p.m., he brings me a big mug of sweet-tasting Greek coffee, a glass of cool water, and some jellied candy. Then he tells me there's a bed available for the night and explains the layout and schedule of the monastery. The general routine at San Grigoriou is similar to most other monasteries. It starts when a monk performs the equivalent of taps on a wooden board called a *talanton* or *simandro* in the courtyard at 3:30 a.m. to wake everyone for services that begin at 4:00 a.m. and end at 7:00 a.m.

It's raining and I'm tempted to call it a day and stay at the comfortable, spacious and welcoming San Grigoriou Monastery. Instead, I let the host monk know that there are four Englishman on the path behind me who asked me to make a reservation on their behalf. Pretending I know that the weather will clear up, I decide to hike on.

After just a few minutes on the hillside trail, I meet a friendly but frail monk who offers to take my picture, tells me that he visited Dayton, Ohio, before monkhood, and says that "Life is like an airport transit lounge." He walks a few steps with me, describes some of his ailments, talks about the Lord, and, clasping my hands, says that "if you walk for me, I'll pray for you."

I seal the deal and quote the god Apollo about the fate of all sentient beings: "Mortals, poor things that they are. Ephemeral as the flame-like budding leaves, men flourish on the ripe wheat of the grainland, then in spiritless age they waste and die."

"Go with God," says the monk.

I'm happy to report that there are a few blemishes on Mount Athos. Trash disposal is a problem near the Agiou Paylou Monastery, and many monks prefer riding mules (hence, mucho mule dung) to walking, though ferries are the most frequent method of transport.

After passing the seaside Agiou Paylou Monastery, I walk uphill to arrive at the smaller and more Spartan Skiti Hermitage Agias Annis. I'm at first rebuffed by the hotel greeter due to my lack of a reservation (Note to self: make reservations next time), but after a few minutes he gives me a room and offers me dinner. The *skiti* (officially the word means "ascetic dwelling" though most *skitis* are not as ascetic as ascetic implies) is an excellent base camp for my climb up Mount Athos.

That night in our four-bed room I chat with a German who works at Cap Sogeti in Dusseldorf. He tells me to travel lightly when climbing up Mount Athos because it's steep and gives me some chocolate bars left over after his climb. I'm pleased to learn that he too did not have reservations at the *skiti* and even plans to overstay his five-day "visa" and illegally spend a few extra days in Mount Athos. Phew! I'm not the only sinner.

During the night, when I didn't think I could hear anything louder than the wailing jackals, I learn that Greek Orthodox pilgrims, who usually share rooms with two to forty beds, snore louder than Buddhists and Catholics.

The next morning I meet a monk who has lived in six different monasteries and hermitages on Mount Athos. He tells me that each monastery and each monk has a distinct personality.

"Each of us is human and we each have our own problems," says the monk, who has heard about Orthodox monasteries in California and Arizona. "We're all different, we're all individuals. But the good monk everywhere prays for everyone, good and bad."

I attend the early morning service at the *skiti* and carry only a light pack when I head up Mount Athos. The steeper-than-I-expected climb to the summit is somewhat slippery, and within 30 minutes everything I'm wearing is wet with sweat. I encounter half a dozen Russians and Serbs coming down the mountain and meet a few Albanian stonemasons at Pagogia, but no one else is going up, presumably because of the light rain and overcast skies.

I make it to the top in four hours. Building material stacked around the existing chapel indicates that it, like almost everything else on and around the Holy Mountain, is being refurbished and expanded. But there are no workers on this Sunday morning. I humbly walk inside the chapel to light a candle amid the colorful icons, cherished relics, and gleaming religious images. Then, although clouds obstruct the view of the peninsula and the sea, I spend an hour on a rock at the peak reflecting about how grateful I am to be alive and sober in such a holy spot.

I catch a glorious rainbow on the easy downhill hike and am again sweaty when I arrive at the *skiti* where, much against the theoretical rules, I'm allowed to spend a second night. On arrival I meet a well-equipped two-Greeks-and-a-German trio at dinner, dressed in US Army fatigues they bought on EBay for their assault of Mount Athos.

They're younger guys but way over-equipped with 10-15 kilogram packs and enough military gear to invade a small country. During breakfast I give them details about the walk up the mountain and learn that they plan to take two days to make the climb.

How did the two eBay-attired Greek twenty-somethings, and a German in his 30s, do on their hike up Mount Athos? Here are some snippets from an email report from Thomas Sidinalsa, one of the hikers, who runs a hotel not far from Mount Athos.

"Greetings Mr. Joel! The five-hour trip to Panagia was exhausting! Too much sweat. Even my boxers were soaked. Robert felt unable to continue after Panagia so he slept for an hour while Jim and I cleaned the place. The Russians that slept there the night before left everything ravaged. The Albanians next door refused to give us two small logs so that we could dry our clothes overnight. Everything stayed wet. The next morning we marched to the top – actually we danced up the mountain – and we made it safe and sound. Jim was literally doing the calypso up there while listening to music and whistling. We're all very tired, but I am up for more and I would do it again next week if someone offered me to! Before leaving we gathered all equipment that we could – including batteries, bandages, solid fuel, and ropes – and left them in a tidy pile by the window to aid the survival of the next hiker."

When I reach the coast after my second night at the *skiti*, I take a ferry around the tip of peninsula to relics-filled Grand Lavra (*lavra* means "alley or street" but also denoted an early monastic community). Grand Lavra, the oldest monastery on Mount Athos, was built by Saint Athanasius of Trebizond, who is buried beneath the huge dome in the church. After an hour there, I catch a ferry back to Daphni and continue walking to Karyes, the administrative seat of Mount Athos that has a population of about 350. Then I continue to Vatopediou, the sprawling monastery dating from 980 where Father Sava had made a reservation for me.

I play follow-the-leader with Father Sava at Vatopediou, the largest monastery on Mount Athos that has a courtyard with a surfeit of Byzantine chapels that reminds me of an Italian Renaissance town. During a four-hour service, when Father Sava lights a candle I light a candle; when he kisses an icon, I kiss an icon; when he chants, I chant; when he crosses himself, I don't cross myself. You get the idea.

Afterwards I meet Father Matthew, an American monk who came to Vatopediou twenty years ago in "order not to worry about the outer world." He gives me an elucidating tour of the grounds, takes me into four of the 37 icon-filled chapels, shows me how to properly venerate numerous miracle-working relics and points out improvements that have been made during the past two decades.

"Vatopediou was a complete ruin in the early 1990s, and Abbot Ephraim gets credit for overseeing an incredible restoration and rebuilding it," says the stocky, grey-bearded Father Matthew.

Abbot Ephraim, who attracted pilgrims like Prince Charles to Vatopediou, is also the focus of a controversial financial scandal involving Mount Athos. But although the controversy created public outrage in Athens and was covered in the pages of *Vanity Fair*, it's been, as you would expect, whitewashed on the Holy Mountain.

Father Matthew doesn't mention that Vatopediou, unlike most other monasteries, has been forced to reduce its foreign workforce and delay its restoration program due to the reduced income it is receiving from the Greek government. "Everyone now agrees that the financial charges were of virtually no merit," is all he says about it.

Father Sava also contends that the scandal, which erupted late in 2008 when the government claimed that Ephraim had swapped a worthless lake for revenue-producing government property, "is just politics by people against the church."

That's obviously not the entire explanation. But it's the usual retort if you're talking to an Athos monk living with one foot in the tenth century during the current religious renaissance on the Holy Mountain.

I ignore the 3:00 a.m. wakeup call but do make it to the 6:30 a.m. services. After breakfast, I'm led up to the trail that crosses the peninsula to Zografou by Patrick, a novice monk from New Zealand. Patrick is in the midst of a personal debate about whether to remain a monk or become a village priest. Our interesting hour-long discussion during our walk touches on his parents, celibacy, desire, pain, prayer practices and sex.

"My friends often wonder why I want to be a monk, and I tell them about the free health care, free food, free bed, the 1,000 year-old monastery overlooking the Mediterranean Sea, and the absolute comfort of being in God's hands," said Patrick, who is undergoing orthodontic work and has a special dispensation to email his mother in Christchurch. "Hermits aren't running away, they're running to God. Maybe I'm not sure how close I want to get."

When we discuss sex, I read Patrick an entry from *360 Days of Tao Meditations* entitled *Lovemaking:* "Making love seems simple, but it is actually a great challenge in these complex times. Too many other layers of meaning have been imposed upon sex. Religions straitjacket it, ascetics deny it, romantics glorify it, intellectuals theorize about it, obsessives pervert it. These actions come from fanaticism and compulsive behavior. Can we actually master the challenge of having lovemaking be open and healthy?"

"See what you don't have to worry about if you stay here?" I smile.

Before we separate I tell Patrick that my entire experience on the Holy Mountain, from MedTrekking on well-tended paths through nearly virginal landscape to participating in lengthy and incomprehensible religious services and quick but healthy meals, has been invigorating, vibrant, exhilarating, illuminating, exotic, serene, and undeniably out of time.

"You're very lucky to be here to continue to experience the miracle," I conclude as I give him my Swiss Army knife, a flashlight, and a personal prayer list that includes my two ex-wives, a few enemies, a few resentments, some friends with problems, and some friends recently departed. "Whether you remain a monk or become a priest, you need a Swiss Army knife and a flashlight."

I breeze through the ten kilometers into Zografou and make it to the ferry to Ouranópoli forty-five minutes early. The first email I read is one of forgiveness from a friend:

"I have concluded that you have done more, read more, learned more, experienced more, remembered more, accomplished more, produced more, thought more, seen more, talked more, written more, known more, recalled more, studied more, researched more, grasped more, WALKED more, pondered more, taught more, pontificated more, retained more, inspired more in five percent of your life than I have in my lifetime," she wrote. "After thinking this over and assessing the situation, I have this to say: I do not hold it against you."

Father Patrick's prayers sure worked quickly.

MedTrek Milestone #9

My last two glorious Greek MedTrek outings enabled me to circumnavigate Crete, climb Mount Olympus, prowl about the Peloponnese, and frolic on Holy Mount Athos. Some monks I meet feel they have found a true home with God and that their earthly odyssey ends at the Holy Mountain.

Not mine, though. I'm now, after being remarkably close to many of the places that Odysseus encountered during his return home, proceeding to Turkey and hope to swim across the Hellespont before marching into Troy. And I have the feeling that my own journey will return me to a home of my own.

The Idiot and the Odyssey II

PART FIVE

TALKING TURKEY AND THE TROJAN WAR

Sweetly Side Trekked

Hellespont Milestone

Homeward Bound

All Roads Lead to Troy

Sweetly SideTrekked

"One should never stop learning, never stop exploring, never stop going on adventures." – Deng Ming-Dao

"Give up learning, and put an end to your troubles." – Lao Tsu

During my MedTrek I learn a lot about Homer, *The Iliad*, *The Odyssey*, the gods, spirituality, and myself when I'm away from the shores of the Mediterranean Sea. That's because I frequently get seriously SideTrekked as Homeric stories, modern myths, and the MedTrek itself create an urge, if not really a necessity, to explore other parts of the planet. My global roaming resembles Odysseus' twenty-year odyssey, Telémakhos' quest to obtain information concerning his father, and further underscores "the goal is the path, the path is the goal" MedTrek theme.

During the past few years I've been fortunate to conduct MedTrek-related research, reporting, promotion and trekking in places as diverse as Bali, Burma, Cambodia, China, Cuba, the Galapagos, Kenya, Mexico, South Africa, and Tibet as well as London, Los Angeles, New York, Paris, and Sydney. To really identify with Odysseus, I even make my own homeward journey to the town where I grew up in Northern California.

These serendipitous SideTreks are part of my own lifelong voyage and provide me with a different and changing perspective of the Mediterranean, the MedTrek, and myself. They expand my own personal progression with varied interests, information, and intrigue.

I particularly enjoy visiting countries on the cusp of change, which is why I went to Cuba during Fidel Castro's last days in power, Burma just before the military dictatorship began introducing a series of gradual reforms, and Tibet, where China continues making great leaps backwards. The journeys to Burma and Tibet not only brought me face-to-face with the extensive repression of the indigenous population by dictatorial regimes, but also allowed me to meditate, practice, and pray with a variety of Buddhist monks. Among other things, these trips enable me to realize how fortunate I am, while I simply put one foot in front of the other, to be healthy, and to have only a few comparatively unimportant problems associated with MedTrekking and a life on the road.

I went to Bali specifically to explore the similarities some reviewers found between *The Idiot and the Odyssey* and *Eat, Pray, Love*, Elizabeth Gilbert's popular memoir. I swam with sea lions in the Galapagos to prepare myself for my swim across the Hellespont. I try to regularly visit informative Greek and Roman exhibits whenever I find myself in a city with a respected museum, and speak to academics and curators about Homer and their own appreciation of the classics.

Not that there's any danger of me becoming a renaissance man. I gleaned from Epeiós in *The Iliad* that "No man can be a master in everything." But it's always nice to add a little more knowledge to my evolving database – and it's fun!

I learned, for example, that Seán Hemingway, the curator of the Department of Greek and Roman Art at The Metropolitan Museum of Art in New York, didn't just uncover the Palekastro Kouros on Crete. He's also playing a major role in displaying bygone Greece in Manhattan.

"People like me who study the Bronze Age are called 'The Ancients' in archeological circles," Hemingway says as he leads me through the expanded Greek and Roman galleries at the Met, where a 15-year, $170 million extension was concluded in 2007. "Our exhibit of Greek and Roman art – more than 17,000 works beginning with the Neolithic era – includes the finest collection of Hellenistic bronzes in North America. There are 7,500 objects on view and another 10,000 have been researched and published on the web."

Shway, as he's known to some friends, shows me a wealth of artifacts relating to *The Odyssey*. They include three terra cotta plaques depicting Odysseus's return, a terra cotta *krater* with an image of Odysseus chasing Circe with a bronze-bladed spear, and a painting of the Cyclops Polyphêmos.

"It's fantastic to see people reconnecting with antiquity when they're here," adds Hemingway, the author of *The Tomb of Alexander,* who studied Greek and Latin in high school and contends that the Met enables each of us to become time travelers. "Even the smallest fragments can create an immediate link to the past, and specific objects enable us to understand how other cultures have suffered but survived."

We discuss the Greek exhibit at the Louvre, and I tell Hemingway, who published a controversial "restored version" of *A Moveable Feast* in 2009, that I never visit the Paris museum without chuckling at the anecdote involving his grandfather. You might remember that Ernest Hemingway took F. Scott Fitzgerald to the Louvre to reassure him that his penis wasn't too small by showing him the modest appendages on the Greek statues.

Cracks me up whenever I think about it.

The Louvre isn't the only place I frequent when I visit Paris, where I lived for a decade, worked for a number of U.S publications and was publisher of a magazine called *The Paris Metro* in the late 1970s.

On a recent visit I invited the Moisan family, with whom I first stayed when I arrived penniless and totally French-speakingless in March 1970, to La Méditerrannée restaurant in the Place de l'Odeon for lunch. Jean Cocteau did the drawings on the original menu, and I asked the restaurant to prepare an *Idiot and Odyssey* menu that I'd concocted. It included *feuillatine de saumon Poseidon, osso buco à la façon d'Odysseus, broccoli de Kalypso* and *crème brûlée de Circe* with bread by Telémakhos, wine courtesy of Dionysus and recycled water from the Styx.

I regularly visit Catherine Domain's *Ulysses* travel bookstore near my old apartment on Île Saint-Louis, most recently with my friend Vincent Meade, who suggested I read Jean-Jacques Rousseau's autobiographical *Confessions* because "he always took off on foot when he was anxious."

"Sound familiar?" Vincent asks.

One of my favorite, and perhaps the most aesthetically pleasing displays of the Mediterranean past, is the Getty Villa in Malibu, California. The 64-acre villa and gardens – dedicated to the study and display of ancient Greek, Roman, and Etruscan cultures and antiquities – has hosted a *Readers of Homer* performance and I once caught a lecture there called "Sex Sells, But Who's Buying? Erotic Imagery on Athenian Vases."

The roomy two-story villa, modeled on a Roman country house called Villa dei Papiri in Herculaneum that was buried when Vesuvius erupted, contains some 1,200 artifacts. It includes a temple of Hêraklês and rooms devoted to gods and goddesses, monsters and minor deities, mythological heroes, stories of the Trojan War, and athletic competitions. Figurines that depict Odysseus and his crew sneaking out of the Cyclops' cave on the underbodies of sheep particularly enchant me and before I leave the Getty I always have a private consultation with Hermês in the garden.

London's British Museum is easily the most controversial depository of Greek antiquity, largely because of the Elgin Marbles. This collection of decorative marble friezes adorned the Parthenon in Athens until Lord Elgin, then the British ambassador to the Ottoman Empire, took them home as souvenirs in the early 1800s and sold them to the British Museum in 1816.

Although the British still like to contend that their museum in Bloomsbury is the best place to preserve and display the stolen treasures, that argument obviously doesn't please the Greeks, especially since the new Acropolis Museum in Athens opened in 2009. That €200 million glass-and-concrete structure designed by New York architect Bernard Tschumi is an airy, light-filled showcase of classical civilization at the base of the Acropolis and is eager to have what the Greeks call the Parthenon Marbles returned.

The five-story Acropolis Museum, designed in the shape and dimensions of the Parthenon, with some 4,000 archaic and classic artifacts, already contains 36 of the 115 panels from the Parthenon frieze, including some bits and pieces returned by museums in Italy, the Vatican, and Germany.

Launching The Great Wall of Europe Project

My SideTrek to China was especially quixotic. I accompanied a high-level-under-the-radar delegation from the European Union to the Great Wall to explore the concept of constructing a similar fortification around the Mediterranean Sea. The fact-finding trip was the result of my repeated suggestions to Brussels officials concerning the numerous benefits of a continuous walking path around the entire Mediterranean. Upon completion, the 16,000-kilometer Great Mediterranean Wall will be three times as long as its Chinese counterpart and adorn the seaside in every country in the Mediterranean Basin.

The discussions in Beijing involved details regarding a long-term €243.45 trillion interest-free loan from China that would enable construction to begin simultaneously in 16 Mediterranean countries as early as January 1st 2020. Chinese labor on the project would be limited to 100,000 workers, and Europeans would maintain, service and patrol the wall after its completion in 2052.

EU delegates enumerated the economic, social, fiscal, environmental, and physical benefits of the Great Mediterranean Wall at a conference at the XiaoXiang Hotel in Beijing. They stressed that jobs created by Europe's largest infrastructure project in the 21st century would stimulate EU economies and have a positive impact on virtually every industry, from agriculture to tourism.

The Great Mediterranean Wall, which would help prevent illegal immigration and make a higher path available on a sea slowly rising due to climate change, would inevitably provide a boost to the long-distance MedTrekking industry. Its promotion of the importance of physical exercise on a spiritual path could reduce healthcare costs in the EU by an estimated 23 percent by 2050. Visitors would pay a €10 daily fee, or €100 annual membership, to MedTrek on the wall.

I can't wait to be among the first!

I SideTrekked to Burma – which was still in the throes of a fifty-year history of a military government that thrived on censorship, corruption, propaganda and surveillance – to determine what empowered the country's Buddhist monks, many of whom were slaughtered in a protest in 2008, to confront the dictatorial regime.

What struck me was the normalcy of the place. No visible military presence, no implicit unrest, no overt feeling of suppression. And that's what made it one of the most Kafkaesque and Orwellian countries on earth. In fact, George Orwell lived in Burma from 1922-27 and wrote *Burmese Days* about his experience. When I visited, Burma seemed to be like *The Trial*, *1984* and *Animal Farm* wrapped into one little package, tied up with a heavy dose of astrology and animism. As with many totalitarian regimes, the xenophobic rulers further avoided their people by creating a surreal Disneyland-like new capital called Nepidaw 170 miles north of Rangoon.

A Burmese student named Ei Phyu Theint took me to the Sule Pagoda, the site of the slaughter of monks during the 2008 Saffron Revolution, and I paid $1 to release two tiny birds to gain merit. The first bird took off into the wild blue yonder, and I felt its freedom and the joy of liberating another sentient being. The second tiny sparrow flew ten feet and returned immediately to its cage. I tried again, same result.

"Opium," said Ei Phyu. "That's how they subdue them – and us."

No longer, I hope.

"You will feel like your mind is sublimed and soul purified as we pass the highest freshwater lake in the world," blared the loudspeaker on the Qinghai-Tibet Railway as I made my way to Tibet. The world's highest railroad, a construction marvel inaugurated in 2006, reaches an altitude of 5,072 meters (16,640 feet) between Xining, China, and Lhasa, Tibet. The train, fortunately, is pressurized.

There are only thirty lamas maintaining the estimated 948 rooms in Lhasa's Potala Palace, the traditional home of the Dalai Lama and the iconic symbol of Tibetan Buddhism. I climbed 365 steps to pay my respects, gawk at myriad treasures, and admire the one-time residence of the 14th Dalai Lama, who grew up here but has lived in exile in India since 1959.

My true goal, however, was to get arrested.

It's illegal, and quite ill-advised, to exhibit a picture of the exiled Dalai Lama anywhere in China, including the Tibet Autonomous Region (where many lamas have a taboo photograph hidden up their sleeves). But I'd been allowed by some courageous Yellow Hat lamas to take photographs of their photographs of His Holiness on display in a number of monasteries and temples. It's impossible to ignore – and also illegal to photograph – the omnipresent Chinese military troops in riot gear on the rooftops and street corners of central Lhasa. I took pictures of them too.

I posted the photos on my blog and am still waiting for the knock on the door.

I appeared at the sprawling World Expo in Shanghai, which attracted almost half a million visitors every day in 2010, to discuss international cultural differences and promote the Chinese edition of *The Idiot and the Odyssey: Walking the Mediterranean.*

Fair-goers, almost all Chinese fascinated by the rest of the world, flocked to the massive Expo site on both banks of the Huangpu River to check out a kaleidoscope of crazy cultures at more than 200 national, corporate, and themed pavilions. And The Idiot was part of the action.

The "Idiot Exhibit," located on a terrace between two silver-sculpted pandas, offered Chinese visitors an opportunity to "talk to an American author about anything." Besides promoting my book, I wound up discussing American obesity, Paris fashion, Italian garbage, Tibetan trauma, Homer's *Odyssey*, Britney Spears and other important topics.

My "(Name of the city) *par* iPhone" albums on Facebook now include shots from Athens, New York, London, the Galapagos, Paris, Istanbul, Rhodes, the French Riviera and Florida. They usually have a Mediterranean twist. My "French Riviera par iPhone" album, for example, captures my ongoing role as a guest guide for tourists on "The Blue Walk" hikes between the Italian border and the Esterel. My "Athens par iPhone" album includes amusing photos from the Acropolis, the

Cycladic Museum, and other places where you'd expect to find a dedicated Athênaphile.

I've been visiting Athens since the 1960s and have fond memories from each decade. In 1968 I slept on a hotel rooftop and wound up in a hospital; in 1976 I went sailing with friends in nearby Glyfada; in the 1980s it was one of my Mediterranean Destinations for a report for *Time*. Since then, I've been making regular visits.

I revere the city named after Athêna, who is considered its protector since she created the olive tree, a symbol of peace and prosperity that is rumored to have sprouted again after the city's sack by Persia in 480 BC. I frequently climb to the Acropolis to pay my respects to various depictions of Athêna, including an altar in the Erechtheion and the imposing Athêna Parthenos at the Parthenon that features the city's patron goddess wearing her iconic triple-crested helmet. The procession depicted on the Parthenon frieze was in her honor and a traditional tribute to Athêna still occurs once a year during the PanAthenaic procession, when residents drape a woven robe, or *peplos*, on the shoulders of their goddess.

I also frequently get SideTrekked on the MedTrek itself, in an effort to connect with local communities and be further exposed to people, places, cultures, cuisine, ideas, and socio-political idiosyncrasies. If I like a particular place, or a particular person, on the sea, or even some distance from it, I'll take a break and go local.

When I hiked onto the "Nudism Obligatory" beach at the world's largest nudist colony in Cap d'Agde, France, I liked the look and feel of the place so much that I stayed a few days. Then I went on a retreat to Sogyal Rinpoche's nearby Buddhist lamasery in the mountains north of Montpelier to recuperate.

One enjoyable SideTrek encounter occurred when three road construction workers invited my son Luke and me to stay with them in Morocco. They gave us beds, made us a fabulous multi-course Moroccan meal, showed us Arabic music videos, let us do our laundry, and even offered to get Luke married. I could have stayed for weeks; Luke, who was given a pair of tennis shoes, could have stayed the rest of his life.

Sometimes I revisit memorable places that I've MedTrekked, especially the Saint Honorat monastery in the south of France, where I stayed on the first night of the MedTrek after walking my initial twenty kilometers, or the home of the Spanish sorceress in Aguilas, Spain, who MedTrekked with me for a month.

Wherever I am, I always do something local. This ranges from a meal and a visit to a church or museum to a facial (except when I run into someone like Big Boris) and a swim (I plan to write a guide to the best swimming holes on the Med).

What breed of locals have I gotten to know best?

Without a doubt it's café waiters, train conductors, bus drivers, and the working-class folk who pick me up hitchhiking to take me back to my base camp at the end of each day. Dozens of brief encounters with people like this teach me everything from compassion and goodwill to social conventions and languages.

"How did you learn Italian?" Eliana asked me when she invited me to lunch at her restaurant in San Stefano di Camastra on Sicily's northern coast.

"From train conductors," I said, only half jokingly.

"Well, they've been very good teachers!" she replied.

I learn on these SideTreks that everyone has his own favored translation of Homer. Don't think so? Just bring up the topic at your next cocktail party.

The Robert Fitzgerald translation seems the obvious favorite for people of my generation.

Paul Richardson, who taught English with me in Hong Kong in 1967 and is now a superior court judge in California, took the same Fitzgerald translation that I read with him on his odyssey, a bike ride across the US.

Eve Siegel still actively compares Fitzgerald with other translations and recalls her introduction to it.

"When I was in high school I found the most marvelous translation of *The Odyssey* by Harvard classicist Robert Fitzgerald," explains Siegel, a San Francisco-based life coach. "His rendering of Homer's epic oral tale had me spellbound immediately because the translation is linguistically clear and fresh, yet palpably conveys its original Greek style, which takes me immediately back into the archaic world of its hero."

Eve pits the opening sentence of Book One in Fitzgerald's 1963 translation against Allen Mandelbaum's poetic version of 1990 and E.V. Rieu's prose version of 1949.

"Mandelbaum's version has a very clear, contemporary poetic quality, but completely lacks the complexity of Homeric rhythmic patterns and the detailed character description of Odysseus himself," she contends. "Rieu's prose rendering is even less true to the original in that, as prose, it completely lacks any attempt at Homeric metric patterns."

"Fitzgerald's emotional engagement of the reader with the nature of Odysseus and the torment of his time in exile – 'the wanderer, harried for years on end'– is how he so masterfully evokes Homer's tale-telling genius in illustrating the human condition and its transformative possibilities" she continues. "Any translation that attempts to convey a sense of Homer's time and place, and convincingly portray the world of *The Odyssey*, needs to use this rich range of rhythm and language."

Kathryn Hohlwein frequently uses the more recent translation by Robert Fagles for many of her *The Readers of Homer* marathon readings "but I like using different translations at the same time – mixing Alexander Pope and Samuel Butler with Fitzgerald and Fagles," she says.

After MedTrekking around Crete I took a SideTrek to luxuriously sail in the Turkish Gulf of Gokova between the Bodrum and Datça peninsulas. One thing I learned very quickly was that the mountainous, unpathed and forested terrain on the 100-kilometer long narrow gulf in southwestern Turkey would be difficult and time-consuming to MedTrek when I later reach this spot on foot.

I was a guest on a 38-foot Sunsail catamaran called *Sam* captained by Gordon Kling, a crayfishing and journalist pal of mine from Cape Town days in the early 1970s. The Canadian-born entrepreneurial skipper motors and sails the high-tech craft to enticing places like Cleopatra's Beach (the fine sand is said to have been imported from the Egyptian desert for Cleopatra's visit), Amazon Creek, the English Harbor (where we sailed past a Copenhagen-like mermaid), and other exotically named coves and crannies.

This mode of travel is much easier than MedTrekking and Odysseus would have made it home in a few weeks, instead of twenty years, if he could have relied on the *Sam*'s array of instruments – including a depth gauge, a wind speed monitor, multicolored ropes, sophisticated cleats, an electronically controlled anchor, and even an autopilot.

Incidentally, there are many sailing metaphors throughout *The Odyssey*. Homer describes warriors returning to the battle in Troy "like a wind, a sailing wind heaven may grant to oarsmen desperate for it at the polished oars, when they have rowed their hearts out, far at sea, so welcome to the Trojans in their longing these appeared."

Bodrum is not only the birthplace of Herodotus and Dionysius, but also the site of the mostly ruined Mausoleum of Halicarnassus, one of the Seven Wonders of the Ancient World. We traipse around the Castle of St. Peter, a showpiece of medieval military architecture, and into the Museum of Underwater Archeology that features treasures from ancient shipwrecks discovered along Turkey's shores. The underwater exhibit inspires me to learn everything I can about the 14th-century BC *Uluburun* shipwreck off of Turkey's south coast.

Skipper Kling and his wife Anne also accompany me on some MedTrek trail testing around Datça, where we meet ace entrepreneur/

fixer/agent/orchestrator Ahmet Ozturk. We are immediately invited onto Ahmet's gulet, his pine-and-hardwood boat that hits a top speed of ten knots an hour and features a beamy master bedroom. Ahmet suggests that I sail around the Turkish coast on his *gulet* and/or buy his donkey when I return to Turkey.

We also visit Ephesus, which still merits its acclaim as another one of the Seven Wonders of the Ancient World. I could have spent many more hours there (and I will when I return on foot) analyzing the plumbing that connects the forty-nine side-by-side latrines (FYI #49 is not the one YOU want!) and studying the instruction manual in one of the world's first "bathhouse exercise rooms" within the intriguing Greco-Roman city, where the Ephesians violently murdered many thousands of Romans one night in 88 BC.

It is during the sailing expedition that I establish one of the more amusing goals of my upcoming MedTrek in Turkey, which is to out-Turk the Turks.

One persistent habit in Turkish restaurants, especially when it's the only one on the dock at a landing in the Gulf of Gokova, is to serve hungry sailors many more *mezes* than they order to inflate the bill. The con is simple: the most handsome waiter approaches the most gullible guest and offers a "gift, only for you."

The extra *meze* that is immediately brought to the table, often without your ordering it, is usually an irresistible succulent octopus in a seductive sauce that's by far the most expensive item on the menu.

"This happens to anybody looking stupid enough to fall prey to the smooth Turkish multiple *meze* con which is a genetic feature of all restaurant-owning Turks," says Ahmet, who calls the Mediterranean the Akdeniz, or "white sea."

"I never give anyone anything they didn't order," insists Tahsin Yasyerli, who has run Husnu Nun Yeri restaurant in the in Gulf of Gokova for twenty-five years.

"I didn't order anything he gave me," retorts Marie-Antoinette Darroll, one of the undesperate South African housewives sailing with us whose husband Roland was in the South African diplomatic service in Italy.

As I pick up the bill (thereby conning myself), I make a vow to out-Turk the Turks in Turkey.

One intriguing aspect of SideTrekking is that a particular place or mode of travel can have a lasting impact. At first I considered the MedTrek itself as just another SideTrek. It certainly didn't appear to be a particularly long or life-changing undertaking when I took my first steps in Antibes, France, on the shores of world's largest inland sea on January 1, 1998.

As a veteran hiker, I considered the expedition a captivating and indulgent 50th birthday present to myself and thought I'd be doing well to make it about 900 kilometers to the Spanish border. I figured a reflective mid-life outing might provide a creative or cosmic uplift in the wake of a melancholy divorce and a decades-long career as a foreign correspondent. An even longer odyssey would allow me to reflect, stay in shape, follow the footsteps of the Homeric characters, and perhaps produce a few dramatic and unpredictable adventures. No big deal.

But within the past few years, it has become apparent that the MedTrek is the principle highlight of my life. I'm having a blast as I continue traipsing through culturally, historically and scenically rich terrain and thrive on myriad physical, spiritual, social, educational, culinary, and mental stimuli. And when I'm not walking or researching, I publicize my book.

As I shamelessly promote *The Idiot* – everywhere from Australia, France and the U.S. to a cruise on the Mediterranean – I am surprised that readers of different ages have unique forms of appreciation for the descriptions of my hike, history, geography, culture and personal ruminations.

I discuss everything, from my alcoholism (I haven't had a drink for over 27 years) and divorces (I've now been through two) to meditation (I've been a student of Buddhism for forty years and practice meditation to remain "physically relaxed, emotionally calm, mentally focused and spiritually aware"), the 1960s (I succumbed to the allure of flower power and free love), Latin lovers (and why I'm not one), the environment (I try, I really do) and French women (whom one critic said I "took off their pedestal").

Some married women buy the book (and I'm not kidding about this) to give to their husbands to encourage them to get out of the house. And some husbands see it as a manual for the moment when they might decide to take a literary, or literal, break from the family. Younger readers like the description of marijuana fields in Morocco and *The Idiot* surprisingly hit a nerve among older men who admire the manner that I realized my childhood dream of walking around the Mediterranean at the age of fifty. "The most fun I've ever had on a trip I didn't make," wrote 80-something Taylor Chambers.

It's always dangerous to believe such positive publicity but Idiot that I am, I let it all go to my head. I forgot that Poseidon at one point in *The Iliad* says "Idiot, but how forgetful you have been."

This mid-life project has even, quite to my surprise, produced an innovative, if somewhat existential and unpredictable, lifestyle. I've become so Zenny about the extended journey that, believe it or not, I'm still enjoying each step and not worrying about whether I'll ultimately complete my circumnavigation of the sea during this lifetime or the next. My birthday present has delightfully developed into a combination of self-employment (I write magazine articles as well as *The Idiot* books), self-examination (I stay at monasteries and nudist colonies to both amusingly and seriously investigate my mind and body), self-cultivation (I practice walking meditation and have run into goddesses, priests and, quite literally, a cow as I continually get to better know myself through ongoing contemplation and an active life), creative living (I've learned how to eat and sleep at little expense), exalting entertainment (I honk at geese and dance with gypsies), completely unforeseen happenstances (I met a delightful sorceress in Spain) and adventurous SideTrekking.

There's no question that my overall physical and mental health has improved. Walking meditation, observed one of my Buddhist mentors, has gradually led me to accept impermanence, develop patience and avoid too much expectation and projection.

Needless to say, I've learned a lot about everything from the works of Homer. I particularly treasure the Robert Fitzgerald translation of *The Odyssey* that I bought four decades ago in college for $6.95, and, like T.E. Lawrence (of Arabia), I also carry a copy of Fitzgerald's translation of *The Iliad*.

When I was SideTrekking in Bali (the one in Indonesia, not the one on Crete) I met a number of pilgrims of various ages who made the trip to the city of Ubud after reading *Eat, Pray, Love*. They were each conducting, at this particular stage of their lives, their own self-examination and, with the benefits of their mistakes and successes up to this point, seeking self-cultivation and new areas to explore.

Many women (and they were mostly women) appeared to be in their 40s and 50s and made the journey after their marriages had dissolved, their children had grown, their jobs had become boring, and/or they were ready for a mature growth spurt. They were, like me at the outset of the MedTrek, having a mid-life "identity issue" (I like to think, perhaps incorrectly, that mid-life crisis is too strong a word) that they hoped to clarify, and maybe even resolve, with or without a mentor or teacher, by spending some weeks or months in Bali's relaxed atmosphere.

I generally recoil from a massive group therapy session but, to my surprise, I enjoyed the vibe and vigor embodied by these seekers of something or nothing in Bali. It reminded me of the 1960s, when identity crisis was easily the preferable phrase and when many of us were at the beginning of an existential and spiritual quest that got us where we are today.

I met a woman named Diana from England and, after describing the MedTrek and the reasons for my own quest, gave her a copy of *The Idiot and the Odyssey: Walking the Mediterranean* and mentioned that one reviewer had compared it to *Eat, Pray, Love.*

The handwritten note I received a month later made me feel pleased that my writing about my walk around the Mediterranean helped someone else on her SideTrek. I was gratified that, in a small way, my book had an impact on her.

"I was at a loose end when we met in Ubud and you gave me a copy of your lovely book with its wisdom, kindness, and gentle philosophy," she wrote. "It's a Godsend! The amusing mix of an easy, accessible voice and learned scholarship – of the big, historical view and the very close, personal insight – is a heady combo that keeps things lively and kept me interested. It made me laugh, feel good, and realize that I won't get anywhere if I don't start by putting one foot in front of the other instead of daydreaming about the pot of gold at the end of the rainbow. What fun!"

Hellespont Milestone

"But all night long Zeus the Profound made thunder overhead while pondering calamities to come, and men turned pale with fear." – *The Iliad*

"I shall lie in the dust when I am dead, but now let me win noble renown." – *The Iliad*

I head towards Turkey and Troy after I bid adieu to Dieu and the monks on Holy Mount Athos. My tentative, not to say ambitious, plan is to emulate Lord Byron by swimming across the Dardanelles Strait – also known as Hellespont – that separates Europe from Asia. However, my first stop involves a meeting with a once blonde Norwegian woman with whom I spent a glorious twenty-four hours in Paris in 1972. We hook up on the Chalkidiki peninsula that, besides Mount Athos, includes the promontories of Kassandra and Sithonia.

Tone Vegheim got in touch with me after reading *The Idiot and the Odyssey* and, during her decades as a teacher in Oslo, has become a great fan of everything Greek. She's staying on the Kassandra promontory in a small village called Nea Skioni.

"Look for me at the beach in the town center by the pier, just down from a *taverna* called Skioni," she emailed. "There are almost no people at the beach, so I will be easy to find in my turquoise bikini on a green towel."

I look forward to a MedTrek walkabout on the cape because Kassandra was one of five names that my wife and I debated calling our daughter. The other four were Petra (because I loved the sunrises at Petra, Jordan); Katya and Larissa (both from Boris Pasternak's enticing *Dr. Zhivago*); and Sonia (which won the contest). I want to make sure that Kassandra isn't as disappointing as the town of Larissa, which I visited recently near Mount Olympus. I also hope to catch a spectacular sunrise over Mount Athos from the highest hill here and a sunset over Mount Olympus when I swim in the sea at dusk.

I arrive in Nea Skioni and see the Hotel Skioni, another called the Olympian Sunset, and one more named Hotel Venus. But I avoid these in favor of a not-too-shabby €30-a-night private room with a sea view, kitchen, and sprawling terrace above a restaurant on the port.

I drop my gear off and have no trouble finding a very tan Tone sunbathing, yes in a turquoise bikini on a green towel, with a friend. We go to their rented flat, where she had two Coke Zeros chilling for me, and discuss our first and last meeting forty years earlier. Following an amusing replay of our Paris tryst (we had stayed out drinking until 5:00 a.m. in Les Halles after I got off my shift as a waiter at Joe Allen restaurant, where I'd invited her for dinner after we met at a café that afternoon), we brought ourselves up-to-date on life (she was still teaching) and kids (we both had two about the same age). After a sunset swim with Mount Olympus in the background, we have a long *taverna* dinner with warm vine leaves and beef stew. And, for my two Norwegian companions, *retsina* and *ouzo*.

"Do you remember that we got married by a gas pump in the Marais at 4:00 a.m.?" Tone asks.

Uh oh! Sounds like a riveting memory from the intoxicating days when my very vague goal in life was to write, drink, and live off women, though the drinking usually came first.

Our dinner in Nea Skioni doesn't last until 5:00 a.m., isn't as romantic as in Paris and we certainly don't get married by a gas pump. But I am delighted to find an enthusiastic fan who adores the Greeks and knows a publisher who might translate *The Idiot* into Norwegian.

"And we'll always have Paris," says Tone.

The next morning I step out just before dawn on a 38-kilometer loop around Kassandra that kicks off on a pebbly-then-sandy beach until I reach a sign that points to "Ancient Skion." I follow a wide dirt road to the highest point on the surprisingly wide promontory for a *bella vista* of the sunrise over Mount Athos and watch the light first hit Sithonia, the headland between Kassandra and Mount Athos, and then Mount Olympus across the glass-smooth sea.

I encounter a few hunters, some dog-guarded chicken-and-sheep farms, lots of olive trees, farmers on tractors, a small monastery tucked in the trees, and not enough vines to qualify this as a stop on the much-publicized Macedonia Wine Route. I'm so amused by a discarded office chair on wheels that I try to ride it down the rocky mountain trail and fall off near a pair of worn and abandoned hiking boots. They remind me that I frequently judge hikers according to their footwear.

The rugged terrain contrasts with the tourist-inhabited seasides on both sides of Kassandra and I continue down the eastern side of the mountain to Pefkohori. There the athletic and hard-drinking Norwegians in Nea Skioni are replaced by typically obese and hard-drinking British sunbathers taking advantage of deals like a fish-or-meat dinner for two with wine for €24 and a Tequila Sunrise or "Sex on the Beach" cocktail for €3.

More importantly, I find and consume perhaps the best olive bread in Greece, even better than in Kalamata. The thinly sliced and unbaked green olives, which pleasantly explode in my mouth at every bite, are remarkably tasty. I also get a new baseball cap (I gave my last one to a Ukrainian laborer on Mount Athos). Recalling how the "Happy Sailor" and "Capri" caps got me in trouble, I choose a bright red one that reads benignly "Chalkidiki." That seems more appropriate than the available alternative, a black one with the moniker "Bad Boy."

Passing the boat-filled lagoon at Cape Klarokavos, I re-enter the forest to encounter hives of buzzing bees, pine trees with plastic bags collecting resin, woodchoppers cutting logs for winter, and a campground with a difficult-looking rock climbing wall and an outdoor Muscle Beach-like weightlifting arena.

Another high point is the presence of pyracantha, one of my favorite plants as a kid. Now, as then, I grab some of the berries from the thorny evergreen shrub and roll them around in my mouth.

As dusk approaches, a ghostly mist covers the sea. What are those gods up to, I wonder? And what's with the Agnantio building complex near Loutra that promises "an individual home for retirement or investment opportunity"? It certainly doesn't look like the units are selling, but I am intrigued by the gigantic SPA written in capital letters on top of the main building in the complex. I enter the spa, and a brochure informs me "the word *thermophylae* relates to the springs that feed the baths here."

I make a reservation to return for swimming, massages, and a facial the next morning before I discover that *thermopylae,* which means "the hot gates that are the entrance to Hades," is also the name of a famous battle between the Greeks and Persians.

I sometimes get a little over-excited when I take a day off. That's what happens after my daylong walkabout on Kassandra as I eagerly look forward to an early morning vigorous swim in the sea, some cleansing hours at the SPA, and afternoon visits to a few archeological sites.

The swim is no problem. It's only a thirty-step walk from my bed to the beach, and I'm the first and only person in the water. I chase darting fish in the crystal clean sea (this is touted as one of the European Union's blue beach award winners) until I smell the aroma of Greek coffee at a nearby café. Then I return to the SPA where I especially want a *soin du visage*, or facial, to open my pores after a month on the road and a deep massage to work out some of the MedTrekking and monastery bed kinks.

The SPA is a rather modern place, opened in 2000, and initially I'm not bothered by the extortionist 2020 prices. I pay in advance for an hour's facial and another hour's rubdown and am ready for action until I realize the SPA is actually stuck in a Black Sea thermal baths time warp circa 1954.

Dozens of older pensioners, wearing tattered and stained blue robes, clomp around in plastic sandals like patients in a cuckoo's nest asylum. The smell doesn't resemble the pleasant herbal odor of a *hammam* in Istanbul, the sulfurous aroma of the thermal baths in Vulcano, or even the stultifying stench of the locker room at the world's oldest YMCA in London. It's a slightly shoey smell complemented by the stink of sweat and bad breath. It has a whiff of death. Hades, indeed.

None of this really bothers me, though, until I meet Big Boris, a Russian who has never heard of a blackhead and was insulted by my proposal that he use steam before delicately cleaning my face. His idea of a facial is a hot towel carelessly thrown over my head until I suffocate. His version of a massage is sitting on my back and giving me a butt roll to crack whatever there is to crack.

I get my money back before it's too late and radically lower my day-off expectations. When I visit the soothing Sanctuary of Zeus Ammon in nearby Kallithea and walk through a sanctuary partially financed by those omnipresent European Union funds, I pray for Big Boris, my perhaps broken back, and my still-uncleansed face.

The sanctuary is touristless and features a carved-from-stone pipe that once carried water to a fourth century BC fountain and a stone staircase that enables me to exit into central Kallithea. Unlike Nea Skioni (Norwegians) or Pefkohori (British), this resort is frequented primarily by Germans. As usual, I determine the nationality of the most prevalent habitués by going to the newsstand and looking at the foreign papers. In

Nea Skioni it's *Aftenposten*, in Pefkohori it's the *Daily Mail* and here it's *Das Bild* . I know I'm right when the salesperson says *"Wie darf ich ihnen helfen?"*

I continue to a village called Olynthos conceived by Hippodamus of Miletus and built on a geometric design known as "the famous Hippodamean system." The ruins reveal a complete city with streets and avenues in a checkerboard square pattern with houses, municipal buildings, drainage conduits, intricate mosaic floors ("These are the earliest known mosaics in the ancient world," says a guide), bathrooms with clay baths, shops and storerooms.

It turns out, I learn as I spend an hour romping around Olynthos, that this is not only the most important ancient cultural center in Chalkidiki but also was inhabited as early as the Neolithic period. Ruled by the Bottiaans from the seventh century BC until the Persians knocked off the place in 479 BC, it was mostly unearthed between 1928-38 by American professor D.M. Robinson from Johns Hopkins and the American School for Classical Studies at Athens.

When I'm sure that Big Boris is cleansed from my spirit and feel that I've walked off his bad karma, I continue along the coast towards Turkey. Although this area has been part of Greece for a hundred years, I begin to feel the Asian atmosphere when I arrive in bustling Kavála – which has been known through history as the port of Philippi (named after Phillip II of Macedonia), Neapolis, Christoupolis, and Bucephalos.

I climb to the citadel in the town's *Paleá Póli*, or old town, and look down on what was once the eastern boundary of ancient Rome's European empire. It was here in AD 49 that Saint Paul addressed his epistle to the Philippian Christians, and I'm surprised that the Muslim Imarét, built in 1817 by Mohamed Ali Pasha and run by Islamic *shaikhs* to house the poor, is now a luxurious hotel. The fact that the airport is named Alexander the Great gets me enthused about heading into Asia as I follow Circe's instructions to "Traipse through Thrace after your meditative stay at Mount Athos."

Encountering Another Homeretic Surprise

I pass numerous minarets and Turkish-y houses distinguished by their inner courtyards in many of the smaller seaside villages on a beeline to the ancient city of Ismara. When I reach the site, a not-too-well known ruin near Maronea, there is no admission charge and no guards. I'm the only visitor in the acropolis and theater before I climb Mount Ismara, which is actually a small hill near an interesting camel-shaped formation called Perota Rock. Then, after strolling three kilometers southeast of the Ismara ruins on a rural along-the-coast road meant for MedTrekkers and four-wheel drive vehicles, I literally stumble upon a sign that proclaims "Ulysses Stream." Just like that. No warning.

I have one of those rewarding "Eureka! Ahh omm, this is why I do this!" MedTrek moments when I reach the stream, because I had absolutely no clue that it was here. And I doubt that many people do because it doesn't seem to be indicated on any of the detailed hiking and archeological maps that I have diagramming the area's *ecotrails* and *geotrails*.

This strip of seaside in Thrace – "that fertile country, billowy grassland, nourisher of flocks" as Homer called it in *The Iliad* – is where Odysseus first landed following the Trojan War and lost numerous members of his crew to the Cicones. It's certainly easy to understand why Odysseus docked here. Although the winds are reputed to be thrashers (one description in *The Iliad* describes "the north wind and west wind wailing out of Thrace in squall on squall, and dark waves crest, and shoreward masses of weed are cast up by the surf"), the sea is calm today, the beach would make for an easy landing and the rolling hills, large boulders, open spaces, and groves of trees are all very pastoral and welcoming.

I visualize the bloody encounter with the pesky Ciconians, a tribe that fought on the side of the Trojans in the war. Things started off on the right foot when Odysseus and his crew "stormed the place and killed the men who fought" while taking the women and children as slaves. But they threw an over-exuberant victory celebration. "Sheep after sheep they butchered by the surf" until "the main force of Ciconians…an army trained to fight on horseback" arrived "with dawn over that terrain like the leaves and blades of spring" and killed six men on each of Odysseus' ships.

It was the first of many embarrassing incidents for Odysseus on his homeward journey.

That battle skirmish seems tame in comparison to my Gallipoli walkabout after I cross the Greek-Turkish border and continue towards the strait that connects the Aegean Sea to the Sea of Marmara – and separates Europe from Asia. As I continue my 11th labor – "MedTrekking through the killing fields of Gallipoli" – I ponder my approaching task, of emulating Leander and Lord Byron by swimming across the Hellespont from Europe to Asia. I may once again be face to face with death.

I have frequently been humbled during the first 8,400 kilometers of my MedTrek. It doesn't take much – a fall off a cliff in Morocco, a robbery by gypsies in Italy, a year with Circe, an encounter with Zeus – to provide a jolt of powerlessness. But there is nothing more sobering anywhere on the Mediterranean than a visit to the beaches and battlefields on Turkey's Gallipoli Peninsula where more than 120,000 soldiers – primarily Turkish, ANZAC (Australian and New Zealand Army Corps), British, French, and Indian – were killed during a barbaric and brief World War I campaign.

"They went like Kings in a pageant to their imminent death," wrote poet John Masefield about the Allied troops who were trying to take over the Turkish passage to Istanbul and the Black Sea.

My two-day, 62-kilometer Gallipoli walkabout takes me onto sandy beaches and former battlefields, through hilly pine forests and fields of sunflowers, and up through harsh terrain to respectfully visit well-tended cemeteries, numerous memorials, a dozen monuments, and two museums. The recollection of battles from Anzac Cove and V Beach on the Aegean seaside to the Lone Pine and Chunuk Bair ridges sends quivers from my fragile Achilles' heel to my lost-in-thought head.

Even with an imagination peppered with vivid scenes from Peter Weir's 1981 film *Gallipoli*, I can't begin to truly fathom the fatal hellhole that existed here between April 1915 and January 1916. Forget, if you can, Odysseus' skirmish with Cicones and even the Trojan War for a sec. The Gallipoli campaign was, without doubt, the most concentrated site of catastrophic carnage in the history of the Mediterranean Sea.

A 127-square mile (33,000 hectares) Gallipoli Historical National Park is now "reserved forever as a resting place for soldiers who fell in the First World War." And there are sanitized but stark reminders of what occurred when enemy forces battled from positions in trenches and tunnels separated by only a few meters.

Although there are scores of wartime cemeteries, the remains of tens of thousands of soldiers have never been identified and many tombstones follow a victim's name with "believed to be buried in this cemetery."

The eeriness is intensified by an incessant ear-cleaning, brain-bashing, howling wind, coupled with the lack of local tourists due to Ramadan. I again feel like Odysseus visiting dead and lost spirits in the underworld as I meander alone on the peninsula.

The terrain itself produces some surreal visions. I climb up one path to find a new Australian flag blowing in the wind and a former killing field covered with sad, solemn, somber and saggy sunflowers, which seems as fitting an image for Gallipoli, which the ancient Greeks called the Thracian Chersonesus, as the current construction of a new museum dedicated to the concept of assimilation.

The assimilation theory was perhaps initially proposed by Kemal Atatürk, a division commander at Gallipoli and Turkey's first president, when he wrote a tribute to ANZAC troops in 1934 that read: "Those heroes that shed their blood and lost their lives…you are now lying in the soil of a friendly country. Therefore rest in peace. There is no difference between the Johnnies and the Mehmets to us where they lie side by side now here in this country of ours."

More shocking and stark reminders of the wounds and reality of war can be found in already-existing museums.

During my walkabout I swim off the beaches and work out in the sea to prepare for my attempt to cross the Hellespont on an upcoming holiday. After one swim practice, I sit on the sand, gaze up towards the erstwhile battlefields, and read the first stanza of a poem I'm carrying called *To A Traveller,* by Turkish poet Necmettin Halil Onan.

> *"Stop wayfarer! Unbeknownst to you this ground*
> *You come and tread on, is where an epoch lies;*
> *Bend down and lend your ear, for this silent mound*
> *Is the place where the heart of a nation sighs."*

When I reach the Helles Memorial at the tip of the Gallipoli Peninsula, where the Hellespont meets the Aegean Sea, it's apparent that swimming across the turbulent strait could be another lesson in humility. It's also humbling, and very appropriate, that each night at 10 p.m., in front of my third floor room facing the Hellespont in the village of Eceabat, taps are solemnly played near a memorial statue called *"Respect History."*

It was Circe, of course, who instructed me to swim across the Hellespont four years – and more than 4,000 kilometers – ago. If I succeed, or perhaps simply if I don't drown, I'll MedTrek into Troy, the site of the decade-long Trojan War that began in 1194 BC, to, as Circe told me, "meet Hektor, the son of King Priam who was slain by quick-to-anger Achilles."

Completing the 4.5-kilometer crossing in the wake of Leander (who, according to the Greek legend and myth as recounted by the Greek writer Musaeus, swam across the Hellespont every night to consort with his lover Hero, a priestess of Aphroditê) could potentially be the most difficult labor that Circe gave me if today's rough water is any indication. Lord Byron (who swam across in May 1810 to prove that Leander could do it) kicked off a swimming mania in 19th-century Europe. Swimming from Eceabat on the European side of the Hellespont to Çanakkale in Asia certainly requires more physical and mental preparation than most of the other footloose tasks.

I trained for the annual August 30 swimming race across the

Turkish strait off-and-on for three months. My rigorous workout regimen included open water swims in Greece, Turkey, France, Ecuador's Galapagos Islands, and Northern California.

I swam amid topless sunbathers on the French Riviera and with turtles, seals, and sharks on the Equator. My most frequent workouts took place in freshwater lakes and rivers in Northern California. Besides daily two-mile workouts in Whiskeytown Lake, these included swimming against the rapids in the Trinity River in Humboldt County. My idiotic theory is that working out in freshwater will enable me to swim faster in the more buoyant saltwater in the Mediterranean that, said President John F. Kennedy, symbolizes "from whence we came." During the three weeks prior to the swim I also ate lots of healthy food, including cod liver which I considered the path to "pure health" when my workout buddy Jim Owens and I got into prime shape in Paris pools and gyms during the early 1980s.

I'm not the first person from Redding to attempt the swim across the Hellespont.

"This was perhaps my favorite open water swim due to the history behind it," lawyer Mark Cibula told me about his successful crossing. "First it goes from Europe to Asia. Second, it is based on Ovid's poem of Hero and Leander. Third, Lord Bryon did it and often said it was the greatest feather in his cap."

Cibula, like Leander and Byron, did it solo.

"I hired a private vessel to follow me and it all went smoothly," he recalled. "The captain was a local named Hussein who became rather famous for guiding someone across in the 60's. Let me know when you make it."

I was glad he said "when" instead of "if."

Why am I making the swim on August 30 and not seeking out my own private Hussein to arrange a solo crossing? After all, a Greek poem claimed Leander was accompanied on his crossing only by "Himself (who was) the crew, the cargo and the ship." My reason is that it's the only day the Hellespont is closed to shipping for ninety minutes for an annual holiday swim to commemorate the anniversary of the Turkish victory over Greek forces in the War of Independence in 1922.

The event has been on the calendar for a quarter century. The overall organization is overseen by the Rotary Club of Çanakkale, which provides detailed technical briefings, hosts spaghetti feeds, supervises the mandatory physicals, and presents medals according to age groups. Simon Murie, an Australian-born Briton, runs a UK-based company called SwimTrek to coordinate foreign swimmers like myself who account for about half the 450 competitors.

The Hellespont doesn't appear too welcoming three days before the race. The wind is blowing at 40-50 kilometers/hour and though I am slightly tempted to jump in and swim a few strokes, I decide it will be a futile, ego-crushing activity. I know I can't make it across with this type of wavy turbulence, and I'm pleased that I spent the last two days galloping through Gallipoli instead of worrying about the open water race conditions. Such concerns, I tell myself, are beyond my control and up to Poseidon and other gods. But I now certainly understand why Homer alluded to the "rip of Hellespont" and contended "all the Hellespont bounds within her riptide straits." Great, riptides! May the currents and tides be with me.

Will I make it across and be able to continue to Troy?

In 2010, almost half of the 400 swimmers entered in the race didn't complete it due to the incessant wind, strong current and turbulent water. I also have some added psychological pressure because my swim is going to benefit a charitable non-profit organization in the United States, and a number of mindful and conscientious people have made donations to the Spondylitis Association of America.

Incidentally if you're not sure about your geography, don't confuse the Hellespont with the 31-kilometer long Bosporus that is also the boundary between Europe and Asia. That strait near Istanbul connects the Sea of Marmara with the Black Sea.

Another favorite challenge for open water swimmers, the name Bosporus does have an intriguing origin. Referred to by the ancient Greeks as the Thracian Bosporus, it means "ox ford" or "ox passage" in Greek. The name comes from a myth about Io's travels after Zeus turned her into an ox for her protection.

I've crossed the Bosporus numerous times by ferry and bridge to get from Europe into Asia Minor, or Anatolia as that part of Turkey is called. The most memorable was during my drive from Paris to Cape Town in 1973, shortly after the bridge was completed. I'd tired of the cold winters in Paris and thought I'd make a two-week sprint drive to Cape Town through Austria, Hungary, Romania, Bulgaria, and along the Black Sea to Jordan. That trip, intended to be a quickie, led me to a fascinating three-year stint in Africa.

This is the first time that I've walked to the Hellespont and, as I approach, I'm thinking of Alexander the Great when he set out from Macedonia to Troy in 334 BC. He was leading a Panhellenic campaign to avenge a Persian invasion of Greece that took place 150 years before he was born to reclaim long ago conquered Greek cities. Unlike me, Alexander wasn't often alone. In fact, historians claim that he was accompanied by 6,000 cavalry, 43,000 infantry, and religiously carried a copy of *The Iliad*, which he regarded as a key to his success.

Alexander too went to Troy, where he paid tribute to the tombs of Achilles and Patróklos, because, wrote Plutarch, "he regarded *The Iliad* as a handbook of the art of war and took with him on his campaigns a text annotated by Aristotle which he always kept under his pillow together with a dagger."

The crossing is a rite of passage that also makes me think of King Xerxes of Persia, who crossed the water on a series of rafts tied together in 480 BC, and Patrick Leigh Fermor, who swam it on his 70th birthday while his long-time mate Xan Fielding waited at the end with a bottle of champagne. The swim not only got these swimmers to the other side but also boosted their reputations and became a key aspect of their personal lore. A statue on the Bay of Spezzia, where Percy Bysshe Shelley drowned, is dedicated to "Lord Byron, Noted English Swimmer and Poet."

Swimming the historic Hellespont is not only a romantic idea but also the definition of poetry in motion. In fact, my friend Janet Holroyd, a teacher in Nice, wrote me the following poem when she heard about my attempt:

> *"Lord Byron may have had the ague*
> *Leander sadly died*
> *But ye of modern fortitude*
> *Will reach the other side*
> *In sterling form and sound of limb*
> *From Asian shore you'll shout it*
> *Then proudly catalogue your swim*
> *And tell us all about it."*

The swim is indeed mythic, and Janet is not the first to extol it in poetry. Christopher Marlowe started his poem *Hero and Leander* by recounting the tale of "Hero the fair" and describing "amorous Leander, beautiful and young" with "dangling tresses, that were never shorn."

> *"On Hellespont, guilty of true-love's blood,*
> *In view and opposite two cities stood,*
> *Sea-borderers, disjoined by Neptune's might."*

Lord Byron, in his poem *Gods, Heroes and Romantics* written after swimming from Sestos to Abydos in May 1810, began his account with

> *"If, in the month of dark December,*

Leander, who was nightly wont
(What maid will not the tale remember?)
To cross thy stream, broad Hellespont!"

He ended it more humbly with:
"For me, degenerate modern wretch,
Though in the genial month of May,
My dripping limbs I faintly stretch,
And think I've done a feat to-day.

But since he cross'd the rapid tide,
According to the doubtful story,
To woo, – and – Lord knows what beside,
And swam for Love, as I for Glory;

'T were hard to say who fared the best:
Sad mortals! Thus the gods still plague you!
He lost his labour, I my jest;
For he was drown'd, and I've the ague.

I have two companions from Antibes with me in the race and make dozens of friends as we prepare for race day. Both Des Baum and Rene Machetti are older than me, as is Lynn Sherr, a former ABC correspondent who is gathering material for a book about swimming.

I've been working out with Des and Rene for more than two decades. Rene and I competed together in French national swimming championships in the 1980s and 90s and he accompanied me on the MedTrek in Spain. I encouraged Des, a decent low-handicap golfer, to get in the pool in the 1990s, and they both eagerly joined me in Turkey.

Lynn has been practicing off Long Island and is doing her first long-distance swim. The other American swimmers include a rugby-playing college student from the University of Washington, a Chicago lawyer (who wears a tiny GPS instrument under his swimming cap) and a mother-and-son combo. Two of Australia's best female open water swimmers, one of them a mother of two in her 40s, have come to Turkey from Perth and the fastest male swimmer is a 26-year-old coach from Switzerland.

Most swimmers feel that the romantic, geographical, mythological, and historical aspect of such an athletic undertaking outweighs the practicality of over-training or being in superb condition. But fortunately there are swim clinics in Çanakkale, on the Asian side of the Hellespont, where we are offered some logistical advice before the race while communing with other swimmers entered from throughout the world.

"Swim towards Istanbul until you sense the strong current from the Sea of Marmara and then turn towards Greece," I'm told by SwimTrek's Simon Murie. "Rock, roll and keep your head down!"

Our technical briefing, swimming workouts and social gatherings make it clear that everyone, at whatever level, is here for one primary reason: fun.

On the morning of the race we are ferried to Eceabat for a staggered start on a small beach. Although the crossing was difficult the year before, today there is almost no wind and the swimming conditions in the strait are perfect. After the first kilometer I feel as comfortable and confident as I imagine Leander, Lord Byron, Patrick Leigh Fermor, and Mark Cibula were.

When I finally get an assist from the strong current moving from the Black Sea towards the Mediterranean, I feel even better with each stroke as Çanakkale and the Asian side of the Hellespont became closer and closer. I reach the finish, become my own Hero, and manage to pick up a bronze medal in my age group.

A few months later I am quoted in Lynn Sherr's book *Swim: Why We Love The Water*: "Joel Stratte-McClure, an adventurer from San Francisco who is trekking the Mediterranean, called his bronze medal 'a walk in the park. I think I compensated too much – went too far to Istanbul (north) before I cut over to Greece (south). But what the hell, I mean it's been a 5,000-mile journey (for me to get here); a couple of kilometers here and there don't matter.'"

Homeward Bound

"Nothing is as sweet as a man's own country."
– *The Odyssey*

"The idea of returning is significant for all of us."
– Deng Ming-Dao, *365 Tao Daily Meditations*

The predominant theme in Homer's *Odyssey* is, of course, the 20-year absence of Odysseus and his effort to return to Ithaka – and everything that his island home meant to him in real, regal, and symbolic terms. That voyage may be responsible for two ongoing trends in Greece: the desire to travel and the homing instinct. Greek emigrants, perhaps influenced by Odysseus' adventurous voyage and painstaking return, still seem genetically programmed to wander worldwide, often on ships and usually to earn money. And then they almost invariably return to their native villages in the autumn or winter of their lives.

My years of wandering make it clear why Circe's twelfth task for me is to "Make your own homeward journey to your own Ithaka and write a heartfelt and cathartic account about the importance of home and friends." After an absence of more than four decades, I am duly returning to the northern California town where I lived as a kid.

My last, and most serious, weeks of training for the Hellespont swim took place in Whiskeytown Lake near Redding. I was at this same spot, with 10,000 others, on September 28, 1963, when President John F. Kennedy dedicated the dam that created this recreational manmade lake. Just before I returned to Turkey to walk through Gallipoli and into Troy, I was in the water every morning to train for my Byronic, if not ironic, attempt to swim from Europe to Asia.

There isn't much similarity, certainly in buoyancy or currents anyway, between the Hellespont and Whiskeytown. But I told Darla Hightower, who used to ride horses with me in high school and now timed my daily workouts while she casually floated on an inflated raft, "my training in so many different types of water throughout the world should make it an easy and enjoyable swim across the Hellespont if the conditions are decent."

I left Redding after high school in 1966 to attend Stanford University and embark on my own forty-year odyssey before making a somewhat quixotic homeward bound voyage to establish a base camp here. Although I spend less than half my time in Redding, it's refreshing, after living outside the United States for over thirty years, to be close to my roots: my feisty 90-something year-old mother and numerous family members; a built-in network of friends that I've made since my family first moved here in 1954; and the mostly unchanged surrounding countryside of lakes, mountains, rivers, creeks and trails, that I know at least as well as the shores of the Mediterranean.

I long ago realized that my comparatively rural upbringing, education, and a childhood filled with adventurous and athletic outdoor activities played an important role in fashioning what I've become. I also gratefully acknowledged how fortunate I am to have gotten out of such a small town.

Admittedly, on my return not everything is to my liking.

The I-recognize-most-of-the-20,000-people-population in a drugstore-on-the-corner friendly downtown with vibe and spirit has been replaced by the distressing desolation of ubiquitous chain stores, the absence of a downtown social scene, and a randomly gathered population of 100,000 located in a rural-urban sprawl lacking, from my perspective, a center or a soul. Besides the destruction of an *American Graffiti*-like town center, the haphazard growth includes the construction of a flashy city hall that looks like a Northern California version of Las Vegas.

A Democratic stronghold in my youth, Redding is now firmly right-wing, fueled by lots of retirees from southern California and a low-income, overweight white (and almost no other races) crowd that seems to excel at perpetuating strange local crimes. Where else could I witness a man getting arrested for mooing and another killed when two men sat on him to keep him from fleeing the scene of a crime?

Wally Herger, the district's former Congressman, refused, to the delight of locals and amusement of the national media, to retract an inflammatory statement that applauded a self-pronounced "right-wing terrorist." Two gays, one a friend of mine in high school, were murdered in 1999, and a polarizing conservative local radio show's signoff is "You're either one of the good guys or one of the bad guys." Even my mother is – let me be polite – a fascist piglet and when we walk in a riverside park at dusk she gleefully lets me record her anti-Obama rants on my iPhone. She even complained about the jeans he wore to an All-Star baseball game. The region is also – and most inhabitants don't think this is a bad thing – fringe Bible Belt, and there's been a proliferation of religious schools.

I shouldn't consider myself an old timer though. Clint Eastwood lived here and has a place that enables him to fish in the Rising River near Burney. When we connected one year at the Cannes Film Festival I mentioned that I was a Redding boy.

"I'll bet you weren't in Redding before Shasta Dam was built (between 1938-1945) like I was?" Eastwood boasted, putting me in my place.

There are a few unchanged physical landmarks from the 50s. I get my mail at the post office on Yuba Street and my hair cut by Mike in the Hotel Lorenz next door. Both buildings still look like they did over half a century ago. The Plunge Swimming pool, where I worked out twice a day as a kid, is now called the Redding Aquatic Center. But it's still fifty meters long, and I still swim with a team there at dawn or dusk during the summer. Other institutions, like Jack's Bar and Grill that has the best steak-and-baked-potato meal in town, the iconic building on Eureka Way where I attended Shasta Union High School, and the annual rodeo grounds don't seem to have aged.

Some things look better. The Cascade Theater has been completely renovated, due to the contributions of Redding-raised film producer Kathleen Kennedy and others, and its original Art Deco ceiling is sparkling. The freestanding $23 million Sundial Bridge, designed by Santiago Calatrava, has been the city's most artistic and inviting landmark since it was completed in 2004. It's almost worth driving over three hours north of San Francisco just to walk across it.

I suppose these memories and mutations are typical of any homecoming, though a Greek village is likely to have changed less, I think, than a Northern California boomtown. Or maybe I shouldn't have stayed away for two decades more than Odysseus did.

Although I wanted to be a doctor when I left Redding ("God knows why in the world you'd want to do that," my stepfather, Dr. Paul Stratte, said. "It's hard work."), I was influenced by the political and social upheavals of the late 1960s and discovered I was destined to be a journalist and adventurer. Forget an office, appointments, surgery, a big house on a hill, and a Barbie Doll wife, though when I was hiking with Ted Loring recently he acknowledged that "Well, you've got one of those today." He was referring to my home on a hill.

Actually, my occupational choice was partly genetic.

My grandfather in Grand Forks, North Dakota, where I was born, was a reporter and manager for the Associated Press before he became a newspaper publisher in 1929. And my father, who was on the business side of the game, became a newspaper publisher in Burlington, Vermont, in 1961. I worked as a reporter for U.S. newspapers and magazines before I became publisher of *The Paris Metro,* where I also wrote a fortnightly column and an array of articles, in 1977.

There's no question that both grandpa and dad passed on their journalistic genes to me. One of my earliest memories is traipsing after Pete, the mailman, at the age of six with a *Grand Forks Herald* newspaper delivery bag slung over my shoulder filled with old papers. I frequently visited the *Herald* offices on Fourth Street in Grand Forks to watch the printing press run, back in the days of classic metal moveable type. I can recall its distinctive and unique smell – an intriguing combination of paper, ink, moving machine parts, and human sweat – even when I'm walking in a Mediterranean breeze.

At the age of ten I attempted to copy, by hand and typewriter, an edition of the *World Book Encyclopedia* (I think I made it ten pages into the A volume) and at twelve began reading the *Encyclopedia Britannica's* 54-volume *Great Books of the Western World* series. I'd like to pretend that I read the *Great Books* version of Homer, but I'd already opted for the condensed Greek tales in *Myths and Legends of the Ages,* my favorite book as a kid.

My grandpa, M.M. Oppegard (aka Oppe or Barney), used to write a column called *"It Seems To Me"* for the *Herald,* and I was amazed at how, when he was staying with us on Riverside Drive in Redding, he'd whip out five-hundred word think pieces with apparent ease and enjoyment. Our genetic relationship was further underlined when grandma would frequently say, after I inquisitioned a stranger on the street or became an immediate friend with a random telephone operator, that my curiosity made me "just like father," which is what she called grandpa.

The last time I saw grandpa, in June 1969, I was driving across the country to work at *The Burlington Free Press* in Vermont. I stopped in Grand Forks to drop off an urn I'd "borrowed" from a hotel in Banff, Canada, as a present for grandma and grandpa. They both said that they would keep it to use as a receptacle for their ashes – and they did. The copper urn was on the plane with me when I brought their ashes to California to spread in the Pacific Ocean in 1996.

I last spoke to grandpa from a public telephone in a muddy field at the Woodstock Rock & Music Festival in New York on August 17, 1969. I am grateful that, just before he died, grandpa knew I was carrying on the family's journalistic tradition and covering a stoned rock concert. In fact, it turns out that we had both written about the moon landing which occurred in July 1969 – the only story we ever covered "together."

I think both my father and stepfather were surprised if not shocked that, after college, I headed to Paris without a job and didn't pursue a more traditional career path. In fact, I didn't even look for a job in the U.S. I "blame" that on the turbulence and tumult of the 1960s when I was among the many teens in the country whose life plan was questioned, if not derailed. It was a time when actively expressing opposition to everything from the Vietnam War to established institutions, and rejecting a traditional life path, was *de rigueur*. I credit the hullaballoo of that era for giving me the opportunity to think outside the box and get outside the country.

I know that my father, James Warren McClure, was very concerned about my lack of a career path and dubious about my own professional choices that included freelancing in Africa and Europe. I was gratified when, a few years into the MedTrek, he said, "No one can duplicate the fantastic experiences you're having. And no one else has had them."

There's something particularly rich, reassuring, and rewarding about resettling in a town where, despite phenomenal growth and a few negatives, the natural landmarks are the ones I grew up with. Just a few steps out my door are the Sacramento River, Shasta Lake, Whiskeytown Lake, the Trinity Alps, Mount Lassen, Mount Shasta, and, a few hours west, the Pacific Ocean.

And this is where I did almost everything, from my first kiss and first broken bone to first swimming competition and first courtship, for the first time during an era that, until 1965, resembled the television shows *Leave It To Beaver* and *Father Knows Best*.

I made out for the first time at the Cascade Theater and lost my virginity on the Sacramento River on an island outside Sloopy's nightclub near Kutras park; I had my first beer in a dusty graveyard on the river and walked drunk, for the first and last time, across the high train trestle spanning the river near the Diestelhorst Bridge; I had my first automobile accident (I was a passenger in a jeep that ran into a chain without any reflectors in the parking lot at Bank of America) and first lawsuit (I lost three teeth and had major facial lacerations as a result of the accident and was awarded $750); I was detained by police for the first time (on suspicion that I'd stolen beer from a freight train), and got my first speeding ticket; I had my first jobs (paper route, drug store delivery boy, bottling mountain spring water) and rode my first horse, caught my first salmon, shot my first pheasant, and bought my first stock (in a local lumber company).

Naturally I'd been back to see my family and attend high school reunions during the past few decades.

I returned in 1968 to give a talk against the Vietnam War to a high school class (I was both applauded and booed); came back to campaign for Eugene McCarthy for president (I bought my first quarter-page newspaper ad in support of the losing candidate); was here when President Nixon resigned (August 1974) and when the embassies in Kenya and Tanzania were bombed (August 1998); and visited shortly before my brother Lars was killed when his air tanker was hit by another tanker while fighting a fire ignited by meth manufacturers just before 9/11/2001.

I celebrated both my 50th and 60th birthdays here. When I turned fifty I took a pack trip up into the Trinity Alps with another childhood friend, Sandy Stewart, and at 60 threw a big party for one hundred at the Riverview Country Club.

But Circe encouraged a more permanent move and I quietly slipped back into the community for a few weeks in early 2009 until Tom Dunlap, a columnist for *The Redding Record Searchlight* (we called it *The Redding Searching Redlight* when I was a kid) reviewed my book with the titillating and irresistible lead: "Joel Stratte-McClure first walked into my life at the local Barnes & Noble Booksellers, and now he goes to bed with me."

"Wait, let me explain," Dunlap continued. "Stratte-McClure is a hometown product, a Shasta High School grad who did time at Stanford and Columbia universities. He loves to read, write, walk and talk, not always in that order. His latest gig is a fun-filled book titled *The Idiot and the Odyssey*. That's what I take to bed."

That gave everyone the idea I was alive, well, and on the market.

I told friends, and was certainly convinced myself, that this was the period of life when I was celebrating my personal liberation after an odyssey that had taken me to live in Palo Alto, New York, Paris, Cape Town, Paris again, the French Riviera and Los Angeles while traveling and covering stories in more than a hundred countries.

This was the first time in thirty years that I'd been without a wife or woman, kids, a big house, dogs, cats, a garden, a pool, or various work commitments. Comparatively free of any external obligations, I rented a modest two-story townhouse that I can painlessly lock and leave to MedTrek for a couple months at time. My hillside home with a suspended terrace looks onto both Mount Lassen and Mount Shasta. Homer's "dawn with rose-red fingers in the east" glows upon me almost every morning.

I reconnected with friends I've known for over fifty years, made new acquaintances and learned during an extensive medical exam that I am afflicted with "abnormally high testosterone," according to Doctor Andrew Solkovits. I realized the problems this would cause the moment I reacted in surprise to the doctor while speaking on my cell phone in a jewelry store, "You're telling me that I have ABNORMALLY HIGH testosterone?" Two women cashiers looked liked they'd just seen a Greek god. They may have also sensed that I'm a textbook Leo and embody the various strengths and weaknesses associated with my July 31 birth date and Zodiac sign.

When I told my mother about my AHT, however, her response was that "you're the only person who didn't know it" and my brother Tryg, a urologist, said "I have to ask most men your age how many times they get up at night. I have to ask you how many times you get it up."

That wasn't my first medical revelation in Redding.

I delivered prescriptions for Owens Pharmacy during my senior year in high school. This was just when the birth control pill became available, and I was very excited because I thought only Playboy centerfold subjects would use birth control. The medical revelation occurred when I delivered the pills to various customers and learned that most of them were mothers of six. The job also enabled me to start a collection of different condoms that my sister Lesle threw out the window of my dormitory when she visited me at Stanford.

I'm not the only one who's returned to Redding after a long session out of town. Darla Hightower came back after a career with the state in Sacramento, Tom Kreider (who said, when he saw me driving my canary yellow Toyota Scion around Redding, "You must be very confident about your sexuality!") returned after a successful financial management career in New York, and journalist Marc Beauchamp, who wrote a story about me entitled "Redding's Odysseus' Finds His Way Home," came back from abroad and worked for *The Searching Redlight*.

Other high school friends have spent most of their lives here. Linda Stewart is a devoted hospice worker, Gayle Guest works with challenged children, Leslie Williams was a teacher, Terry Hansen designed a top-notch river trail network, Greg Beale calls himself the

Lone Liberal on his blog, and Paul Hughes, my liberal English professor, is still a progressive beacon in his eighties. Paul, who claims to be a "non-theist," spoke about death recently and proclaimed that "I'm a Greek. There's nothing after life...eternal rest."

The Sacramento River, on which I was raised and where I spent a lot of time fishing for salmon and hunting for quail along the banks, isn't quite the Mediterranean. But there are some Mediterranean touches here.

There's a Greek orthodox monk from the monastery in nearby Platina who hangs out at the library and I can keep in shape for the MedTrek on the local trail network, from a little six-mile river trail loop to the twenty-five mile descent from Shasta Dam to downtown Redding.

Even my volunteer gardening at Turtle Bay's McConnell Arboretum and Botanical Gardens has a Greek twist. When we cut back Teucrium (aka germander) I'm told by Marie Stadther, the head gardener whose blog tag is *The Tree Goddess*, that "the genus name, Teucrium, is derived from the legendary first king of Troy, Teucer, who pioneered the medicinal use of these plants. Teucer was an ancestor and king of the Trojans."

Who knew?

One summer solstice I read from *The Odyssey* in Sacramento at a performance by *The Readers of Homer,* and I meditate with my former high school classmate Leslye (now Layne) Russell and her luthier husband James (he adopted her last name when they married). I frequently make the three-hour drive across the Trinity Alps to the Pacific Ocean, where we have a family house in a little fishing village called Trinidad, to hike in the redwoods. I've done the 16-mile round-trip Redwood Creek hike to the world's tallest trees scores of times.

I even had an experience with garbage in Trinidad. I innocently put some household garbage into the parking lot trash bin at the Larrupin Café after I bought dinner for four. When I came home from a hike the next afternoon, the contents were strewn across our front yard.

Nearby Arcata, home to Humboldt State University and the capital of the area's proliferating marijuana industry, is one of my favorite downtowns in the country. Arcata is centered around a popular town plaza and features some treasured institutions, like the quaint Finnish Country Spa and Hot Tubs, where I had my first non-Indian chai when it opened in 1984. I continue to eat the excellent carrot cake at Bon Boniere, shop at the hip Wildberries Market, and I've accompanied my college pal Annette Holland and her radiologist husband Greg for Lindy dancing at the former dairy.

I have many more female than male friends in Redding, and I attribute this to the fact that aging men seem to burnout more rapidly than maturing women, who often get a second wind at sixty.

I've known Leslie Williams since the first grade when we co-starred (or that's how we prefer to recall it) in *The Little White Duck*. I've been admiring Gayle Guest since we were on the Redding Aquaducks Swim Team together in the fifth grade. I regularly compare notes on life with Beth Harral. Beth, Leslie, Darla, and I frequently walk the river trail together and often arrange coffee klatches with our classmates at a local coffee house called Yaks. I relish being, usually, the sole guy.

We frequently walk through a Peace Labyrinth on the river trail. It's a short and simple but peaceful meander, and it's customary to leave a stone, either in decoration or to increase the length of the path, on each visit. Before one walking meditation I shared a bit of knowledge picked up on the Med from archeologist Sandy MacGillivray on Crete.

"To the ancient Greeks the labyrinth was a metaphor for life," Sandy told me. "It's a complex of twists and turns, deceptive dead-ends, double-backs, and long meandering diversions, through which the explorer, having entered, had to find his way in order to confront the monster, half-human/half-divine, which lurked there."

As strange as it seems, some of us are more like teenagers now than we were fifty years ago. In fact, when I meet Susie Letsinger, my first real girlfriend in the third grade, at the YMCA we go totally bananas.

Heck, I still even fall in love and go steady with eighth-grade enthusiasm. I truly appreciate women my own age because of our shared experiences and very much value many of the relationships and friendships that I rekindled when I returned to Redding. After two marriages and being engrossed in a project as time consuming as the MedTrek, I wasn't looking for a third wife, but I found very valuable companionship.

Twenty years ago I had a male friend in his 70s who acted like a kid when he fell in love with a woman his age. My reaction was "I sure won't be that immature when I'm in my 70s." In fact, it looks like I might be.

There must be something in the Redding water, if the experiences my friend Eastwood, who has at least seven children by five different women, and I have had with women are indicative of any local influences.

I wound up in France because of a woman. I flew to Paris in 1970 to meet a Stanford co-ed attending Stanford-in-Tours, only to learn that her father "encouraged" her to return to the U.S. on the day of my arrival to avoid meeting me. Thirty-five years later I returned to Hollywood to resume life with another woman, only to learn that I should have stayed in France.

"I left for a woman and returned for a woman," I told one friend when I summed up my life. "Almost no progress in four decades."

I like to think I brought the *je ne sais quoi* sensibility that I'd picked up in France back to Redding with me. This includes my uncanny ability to "read" a woman the second I see her and, among other things, determine her nationality by her dress and demeanor.

For example, there's a woman in my 90-minute butts and guts class at the local YMCA, where I regularly swim and exercise, who looks just like Kalypso. Off and on, whenever I am in town, I observe this somewhat unapproachable, almost mysterious, seemingly arrogant, generally unsmiling woman with long hair. As I watch her in class, captivated by her movement and appearance, I'm sure she is either a French *femme fatale* or a Greek goddess.

I consider women in a gym off limits, but when I ask if she's French, telling her that her distant demeanor and aloof character are typically French (and I mean that as a compliment in let-it-all-hang-out Redding), she tells me she comes from Ferndale, a little town on the California coast.

There goes my theory about my ability to "read" a woman.

Incidentally, not everyone thought I was ready to come home.

"I don't think that in your mythological (archetypal) journey you are actually in the 'coming home' phase; but, rather, still in the 'going to war' phase," said Gayle Guest. "You still enjoy finding yourself apart from your family and wives and girlfriends."

Another friend contends I came back to Redding for a woman.

Gloria Ackley, who lived with me in Paris in the 1970s, pointed out that "upon your return to Redding/Ithaka, there was no Penélopê waiting, but there was a Helen."

Indeed my mother's name is Helen, and, for the record, her mother's name was also Helen. My mom, still a social butterfly in her 90s, is as responsible as Helen of Troy for giving me the elements required for my meander around the Med.

It started, of course, when she gave birth to me in 1948 and continued when she gave me a copy of *Myths and Legends of the Ages* in 1957, encouraged me to compete in swimming at the age of ten, stressed the comparative importance of academics in high school between 1962-66, and prompted me to apply to Stanford in 1965.

Both my mother and grandmother, whom I described in my first book when I was MedTrekking in Spain (she died at 96), were responsible for providing me with the confidence to travel, take risks, try new things, and adopt the classic American attitude (actually it was first expressed in a proverb by William Edward Hickson in Britain in the mid-1800s) that "if at first you don't succeed, try, try again."

I'd say that, while I learned a great deal from both my father and stepfather, my mother and other women have been more influential, genetically and environmentally, in encouraging me to stray a bit from the beaten path of life.

My mother raised six kids, but before all that she was the class valedictorian and on the soccer team in high school (who the hell played soccer in North Dakota in the 1930s?), claims she should have been valedictorian of her University of North Dakota Class of '39 (she minored in French and, based on the way she speaks it, I can see why someone else got the nod), and got a graduate degree in journalism from Northwestern in 1940.

She was employed by CBS Radio in Chicago in the early 40s and has told me (many times) that she was among the first to break the news of Pearl Harbor on the air from the CBS studios in the Wrigley building. She worked for newspapers (she refused to be society editor on the Columbus Dispatch in Ohio because it wasn't considered a "real" reporting job), in public relations (for the American University in Washington, DC), and taught freshman English at the University of North Dakota "because everyone else was at war." Even after I was born and she concentrated on motherhood, she did the books for my stepfather's medical practice, made a number of shrewd investments, became an expert dove huntress and trout fisherwoman, amassed a large library, was an avid golfer, and went to Europe every year for thirty-five years.

Naturally no one goes through life unscathed, and my mother is scarred by her die-hard, right-wing political outlook. She's not alone in Redding and I'm easily outnumbered by her like-minded friends when we have our weekly dinners at the Riverview Country Club.

It's hard, after more than sixty years, to boil down the importance and impact of my mother. There's so much learned and inherited influence that I have to struggle to find the best advice she ever gave me. It took me months in Redding to realize what it was: always unpack the second you get someplace. Her last wish is to "come back to haunt you if you publish a paid obituary in the *Searching Redlight*."

Tackling a Mountain on My Home Turf
I do a lot of hiking around Redding to stay in MedTrekking shape, but the snow-covered pathless ascent up the 14,162-feet (4,317m) magic, majestic, and mythical Mount Shasta, which may or may not have been calling me for over 60 years, is an arduous delight and glorious grind (if the words aren't contradictory). I attempt to reach the summit

with Reinhard Hohlwein, the son of Kathyrn Hohlwein who founded *The Readers of Homer.*

It's Reinhard's ninth time tackling the mountain, which is why I chose him to lead me up the West Face and the aptly named Misery Hill. Outfitted with crampons, helmets, and ice axes, we proceed with caution due to a number of recent accidents, helicopter rescues, and the omnipresent threat of avalanches, rock falls, hidden crevasses and boilerplate ice. We spend two nights on the mountain and when we reach the summit are alone for an hour, relishing the 360-degree views (I can't see my deck in Redding from which, somewhat paradoxically, I can clearly see the summit) and listening to the stunning silence as a gigantic ravenous bird (an auspicious or ominous omen, as any Homerphile knows) flies over.

I dedicate the hike to Leisha Graves, the daughter of a friend. "I waited 63 years to get to the top of Mount Shasta and dedicate this summiting to Leisha Graves, who died too young to do it," I write in the logbook at the top.

"Taking her to the top with you is such an honor," her mother Judy tells me when I descend, noting that some of her daughter's ashes are in the abbey at the base of the mountain. "I always think of her when I see Mount Shasta, and now she stands at the top. Thank you."

I also make the climb on behalf of my friend Don Mangrum, who says that climbing Shasta "was among the things I always wanted to do and put off. Now, I am physically unable."

I am thinking of Leisha and Don as I cautiously enter a rabbit-sized tunnel at the summit and descend into the secret city of Lemuria for thirty minutes. The inside of the mountain consists, as novelist Frederick Spencer Oliver correctly describes it, of "walls, polished as by jewelers, though excavated by giants; floors carpeted with long, fleecy gray fabric that looked like fur, but was a mineral product; ledges intersected by the builders, and in their wonderful polish exhibiting veins of gold, of silver, of green copper ores, and maculation of precious stones."

"This is an inspirational trip and one of the very best climbing days in memory," Reinhard tells me when I return to the surface. "We really got the blessing of the powers and gods that be in every way."

"I'll bet you came down a wiser, wilder, and woolier man, knowing you answered the challenge of the peak that has been calling to you since childhood," writes Gloria Ackley a few days later.

That reminds me to return to the MedTrek before I start looking like one.

All Roads Lead to Troy

"Sing that wooden horse Epeios built, inspired by Athêna
– the ambuscade Odysseus filled with fighters and sent to
take the inner town of Troy. Sing only this for me, sing
me this well, and I shall say at once before the world the
grace of heaven has given us a song." – *The Odyssey*

I say goodbye to one gigantic fake Trojan horse – the prop used
in *Troy* starring Brad Pitt, the 2004 film that was actually shot in Malta
and Mexico – on the beachfront promenade in Çanakkale. Then I
MedTrek along the mirror-smooth Hellespont through richly cultivated
countryside and across the legendary Skamánder River to arrive at the
generally agreed-upon site of the famed city of Troy.

My pleasant 25-kilometer stroll from Çanakkale to the Aegean
Sea is an ideal transition from SwimTrekking and socializing to
MedTrekking solo, one step at a time. A mix of seaside beaches, trails,
tarmac, and dirt roads takes me near the mouth of the Hellespont. There I
cut cross-country for seven kilometers through the village of Kumkale to
now-inland Troy.

When I climb a hill and enter the ruins of Truva, as the Turks call
Troy, I immediately encounter another gigantic fake Trojan horse.

The legend of the Greeks sneaking into Troy inside the Trojan horse to conquer the city after a ten-year battle is mentioned in *The Odyssey*, but never in *The Iliad*. Still, the incident has become one of the most enduring symbols of Greek chicanery, cunning, warfare, and wile. It captivated the psyche of ancient Greece and boosted the reputation of Odysseus, who came up with the Trojan horse ploy. In classical Athens, there were numerous replicas of the Trojan horse, including a bronze statue on the Acropolis.

More important than encountering another Trojan horse in Troy is the fact that I again meet Athêna and get the lowdown on a variety of issues relating to the city's history, the lengthy war, and my remaining steps on this portion of the MedTrek. Athêna, as she did in Rome some 4,157 kilometers ago, appears in the guise of a tour guide.

This time her earthly name is Mustafa Askin, one of the best-known guides in Troy whose family owns the nearby Hisarlik (it means "castled place") Hotel. Just to complicate things, Mustafa contends that he is also a reincarnation of Hektor, the son of King Priam of Troy, who was killed by Achilles in vicious face-to-face combat and whose funeral rights conclude *The Iliad*. This human guide/goddess/warrior composite comes up with all sorts of surprising statements, and I try to take what I learn in my stride during our extensive conversations.

Mustafa/Athêna/Hektor delivers some attention-grabbing buzz, and dispels a few Trojan tales, the moment I check into my €30-a-night room, half a kilometer from the entrance to the ruins. I'm in Room 7, which is named after King Priam who reigned over the "god-built bastion" on a steep and windy plateau.

First of all, Mustafa/Athêna/Hektor claims that the legendary Helen of Troy was "the first real WMD, or Woman of Mass Destruction" and contends that "in reality there's no way that the Greeks and Trojans, or anyone else, would fight for ten years over a woman. Even the idea of a single ongoing ten-year siege is impossible."

"They were fighting for control of the Hellespont and its trade routes," he insists as we casually sip strong Turkish coffee on the hotel terrace. "Seriously, would you fight for one woman for ten years? Ah, but access to the Black Sea is another matter."

Mustafa/Athêna/Hektor informs me that Helen had two kids fathered by her lover Paris when she was in Troy, which then had 6,000 inhabitants speaking many different languages. He goes on to totally wreck my day by challenging an image emblazoned in my mind since I first read about the Trojan horse at the age of nine. He says there's no truth to the iconic ruse.

"There was certainly a Trojan horse but it was a religious symbol, not wartime trickery," he continues, as we stroll into Troy, where we see kids climbing the stairs into the stomach of the gigantic, albeit fake, wooden horse. "The Greeks like to think it was an innovative invasion tactic, but do you really think the Trojans were so incompetent that they'd let a wooden horse, even one considered a holy symbol, into town without searching it? Their guards could give us more tips about efficient border control than your Transport Security Administration."

And, he adds, "the Trojan horse wouldn't have been built from wood from Greek ships, as Homer claimed, because there were adequate forests here then. Don't believe everything you read."

Mustafa/Athêna/Hektor, who in his current incarnation was born in Troy and has been a multilingual guide for 32 years, continues with a barrage of other surprising suppositions as he leads me through the multilayered ruins.

"The academics are also all wrong about the date of the war, simply because it's impossible to date," he says, pointing out that Troy's original walls were already built at a slant 5,000 years ago to mitigate damage from earthquakes.

Then he moves into Trojan War mode.

"Every time I walk around Troy, I imagine the battle occurring in front of my eyes on the plain below with the cast of thousands that Homer describes in *The Iliad*, which I read in Turkish, though Homer originally wrote it in the Ionic dialect.

"When I visualize the war I feel, as a true Turk, a sense of pride, honor, love, and a variety of other emotions, including anger and aggressiveness," he continues as we stop to chat under a fig tree. "Incidentally, *The Iliad* is a much more important poem than *The Odyssey*, which is just an adventure novel. *The Iliad* is about war, tragedy, friendship, grief, honor, drama, and existence itself."

In case you've forgotten, let me remind you that the main players in *The Iliad* for the Akhaians/Argives/Danäans, as the Greeks were called at the time, include the fearless and proud warrior Achilles, the haughty commander Agamémnon, and Achilles' best pal Patróklos. On the Trojan side, Hektor has the lead with key supporting roles by Helen, Paris, and King Priam.

Mustafa/Athêna/Hektor discusses the relationship between Achilles and Patróklos to illustrate friendship, grief, bravery, and tragedy.

"When Patróklos, garbed in Achilles' armor of war, dies at the hands of Hektor it's not just the turning point of the war but provokes a powerful expression of love and loss," he says, with some emotion. "It also, of course, leads to Hektor's, or my own, honorable end."

Achilles describes the death of "my greatest friend, a comrade in arms whom I held dear above all others, dear as myself" in *The Iliad* as "the last twist of the knife. Groaning shook his heart and he gave a dreadful cry that his mother, the silvery-footed, Thetis heard in the depths of the offshore sea."

"No burden like this grief will come a second time upon my heart, while I remain among the living," Achilles moaned.

Mustafa/Athêna/Hektor jumps over a barrier to pick some figs for us to eat as we approach the West Gate that faced the battleground and, he says, was the site of a spring where Trojan women washed clothes. He points towards the sea and continues, reflectively, "This is where I (Hektor) was killed by Achilles in front of King Priam and my family and then dragged around by a chariot."

"It was windy then and it's windy now," he adds as a northeasterly breeze wafts over us. "The wind brought wealth to Troy because boats had to wait for a south wind to proceed up the Dardanelles in an era before tacking was invented. That made this a popular trading post."

Mustafa/Athêna/Hektor enumerates vivid descriptions of the savagery of the war by cherry picking a number of descriptive phrases from *The Iliad* and recites them as though providing confessional details to Homer. The Trojans, he adds, were like "cranes at dawn descending, beaked in cruel attack" while the advancing Greek army resembled a swarm of "geese, cranes, and long-throated swans in the Asian meadow" as they "came on in silence, raging under their breath" while "yanking the horse's heads, lashing their flanks."

As I listen to his personal account, it becomes increasingly easy for me to visualize the conflict. I picture chariot skirmishes while "dust rose underfoot as thudding hooves of horses shook the plain and men plied deadly bronze" and make out Patróklos putting on Achilles' flashing bronze and outfitting himself with greaves, a cuirass, a solid shield, a plumed helmet, two shining spears, and a silver-studded blade as he rode off towards Hektor and his undoing. I clearly hear Patróklos's last words to Hektor before he dies: "No long life is ahead for you. This day your death stands near, and your immutable end, at Prince Achilles' hands."

Then I envisage Achilles entering the battle "mad with rage for his friend's death," knowing full well that both he and Hektor "were destined to stain the same earth dark red here at Troy." Achilles looks "for the destroyer of my great friend" and confesses that "I must reject this life, my heart tells me, reject the world of men, if Hektor does not feel my battering spear tear the life out of him, making him pay in his own blood for the slaughter of Patróklos."

I also hear Achilles call Agamémnon, the Greek leader, the "most insatiate of men," a "thick-skinned, shameless, greedy fool," and a "sack of wine" with a "cur's eyes and antelope heart." Then, for good measure, he adds that Agamémnon is a "commander of trash" who "pays for his behavior with his blood."

As a young boy in Redding, I was particularly touched by one moving scene during the Trojan War that occurs when Hektor and the Greek warrior Aías, after a particularly ferocious hand-to-hand combat, call it quits for the day, give each other gifts, promise to meet again and fight another time, and return to their respective camps unharmed.

"Let us make one another memorable gifts, and afterward they'll say, among Akhaians and Trojans: 'These two fought and gave no quarter in close combat, yet they parted friends.'"

Noble, very noble.

When I come back to reality, Mustafa/Athêna/Hector quotes Agamémnon about how well Hector fought during the war: "In my lifetime I have not seen or heard of one man doing in a day's action what Hektor did to the Akhaian army – one man, son of neither god nor goddess, in one day's action – but for years to come that havoc will be felt among the Argives."

"Isn't that a nice line?" Mustafa/Athêna/Hector asks me as he reads it again.

He then turns to Book Four of *The Iliad,* and I'm hit with more vivid descriptions of the battle. The two sides were "going for one another like wolves whirling upon each other" and "when long lines met at the point of contact, there was a shock of bull's hide, battering pikes, and weight of men in bronze" before "a great din rose, in one same air elation and agony of men destroying and destroyed, and earth astream with blood."

Many of the phrases he recites bring the Trojan War to life and are lyrically evocative, like "on his shield and helm she kindled fire most like midsummer's purest flaming star in heaven rising, bathed by the Ocean stream."

Then my guide recalls what Helen told King Priam when he asked her about a certain enemy officer.

"That is Laërtês' son, the great tactician, Odysseus," Helen told the king. "He was bred on Ithaka, a bare and stony island – but he knows all manner of stratagems and moves in war."

There are numerous phrases in *The Iliad* promoting Odysseus. He's the "hero of battle guile and greed," "the wily field commander," "that rugged man bold for adventure," "shrewd, cool and brave, beyond all others in rough work," "great in all men's eyes, unwearying master of guile and toil," and had "no rivals at the tricks of war." There are also colorful descriptions of Odysseus at war as he "kept his lance in play, and made the Trojans facing him recoil....Full of rage over his dead companion, Odysseus speared him in the temple, and the spearhead passed clean through his head from side to side so darkness veiled his eyes."

"No man knows war as he does," Diomêdês said of Odysseus.

This type of vibrant prose has kept *The Iliad* on the best-seller list for 3,000 years, as have numerous existential themes dealing with honor, heroism, war, mortality, companionship, and the loss of the "bloom of youth that is the greatest strength of all."

Many of its stories and themes even have contemporary parallels. The image of Achilles dragging Hektor's body behind his war chariot (he lashed the body to his chariot with rawhide cords, "whipped the team ahead into a willing run" and "chariot horses at a brutal gallop pulled the torn body toward the decked ships...full-length in dust") was eerily resurrected when a U.S. Army soldier was dragged around the capital of Somalia after the Battle of Mogadishu in 1993.

Even current preoccupations like insomnia are discussed.

One night during the Trojan War, Agamémnon "lay beyond sweet sleep and cast about in tumult of the mind" and on another he walked around camp "because no sleep will come to settle on my eyes; the war stays with me."

Grieving Achilles too was tormented by a lack of sleep for eleven nights after the funeral of his friend Patróklos on a blazing pyre.

"Achilles thought of his friend, and sleep that quiets all things would not take hold of him," Homer wrote in the final book of *The Iliad*. "He tossed and turned remembering with pain Patróklos' courage, his buoyant heart...With memory his eyes grew wet."

And what, prior to the advent of the pharmaceutical industry, was the panacea suggested for his insomnia in Troy? Achilles' mother Thetis suggests "it would be comforting to make love to a woman."

Mustafa/Athêna/Hektor says I owe the Troy I'm seeing today to the efforts of Heinrich Schliemann, the German archeologist who also uncovered Ithaka and the "strong founded citadel" of Mycenae. He calls Schliemann "a treasure hunter, romantic, hero, villain, and passionate idealist who spent his wealth and suffered from malaria while he tried to prove the existence of Troy."

Reminding me that his great-grandfather arrived here shortly after Schliemann's discovery, Mustafa/Athêna/Hektor explains that there were fossils, fishhooks, and other artifacts found within Troy's first three layers that prove it was once located on the seaside. Then, he adds, primarily due to siltation from two rivers the surrounding flats became a swamp then, finally, *terra firma*.

"Nine different levels of Troy were constructed between 3000 BC and the early fourth century AD, when it was the Roman city of New Ilium," he explains as he points out remains from the different epochs and describes some of the discoveries of the dig, including a chest-protecting, oxhide-aproned shield and helmet similar to the one worn by Odysseus.

"The different walls, dated by the workmanship and construction, are the easiest way to assess the evolution of Troy," he continues. "Small rocks were used in early walls and these were replaced with larger, vertically cut stones during the Bronze Age."

He tells me that today there's a 20-meter difference between the levels of Troy 1 and Troy 9, but that they were built on the same spot "because this was such a strategic location and the gateway to both the Aegean and the Black Sea."

"This was an active city for 2,000 years before the Trojan War, which probably occurred in the 6th or 7th layer of Troy," he goes on, adding that the Greek period of Troy accounted for its 8th layer. "The battle Homer describes was not the first war here, because arrowheads and *pithoi* were found from earlier periods when this was known as Wilusa, the Hittite name of Troy."

"Ninety percent of Troy has still not been excavated, and it's possible that we haven't seen anything yet," my mentor adds as he points to a slanted entry ramp from Troy II constructed in 2500 BC. "I think the most exciting discovery would be the graveyards of Homeric Troy and further proof that Troy was an important city – smaller than Babylon or Hattusa but bigger than Mycenae."

Mustafa/Athêna/Hektor enumerates improvements that could make Troy a more impressive destination for half a million visitors annually. He also purports to know where Homer was really born.

"Troy will be improved by reconstructions and additions that make it more attractive and comprehensible for the common visitor," he explains. "A Troy lover like you can come here and immediately sense the riveting atmosphere of the past, but normal people need something more eye-catching. A new museum is slated to be built, and that's a step in the right direction."

Then he discusses Homer and anticipates my next question – "Now that I'm in Troy, where should I go and what should I do next?" – before I ask it.

"The Greeks are completely mistaken when they say Homer was born in Chios, because he was born in Turkey," he states unequivocally. "Continue MedTrekking until you reach Homer's birthplace at Homeros near İzmir."

"It's not just Homer's birthplace that makes me encourage you to keep walking," Mustafa/Athêna/Hektor explains, now with the bemused and ethereal smile that brings the Athêna in him to the forefront. "You still have to MedTrek a bit more to exactly equal the 4,401 kilometers you wrote about in your first book, and I'm going to give you a few Turkish tasks to keep you on the path."

"Why should I have to MedTrek the exact distance that I did for the first book?" I ask. "Is there something special about 8,802 kilometers?"

"Symmetry, or συμμετρεῖν, is what it's all about," he/she says, using the Greek word *symmetria* that means "measure together." "How odd it would look if you MedTrekked anything but 8,802 kilometers. Here's what you should do next:

1. Cross the Skamánder River to the shores of the Aegean Sea and visit Besik Bay where the Greeks camped during their attack on Troy.

2. Continue along the coast to Allos to pay your respects to my temple.

3. Climb to the summit of Mount Ida where the Trojan War was scripted and directed by teams of gods working against each other. Zeus wants to have a word with you.

4. Visit Homeros.

5. Remember the gods are on your side and more will be revealed during your walk.

The next morning I sit reflectively on a crumbling wall overlooking fields of sunflowers and gaze towards the Skamánder and Xánthos Rivers. Homer described the blue Xánthos as an "eddying and running, god-begotten wondrous river" but at one point during the war the Skamánder could not "spend my current in the salt immortal sea being dammed with corpses." The Skamánder starts on Mount Ida – where, it's written many times in *The Iliad*, things were controlled by "O Father Zeus! who rul'st Ida's height" – and flows into the Hellespont north of Troy.

I take a photograph of the now-serene Skamánder River as I casually walk through tomato, corn and melon fields, and fig and olive orchards, to the wine-dark sea. The pastoral morning ends when I confront a monstrous cement plant. It looks like a gigantic ship from the distance, overshadowing any beauty that might once have been related to Besik Bay, about 15-kilometers away from Troy.

"Is this the lovely bay where Achilles and the Greeks kept their deep-sea ships and bivouacked during the war?" I wonder.

It meets the description, and, though blemished by the cement factory, I'm able to imagine the time that "Achilles wept, and sat apart by the grey wave, scanning the endless sea," when "from the deep water, girdler of earth and shaker of earth, Poseidon, came to arouse new spirit in the Argives," and, one night, "the lightning glare of a ship ablaze" appeared.

The next day I pass the chic island of Bozcaada and a few hours later enter the Temple of Athêna atop a crag near Assos. I'm delighted, as though stumbling upon a long-lost girlfriend, to see the island of Lesbos glimmering in the Aegean Sea. The view accentuates the beauty and tranquility of this serene hilltop tribute to Athêna, and I spend a couple of hours in contented contemplation high above beaches packed with post-Ramadan revelers.

A brochure informs me "the buildings in the ancient city of Assos, founded in the sixth century BC on a dormant volcano, were made of andesite, which is a volcanic rock difficult to process but very stable. The sarcophagi made in this city were very famous in the ancient world and became a top export because they were called 'flesh-eating sarcophagi' since they were rapidly consuming the bodies placed into them."

Flesh-eating sarcophagi (it's from the Greek word *sarcophagus,* which actually means "flesh-eating)?" Now that's what I want to get as a lasting MedTrek souvenir!

Aristotle, the Greek philosopher, lived here from 347 to 344 BC and established a school of philosophy, though I'm unable to find any notable commentary by him about flesh-eating sarcophagi. Athêna's temple, built on the highest point of the city and the first and only Doric temple in Anatolia, is a tribute to her role as city protector.

While I calmly explore Assos, Athêna again appears, this time in the body of an Austrian tourist who winks and pretends she wants to chat about Paul Theroux's *The Pillars of Hercules.*

"That was a bad joke," Athêna said in Viennese Deutsch. "I now want you to MedTrek along the Olive Riviera to the delightfully named town of Küçükkuyu and awaken at sunrise to visit the Altar of Zeus at the nearby hilltop town of Adatepe. Then MedTrek deep into the hills to swim with the nymphs at the Milhi waterfall before climbing to the highest peak on the western side of the Mount Ida range and looking down on distant Troy, just as Zeus and company did during the Trojan War."

I recall how Zeus, benched high on Ida, made it clear that he ruled that particular roost when Homer quotes him addressing the gods during the war.

"If I catch sight of anyone slipping away with a mind to assist the Danääns or the Trojans, he comes back blasted without ceremony, or else he will be flung out of Olympus into the murk of Tartaros that lies deep down in the underworld," Zeus said in an attempt to briefly let men fight their own battles. "You may learn then how far my power puts all gods to shame."

Everybody, gods and men, respected Zeus, and soldiers often prayed to him on "Ida looking out for us all." One of the 24 books in *The Iliad* is entitled "The Battle Swayed by Zeus," and his power is continually underscored.

"I would not dream of pitting all the rest of us against Lord Zeus," Poseidon told Hêra. "He overmasters all."

"Easy to see how men get strength from Zeus," Prince Hektor said. "On the one hand, when he gives them glory, on the other, when he saps their enemies."

In the end, adds Agamémnon, "troops of soldiers are worth no more than one man cherished by Zeus."

Turkey Trotting After Troy

When I leave the temple I run into four young European college kids in the Erasmus Program at Istanbul University and then meet a forty-something Turkish woman living in New York and teaching Pilates at a local resort.

The flashily dressed and sassy gym instructor, who's been in New York for 25 years and has *K. Ataturk* tattooed on her left arm, is wearing a bright yellow sarong and tiny bikini top. She's traveling with a Turkish friend who teaches English in İzmir and the pair illustrate that Turkey – where little English is spoken in the rural countryside, and there's a pronounced fashion and cultural gap between simple peasant garb and chic, touristic beachwear – is in transition, though in which direction is unclear.

"If my friend and I dressed like this in her neighborhood in İzmir, we'd be beaten by fundamentalists," admits the New Yorker. "Here everyone just thinks we're foreign tourists."

"It'll take one more generation for people to start speaking English," adds the English teacher. "There's no way to predict whether Turkey will become more or less secular than it is today, or whether it will ultimately join Europe."

Who wouldn't stop in a place with a name like Küçükkuyu,

perhaps the best-named town on the entire MedTrek, to set up a base camp southeast of Troy? The name keeps me excited as I stroll on the delightfully quiet coastal road from Assos along the Olive Riviera through olive trees, campgrounds, beaches, and one little *antik*, or unmodernized, village with a mosque.

I chat with a 17-year-old high school student at a campsite who, presumably to practice her English, wants to discuss the various social and cultural transitions underway in contemporary Turkey. She tells me there's no rift between bikini'd and clothed Turks, though she's upset that I've taken a picture of garbage near the campsite.

"That's because of the Ramadan holidays," she apologizes. "It's not a usual sight."

A woman fully dressed in pink from head-to-toe is "sunbathing" at the beach near Küçükkuyu, where I take an afternoon dip amid dozens of young girls in bikinis. While I'm there she steps, fully-clothed, into the water. I'm the only one who seems to think that picture is worth a thousand words.

Küçükkuyu is located on the Gulf of Edremit at the base of Mount Ida, and when I enter town I visit the *Adatepe Zeytinyai Müzesi* (Olive Oil Museum), even before I find a decent €17 room at the Ali Baba Hotel.

That night, as I linger over a dinner of fresh sardines straight from the grill, I'm told that the Greek word for fish, *ichthys*, is also an acronym for the expression *Iesoûs Christòs Theoû Hyiòs Sotr,* which means "Jesus Christ, Son of God, Savior." This is another explanation, I presume, why the image of a fish is often used as a symbol of Christ. I take an after-dinner stroll, buy a banana waffle dessert, and eat it on a bench looking out at the Aegean and Greek islands.

Ushered Up Mount Ida

The next morning, I'm up before the 5:38 call to prayer by the *muezzin* at the nearby mosque and out the door early in an attempt to make it up and down Mount Ida in one day. I wander through the port hoping to find a coffee and meet the English-speaking owner of the Hêra Butik Hotel, who has one of his staff make me two strong ones. We talk about the image of Turkey (he seems to think everyone hates the country and/or the people) and the various trails heading up the mountain.

Awakening at sunrise was easy, but I wonder if Athêna is aware that someone has written the word "FAKE" at the Altar of Zeus in nearby Adatepe, about four kilometers north of Küçükkuyu on Zeus Street. It's so rare to see any English words in rural Turkey that this one definitely stands out, and some archeologists are indeed dubious about the altar's authenticity. Zeus might be slightly placated that visitors still tie "wishes" to a tree near the altar.

I continue to the Milhi waterfall, where it costs three Turkish lira to swim and 20 more to picnic. I take a quick nymphless dip before sweating profusely during a 38-kilometer daylong MedTrek in the grueling early September heat. It takes me through fields – where I energetically pick and eat dozens of figs – and pine forests to the top of a peak that affords a view west to distant Troy and east to the summit of Mount Ida in the *Kazdaği Milli Parki*, or the Kazdağı National Park (KDNP). *Kazdaği* means "Goose Mountain," and in ancient times this part of Anatolia was known as the Troad, or "land of Troy."

I've been excited about getting to the top of Mount Ida for years because of an enticing paragraph in *The Iliad:* "At full stretch midway between the earth and starry heaven they ran toward Ida, sparkling with cool streams, mother of wild things, and the peak of Gárgaron where are his holy plot and fragrant altar. There Zeus, father of gods and men, reined in and freed his team, diffusing cloud about them, while glorying upon the crest he sat to view the far-off scene below – Akhaian ships and Trojan city."

It's right up there with Olympus and I give the gods my thanks for locating their earthly homes in such heavenly spots.

Sometimes Athêna cracks me up.

You'll recall that she politely ordered me to go have a consultation with Zeus at the top of Mount Ida, though I would have climbed it anyway because the tree-covered, multi-flowered, bee-hived national park is rumored to be the best source of oxygen in all of Turkey.

In addition, the world's first beauty contest was held here between Aphroditê, Hêra and Athêna. Zeus told them to go to Mount Ida where Paris was a shepherd and the Trojan prince would pronounce the winner. The goddesses each tried to bribe him in order to win: Hêra promised to make Paris the Lord of Europe and Asia, Athêna said she'd enable him to be a victor in war, and Aphroditê promised that the fairest woman in the world would be his. Aphroditê won the contest known as the Judgment of Paris. The fairest woman in the world was Helen of Troy and the beauty contest led to her affair with Paris and the Trojan War.

I obey Athêna but when I get to the main entrance of the KDNP I'm told that I can't enter without a guide because, says the guard, "we don't want people picking flowers." The only solution is to make arrangements to climb Mount Ida with a guide the next day but I am pretty sure I know what Athêna is up to. The wily and wise goddess would invariably again appear in the guise of a tour guide and, for a charge of €40, safely lead me on a 25-kilometer saunter up the 1,774-meter (5,820 ft) mountain to Zeus' lair.

Yet when the tour guide arrives at the entrance to the gigantic national park the next morning at 8:00, I am astounded to see not a disguised and winking Athêna but rather a mortal called Usher (a corruption of his Turkish name Asir) Altinoz, a 48-year-old former biology researcher/translator and English-speaking guide, who's writing a book containing "everything you always wanted to know about Mount Ida but were afraid to ask" and other bits of wisdom.

That cracks me up too, but Usher turns out to be a fountain of information and advice during our six-hour hike up Mount Ida. He describes the influence of women (including the white-armed goddess Hêra, the Magna Mater and the Blonde Legend) in the mountain's history and gives me his take on Aphroditê's win in the beauty contest. He mentions that Mount Ida inspired Koranic verses and that contemporary religious and spiritual ceremonies frequently occur on the holy ground and shrine on the mountain's broad, table-top summit, where there are the remains of an unexplained circular stone wall that was once four kilometers in circumference.

An ardent hiker who climbs Mount Ida a hundred times a year, Usher (with a name like that, he was destined to be a guide) chatted about the KDNP's wildlife (black and brown bears, wild boar, roe deer, wolves, rainbow trout, and jackals); flora, including 40 different wild herbs, scores of flowers that blossom in May and June, and everything from pine, pistachio and plum trees to figs, olives, and porcini; four different micro-climates (Mediterranean, Black Sea, Marmara Sea, Alpine) on a mountain range that's 70-kilometers long and 30-kilometers wide; abundant fresh water on the "mountain of 1,000 springs"; watchtowers for fires; a NATO radar for defense and the extraordinary quality of its oxygen.

"The oxygen makes everyone feel young again, and there are amazing fresh and unique smells on this mountain mecca that is an altar for women," Usher says as he hands me some seductively scented samples of oregano and thyme. "Hêra was able to seduce Zeus here and influence the outcome of the Trojan War because she created her sensuous smell with oils from herbs like these. And did I mention that any wish you make on the holy ground or in the shrine at the top of Mount Ida will come true?"

Usher is sure that I'll meet Zeus and that one day he (Usher) will win the lottery.

"Just go into the shrine, light the candles, meditate or pray, and it will happen," Usher told me when he stopped to have a drink of *raki* mixed with fresh stream water.

Athêna, it turns out, had supplied me with a human guide who was perhaps more experienced than even a goddess.

She cracks me up. She really does.

Several mythic events in the works of Homer occur at the summit of Mount Ida where the Olympian gods watched the progress of the epic battle around Troy. It was here, in my favorite book of *The Iliad,* that Hêra seduced and distracted Zeus long enough to enable the Greeks to temporarily take the initiative in the war. The delightful passages describe how Hêra conceived, executed and succeeded in her plan to overpower the god of all gods, using one of the oldest weapons on earth: sex.

"Her ladyship of the wide eyes took thought how to distract her lord who bears the stormcloud," Homer writes. "Her best plan, she thought, was this: to scent and adorn herself and visit Ida, hoping hot desire might rise in him – desire to lie with her and make love to her nakedness – that so she might infuse warm slumber on his eyes and over his shrewd heart."

Now get prepared for one of the hottest sex scenes in classical literature that is a textbook example for contemporary women who want to get a man to ignore anything from the Trojan War to a dent in the car. Of course, who would expect anything less from Hêra who ranked in "two respects highest of goddesses – by birth and by my station, queen to thee, lord of all gods."

"Those shining doors the goddess closed behind her, and with ambrosia cleansed all stain away from her delectable skin. Then with fine oil she smoothed herself, and this, her scented oil, unstoppered in the bronze-floored house of Zeus, cast fragrance over earth and heaven. Hêra, having anointed all her graceful body, and having combed her hair, plaited it shining in braids from her immortal head. That done, she chose a wondrous gown, worked by Athêna in downy linen with embroideries. She caught this at her breast with golden pins and girt it with a waistband, sewn all around with a hundred tassels. Then she hung mulberry-colored pendants in her earlobes, and loveliness shone round her. A new headdress, white as the sun, she took to veil her glory, and on her smooth feet tied her beautiful sandals."

Each time I read these lines I have to agree with some academics that believe that Homer might have been a woman, or a very sensitive man who appreciated women. That seems especially true when Hêra goes to Aphroditê for assistance in her connivance. Seriously, could a blind male poet come up with this?

"Lend me longing, lend me desire, by which you bring immortals low as you do mortal men," Hêra, whose arms shone white as ivory, requests of Aphroditê.

To further seal the deal Hêra went to Sleep (that's with a capital S), the brother of Death, and asked him to "lull to sleep for me the shining eyes of Zeus as soon as I lie down with him in love."

With that she was ready and, a possibly female Homer writes, "her enchantments came from this: allurement of the eyes, hunger of longing, and the touch of lips that steals all wisdom from the coolest men."

Zeus took the delectable bait hook, line and sinker, though he attempts to make it look like going to bed is his idea. That, of course, was also part of Hêra's cunning plan.

"We two must give ourselves to love-making," Zeus says. the second Hêra arrives on Mount Ida. "Desire for girl or goddess in so wild a flood never came over me...No lust as sweet as this for you has ever taken me."

He enshrouded them both in a vapor of golden cloud, and as Zeus was wrapped in a night of sleep, "Hêra beguiled him into making love." While he was sidelined, various gods, including Poseidon, tried to alter the course of the Trojan War in favor of the invading Greeks.

As you can imagine, Zeus wasn't too pleased with Hêra's ploy when he "by Hêra's queenly side awoke and rose in a single bound."

"Fine underhanded work, eternal bitch!" Zeus bellowed.

When Hêra returned to Mount Olympus she told one of the other immortals "Oh, what mindless fools to lay plans against Zeus! And yet we do, we think we can be near him, and restrain him, by pleading or by force. But there he sits apart from us, careless of us, forever telling us he is quite beyond us all in power and might, supreme among the gods."

And in the end, even Hêra gives in.

"Let him be arbiter, as he desires, between Danáäns and Trojans," she told Athêna about Zeus. "It is due his majesty."

The gods often argued among themselves at top of Mount Ida as they debated and decided the fate of warriors in the battle in Troy. Hêphaistos was especially fed up at one point.

"Ah! What a miserable day, if you two raise your voices over mortal creatures. More than enough already!" Hêphaistos said to Hêra using, for the first time in literature, the phrase "Enough already!"

And sometimes cloud-massing Zeus stepped in to criticize them or curb their enthusiasm.

"Do not come whining here, you two-faced brute, most hateful to me of all the Olympians," he said to Arês. "Combat and brawling are your element. This beastly, incorrigible truculence comes from your mother Hêra, whom I keep but barely in my power, say what I will."

"Warfare is not for you, child," he told Aphroditê because she liked to "beguile the women of Akhaia to elope with Trojans...Lend yourself to sighs of longing and the marriage bed. Let Arês and Athêna deal with war."

The gods also had revealed their favorites among men. Although he was killed, it was said about Prince Hektor that "one of the gods goes with him everywhere to shield him from a mortal wound. Look! There, beside him – Arês in disguise!"

According to ancient legend, all sorts of divine goings-on took place on Mount Ida, as the gods charmed, seduced, tricked, married, and betrayed one another. There were also times that they compromised.

"I am immortal, too, your stock and my stock are the same," Hêra told Zeus. "Come, we'll give way to one another in this affair: I yield to you and you to me; the gods will follow."

She even counsels him to use a softer tone.

"Fearsome as you are, why take that tone with goddesses, my lord?" she said. "We are well aware how far from weak you are."

After I send a GPS location from the summit and have long enough admired the view of Troy and the Hellespont from magical, mystical, mythical, and holy Mount Ida, I hike across the broad hilltop to the altar to meditate, pray and prepare for my meeting with Zeus.

I am looking forward to meeting Zeus again: the gatherer of cloud and the lord of storm and lightning who didn't take too much time to chat with me at the top of Mount Olympus. I plan to give him the lowdown on my recent visits to his caves on Crete, my not-so-wild engagement with Helen of Troy, and my appreciation of Athêna's help throughout the MedTrek. I also expect to learn a few things from the god of glory and power reigning from Ida about Odysseus, the Trojan War, good and evil, seduction, thunderbolt tossing, my own existence, and immortality.

I enter the shrine and admire the multicolored scarves, icons, and candles left by pilgrims and visitors. I sense Athêna's presence and expect her to lead me to the undying ruler of gods and men who drives the clouds of heaven.

"My father, the king of all gods benched high on Ida, is looking forward to sitting with you and speaking about anything you desire," she says as she leads me to his throne. "Everything is on the record."

The first question Zeus asks me is not the first question I thought he'd ask me.

"You've been to the cave of my birth on Crete, to the top of Mount Olympus across the Aegean Sea, to everywhere in between, and now you're here on Mount Ida. Welcome!" he pronounced royally. "But I have one question: May I see your pedometer?"

I detach the small black plastic pedometer from my gray shorts and hand it over.

He beckons Hermês, the messenger god, and gives him the instrument.

"See how many kilometers you can do in an hour," Zeus tells him.

"I average five on good terrain," I pipe in to absolutely no response from either Zeus or Hermês, who takes off at the speed of light.

I haven't seen Hermês or that particular pedometer since.

For lack of a better comparison, Zeus resembles Charlton Heston in the 1956 version of *The Ten Commandments*. He is earthshaking, eye opening and ear splitting. He covers a variety of topics as we stare beyond Troy until "the sun dips and starry darkness comes."

In a conversation that was at least as valuable as my four years in college and fourteen years on the MedTrek combined – heck maybe even all my life up to this point – Zeus tells me about the pros and cons of immortality, what it's like to sleep with unblemished women who never age, and how he copes with the idiosyncrasies of the various gods. He describes how detached he is when it comes to most individual humans, though he, too, liked Hektor during the Trojan War.

"I've got to let my children, the other gods, exert more influence over specific events and certain people while I orchestrate the bigger picture," he says.

I ask him about how, if he's so darn smart, Hêra tricked him into taking his eye off the ball during the Trojan War by sleeping with him.

"Nobody's perfect, even up here," he says. "I may be immortal, but I make mistakes. All gods make mistakes; we just don't have to suffer for them. But don't tell anybody that."

As we enter the baths, attended by various nymphs, Zeus discusses where I should go on the MedTrek in the years ahead.

"Follow in the tracks of that *Iliad* lover and Homerphile, Alexander the Great, who went south from Troy," he says. "But instead of going to Persia, simply continue along the windy and difficult coast in Turkey and follow the shores of the Mediterranean through Syria, Lebanon, and Israel to enter Egypt. End your next 4,401-kilometer MedTrek in Alexandria where your 20-year odyssey is destined to come to an end. Don't worry, we gods will look after you. We frequently like happy endings and, as you've so successfully learned, the path is the goal and the goal is the path."

It won't be easy to follow in the footsteps of Alexander, the son of Philip II, the shrewd and forceful king of Macedonia, and his bacchante mother Olympias, a proud princess from Epirus. At 18, the short and stocky Alexander was tutored by Aristotle and began a 14-year-quest from Pella, just outside Thesssaloniki, to successfully conquer the known world on three continents. He changed the course of history before he died in Babylon in 323 BC at only 33.

Incidentally, according to erudite author Anthony Burgess, the name Alexander means "the defender of men." Burgess named Alex, the main character in *A Clockwork Orange*, after Alexander the Great, calling his character "a comic reduction of Alexander the Great slashing his way through the world and conquering it."

Why should I identify with Alexander the Great?

Because Alexander, like some other people I know, believed he was a descendant of Achilles and traveled with his dog, Peritas, who, according to some, saved his life at Gaugamela by leaping in front of a Persian elephant and biting its trunk.

Maybe I'll find a dog to join me, perhaps a reincarnation of Bogart who was with me on the MedTrek when I set out from Antibes.

At sunrise, Athêna enters the shrine, wryly smiles, gives me a knowing wink, and takes me outside to meet Usher. It turns out that, in human time, my meeting with Zeus only lasted five minutes. She sends me down the mountain with instructions to not "worry about Egypt, but end your current MedTrek when you've reached 8,802 kilometers at the place the Turks claim Homer was born."

Have I Become Homer?

More wiped out than I thought I'd be after the Mount Ida excursion and exposure to Zeus, to recuperate I take a SideTrek to the ancient Greek city of Pergamon, now known as Bergama. I spend a couple of hours exploring the Sanctuary of Athêna at the hilltop Acropolis, where I tell one Japanese tourist that she looks like the goddess Athêna, and she swoons, covering her mouth with her hand in embarrassment as Japanese women frequently do. Then I have a muscle-stretching, bone-cracking, head-relaxing massage and soapy bath in the local *hammam* that puts me in the mood for a long afternoon nap. Go with the slow flow, I think to myself as I notice that every other hotel in Bergama has *butik,* or boutique, in its name. And that every male in town has learned the same phrase in English: "Where are you from?"

When I'm restored two days later, I gamely walk in the direction of İzmir along the Mediterranean seashore through the towns of Ayvalik, Dikili, Candarli and Denzikoy.

In Dikili, I get a third floor room at the seaside La Perla Hotel and enjoy a splendid sunset over Lesbos. Candarli is a luscious and quiet day's walk along a still-smooth sea and when I continue to Denizkoy it's

9/11, and I MedTrek in memory of the American dead. There's no contemplation of that event by the Turks who casually play backgammon and cards at outdoor cafes on the port. I notice the fashionable colors for fully clothed women on Sarimsakli Plaj are light grey, turquoise and pink and one local innovation is the use of sandbags as steps over offshore rocks to permit bathers to get into deeper water.

When I make it to İzmir, a large and busy seaside metropolis, I head through the northeast suburb of Bornova to an idyllic, isolated, and peaceful park in the hills that was created in 2008 in homage to Homer's purported birth there.

The aptly named Homeros is located at the top of the 3.5-kilometer-long Homeros Valley near the village of Kayadibi and features three natural caves, oak-and-pine tree forests, hiking trails, man-made ponds and reservoirs, a large picnic area (*piknik alani*), a Vitamin Bar café, and the occasional whiff of livestock.

This homage to Homer's birth is much more distinguished than anything the Greeks have created on the nearby island of Chios. It's a definite PR win for the Turks, although quite a way from the poet's native Meles River, which obviously makes this a contestable choice. However, what do I know? Homer could have been a Turk. And I could be Homer.

This thought makes more sense when I receive an email from Usher who writes: "İzmir is a beautiful city. Homer was born in İzmir. You are on the right track. You can be Homer, nothing less nothing more. When I was a young man, I didn't know any better and was just like Paris of Troy. In fact, I have the same life story as Paris of Troy. I lived on Mount İda as a boy. And fate took me to Troy, Alabama, where I met a lady as beautiful as Helen of Troy on the Troy Highway between Troy and Montgomery. She was a married woman. I cannot tell more."

The next morning, as I walk along the buzzing and busy İzmir seafront before catching a train-and-ferry to Istanbul, I ask passersby if they think I'm Homer. Some of them cross to the other side of the street. I finally tell a restaurant owner that I'll buy lunch at his place if he simply tells me I look like Homer. He does, and I have aubergines with lamb and spinach followed by a Turkish *kahve*, or coffee. Then I get a luxuriously lathered shave at a barber shop.

Now, with precisely 8,802 kilometers on my pedometer, I'll follow the final instruction Athêna gave me just before we parted at the summit of Mount Ida and take into account Deng Ming-Dao's adage that "the time to contemplate the ending is before the ending." Alluding to Odysseus's two-decade journey back to his home in Ithaka after the Trojan War, the cunning and crafty goddess told me to return to Redding, California. "Don't return to the Mediterranean until you've written the last word of *The Idiot and the Odyssey II: Myth, Madness and Magic on the Mediterranean*," said the spear-carrying wily and wise goddess.

MedTrek Milestone #10

As you well know, I have finished writing the second book about my walk around the Mediterranean and am ready to resume the MedTrek from İzmir to Egypt. First, though, I'm returning to Alexander the Great's birthplace in Pella, the capital of the ancient kingdom of Macedonia, to walk from there to the sea. I may even run in the annual Alexander the Great Marathon that ends at the White Tower in Thessaloniki, the last capital of ancient Macedonia. Then away I go back to Turkey and down the shores of Syria, Lebanon and Israel into Egypt.

See you in
Alexandria!

Hiking Addendum
Twelve Commonsense Tips for Mindful MedTrekking

One of the reasons that I have such a delightful time walking around the Mediterranean Sea is because I keep it simple. Here are twelve commonsense tips that will enable you to have an equally pleasant and unencumbered stroll.

Adequately prepare and train to avoid, or lessen, aches, pains and injuries.

It's very difficult to get lost if you stay as close as possible to the sea. It will always be on your left or right.

There's no hurry. Start slowly and walk at the speed of the slowest member of your party. For the record, I walk an average of 33 kilometers

Fresh water is the most important item in your backpack. Don't worry, the load will get lighter after you over pack on the first few days out. You are what you carry.

Practice walking meditation, pick up litter, smile at strangers, don't argue (too much) with security officials and walk on behalf of all sentient beings.

There's nothing more delightful than meeting strangers on the road.

Many things beyond your control – weather, logistics, illness, injury, topography, and security officials – come with the territory. Accept that and don't worry about time.

There's more daylight during summer months but it's hot, tourists are everywhere and accommodation is more expensive and sometimes difficult to find. Try April/May/early June and September/October.

It's fun to hike with friends but it's essential, and often much more interesting, to hike alone from time to time.

Never reserve a room in advance and always be prepared to stay on the beach, in a monastery, at a nudist colony or almost anywhere else. It's part of the game.

Forget the destination, take it a step at a time and don't worry about what's around the next corner (actually, there aren't many corners). The goal is the path, the path is the goal.

Try to practice the relaxed attitude of the MedTrek in other parts of your life.

Acknowledgements

Walking around the Mediterranean Sea is my mid-life passion and it's a continual joy to share the path with Greek gods, contemporary mortals and anonymous readers. Once again, this adventurous project would not have been possible without constant inspiration from Homer vis-à-vis Robert Fitzgerald's well-thumbed translations of *The Iliad* and *The Odyssey*, which are the source of most quotes from the gods, the Greeks, the Trojans and Homer throughout this book.

I would not have been able to compile this account without the generous assistance of a variety of people both on and off the path. A number of readers have discussed the project with me and patiently read drafts of the text at different stages of its evolution. I would like to again thank Gloria Ackley, Liz Chapin, Lex Hames, John Keeney, Alexander "Sandy" MacGillivray, Carlo Roberts, Martha Shulman, Helen Stratte, Luke Stratte-McClure and Robin Thompson for their critical assessments and astute observations.

Classics professor Vince Tomasso deserves to be singled out for patiently reviewing the manuscript for mythical errors and my editor, Michael Knipe in London, tended to the text "as if I'm in the role of midwife at birth following your long and arduous pregnancy." Judy Barnett deserves a rousing round of applause for the work she did as my publicist throughout the world and on various social networks, the book's website and my blog.

I want to thank John Keeney for his recollections regarding our long-ago underwater cave dive on Capri, Gordon Kling for taking me sailing off the coast of Turkey and Travel Dynamics for permitting me to voyage on the *Corinthian II*. My appreciation also extends to a number of authors, curators, professors and scholars who allowed me to interview them. This group includes Kathryn Hohlwein, who created *The Readers of Homer* and permitted me to participate in two readings of *The Odyssey* on the Mediterranean and in Sacramento, California. Thanks also to many high school teachers, especially Jim Owens in Florida, who invited me to give pep talks about the MedTrek to their classes.

I'm deeply indebted to Luke Stratte-McClure and Judy Barnett for their extensive photographic work in Italy and to Des Baum (Turkey), Darla Hightower (California), Toby Lorenzen (Sicily) and Reinhard

Hohlwein (California) for other snapshots from the path. Thanks also to numerous acquaintances and strangers who politely took photographs of me in some admittedly idiotic poses. As I mentioned, my small Canon camera died in the Peloponnese and all of the photographs after it's demise were taken with an iPhone.

My agent, Felicia Eth, has been particularly patient with my steady progress and the Slingshot Marketing design team -- who took my written words to a new level by integrating maps, photographs and various links in the online version of the book – have been especially creative.

A number of friends and strangers joined me on the path and helped me on the road. But I particularly want to thank the anonymous women who, often in the middle of nowhere and busy with their daily chores, graciously stopped simply to inquire if I needed any assistance. Thanks too to the gypsies who chose not to take my right arm, or my life, when they attempted to rob me.

Ever walk omward!

Redding, California, July 31, 2013

Bibliography

Partial Bibliography of Publications Cited in "The Idiot and the Odyssey: Walking the Mediterranean" and "The Idiot and the Odyssey II: Myth, Madness and Magic on the Mediterranean."

"365 Tao Daily Meditations," Deng Ming-Dao, Harper San Francisco, 1992.

"Barcelona," Robert Hughes, Alfred A. Knopf, 1992.

"Be Still and Know: Reflections from Living Buddha, Living Christ," Thich Nhat Hanh, Riverhead Books, 1996.

"Bullfinch's Mythology: The Greek and Roman Fables Illustrated," Thomas Bullfinch, The Viking Press, 1979.

"Celebrating Homer's Landscapes: Troy and Ithaka Revisited," J.V. Luce, Yale University Press, 1998.

"Coastal Pleasures: Perusing the French Coastline," Elizabeth Billhardt, Editions PC, 1999.

"The Colossus of Maroussi," Henry Miller, New Directions Books, 1941.

"Chronicle of Tao: The Secret Life of a Taoist Master," Deng Ming-Dao, Harper Collins, 1993.

"D'Aulaire's Book of Greek Myths," Ingri and Edgar Parin D'Aulaire, Yearling Books, 1962.

"The Dictaean Cave," Georgios I.Panagiotakis, Lassithi, 1988.

"The Eternal Drama: The Inner Meaning of Greek Mythology," Edward F. Edinger, Shambhala, 1994.

"The Great Sea: A Human History of the Mediterranean," David Abulafia, Oxford University Press, 2011.

"Greeks Gods and Heroes," Robert Graves, Doubleday & Company, 1960.

"The Greek Islands," Lawrence Durrell, The Viking Press, 1978.

"Homeric Moments: Clues to Delight in Reading The Odyssey and The Iliad," Eva Brann, Paul Dry Books, 2002.

"The Iliad," Homer, Translated by Robert Fitzgerald, Farrar, Straus and Giroux, 1974.

"A Literary Companion to Travel in Greece," Edited by Richard Stoneman, Penguin Books, 1984.

"The Long Road Turns To Joy: A Guide to Walking Meditation," Thich Nhat Hanh, Parallax Press, 1996.

"A Mediterranean Feast," Clifford A. Wright, William Morrow, 1999.

"The Mediterranean in History," David Abulafia, J. Paul Getty Trust Publications, 2003.

Michelin Country Green Guides (France, Spain, Italy, Greece), Michelin Travel Publications.

"Middlesex," Jeffrey Eugenides, Picador, 2002.

"Myths and Legends of the Ages," Marlon N. French, Hart Publishers, 1951.

"No-Man's Lands: One Man's Odyssey Through The Odyssey," Scott Huler, Crown Publishers, 2008.

"Odysseus Unbound: The Search for Homer's Ithaka," Robert Bittlestone, Cambridge University Press, 2005.

"The Odyssey," Homer, Translated by Robert Fagles, Penguin Books, 1997.

"The Odyssey," Homer, Translated by Robert Fitzgerald, Doubleday & Co., 1961.

"The Odyssey: A Modern Sequel," Nikos Kazantzakis, Translation by Kimon Friar, Simon and Schuster, 1958.

"The Odyssey For Boys and Girls," Alfred J. Church, The Macmillan Company, 1949.

"On The Shores of the Mediterranean," Eric Newby, Harvill Press, 1984.

"Pan Am's Insider's Rome," Random House, 1972.

"The Pillars of Hercules: A Grand Tour of the Mediterranean," Paul Theroux, Hamish Hamilton, 1993.

"Route 66 A.D. - On The Trail of Ancient Roman Tourists," Tony Perrottet, Random House, 2002.

"Sicily: Three Thousand Years of Human History," Sandra Benjamin, Steerforth Press, 2006.

"Siddhartha," Herman Hesse, Translated by Hilda Rosner, New Directions, 1951.

"A Simple Path," The Dalai Lama, Thorsons, 2000.

"The Story of *The Iliad*," Alfred J. Church, The Macmillan Company, 1904.

"Swim: Why We Love The Water," Lynn Sherr, Public Affairs, 2012.

"Tao Te Ching," Lao Tsu, Translated by Gia-Fu Feng and Jane English, Vintage Books Edition, March 1997.

"A Thousand-Mile Walk to the Gulf," John Muir, Houghton Mifflin, 1916.

"The Tibetan Book of Living and Dying," Sogyal Rinpoche, HarperCollins, 1993.

"Three-Way Mirror: Istanbul, Athens, Rome," Michael Kuser, Citlembik/ Nettleberry Publications, 2010.

"The Tomb of Alexander," Seán Hemingway, Hutchinson, 2012.

"Travels With Herodotus," Ryszard Kapuscinski, Translated by Klara Glowczewska, Alfred A. Knopf, 2007.

"Ulysses Airborne," Mauricio Obregon, Harper & Row, 1971.

"Ulysses," James Joyce, Modern Library, 1934.

"The War That Killed Achilles: The True Story of Homer's Iliad and the Trojan War," Caroline Alexander, Viking, 2009.

"Who's Who in Greek and Roman Mythology," David Kravitz, Clarkson N. Potter Inc., 1976.

"The World of Odysseus," M. I. Finley, New York Review Books, 1954.

"Zen and the Art of Motorcycle Maintenance," Robert M. Pirsig, Bodley Head, 1974.

Various articles by author Joel Stratte-McClure in "Time," "The International Herald Tribune," "European Travel and Life," "People," "The Paris Metro" and other publications.

About the Author

Joel Stratte-McClure

Joel Stratte-McClure, an American journalist/ adventurer who lived in France for over three decades, has been writing about his global trekking and hiking adventures since the 1970s. His work has taken him to over 110 countries and his articles on a variety of subjects have appeared in *The International Herald Tribune*, *Time Magazine*, *The Times of London*, *People Magazine* and numerous other publications. He is currently based in Northern California but regularly travels to the Mediterranean to gather anecdotes and add kilometers for his third book in this series: *The Idiot and the Odyssey III: Alexander the Great Walks the Mediterranean*.

www.ingramcontent.com/pod-product-compliance
Lightning Source LLC
Chambersburg PA
CBHW051933090426
42741CB00008B/1165